Ireland: A Reference Guide from the Renaissance to the Present

Facts On File, Inc.
An imprint of Infobase Publishing
132 West 31st Street
New York NY 10001

Library of Congress Cataloging-in-Publication Data
McCarthy, John P.
    Ireland : a reference guide from the Renaissance to the present / John P. McCarthy.
        p. cm. — (European nations)
    Includes bibliographical references (p.) and index.
    ISBN 0-8160-5378-2 (acid-free paper)
    1. Ireland—History—Handbooks, manuals, etc. 2. Ireland—Civilization—Handbooks, manuals, etc. 3. Ireland—Politics and government—Handbooks, manuals, etc. 4. Ireland—Encyclopedias. I. Title. II. Series.
    DA911.M34 2006
    941.5′003—dc22   2005016259

Facts On File books are available at special discounts when purchased in bulk quantities for businesses, associations, institutions, or sales promotions. Please call our Special Sales Department in New York at (212) 967-8800 or (800) 322-8755.

You can find Facts On File on the World Wide Web at http://www.factsonfile.com

Text design by David Strelecky
Cover design by Semadar Megged
Maps by Dale Williams © Infobase Publishing

Printed in the United States of America

VB Hermitage 10 9 8 7 6 5 4 3 2 1

This book is printed on acid-free paper.

In memory of my uncles,
John and Michael "Mickey" McCarthy

CONTENTS

INTRODUCTION

Until relatively recently, the study of Irish history in most American universities was part of the study of British history. This was because Ireland was until 1922 united with Britain (and the northeast corner of the island remains linked to this day) and until 1949 a member of the Commonwealth. In addition, the American academic establishment tended to have an Anglophile bias.

Much has changed, not only with the appearance of specific courses in Irish history in many universities, but also with the formation of institutes of Irish studies whereby students can major, minor, and even pursue graduate degrees in the history, the social order, the culture, or the literature of Ireland. This American academic development has happened because of several things. A thoughtful ethnic consciousness on the part of millions of Americans who have Irish ancestry has come about. Ireland has come to play a significant international role by its participation in the European Union and the United Nations. Irish writers, actors, and popular entertainers have achieved an extraordinary degree of regard and celebrity from Nobel Prizes to Academy Awards to the sale of millions of recordings. The astonishing economic prosperity of recent years has put Ireland among the leading nations of Europe and the world in terms of per capita income. The extensive observance of the sesquicentennial of Ireland's historic nightmare, the Great Famine of 1845–49, has served to stimulate interest in Irish history as well as to remind people of the reality of starvation and disease afflicting so much of the contemporary world. Understandably, it may well have been the tragic struggle in Northern Ireland since the late 1960s, with all its features of terrorism, state repression, sectarian hostility, and irredentist aspirations, that has possibly done more than anything else to make the world aware of Ireland. It is hoped that struggle is near resolution.

The fascination with Ireland contrasts with the situation a half century ago. Although Ireland had attained its political independence and had developed successful constitutional and democratic political institutions, two achievements not frequently combined in the twentieth century, the nation drew little world attention, never mind academic interest. Many things accounted for this. One was Ireland's self-imposed economic and cultural isolation ranging from severe economic protection to strict literary censorship. Irish society seemed resigned to economic stagnation and high emigration. The nation's neutrality in the Second World War made some invalidly suspect an Irish bias toward the Axis powers. Many observers became dismissive of any Irish matter when her government launched a campaign to draw world interest to her aspirations for the political unification of the island immediately after the war, a time when the world was witness to millions of refugees, massive reconstruction, and the onset of the cold war. The world's indifference to Ireland was matched by Irish adherence to the attitudes that had brought on their isolation: a sense of moral superiority and a notion that Ireland was a poor and small nation. Postwar poverty remained endemic but many Irish then failed to appreciate that Ireland, even excluding Northern Ireland, is a relatively large European nation in terms of area. Its 32,595 square miles exceeds each of the areas of Belgium, the Netherlands, Luxembourg, Albania, Switzerland, Denmark, Malta, Estonia, Latvia, Lithuania, and the Czech and Slovak Republics.

The history of Ireland in the modern era must be read in terms of its relationship to the neighboring island, from political and cultural colonization to varying efforts at autonomy to actual independence. Since the beginning of the sixteenth century the modernization of the English state has involved the absorption of Ireland, as well as Scotland and Wales. The aim to Anglicize Ireland was further spurred by Ireland's religious identity with England's continental enemies.

Another immensely important aspect of Irish history is the record of millions in the Irish diaspora, particularly those immigrating to the English-speaking world. In a way, Irish talents required a stage bigger than the island itself. These were displayed in the socio-cultural-political achievement of the Irish and their descendants in the United States, in Canada, and in Australia. The Irish also played a significant religious role in foreign places. They tended to dominate the Catholic Church in the above-mentioned areas, despite millions from other Catholic lands settling there. Great numbers of Irish became missionaries, especially to the former British imperial territories in the developing countries of Asia and Africa. Many continue today in this nonconquering and benevolent role, although now increasingly in a secularized form as participants in relief agencies.

Political nationalism is a relatively modern phenomenon, dating primarily from the late eighteenth century, while ethnic identity existed long before. There was an Ireland and an Irish people long before there was nationalism. In the medieval era, when all of Europe formed part of the same Christendom and monarchical authority did not correspond to ethnic boundaries, the king of England had accepted the title of Lord of Ireland. Much earlier, Europeans, many of whom had been converted to Christianity by Irish missionaries, had come to Ireland to study in monastic settlements that played a significant role in preserving classical learning during the "Dark Ages." Perhaps the Irish story is best appreciated not so much as the struggle for and attainment of independence as the participation of the country in a broader theater, whether within the Christendom of old, the British Empire, or, presently, the European Union and the United Nations.

The rightfully deserved attention being given to Irish studies also serves a pragmatic purpose for the world at large. Ireland offers itself as a unique example of being both a modern Western state and an ex-colony. Such credentials enable the nation both to identify with and to guide and assist ex-colonies in the developing world that might have a reluctance to accept the tutelage of other Western powers. The Irish historical experience of absorbing various settlers, even conquerors, ranging from the Vikings to the Normans to the English, and drawing from their strengths, especially in such matters as urbanization, commerce, agricultural modernization, and constitutional institutions, should provide insight to other relatively recently independent nations. One of the crowning glories of modern Ireland is its achievement of and maintenance of constitutional democracy after independence and after a civil war more brutal than the war of independence. That achievement had few parallels in the twentieth century, whether in Europe or elsewhere. Even the incompletely resolved crisis in Northern Ireland provides extraordinary examples of creative efforts at resolution of community conflict. One example is the unique mechanism of power sharing, which guarantees cross-community participation in government even when the same group retains the majority permanently. That may well be an appropriate instrument for resolving community conflict in so many other parts of the world.

HISTORY OF IRELAND

EARLY AND MEDIEVAL IRELAND

The first consideration in examining Ireland is its geography. It is a large island off the rim of Europe with a larger island between it and the continent. Ireland separated from the continental landmass as the Ice Age was receding, but before Britain had separated. This explains the relative paucity of wildlife species. That fact, rather than their banishment by St. Patrick, explains the absence of snakes in Ireland. Topographically, Ireland is like a saucer, that is, it consists of a mountainous rim and a lower level of land in the center, but with one bit of the rim broken, which opens to the island's richest plain: the Boyne valley, whose central river empties into the Irish Sea on the east and which was the inevitable path taken by many invaders.

The earliest human inhabitants of the island were hunter-gatherers living more than 8,000 years ago. Several millennia later, in the new Stone Age, settlers arrived who planted crops and raised animals. Extensive relics of this era in the form of houses, pottery, and tools survive. These Neolithic farmers were more than self-sufficient, as they constructed megalithic tombs, such as that at Newgrange in County Meath, which indicate a remarkable degree of engineering and astronomical knowledge. The passageway in it is angled in a way to allow the inner chamber to be illuminated by the rays of the Sun only at daybreak of the shortest day of the year. Within the next two millennia, Bronze Age settlers came with weapons, jewelry, and tools, and they built artificial islands or *crannogs* within lakes as dwelling places.

THE CELTS

Undoubtedly the most significant ancient settlers of Ireland were the Celts, who arrived during the Iron Age beginning about 500 B.C. They were an Indo-European people who had emigrated from central Europe to the westernmost parts of the continent. While it is still unclear whether they came to Ireland in large groups or in smaller bands of conquerors, their culture and language became ascendant. Their oral literary tradition has given us greater knowledge of their society and culture than of the earlier settlers. Celtic folklore, especially the folk epic the *Tain*, which deals, among other things, with the warrior hero Cuchulain, not only has provided knowledge of Celtic society but also has served in modern times to fuel and inspire political nationalism, including the naming of modern political parties and government positions.

A similar culture and language, however, did not bring political unity to Celtic Ireland. Instead there were several score *tuatha*, or small kingdoms. Groups of these would be subordinate to a stronger kingdom, which in turn would be subject to one of a handful of even greater kingships, but the alliances and positions of dominance would continually shift. Each *tuath* had a king, or *ri*, and occasionally kings who led large alliances would claim the title of *ard-ri*, or high king. A limited electorate of relatives selected the king of a *tuath*, with the choice limited to near relatives, not necessarily sons, of the last king. The druids (priests) and the brehons (judges) also played significant roles. Law was more a matter of arbitration. More fines were meted out than severe forms of punishment or imprisonment. There was no currency and wealth was measured in terms of cattle. The society was not democratic—many were held in slavery or other forms of servitude. Although their society was relatively developed and complex with a system of laws, intricate inauguration or coronation rituals, and refined art, the Celts had not developed the art of writing aside from *ogham*, a system of strokes on stones, many of which still stand in rural Ireland. The lack of written records enhanced the position of the *fili* or poets, whose task was the committing of royal genealogies, the significance of sacred places, the privileges and obligations of aristocrats, and the laws to memory. The *fili* also acted as social commentators, utilizing their poetic talent to celebrate a patron or disabuse someone who had fallen out of their favor.

CHRISTIANITY

Ireland had not been a part of the Roman Empire as had Britain, but commercial contact had existed. There were also occasional Irish raids on Roman Britain, especially in search of slaves. One such slave captured in the early fifth century was a young man named Patrick, of Roman-Briton background, whose father was a deacon in the Christian Church. Patrick spent six years in captivity during which he regained the religious faith of his youth. Following a voice in a dream alerting him that a ship would take him home, he escaped, traveled twenty miles, came upon the ship, and did ultimately return home. Then a message in another dream urged him to return to Ireland. Before doing so he studied for the priesthood and became a bishop. He came back to convert thousands of the Irish to Christianity. Patrick was not the only Christian missionary to Ireland and there were Christians in Ireland before him. Furthermore, he scarcely converted all the Irish—large numbers, even some nominally Christian converts, continued to adhere to pre-Christian beliefs for sometime afterward. More than likely, his mission was concentrated in the northern half of the island as the present provinces of Munster and Leinster probably had Christian communities preceding Patrick. But his impact must have been of some significance to warrant the subsequent hagiography, which titles him Apostle to the Irish. The island would never be the same. Within a few centuries Ireland became a major center for the study and preservation of religious and classical thought in a Europe where the Roman Empire had disintegrated, to be replaced by political and social disorder and economic retrogression.

The Bard, with harp, kneeling in front of St. Patrick. Engraving by Joseph Hoey *(Library of Congress)*

Important social factors inhibited the effort of churchmen to duplicate in Ireland the institutional and disciplinary structure of the European continent. There the leaders of the church were the bishops, who ruled dioceses centered in cities, as had the local political authorities in the Roman Empire. Because Ireland had no cities, it was difficult to apply the same pattern. The territorial boundaries of the *tuatha* were often in flux as their people were relatively mobile or migratory. Such a situation was not amenable to a diocesan ecclesiastical structure. In addition, *ri,* the local rulers, were amenable neither to alienating property within the *tuath* to outsiders nor to allowing outsiders to occupy positions within. It was expected that the occupants of church property and office should come from within the *tuatha* and be kinfolk of the previous occupant. Rulers found it more to their liking to endow monastic settlements as a means of guaranteeing the exclusion of outside influences. Furthermore, to the degree both that monasteries were located within a *tuatha* and that the founder or leader enjoyed celebrity status, abbots began to assume a position of significance or importance in the church exceeding that of the bishop, who became more confined to the sanctifying rather than the ruling functions of his office.

Irish monasticism was eremitic, similar to that found in the eastern Mediterranean in its emphasis on asceticism and isolation, and unlike the highly disciplined settlements that would draw their founding inspiration during the late sixth and early seventh centuries from the rule of St. Benedict. Paradoxically, that very isolation drew followers that led inevitably to communities, but communities of individualized cells. A classic example of this pursuit of hermitage and closeness to God in a remote and inaccessible place was the celebrated Skellig Michael, a monastic settlement whose cells remain intact today 700 feet above sea level on a remote rocky island seven miles off the coast of Kerry in southwest Ireland. Irish monasticism retained this character until the arrival of continental influences during the High Middle Ages. The sixth century saw the appearance of a multitude of these monasteries, among the more notable that of Clonard, Clonmacnoise, and Clonfert.

Other distinguishing features of the Irish church included variations in the liturgical calendar and a different tonsure for clergy (the Irish would shave the front half of the head rather than the rear top like the continental monks). Centuries later this would lead a reforming papacy to harbor serious anxieties about the Irish church, especially in view of the persistence of pre-Christian attitudes, particularly with regard to marital codes.

A remarkable feature of the hermetical impulse driving the monks was the inclination to undertake the *peregrinatio,* that is, a pilgrimage for Christ, which would entail wandering across the ocean away from Ireland. One example was the voyage of St. Brendan, which some claim went as far as North America. More significant in their historical impact were the peregrinations of Colm Cille and Columbanus. Colm Cille, a member of the Ui Neills, one of the ruling families of ancient Ireland, led a handful of followers from Derry to Scotland, where he played the same role there as Patrick had in Ireland. Some argue than he, rather than St. Andrew, should be the patron saint of Scotland. His influence would extend down to northern England in contributing to the conversion of the Anglo-Saxons, although at the Council of Whitby in the mid-seventh century the Anglo-Saxon church deferred to the tradition that had emanated from St. Augustine in adopting the Roman model in terms of church organization, liturgy, and discipline.

In the same sixth century that Colm Cille had gone to Scotland, Columbanus led his followers on a pilgrimage to the Continent. His group traveled through Gaul and ultimately reached Bobbio in Italy; Their influence and their settlements also developed in Belgium, Germany, and Switzerland.

The Irish monasteries were noted not just for asceticism but also for learning. They became renowned as schools abroad as well as at home. Bede, the great historian of Anglo-Saxon England, noted how many English went to Ireland to study. The Irish monks became masters of classical Latin, but they also began to write down the Celtic folklore, although blending it with a Christian perspective. The monasteries became the great centers for artistic work, noted especially for producing illuminated manuscripts of the scriptures like the *Book of Durrow* and later the Book of Kells. Perhaps the most famous product of Irish schools who made his way to the continent was John Scotus Eruigena, who remained for a quarter of a century as the chief professor at the school of Emperor Charles the Bald, and who was regarded as one of the leading intellects of the post-Carolingian renaissance of the ninth century. He was pictured on the five-punt note in the Irish currency that was replaced in 2001 by the common European currency. His work included commentaries on the Gospel of St. John and the theology of Boethius. Some suggested his speculative work was heretical, but he insisted on his orthodoxy and his work provided the first great synthesis of theology, one that would not be rivaled until that of Thomas Aquinas in the 13th century.

As mentioned earlier, the monasteries became intertwined with ecclesiastical and political ambitions, as various kings and bishops sought to assert their rival claims of ascendancy. St. Patrick's hagiography developed in connection with the efforts of the See of Armagh to claim ecclesiastical primacy over Kildare and with the Ui Neill claim to the high kingship on the basis of their connection to Tara, a site of remarkable apostolic achievement by Patrick. On a more local basis, patrons of monasteries obviously supported efforts to celebrate saintly figures whose remains were interred on the grounds within their political domain. An inevitable consequence of the development of such secular interests was a certain corruption of the monastic ideal, as evidenced by the tendency of abbots to succeed by inheritance, suggesting that celibacy was not always the rule.

Politically, Ireland remained divided into scores of small kingdoms. But there were various alliances of smaller kingdom under great kings, some of which made rival claims for the high kingship of Ireland. But much of the authority of the greater kings was symbolic and significant only for genealogical reasons. The topographic conditions of the island, with its mountains, forests, and bogs, inhibited much effective and regular communication, never mind political centralization. Ireland lay exposed and, like much of the rest of Western Europe, would fall prey, by the end of the eighth century, to the incursions of the Vikings.

THE VIKINGS

The Scandinavians raided Lambey Island in Dublin Bay in 795 and persisted in their assaults for another half century. A primary objective were the monasteries, where they sought precious metals and jewels. Attaching no value to books, they destroyed them. When they found no treasure, they took food and slaves. They also took venerated items, such as relics, and individuals for ransom. They had attacked Colm Cille's settlement, Iona, in northern Scotland, Bangor, and Skelligs. They even traveled inland, attacking and sacking places like Armagh. Norse fleets appeared on the Boyne, the Liffey, and the Shannon. Dread of the Vikings prompted lamentations and prayers such as "From the fury of the Northmen deliver us O Lord," which evocation would be repeated elsewhere in Western Europe for more than a century. The destruction of so many monasteries in Ireland by the Vikings forced many Irish monks to transfer to the Continent, where, like John Scotus, they assumed positions of importance as scholars and missionaries. This flight to continental Europe might have diminished the glories of monasticism in Ireland itself. Significantly, the Irish monks on the Continent began to accept the Benedictine rule and the ascendancy of the episcopacy.

By the middle of the ninth century, the Vikings began to winter in Ireland and establish permanent settlements. Those who arrived first concentrated along the east coast in primarily military outposts from which to launch raids elsewhere. In some cases the Vikings brought their own women to these settlements, but eventually there was a certain amount of intermarriage with Irish women. Likewise, there was even a certain degree of cooperation or collaboration with Irish chieftains who did not feel necessarily loyal to other Irish chieftains, especially if they believed alliance with the Vikings would be to their individual benefit in terms of expansion of territory or riches. The final stage of integration or permanency would be the Vikings' acceptance of Christianity. Possibly the most significant or lasting contribution of the Vikings to Irish history was the gradual transformation of their military settlements into the first Irish cities. Places like Dublin, Limerick, Waterford, Wexford, and Cork owe their origins to the Vikings. Traders, who brought commercial life to a primarily agrarian island, came after the Viking raiders. Significantly, the use of coinage followed the Viking settlement. On the other hand, the cultural contributions were minimal. Few words of Viking origin remain, and there were not significant Viking influences in artistic work.

Paradoxically, the greatest contribution of the Vikings might well have been the reaction to them by some Irish kings, who utilized the struggle against them to enhance the concept of high king and even the idea of an Irish nation. This occurred at about the end of the first millennium when the Vikings had increasingly accepted the Christian religion of the Irish. The central figure in this development was the heroic figure Brian Boru, whom legend and history have combined to magnify as someone comparable to Alfred the Great of Anglo-Saxon England as the savior or liberator of the nation from the Vikings. Of course, the story is somewhat more complex and less ideal. Brian Boru was of the Dal Cais, a Munster royal family that challenged the power of a Viking ruler in Limerick as well as the Eoganacht kings of Cashel, who traditionally had been matched only by the Ui Neill of the North in rank. Brian's ambitions might have been prompted by the treacherous murder of his brother, whom he had succeeded. At any rate, during the last quarter of the 10th century he had gained such ascendancy over various other kingdoms in Ireland that even the Ui Neill formally acknowledged him as the over-king of the southern half of the island, and ultimately as the high king of all Ireland, noting in the precious Book of Armagh, on the occasion of Brian's visit there in 1005, that he was the emperor of the Irish.

In 1014 Brian went on the offensive against the king of Leinster and a Viking king, both of whom refused to acknowledge his supremacy. In the fierce Battle of Clontarf on Good Friday 1014, in which there were many casualties and in which most of the leaders, including Brian himself, were killed, the Irish won. That victory might well have inhibited a possible renewed Viking assault on the island, as the year before the king of Denmark had conquered England (his son Canute would later be king of England), and a great Viking fleet had raided Munster. Also, although the high kingship remained more theoretical than real, it was on the way to becoming a reality. In less than two centuries that reality would come about, but it would be exercised by King Henry II of England. Before then the Irish church would experience the reforming currents then at work in the continental church.

Earlier, in the seventh and eight centuries, Ireland was in the forefront of intellectual and cultural development in a retrogressive Europe. However, by the 11th and 12th centuries, the island had become a backwater to which the creative and reforming energies of the Continent were barely making their way. Central to what was happening in Europe was the growing ascendancy within the church of the reform party, which sought, in the spirit of the monk Hildebrand, later Pope Gregory VII, to free the church from secular dominance, that is, from private or familial control of church offices and property. The specific offenses fought against were simony, the sale of offices, and lay investiture, the awarding of church offices, such as bishoprics and abbacies, by political figures rather than by church authorities. A reinvigorated papacy, no longer selected by the nobility of Rome, but instead by a more universal electoral body, the College of Cardinals, was able to assume the reforming task. However, to rid itself of control by secular leaders, the church had to rely on other secular leaders, who, over time, would prove as troublesome to the church. At the time, the leaders most likely to respond to the desire to free the church from control by local leaders were kings or national monarchs who were increasingly asserting their own authority against more localized feudal lords. Unfortunately, despite Brian Boru's achievements, the high kings of Ireland, or any of the rival claimants to the title, were nowhere near neither the kings of France or England nor the Holy Roman Emperor in being able to assert any centralized authority.

The church in Ireland also languished in a pattern of weakened bishops and abbots greatly dependent on local kings and holding titles by reason of family. In addition, the century and a half of Viking plunder had diminished the spiritual and cultural grandeur of Irish monasticism. Significantly, the earlier moves in the direction of the continental reform movement within Ireland occurred in dioceses, such as Dublin and Waterford, that were settlements of by now Christian Vikings. There the reforming archbishop of Canterbury, Lanfranc, and his later successor, Anselm, had consecrated the bishops. The ascendancy of the reforming party in England had followed the conquest of England by William the Conqueror of Normandy in 1066. That conquest began the completion of feudalization in England, but in a manner that augmented the centralizing authority of the national monarch. In the 11th century the reforming party advanced in Ireland. The reform cause benefited from the sympathy of Turloch O'Connor, the king of Connacht, who now wielded as much ascendant power as high king as had Brian Boru a century and a half before. He presided over the Synod of Kells in 1152, which advanced the organizational and disciplinary reform of the church in Ireland in accord with the spirit desired by the papacy.

The churchman most connected with this was the archbishop of Armagh, Malachy (St. Malachy), who had gone to Rome several years before seeking formal papal acceptance of his title to the office. On his way to Rome he met St. Bernard of Clairvaux, the leader of the reforming monastic order of Cistercians, whom he informed of the church's situation in Ireland. The pope, Innocent II, was willing to acknowledge Malachy's position, but only after a national synod in which the reforms would be implemented. That synod, which occurred after Malachy's death, finally took place with Turloch O'Connor's approval. It organized the Irish church into 36 dioceses and four archbishoprics, Armagh, Cashel, Tuam, and Dublin, and the administrative arrangement was acknowledged by Rome. Even before the synod, Malachy had brought with him a band of Cistercians who established their monastery in Mellifont, the first Gothic structure in Ireland. From then on European-style monastic organization began to take hold in Ireland.

THE NORMANS

However, a strong central political authority, which usually accompanied the triumph of the reforming party of the church elsewhere, did not exist in Ireland.

Murcertach MacLochlain of Ulster successfully challenged Turloch's son, Rory, for the high kingship. However, when MacLochlain was killed in a battle with some of his discontented subkings, O'Connor raised his claim again in 1166. This disorder gave the occasion for Dermot MacMurrough, the king of Leinster, who had supported the MacLochlain claims, to seek satisfaction against an antagonist, Tiernan O'Rourke, king of Breifne (Leitrim), whose wife MacMurrough had earlier abducted. He went abroad seeking allies, first in the person of Henry II, the king of England. Henry, whose domain included more than a third of France, and who was the great-grandson of William the Conqueror, had too full a plate at the time, including difficulties with his own churchman, Thomas à Becket. However, MacMurrough secured assistance from Richard FitzGilbert de Clare (Strongbow), a vassal of Henry's in Wales. He sent some Norman-Welsh knights with names like FitzGerald and Barry back to Ireland with MacMurrough and came himself three years later, in 1170, with 1,200 men. Part of the price for his coming was the hand of MacMurrough's daughter, Eva.

FitzGilbert was a marcher lord in Wales, which meant that he and his like, while vassals of Henry II, had much greater autonomy than their counterparts in England because Wales was viewed as a separate territory, still in the process of being conquered. That autonomy would later worry Henry II when this vassal would have great success in Ireland, successfully defending MacMurrough and, upon his death, succeeding him as king of Leinster. This fact, coupled with the autonomy of Wales, caused Henry to suspect that FitzGilbert might turn his conquests in Ireland into something comparable to what Henry's great-grandfather, William the Conqueror, had done a century before. William had transformed himself from being the duke of Normandy and a vassal of the king of France into becoming king of England, which position would in time seriously challenge the French monarchy. Rather than allow history to repeat itself, Henry II decided to come to Ireland himself in October 1171, with a force of 3,500 men.

The Irish kings soon received Henry as "Lord of Ireland," who could protect them against the Norman-Welsh. Henry was able to base his claim to the title on a bull issued by Pope Adrian IV (the only English pope in history) authorizing him to assert his position over Ireland in order to control the undisciplined church of the island. Significantly, even Rory O'Connor, in the treaty of Windsor of 1175, which was promoted by Lawrence O'Toole (St. Lawrence O'Toole), the archbishop of Dublin, accepted Henry as his lord, while Henry acknowledged Rory's position as *ard-ri,* which gave him the authority to collect from the other Irish kings tributes that were due annually to Henry. Henry's minimal interest in Ireland, other than inhibiting his Norman-Welsh vassals there from becoming too powerful or independent, was manifest in his transfer of the lordship to one of his sons, John, while he was still a child. John made only two visits to Ireland: in 1185, 14 years before he acceded to the throne, and in 1210, when he sought to contain his barons in Ireland. He was less successful when he attempted to do the same four years later in England and had to acquiesce, in the Magna Carta, to baronial restrictions on his powers.

The visit to Ireland in 1210 by John was to be the last by an English king or "Lord of Ireland" until Richard II came over in 1394. This would suggest that

English authority over Ireland was more nominal than real. However, within Ireland, the power and domain of the Normans was extending itself. Theoretically the territory under their domain was to be governed by English law. That legal system and its various institutions, such as parliament, had developed in England at the behest of the kings. It replaced traditional, customary, or folk law with a mixture of feudal and royal law. Ultimately, the law and its institutions would be employed to restrain the king.

To some degree this constitutional evolution was copied in Ireland, including even the formation of an Irish parliament. But this occurred only in the areas under Norman control, and often only in a limited portion of that area, specifically the territory extending a few score miles out from Dublin. Significantly, the first Irish parliament, summoned in 1297, drew its members from the Normans and its will was effective only in the territory they controlled. Within that territory, areas were divided into shires or counties, as in England, with sheriffs, shire courts, and itinerant justices applying the "common law." There was substantial immigration of many Normans to Ireland, accompanied by significant development of towns, castles, cathedrals, and roads, as well as commerce.

LATER MEDIEVAL IRELAND

In effect, the island was developing into two separate communities, the Irish and the Normans. Nonetheless, many of the Norman barons who had persisted in further conquest loosened themselves from the English law, intermarried with the natives whom they had conquered, and soon became "more Irish than the Irish" with regard to English law, and even began to adapt the existing Gaelic system for their own purposes. Many territories still remained under the dominance of Irish kings and there the Irish law and custom prevailed. But within some Norman communities, specifically what became known as the "Pale," a territory of varying size at different periods of history, there was a general disregard for the Irish, who were regarded as less than civilized. There the benefit of the law was not extended to the Irish, even if they were of a free status. Even within the church there was internal segregation in the religious orders between Irish and Norman congregations. The older Celtic system of monasticism was declining before the influx of the orders structured on the Benedictine model and the new mendicant orders, such as the Dominicans and the Franciscans, to which both the Irish and the Normans were drawn.

The Anglo-Normanization of Ireland, with the appearance of counties and officials such as sheriffs, received a setback in 1315 when Edward Bruce, the brother of the king of Scotland, landed in Antrim. Donal O'Neill, the king of Ulster and claimant for the title of high king of Ireland, deferred to Bruce's claim. During the severe warfare that ensued, Bruce's forces won many battles, but the lack of unity among his allies, some of whom sought to enhance their own claims against either other Irish or the Normans, inhibited it from becoming a national resistance. Bruce himself was killed three years later.

Forestalling the threat from Bruce was not followed by an enhancement of the Norman position in Ireland. Gaelic chieftains reconquered some territory and more Normans, such as the de Brughs in Connacht who became Burkes, were Gaelicized. Social disorder and the onset of the Black Death, the plague that decimated the European population in the 14th century, discouraged immigration and even encouraged reverse migration back to England. The phenomenon, so frequent in Irish history, of absenteeism began to develop. Vassals of the king who had been given territories in Ireland remained aloof from them, other than securing their own personal profit, but they abandoned any effort at exercising their public duties, especially that of gathering revenue for the crown.

So serious was the situation that an Irish parliament, moved by fear and a sense of siege, met in Kilkenny in 1366 and passed a series of celebrated, notorious statutes, which from a modern perspective appear racist and exclusivist. The laws forbade Normans from engaging in private warfare within the Norman (or English) area, entering into marriage alliances or alliances based on fostering of children between the Normans and the Irish, using Irish names, dress, or law, and speaking the Irish language within Norman territories. The segregation pattern was also reinforced within the church. Normans who had adapted to Irish customs and language were regarded as "degenerate English."[1] But even the Normans, or English in Ireland, began to be looked on as different from the English in England, where a distinction was increasingly drawn between the English born in England and those born in Ireland, which worked to the disadvantage of the latter.

The English nobility in Ireland were pulled two ways. On one hand, they emphasized their distinction from the Gaelic Irish and continually expressed disappointment at the failure of the king and the authorities in England to give them needed monetary and military support. On the other hand, they had a sense of autonomy and were resentful at any English interference. In a very premature way they were formulating a constitutional theory of a distinct kingdom of Ireland.

An example of some royal interest in Irish developments was Edward III's designation of Lionel, the duke of Clarence, his second son, as lieutenant and supreme governor for Ireland. He arrived in 1361 with a thousand men, the cost of which was born by the English exchequer. He had success in regaining some territories lost to the Gaelic kings. It was during his sojourn in Ireland that the ominous statutes of Kilkenny were passed. For the rest of the 14th century the English monarchy continued to supply substantial subsidies and armed men to Ireland.

In 1394 and 1399 King Richard II came to Ireland. His first visit brought significant military victories. Many of the Irish chieftains swore oaths of "liege homage" to him, and some were knighted. Richard categorized the factions in Ireland into three groups, "the wild Irish our enemies, Irish rebels, and obedient Englishmen." The middle group consisted of the great majority of the Irish chieftains who had submitted, while the wild Irish were those few, like O'Donnell, who had not submitted. Many of the Irish chieftains even visited the king

---

[1] From this point we will refer to the Normans, their descendants, and others who followed them to Ireland as English. We will reserve the use of the term Anglo-Irish until dealing with those whose roots in Ireland start in the 16th and 17th centuries.

in England when he returned there. However, not long after, English nobles in Ireland attacked many of the Irish leaders. The king aimed to return to Ireland to resolve the difficulties. However, his return was delayed until 1399 because of threatened rebellion in England. When he did come with a large and well-equipped army, he still met considerable opposition. Then an invasion of England by the supporters of Henry, duke of Lancaster, drew him home again. The invaders were successful and Richard was executed.

Preoccupation with continental wars, in which the English king ultimately lost title over all territory except Calais, inhibited the Lancastrian monarchs from devoting much attention to Ireland. During the period from 1399 to 1461, Gaelic chieftains made a significant reassertion of their position. The territory where "English law" prevailed was significantly reduced. That territory, the "Pale," had shrunk to the area emanating from Dublin northward only to Dundalk, westward to Kells and Trim, and southward to just below Dublin. Significant territories outside the Pale were under the control of English lords, such as FitzGerald of Desmond in Munster, Butler of Ormonde in Kilkenny, Burke of Clanricard and Burke of Mayo in Connacht, who had integrated into Gaelic society. The drawn out Wars of the Roses, that is, the rivalry for the English monarchy between the houses of Lancaster and of York, made the claimants

Kilkenny Castle is one of the most recognized buildings in Ireland. The Butler family bought the castle in 1391 and lived there until 1935. They were the earls and dukes of Ormonde.
(Library of Congress)

for the throne heavily dependent on certain great lords and the substantial military forces they could provide. It was a reversal of the feudal ideal whereby the king's vassals were expected to provide designated amounts of warriors when needed. Now, the claimants for the monarchy had to beseech the support of mighty vassals who were virtually monarchs in their own right. The same situation applied in Ireland, and those who particularly gained from the turmoil in England were the Butlers of Ormond, who identified with the Lancaster side and the FitzGeralds, especially the FitzGeralds of Kildare, who generally supported the Yorkists.

Edward IV, the first Yorkist king, in 1467 sent John Tibetot, the earl of Worcester, as lieutenant in Ireland with the task of reasserting Edward's title as Lord of Ireland, and subduing even the semi-independent lords who had supported him. For instance, the earl of Desmond was attained and beheaded. The execution backfired as the Desmond Geraldines henceforth permanently identified with the Irish rather than the English. Subsequently, Edward was confronted by a Lancastrian revival in England. He retained control but became more conciliatory in his Irish policy, relying increasingly on the FitzGeralds of Kildare, who subsequently became more powerful than the nominal lieutenants. Perhaps the greatest of these was Gerald, or Garret, Mor, almost the virtual king of Ireland from 1477 until 1513.

In that period changes in the English monarchy would result in the appearance of a modern national monarchy and state, both in England and in Ireland. Centralization in Ireland would clash with the traditional Gaelic social order. But the English in Ireland would also be hostile to modernization and its agents, the "New English," especially since the Protestant Reformation was an integral part of the modernizing process. England's acceptance of the Reformation and her growing international power put her at odds with Catholic continental powers. The latter would consider the feasibility of employing Ireland as a backdoor to assaulting England, which prompted greater English assertion of control in Ireland. Some in England also championed aggressive colonization, that is, plantation and resettlement of Ireland, as would be done in America, with the native Irish being depicted as savages.

ANGLICIZATION OF IRELAND
1485–1603

THE KILDARE ASCENDANCY, 1477–1535

The earls of Kildare, especially Garret Mor (1477–1513) and his son, Garret Og (1513–34), were regarded in some ways as the virtual rulers of Ireland. But if so, it was the triumph before the fall, as immediately after their deaths the process of complete colonization by the English monarchy began. As indicated in the previous chapter, Kildare had benefited from the internal disorder in England that inhibited any extended effort by English monarchs to assert greater authority in Ireland. On the other hand, the English kings realized that what degree of authority they might have could be exercised only with the connivance of Kildare. Kildare was able to provide such assistance because of the remarkable authority and following he had among both many of the English nobility in Ireland and many of the Irish chieftains.

Soon after Garret Mor had succeeded his father Thomas in 1477, King Edward IV, now very much the successful master in England after the decisive defeat of the Lancasters a few years earlier, sought to appoint lieutenants to act for him in Ireland in place of Kildare. However, Kildare's dominance of the Irish council made the efforts of the king's appointee futile and the king acquiesced in Kildare's remaining deputy. In his short reign, King Richard III sought seriously to undermine Kildare by attempting contacts with other Anglo-Irish lords and even Irish leaders. However, the success of Henry Tudor at the Battle of Bosworth removed Richard's threat to Kildare's position. The new king, Henry VII, despite his familial ties to the Lancasters and his marital ties to the Yorkists, was not without serious challenges to his claim to the throne. Even though the king had recognized him as deputy, Garret Mor agreed in 1487 to support the claim to the throne by one of those pretenders, a 10-year-old boy named Lambert Simnel, who was purported to be Edward, earl of Warwick, and true heir to the throne. A large German mercenary force had come to Ireland in support of the pretender and was augmented by substantial Irish forces. The pretender was formally crowned in Christ Church Cathedral, Dublin, as Edward VI, king of England and Ireland (in contrast to the title Lord of Ireland). However, his forces were defeated when they invaded England. Garret Mor's brother lost his life in the battle. Nonetheless, Garret Mor was able to maintain his deputyship, even being entertained by the king in England (where it was claimed the young pretender, who was consigned to work in royal kitchens, waited on the table).

Several years later another pretender, Perkin Warbeck, appeared in Ireland claiming to be the duke of York. The earl of Desmond, and possibly Kildare, supported him for a while, but he was ultimately unsuccessful, being captured in 1497 and executed two years later. Henry VII had clearly become determined to inhibit Ireland from becoming a base from which to challenge his throne. He continued to work through Kildare, as well as the earl of Ormond (Kildare's rival), but he also appointed an Englishman named Edward Poynings as deputy. Poynings, with the aid of Kildare, won military successes against some Irish leaders. More permanent were his political achievements. He convened an Irish parliament, which it was hoped would make Ireland pay for itself, that is, support the English military presence. This proved futile, but more significant, a parliament in Drogheda in 1494 passed what became know as Poynings' Law, which required royal consent for the calling of any Irish parliament and required approval by the king and his council before any bill could be introduced for consideration by an Irish parliament. Afterward, the parliaments began to meet infrequently, often years between sessions, in contrast to an initial pattern of almost annual gatherings. It must be remembered, of course, that the parliaments were scarcely democratic institutions, but rather were drawn from a limited portion of the island's population and selected by a very limited electorate.

However, Henry VII, always financially prudent and disinclined to make great demands on the fiscal resources of England (where his own title was on possibly questionable grounds) and aware of the enormous cost of direct military control or conquest of Ireland, fell back on the policy of relying on Kildare as his agent in Ireland. Garret Mor was reappointed deputy in 1496. Henry even gave his own cousin, Elizabeth St. John, as a wife to the widower Kildare, as he realized that "since all Ireland cannot rule this man, this man must rule all Ireland." Kildare himself practiced the technique of diplomatic marriages as his sister was married to one of the leading Irish chieftains, Conn More O'Neill, and his daughters were married to a mixture of English and Irish lords, including even a Butler. Garret Mor was more than just a warrior leader of rival chieftains in a politically disunited Ireland. He was also a man of some culture as manifested by his library and his patronage of various churches and cathedrals. He died from gunshot wounds in 1513 and was succeeded by his son, Garret Og. The son had spent his formative years at the English royal court in an arrangement not very different from the Irish practice of fosterage. Also he was married to a royal ward.

The young king Henry VIII, who had been crowned in 1509, confirmed Garret Og as deputy. However, before long, the king, prompted especially by his adviser, Cardinal Wolsey, began to be suspicious of the "Irish" practices being tolerated by his deputy. Several times he summoned Garret Og to England to explain why he made concessions to certain Irish practices in the governance of Ireland. Henry was particularly anxious about reported contacts between the earl of Desmond and continental rulers, especially since Garret Og had contact with Desmond. Accordingly, he sent Thomas Howard, the earl of Surrey, to Ireland as lieutenant, a post not occupied since 1460, to bring the Irish lords to "obedience" and "observance of our laws." Surrey brought with him 700 soldiers and was able to quickly secure submissions from several Irish chieftains, including O'Neill and O'Donnell in Ulster. Ultimately, he realized his task was impossible except by conquest, which could require 6,000 men, the construction of new towns, castles, and a program of colonization by English settlers. This was more than Henry was willing to attempt at the time, given various continental preoccupations. Accordingly, Surrey returned to England.

For the next decade the king deferred taking any direct action regarding Ireland. Instead, he played upon the rivalry of the Geraldines and the Butlers by having them serve alternately as deputy. The king became enamored of Anne Boleyn, a relation of the Butlers. Her father had gained the title of earl of Ormond, which required the resident Butler, Piers Roe, to accept compensation in the form of the title of earl of Ossory. The king's infatuation would set in motion a chain of events, including his suit for an annulment of his marriage with Catherine of Aragon, the replacement of his chief minister, Cardinal Wolsey, who had failed to secure papal agreement for the annulment, the rise to power of Thomas Cromwell, and Henry's break with the Church of Rome. Cromwell was an advocate of firmer assertion of royal authority in Ireland, as it had been developed in England. In other words, he espoused the "new politics," which called for governance by royal servants, rather than the occasional cooperation of quasi-independent lords kept somewhat in line by almost autonomous deputies like the Geraldines of Kildare.

In February 1534, after Henry had married Anne Boleyn and had broken with the church, Garret Og came to England in response to a summons for

Lord Thomas Fitzgerald renounces his allegiance to Henry VIII, 1534. *(Mary Evans Picture Library)*

allegedly plotting treason. His cousin, James, the earl of Desmond, was already communicating with the kings of France and Spain. Garret Og designated his son Thomas to act as his deputy in his absence. A few months later the impetuous Thomas, hearing that his father was liable to be killed, threw down the gauntlet by resigning his office of state, denouncing Henry VIII as a heretic, ordering all Englishmen from his territory, and demanding oaths of allegiance to the Holy Roman Emperor, the pope, and himself. When word came to London, Henry had Garret Mor imprisoned in the Tower, where he died three months later. By then outright rebellion was well underway in Ireland with the king's authority almost destroyed. Then Sir William Skeffington, whom the king had sometime earlier made the deputy for Ireland, arrived with an army of 2,300 men.

The confrontation then assumed a new character. No longer was it simply an attempt to reassert the authority of the king as "lord" of Ireland over various Irish lords, whether English Irish or Irish. Instead, it was an attempt to impose the engines of the modern state on the hitherto loose, almost anarchic, system with its shifting arrangements of authority and uncertain patterns of succession. The English state now committed itself fully in terms of money and manpower to the achievement of control. This time the goal was not to look to the eventual acquiescence or submission of Irish lords, who in turn would be restored to authority as the king's men. Rather, new English servants or officials would enforce his will and his law.

The war lasted about a year. Skeffington's modern weaponry, especially artillery, was telling in the outcome. Many of Thomas's allies withdrew from the campaign. His own fortress, Maynooth, fell and he surrendered the following August. This time the traditional practice of pardon and reinstatement was not followed. Instead, a year and a half later, after things in Ireland had calmed and royal authority was in the ascendancy, Thomas, his five uncles, and nearly 100 others were hung and beheaded. However, a Geraldine resistance persisted for a few years after. Its instigator was Manus O'Donnell of Donegal, whose wife was a FitzGerald and aunt of Gerald, the youthful nephew of Silken Thomas and Kildare heir, who was on the Continent. A new alliance of many Irish lords had successfully invaded the Pale. However, they were routed by the forces of the new deputy, Lord Leonard Grey, when they withdrew with substantial booty in cattle. An ideology, which envisioned O'Neill as high king of Ireland and a restored earl of Kildare as his vassal, had inspired this movement. There was also opposition to Henry's attempt to extend his policy of religious reformation to Ireland. However, the criticism of the English as "heretics" might have been leveled more for popular consumption than real concern.

THE NEW TUDOR MONARCHY IN IRELAND

By 1541 Henry, convinced that his ascendancy in Ireland would be advanced more by conciliation than by conquest, replaced Grey with Sir Anthony St. Leger as deputy. However, the conciliation would be on his terms rather than on Irish terms. An instrument used by the king in winning over the Irish chieftains, as well as the "Old English"[2] lords, was the availability of land that had been taken from Kildare and other Geraldines still in rebellion. As he did in England, Henry used parliament to ratify his designs. A new Irish parliament met in 1541. In attendance in its House of Lords were representatives from families that had long been absent as well as native Irish lords, who hitherforce would not have been eligible to attend. This parliament acknowledged Henry, and his successors, to be "for evermore Kings of Ireland."

The same parliament passed legislation governing the policy of "Surrender and Regrant," by which a Gaelic lord would acknowledge the king's authority over his territory. In return he would be regranted the territory and awarded a title. This situation would put the Irish lords in the same relationship with the king and his law as the Anglo-Irish lords, with right to his courts and the full protection of his law. It would replicate in Ireland the situation in England whereby all land in theory was the king's, but by which the individual occupier held title in return for fulfilling certain obligations to the king, originally military but increasingly financial. Succession to the land was by primogeniture, that is, to the eldest male as heir.

This system contrasted with the native Irish, or Brehon, law concept that the land belonged to the family, or sept, and succession to it was determined by election from among the near relatives of the incumbent. As so often happens in history, acceptance of the new arrangement was often nominal, or at least until a serious dispute of inheritance would arise whereby one party might claim the traditional system to enhance his claim. However, at first, the policy seemed to be effective, as most Irish lords accepted it. Conn O'Neill, the Ulster ruler who held pretensions to become high king of Ireland, accepted the title of earl of Tyrone; Murrough O'Brien became earl of Thomond and Baron Inchiquin, and even James Fitzmaurice FitzGerald, a future earl of Desmond, served for a time as court page at Windsor, where he was educated.

Several years before, that other component of the Henrician revolution in government, the religious reformation, also obtained sanction from an Irish parliament. Meeting in 1537, the Act of Supremacy was passed declaring the king to be the supreme head of the Church of Ireland, which all church and state officeholders were required to accept. Probably a majority of the bishops took the oath of supremacy, but most of the faithful remained unaware of the full implications of what was happening. In most places, aside from the Pale, the liturgy and religious practices remained the same, including the Latin liturgy. However, another aspect of Henry's Reformation policy, the dissolution of the monasteries, was not as easily put in motion in Ireland. Opposition was based as much on private or familial interest in monasteries as on religious scruples. Individual families often controlled monasteries, and some abbots held their position by hereditary succession, as many clergy were not particularly observant of church rules of clerical celibacy.

The Reformation in Ireland differed from that in England, and elsewhere. Ireland had not experienced outbursts of heretical thought and agitation, nor were church or clerical abuses a source of popular displeasure, not that they

---

[2] With the arrival of so many "New English" as royal officials and settlers in Ireland, it is appropriate henceforth to refer to the descendants of the Normans and other medieval arrivals in Ireland as the "Old English."

did not exist. This meant that a reformation, if it came about, would have to be something imposed from above and outside rather than based on any domestic, even if minority, demand. But while there was no or minimal zeal for religious change, the opposition to change was not particularly founded on religious enthusiasm, but possibly more on self-interest. To the degree that the Reformation remained superficial and did not really affect everyday life it met little resistance. After all, had not the popes historically been supportive of the assertion of English authority in Ireland as a means of advancing church reform? Was there any difference now, other than that the reform program of the English sought to disconnect the church in Ireland from the papacy?

However much he challenged papal ascendancy, Henry VIII was a very orthodox Catholic in terms of doctrine. It would be during the short reign of his son, Edward VI, still a minor but under the direction of Edward Seymour, the duke of Somerset, that a more substantial church reformation would be extended to Ireland, such as the attempt to put in use the 1549 Book of Common Prayer. The latter provoked the resignation of George Dowdall, the pro–royal supremacy archbishop of Armagh, who equated the new prayer book with the abolition of the Mass. Only a few reforming enthusiasts were supportive, such as the Englishman who was archbishop of Dublin, George Browne, whereas most nobles, whether Old English or Irish, stood in opposition.

In Edward's reign, St. Leger, who had successfully applied, at least superficially, the "Surrender and Regrant" policy, was replaced by Edmund Bellingham, a soldier committed to a military solution for Ireland and supportive of further religious reformation. To the latter end, the Book of Common Prayer was made available for the abolition of "idolatry, papacy and the like." A more Protestant Second Book of Common Prayers in 1552 called for substantial changes in liturgy and rites. Bellingham used his military energies to combat renewed rebellion by two of the Irish chieftains, O'Connor and O'More, both of whom, after fighting in Kildare, Leix, and Offaly, were forced to surrender. Their territories in Offaly and Leix were confiscated, which would allow the introduction of a new approach to the treatment of Ireland: plantation, which meant the occupation and resettlement of land taken from the Irish.

The process of plantation was slowly being readied when Edward died and was succeeded by his half sister, Mary, a Catholic and the daughter of Henry's first wife, Catherine of Aragon. The superficiality of the reformation in England, as well as Ireland, was shown by the readiness with which she was accepted. However, for her part, she shrewdly did not undo reformation measures, such as the dissolution of the monasteries, which had created new special interests on the part of those who had gained what had been church properties. But she did allow the prosecution of many radical Protestants, which created a martyrology for Protestantism in Britain. Within Ireland she was as concerned as any of her predecessors with asserting her authority. She did reappoint St. Leger as deputy, removed the diehard Protestant Browne as archbishop of Dublin, and even allowed the exiled pretender to the earldom of Kildare, Gerald, to return, although the Kildare Geraldines never recovered their old political ascendancy.

However, it was under Mary that the system of plantation was first implemented. Surveys were made of the O'Connor and O'More territories of Offaly and Leix, and a grand jury declared the lands of "traitors" to be forfeited and vested in the Crown. The procedure of plantation, which would be repeated for the next century and a half in Ireland, allowed native owners to retain one-third of the territory with the remainder being made available to settlers, who were to be Englishmen or Englishmen born in Ireland, on specific terms, such as recruiting English servants and providing troops to the deputy. It must be remembered that the displacement of owners involved the aristocratic class and not the ordinary people, who remained as peasant laborers in varying degrees of servitude. The territories of Offaly and Leix so planted were renamed Kings County and Queens County, respectively, in honor of Queen Mary and her husband, Philip, the king of Spain. Even the ousted Irish chieftains were not entirely displaced as landowners. However, the position of being landlord, holding land according to English law, was a far cry from having been a local king, ruling a whole sept, and having a title subject to Brehon rules of succession rather than primogeniture. Naturally, they persisted in intermittent opposition to the new order for decades after.

ELIZABETHAN REFORMATION

Mary died in 1558 and was succeeded by her half sister Elizabeth, Henry's child by Anne Boleyn. Elizabeth was a *politique,* that is, she was someone who placed royal prerogatives in the political order above religious or traditional considerations. While she was not moved by Protestant principles and could tolerate accommodation with Catholics, the maintenance of her ascendancy in all her realm was her first concern and that required her maintenance of supremacy in the church. Accordingly, in Ireland she had the lord lieutenant, the earl of Sussex, summon a parliament, which in less than a month imposed the complete reformation on the church in Ireland. Significantly, unlike the Irish parliaments in Henry's time, there were almost no Gaelic peers in attendance and a substantial number of the bishops were absent. Even the territorial representatives who made up the House of Commons came largely from only 10 counties, primarily in Leinster, and 28 towns. Ulster and Connacht were all but unrepresented. The parliament passed an Act of Supremacy, which stated that the queen was the head on earth of the Church of Ireland. All officeholders in church and state, all mayors of towns, all those taking university degrees, and all tenants in chief of the queen (that is, all lords including those who had gained their land and title as a consequence of "Surrender and Regrant") were required to take an oath acknowledging her status. Also passed was an Act of Uniformity, which imposed the new Book of Common Prayer on all the clergy, made English the language of the prayer book, and made attendance at the state church compulsory on pain of a fine.

These developments worked to change the landscape of loyalties in Ireland and would ultimately draw together, in their allegiance to Catholicism, the Irish and the Old English who had been contesting against each other for centuries. The Old English were especially incensed, as they had been loyal to the Crown, basing their own position on their adherence to English law. The Gaelic chieftains had given periodically their allegiance to the king as "lord" of Ireland, and had gone through the motions of "Surrender and Regrant," but they remained temperamentally committed to the Brehon tradition, with the implications that their holdings belonged to the sept or family and that election rather than primogeniture was the basis of succession. They were warrior chieftains who drew on the feudal contributions and military services of both their subordinates and the common folk, who possessed varying degrees of freedom. In many ways their system was an anachronism, a throwback from the modern world of commerce and settled agriculture that the "New Monarchy" had brought to England and was attempting to bring to Ireland. The Anglo-Irish were better adapted to implement the new system, except for the religious question. Accordingly, their place in public life would increasingly be taken by the "New English," settlers who arrived as civil servants sent over from England and who in course of time became officials, churchmen, and landlords.

This was the period in which the energies of the Counter-Reformation, the Catholic attempt to reform the church and undo the spread of Protestantism, was well underway in Europe. The instrument that was especially employed to that end was education, as it was primarily Catholics who began the schools in Ireland that had been called by an act of 1538 to be set up to promote the English language. In addition, attendance at Catholic colleges on the Continent began, which became a regular pattern for Irish Catholics seeking higher education, especially in preparation for the priesthood. A persistent number of missionaries, especially Jesuits, began to make their way to Ireland to defend the "True Faith," although an earlier Jesuit mission to Ireland in the 1540s had met little response and had to be diverted to Scotland. The work of the other friars, the Franciscans, Dominicans, and Augustinians, also persisted and did much to make Ireland the intensely faithful Catholic nation it would become. The general effect was to make the Act of Uniformity unenforceable in most cases.

SHANE O'NEILL

When Conn O'Neill, one of the more recent claimants to be high king of Ireland, but who had also received the title of earl of Tyrone, died in 1559, his son Shane was the logical successor since his brother Matthew, the designated successor, had predeceased the father. However, Shane refused to hold tenure as vassal to the English Crown, the situation which his father had accepted, preferring instead to be an Irish chieftain. The queen would have preferred therefore that Matthew's son, the baron of Dungannon, receive the title. However, the earl of Sussex, who had been deputy and then elevated to lord lieutenant, suggested first trying diplomacy, even having O'Neill entertained at the royal court in the early part of 1562. Although he gave his submission to the queen, O'Neill, upon returning to Ireland, was unremitting in his adherence to the old ways. Accordingly, three years later, Sir Henry Sidney, who had succeeded Sussex, his brother-in-law, decided a campaign had to be undertaken to bring O'Neill down. He sent a large army into Ulster after him, which had great success but did not capture him. What brought him down in the end was defeat by a rival Irish force, that of O'Donnell of Tyrconnell. When he sought protection from the MacDonnells of Antrim, whom he had defeated a few years earlier, they murdered him. With his death, which was followed by the attainment of his lands by the queen, a second cousin, Turloch O'Neill, the Tanist, succeeded as the Gaelic chieftain. The queen also acquiesced to his ascendancy in Tyrone, although Shane's young nephew, Hugh, who had been rescued and brought to London after Turloch had killed his brother Brian, remained her ultimate favorite for the earldom. Paradoxically, several decades later, he would come to lead the last great stand of the Gaelic order against her policy of Anglicization.

SECOND GERALDINE REVOLT

Government attention was next directed to the province of Munster, and in particular to the rival Anglo-Norman earls, Ormond and Desmond. At this point the government had to contend with a strengthening of Catholic enthusiasm on the part of many of the Old English. Led by Sir Edmund Butler, they utilized their position in the Irish parliament to weaken anti-Catholic legislation, often at the price of strengthening the process of political centralization and dilution of Gaelic custom. However, when a new step in the Anglicization began, that of establishing presidencies in Connacht and Munster to implement the direct rule of the heretofore quasi-autonomous regions, a second Geraldine revolt ensued. The revolt was provoked both by a combination of land grabbing by English adventurers, such as Sir Walter Raleigh, Sir Humphrey Gilbert, and Sir Peter Carew (who based his claim on a very distant Irish antecedent) and by an enthusiasm for the Catholic Counter-Reformation fueled by papal excommunication of Elizabeth and encouragement to her Catholic subjects to disavow her.

Gerald, the earl of Desmond, was detained in England at the time following his defeat in a struggle over land with the earl of Ormond. His more zealous Catholic cousin, James Fitzmaurice FitzGerald, took his place at home. The previous parliamentary opponent of the reformation, Edmund Butler, joined him in an uprising against both the religious policy and the land grab. Although they were joined in the revolt by other discontented Gaelic families, the rebellion was unsuccessful. The earl of Desmond was allowed to return to Ireland and his cousin went off to the Continent. Sidney had been recalled as lord deputy and resumed a policy of pacification, seeking in particular the consent by the Gaelic and increasingly Gaelicized Old English lords of Connacht, such as the Burkes and Prendergasts, to the new system of laws and titles. Within Connacht, a special court dominated by New English appointees came to dominate the government at the expense of the power of the Anglo-Norman or old English lords of the Pale.

However, on July 18, 1579, James Fitzmaurice FitzGerald landed back in Dingle in Kerry with some soldiers, money, and promises of further assistance from the king of Spain (whose primary attention at the time was taken up in contending with rebellion by Protestants in the Netherlands, who were aided by the English). Basing the rebellion on Pope Gregory XIII's bull of excommunication, he gained the endorsement of the same Gaelic and some Anglo Norman allies who had earlier rebelled. This time the revolt was again suppressed, but more brutally. There was only one instance of Spanish assistance—a force of 700 landed at Smerwick harbor, also in Dingle, in October 1580 and occupied a fort. The new lord deputy, Leonard Grey, and Sir Walter Raleigh successfully besieged the fort and the Spanish were forced to surrender, after which they were massacred. James Fitzmaurice FitzGerald had been killed earlier in the revolt, as were many of the other leaders. Even his cousin, the earl of Desmond, a reluctant participant, lost his life on November 11, 1583.

The suppression of the second Geraldine revolt was followed by a series of Acts of Attainment whereby the lands of Desmond were taken and the province of Munster subjected to plantation. A half million of the 5 million acres of Munster were to be made available to new settlers, who were required to be English. "Undertakers," who were to be granted up to 12,000 acres each, were to recruit English tenants. Much of the awarding of land for plantation was done quite arbitrarily and exploited native and even Anglo-Norman unfamiliarity with the law. However, the poverty of Munster, consequent to the devastation wrought by the war and an ensuing famine, frustrated the major aim of establishing an English population. Many of the Undertakers were unable to recruit English settlers and, instead, they sublet holdings to the native population. In addition, some of the English, such as Sir Nicholas Browne, an ancestor of the future earls of Kenmare, were themselves Catholics.

THE COMPOSITION OF CONNACHT

The implementation of the "Surrender and Regrant" policy was achieved more peacefully and more successfully in the province of Connacht and County Clare during the Lord Deputyship of the same Sir John Perrot, who had been so brutal in his repressive policies while president of Munster. Following the work of a commission and the decisions of local juries, awards were made to various local Old English lords and Irish chieftains enabling them to hold their land securely from the Crown in return for a fixed fee and occasional military costs or service. They continued to receive certain rents and services from their own tenants. The English system of primogeniture was to apply with regard to succession and certain Irish titles, such as the "O'Connor Don," were abolished. The general effect was that Connacht and Clare remained Gaelic in character. This would continue even after the Cromwellian conquests in the following century when the area was reserved for the Catholic leaders expelled from elsewhere in Ireland.

In 1585 the last of the three Irish parliaments of Elizabeth's reign met. The first, in 1560, nominally confirmed Elizabeth's religious settlement of Ireland. The second, in 1569, approved the attainment of Shane O'Neill and his property. The members of the third was more reflective of a greater territorial portion of the country than earlier parliaments. This was because "Surrender and Regrant" and extensions of English law and institutions throughout the island resulted in more areas being designated as shires or counties with entitlement to representatives in the House of Commons. Also, increasing numbers of towns were incorporated and thereby entitled to representation in parliament. But the membership was predominantly either New English or Old English.

The Catholicism of the latter provided a focus for opposition, especially on measures against their religion.[3]

In recounting the sad tale of conquest and brutality there is a tendency to overlook certain modernizing consequences of the Tudor governance, which would have been much longer in coming had the existing Gaelic order been allowed to prevail. These included the planning and development of new towns and roads, increased commerce, architectural development, such as the construction of windowed homes rather than forts, land drainage, and map making. Many of the beneficiaries were new English planters, but much of the planting remained superficial as few settlers were drawn from England. Most of the incumbent natives continued as laborers and tenants of the new aristocracy, and often of the old aristocracy who held new titles. Economic conditions, especially the material conditions of those at the bottom of the social ladder, might even have improved significantly. However, the cultural upheaval, and the consciousness of it that was reinforced by the poets of the older order, who continued to be patronized by the heirs of old Gaelic titles, outweighed the material improvements and left an abiding sense of having been conquered and dispossessed.

The Protestant archbishop of Dublin, Adam Loftus, was outspoken in his criticism of Deputy Perrot for having allowed so many Catholics into the 1585 parliament. Perrot was charged with various offenses, dismissed as deputy, returned to England, and committed to the Tower, where he died in 1592. In the same year, an effort to invigorate the secession of Irish Catholics from Rome was undertaken with the formation of a seminary for the clergy of the Church of Ireland, which became Trinity College. But by this time the spirit of the Counter-Reformation was very much alive in Ireland. A number of papal-appointed bishops had arrived as alternatives to the hierarchy of the official church appointed by the Crown. Also, numerous Catholic clergy educated on the Continent, particularly members of the older orders of friars as well as the new elite champions of the pope and Catholic orthodoxy, the Jesuits, had come to Ireland.

ULSTER

In the latter part of the 16th century, the one great area of Ireland that had not been subordinated to Anglicization, by either plantation or "Surrender and Regrant," was Ulster. However, adventurers had set their eyes on its real estate. A major figure in Ulster was Turloch O'Neill, whose succession to Shane O'Neill, to whom he was Tanist, had been acquiesced to by the Crown. Another was his cousin, Hugh O'Neill, whom the queen had protected as a youngster and who had spent much of his youth in England, had served the Crown as a

[3] Significantly, the territorial division of Ireland into shires or counties, a process that had begun in a very limited way in the Pale in the medieval times, came near to completion in Elizabethan times. It constituted one aspect of Anglicization that would persist in Ireland even after independence was gained in the 20th century. The Irish automatically have a consciousness of county identity. This is partly the result of sports rivalries among the counties but also because political constituencies are based on county lines. Ironically, in the part of Ireland still linked to Britain, Northern Ireland, the counties have only a geographic and social significance, but no political meaning as representation and local governmental lines cross county borders.

soldier in Munster, had attended the 1585 Irish parliament, and had been designated Baron of Dungannon.

However, for all his training and experience in the new Anglicized order, Hugh O'Neill felt the stirrings of the old order, aspiring to be "The O'Neill" as much as the earl of Tyrone. His determination to revive the old system was further enhanced by the execution and attainment of the lands of the McMahon of Monaghan when the chieftain had exercised customary rights, rather than the rules called for by the "Surrender and Regrant" arrangements. (Afterward, several minor figures among the leading family of Monaghan were given estates under English law. This development would spare Monaghan, although part of Ulster, from the Ulster Plantation two decades later.) Earlier instances of English aggrandizement of which O'Neill would have been aware included the seizure and execution of Brian O'Neill of Clandeboy, his wife, and 200 followers at negotiations in 1574 and the massacre of the population of Rathlin Island, off the Antrim coast, in the following year as part of the territorial ambitions of the earl of Essex.

In 1595 O'Neill attacked and defeated the Crown's army, which was commanded by his brother-in-law, Sir Henry Bagenal, at Clontibert in County Monaghan. Several months later, when Turloch O'Neill died, Hugh succeeded him as "The O'Neill." Soon after, he was leading a confederacy of Ulster chieftains. Most prominent was Hugh Roe O'Donnell of Tyrconnell, whose own experience of having been captured by Perrot in 1587 and cruelly imprisoned in Dublin for four years until he dramatically escaped, as well as the influence of his wife, a niece of Sorley Boy MacDonnell, who had been a rival of the O'Neills but also an opponent and victim of Anglicization, emboldened him to fight the new regime. The politically astute Hugh O'Neill accepted O'Donnell's claim as "The O'Donnell" and formed the alliance, which grew into a national rebellion.

O'NEILL ON THE OFFENSIVE

After Clontibert and after having proclaimed himself the O'Neill, Hugh O'Neill was branded a traitor and "the principal and chief author of this rebellion and a known practiciser with Spain and her Majesty's other enemies." The events in Ireland soon had an international dimension. Seven years earlier the Spanish Armada had posed a severe threat of invasion from which England was spared only by stormy weather. Accordingly, any indication that rebellious elements in Ireland might invoke the assistance of the Spanish, as had the Munster Geraldines, was regarded as a major threat to England, as well as to the English law and institutions imposed on Ireland. O'Neill was undoubtedly reaching out to both the Spanish king, Philip II, and to the pope, Clement VII, for support in what was presented as a struggle for Irish Catholicism. In 1595 he had appointed the bishop of Killaloe to champion O'Neill's case before the pope and to ask that he repeal the 12th-century papal bull that had granted dominion over Ireland to Henry II. The bishop claimed that the princes and bishops of Ireland were willing to regard O'Neill as their rightful king by right of descent.

O'Neill and his associates made clear the religious character of the impending struggle by an appeal of July 6, 1596, to the chieftains in Munster to join in making war on the English in defense of "Christ's Catholic religion." However, the Old English did not respond, as they were uncertain of the sincerity of O'Neill's religious claims. The same reasoning inhibited papal endorsement until late 1599, when Peter Lombard, the Irish scholar in Louvain, as O'Neill's personal representative in Rome, succeeded in persuading Clement VII of the validity of the cause. The following year the pope offered a plenary indulgence to anyone assisting O'Neill in what was regarded as a struggle comparable to the European wars against the Turks.

Another intriguing component to the story was O'Neill's having visited and been received kindly by James VI, king of Scotland, whose nation was independent of England at this time, even though he was the probable successor to his cousin Elizabeth as English monarch. James had hinted he would favorably treat O'Neill after the death of Elizabeth. The fact that James was the son of Mary, Queen of Scots, the candidate of the Catholic opponents of Elizabeth's reign, made him appear to O'Neill, and probably the pope, as a potential ally regardless of James's own uncertain religious position.

O'Neill took advantage of a lengthy truce to increase his forces and seek foreign assistance. But by the middle of 1597 the government went on the offensive, making a three-pronged march on O'Neill. Both Irish and Old English, such as Donough O'Brien, earl of Thomond and Baron Inchiquin, and Ulick, earl of Clanricard, led other forces in the march. But O'Neill's armies defeated all three movements. After another truce the government went on the offensive again in July 1598, as Sir Henry Bagenel, O'Neill's brother-in-law, led an army of 4,300 northward. On August 15, 1598, O'Neill and O'Donnell, commanding 8,000 men, completely defeated the English, killing a third of their army, included Bagenel. All appeared open for O'Neill to sweep to total victory as supporters from among those defeated in Munster two decades previously rallied to his banner.

However, many, especially those in Connacht and Clare and including some in Munster, appeased by the composition policy, remained unsympathetic. Apprehensive about the situation in Ireland, the queen sent her favorite, Sir Robert Devereux, the earl of Essex, who had promoted the colonial policies that included the brutal slaughter on Rathlin Island in 1574, as lord lieutenant in Ireland. He arrived in April 1599 accompanied by a force of 17,000. But Essex dissipated his forces in a number of different moves and was routed in all engagements, including near Maryborough in Queens or Laois County, in Glenmalure in Wicklow, and in the Curlew Mountains in Connacht. After a further encounter in Monaghan-Louth, he entered into a truce with O'Neill. The outraged queen ordered his return to England in September and a year later he was beheaded.

MOUNTJOY AND KINSALE

As far back as 1596, Spanish arms and ammunition had come to Donegal in support of the O'Neill forces. More came again in 1599 and 1600. But what was most wanted was a Spanish army. Only in early 1601 was the new king, Philip III, able to approve sending 6,000 men to Ireland. O'Neill's ability, a year and a half before after the departure of Essex, to move triumphantly about Leinster and Munster, had helped persuade the Spanish monarch to send him support. Actually, only 4,400 were assembled in Portugal in August and set sail for Ireland. A storm detached four ships with about 600 men. The main force arrived in Kinsale, County Cork, on September 21, although disease and injury left only about 2,500 fit for battle.

However, another player had arrived on the scene who would change the picture dramatically. Sir Charles Blount, Lord Mountjoy, had been appointed lord deputy. He arrived in Ireland in February 1600 with an army of 20,000. His strategy was to avoid general battles, but rather wreak enough destruction so as to inhibit any support among the populace for the O'Neill cause. The regime's determination was manifest in the queen's giving him absolute power, but not the power to grant "the pardon of the archtraitor" (O'Neill). Mountjoy was assisted by the appointment as president of Munster of Sir George Carew, cousin of the land claimant of the 1560s. Within weeks Mountjoy's forces had savagely overwhelmed the Irish in Leinster and Munster, as James FitzThomas, the claimant to be earl of Kildare, and Fineen McCarthy, "McCarthy Mor" were imprisoned in the Tower of London, and the leaders of the O'More sept in Leix were killed. While O'Neill's territory in the north was not overrun, 4,000 soldiers had landed in Derry, and a scorched earth policy of raids by Montjoy into Ulster had resulted in cousins of both O'Neill and O'Donnell capitulating.

The Spanish came to the wrong place when they landed in Kinsale, since the Crown's forces had already overrun Munster. It would have been better for the Irish cause had they come to Ulster. When word came of their landing, Mountjoy immediately undertook to besiege Kinsale by sea and land. He withdrew forces from his Ulster campaign to use against Kinsale. O'Neill and O'Donnell also decided to march immediately south to join forces with the Spanish in what was to be perhaps the most fateful battle in Irish history, for an Irish-Spanish victory would have been followed by even more Spanish forces being sent with all of the ultimate implications that such might have had for the whole of modern European history. The battle took place on Christmas Eve, 1601. There were 6,500 men under O'Neill and O'Donnell besieging a comparable number under Mountjoy, who were besieging the town in which there were about 3,000 Spanish. Tactical miscalculation and bad management resulted in a rout for the Irish and Spanish, as the Irish lost between 1,000 and 2,000. The Spanish under their commander Don Juan del Aquila were allowed to leave for Spain intact. O'Donnell panicked at what had happened and fled immediately to Spain, where he died the following year.

O'Neill let a forced retreat back to Ulster in which he lost great numbers as well. Even in Ulster, where he was ready to make his last stand, joined by Hugh O'Donnell's younger brother, Rory, he suffered numerous defeats, as the virtual seat of the O'Neill's, Dungannon, was overtaken and the O'Neill inauguration chair at Tullahogue was destroyed. Mountjoy's policy of destruction had made O'Neill's retreat into the woods of Ulster impossible, as the starving populace was unable to give sustenance to his forces.

Accordingly, O'Neill began negotiations with Mountjoy, formally submitting on March 30, 1603, at Mellifont under relatively generous terms, but terms that marked the end of the Gaelic order. He remained earl of Tyrone, but now held his lands as a private possession from the Crown rather than as ancestral familial lands. Ulster was divided into nine counties or shires and endowed with all of the appropriate officialdom, including sheriffs. All inhabitants were to be regarded as subjects of the Crown and of no other lord. The same terms were given to Rory O'Donnell, who was made the earl of Tyrconnell. Unknown to O'Neill, Queen Elizabeth had died on March 23, but he was not made aware of that until he had made his formal submission. Obviously, he had assumed that the Scottish king, James, who succeeded his cousin Elizabeth, might have been more generous in his new role as king of England, Scotland, and Ireland. The subsequent record, however, did not bear out such expectations.

FLIGHT OF THE EARLS

O'Neill and O'Donnell accompanied Mountjoy to London where they were graciously received by James I (VI of Scotland). But when they returned to Ireland their position was different from what it had been. O'Neill was in a position to become a substantial landlord in large areas of Ulster, but he was no longer the chieftain. It had become obvious in cases affecting other chieftains that their authority over their underlings had been removed with the latter having become freeholders able to exercise English law to assert their position. Ultimately, the application of English law in a society previously governed by the traditional Brehon code would give outsiders, better aware of the new law, an advantage in asserting claims for territory previously held unquestioned by the Gaelic lords. This troubled O'Neill. He was also aware of suspicions harbored against him because his son served as colonel of a Spanish regiment in the Netherlands. In July 1607 he was summoned to London over a land dispute. Aware of the fate of others who had gone to London and never returned, he decided to board a ship that had come to Lough Swilly to take O'Donnell and other chieftains to the Continent. They ultimately made their way to Rome, where they were received with honor. However, O'Donnell died a few months after arrival. O'Neill survived until 1616, but never set foot in Ireland again. Such was the end of the Gaelic order in Ireland. While there would be brief efforts at recovery during the 17th century, such would only be a part of a general alliance of Catholics in Ireland and scarcely a struggle for the restoration of the old order.

STUART ERA

1603–1691

Had the northern earls not taken flight in September 1607, Irish history in the rest of the 17th century might have been quite different. Admittedly, the earls no longer held their old position as virtual rulers of independent septs, but they remained formidable landlords over vast areas with as much, if not more, power and influence than any of the other Gaelic chieftains, such as those in Connaught and Clare who had abided by the Composition, and the various Old English Catholic lords, especially, but not exclusively, those of Leinster. As it was, Catholics, not as chieftains, but as landlords, still controlled over 80 percent of the land of Ireland, dominated many of the old towns, and would make up a substantial portion of any Irish parliament that might be called. Whatever expansion in the ranks of Protestantism took place was almost entirely of newcomers to Ireland, the New English, who were very often public officials. There remained an unwarranted conviction that the Catholicism of King James's mother would reassert itself in the new king, James, or that he would at least be more appreciative of the grievances of his Catholic subjects. Even the lord deputy, Mountjoy, although having been a brutal conqueror, had upon peace taken a more conciliatory line. But Mountjoy was replaced by Arthur Chichester in 1604, and he was dead by 1606. Other servants of the king had other designs on Ireland.

One such was the extremely talented attorney general for Ireland, Sir John Davies, who saw the flight of the earls as achieving something that the best army in Europe had not been able to achieve: an opportunity for colonization that would make Ireland a new England in all but name. Within two weeks of the flight, Chichester submitted to the English Privy Council a proposal regarding the disposal of the lands of those who had left. Surveys and mapmaking of six Ulster counties (Armagh, Cavan, Coleraine (Derry), Donegal, Fermanagh and Tyrone), were undertaken during 1608, 1609, and 1610, readying the province for plantation.[4]

---

[4] In a settlement of 1590, Monaghan had been left to the Irish landlords, and Antrim and Down were held by Scots lords, one of whom was the son of Sorley Boy McDonnell, a sometime ally of the O'Neills, who controlled the celebrated Glens of Antrim, and other native chiefs like O'Neill and a Magennis, as well as a substantial Scots settlement recruited by two adventurers, Sirs James Hamilton and Hugh Montgomery, who had induced imprudent Irish chieftains to sell their lands.

PLANTATION OF ULSTER

A half-million acres of the best land in the six counties was to be made available to either "Undertakers" or "Servitors," who would hold their land from the king for a specified rent. The former were ideally English or Lowland Scots, while the latter, whose terms were less generous, were usually Scots. Naturally they had to take the Oath of Supremacy recognizing the king as head of the church. They were expected to recruit settlers from England and Scotland as their tenants on the land. Plans were made for the formation of a number of towns. The incumbent native landowners, whether owners themselves or tenants of the exiled earls, were dispossessed and less attractive parcels of land were given to them. Several thousand settlers came in the next few years, primarily from Scotland, and several new towns were established.

However, the colonization was never complete. Many of the undertakers or servitors found it easier to recruit natives, especially if they wound up with more land than expected because of inaccurate mapping. In addition, many settlers did not remain on the sites to which they had originally come, but moved on elsewhere gaining more land by various legal and not so legal manners. This left a religiously mixed population in many areas, which would become the root of difficulties that have persisted to the present time. One undertaker was the city of London, whose territory of settlement included the town and the county of Londonderry. Another side of the story was that of the dispossessed. Many had acquiesced to being confined to less favored areas. Others, especially if they had been the warriors for the chieftains, became embittered and took to the mountains and the substantial woods of the time to pursue a populist outlaw, or "Robin Hood," role in anticipation of an eventual return of the earls.

THE OLD ENGLISH

Despite the Ulster Plantation, most land in the island of Ireland remained in the possession of Catholics, especially those Catholics who were descendants of the Anglo-Normans. These "Old English" still retained a sense of distinction from the Gaelic Irish and were particularly adamant in their loyalty to the Crown. Also, they had firmly accepted the reforms of the Council of Trent, which reforms had not gained the same adherence among the Gaelic Catholics. In addition, they espoused a premature sense of parliamentary nationalism, that is, a sense of the autonomy of the Irish parliament from that of England, regardless of the inhibitions on it imposed by Poynings' Law. Catholicism thrived in Ireland in the early decades of the 17th century as a resident episcopacy had been reestablished and numerous parishes set up. Catholics formed the majority of the aldermen in Dublin, and the number of Franciscan friars on the island increased fivefold to 1,000 within several decades.

On the other hand, repressive measures still existed and more were being considered or advocated. In theory, priests were supposed to be banished and nonattendance at the Protestant Church of Ireland was subject to a fine. Outrage at the "Gunpowder Plot" of November 1605, an alleged attempt by some Catholics in England to supplant the monarchy, led to demands for more repressive measures in Ireland. A Catholic bishop of Down and Connor was hung for treason in 1612 and a Catholic alderman died after seven years imprisonment in 1621. A special court, the Castle Chamber, which played the same role in Ireland as that of the Star Chamber in England, of bypassing the common law, was often employed against Catholics. Because of their "Englishness," the Old English Catholics were better adapted than the Gaelic Catholics to employ such English institutions as Parliament to defend their religious rights. They tried to overcome restrictions on their religion, whether impediments to church building, establishment of educational institutions, movement of clergy, or exclusion from certain offices or professions because of religion. They also had to contend with assaults on their property. A mixture of use of special courts and intimidation of common law court juries often worked to challenge their title to various lands. These tactics were especially effective when applied against the Gaelic lords, whose original claims were based on traditional and Brehon law concepts.

Differences between James I and the English parliament gave the Old English Catholics an opportunity to improve their position. Irish history in the 17th century was inexorably drawn into the domestic struggle in England between the king and parliament. The Irish sought concessions from the king at the time of his difficulties with his parliament. This, in turn, made the parliamentary forces severely condemnatory of real or imagined royal collusion with the Irish against the interests of the English parliament and Protestantism.

Two matters were at the root of the clash between the king and parliament: one was the parliament's growing consciousness of what it thought should be its powers, the other was the severe revenue shortfall confronting the king. Adding to the difficulty was the fact that James was a "foreigner," that is, a Scot. His own experience as king of Scotland and his dealings with the elected kirks of the Presbyterian Church had made him increasingly suspicious of elected bodies that could inhibit royal power. Adhering to the concept of the divine right of kings, he was emboldened in his new position to take steps that would inhibit the English parliament from behaving the way in which the Scots had. A clash became inevitable when the dispute moved beyond simple requests for revenue to the theoretical questions about whether parliament had the right to exist without the king. James's depreciatory remarks about Calvinist elements (the source of his difficulties in Scotland) within the English church, still a minority, transformed these adherents into martyrs, which scarcely helped his efforts to sustain the Episcopal character of the church, that is, one with bishops appointed by the monarch.

The king hoped Ireland might provide assistance in the financial difficulties caused by his own parliament's reluctance to give him additional revenues. Accordingly, the lord deputy, Chichester, summoned a parliament in 1613. Old English Catholics made up a substantial portion of the upper house, the House of Lords. Catholics were a minority in the House of Commons, whose members represented the counties and the incorporated boroughs, because of the careful management of the county elections by the royally appointed sheriffs and the creation of 39 new boroughs that were certain to return Protestant members. Catholic members were outraged at the substantial Protestant major-

ity so created and withdrew from the parliament. An inquiry partially rectified their grievances, leaving the Protestants with a much narrower majority
when the parliament reassembled in 1614. The government secured post-facto
parliamentary sanction for the attainder of the land of O'Neill and O'Donnell
in Ulster, but it was unsuccessful in its revenue requests and in measures to
inhibit the Jesuits in Ireland. The major difficulties for Catholics included the
Act of Supremacy, which required the oath acknowledging the king as head
of the church, and recusancy fines, which, when enforced, could penalize those
who did not attend the official church. However, these were not as rigorously
enforced in Ireland, although many of the New English, including the hierarchy of the church, were outraged at this "sinful" toleration of Papists.

When he failed to get the desired revenues from Ireland, James resorted to the
same tactic he had employed in England. He invoked certain feudal rights as first
lord of all property and made use of special royal courts as enforcers. In addition
to legal challenges to the land title of many Catholic lords, James employed a
Court of Wards to administer the estates and oversee the education of minor children of a tenant in chief, that is, a lord who had died without a male successor
who had come of age. The effect was to exploit the property for the revenue interests of the government and to guarantee the Protestant education of the minor
children. It was in such circumstances that James Butler, later earl and ultimately
duke of Ormond, became a Protestant. During the 16th century the Butlers had
proved more loyal than had their Geraldine rivals in Kildare or Munster.

Even if they were not minors, heirs of tenants in chief could also be required
to take the Oath of Supremacy when coming into their inheritance. This was
a further instrument to induce religious conversion or to gain financial or property concessions. Lastly, there were the continuing title challenges to Catholic
landholders, especially Gaelic lords, that resulted in acquisition of extensive
property by many New English. Typical of the latter was Richard Boyle, who
had arrived in Cork as a penniless settler in 1588 and, having been created earl
of Cork in 1620, built several towns and started industries.

CHARLES I AND THE GRACES

Charles I, who succeeded his father in March 1625, also started his reign with
a difficult relationship with parliament. His problems stemmed from foreign
affairs. His father had been able to stay out of the religious warfare that was
sweeping continental Europe at the time, in what would be called the Thirty
Years' War. More zealous Protestant elements in England, namely those members of the Church of England with a more Calvinist disposition, desired English
entry on the side of the Protestant alliance, which counted among its members
at various times Brandenburg (ultimately Prussia), the Netherlands, and Swe-
den. However, the same interventionists were usually reluctant to provide the
monarch with the financial resources for warfare. Charles had entered into war
with Spain following the failure of efforts to win the hand of the Spanish
princess. In this way England found itself partially backed into the Thirty Years'
War, since the Hapsburg rulers of Spain were important members of the
Catholic alliance.

Charles eventually married the French princess, Henrietta Maria, but that did not deter him from entering into war with France as well. Both the historic close links of Spain with the Irish Catholics and the failure of an English effort to assist French Protestants in the siege of La Rochelle raised the perennial fears about Ireland as the backdoor for England's continental enemies. Demands rose to raise an army to defend Ireland from foreign invasion as well as to secure the funds to support that army.

Charles saw a source of support in the Old English of Ireland. Many in the government had been convinced that relieving their grievances might result in their supplying and supporting soldiers. In 1627 Charles met a delegation from Ireland, eight Catholics and three Protestants, who agreed to provide him with a subsidy of £40,000 annually in return for concessions, which he instructed his government in Ireland to give. These "instructions and graces" which amounted to 51 items in all, included replacing the Oath of Supremacy with one of allegiance that would allow uninhibited Catholic inheritance and admission to legal practice, the appointment of some Catholics as army commanders, and the guarantee of security of title for all landholders of more than 60 years standing. The "Graces" were to be confirmed by an act of the Irish parliament, which was summoned for the first time since 1615 in 1628 by the lord deputy, Viscount Falkland. However, because the summoning of the parliament had not received the sanction of the English Privy Council as required by Poynings' Law, the parliament was postponed. Several months later peace was made with France and then Spain, ending the sense of crisis that had prompted the generosity of the "Graces." There was no need for a parliament, nor the implementation of the "Graces," even though the first subsidy of £40,000 had been advanced.

WENTWORTH

In January 1632 Thomas, Viscount Wentworth was appointed lord deputy in Ireland. Wentworth was the instrument whereby the policy of "thorough," which the king sought to apply throughout his realm, was to be enforced in Ireland. "Thorough" was a policy that sought to employ effective administration and so to enable the king and his government to operate without having to go to parliament for resources to enforce his will and implement his programs. One aspect of "thorough" dealt with church policy. Through William Laud, the archbishop of Canterbury, he sought to enforce the more orthodox high church ritual and doctrine and inhibit the growing Calvinist or low church influences. A high church theological perspective was usually supportive of monarchical prerogative. Significantly, many of the New English in Ireland were of low church attitudes in addition to the great number of outright Presbyterians in Ulster.

Wentworth's strategy for Ireland was to ensure that the island would provide a return for the king considerably in excess of the cost to the monarchy in maintaining power there. In addition, he sought to guarantee that neither the Gaelic Irish, the Old English, nor the New English would be able to seriously impede royal governance. In doing so, Wentworth also acted to guarantee for himself an income that made him one of the richest men in the kingdom. Over the Catholics, especially the Old English Catholics, he held the threat of enforcing the Recusancy Laws, which could be avoided by making substantial contributions to the exchequer. He imposed the orthodox Thirty-nine Articles on the Church of Ireland and imposed an Act of Uniformity whereby church property or income could be recovered from dissenting clergy.

He summoned a parliament in 1634 in which the creation of new peerages and the presence of their bishops gave a majority to the Protestants in the House of Lords as well as in the Commons. Catholics were induced to make further subsidies to the government by the promise of making the "Graces" statutory. In fact, the concessions gained were minor, such as allowing limited practice of law. On the other hand, rather than confirm land holdings of 60 years, Wentworth secured parliamentary acquiescence in establishing a Commission for Defective Titles whereby more holdings could be taken from Gaelic, Old English, and even New English for the advantage of the Crown. With that accomplished, he dissolved parliament in 1635, hoping, as the king had been able to do in England, to rule without it. Wentworth had no theological hostility toward Catholics, whom he realized were temperamentally disposed toward monarchy, and he granted them general tolerance to practice their religion. But they remained disqualified from public office and they were denied real security of land tenure.

In many ways, Wentworth's administration in Ireland was remarkable, measured by the revenues he obtained, often by intimidation of juries or threats of attaining land with possibly defective titles. He encouraged commerce and industry in the towns, built up merchant shipping, and aimed at further colonization by the English. However, events outside of Ireland would begin a process that would energize all those whom he had antagonized in Ireland, leading to his removal from the scene.

In 1638 Charles, encouraged by Archbishop Laud, sought to extend the policy of religious uniformity to his other kingdom, Scotland. Rather than accept the high church orthodoxy in doctrine and ritual the Scots took the famous Solemn Oath and Covenant to resist violently the imposition of prelacy on them. Eventually war ensued between the two kingdoms. Significantly, Wentworth had begun to implement a similar policy of religious conformity against the many Scots in Ulster, including asking all males over 16 years of age to take an oath of loyalty. Then early in 1640 Charles summoned his faithful and effective servant in Ireland to come to London to advise him of the situation. He was raised to the title of the earl of Stafford and given the higher title of Lord Lieutenant of Ireland. Wentworth had already called an Irish parliament, at which he asked for subsidies with which to raise an army of 9,000. The parliament had complied with his request by the time he returned to Ireland in March. The following month, he returned to England where he hoped similar acquiescence would come from a parliament that was being summoned for the first time since 1629. The parliament refused to meet the king's request for assistance against the Scots. The noncompliant parliament, known in history as the "Short Parliament," was dissolved within three weeks.

That summer the Scots went on the offensive, defeating a royal army at Newcastle, forcing the king to summon yet another parliament. This parliament, historically known as the "Long Parliament," some of whose members were in league with the Scots, proved just as obstinate, concerning itself with redress of grievances before tending to the royal requests for subsidy. The members asserted remarkable control over the monarch, his officials, and even his family, and they began the process that would result in civil war, the end of which would see the execution of the king and more than a decade of republican rule in England, Scotland, and Ireland. One issue that particularly excited the parliament was suspicion that Wentworth was in connivance with Irish Catholics in support of the monarchy. There was a large number of Catholics among the army of 9,000 raised by the subsidies of the Irish parliament. Many in the English parliament feared that this army might be employed in England. The ouster of Stafford became their primary objective. The Irish parliament, meeting in January 1641, also issued a bill of particulars against the man. However, there was never formal impeachment; instead, the parliament of England passed a bill of attainder against him and secured his execution in May 1641.

INSURRECTION IN IRELAND

Charles appointed an absentee, the earl of Leicester, in Wentworth's place as Lord Lieutenant of Ireland, but left real power to two lords justices, Borlase and Parsons, who sided with the parliamentary opposition to the monarchy in England. They used their position in Ireland to advance the interests of the New English, in terms of political power, economic advantage, and religious attitudes (low church, antiepiscopal, and vehemently anti-Catholic). They suspended the Irish parliament and blocked an issuance of further "Graces" that would benefit the Catholics. When the parliament met again in March 1642 there were no Catholics present.

In view of the developments in England and Ireland, which augured so poorly for the position of the Catholics in Ireland, many were attracted to the idea of a rising. Leading figures were Rory O'More, of the Leix family, who had been ousted from their holdings in the 1550s and Sir Phelim O'Neill, a member of the Irish parliament. Encouragement came from many Irish in the military service of continental kings and many Irish clergy on the Continent. A planned seizure of Dublin Castle on October 23, 1641, failed when a drunken participant revealed the plot.

A rising did take place in Ulster that was directed at the settler population who had arrived since the Ulster Plantation. These Presbyterian Ulster Scots had earlier been under threat from Wentworth with his religious conformity policy. Now the native Irish Catholics had turned on them. Despite the admonitions of the Catholic leaders, such as Turlough O'Neill that no harm should come to the Scots, there were, as in many popular uprisings, numerous atrocities. Modest estimations would put the number killed at 4,000, but possibly twice that number died from exposure or lack of sustenance. The Catholics drove the Scots from holdings, which had been occupied by Catholics in the previous generation. The Catholic "gentry" leadership obviously hoped the uprising would result in their being restored to lands under familial control in earlier times. However, the refugees were able to obtain shelter in towns like Enniskillen, Coleraine, Londonderry, and Lisburne, whose fortifications held out against the rebels who tended to dominate the open country of the province. News of the uprising, and tales of the woes of refugees who came to Dublin and Drogheda, quickly made the tragedy appear even worse. It was not long before the number of victims in popular accounts exceeded by tens of thousands the total number of Protestants actually living in Ulster at the time. Over decades and even centuries the horrors of the uprising would be a major element in popular Ulster loyalist historiography.

CONFEDERATION OF KILKENNY

The relative success of the Ulster insurrection and the increasing disregard for Catholics by the government in Dublin, which identified with those in the English parliament seeking to weaken the position of the monarch, drew the Old English Catholics into alliance with the Gaelic Catholics. Both wings of Catholicism continued to profess their loyalty to the king, although there were popular rumors about continental kings extending recognition to Phelim O'Neill as king of Ireland. Those rumors strengthened English determination to suppress the Irish insurrection. But the loyalty of the Catholics in Ireland to Charles I also intensified parliamentary hostility to both the Catholics and the king, who were invalidly suspected of being allies. The English agreed to finance the sending of a Scottish army of 10,000 men to Ireland under Major General Robert Munro to repress the rebellion. Charles also gave his assent in March 1642 to an Adventurers' Act passed by the English parliament, which called for the confiscation of two and a half million acres in Ireland from anyone disloyal. The confiscated land would compensate those who advanced money to finance the war effort against the Irish (and also against the monarch). It would serve a decade later as the basis on which Oliver Cromwell implemented his plantation of Ireland. The Irish Catholics consequently found themselves opposed by the supporters of both monarch and parliament, a situation that would persist even after outright civil war had broken out in England in August 1642 between king and parliament.

In March 1642 the Catholic hierarchy of Ireland gave their sanction to the formation of a confederation of Catholics, which became in October the Confederation of Kilkenny. In this government, which was a substitute for the Irish parliament from which they had been excluded, the united Gaelic and Old English Catholics committed themselves to restore the rights of the church, to defend the liberties of the nation, and to maintain the prerogatives of the Crown, with the motto of *"Pro Deo, pro rege, pro patria Hibernia unanimis"* on their seal. However, despite the proclaimed unity, differences in temperament and strategy persisted between the Gaelic and the Old English. The former had already lost much more in terms of their holdings and were accordingly less inclined toward compromise, while the later persisted in a confidence that they might come to some kind of alliance with the English monarch against the parliamentary forces. These differences carried even to the rivalry between the two leaders who had returned from serving the Spanish king on the Continent to lead the "Catholic Confederates." One was Thomas Preston, the brother of Lord Gormanstown, an Old English peer, and the other was Owen Roe O'Neill, the nephew of Hugh, the earl who had fled Ireland in 1607.

There were also divisions on the other side between royalists and parliamentary supporters. Munro and his forces identified with the parliamentary (and low church) cause, as did many New English commanders, like Lord Broghill (son of Robert Boyle, earl of Cork), and the Gaelic leader (but also committed Protestant), Murrough O'Brien (Lord Inchiquin). The earl of Ormond, a loyal monarchist, served as commander of the army and Lord Lieutenant of Ireland. He had to contend with the parliamentary sympathies of many in the government. To add to his difficulties, the king directed him in early 1643 to deal with the Confederates in the hope of bringing them over to the royalist side.

At that stage the Confederates were strongest in Connacht. O'Neill had formed a strong army among the Gaelic in Ulster, but Preston had suffered a serious defeat at royalist hands in Wexford and the Old English had not much success in Munster. The Confederates feared that the king and parliament might ultimately come to terms, which would be to the detriment of the Catholic position. Some argued that their best strategy was to play for time with expectations of continental support. That view was more characteristic of the Gaelic leaders, whereas the Old English believed the Catholics had a better chance with a royalist success and that any reasonable arrangement with the monarchy would be wise. A papal envoy, Pietro Scarampi, who brought some money and supplies, had urged the continuance of the struggle. However, the Old English prevailed and agreed to a cessation of violence for a year in September 1643. However, the parliamentary side did not accept the cessation signed by the royal side, and Munro continued the war in Ulster, as did Lord Inchiquin a few months later.

However, negotiations between the Confederates and Ormond continued with the goal to secure a permanent settlement, although Ormond was reluctant to surrender anything that was vital to the interests of Protestantism. The king, anxious to draw upon the Confederate military forces to support his campaign in England, called upon an English Catholic, the earl of Glamorgan, to negotiate for him. Unknown to Ormond, he obtained a treaty in August 1645, which gave complete freedom to the Catholic Church in Ireland, including restoration of all churches and church property not actually being used by Protestants, in return for the supply of 10,000 men for the king in England. When it became publicly known, the king had to repudiate the treaty. Negotiations between the Confederates and Ormond continued, however, with the former hoping to win generous terms and the king, suffering from a severe defeat in July 1645 at Naseby, anxious for additional troops. In the following year, the Confederates accepted a deal less favorable, but still substantial. Similar to the earlier "Graces," it abolished the Court of Wards whereby the king had been able to assert authority over the minor offspring of a deceased Catholic lord and raise them as Protestants (as had happened to Ormond), substituted an oath of allegiance for the Oath of Supremacy, admitted Catholics to public office, and ended restrictions on Catholic education. But nothing was agreed on relating to church property.

Before the treaty had been negotiated, another papal emissary, the papal nuncio, Bishop Giovanni Battista Rinuccini, had come to Ireland. When the treaty was published he condemned it as a betrayal of the original terms of the Confederation of Kilkenny in that it did not secure the full rights of the church. He preached against it and threatened its proponents with excommunication. The clergy and the rank and file tended to support him, as did Owen Roe O'Neill. The latter had triumphed a few months before over Munro in the Battle of Benburb near Armagh, destroying half the forces that he had hoped to employ in the south against the Confederacy. But instead of mopping up the remainder of Munro's forces, O'Neill's army marched south relishing their triumph. On the basis of the Benburb victory, even Preston acceded to Rinuccini's wishes and rejected the treaty.

With the peace efforts having failed, the Confederates hoped to take Dublin, but further disagreements among their leaders inhibited their chances. But the Confederacy itself remained committed to Rinuccini's insistence on full restoration of the position of the Catholic Church in Ireland. Therefore, Ormond turned to the parliamentary side and agreed to surrender Dublin and the forces under his command to the parliamentary forces and withdrew from Ireland himself in mid-1647. From then on matters soured for the Confederate cause. Colonel Michael Jones, who had arrived from England with his Roundhead army of 8,000, overwhelmingly defeated Preston, who lost 5,000 men. In addition, Inchiquin swept all before him in Munster. The Confederates began to dispute among themselves. They dismissed O'Neill, appealed over Rinuccini to Rome, and came near to battle against each other. Ormond returned to Ireland and signed a new treaty with the Confederates, but by then all had changed as the king had been tried and executed by the English parliament.

O'Neill, now independent from the other Confederates and Ormond, entered into a temporary truce with the parliamentary forces. But on the other side, the Ulster Scots and Inchiquin turned against the parliamentary forces. Now a loyal monarchist, Inchiquin had captured Drogheda and Dundalk, but Ormond was unsuccessful in his assault on Dublin where the forces of Michael Jones triumphed on August 2. Two weeks later Oliver Cromwell, "Lord Lieutenant and General for the Parliament of England," arrived in Dublin with 20,000 men. The way was clear for a complete conquest of the island.

CROMWELL

Although he was present in Ireland for less than a year, and exercised control over the island for less than a decade, Cromwell made an impact on Irish society and history that has had few rivals. To the present he remains a figure of dread and tyranny, having the same ominous significance to the Irish that Hitler would have for the Jews of Europe. Even after his system was replaced and the monarchy restored in England and Ireland, the permanent social upheaval he imposed remained until the 20th century, for he guaranteed that the property and political power in Ireland would be in the hands of the "New English."

Within a few weeks of his arrival, Cromwell's army laid siege to the royalist position in Drogheda. The entire garrison, mainly royalists and high church Protestants, was slaughtered, as were any Catholic priests who were found and many among the civilian population. Fired by ideological zeal, directed particularly at Roman Catholicism and at Irish rebels, Cromwell regarded the massacre as an act of divine retribution. At this point O'Neill and Ormond finally formed an alliance, but it was much too late, as O'Neill died a few weeks after, and Cromwellian forces gained dominance in most of Ulster. Cromwell himself moved south, taking Wexford, New Ross, Cork, Youghal, Kinsale, Kilkenny, and Clonmel over the next few months. On May 26, 1650, Cromwell left Ireland, leaving what would amount to a mopping-up operation in the hands of his son-in-law, Henry Ireton. Resistance of one sort or another persisted until the summer of 1652, although Ormond left Ireland in December 1650. Waterford surrendered in August of that year; Limerick, after a long siege, in October 1651; and Galway in May 1652. Many of the defeated soldiers retreated into the countryside and became guerrilla warriors, playing a "Robin Hood" role that would be invoked by later popular irregular forces in Irish history. Ironically, the nickname given to these "outlaws" by the authorities was "Tory," a name later associated with the "King's Friends" in England and to this day with the British Conservative Party. To inhibit a rebel presence as much as possible, the Cromwellian forces allowed many of those who had surrendered to leave the island and accept service in the armies of other nations. However, as will be seen, the treatment accorded the rest of the population, especially the Catholic landowners, was not as generous.

Ireton, who directed the military conquest, had been made lord deputy. For the civilian governance of the island four commissioners were appointed. Their main task in a land devastated by a decade of continuous warfare, undergoing famine in many areas and completely devoid of the structures of law and order, was to propagate the gospel, suppress popery, advance education, inquire about law enforcement, and secure public revenue. They eventually divided the country into a dozen regions under command of military governors, who imposed orders, raised revenues, and appointed preaching ministers. When Ireton died in 1651, the offices of lord lieutenant and lord deputy were abolished and the commissioners assumed full authority. However, by 1654 the Lord Deputyship was reestablished as Charles Fleetwood, the then military commander in Ireland, was appointed and the commissioners were replaced with a council.

The ultimate goal of the conquerors was plantation of the entire island with a thorough colonization. The drastic reduction of the population by almost a third because of the destruction and turmoil had created an opportunity to achieve this. The main instrument for plantation was an Act of Settlement passed by the English parliament in August 1652. This act would fulfill the Adventurers' Act of a decade earlier, which had allowed for private financing of the army of the parliamentary cause. Now the supporters were to be reimbursed with land seized in Ireland. Not only were the investors in the army to be reimbursed, but the soldiers had to be compensated as well. Lands that would be left would be available for the government's purposes. William Petty played a major role in the complicated process of determining what property was to be taken and how it was to be allocated, as he produced "the Down survey" of Ireland, the first scientific mapping of the island. He would be rewarded with substantial land himself in Munster, and his descendants would be elevated as the earl of Shelburne and later the marquis of Lansdowne.

Cromwell besieges
and takes
Drogheda, 1649.
*(Mary Evans
Picture Library)*

The property of all who had taken part in, assisted, or supported the rebellion, that is, those who had supported either the Confederates or the Royalists
in the decade long war, was to be seized. Certain named individuals, such as
Ormond, were subject to execution and ineligible for pardon, as was anyone
active before November 10, 1642, when the Confederation of Kilkenny was
formed. Others might be pardoned, but they would lose their lands, although
they could be compensated with a proportionate share of seized land being made

available in Clare or Connacht. Any Catholic landowner, even if a nonpartici-pant in the war, would receive similar treatment. Naturally, those who were landless laborers, probably the vast majority, and certain specified skilled work-ers essential for the working of the lands, were exempt from this expulsion pro-cess. On the other hand, certain tenants and servants of the dispossessed preferred to follow their old masters to Connacht. The total amount of landown-ers punished was about 3,000, and probably about 45,000 actually moved. The bulk of the population remained in place, although a certain number, particu-larly those apprehended as vagrants or beggars, were subject to transportation in various degrees of indenture or servitude to America or to the West Indies.

The effect of the Cromwellian settlement on the island was immense, for it meant that the landownership had changed from having being nearly 60 per-cent in Catholic hands in 1641 to less than 22 percent by 1660, and that pri-marily in Clare and Connacht. Furthermore, Catholics were excluded from the governance of towns in which they had played a large part. It was hoped that a large portion of the 35,000 soldiers of the Cromwellian army would settle on the land they received as compensation. However, not as many as had been expected did so, opting instead to sell their holding to speculators, who already held land in Ireland and thereby increased their holdings, or to remain absen-tees with all of the ominous implications that entailed in terms of fruitful land management. Many of the soldiers who did settle married local women and either they or their children assumed the Catholic religion of their wives or mothers.

The number of new settlers who came to Ireland was much smaller than had been hoped. The major beneficiaries of the transformation were not new set-tlers, but rather the "New English," that is, those with roots in Ireland from ear-lier in the 17th century. Many, even if adherents to the Church of Ireland, were not high church and were compliant with the religious revolution imposed by the Cromwellians. The Catholic Church was outlawed and priests were subject to execution, although their numbers, even as outlaws, continued to grow. But the property of the Church of Ireland was seized and most of its bishops, who had been appointed by the beheaded king, were dead or in exile. Some of its clergy agreed to accept positions as preachers in the state-established "Inde-pendent" church, while other preachers were recruited from England. The offi-cial "Independent" religious policy opposed both Papism (or Catholicism) and prelacy (what had been the Church of Ireland) and also Presbyterianism. There were also theological differences between the more congregation-based Inde-pendents (or Puritans) and the Presbyterians, who, while not Episcopal, had a more centralized church. There were serious political differences as well, as the Presbyterians of both Scotland and Northern Ireland had disapproved of the extremes to which the parliamentary revolution in England had gone, includ-ing the execution of the king. Some Presbyterian ministers were jailed, but tol-erance was ultimately granted.

In economic and agricultural terms, the plantation had other significant effects. The process, which commenced with the New English in the early plan-tations, of enclosing property and increasingly resorting to tillage continued. There was also extensive deforestation of Ireland both to inhibit sanctuaries for outlaw groups and to provide charcoal for the industrial furnaces, such as those of the iron industries of the Blackwater in Cork and the Lagan valley near Belfast. That deforestation remains a landmark quickly noted by visitors to contemporary Ireland.

Another important characteristic of Cromwellian Ireland was Ireland's formal unification with Scotland and England under a united parliament. Since Cromwell had declined the Crown, an essentially republican form of government, the Protectorate, was set up and was governed by a written constitution. Cromwell was named Lord Protector. The Irish were allotted 30 members in the parliaments that met in 1654, 1656, and 1659, although most of the members were army officers. Paradoxically, Cromwell brought to Ireland for a brief time the two contradictory objectives that would be aspired to by the rival groups of later Irish history: union, championed by the predominantly Protestant unionists of the 19th and 20th centuries, and republicanism, the goal of the Fenians and Sinn Féin in the same periods.

RESTORATION IRELAND

Cromwell died on September 3, 1658, and was succeeded as Lord Protector by his son, Richard. In Ireland his other son, Henry, had succeeded Fleetwood as lord deputy and then lord lieutenant. However, within a few months Richard resigned as sympathy increased in England for the restoration of the Long Parliament whose place had been taken by the Protectorate parliaments. Similar sentiment was developing in Ireland for the restoration of the parliament that Wentworth had called in 1640, and Henry Cromwell also resigned. The military under General George Monck forced the rump of the Long Parliament to restore its full membership, which body then dissolved and allowed a representative Convention Parliament to assemble, enabling the monarchy to be restored in the person of Charles II, the son of the executed king. A similar pattern occurred in Ireland where a military group headed by Sir Hardress Waller proclaimed their support of the restoration of the earlier parliament. Soon after, Lord Broghill (Boyle), Sir Charles Coote, both of whom were former royalists, and Major William Bury, a devout Presbyterian, all men who had done well out of the Cromwellian settlement, were appointed commissioners for Ireland. On May 14, Charles II was proclaimed king of Ireland.

The major problem confronting the restored king was to satisfy, both in England and even more in Ireland, the property aspirations of those who had been supporters of the monarchy while in exile, including Catholics, and those who had gained from the revolution, but who had not wanted to go any further in political or religious radicalization. In Ireland the latter included many of the New English, who earlier had supported the monarchy, but who had accepted the Protectorate and even its religious settlement in spite of their Episcopal or Presbyterian beliefs. Charles attempted to bridge the gap by issuing a declaration in November 1660 confirming the holdings of the Cromwellian soldiers, but also providing for "innocent" Catholics who had supported the monarchy. Thirty-six commissioners were appointed to give effect to the insurmountable task announced in the declaration. Then, more than a year and a half later, the Irish parliament passed an Act of Settlement to resolve the conflicting claims.

The act confirmed the holdings of the soldiers and the adventurers. It also allowed certain owners dispossessed of their lands to make claims for restoration to a court of commissioners appointed for that purpose. Should any lands being restored have come into the possession of the adventurers or soldiers they would be restored to the original owner with the latter receiving compensation with other land. Various categories of eligibility for having land restored existed: ensignmen, who had served the king abroad; article men, who had accepted the 1646 or 1649 treaties between the Confederates and Ormond; and innocents, who had not taken part in rebellion. In fact, awards were made only to "innocents," and, among the thousands of applications, only a few hundred received awards. Even at that, the task of compensating the Cromwellian soldiers, who had to return land to the innocents, with other land was almost insurmountable. A failed conspiracy in March 1663 of resentful soldiers led by Colonel Thomas Blood illustrated the strong animosity among many at Charles's efforts to satisfy the Catholics.

Finally, in December 1665, the Irish Parliament passed begrudgingly an Act of Explanation, which required the soldiers and adventurers to give up one-third of their lands to be restored to the innocents, but that no further claims of innocence were to be heard. In addition, certain named individuals were also given back their lands. The general effect was that the percentage of land owned by Catholic, which had dropped from 60 percent in 1640 to 8 percent in 1660, climbed back to 20 percent. However, almost all the Catholics receiving land back were Old English. Dispossessed Gaelic owners often acquiesced in being the stronger tenants of the Old English, or they turned to outlawry.

Charles appointed an old Cavalier ally, Ormond, as Lord Lieutenant of Ireland, just as he had appointed Edward Hyde, the earl of Clarendon, as chancellor in England. However, in Ireland, as in England, he had to contend with the reality of a parliament that had assumed much greater power for itself, especially with regard to royal revenues. The king acquiesced in abandoning traditional prerogative or feudal revenues, such as the Court of Wards, in return for a parliamentary allocation of revenues for life. In fact, those revenues would not amount to as much as would be needed. In Ireland, the revenues given to the king included customs and excise duties, a hearth tax with a retrogressive character especially onerous to the poor, and a quit-rent on the lands restored by the Acts of Settlement and Explanation. Despite later needs for increased revenue, Charles did not call another Irish parliament for the rest of his reign after the first had been dissolved in August 1666.

Restoration Ireland was marked by a degree of religious toleration, reflective of weariness at the religious turmoil that had fueled the wars of the previous generation. Charles himself was tolerant and even anxious, if possible, to treat his Catholic subjects equitably. The Episcopal character of the Church of Ireland was restored, as were its properties. The primacy was given to John Bramhill. Twelve other bishops were appointed, all high church in attitude. At first religious uniformity within the church was sought, including even the dispossession of Presbyterian-minded ministers in Ulster. The heart of the problem was the

Presbyterian wish to be the established religion, while the more orthodox of the restored hierarchy did not want to allow Presbyterians to serve as ministers within the established church. There was also suspicion that many Presbyterians had been implicated in the attempted coup of Colonel Blood in 1663.

In 1666, several months before it was dissolved, the Irish parliament, like the English parliament, passed an Act of Uniformity imposing the Book of Common Prayer on the established church, mandating ordination of clergy by bishops, and requiring schoolteachers to be licensed by the bishops of the established church. The Presbyterians were not interfered with in their own church system, but they were excluded from the established church and they lost posts they had held within it. However, in a sign of political pragmatism prevailing over religious dogmatism and of the hope to abate religious and political extremism, in 1672 a *regium donum*, that is, an outright gift to Presbyterian ministers, which would be given irregularly in lieu of their presence within the established church, was first awarded.

In a sign of confidence by Catholics that things would improve, Edmund O'Reilly, the archbishop of Armagh, felt confident enough to return to Ireland in October 1659, months before the restoration. In an attempt to gain greater sympathy for the Catholics and overcome the suspicions of their loyalty that had stemmed from the papal excommunication of Elizabeth in the previous century, Peter Walsh, a Franciscan priest, an agent for the Catholic hierarchy, drafted a "remonstrance." It declared the allegiance of the Catholics to the king and disclaimed any papal authority to absolve them from allegiance. A statement by an assembly of Catholics in 1666 denied papal power of deposition and acknowledged the king's divine right in temporal matters. But the papacy and the Irish hierarchy refused to accept the full implications of the remonstrance or the declaration. The government continued to regard Catholics as undeserving of legal toleration. But whatever their legal position, the Catholics in fact received significant toleration as evidenced by O'Reilly's having visited Ireland several times, by the other exiled bishops being able to maintain contact with their dioceses through vicars, and by a general functioning of the church and its schools.

Population estimates for Ireland in the first decade of the restoration are put at about 1,200,000, of whom 800,000 were Catholics and the other 400,000 were split primarily between members of the established Church of Ireland and the Presbyterians, but with some Independents, Anabaptists, and a growing number of Quakers, which variety would make informal tolerance almost requisite. The economy had improved, evidenced by the growth of Dublin and other towns. Cattle become a major source of income, assisted by the ideal grazing character of the Irish landscape and the minimal amount of labor required. So successful was the export of cattle to England that navigation legislation—the forms of protective legislation that would plague Anglo-Irish relations for more than another century, as well as provoke the American Revolution—began to be employed. In July 1663 the English parliament passed an act restricting both importation of Irish cattle into England and Irish trade with the colonies. Four years later further legislation forbade the importation of Irish cattle into England. In 1671 direct imports from the colonies to Irish ports were prohibited. Disappointment at the failure of Ireland to provide a greater positive cash flow to the monarch, already restricted by an impecunious English parliament, prompted Charles to replace the ever-faithful Ormond as lord lieutenant with John Robartes in 1669.

THE POPISH PLOT

For the next decade and a half, Irish history again became inseparably intertwined with crises in English politics, both foreign and domestic. Central was Charles's desire to reassert his sovereignty against the jealousies of parliament. He had already lost his feudal or hereditary revenues and was confined to revenues granted for life by parliament. When those revenues were insufficient he would have to turn to parliament for more revenues, which would mean summoning the members into session. At that point parliament might make demands on or criticisms of royal policy in domestic or foreign matters. All of this might seem perfectly normal in parliamentary democracies of the 19th, 20th, and 21st centuries, but it was something quite irregular in an earlier age, especially in the 16th and 17th centuries, which were characterized by royal absolutism.

The parliament of the 17th century, whether in England or in Ireland, was scarcely a democratic body. One house, the Lords, was composed of hereditary members and bishops of the established church. The other house, the Commons, consisted of representatives from the counties or shires, elected by a restricted franchise, and members selected from assorted towns or boroughs by varying electorates, usually extremely limited. In a sense, the impending struggle was between the friends of the king, who later would be nicknamed the Tories, after the Irish Catholic outlaws, because of allegations of the king's softness toward Catholics, and those who hoped to further augment the authority of the parliament against the power of the monarch, labeled the Whigs after more extreme Calvinists in Scotland. The Whigs were usually people of enormous economic strength and disposed toward a Calvinistic attitude toward religion, even if they nominally conformed to the established church. The Tories, on the other hand, were loyal adherents to the church and suspicious that the Whigs and religious nonconformists were at heart potential "republicans," as had been the Cromwellians.

Charles's difficulties with parliament, especially in getting revenues, led him to secretly agree to accept direct subsidies from his cousin, Louis XIV, the most Catholic king of France, in return for supporting certain of Louis's territorial aspirations against the Netherlands, with whom England had successfully warred in the 1660s, gaining New York. Charles also promised certain concessions to the Catholic population of England and Ireland, and to ultimately become a Catholic himself. One specific action taken by Charles that caused immediate outrage was his issuance in March 1672 of a Declaration of Indulgence suspending penal laws against Catholics (or recusants) and nonconformists. These were laws that had imposed penalties for nonconformity to the established church. The following year the House of Commons declared the declaration invalid and a Test Act was passed requiring all officeholders to take communion in the established church. These actions were to be applied in Ireland as well. In October of that year all Catholic bishops and clergy who were members of religious orders were ordered to leave the country. However, the measure was not strictly enforced. Persistent fears of Catholicism were stoked by the marriage of the king's brother, James, the duke of York and his probable successor in view of the king having no legitimate heir, to Mary of Modena, a Catholic to whose religion James would convert.

The several successors to Ormond as lord lieutenant of Ireland all failed to provide the desirable revenues and Charles reappointed Ormond in 1677. A certain amount of Ormond's energies in the first year of his reappointment were taken up with military preparation in fear of a militant Presbyterian uprising in Ulster stimulated by zealots in Scotland. The crisis passed. His next major problem was the extension to Ireland of the "Popish Plot" hysteria. An allegation was advanced by Titus Oates that there was a Catholic plot to assassinate Charles and replace him with their coreligionist, his brother James. The theory fueled efforts by the Whigs to pass exclusion legislation that would bar the succession by the Duke of York. The anti-Catholic fears occasioned the imprisonment of great numbers. In Ireland, Oliver Plunkett, the archbishop of Armagh since 1669, was arrested in 1679 on grounds of aiding an alleged Catholic plot. Peter Talbot, the Catholic archbishop of Dublin, was arrested in 1678 and detained in Dublin Castle for two years until his death. Plunkett's trial in Ireland ended without his being indicted, but he was then charged for high treason before the court of the King's Bench in London, where, on the perjuring testimony of disgruntled priests, he was convicted and executed on July 1, 1681.

JAMES II AND IRELAND

The fanaticism of the anti-Catholics eventually backfired to the advantage of the monarchy. Efforts to exclude James, the duke of York, from succeeding Charles failed and, in February 1685, he became king. A paradoxical situation therefore existed whereby the king, the de jure head of the Church of England (and Ireland), was a Roman Catholic. This can be seen as a classic example of English political pragmatism whereby theoretical consistency was disregarded in favor of political stability. The Tories, who were high church in their religious sentiment and hostile toward concessions for Catholics, feared that any interference with the natural hereditary succession would open the door for parliamentary selection of a monarch, which could ultimately lead to republicanism, the very thing from which they had escaped with the demise of Cromwellianism. They were also confident that a Catholic reign would be confined only to James's lifetime, as his Catholic wife was assumed to have entered menopause and so be unlikely to bear him a successor son, and his daughters by his late first wife, who would be his successors, were both Protestants.

Suspicions of James by Protestants in England were roused when his cousin, Louis XIV of France, revoked, in the same year that James had ascended the throne, the Edict of Nantes, the award of partial religious toleration to French Protestants granted a century before by his ancestor, Henry IV. The revocation required French Protestants to either conform as Catholics or leave the kingdom. Not only were English and Irish Protestants disturbed by Louis's policy, they were also turned off by James's very impolitic advancement of the position of his co-religionists, especially in Ireland. The complications of the situation were magnified when the queen, Mary of Modena, gave birth to a son. He would take precedence over his half sisters in succession and be raised a Catholic. The implications were that the royal family henceforth would be Catholic with the probability of Catholicism being reestablished.

With regard to Ireland, James gave signs of leaning toward the Catholic interest in dismissing Ormond as lord lieutenant. Earlier he had given command over army regiments in Ireland to Richard Talbot and Justin MacCarthy, both Catholics, who were exempted from taking the Oath of Supremacy. Protestant suspicions might have been partly allayed by Michael Boyle, the archbishop of Dublin in the established church, and Sir Arthur Forbes, the earl of Granard, both lord justices, being designated to take over the government in Ormond's place. However, significant political influence fell to Talbot who was elevated as earl of Tyrconnell (the title held earlier by the O'Donnells). The following year he was placed in command of the Irish army in which increasing numbers of Catholics were not only recruited to the ranks but also commissioned as officers. Catholics were also appointed as judges, admitted to town corporations, and given seats on the Privy Council. That same year Tyrconnell accompanied a Catholic lawyer, Richard Nagle, to England, petitioning for readjustment of the land settlement of the Cromwellian era. In February 1687 he replaced Clarendon, who had advised against any alteration of the land settlement, to become lord deputy. In June he received a royal warrant authorizing him to issue new charters to cities and incorporate towns with large Catholic populations. This insured that many more Catholics would be returned to any future parliament. Catholics were appointed as sheriffs in nearly every county, which would also guarantee the election of Catholic members from the counties. In August Tyrconnell met with the king to discuss prospective legislation for a future parliament.

Many Protestants in Ireland panicked and great numbers fled to England. Their fears had been fired by the publication a few years earlier of Edmund Borlase's *History of the execrable Irish rebellion* with its exaggerated account of the 1641 uprising. In 1687 a satirical song critical of the "Teague" (Irish Catholic) lord deputy and his intention to "cut all de English throat, Lillibulero bullen-a-la," gained rapid popularity among the Protestant population in Ireland.

In England James issued a Declaration of Indulgences granting religious toleration and exemption from the existing statues penalizing Catholics and nonconforming Protestants. The declaration was extended to Ireland as well. This exercise of royal prerogative in overturning parliament's will annoyed even the Tories, the king's natural allies, as several bishops refused to have the declaration read in their churches. James responded by having the bishops charged and tried. Although the bishops were acquitted, the very trial and the birth of a male child to the queen a few weeks before prompted a coalition of leading Whigs and Tories to invite the husband of the king's daughter Mary, William of Orange, the ruler of the Netherlands, to invade England. To assist James against the prospective invasion, Tyrconnell sent a regiment of Irish troops to London. The presence of these largely Catholic soldiers confirmed English suspicion of

James's ultimate Catholicizing plans for the nation. Ironically, in view of later events, these troops had been removed from Ulster where they would have been most needed.

William landed in England in November and James had fled to France before Christmas. In February William and Mary were recognized as monarchs upon their acceptance of a Bill of Rights limiting the royal prerogative and asserting parliamentary powers, legal due process, and religious tolerance (except for Catholics). This was the Glorious Revolution, so benevolent in Anglo-American history, but so deleterious in its immediate effect on the Catholic population of Ireland. William and Mary's accession to the monarchy meant that James was regarded as king only by the authorities in Ireland. Even here, there were many, especially among the Presbyterians in Ulster, who rejected him. For instance, in December the gates of the city of Londonderry were shut before the regiment of the Earl of Antrim, one of James's commanders in Ireland, and Protestants in Bandon, County Cork, attacked a Jacobite (pro-James) garrison.

The Irish situation must be seen in the context of the broader European scene. The League of Augsburg, in which William was a major mover, had been formed three years earlier to inhibit the threatened expansionism of Louis XIV of France. Among William's allies in the alliance were the Catholic Holy Roman Emperor and the pope. Louis, on the other hand, was the solitary international champion of James, whom he hoped to use to distract his opponent William. With Louis's blessing, James returned to Ireland in March accompanied by the French ambassador and French officers. A Jacobite army defeated Ulster Protestants in County Down on March 21, and three weeks later confronted them at Clady in County Derry. However, the city of Londonderry, to which many Protestants had fled, refused entry to James's forces, and a siege of the city began. The following month the Irish parliament, for which Tyrconnell had been preparing, met.

THE PATRIOT PARLIAMENT

James's Irish parliament met from May 7 through July 18. Significantly James had invited the hierarchy of the Church of Ireland to attend, but only four of them, along with four Protestant lay peers sat as members while the 27 others in attendance were Catholic and predominantly Old English. Catholics also made up 226 of the 230 attending the House of Commons to which 300 could have attended. About two-thirds of them came from Old English stock, but there were some Irish members. Their main objective was to undo the Act of Settlement, which had taken land from them in the previous generation. James had some reservations about completely alienating the Protestant population in Ireland, but the parliament nonetheless repealed both the Act of Settlement and the 1663 Act of Explanation, which had enabled some land to be restored to Catholics. In addition, taking a cue from what the Cromwellians had done to them, the parliament passed an Act of Attainment against those Protestants who had absented themselves by going into exile. Their lands became vested in the Crown and would be restored only if they returned to prove their loyalty. Another act required Catholics and Protestants to pay tithes to their own respective clergy rather than solely to the established church. One measure, which James opposed and which therefore had to be dropped, was the repeal of Poynings' Law. James also opposed any mercantile measures, such as that prohibiting the export of wool to England.

Titled the "Patriot Parliament" by the 19th-century Irish nationalist Thomas Davis, the body was hailed by Catholics and nationalists as a generous assemblage committed to religious liberty. However, Protestants saw it as having been engaged in a land grab of their property. Its ambitious agenda would be grounds for Protestant retribution after the Jacobite cause failed.

LONDONDERRY, THE BOYNE, AND THE TREATY OF LIMERICK

The parliament sat in session simultaneous with the siege of Londonderry. More than 30,000 Protestants had taken refuge behind its walls and were defended by a force of 7,500. French engineers allied with the Jacobite army had constructed a boom about two miles north of the city on the river Foyle, which made it impossible for relief troops or supplies to reach the defenders. Soon starvation as well as disease seemed imminent. A French commander among the Jacobites threatened to force other Protestants to seek refuge in the city and thereby increase the risk of starvation. The defenders refused to admit them, but instead indicated that they would begin to hang any prisoners in their control. The French commander relented and abandoned his gesture. However, the siege continued with unrelenting bombardment and thousands of deaths from starvation and disease. Finally, on July 28, two ships with relief supplies were able to break the boom and reach the city. Three days later the Jacobite besiegers withdrew.

On the same day at Newtownbutler, County Fermanagh, a Jacobite army under the command of Justin MacCarthy was decisively defeated by supporters of King William based in Enniskillen. Two thousand of MacCarthy's 5,500 men were killed and another 500 taken prisoner. Two weeks later a large Williamite force under Marshall Schomberg, a French Protestant refugee from Louis XIV's revocation of the Edict of Nantes, landed in Bangor, County Down, and soon after captured Carrickfergus. His forward march toward Dublin, however, was stopped by an outbreak of disease, which decimated his army. James led an army of 20,000 toward him at Dundalk, but mysteriously he did not attack, allowing Schomberg to retreat deeper into Ulster for the winter.

The international, often contradictory character of the struggle was obvious the following year when Dutch Protestants arrived in Cork to support the Jacobites, while Danish mercenaries arrived in Belfast to support William. Louis XIV's requirement that James send a comparable number of Irish soldiers under Justin MacCarthy to France a month later revealed that his motives in supporting James were not entirely selfless. William himself arrived in Ireland on June 14 and soon after doubled the *regium donum* subsidy to the Presbyterian clergy. In command of 37,000 men, William engaged James and his 25,000 men at the famous Battle of the Boyne, where James hoped he held an advantageous position for making a stand against William's march south toward Dublin.

Londonderry is besieged by King James II's forces, 1689. (Mary Evans Picture Library)

However, William's forces triumphed in the battle on July 1.[5] Within three days James set sail for France and two days later William entered Dublin. The victory was hailed in the courts of Europe allied with William in the League of Augsberg, including reportedly the papal court in Rome. It was regarded as especially fortuitous in view of the naval triumph of Louis over a combined Anglo-Dutch fleet off Beechy Head the day before the Battle of the Boyne.

After the Boyne the Jacobite forces in Ireland were confined almost entirely west of the Shannon River, where they were able to resist successfully Williamite sieges of Athlone and Limerick in July and August. The following month William himself left Ireland, giving command of his forces to Dutch general Godbert de Ginkel. The Jacobite forces rejected William's demand for unconditional surrender. On the orders of Louis XIV, the French forces under General Lauzun left Galway for France. Tyrconnell accompanied them, leaving Patrick Sarsfield as the leading commander. His role in resisting the siege of Limerick was rewarded by his elevation as earl of Lucan by James. On another Irish front, a Williamite army commanded by Winston Churchill, the earl of Marlborough, captured Cork and Kinsale in October.

Tyrconnell returned to Ireland in January and, in May, a replacement French force under Marquis de Saint-Ruth landed in Limerick. The next month Ginkel's army took Athlone. Two weeks later, on July 12, his forces defeated

[5] The memory of the Williamite and Protestant victory at the Boyne is still celebrated in Northern Ireland with contentious parades. However, the celebration is on July 12 rather than the date of the battle according to the old calendar then in use in England and Ireland.

the Jacobite army at Aughrim, County Galway. Seven thousand Jacobite soldiers, including their commander Saint-Ruth, were killed in contrast to only 700 on the Williamite side. Galway subsequently surrendered. In late August Ginkel began a siege of Limerick, where Tyrconnell had died. At this time, Sligo surrendered to the Williamites. On October 3, after a few day's negotiations, the Treaty of Limerick was signed, allowing the Irish army to depart for France, where they could continue to serve James, and promising Irish Catholics who accepted the rule of William all the privileges they held under Charles II and a guarantee of their property to "all such as are under their protection in these counties" (that is, the counties still under Jacobite control: Limerick, Galway, Mayo, Cork, Kerry, and Clare). In other areas of Ireland, indictment of Jacobites, especially landowners, did take place and resulted in the confiscation of 1,700,000 acres, leaving less than 14 percent of the land in Catholic hands. However, William also granted pardons and restoration of land to 24 other leading Jacobites, including Richard Talbot and the earl of Antrim.

This suggests that William's first impulse on victory was to treat the defeated generously. However, the Protestant population of Ireland, which had seen its position of dominance threatened by the Jacobites, harbored less kindly attitudes toward the Catholics. In the Irish parliament, which had now become exclusively Protestant, legislation was passed of an uncompromising and discriminatory character, to which William had to acquiesce. In a gesture of displeasure at what was happening, William wrote back into the ratifying legislation words in the Treaty of Limerick accommodating to Catholics (quoted in the previous paragraph) that had been omitted. However, political pragmatist that he was, he accepted as part of the price of retaining his kingship in England, and of inhibiting the ambitions of Louis XIV internationally, an assertion of ascendancy by the "New English" Protestants of Ireland over the vast majority of the inhabitants of the island. The situation of the minority was further reduced because so many of the natural leaders, who were Old English and Gaelic aristocrats, went into exile. The new rulers of Ireland, determined that Catholics would never again pose a threat to their property and ascendancy, set out to inhibit their socioeconomic significance and place severe restrictions on their religious observance.

ASCENDANCY IRELAND

1691–1800

The history of 18th-century Ireland is the history of two distinct societies: the Protestant Ascendancy, which presided over remarkable economic and cultural development, and a Catholic majority, which was legally relegated to second-class status with restrictions on religious liberty and socioeconomic advancement. Within the Protestant community itself, the Dissenters, that is, those not conforming to the established Church of Ireland, suffered political disabilities and other exclusions, although not to the degree experienced by the Catholics. A remarkable feature of the time was the development within the Ascendancy of an Irish patriotism that identified with the claim of Irish nationhood made in earlier centuries by the Anglo–Normans and the Old English. The claim regarded Ireland as one of the jewels in the monarch's crown, but a jewel that ought to be its own master and not subject to the English parliament.[6] Yet the same Ascendancy, which called itself the Irish nation, held sway over the overwhelming majority of the inhabitants of the island because of the support of the very English government whose restricting hand it wished to remove. The century would see the Protestant Irish nation gain a degree of political autonomy, which was partly inspired by and to some degree facilitated by the American War of Independence. There would also develop a more radical separatist republican nationalism, inspired by the French Revolution. Irish republicanism appeared primarily among Ulster Presbyterians. However, many Catholics, whose perspective until then was shaped primarily by a romantic conservative longing for the return of the defeated Gaelic society, would also join the cause.

THE PENAL LAWS

The Protestant Ascendancy in Ireland was solidified by the defeat of the Catholic or Jacobite cause in 1691. Much of the natural Catholic leadership had taken advantage of the option offered by the Treaty of Limerick to follow King James in exile on the Continent, a pattern that would be continued for several generations among the young of the increasingly restricted Catholic aris-

---

[6] *It is from this period on that we can properly refer to the members of the Ascendancy, whether the "New English" with roots in Ireland less than a century old or both Gaelic or "Old English" conformists to the established church, as the Anglo-Irish.*

tocracy of Ireland. Those who departed, whose exile would be permanent, became known in history as the "Wild Geese."

The Catholics who did not opt for exile found themselves subject, in violation of the spirit as well as the letter of the Treaty of Limerick, to a series of laws that would be known as the "Penal Laws." That legislation was designed to ensure that Catholics remained the subjected underclass of the island. Catholics were denied the means of socioeconomic advancement, and distinct inheritance rules inhibited the preservation of any substantial Catholic holding. The process started with the meeting of the Irish parliament in 1692. There were no Catholics in attendance because of the application of the act governing the English parliament requiring members to take an oath repudiating significant Catholic religious doctrines.

Ironically, the Glorious Revolution, which had done so much to advance the position of the parliament in relation to the monarchy within England, did not advance self-governance in Ireland, even for the dominant Protestant minority. Poynings' Law still applied making the agenda of the Irish parliament dependent on approval of the royal council in England. One slight advance was a practice whereby the heads of prospective legislation could be sent by the Irish parliament to the royal council for their approval. However, when approved, it had to be either accepted or rejected in total without option of amendment by the Irish parliament. To the degree that an English monarch, who was also the king of Ireland, might be generously inclined to either the Catholic majority or the Ascendancy minority, he or she would have to contend with the less sympathetic attitude of the English parliament to either group in Ireland. Obviously, if a choice had to be made both the parliament and the monarchy would favor the Ascendancy, which had supported the Williamite cause against the Jacobites.

This was demonstrated by William's acceptance of the penal legislation, which contradicted the Treaty of Limerick, and even though he had Catholic continental allies in his struggle with Louis XIV. In 1695 he accepted the first of the Penal Laws, an act denying to Catholics, or "Papists," the right of a gentleman to bear arms for self-defense or for fowling. Other legislation forbade Papists from going abroad to be educated or to run schools in Ireland, where they had already been excluded from Trinity College. All this was in keeping with the aim to reduce the leadership potential of Catholics, who would not conform to the established church, and to keep them confined to peasant status. Within a generation or two, Catholics would be the "hewers of wood and the drawers of water," with leaders either in exile or having conformed. In 1697 William even accepted the Irish parliament's belated approval of a version of the Treaty of Limerick in which the clause favorable to Catholics that William had earlier sought to include was omitted. This paved the way for further penal legislation that would continue to be expanded until 1727. In the same year, Catholic bishops were banished from Ireland with the hope that in time there would be no one to ordain priests. In 1698 Catholics, other than those who had practiced under Charles II, were barred from the practice of law.

The penal spirit prevailed under William's successor, his sister-in-law, Queen Anne, the second daughter of James II, even though her lord lieutenant in Ireland, the duke of Ormond, was amenable to treating the Catholics more generously. A 1703 act banished regular priests, that is, those who were members of religious orders, as well as bishops. However, the ordinary clergy were allowed to say Mass undisturbed if they would register and take an oath of allegiance. In 1704, in an effort to further reduce the socioeconomic position of Catholics, an act was passed that disallowed property owned by Protestants from coming into the hands of Catholics by sale or inheritance. Nor could Catholics take a lease on land for more than 31 years. Another act did not allow the English practice of primogeniture, whereby the eldest son automatically inherited an estate, to apply to Catholics. In their case the estate had to be divided equally among all sons, unless the eldest son would conform to the established church. Later legislation excluded Catholics from state office, the local corporations (town governments), the army, and grand juries, from having more than two apprentices in their trade, and, finally, in 1727, from voting for members of parliament even if otherwise entitled.

The non-Episcopal Protestants, especially the Presbyterians in Ulster, suffered some disabilities as well, but not to a degree as severe as the Catholics. Their clergy were not regarded as legitimate and the law did not recognize marriages performed by them. Like the Catholics, they had to pay tithes to the established church. However, their own clergy continued to receive the *regium donum,* or royal subsidy, under William. Then, during a period of strong sentiment against Dissenters in England in the reign of Queen Anne, that subsidy was ended and religious Dissenters were excluded from public office unless they would agree to take the sacraments in the established church. Unlike their nonconformist counterparts in England, Irish Presbyterians were too strong in their religious commitment to perform the requisite acts of "Occasional Conformity" to the established church. Consequently, they lost positions in parliament and in local boroughs. The sacramental test continued until the 1780s, although there were occasional indemnity acts allowing specific exceptions. One factor that moderated Ascendancy hostility toward dissenting Protestants was the realization that the Dissenters were as anxious as the Ascendancy to keep the Catholics in a secondary position.

THE POLITICAL STRUCTURE OF 18TH-CENTURY IRELAND

As indicated earlier, the advances in parliamentary power gained by the Glorious Revolution did not apply in Ireland. The parliament, now exclusively Protestant and soon exclusively Church of Ireland, was still subordinate to English interests. Since the hereditary revenues received by the monarch in Ireland were insufficient to meet public expenses, part of which were for the maintenance of an army almost twice the size of the army in England, the parliament had to be summoned into session biennially to appropriate additional revenues. The agenda of that parliament was governed by Poynings' Law, which meant that legislation had first to be approved by the English Privy Council before receiving consideration by the Irish parliament. In addition, the administration of Ireland was in the hands of English appointees who were automatically members of the cabinet form of government that was beginning to congeal in 18th-century England. That cabinet, while not yet the product of a majority in parliament, had to at least be responsive to that majority. The English government named the Irish lord lieutenant, who usually would reside in Ireland only for the biennial parliamentary session, and his secretary. They approached their work as members of that government rather than as the governors of Ireland. Appointments within Ireland and the management of political developments, particularly the securing of consent by the Irish parliament to legislation and revenue measures, were primarily influenced by English political considerations.

The structure of the Irish parliament itself was unlikely to trouble the system, as there was no element of democracy present. As in England, suffrage was very limited in the countywide constituencies, and even more so in the many borough or town constituencies. Some of the latter were "rotten," that is, purely nominal corporations in which only a handful of votes existed. None of the acts governing the duration of a parliament, whether the earlier Triennial Act passed in the post–Glorious Revolution zeal, or the more conservative Septennial Act passed in 1719 to perpetuate Whig and pro-Hanoverian dominance, applied to Ireland. There, a new parliament need be elected only if the monarch died. The main consideration of the government was to manage the various private interests of individual members or of groups of members, who usually could be satisfied or "bought off" with favors or positions.

In 1715 James III, the son of James II, tried unsuccessfully to oust his Protestant cousin, George I, who had succeeded Anne thanks to the 1707 Succession Act, which had specifically excluded Roman Catholics from inheriting the crown. George was aware that many Tories in England retained a degree of sympathy for the Jacobite cause. Accordingly, he gave greater preference to the Whigs, who in turn took advantage of the king's foreignness, extensive absences in his native Hanover, and general unfamiliarity with the intricacies of English politics, to make him increasingly dependent on them. Out of this would gradually emerge the concept of a prime minister, who would be the leader of the majority in parliament. He would chair the cabinet that would control the regular management of government. However, the first minister and the cabinet remained dependent, first, on the approval of the king and, second, on their ability to command a majority in parliament.

The Whigs were more sympathetic to the dissenters in England and Ireland, possibly because many of them were closet Dissenters themselves. In such an atmosphere the appointment of bishops for both England and Ireland was prompted more by political than religious considerations, and, accordingly, the hierarchy consisted of men less filled with religious enthusiasm and more ready to accommodate an increased tolerance for dissenters and, ultimately, Catholics. The same "political" bishops could be counted on to generally support the government as members of the House of Lords in both kingdoms. There was also an increasing disposition to mitigate the burdens on Catholics because many Irish Catholics had not identified with the Jacobite cause in 1715 nor again in 1745, when James II's grandson, Prince Charles Edward, staged an unsuccessful rising in Scotland that penetrated even into England until brutally repressed at the Battle of Culloden.

Significantly, to guarantee the maintenance of Whig dominance of the parliament, a Septennial Act was passed in 1719 to replace the Triennial Act. This act lessened the number of elections and worked to discourage the formation of an opposition or the challenging of incumbents in most constituencies. In the same year, the parliament passed the famous "Sixth of George I" in which the Westminster Parliament formally asserted the power, which it had in fact been exercising, to legislate when it saw fit for Ireland. It also abolished the judicial appellate power of the Irish House of Lords, insisting that such power resided only in the Westminster Lords.

EARLY PROTESTANT NATIONALISM

In spite of such inauspicious circumstances for the expression of popular feelings of opposition, occasions and issues did arise in which they did come to play a significant role. A major issue even during William's reign was the effect of British mercantilism on Ireland. Legislation in 1697 was considered by the English parliament to prohibit the export of wool from Ireland because it threatened the English woolen industry. The measure did not pass, but it prompted William Molyneux, a representative for Trinity College in the Irish Commons, to write a celebrated critique of the English claim to legislate for Ireland. Molyneux, who was a friend of John Locke, the major theorist for the Glorious Revolution, based his critique of the English claims on medieval precedent and on the general principle of the unnaturalness of taxation without consent or legislation without representation, a theme that would be uttered three-quarters of a century later in the American colonies. Regardless of Moyneux's rhetoric, the English parliament in 1699 passed legislation prohibiting the export of wool from Ireland except to England, where the levy of severe duties made it uncompetitive.

Another instance of a popular opposition to the government and an assertion of the right of self-governance for Ireland, or at least, for the Ascendancy in Ireland against the English, was the celebrated issue of "Wood's ha'penny." Wood, a friend of a former mistress of King George I, had been issued a license to mint copper half-pennies and farthings. There was criticism within the Irish parliament as well as from officials in government in Ireland, not to mention a certain degree of popular public outrage. The issue prompted the dean of St. Patrick's Cathedral in Dublin, Jonathan Swift, to write pamphlets attacking the mercantile restrictions that the English were imposing on Ireland. Swift wrote not just from the perspective of Irish entrepreneurs but also from that of the Irish poor, who were faced with unemployment. His pamphlets on the ha'penny issue were called the *Drapier's Letters,* and asserted that "the whole people of Ireland," by which he meant, the Irish members of the established church, "are and ought to be as free a people as your brethren in England." The implication of this Ascendancy nationalism as asserted by Molyneux and Swift was that the Ascendancy succeeded to the Normans, who had a parliament in the medieval Irish kingdom and, as such, constituted a country distinct from England. The complication to this argument was that the position of the Ascendancy over the overwhelming majority of the people of Ireland was due to the English connection. The other logical alternative to asserting legislative independence was to accept formal union with England in a single parliament, as had occurred between England and Scotland in 1707. However, that option would be considered only at the end of the century and only after traumatic social upheaval.

THE UNDERTAKERS

The popular outrage over Wood's ha'penny and the necessity to withdraw his license, as well as the need to recall the lord lieutenant, suggested that governance of Ireland, or more specifically, the ability to guarantee that the Irish parliament would provide the requested supplies, that is, revenues, required another method to guarantee complicity with government wishes greater than simply the lord lieutenant's biennial presence in Ireland. The device employed was to select two or three formidable Irish parliamentary figures with great following among their colleagues. These men, nicknamed the "Undertakers," would guarantee majorities for government business in return for their command in awarding patronage in Ireland. Given the infrequency of election, the minimal amount of opposition, and the oligarchic character of the electorate, the probability of their success was inevitable. It continued after the election in 1727 necessitated by the succession of George II as king. Foremost among these Undertakers were William Connolly and Henry Boyle, successively Speakers of the Irish House of Commons between 1715 and 1752. Connelly was a man of relatively humble origins who was transformed by land speculation into one of the richest men in Ireland. Besides the Speakers, the lord lieutenant could always engage as an Undertaker the archbishop of Armagh, de jure a member of the Irish House of Lords, inevitably an Englishman and appointed more for political than for religious reasons.

GEORGIAN IRELAND

Ireland under the Hanoverian kings, George I, II, and III, was a colonial society dominated by a minority whose position was entirely dependent on the support of the English government, and in which religious disabilities severely restricted the social advancement of and even the proper adherence to religious practices by the majority. However, it was also a society of remarkable creativity and development, at least for the ruling elite. The existence today of a Georgian Society committed to the preservation of the architectural masterpieces of the era is evidence of the period's accomplishment. Urban development was especially noteworthy; most prominently in Dublin, which was viewed as the second city of the British Empire after London, and, as its population grew, broad new boulevards were laid out and extensive and magnificent buildings were constructed, including the House of Parliament, the Four Courts, and the Customs House, all of which remain as central sights of the contemporary city. There was extensive road building, canal construction, and river drainage, which fostered economic development in spite of the mercantile restrictions imposed by England. Evidence of the wealth that was amassed, at least by some, were the numerous palatial residences built throughout the countryside by the ruling elite, comparable to what was being done by their counterparts in England.

Other noted cultural features of the era included the first public performance of Handel's *The Messiah* in Dublin in 1741, the formation in 1750 of the Dublin Society, which would become the Royal Dublin Society, to encourage horticulture, agriculture, and animal breeding, the formation of the Rotunda Maternity Hospital in 1756, and the founding of the Guinness Brewery in 1759.

The virtual doubling of the population in the period, despite penal legislation, severe famine, and disease between 1725 and 1745, and elitist domination of landownership, suggest that some degree of well-being did trickle down to what would be called "Hidden Ireland," that is, the Catholics.

However, there was an ugly side to Georgian Ireland that often accompanied the architectural and material splendor. Many among the landed wealthy were completely irresponsible in their attitude toward their land for which they sought only rental income. They paid minimal attention to improvements. Their personal conduct displayed the worst features of nouveau riche extravagance and coarseness. Dueling was a common practice. Abusive treatment of women, including kidnapping of prospective mates with fortunes, was frequent. Naturally, there was an inordinate consumption of alcohol.

HIDDEN IRELAND

Catholic Ireland had remained rather passive for most of the 18th century. This can be partly explained by the fact that so many of the natural leaders had opted for the path of the "Wild Geese," or exile. That path, taken by so many after the Treaty of Limerick, continued to be followed throughout the next century in view of the restrictions on Catholics in terms of educational opportunities, professional possibilities, social advancement, or public position. Many of those who went abroad to be educated stayed abroad. Many who held aristocratic or gentlemen status opted to serve as officers in foreign armies. The practice continued for generations, as uncles or cousins abroad would serve to attract the rising youth of the family still in Ireland.

Another factor was that a not insignificant number of Catholics, for the sake of either professional advancement or to maintain familial lands intact, opted to conform to the Church of Ireland. The amount doing so has been estimated at about 5,000, which is significant when the social status of those doing so is taken into account.

Other Catholics did not apostatize, but they did maintain a low profile. They hoped that by not drawing attention to themselves they would receive, to a certain degree, a remission in the severity of the penal legislation, or at least its enforcement. Some Catholics turned successfully to other channels of opportunity still open to them, specifically middle-class activities in commerce, especially as victuallers or meat dealers. Some Catholics became so prosperous that they held considerable influence in some cities, even though they were politically disqualified.

The disinterest of the Irish Catholics in the Jacobite risings of 1715 and 1745 furthered the increasingly tolerant attitude of many in the Ascendancy. The era, influenced by English and continental Enlightenment thought, was marked by suspicion of religious enthusiasms, including that which would prompt persecution of religion, even Catholicism. Most members of the Church of Ireland hierarchy, who were more political than religious, were disdainful of the religious zealotry of their predecessors.

Accordingly, despite the Penal Laws, the Catholic religion thrived in Ireland with its many "chapels" functioning openly and being well attended. The numbers of its clergy continued to remain high, including members of the orders that were ostensibly proscribed. Significantly, aside from the allurements of advancement and property retention that could ensue conforming to the established church, efforts at converting Catholics were minimal. There was a diminution of the religious enthusiasm that might have inspired proselytizing efforts aimed at Catholics. It was assumed that the restriction of Catholicism to the lower social orders would work toward its ultimate disappearance.

Among the Catholic masses and among many members of the old Catholic gentry and aristocracy, now in diminished social status, there remained a Gaelic culture, particularly poetic. In earlier times the poets had celebrated the victories and the glories of kings and chieftains. In the 18th century their theme was one of lamentation for lost things and a prayerful wish for restoration that might come from allies and exiles abroad. The poetry, however, did not go much beyond expressing wishes or laments, as efforts to actually advance such liberation or restoration were virtually nonexistent. The Gaelic language was the predominant language among most of the Catholics. Since English was the tongue of the ruling ascendancy as well as the language prevailing in the world of commerce, Gaelic became increasing identified with the lower class peasantry. Nonetheless, remarkable verse continued to be produced.

UNDERTAKER INDEPENDENCE AND REVIVED PATRIOTISM

In the early 1750s the lord lieutenant, the duke of Dorset, found himself in the awkward position of his Undertakers being unable to deliver and indeed in active opposition. The issue was the Irish parliament's claim that it controlled the disposal of a revenue surplus that had accumulated. The government insisted that the Crown had the power to use it to reduce public debt. The Speaker, Henry Boyle, joined by Anthony Malone, the prime sergeant, and by the Earl of Kildare, led the opposition to the government. This "Undertaker" patriotism was short-lived, however, as all three were won over to the government side with titles and pensions, Boyle becoming the earl of Shannon, Malone becoming the chancellor of the exchequer, and Kildare becoming the duke of Leinster. But the seeds were set for future parliamentary "Patriotism." Within a decade outspoken champions of Irish constitutional liberties were elected to parliament. They included Henry Flood and Charles Lucas. The latter had a long career of agitation against public abuses and was elected for the city of Dublin. The specific objectives of these new patriots included security of tenure for judges, a habeas corpus act, a national militia, and a limit to the life of a parliament, objectives in existence in England.

There had been an election upon the death of George II in 1760. His grandson and successor, George III, desirous of more effective government, sought to have the lord lieutenant directly lead the Irish parliament, rather than rely on the patronage mongering Undertakers. To that end, approval was given to an Octennial Act in 1768. This concession to patriot sentiment would hopefully make independent members more amenable to the wishes of the new lord lieutenant, George Townsend, who hoped to directly manage the parliament, control patronage, and bypass the Undertakers. He would also be a continuous rather than occasional resident in Ireland and make the viceregal court a center of social attention.

TOWARD PARLIAMENTARY INDEPENDENCE

Townsend succeeded in breaking the Undertakers, but the spirit of patriotism was also invigorated, and it would have to be contended with by his successors, Lord Harcourt (1772–76) and Lord Buckinghamshire (1776–80). Adding to the government's difficulties and inspiring Irish determination were the difficulties that had developed in the American colonies. The issues were much the same. In both places the rights of Englishmen were being asserted: by the Englishmen in the American colonies who resented the restraint on their trade caused by English navigation laws, the imposition of taxes by a parliament in which they had no representatives, and the efforts to govern by executive mandate; and by the Anglo-Irish ascendancy, or English, in Ireland, who resented the absence in Ireland of many of the gains of the Glorious Revolution in England in 1689, the restraint on Irish commerce by English navigation laws, and the inhibitions on their self-government because of Poynings' Law and the Fourth of George I. An added factor that prompted sympathy with the Americans was the considerable numbers of Irish, especially Presbyterians from the northern counties, who had immigrated to America in search of economic opportunities not available because of economic restrictions resulting from English laws. In addition, the civil disabilities that the non-Episcopal Irish Protestants experienced made them sympathetic to the somewhat freer atmosphere of the American colonies. Naturally, in both situations, there was also a massive native and/or unfree population. In the American colonies it was the Native Americans and African slaves. In Ireland it was the Roman Catholics.

The specific question facilitating the Patriot cause was the matter of the defense of Ireland. In 1772 the Irish parliament had approved raising an army of 15,000 men, 12,000 of whom were to stay in Ireland. However, as the American situation developed from an insurrection to an outright war in which France had come to the assistance of the rebels, the Irish parliament acquiesced in sending several thousands of the army in Ireland to America in defense of the empire. But the very entry of France on the American side raised anew the apprehensions of previous centuries that Ireland might be invaded by a continental enemy of England. Adherents of the Patriot party, while sympathetic to the grievances of America, were still members of the Anglo-Irish ascendancy and could look with nothing but dread on a French invasion. Accordingly, they proposed and received government consent to the formation of an Irish Volunteer Corps, to which 80,000 joined and received arms from the government.

The movement captured the public imagination, as the members were adorned with brilliant uniforms and staged numerous marches and drills. The membership was almost exclusively Protestant, although some Catholics had given financial support. Leading Patriot political figures assumed senior rank in the movement, with the duke of Leinster commanding in Leinster and the earl of Charlemont commanding in Ulster. The logical conclusion drawn from the development was that the existence of this large volunteer force, ostensibly formed to inhibit foreign invasion, could as easily be used to pressure the government to make concessions to the Patriot program.

Their opportunity came with the parliamentary session in October 1779. Henry Flood, even though somewhat out of grace with the Patriots because he had accepted a position as vice-treasurer in 1775, had always championed free trade for Ireland and removal of the restrictions imposed by the English parliament. When the Irish Commons voted supplies only for six months, the government had no choice but to grant the free export of Irish wool and manufactured glass and to allow free trade with the colonies. This victory only emboldened the Patriots to ask for more. Henry Grattan, who entered parliament in 1775, had emerged as one of the leaders, along with the earl of Charlemont, in pushing for constitutional change that would entail actual parliamentary independence for Ireland. Together with Flood, they prompted a convention of the Irish Volunteers meeting in Dungannon, County Tyrone, on February 15, 1782, to pass a motion that the constitutional independence of Ireland was a leading Volunteer aspiration.

The next month the government of Lord North stepped down in England following the success of the Americans. The new government of the Marquis of Rockingham was sympathetic to conciliation with both the Americans and the Irish. A new viceroy, the duke of Portland, was instructed to make concessions to the Irish when he arrived in April. Grattan hailed the development with the celebrated words, "Ireland is now a nation. . . . *Esto perpetua* (be it so forever.)" The following month both parliaments repealed the Sixth of George I, which had asserted the English parliament's right to legislate for Ireland and modified Poynings' Law. However, the Crown of Ireland remained inseparably linked to the Crown of Great Britain.

The Irish parliament voted a sum of £50,000 to Grattan in gratitude for his leadership in the struggle for parliamentary independence. Such a public gift to a political leader might seem extraordinary today, but it was less outrageous in an era in which members received no salaries and where the quest for pensions, sinecures, and so forth was standard. Furthermore, Grattan was a man of relative impoverishment compared to many of his contemporaries.

The following year Henry Flood, whose role in the cause had been obscured by his earlier acceptance of a position and by the emergence of the articulate Grattan, proposed a measure that would eliminate the need for reliance on English goodwill in the maintenance of parliamentary independence. He sought and received a formal declaration by the British parliament that henceforth the only laws governing Ireland were to be those approved by her own parliament and by the king. He suspected that the same parliament that had modified Poynings' Law and the Sixth of George I could as easily reinvigorate them again.

PARADOXES UNDER
PARLIAMENTARY INDEPENDENCE

Nineteenth and early 20th-century Irish nationalists, seeking to end the Act of Union of 1800 that absorbed the Irish legislature into that of Britain, would idealize the short-lived era of parliamentary independence, that of "Grattan's parliament." However, the situation in Ireland in that era was scarcely ideal in view of extraordinary institutional contradictions, the varying agendas of different champions of independence, and the continuing gulf between the two nations within Ireland, the Protestant Ascendancy and the Catholic masses. The institutional contradiction lay in the fact that the administration in Ireland, under the lord lieutenant and his chief secretary, remained under the direction of the British cabinet, of which both were members. They would seek to advance policies and legislation through the Irish parliament that were decided by, and were in accordance with the wishes of, the British government.

The champions of independence began to differ among themselves as to the next step on their agenda. Some advocated further relaxation of the political and

The last parliament of Ireland, elected in 1797, Dublin *(Library of Congress)*

social restraints on Catholics, whereas others saw any involvement of Catholics in governance as an ultimate threat to the benefits of the Glorious Revolution and to the Ascendancy. Some spoke in terms of moving beyond parliamentary independence to the issue of parliamentary reform, that is, to reorganize the way in which members were selected away from the oligarchic constituencies of varying sizes and extremely limited electorates toward a system of equal constituencies with broader franchise and more frequent elections. Others talked of reform in more limited terms, thinking primarily of inhibiting the awarding of patronage to members of parliament by the government as a means of influencing their votes. In addition, while there had been some modifications of the Penal Laws and mitigation in their enforcement, the fact remained that the overwhelming majority of the population were excluded from its governance and were subject to disabilities because of their religion. Lastly, the land system of most of Ireland was settling into the disaster-prone character of oligarchic ownership, characterized by large-scale absentee ownership, numerous exploitive middlemen, and millions of peasant tenants who held small holdings of very short tenure or who were employed as cottiers or laborers, who paid for their homes with their labor.

CATHOLIC RELIEF

As mentioned earlier, Irish Catholics were generally disinterested in the Jacobite risings in Scotland and England in 1715 and 1745. There was a decline of religious enthusiasm and an acceptance of philosophical Deism by many in the established church. Both factors served to promote a more liberal and generous attitude toward the Catholics of Ireland. A formal declaration by many of the Catholic hierarchy that the pope had no civic or temporal authority in Ireland was also helpful in this regard. The relief began with the admittance of Catholics to the lower ranks of the army in 1750. In 1771 Catholics were allowed to take leases of 61, rather than only 29, years on up to 50 acres of "unprofitable land." This was a "toe in the door," followed in 1778 by Gardiner's Relief Act, which allowed Catholics to take leases of indefinite tenure, but not obtain outright freeholds. The same inheritance laws were to apply to Catholics as to Protestants, ending the punitive insistence on gavelkind (equal inheritance to all male heirs), which had been designed to dilute the size of Catholic holdings after each generation. Then, in 1782, in the midst of the enthusiasm over the attainment of parliamentary independence, the Irish parliament passed a second Gardiner's Relief Act, which allowed Catholics to purchase, hold, and bequeath freeholds on the same terms as Protestants. Laws against the regular Catholic clergy and the required registration by any other priest were done away with, as were laws against the Catholics establishing schools. But efforts by Grattan to go even further in gaining liberties for Catholics were opposed by his allies Charlemont and Flood. In fact, fear of whetting Catholic appetites for lands held formerly by their ancestors prompted the passage by the same parliament of Yelverton's Act, which reaffirmed the land awards by the English parliament since 1642.

The limits to which the generosity could go before it was seen as threatening the Ascendancy became apparent in November 1783 at a convention of the Irish Volunteers in Dublin. A motion by the Episcopal bishop of Derry, Frederick Harvey, to give Catholics the vote was defeated. When the same convention forwarded motions to reform parliament in the direction of more equitable representation, the Ascendancy apprehensions were alerted in parliament. John Fitzgibbon, who would become the Earl of Clare and a dominant figure in the government, warned "I do not think life worth holding at the will of an armed demagogue," by which he meant Henry Flood and his Volunteer-sponsored reform resolutions. With the decisive defeat of the resolution, the centrality of the Volunteers in Irish politics ended, although many of its members would eventually be drawn in more radical directions.

But sympathy for further Catholic relief did not disappear, and Catholics themselves were emboldened to advance their cause. A Catholic Committee, composed primarily of Catholic aristocrats like Lord Gormanstown and Lord Kenmare, continued to press their grievances and had as an ally the Irish-born parliamentary figure, Edmund Burke.[7] Subsequent British governments were less sympathetic to Irish parliamentary aspirations, although remaining more generously disposed toward Catholics than the Irish parliament.

Many rank-and-file Catholics were drawn into the "Defenders," a peasant organization not inhospitable to violence that nurtured a romantic idealization of a former past and an aspiration for an undefined liberation from abroad, either through the "Wild Geese" or sympathetic foreign sovereigns. Defender involvement often overlapped with participation in irregular peasant groups such as the Whiteboys who resorted to violence, including cattle-maiming and arson, in protest at landlord maltreatment of tenants.

STATE OF POLITICS DURING PARLIAMENTARY INDEPENDENCE

As mentioned, the champions of independence began to divide among themselves on the next moves for reform. Flood advocated more thorough reform in the direction of equal constituencies and a broader franchise, while Grattan, like Burke in England, wished primarily to curb executive use of patronage to influence parliament. Significantly, the advocate of more thorough reform, Flood, was less sympathetic to completing the process of Catholic liberation than was Grattan, the more conservative reformer. At any rate, the dominance of the British government by ministries less sympathetic to Irish autonomy would see neither wing of the Irish Patriots satisfied. This was especially the case when William Pitt the Younger became prime minister in 1784 and retained that position for nearly two decades. His resident lord lieutenants employed the traditional devices of patronage to inhibit legislation opposed by the government and to promote measures and/or revenues desired by the government. In this task, the government headquarters, Dublin Castle, had the ready support of a group of particularly talented members of the parliament who were convinced the British connection was essential for the survival of the

---

[7] Burke was a major Whig spokesman for the reform, that is, the ending of executive use of patronage. But he did not go along with more radically minded Whigs who wanted constituency equality and a broader franchise. Burke's patron had been the Marquis of Rockingham, in whose short-lived ministry Irish parliamentary independence had been obtained.

Ascendancy. Nicknamed the Junta, the group included John Fitzgibbon, the future earl of Clare; John Beresford, the son of the earl of Tyrone; and John Foster, the Speaker of the House of Commons.

One issue that Pitt espoused was a commercial treaty between Britain and Ireland that would give Ireland full access to the markets of the British Empire and allow free trade between Ireland and Britain. In return Ireland would give of her surplus public revenue to support the Imperial Navy. The Irish parliament passed the measure in 1785, but opposition by English commercial interests prompted extensive amending of the measure in the Westminster parliament that excluded Ireland from much of the imperial overseas trade. Irish reaction was strong, especially when some Irish interests feared free trade with England would hurt some domestic industries. Accordingly, the amended measure was not approved.

Another issue over which the British government and the Irish parliament divided was the Regency Question. King George III in 1788 gave signs of losing his mind. The opposition party, the Whigs, wanted a Regency to be established whereby the prince of Wales, who allied himself with the Whigs against his father and Pitt, would be the sovereign. Pitt sought to inhibit the potential regency with restraining legislation, whereas the Whigs wanted no limits on a regent who could have them form a government. British constitutional practice had not evolved to the point whereby a parliamentary majority would determine the government. The king's wishes remained an essential ingredient in making the selection of a ministry that could manage parliament. Irish Patriots hoped the potential regent would work against the Junta. Accordingly, they passed a resolution urging the prince of Wales to assume the Regency, and, when the lord lieutenant refused to forward the measure to London, they sent a deputation to see the prince. The parliament also accepted a motion of Grattan's censuring the lord lieutenant. He also moved that the Regency motion constituted an undoubted right of the Irish parliament.

Fitzgibbon braved the outrage of the parliamentary majority by reminding them that if they were "duped into idle and fantastical speculations under the pretence of asserting national dignity, they will feel the effects to their sorrow." He reminded them also of their absolute dependence on England and the Act of Settlement, which gave them title to their lands at the expense of the earlier holders. He was frankly honest as he proclaimed: "The Act by which most of us hold our estates was an Act of violence—an Act subverting the first principles of the Common Law in England and Ireland." He went on to remind them that if their parliament could claim the independence to invest the Prince of Wales with royal power in Ireland (against the wishes of the British government), then they could also "convey the same power to Louis XVI (then king of France), or to his Holiness the Pope." His revelation of the family secret and his warning of the implications of departing from it made him as expected, unpopular, but also understood.

CONCESSIONS TO CATHOLICS

The revolutionary spirit in France in the summer of 1789 that would ultimate topple the monarchy infected Ireland soon after. Sentiment in favor of the revolution was very common among the dissenting Protestants, especially in Ulster, who, like liberal radicals in England, saw the agenda of liberty, equality, and fraternity as the appropriate corrective for their own society with its established church, hereditary aristocracy, inequitable representation in parliament, and substantial disabilities on religious nonconformists. The fact that the spearhead of the revolutionary enthusiasm appeared in France, which was the bête noire of Calvinist Protestantism—a Catholic society with an absolute monarchy and a powerful church—solidified their sympathy with it. Many of the Irish Patriots, particularly those who had desired a root and branch reform in the sense of equal constituencies and a broader franchise, shared the approbation of many English Whigs, such as Charles James Fox, for what was happening in France.

Significantly, the most celebrated Irish-born politician of the 18th century, Edmund Burke, broke with his Whig allies in parliament over the French Revolution, which he interpreted in his *Reflections on the Revolution in France* as the beginnings of an assault on the foundations of Western civilization. For the remainder of his life, he urged resistance against it. However, in Ireland, a book more widely read—it was reprinted in four Irish newspapers—was Tom Paine's *Rights of Man,* written specifically to counter Burke.

Paradoxically, even though the French Revolution was directed against His Most Catholic Majesty, the king of France, the historic patron and ally of the Irish Catholic cause, the revolution emboldened many Catholics in Ireland and their sympathizers to be more forthright in demanding relief of their disabilities. A more vigorous and middle-class group replaced the more conservative and aristocratic leaders of the Catholic Committee, who had tended to be more restrained in advancing their cause. The Catholic Committee engaged Wolfe Tone as an agent for their cause. Tone, a Dublin barrister, had written a pamphlet in 1791, primarily for Presbyterians, that urged the granting of rights to Catholics, who could then work in harmony with others in advancing reform of "the present despotism."

The more activist leadership, led by John Keogh, a Dublin tradesman, then decided to bypass the conventional manner of petitioning the lord lieutenant for relief of their grievances and instead organize a national convention, whose members would be selected in the various parishes, to present demands that would claim to speak for "Catholic Ireland." The resolutions of the convention, which met in Dublin in December 1792, were taken by a delegation directly to King George III, although they stopped first in Belfast where they were well received by Protestant sympathizers. Other champions of their cause in London, where the king graciously received them, were Burke and Grattan. Their efforts succeeded in many ways. In 1793, in response to the king's wish that the situation of his Catholic subjects be dealt with, a Catholic Enfranchisement Act was passed allowing Catholics to vote on the same terms as others. Catholics were also allowed to bear arms, become members of corporations (that is, town governments), act as grand jurors, take degrees at Trinity, hold minor offices, and take commissions in the army below the rank of general. However, they still could not serve in parliament.

For all the advances obtained, more radical elements still wished for a more thorough all around reform, rather than just the admission of Catholics to an unreformed system. On the other hand, the passage of Catholic relief coincided with the guillotining of the French monarch and increasing likelihood of Britain going to war with revolutionary France. The British government found itself increasingly in alliance with the Roman Catholic Church in opposing the forces of revolution and, accordingly, more understandably disposed toward its own Catholic subjects in England and Ireland.

Two years later conservative Whigs, sharing Burke's perspective and led by the Duke of Portland, joined William Pitt's government, which was committed to warring against revolutionary France. One of them, Lord William Fitzwilliam, was made lord lieutenant of Ireland. He had been instructed to act favorably toward Catholic emancipation, that is, the admission of Catholics to parliament, if such would be brought forward, but not to raise the matter himself. In fact, he began to take steps soon after his arrival early in 1795 to topple the Ascendancy junta that was the major barrier to Catholic emancipation by dismissing Beresford and proposing to dismiss Fitzgibbon and others from their public offices. But this was more than Pitt, whose governance of Ireland was dependent on the junta, could tolerate and Fitzwilliam was recalled and replaced by Lord Camden, with instructions to oppose emancipation.

However, the government was not averse to appeasing Catholics. To that end an endowment of state funds was made to facilitate the establishment of a Catholic seminary at Maynooth where Catholic clergy, unable now to be educated in revolutionary France, could be trained and hopefully prove well disposed toward the regime that supported them. Anticlerical Irish nationalists have argued that the antirevolutionary attitude of the Catholic Church in Ireland stems from this grant. However, the church has been historically antirevolutionary (as opposed to being antiseparatist or antinationalist). In fact, the education of most of the Irish clergy at home in Ireland probably made them more sympathetic to nationalist attitudes than would have been the case if their training had been at the hands of conservative continental churchmen.

THE UNITED IRISHMEN

In October 1791 Wolfe Tone and a group of well-educated Protestants formed and established a headquarters in Belfast for the "Society of United Irishmen." Their objective was to unite Irishmen regardless of creed in the cause of lessening British influence and reforming the national parliament so as to be truly equitable and representative. Early associates of Tone included Napper Tandy, a radical with Irish Volunteer roots, Rowan Hamilton, and Thomas Addis Emmet, all from Dublin, and Henry Joy McCracken and others from Belfast. The next year a journal, *The Northern Star,* appeared in Belfast championing the views of radical Protestantism against the existing establishment. The movement rapidly developed a system to disseminate propaganda, distributing pamphlets, holding meetings, and organizing numerous local chapters. The movement in its earlier stages was not necessarily separatist, or revolutionary. Most of its following came from the Presbyterian lower middle class, that is, shopkeepers, skilled tradesmen, teachers, and clergy. Ideas that it considered, such as equitable representation in parliament, broader franchise, more frequent elections, were similar to ideas being championed by the more radical wing of the Whigs, especially by those who sympathized with what was happening in France.

Things began to take a different tone by late 1794 and early 1795, as the United Irishmen rhetoric began to concern itself with issues such as tithes that had to be paid to the established church, rents to landlords, and general social inequity. The authorities, likewise, grew concerned about the movement, some of whose sections had begun organizing themselves along military lines. In 1794, the organization was made illegal. Approaches by some United Irishmen began to be made to the Defenders, the Catholic popular secret society whose ideology, to the degree it had any, was in ways antithetical to the progressive United Irishmen, as it was romantic and conservative in perspective, idealizing an Ireland of the past.

Allegations developed that Tone was providing information to the French as to the degree of support a French invasion might have in Ireland. The go-between for Tone with the French was an Anglican clergyman named William Jackson, who committed suicide when facing sentence of treason. Tone negotiated with the authorities to be allowed to leave the country, which he did, sailing to America in June 1795, although he departed for France the following year, where he began decisively to advance the prospects of a French invasion in league with an Irish uprising.

THE ORANGE ORDER

Another side to the popular 18th-century Irish history than the professions of religious tolerance proclaimed by the Presbyterian United Irishmen existed. Sectarian hostility was endemic, particularly in the Ulster counties where the population numbers of Catholics and Protestants were close in numbers. The widespread phenomenon of agrarian violence, usually directed at landlords or their agents because of rent increases, enclosures of commonages, evictions, and so forth, assumed a sectarian character in Ulster where Protestant tenants feared Catholic tenants would replace them by their willingness to pay higher rents and accept lower conditions. A popular Protestant group was the "Peep o' Day Boys" while the Catholics counted on the Defenders. Both groups engaged in numerous confrontations in the latter decades of the century. One severe encounter between the groups, at which the Protestants prevailed, the "Battle of the Diamond" in Loughall, County Armagh, on September 21, 1795, prompted the formation of a more formal Protestant defense organization, the Orange Order, which was encouraged by government authorities as an antidote to the many Protestant United Irishmen. In the original oath of membership, prospective members promised "to the utmost of my power, support and defend the king and his heirs as long as he or they support the Protestant ascendancy." Note the conditional character of Orange loyalism: loyalty depended on the sovereign's defense of the Protestant Ascendancy. Such conditional loyalty reflected an element of Whigism in the Orange Order that was nonexistent in Tory monarchism, or in the support of continental absolute monarchy. The Orange Order grew in numbers in the next few years to more than 170,000 members, and it existed throughout the country. Its tactics of intimidation forced the flight of thousands of Catholics from several Ulster counties.

THE REVOLUTION

Apprehension about the increasingly revolutionary character of the United Irishmen and of possible French invasion in their support prompted the passage in February 1796 of an Insurrection Act. It was made a capital offense to administer an illegal oath. The lord lieutenant was empowered to proclaim an area as disturbed and give special powers of search and arrest to magistrates in the locality. The following November the Irish parliament approved by a vote of 157 to 7 the suspension of the Habeas Corpus Act.

Government fears were given validity in December when Wolfe Tone's efforts to secure French assistance saw a French fleet set sail for Ireland. Bad weather drove many of the ships out to the Atlantic so that they were unable to approach Ireland. A portion with about 14,000 men on board sailed into Bantry Bay, but the same bad weather inhibited an attempt at landing. In 1797 the government directed General Gerard Lake to undertake the disarming of Ulster, where the United Irishmen had originated and where there were many weapons stored, some dating from the Irish Volunteer period and others newly made in forges throughout the country. Despite the appeals to resist by United Irish leaders such as Henry Munro and Henry Joy McCracken, Ulster remained relatively passive during the disarming, which was often brutal. Some suggest there was a popular disenchantment with the French, whom the inhabitants still regarded as papists despite the anticlerical revolution in Paris.

In other parts of the country United Irish militancy intensified, especially as formal membership was assumed by two sympathetic members of parliament, Arthur O'Connor and Lord Edward Fitzgerald, the younger son of the Earl of Kildare. Fitzgerald, in spite or perhaps because of his aristocratic background, was an enthusiast for revolution. He quickly became the military commander of the movement. Reaction to Orange intimidation heightened popular Catholic fears and made them susceptible to Defender appeals. The militant United Irishmen did not let their secularist beliefs inhibit intensifying contacts and collaboration with the Defenders, regardless of their specifically Catholic character. Plans were made for an uprising on May 23, 1798, with expectations of French assistance.

However, the movement was replete with informers and spies. The authorities acted swiftly on March 12, apprehending a number of leaders. Shortly after they captured O'Connor and Fitzgerald. The latter was wounded during arrest and died while in prison. Martial law was proclaimed and the Militia, a regular auxiliary military force many of whose members were Catholics, and the Yeomanry, a volunteer force drawn largely from Orange Lodges, were employed to suppress the United Irishmen–Defenders and collect weapons. They were given license to use all manner of methods, including taking no prisoners, employing torture, and retaliating on whole communities, which effectively broke the back of the movement in the counties of Dublin, Kildare, and Carlow where it had been very strong.

But the reaction to what was happening in those counties had an opposite effect especially in Wexford, where general Catholic fear of a mass pogrom prompted a popular uprising in which some clergy played a central role. For a few weeks the peasant army seemed to sweep all before it, taking Wexford town and Enniscorthy and putting the militia and the yeomanry to flight. The uprising was accompanied by a number of sectarian brutalities, including the burning of a barn containing over 200 local Protestants. By mid-June 1798 the regular army had gained control of the situation, and 20,000 insurgents were routed at Vinegar Hill by Lake's well-armed 10,000 troops on June 21. Fortunately, a new lord lieutenant, Lord Cornwallis, withheld the expected vengeance. His offer of a general amnesty to rebels who would turn in their weapons brought calm to the area.

That same month the primarily Protestant United Irishmen in Antrim and Down, led, respectively, by Henry Joy McCracken and Henry Munro, rose in rebellion. McCraken led 6,000 in an abortive attack on Antrim town on June 7, and Munro's 7,000 were defeated in a battle at Ballinahinch on June 13. Both leaders paid for their efforts by being executed, as were a number of other sympathizers, as examples to other potential rebels.

Two months later, well after the back of both United Irishmen and Defender strength had been broken in Dublin, Kildare, Carlow, Wexford, and Ulster, a French force of about 1,000 men finally landed in Killala, County Mayo, on August 27 under command of General Humbert. The local peasantry looked on them as liberators and many joined them as they advanced further into Mayo. The anticlerical French Republicans were confused by the welcome accorded them by the pious Catholic Mayo peasantry. Nonetheless, the advancing mixed force prompted the defending army garrison at Castlebar, commanded by Generals Lake and Hutchinson, to flee to Tuam. The rebels established a provisional government in Connacht. However, Cornwallis was assembling substantial forces to deal with the insurgents. He was ready when he met Humbert's forces and a smaller number of local rebels at Ballinamuck, County Longford, on September 8. After a token resistance, Humbert surrendered. He and his French forces were allowed to return to France. The Irish rebels were not treated as graciously. Within the next few weeks they scattered throughout Mayo and many of those captured were executed.

On October 12 a superior British naval force captured another French expedition carrying 3,000 troops. Wolfe Tone was apprehended on the flagship, wearing the uniform of a French officer. He was taken to Dublin to be tried by courts-martial, but he committed suicide while awaiting trial, dying on November 19.

The rebellion cost Ireland at least 30,000 lives, not to mention property damage. Its failure can be attributed to a variety of factors. Foremost was the inherent contradiction between the secularist United Irishmen ideology and the traditional Catholicism of the Irish people. The natural Catholic leadership, the surviving Catholic aristocrats and the hierarchy, was suspicious of the secular United Irishmen, and most Irish Presbyterians, from among whom came most of the original support of the United Irishmen, were inhibited from supporting a movement that had so many Catholic allies, even if revolutionary. Even liberal elements within both Irish Catholicism and Irish Protestantism, especially the middle class, while sympathetic to objectives such as Catholic emancipation and parliamentary and electoral reform, had became apprehensive at the radicalization of the United Irishmen, especially the appeal to class war-

Rebels with pikes fight soldiers with rifles and cannons in the Battle of Ross, 1798. *(Mary Evans Picture Library)*

fare that was entailed in their approach to the Defenders. Finally, French assistance came too little and too late.

THE ACT OF UNION

The prime minister, William Pitt, soon after the suppression of the rebellion, began to act on an view he had entertained for some time, that the well-being of both Britain and Ireland would best be served by their formal unification, as England and Scotland had done in 1707. The unification of the two separate kingdoms would expedite commerce, lessen political complications and expenses, and facilitate defense against foreign enemies. Under unification the paradox of an established church in Ireland having a minority of the population as its adherents would be resolved. The Church of Ireland would then be part of the wider Church of England and its adherents would compose part of the majority of the united kingdoms. On the other hand, Pitt believed it could be feasible to make further concessions to Catholics, such as membership in parliament and public subsidization of their church, since they would be only a small minority in the united kingdoms, unlike the overwhelming majority position they had in Ireland alone. Under union the Protestant Ascendancy, in terms of its landed position and social eminence, would continue, but the bribery and patronage that characterized the separate parliament would be no more.

There was minimal opposition to the idea of union within Britain, but there was a considerable degree of opposition in Ireland from diverse quarters. Naturally the now scattered and underground United Irishmen, now completely committed to the idea of a separate Irish republic, were opposed. But the Orange Order, apprehensive at the prospects of Catholic emancipation, was also opposed. Many Irish commercial interests, who had benefited from protectionist tariffs, feared the free trade that union would bring. The business classes of Dublin were anxious that the end of the Irish parliament and the city's subsequent loss of political importance would have dire economic consequences. The legal profession, including both barristers and judges, was concerned at the possible ending of their domains. Lastly, and possibly the most important, the members of the Irish parliament, particularly the placeholders, that is, the recipients of patronage in return for their votes, and the occupiers or owners of the numerous "rotten boroughs," those constituencies with very few voters, were reluctant to lose what they regarded as virtually private property.

When Lord Cornwallis had the measure for union presented to the Irish parliament for consideration the first time in January 1799 a motion opposing it carried by five votes. Among the opponents were some members of the pro-government "Junta," such as John Foster and John Parnell, as well as Henry Grattan and the Patriots. The measure did pass in the Westminster parliament with ease. Cornwallis and his chief secretary, Robert Stewart, Viscount Castlereagh, and John Fitzgibbons, the earl of Clare, undertook the task of persuading a sufficient number of Irish MP's to accept union. This required threatening placeholders with dismissal if they acted independently and offering substantial compensation to owners of rotten boroughs for the loss of their "property." Their efforts were sufficient to enable the Act of Union to be passed the following year and go into effect at the beginning of 1801.

The terms of the Act of Union were as follows. Four of the Irish bishops and 28 of the other Irish peers would represent their colleagues in the Westminster House of Lords. Ireland would have 100 members in the House of Commons, most of whom would be county representatives selected by the forty-shilling freeholders, of which there were many Catholics. Common budget expenses, such as defense, would be apportioned between Ireland and the rest of Britain at a rate of two to 15. Free trade was established, but certain tariffs and duties were allowed to continue for 20 years to allow adjustment. Ireland would have a separate exchequer with responsibility for its own national debt. The established churches of England and Ireland would be unified. Existing statutes in both countries would continue and could be changed only by the Westminster parliament.

One of the items Pitt had hoped would ensue from the act was Catholic emancipation. However, when he pressed the idea King George III reacted most vigorously in opposition, as he regarded allowing Catholics to sit in the parliament as a violation of his coronation oath. Since Pitt did not want the king to lapse into a bout of insanity, such as had brought the Regency crisis of more than a decade before, he dropped the matter, although the Catholics had been given to believe that it was imminent. However, he was honorable enough to resign his office. The effort to repeal the Act of Union would become the persistent overriding issue in Ireland for the next 120 years and in Northern Ireland to this day. It would be primarily the Catholics of the island who would seek its repeal, whereas Protestants would overwhelmingly come to support the union. Had Pitt persisted in pushing Catholic emancipation against the king's wishes and had he succeeded, one wonders if Irish history might have evolved differently.

NINETEENTH-CENTURY IRELAND

The three major phases in 19th-century Irish history are those of O'Connell, the Famine, and Parnell. All three have to be read in the context of a world, especially the European world, undergoing industrialization, political liberalization, and democratization, and experiencing a parallel rise of nationalism and imperialism. The political issues, which dominated Ireland in all three phases, were the quest for equality for Catholics, the undoing of the Act of Union, and land reform.

IMMEDIATELY AFTER THE ACT OF UNION

Pitt did not try to bring his cabinet along in challenging the king's opposition to Catholic emancipation. Instead, he soon after resigned from office. Those of the old Patriots who had opposed the Act of Union in Ireland became reconciled to its seeming permanence and some even took executive office under it. The masses of the population, more taken up with local grievances, such as evictions, rents, and tithes, did not give much thought to the constitutional status of Ireland. Generally not politically enfranchised, they were likely to turn to very local secret societies that resorted to occasional violence to express grievances. The Catholic hierarchy and the older aristocratic and landed leaders remained confident that Union would ultimately bring redress of Catholic grievances, particularly in view of the long collaboration of the British government and the Papacy in combating the French Revolution and subsequently Napoleon. The Act of Union had not disturbed the Protestant Ascendancy, other than the loss of a local parliament, whose patrons and members had been adequately compensated. The executive branch of government in Ireland—an aristocratic lord lieutenant who now resided permanently in the country, the chief secretary who visited Ireland periodically while serving in the British cabinet and in the House of Commons, and the undersecretary who was the major day-to-day administrator—drew the remainder of officials from within the Ascendancy, and Ascendancy feelings, registered by the hierarchy of the established church, various judicial officials, the provost of Trinity College, and major landlords, were dutifully served.

A last gesture of United Irishmen defiance occurred in 1803 when Robert Emmet, the brother of exiled United Irishmen leader Thomas Addis Emmet, staged an abortive uprising in Dublin. He was tried, convicted, and executed. But after sentencing he gave a striking oration at the dock, asking that no one write his epitaph until "my country takes her place among the nations of the earth." Those remarks, much more than his revolutionary efforts, contributed to the persistence of a revolutionary nationalist heritage in Ireland.

The effect of the union on Ireland economically was scarcely benevolent. Ireland's portion of what would be called the imperial debt was only two-seventeenths. But the Napoleonic Wars had occasioned such a massive expenditure that the Irish portion greatly exceeded anything imagined when union was formulated. Ireland's financing of her portion meant an enormous drain on Irish resources. Furthermore, the free trade that had ensued with union put the fledgling Irish manufacturers at a disadvantage when competing with the more developed ones in England. The absence of coal and iron in Ireland was a further disadvantage. While Irish agriculture gained from the requirements occasioned by the wars, the fact that so many of the Irish landlords were absentees living in England meant a further draining of resources, as they invested much of their increasing rental income outside of Ireland.

DANIEL O'CONNELL

This was the Ireland in which Daniel O'Connell would emerge as one of the earliest leaders of a constitutional and democratic mass movement. Born in 1775 near Cahirciveen, County Kerry, O'Connell's family were old Catholic gentry that had been able to maintain a certain degree of well-being through the cooperation of relatives and some Protestants, who connived in evading the full implications of the penal law restrictions on the amassment of land by Catholics. O'Connell's very close roots with Gaelic Ireland are evidenced in his father's fostering him as a very young child to a tenant family, much like a pattern in earlier times where alliances and solidarity between families was secured in such a manner. The family to whom the young boy was sent spoke only Irish and O'Connell only learned English when he returned to his parents. As a teenager he went to live with his wealthy uncle, Maurice, who had an estate at nearby Derrynane and who had amassed a fortune, in no small part through smuggling, especially wines and cognac from France, as well as grazing. His uncle sent O'Connell to Catholic schools in France during the early years of the French Revolution. The oppression of those institutions by the new regime required O'Connell to flee France and continue his studies in England. He began to read for the bar, to which Catholics had become eligible for admission, at Lincoln's Inn in 1794.

The frightening experience of the revolution in France made a permanent impression on the young man and would inhibit him from sympathizing with violence as a means for righting injustice in Ireland. His study in London weaned him from his Catholic beliefs, but not in the direction of accepting the established church. Rather, he was drawn toward the secular or at least Deist ideas of the Enlightenment, particularly the thought of William Godwin and Jeremy Bentham, both critics of traditional institutions and advocates of liberty and democracy. Bentham's theory of utilitarianism, however, was also condemnatory of violent uprisings, as, he affirmed, they stem from emotion rather than reason and would not adequately advance what would be in the best interests of most. O'Connell later returned to Catholicism and, indeed, become a particularly devout adherent, but he never shed the political liberalism he had accepted as a law student. Later in his career, while championing the rights of his fellow Catholics in Ireland and earnestly adhering to his religion, he advocated religious disestablishment, even in countries where Catholicism was the established religion.

Called to the bar in 1798 in Dublin, he had sympathized with the reform aspect of the United Irishmen program, but he disapproved of the violent direction the movement ultimately took. He even served on a lawyer's yeoman corps against further violence. But while he condemned the insurrection of 1798 as a useless waste of life and property, he was not one with the more conservative Catholic elements, including the hierarchy and the landowners, including his own uncle-patron, in looking to the Act of Union as a means of gaining concessions. He committed himself to the restoration of an Irish parliament quite early in his career. However, Catholic emancipation, that is, the right of Catholics to sit in parliament, would be his first item of consideration.

Within a decade the British government had forwarded the notion of combining Catholic emancipation with the semi-establishment of Catholicism through state financing of the hierarchy and clergy. In return the government would receive a veto power over the appointments of bishops, something common in Catholic nations at the time. Henry Grattan, a longtime champion of relief for Catholics, introduced legislation in 1813 giving Catholic emancipation in return for a governmental veto over church appointment. The English Catholics were supportive as were many in the Irish Catholic upper class, and the concept had tentative papal approbation, but O'Connell was vigorously opposed. Even the Irish Catholic hierarchy came around to agree with him, which prompted the pope to defer to that opposition. Subsequently, the chief secretary, Robert Peel, in 1814 ordered the dissolution of the Catholic Board whose older aristocratic leadership had been replaced by O'Connell and middle-class members.

During these years O'Connell achieved extraordinary success in his legal career, bringing in a formidable income. Relations with his uncle, who had disinherited him because of his "improvident" marriage to a distant cousin and also probably because of his political radicalism, were rectified and he again became a beneficiary, although not of the entire legacy. O'Connell used his legal talents to serve many Catholic defendants in various cases, particularly in cases where judge and jury were inclined to be unsympathetic to the accused. He often used the courtroom to denounce the injustice of the system. Sometimes his rhetoric infuriated officials, one of whom was Robert Peel, whom he labeled "Orange Peel . . . squeezed out of the workings of I know not what factory in England" (a play on Peel's middle-class, rather than landed, background). At one point they came close to actually dueling. It was tragic that O'Connell and Peel developed such enmity, as many of Peel's policies on Ireland were benevolent, such as establishing a police force as an alternative to the sectarian posses recruited by local grand juries consisting of landlords. Later, while prime minister, Peel would undertake relief measures at the outset of the Irish famine that would not be continued by the succeeding government of Whig allies of O'Connell.

CATHOLIC EMANCIPATION

Daniel O'Connell on trial for sedition, Dublin, 1844. Lithograph by J. H. Daniels *(Library of Congress)*

A further attempt at legislating for Catholic emancipation, again with the power of veto over episcopal appointments, passed the House of Commons in 1821 but failed in the House of Lords. At this point O'Connell decided to employ a new tactic, the enlisting of mass popular support, rather than simply petitioning for redress through select committees. In May 1823 he formed a new Catholic Association to advance political rights for Catholics and their general interests in all issues. The new group, which had annual dues of one guinea, would hold weekly meetings open to the press. The following year O'Connell broadened its support by establishing a new kind of associate membership whose dues were one shilling a year, a penny a month, or a farthing a week. This brought in mass participation, as the rank and file Catholic clergy became the primary local organizers, encouraging the faithful at weekly Mass to make the affordable contribution. The first week drew in £8, which meant 7,680 subscribers, and within a year the weekly returns were averaging £1,000, which meant 960,000 subscribers. In essence, virtually every Catholic family in Ireland had subscribed.

The role of the local clergy was central to the success of the movement. The local clergy, in contrast to the hierarchy who tended to come from landed families, were middle class or lower in their social origins. Less likely than the hierarchy to have been trained on the Continent, they had a more parochial perspective on issues and were less appreciative of the hierarchical disposition to compromise with political powers on matters such as allowing veto over church appointment. It was the original state grant of a subsidy for a Catholic seminary at Maynooth, followed by the formation of more seminaries, which allowed clerical training to take place in Ireland, thereby forming a more populist-minded clergy drawn from the rank and file of the population. The original grant was designed to inhibit potential Irish priests from being infected with French revolutionary attitudes. While they did not get the Jacobin virus by being trained at home, they did maintain a closer identity with the native populace from whose ranks they came and would be the ready agents for mass political activism reflective of popular sentiment. The only educated members of the Catholic community, aside from teachers and a few professionals, priests easily assumed a leadership position, which they would retain well into the late 20th century, and to which their community readily acceded. This clerical leadership of a mass movement finds a parallel in the role of the Afro-American ministry in the American Civil Rights movement and beyond in the second half of the 20th century.

The zeal with which the Catholic clergy took to the movement was partly prompted in reaction to a vigorous campaign of Protestant proselytism that had been launched by important figures in the Church of Ireland and that had some success among Catholics in very impoverished areas on the western coast of Ireland. This aggressive proselytism, which was encouraged with financial or material reward and framed in depreciatory rhetoric about the "Church of Rome," would leave a permanent apprehension in the Irish Catholic mind and explain much of the church's tardiness in rushing into ecumenical involvement in the more tolerant 20th century.

From the perspective of the Ascendancy, as well as from the rank-and-file Protestants, especially in Ulster, the vigor of the new Catholic Association sparked fears. They did not interpret the movement as a democratic effort to gain political rights, but rather as a new version of the threat posed by the Defenders in 1798 of political and social revolution. Their awareness of the adherence by some Catholics to some prophecies by a continental clergyman that Protestantism was about to be annihilated made them even more anxious. Accordingly, the movement launched by the liberal O'Connell to achieve civil and political equality for his fellow Catholics would be marked from the onset by a fear that it constituted an effort to achieve a Catholic ascendancy.

Significantly, Catholic emancipation was viewed sympathetically by the prime minister, Lord Liverpool, and the lord lieutenants, Lord Wellesley and later Lord Anglesey, but not by the chief secretary, the undersecretary, nor the lord chancellor. O'Connell's opponents in government tried unsuccessfully to have him prosecuted for sedition, and then sought to disband the Catholic Association by legislation restricting political associations. O'Connell and his allies shrewdly got around the last challenge by disbanding their organization and reconstituting it with a new name.

The general election of 1826 gave O'Connell the opportunity to use his organization to achieve political ends. Its members were encouraged to support any candidate for parliament who was sympathetic to Catholic emancipation. Most of those who had made their contribution to the "Catholic rent," as the weekly contributions were nicknamed, were not eligible to vote. They were not being enfranchised because the age was one in which few could vote, rather than because of their Catholicism. There were many Catholics among the nearly 100,000 40-shilling freeholders who could vote in the 32 county constituencies, each of which returned two members to parliament. These freeholders owned their own land, but also rented land from landlords. Consequently, their political independence was subject to considerable pressure, especially since the secret ballot had not yet been introduced. Accordingly, O'Connell had to organize considerable effort and local agitation, in which the Catholic clergy would play a significant role, to get the Catholic freeholders to endanger their economic position and face local landlord hostility.

The Catholic Association concentrated its efforts on four constituencies in particular where pro-emancipation candidates were running, Counties Waterford, Louth, Monaghan, and Westmeath. Elections in the constituencies were not all held on the same day, which would have added to the drama and to the formation of a momentum. The first contest was in Waterford, where a powerful local family, the Beresfords, had dominated the scene for generations. A pro-emancipation candidate named Villiers Stuart appeared as a challenger. Massive campaigning, including a week of speeches by O'Connell, resulted in Stuart's victory. The pro-emancipation candidates were subsequently successful in the other three constituencies.

In Britain the lengthy premiership of Lord Liverpool ended in 1827. His successor, George Canning, died within months, and an interim successor, Lord Gooderich, stepped aside to allow the duke of Wellington to serve as prime minister at the beginning of 1828. O'Connell's nemesis, Robert Peel, became home secretary. Both agreed with King George IV that Catholic emancipation ought not to be allowed. Wellington named Vesey Fitzgerald, a member for Clare and a "liberal" landowner and sympathizer with emancipation, to the presidency of the Board of Trade. In accord with the practice of the time, his appointment required that he resign his parliamentary seat and seek reelection. This gave O'Connell the opportunity to bring the issue to a head by running for the seat himself. If elected he would refuse to take the offensive oaths condemnatory of various central Catholic beliefs that inhibited Catholics from taking a place in parliament. The Catholic forty-shilling freeholders of Clare were well disciplined and reinforced with massive community demonstrations of support so as to guarantee O'Connell's overwhelming victory.

The almost military type demonstrations of celebration that took place throughout the country following the electoral victory made Wellington and Peel fear the possibility of a violent insurrection in Ireland if O'Connell were refused his seat for not taking the oath. Accordingly, when parliament reassembled in February 1829, they induced the king to include in his address a promise of Catholic emancipation, which was in fact passed several months later. However, O'Connell was not allowed a complete victory. He was required to stand again for election, as he had not complied with the existing rules inhibiting Catholics when first returned. Also the 40-shilling freehold franchise was abolished in Ireland, taking the votes away from the electors who had put O'Connell in office.

The passage of the act must be seen as one of the first examples in history of peaceful mass democratic agitation bringing about constitutional reform. Many later Irish nationalists condemned O'Connell's acceptance of the disenfranchisement of the forty-shilling freeholders, but his view was that the momentum of political independence among them was unlikely to be maintained in view of a nonsecret ballot and continued landlord pressure. O'Connell's absolute commitment to nonviolence, coupled with his awareness of the potential for violence, especially if in future elections the forty-shilling freeholders were to be torn between popular secret society and landlord pressure, might also have made him acquiesce in the disenfranchisement. He regarded the gains of the emancipation legislation, which opened every office in the kingdom to Catholics except lord chancellor or lord lieutenant, as having made the sacrifice worthwhile. While it would take some years to come about, the door was open for the attainment of government office by middle-class Catholics. Another factor to be borne in mind was that members of parliament were not paid. This practice was based on the assumption that only people of sufficient means as to not need remuneration should serve. Very few Catholics in Ireland possessed such means, and prospects of future redress of grievances would continue to depend on the sympathy of wealthy non-Catholic members of parliament.

O'CONNELL AND THE WHIGS

With the achievement of Catholic emancipation O'Connell fell back on the cause that was his perpetual goal, the repeal of the Act of Union. Probably he realized the unlikelihood of its being attained, but he used it as an issue with which to rally mass support and to pressure the authorities for reforms short of repeal. In early 1830 he formed a Society for the Repeal of the Union. Like the Catholic Association, the new group held collections, part of whose proceeds went to subsidize O'Connell, who had to forsake a formidable income as barrister while pursuing political agitation and while serving in parliament. Enemies would make much of this "O'Connell Tribute."

In a general election that year, necessitated by the succession of King William IV upon the death of his brother, George III, O'Connell was returned along with 30 others committed to repeal of the union. At the time Europe was again experiencing revolution. In France the Bourbon king had been forced from the throne and replaced with his liberal cousin, Louis Philippe. Uprisings occurred in various German states, and Belgium seceded from its unification with the Netherlands imposed by the Congress of Vienna. Within Britain, agitation was afoot for long-sought parliamentary reform. Reform would entail eliminating or at least lessening the number of "rotten boroughs," that is, those constituencies that had very few electors and, for that matter, few residents. This situation contrasted with that of many newer cities, which had grown in conjunction with the Industrial Revolution and which did not have specific representation, aside from the countywide member elected primarily by rural 40-shilling freeholders. Reform would also broaden the franchise in the boroughs.

The Whigs in parliament were sympathetic to a certain degree of reform, while a few radicals, inspired by the writings of those such as Jeremy Bentham and John Stuart Mill, sought broader reforms. The attempted opposition of the House of Lords and the king caused a Whig ministry that reflected the majority in parliament to be replaced by the Tories under Wellington. But Wellington and the king quickly realized that the time had come when government would have to reflect the majority in the House of Commons and so they allowed Lord Grey and the Whigs to return to power. The Tory-dominated House of Lords accepted the Reform Act in 1832 when faced with the prospect that the king would use his prerogative to appoint sufficient new members to guarantee passage if they would not accede.

The Reform Act, which eliminated a few rotten boroughs and established a uniform franchise requirement for the others, scarcely brought in democracy, as the electorate remained a very small percentage of the population, but it now included a greater proportion of middle-class and professional people. As far as Ireland was concerned, it left the forty-shilling freeholders disenfranchised, but it did add five more members who could be elected from Ireland. The act, which launched a move away from the old Tory notion of viewing parliament as a grand jury whose members ought be seen as acting on their own rather than as representatives of constituencies, made inevitable future gradual broadening of the franchise until democracy was attained. In all this O'Connell and his following from Ireland were allied with the radicals desirous of broader reform.

An immediate issue that O'Connell hoped the more reform-minded Whigs would take on in Ireland was the matter of tithes, that is, the compulsory taxation paid to the established Church of Ireland to which only about a tenth of the population belonged. Naturally the Catholics, and non-Episcopal Protestants, preferred the complete abolition of tithes. The government was less inclined to abolish them, but sought rather to rationalize them. For instance, one grievance had been that tithes had been based on tillage rather than pasture income, which placed the burden more on small tenants than on large landlords. Another source of complaint was the surplus number of bishops and churches, most of which had virtual ghost congregations in overwhelmingly Catholic areas. A complication in any reform was the fact that many of the tithes had been passed from the church to private individuals, who regarded them as a form of private property.

The demand for tithe reform came from O'Connell, the Catholic bishops, and middle-class liberals who regarded it as an anachronism. It was also sought by the rank-and-file Catholic peasantry who bore the brunt of the tithes, even if disguised as part of the rent to their landlords, and who were drawn to the still very strong secret societies that were inclined to agrarian violence ranging from cattle-maiming to murder. Ireland in the 1830s experienced a very high incidence of violence. O'Connell realized that incendiary agitation could provoke the very upheaval he most wished to avoid. Awareness of this danger prompted the government to pass coercion legislation allowing the lord lieutenant to suppress public meetings and to designate certain counties as being in a state of insurrection where ordinary courts could be replaced by martial law.

While O'Connell's followers among the Irish parliamentary representation had increased in the 1832 election to 39 (which suggests the loss of the forty-shilling freeholder votes was not disastrous), the Whig government of Lord Grey, especially its chief secretary for Ireland, Edward Stanley (later Lord Derby), was unwilling to go the whole way in appeasing the tithe agitation. They did put forward an Irish Church Temporalities Act, which eliminated a number of bishoprics and taxed a number of church benefices. The revenue gains from the reduced costs of the establishment were put at the discretion of commissioners for ecclesiastical use. The government viewed this approach as a compromise between the expectations of the O'Connellites and English radicals that the financial gains should go for secular purposes as a first step toward disestablishment and the outrage of high church supporters at what was seen as a statist assault on the church itself.[8]

His dissatisfaction with the inadequacy of the church measure and his displeasure at the coercion legislation prompted O'Connell to raise the issue of repeal of the union. This assertion of the ultimate demand in his program, however, fell on deaf ears as the House of Commons voted 523 to 38 that the union be maintained as it was. O'Connell continued to advocate repeal in his campaigning in Ireland, but political movement within Britain would soon create an opportunity for him to advance more immediate and practical goals. A split in the government on the issue of appropriating some church revenues for secular purposes led to the prime minister's resignation. The reconstituted ministry led by Lord Melbourne had to ultimately give way to a Tory ministry headed by Robert Peel before the end of the year. During the general election of early 1835, O'Connell continued to invoke "Repeal," but soon after, in what was called the Lichfield House compact, he came to an understanding with Melbourne, who would become prime minister, and Lord John Russell, who would become home secretary, to collaborate in driving Peel from office in return for significant reforms within Ireland, particularly the advancement of the position of Catholics.

While O'Connell's faction in parliament declined in the 1835 election to 32 and in the 1837 election (occasioned by the succession the throne of the young queen Victoria) to 31, the second half of the decade brought significant advances for Catholics in accord with the Lichfield House compact. The person most closely connected with these was the undersecretary for Ireland, Thomas Drummond, a Scotsman who advocated impartiality of governmental administration in contrast to the prevailing Protestant Ascendancy bias. He expanded Peel's earlier police force by establishing a national constabulary, which became the Royal Irish Constabulary (RIC), to which great numbers of

---

[8] *Amazingly, the Irish Church Temporalities Act helped provoke the Tractarian Movement of high church clergy at Oxford, one of whose members followed his high church logic all the way to actually entering the Roman Catholic Church. That individual was John Henry Newman, later Cardinal Newman. Another young Tory politician who was very outspoken in criticism of the measure was William Gladstone, who later in the century as prime minister would bring about the disestablishment of the Church of Ireland.*

Catholics were recruited. He appointed paid magistrates who would be free from local landlord pressure and included Catholics among the unpaid magistrates. He moved against the Orange Order, using the same instruments that earlier had been employed against both the Catholic Association and the Repeal Association to inhibit its demonstrations and minimize its dominance of local judiciaries. There were significant appointments of Catholics to senior positions in the public service. Drummond is remembered for his remark that "property has its duties as well as its rights," when suggesting to landlords that they were partly to blame for the degree of agrarian crime in Ireland. The impartial law enforcement he advanced helped to lessen that crime.

While tithes were not abolished, they were greatly reduced and imposed only on the landlords, while arrears were written off. The government also advanced to Ireland two other Whig-Radical reforms that had been established in Britain in the first half of the decade: poor law and municipal corporation reform. Both were reflective of the liberal-utilitarian principles of weakening privilege and advancing impartial government.

The "New Poor Law" of 1833 in England had replaced the centuries-old system of poor relief administered on a parish basis by the local vestry board, under which system landlords were able to supplement the inadequate wages they paid their laborers with poor relief. Under the new system, relief could be obtained only by taking up residence in a poor house, administered by poor law boards governing relatively equal territory not parallel to the old parish boundaries. The receipt of poor relief was to be almost punitive, as the conditions of the recipients were supposed to be worse than those of the lowest paid person actually employed. While "new," the logic of the poor law failed to appreciate the absence of personal responsibility for unemployment in an industrial age confronted with periodic recession.

Like many reforms that are temporarily fashionable, the extension of the measure was completely inappropriate for Ireland where there was no existing poor law system subject to the abuses of the older English system in Ireland and where poverty was so widespread that a punitive poorhouse system would barely touch the surface of the problem. However, one benevolent consequence was the creation of another layer of authority on a local level that would be elected, in contrast to the grand jury system where the landlord interests co-opted from within their own ranks the members who would determine most matters of local governance, whether roads or public contracts, never mind judicial indictments.

The other measure was the Irish Municipal Corporations Act of 1840, which extended the same general principles of an 1835 act governing English borough governance to Ireland. The cities and towns of Ireland were almost entirely dominated by a single patron or a very limited electorate and almost entirely Protestant. The new law was not as generous as the English legislation, which allowed all ratepayers to vote for the towns' governors. It granted the franchise for municipal elections to a more limited electorate and restricted the elected councils' authority over the police. However, it did bring most of the town corporations under Catholic control. Significantly, O'Connell himself become lord mayor of Dublin in 1841.

Drummond's death in 1840, the weakening position of the Whigs under Lord Melbourne, and his anxiety that his movement not dissolve with the achievement of a limited number of reforms, prompted O'Connell to again raise the ultimate issue of repeal. As early as 1838 he had started a preliminary organization and in 1840 formed the National Repeal Association. The next year the Tories, now headed by Robert Peel, who had formulated the new label "Conservative" for the party, were in power. In the elections of that year the number of O'Connellites returned to parliament had shrunk to 18. The end of collaboration with the Whigs paved the way for O'Connell to return to mass movement politics, this time, for repeal.

THE REPEAL CAMPAIGN

The repeal movement took a full year before it assumed the proportions of the Catholic emancipation campaign. Furthermore, there were significant differences in this campaign. Some British and some Irish Protestant had been sympathetic to Catholic emancipation, but virtually none sympathized with repeal. O'Connell's allies included, most significantly, Archbishop John McHale of Tuam, whose endorsement was soon followed by many fellow Catholic bishops and by most of the lower clergy. The Catholic middle classes went along, probably more out of disapproval of the Tory or Conservative government than enthusiasm for repeal. The Catholic peasant masses were supportive, although a rival claimant on their loyalty were the still continuing secret societies whom O'Connell occasionally had to outbid by provocative oratory. An added ingredient to the movement was the support given by a group of young journalists and intellectuals, many of whom were Protestants, who championed a romantic nationalism based on language and ethnicity. Their weekly paper, the *Nation*, which started in October 1842, was a major instrument for advancing the cause of repeal.

O'Connell had proclaimed 1843 as "the repeal year" and he held a series of enormous meetings at various sites, usually places of historical significance, to which tens of thousands came. His meeting strategy coincided with a massive temperance campaign undertaken by a Cork Capuchin priest, Theobald Mathew, in which thousands of the peasantry "took the pledge" against alcoholic drink that so many had used as an escape from the misery of their socioeconomic situation. However, the implications from O'Connell's rhetoric, as well the overwhelming popular Catholic character of his audience, further frightened the Protestant population, some of whom feared they were witnessing a prelude to another 1798, but one that would be even more sectarian. Peel's government wanted to respond to the fears and put a dint in O'Connell's momentum, but they had to contend with the reality of the comparable mass movement in England in favor of the repeal of the Corn Laws, protective tariffs that the middle classes opposed because of their belief in free trade. But besides strengthening the military in Ireland, Peel did not have many options.

When O'Connell called the last meeting of the year for October 8 at Clontarf, north of Dublin, the site of Brian Boru's defeat of the Danes, the government was able to use the military character of the notices announcing the meeting as grounds for declaring it illegal. O'Connell immediately capitulated and issued a proclamation canceling the meeting and directing his supporters not to come. They obeyed and there was no confrontation. Later revolutionary nationalists condemned O'Connell for not calling Peel's bluff. O'Connell was opposed on principle to using violence in advancing his causes, but he was also aware of the futility of insurrection by masses of people against a well-trained army. The government was not satisfied with its victory, which inevitably worked to dampen enthusiasm for O'Connell. Authorities rescued his popularity among the Irish by charging him and a number of his associates with sedition the following May. He spent a number of months in comfortable imprisonment, being entertained as a dinner guest by the governor of the prison, until the House of Lords overturned the charges in September.

CLASH WITH YOUNG IRELAND

The circle about the *Nation*, who would come to be called the Young Irelanders, accepted O'Connell's decision to call off the Clontarf meeting. However, there were inherent differences between them and O'Connell that would become manifest in the years that followed. Many of their leaders were Protestants, such as the poet and editor Thomas Davis, the landowner William Smith O'Brien, and the Ulster Presbyterian John Mitchel. They and their Catholic colleagues, John Blake Dillon and Charles Gavan Duffy, adhered to a romantic and primarily linguistic and ethnic vision of nationhood, similar to the various romantic nationalisms espoused in continental Europe at the time, including among the Italians and Germans, the aspirations for national unification expressed by assorted principalities, and in the case of Eastern Europe, the aspiration for national liberation from domination by a larger neighbor. O'Connell, on the other hand, for all of his close roots to the Gaelic world, was a political liberal and a pragmatist, willing to espouse nationalist goals, but to accept in their place substantial reforms fostering judicial, administrative, and political equity. O'Connell's pragmatism made him realize that the cooperation of the Catholic Church, the faith of 80 percent of the Irish people, and rectification of its grievances had to be a central part of his mass appeal. The Young Irelanders believed in the United Irish ideal that religious conviction should have no part in the definition of Irishness.

A central issue that divided them was related to education. In keeping with the pragmatic character of British political institutions, there was no consistent policy of support for education from the government in Britain or in Ireland. Subsidies had been given to the Catholic seminary at Maynooth, while the only university on the island was Trinity College, originally a seminary for the Church of Ireland, which still retained its high church character and limited its scholarships and fellowships to members of the established church. The Kildare Place Society had received annual public grants for the promotion of nondenominational elementary education since 1815, but in fact its direction was in the hands of Protestants. Penal Law restrictions on Catholic-run schools had been removed, which enabled new religious orders, such as the Irish Christian Brothers, to establish schools, including secondary schools, for Catholics. However, their efforts reached only a small minority.

In 1831 the same chief secretary, Stanley, who inhibited the complete removal of tithes for the established church, sought to overcome the sectarianism of the Kildare Place Society by establishing a national board of education with members who were Anglican, Presbyterian, and Catholic. This marked the beginning of national popular education in Ireland. The original goal of fostering nondenominational and mixed schools met with criticism from Protestants. Attempts to appease them irritated the Catholics. Ultimately, concessions were made to all and the national system evolved into one in which most schools were in fact denominational, dependent on the predominant faith in the district, and few were mixed. Such a pattern has characterized Irish education to the present. Thus a national school system came into being in Ireland more than a quarter of a century before the same would develop in Britain. It succeeded marvelously in catapulting the Irish population ahead of much of Europe in terms of popular literacy. As a side effect, however, it contributed to the decline in popular use of the Irish language, which by the end of the 19th century was confined to a very small percentage of the population.

As prime minister, Robert Peel sought to combine his hostility to O'Connell's repeal movement with promotion of actual reform, a pattern that would be followed by later Conservative governments between 1886 and 1906. In 1845 he broadened the award to Maynooth College. He also sought to build upon the example set by the national school system and create a national university, the Queen's University of Ireland, which would be a federation of four "Queen's Colleges," in Belfast, Cork, Dublin, and Galway, all of which were to be nondenominational, charge low tuition, and furnish ample scholarship funds. The Young Irelanders were enthusiastic about the project as a means of enhancing their goal of an Irish identity free of denominational ties. Religious leaders, however, were critical of the "Godless colleges," although provision was made for the various faiths to instruct their own adherents at the schools. Catholic criticism persisted the longest, as the bishops, led by McHale of Tuam, advocated support for a separate Catholic higher educational system in insisting on Catholic instructors for Catholic students in a variety of subjects, including history, philosophy, and some sciences, that could effect their faith and morals. Although condemned by the bishops, the colleges were established, but, aside from Queen's College, Belfast, they would have relatively small attendance for many decades.

O'Connell took the same line as the bishops on the issue, while the Young Irelanders and the *Nation* challenged the demand for separate education for distinct denominations. Despite these differences, a formal break between them would not occur until 1846, several months after Thomas Davis had died. O'Connell forced the issue by insisting on the expulsion from the Repeal Association of anyone who would not take an oath rejecting the use of physical force in advancing the association's aims. The Young Irelanders, while not at the time advocated physical force, opposed rejecting its employment in principle and resigned or were expelled from the association. Since his old allies, the Whigs, were back in power, following massive Tory desertion of Peel when he endorsed the Whig-Radical cause of Corn Law repeal, O'Connell found himself switching gears by seeking more immediate concessions and de-emphasizing the absolute goal of repeal of the Act of Union. By this time Ireland was already into the great natural disaster of the potato famine, which would make any issue other than feeding the people irrelevant. O'Connell himself, after a last impassioned appeal in parliament for further relief for his suffering people, died on his way to Rome.

THE FAMINE, 1845–1849

The potato blight effected other European nations besides Ireland, but the nature of the Irish agricultural system, its overall economy, and the size of its population caused Ireland to undergo a disaster of immense proportions. Within a decade the Irish population fell by a quarter, as probably close to a million died of a mixture of starvation and disease consequent upon malnourishment. Another million and a half emigrated to Britain and, for the first time in impressive numbers, to North America.

There were many reasons for the magnitude of the disaster. One was the massive population growth Ireland experienced in the previous century, a growth that had slowed down in the years immediately preceding the famine. Another was minimal development of industrialization in Ireland, which was partly the consequence of the absence of protection from more substantial British competitors, partly the disinclination to invest within Ireland, even on the part of Irish possessed of capital, and, partly, the absence in Ireland of the raw materials essential to large-scale industrialization, such as iron and coal. But probably the greatest factor was the inclination of the population to follow the simplest and most readily available path for sustaining themselves, which was to rely on the easily and intensively grown potato, a plant that needed minimal acreage. Accordingly, hundreds of thousands of heads of families were able to remain in the neighborhoods where they were born by accepting work as day laborers for a landlord or large farmer in return for a small plot of land, on which they could grow the absolutely essential potatoes and erect a cottage. Others might have smallholdings of less than five acres, for which they paid as rent whatever cash they received laboring for others. Everything was dependent on the potato, as few had cash with which to buy other food. Those who did have cash had to use it to pay the rent, which others paid with their labor.

The ownership of much of the land by absentee landlords, who left it unimproved, helps to explain the development of such a system. Such owners looked to their property solely as a source of rental income. Intermediaries, either middlemen or slightly larger farmers ready to sublet portions of their own relatively small holdings, worsened the situation. Lastly, most holdings were held on very short-term leases, which discouraged the occupants from making improvements, either agricultural or residential. Many among the landlord class were descendants of what could be regarded as conquerors or colonizers. Some had ancient Irish roots but their ancestors at some stage had conformed to the religious tests of the Ascendancy in order to maintain their holdings. This religious divide created a gulf of disinterest and often contempt toward the tenancy.

Scene of charity during the distress caused by the Great Famine, 1849 *(Mary Evans Picture Library)*

The famine occurred primarily in the western counties of Ireland, from Donegal down to Cork. Those were the regions where the Irish language was predominant and where extensive smallholdings prevailed. Other areas, where there was greater variety of crops or primarily pasture, were not as badly affected. The blight first hit in 1845, and repeated itself in 1846. It was not as bad in 1847, but the use of so much of the seed potato for food the previous winter prevented an adequate number being set for harvest. The blight resumed with full fury in 1848 and 1849.

The response of the government of Robert Peel was rapid and interventionist. A vast amount of Indian corn was purchased from the United States to provide cheap food to offset any profiteering in view of shortages. The Board of Works was directed to undertake the construction of new roads to provide employment. However, Peel fell from power in 1846 when his own party deserted him for his advocacy of free trade. He was defeated on an Irish Coercion measure prompted by increased agrarian violence in the despairing land. The Whigs and Radicals whom he had joined in pushing free trade deserted him on a coercive measure for Ireland, as did the O'Connellites.

The succeeding Whig government led by John Russell, toward whom the politically active Irish were better disposed, took a completely different approach in dealing with the famine. Russell's government was driven by the principles of economic laissez-faire, which discouraged any governmental intervention in the free operations of the market. The authorities argued that the burden of relief should be borne by the nonimproving landlord class, whose rates should finance assistance. Most assistance was directed toward public works, but those works could not consist of projects that the market would ordinarily provide. Hence, after long delays, futile projects such as the building of roads to nowhere and docks where there were no boats were undertaken. Chancellor of the Exchequer Charles Wood and the permanent secretary at the treasury, Charles Trevelyan, held absolutist views regarding fiscal rigidity. Their anxiety to minimize waste impeded much of the relief that had been given. Trevelyan took a Malthusian perspective on the disaster as one that was inevitable, if not divine, retribution on a population seen as wastrel.

The course of events worked to achieve clearances of vast numbers of people from the blighted areas. Much was by death, but certain policies, such as the requirement that the landlord assume the rate burden of any holding on his property of less than four pounds valuation, or the denial of eligibility for public relief to anyone in occupation of more than one-quarter of an acre of land, induced evictions in the first case and voluntary removal in the second. Not surprisingly, the number of holdings of less than five acres declined in Ireland between 1841 and 1851 from 310,000 to 88,000, whereas holdings over 30 acres increased from 48,000 to 149,000.

In spite of its economic rigidity, the government had to accept departures from market orthodoxy and institute a program of soup kitchens, which by August 1847 were feeding three million people daily. Public works projects employed more than 700,000. In 1848, 800,000 received outdoor relief, that is, direct assistance, while the overburdened poor houses, where theoretically recipients of aid should have gone, had to deal with more than 930,000 at different times throughout 1849.

The private response to the disaster was mixed. There were large funds gathered in England, including a donation from the queen, and from other parts of a world, such as a contribution from an American Indian tribe. On the other hand, some Evangelical Protestants combined offering private assistance with proselytizing efforts. However, others made no conditions for receipt of their aid. The Quakers were particularly laudable in this regard. Many volunteers, clergymen, and medical personnel placed themselves in danger and often lost their own lives in trying to bring relief to starving and diseased victims. Some landlords were solicitous and caring, often sponsoring emigration by their impoverished tenants. Others were concerned only with clearing their land of the surplus tenants unable to meet rent obligations. Some landholders, their own position only slightly above the impoverished, whose holdings they were able to absorb, oftentimes displayed similar or worse heartlessness.

A popular view is to label the famine as genocide by Britain toward the Irish. However, in view of the very clear acts of genocide that the 20th century has witnessed, when there was a conscious attempt to eliminate a specific race or people by positive action of governments, the term seems inappropriate to apply to the Irish famine. Admittedly the British authorities did not respond with the vigor that ought to have been expected from the world's then strongest power to immense suffering in a neighboring island under its political authority. Also, Britain's insufficient response was partly prompted by prejudice against the people who were suffering. But the needed response would have required a degree of state action and coercion, such as price controls, embargoes, and conscription of property and materials, that political authorities began to employ only in the 20th century and for the purpose of waging total war. Even in the modern age, where communications are such that the whole world knows of disasters immediately and where the transportation facilities allow almost instant response, disasters of comparable proportions to that of the Irish famine have been allowed to persist and have received inadequate assistance.

One response by the government to the famine, aimed at a landlord class that was seen as largely responsible for the inefficient state of the Irish agricultural system, was the passage of an Encumbered Estates Act of 1849, which facilitated the sale of estates tied up with restrictive inheritance clauses. It was hoped that the new purchasers would be progressive, as was characteristic of many English landlords. In fact, the purchasers more often than not turned out to be local speculators, many with roots in the peasant class, whose approach to the property was not much different from that of their predecessors.

A significant long-range consequence of the famine on those who had survived it was the acceptance by most Irish rural families of the inevitability of most of their offspring having to emigrate. A desire to avoid the dangerous situation of being dependent on a small piece of land made small farmers anxious to increase the size of their holdings, or, at least, to keep as a unit the land they did have. Accordingly, only one of their children, usually the eldest son, would inherit the holding.[9] Most of the other sons would accept the prospects of emigration to Britain or, increasingly more likely, North America. Daughters either married locally or also emigrated. Siblings who did not leave usually accepted an unmarried life as almost a domestic on the family farm. Since the inheriting son was unlikely to bring a bride to the homestead until his parents were quite aged, a tendency set in for men to marry women considerably younger than themselves. This practice guaranteed the continuance of the same pattern for generations, especially since there would be so many vigorous young widows whose presence would inhibit their sons bringing a bride to the land. The demographic consequence was that Ireland, for more than a century, would have a very high birth rate, a very large number of unmarried adults, and a continually declining population.

As is nearly always the case historically, a suffering people are least likely to take part in rebellion when their suffering is most acute. Ireland was relatively peaceful during the years of the famine, aside from the very brief Young Ireland uprising in August 1848. John Mitchel in 1847 had started a separate journal, the *United Irishman,* which championed land reform. His ideas were comparable to those of John Fintan Lalor who saw the landlord system as the

---

[9] *Admittedly, most farmers were still tenants as land purchase programs would not start until the 1880s, but there had developed some continuity in tenancy, especially as holdings on the average increased in size.*

cause of Ireland's problems and who advocated the awarding of permanent security to the tenants. By the early part of 1848 many Young Irelanders, who earlier had apprehensions about aspects of Mitchel's radicalism, including armed insurrection, became more sympathetic. The government reacted swiftly, convicting Mitchel of sedition and having him transported to Australia. In August, the Young Irelanders staged what would be a purely symbolic uprising on a single farm in South Tipperary; Smith O'Brien and colleagues were arrested, convicted, and condemned to death, then transported to Australia. Others escaped. The revolution had not amounted to much. But its progenitors were able subsequently, especially while in exile in America, to promote a vigorous Irish separatist nationalism among the hundreds of thousands who had fled the famine. In addition, several lower ranking members of the movement would, a decade later, form a secret organization dedicated to armed insurrection on behalf of a separate Irish republic.

Irish emigrants leaving their home for America, 1866 *(Library of Congress)*

IRISH TENANT LEAGUE

An 1850 Irish Franchise Act had nearly tripled the electorate of Ireland, primarily in the county constituencies, thereby undoing the disenfranchisement of the 40-shilling freeholders. In these circumstances, Gavan Duffy, a Young Ireland member and editor of the *Nation,* who had successfully defended himself against prosecution, joined with two other editors, John Grey of the *Freeman's Journal* and Frederick Lucas of the *Tablet,* an English Catholic weekly, to promote an Irish Tenant League. The organization would support candidates who would champion tenant rights, or, what would be called, the three "F's," that is, fixity of tenure, fair rent, and free sale.[10] Forty-eight members elected in 1852 committed themselves to these principles and, by joining their votes with the Whigs, Radicals, and former Tories who had remained loyal to Robert Peel, brought down the Conservative government of Lord Derby (the same Edward Stanley who was chief secretary for Ireland in the Whig government of the early 1830s). The Catholic hierarchy and a Catholic Defence Association had supported their election.[11] Two of the tenant rights MP's, William Keogh and John Sadleir, took office in the new government headed by Lord Aberdeen against the group policy of remaining independent.

The hierarchy regarded their taking office as an effective means of promoting concessions on education to the likings of the church, but the break in party unity started the demise of the movement, especially as the new government was disinclined to yield on the tenant rights issue. Gavan Duffy withdrew from involvement and moved to Australia, where he achieved considerable political distinction before returning to Ireland in later years. A. M. Sullivan, a young Cork-born journalist, replaced him as editor of the *Nation.* The number of members of parliament linked to the independent Irish group had shrunk by the end of the decade to 12.

The movement was scarcely encouraged by archbishop Paul Cullen, who was archbishop of Armagh between 1849 and 1852 and of Dublin until 1878. This son of strong farming stock had spent most of his earlier clerical life in Rome and shared papal misapprehension of nationalist revolutionaries. He directed his energies to asserting the rights of the Catholic Church in Ireland, especially in terms of education, and he called for the disestablishment of the Church of Ireland. Within the Catholic Church, he completed the bringing to Ireland, three centuries afterward, of the centralizing and standardizing reforms of the 16th-century Council of Trent. He worked hard at gaining the loyalty of most of the rest of the hierarchy in curbing folk religious practices that the church held to be superstitious, irreverent, and sometimes licentious. He encouraged more formal religious devotions such as novenas and missions. His objectives coincided with growing literacy among the masses of the Catholic population together with a certain degree of social and economic improvement.

---

[10] *Free sale meant that a tenant leaving a holding would be entitled to payment from the person who would replace him, implying that the tenant had a proprietary claim to the holding.*
[11] *They were perturbed by the anti-Catholic implications in Lord John Russell's advancement of a Church Temporalities Act. That measure prohibited a Catholic hierarchy, which the pope hope to reestablish in England, from assuming the same territorial titles as the hierarchy of the established church.*

THE FENIANS

The weakening of constitutional politics in the Catholic and/or antirepeal camp enabled the violent revolutionaries to flourish. The Fenian movement, as it would be popularly called, was started by lower ranking participants in the Young Ireland uprising of 1848 who had escaped apprehension. James Stephens and John O'Mahony had gone to Paris, where, amidst various continental political exiles and revolutionaries, they began to formulate their concept of how to promote an independent Irish republic. Stephens worked in Britain and Ireland while O'Mahony went to the United States, promoting an Irish Republican Brotherhood (IRB), a secret organization, made up of cells whose members were unknown to members of other cells, aside from leaders, who would be part of other cells in a pyramidal structure. Their tactic was armed insurrection and their exclusive goal was the establishment of an independent Irish republic. Other issues, such as land reform or concessions to the church, were regarded as distractions from that main goal.

Significantly, Stephens was able to recruit mainly among urban shop workers and artisans, while the farmers and the bourgeoisie, the usual followers of the earlier constitutional movements were indifferent. O'Mahony found a ready audience among the Irish-Americans, where an elaborate support organization was formed. Calling itself Clan na Gael, it would raised immense sums of money for decades after, and has had, in greatly diminished form, organizational continuity to this day. Inevitably divisions developed in America, as one wing advocated, especially after the American Civil War in which so many Irish-born had obtained military experience, attacking the British in Canada. When Stephens went to America to try to resolve the differences, he was overthrown as leader and replaced by an Irish-American, Colonel Thomas Kelly. An unsuccessful attack was made into Canada across the Niagara River on the New York–Ontario border. Afterward, the Irish-American "Fenians" readied themselves for action in Ireland. That uprising, which took place in 1867, was a failure, as a mixture of indiscretions by some members in losing important documents and significant infiltration by police agents doomed it from the beginning. A shipload of volunteers from America sailed straight into the arms of arresting authorities. A rising in Tallaght, outside of Dublin, was easily put down, as was another in southern Kerry. In addition, the movement was subject to severe hierarchical condemnation, as it was feared it would provoke a backlash in England that would inhibit any future concessions to the Catholics.

Oddly enough, the Fenians found their greatest success in their failures, or better, in their martyrs. Efforts by three members to rescue the imprisoned Colonel Kelly from a police van in Manchester resulted in the death of a police officer. The three in turn were executed, provoking massive outrage in Ireland and stimulating the writing of the evocative tune, "The Manchester Martyrs." As is frequently the case, severe state reprisal backfired. One person who was prompted to do something that would mitigate the prospects of violence in Ireland was William Gladstone. Originally a die-hard Tory who had entered politics opposing Catholic emancipation, Gladstone had followed Peel out of the Tory-Conservative Party, and by the late 1860s he had become leader of that alliance of Whigs, Peelites, and Radicals that had become the Liberal Party. His party came to power following the second great electoral reform act, that of 1867, which brought Britain and Ireland one step closer to democracy. To offset the appeal of Fenianism, he advanced a number of reforms for Ireland.

The first was the disestablishment of the Church of Ireland, which the 1869 legislation mandated to take place in 1871. Disestablishment meant that the church's law and its courts would no longer have coercive force. Its property, aside from the churches themselves, would go to a public body that would distribute the same as an endowment for the support of the present clergy and church employees, as well as Presbyterian recipients of the *regium donum* dating from Stuart times, and grant a final lump sum gift to Maynooth College in place of the annual grant. The remainder of the property was to be used for the people of Ireland, especially for socially ameliorative purposes.

The second was the Land Act of 1870, which called for compensation to any evicted tenant for any improvements on the land, with the presumption that the work was done by the tenant unless the landlord could prove otherwise, and compensation for disturbance based on the value of the holding. It also called for public assistance in buying out a holding from a landlord, but at what were, for most prospective purchasers, relatively high borrowing terms of one-third down payment and interest of 5 percent for 35 years. The Land Act did little to settle the grievances of the Irish farmer-tenants, but it is significant in that it marked the beginning of recognition of a proprietary right of the tenant to the land he worked.

Both gestures, the disestablishment and the land act, can be seen as steps in the direction sought by the Irish Tenant League and the Catholic Defence Association, but they had come about in reaction to Fenian outrages.

ISSAC BUTT AND HOME GOVERNMENT

The reforms imposed on Ireland by Gladstone's Liberal government caused some Protestants and supporters of the union to look again at the idea of a self-ruled Ireland. Foremost among them was the Donegal-born barrister Issac Butt. Having started as a firm supporter of the union and an opponent of O'Connell, his experience as a defense attorney for Young Irelanders softened his attitude on the grievances of tenants and Catholics. As a Conservative member of parliament he doubted the benefit to Ireland of free trade. In 1870 he formed a Home Government Association, most of whose members were originally Protestants. He was convinced that a local Irish government could better satisfy Catholic and tenant grievances and thereby promote Anglo-Irish accord. This curious vision of conservative Protestants and aggrieved Catholic and tenants collaborating to oppose the influences of British liberalism seemed unrealistic. However, very rapidly, numerous political organizations, including local governing authorities, endorsed the idea and within a few years there were 14 members of parliament attached to the Home Government movement and the appearance of chapters in England and Scotland lead to the formation of a Home Rule Confederation with Butt as its president.

In 1872 Gladstone secured legislation establishing the secret ballot, a development that would have substantial consequences for Irish politics. But in 1874 he began to lose the not very deeply felt sympathy of the Irish Catholic hierarchy. Their alliance with English liberalism was temporary and prompted solely by issues such as the disestablishment of the Church of Ireland and the advancement of reforms as an alternative to violent Fenianism. The particular issue on which the bishops turned on Gladstone was that of the universities question.

When Peel's Queen's Colleges had been set up in the 1840s the bishops had disapproved of their secular character, especially since Trinity College would continue to be sectarian under the Church of Ireland. While the Queen's Colleges of Belfast, Cork, and Galway had been established, with only the former really thriving, a Catholic university had been established in Dublin privately with Cardinal John Henry Newman as its first president.[12] But that university was not allowed to give degrees and it received no endowments. The bishops continued to hope for public assistance for this distinctly Catholic university. Gladstone's 1874 university's bill proved to be quite disappointing to them, as it would simply include the Catholic university in a new national university along with Trinity (which was in the process of removing its religious tests for fellowships or scholarships) and the Queen's Colleges, but would not give it an endowment. Gladstone did not want to offend secularist Liberals within his own party by subsidizing a Catholic university nor alienate Protestants by being too favorable to Catholics. Ultimately, Gladstone alienated everyone and when his measure was defeated he dissolved parliament.[13]

In the subsequent general election, the first held with a secret ballot, the results in Ireland were astonishing. The Home Government Association had been dissolved the previous year and replaced with a Home Rule League. The movement came under the control of men sympathetic to Home Rule, but also to advancing denominational education and tenant rights, in other words, to becoming more Catholic. The hierarchy that had earlier been indifferent became more sympathetic. Home rule supporters were elected to 59 seats, only two of which were in Ulster. Those elected met afterward and committed themselves to presenting a disciplined and united front in parliament, which would be adhered to by most members elected from Ireland for almost the next half century.

While still the leader, Butt found himself in an increasingly uncomfortable position as some of the new members began to advocate a policy of obstruction, that is, using parliamentary rules in a way to impede any business being conducted unless that desired by the obstructionists would be heard. The champions of the obstruction tactic included a Belfast provisions merchant, J. A. Biggar, a Protestant who had become a Fenian, and Charles Stewart Parnell, also a Protestant and a County Wicklow landlord whose great grandfather had been

---

[12] *It was while serving as its president that Newman delivered the lectures that became his classic* The Idea of a University.

[13] *Legislation passed under the Conservative government of Benjamin Disraeli in 1879 would establish a Royal University of Ireland that could grant degrees to students of the Catholic University upon taking required exams. It also allotted fellowship to the Catholic University, which in 1882 became known as University College, Dublin. The year before, legislation allowed the awarding of grants to previously exclusively private secondary schools on the basis of the performance of their students on nationally administered exams.*

a major parliamentary defender of the Ascendancy in the late 18th century and who had opposed concessions to Catholics and the original Act of Union.

Butt continued to espouse tactics in conformity with the gentlemanly spirit of parliament as the best means of winning support for Home Rule rather than employing provocative obstruction. He remained the leader of the Home Government Association, but the obstructionists gained increasing popular support in Ireland. While the Irish Republican Brotherhood expelled Biggar for his involvement in constitutional politics (he became a Catholic soon after), it is unlikely that he had shed his Fenian beliefs nor they their regard for him. But it was Parnell to whom popular attention was most drawn. The Home Rule Confederation of Great Britain, whose members were mainly Irish in Britain, replaced Butt as its leader with Parnell in 1877. But Parnell did not yet challenge Butt's leadership of the parliamentary group.

PARNELL AND THE NEW DEPARTURE

The Fenian movement regarded any other issue, whether Home Rule, tenant rights, or church grievances, as distractions from the goal of an Irish republic. However by late 1878 more realistic minds in the movement, prompted primarily by its American support organization, Clan na Gael, in which the exiled former Fenian prisoner, John Devoy, played a leading role, began to think of cooperating, at least temporarily, with other popular forces in Irish politics.

One such force was the land movement started by Michael Davitt, whose family was evicted in County Mayo when he was a young child. He had been brought up in Lancashire, where he lost an arm in an industrial accident, and had been imprisoned for Fenian activism. Conditions were ripe for land agitation in the later 1870s as Ireland, like Britain in general, experienced a great agricultural depression consequent to significant declines in agricultural income following the import of American grains via faster shipping. The old Tory fears of free trade were coming home to roost with major long-range implications for the landed establishment in Britain and Ireland. In Ireland the most immediate effect was the increasing inability of farmers to pay their rents at the very time the landlords themselves were feeling economic pressure. Modern statistics suggest that farms of medium size, still rented, had done relatively well in the decades following the famine. It could be argued that the interruption of improvement, their inability to meet rent demands, and their fear of eviction stimulated their response to the appeal of Davitt for land reform.

Parnell, a landlord, was not especially drawn to the idea of alleviating tenants, never mind redistributing land. However, in late 1878 and early 1879, contacts between him and Clan na Gael resulted in the irregular alliance that would be called the "New Departure." It would consist of a suspension of the violent republican campaign and support for the parliamentary party, which would place its major emphasis on the settlement of the land question, that is, "on the basis of a peasant proprietary," after which home rule and then a republic would fall in place. It was an ingenious subordination of varying long-range and possibly contradictory roles so as to unite energies in the pursuit of a broadly popular goal.

In February 1879 Butt suffered a defeat at a meeting of the Home Rule Confederation on a motion calling for the parliamentary members to act more vigorously, that is, involve themselves in obstruction. Rebuffed by his support organization, Butt died the following May. A Cork Protestant, William Shaw, was elected as the parliamentary leader of the home rulers, but Parnell was amassing support and strength in other areas. Following negotiations with John Devoy and Michael Davitt, Parnell accepted the presidency of the Land League that Davitt had organized in October 1879. Early the next year Parnell was in the United States, where he addressed a joint session of Congress, cementing the New Departure and amassing funds for a forthcoming general election.

In that election the Home Rule Party elected 61 members, and in a caucus of the elected members, replaced Shaw with Parnell as leader. Shaw's supporters thereafter separated from the Home Rule group, identifying themselves with the Liberals. At the next general election in 1885, most of them lost their seats to Parnell supporters.

Print shows clusters of tenants with their belongings after being forcibly evicted from their homes on land owned by British absentee landlords. Lithograph by W. H. Powell *(Library of Congress)*

THE LAND LEAGUE

William Gladstone had again become prime minister following the 1880 general election. He was committed to further land reform in Ireland, but even before he could present proposals in parliament, the Land League proceeded with an intensified campaign of withholding rents, massive rallies and marches, and the new tactic of boycott. Parnell himself called for the last tactic in a September 1880 speech in Ennis, County Clare, in which he asked that anyone taking a farm from which someone had been evicted be placed in a moral Coventry, that is, be shunned by the whole community. In County Mayo the agent for the property of Lord Erne, a Captain Boycott, was subject to this tactic in response to evictions. So complete was the process that the only way in which domestic servants or farm hands could be hired to work the property was by importing them from Ulster counties. The name of the object of the tactic became a common word in the English language for the tactic itself.

The Catholic hierarchy, although not necessarily the rank-and-file clergy, was somewhat apprehensive about the potential of the Land League campaign turning violent. However, a rising Catholic middle class, primarily shopkeepers and publicans, with close familial and commercial ties to the farmers, was supportive. Violence did increase, with some fatalities and considerable destruction of property.

Gladstone had to balance his own sympathy with further land reform with the strong links to landlords and concern with property rights held by the aristocratic Whig component of his government, which was made up of not just Liberals and radicals. In 1881 he put through two measures. One was coercion legislation, allowing extraordinary police powers and martial law in certain situations. The other was a land act granting the essence of what the Land League demanded: the three "F's," fixity of tenure, fair rent, and free sale. It also increased the amount of state assistance in land purchase by tenants from two-thirds to three-quarters of the sale amount with a 35-year term for repayment. But because the down payment and the interest were too high, few took up the opportunity. Since the three "F's" part of the legislation did not apply to those in default on their rent, who constituted about a third of the farmers in Ireland, the Land League continued its campaign after the legislation was enacted.

Parnell, having had no choice but to keep ahead of the more extreme elements in his movement, including major financial supporters among Irish Americans, complained of the act's inadequacies. The chief secretary, William Forster, responded by having Parnell and Davitt arrested under the Coercion Act and imprisoned in Kilmainham Jail in Dublin. This gave Parnell excellent cover from criticism by the more extreme among his supporters, who responded to his arrest by launching another "no-rent" campaign. The Coercion Act was enforced in order to suppress the Land League for this activity, but that spurred more violence. In April informal agreement between Parnell and the government, known as the "Kilmainham Treaty," resulted in his release, amendment of the land legislation to extend its benefits to those in arrears, relaxation of the coercion policy, and a promise by Parnell to use his influence to gain popular acceptance of the law and cessation of violence. The settlement was immediately thrown into danger a few days after Parnell's release when an extremist wing of the Fenians assassinated Lord Frederick Cavendish, who had replaced Forster who had resigned over the concessions to Parnell, and the undersecretary, T. H. Burke, in Phoenix Park, Dublin. But Parnell's immediate condemnation of the killings won him respect in Britain and opened the way for increased cooperation with the government.

FIRST HOME RULE BILL

Parnell received credit for the subsequent improvement in things all around, including the lessening of violence, the decline in rents, and satisfaction with land reform. In 1882 he formed a new organization, the National League, as a support group for his followers in parliament. Two years later he tightened discipline in his party by requiring any of its candidates for office to take a pledge that they would follow party direction in parliament or else resign their seat. The presence of the Irish party in parliament had already caused significant changes in the character and operation of that body. Irish obstructionist tactics had forced the formulation of stricter rules governing parliamentary procedure to allow cloture against delaying tactics by a minority. The general effect was to give the incumbent government greater control over the agenda and to lessen the role of the independent member unattached to any party, which had been characteristic of a significant number of members earlier in the century.

Parnell's discipline over his own members would parallel to some degree the pattern in the major parties, the Conservatives and the Liberals. Reform legislation governing individual expenditure by candidates for seats made them more dependent on the expenditure of funds by the party itself in campaigning. In addition, the increased size of the electorate, especially following an 1884 act, made voters less likely to know or vote for the individual candidates and more likely to vote for their party label. Hence, candidates became anxious to retain party designation by not acting too independently in parliamentary matters. If this was the situation within the major parties, where most of the candidates were men of substantial means, it applied even more to the Irish party, most of whose candidates were relatively impoverished, many being journalists or young political activists and entirely dependent on party funds to support themselves in London during sessions as members of parliament were still neither paid nor allotted expenses.

The 1884 franchise act extended to the county constituencies the same substantial lowering of the franchise that the 1867 act had done for the boroughs. Then the next year a redistricting act organized constituencies along territorial lines, abolishing the distinction between counties and boroughs, with the constituencies being approximately equal in size in terms of electors.[14] All of this advanced the process of democratization and would guarantee extraordinary success for Parnell's party in the next general election. Accordingly, he worked with the Conservatives and other critics of Gladstone's ministry to bring about a parliamentary defeat that would result in a new election. The administrative changes required by the franchise and redistribution acts delayed an election for several months, allowing a Conservative ministry to govern in the interim.

This government passed a land purchase act, named the Ashbourne Act after the Irish lord chancellor, that was very generous in comparison to earlier

[14] An exception would be the university constituencies.

attempts, as the government would advance the entire cost of the land, with the tenants having 49 years to pay off at only 4 percent interest, which amounted to only 70 percent of the rent a tenant was paying. So great was the response that the funds authorized were exhausted in a few years, requiring further appropriations. This was the first major step in the transformation of Ireland from a society of landlord owners to a nation of peasant proprietors.

With the approaching election, Parnell tried to advance the position of his party as the power broker in the future parliament. He urged supporters in Britain to vote for the Conservatives so as to inhibit too overwhelming a Liberal majority. He even bargained with the Conservatives as to their amenability to his primary agenda, Home Rule, that is, a distinct Irish parliament. The results of the election gave 335 seats to the Liberals, 249 to the Conservatives, and 86 to Parnell's party, putting him in the position of being able to keep the Conservatives in power should they be amenable to Irish self-government. In the interval between the election and the sitting of parliament, Gladstone's sympathy for Home Rule was made public by his son, which allowed Parnell to swing to the Liberals. Gladstone formed a government, which introduced a Home Rule bill.

The terms of the legislation included creation of a two-house Irish legislature, with the upper house to consist of 28 appointed members and 75 elected by a very restricted franchise and a lower house with 204 popularly elected members; an Irish executive responsible to that legislature; restrictions on the legislature's power with regard to foreign affairs, defense, and customs and excise; temporary continued control over the police by the British government; appellate review of the Irish courts and of the constitutionality of Irish legislation by the Privy Council in London; continued Irish contribution of one-fifteenth of the imperial budget; and the loss of Irish representation at Westminster other than for reconsideration of the Home Rule legislation. From an Irish nationalist perspective the legislation might appear disappointing as it fell short of full sovereignty, enshrined deference to the upper classes, and allotted a disproportionate share of the imperial budget to Ireland in view of the increasing difference in population between Britain and Ireland. On the other hand, it was the most advanced step toward undoing the Act of Union that had yet appeared.

However, opposition to the measure developed within the Liberal Party. The Whig faction viewed it as a capitulation to the Land League, which they had seen as a form of land communism. Also opposed was the former Radical lord mayor of Birmingham, Joseph Chamberlain, a member of the cabinet, who saw it as a step toward the dismemberment of the British Empire. He preferred imposition of social and democratic reform in Ireland from Westminster rather than through an Irish parliament. During its second reading the measure failed by a vote of 343 to 313, as 93 Liberals broke with Gladstone.

THE FALL OF PARNELL

Gladstone then prevailed on Queen Victoria to dissolve the parliament and call another general election. The results gave an overwhelming rejection to Home Rule, as 316 Conservatives and 78 anti–Home Rule Liberals were returned as opposed to only 191 other Liberals and 85 members of the Irish party. The anti–Home Rule Liberals would ultimately be formally linked with the Conservatives in what would be called the Conservative and Unionist Party. The issue galvanized pro-unionist feelings among the Protestants of Ireland, especially those in northeastern areas. A leading Conservative, Randolph Churchill, played upon these sentiments when he visited Ulster and proclaimed "Ulster will fight; Ulster will be right." The strong resentment toward Home Rule was based on a variety of factors. They included apprehension among the business classes of Ulster, the more industrialized sector of Ireland, that a separate Irish parliament, regardless of restrictions on its power to impose excise or customs duties, would move toward some type of protectionism and impede the close economic ties with Britain on which Ulster had thrived. Others saw their careers entirely linked to the British connection, as a great number of Ulsterites served in the British army and the public service and feared these doors would be closed following any degree of Irish autonomy. But probably religion proved the greatest source of anxiety. Many remained committed to the old idea of the Protestant Ascendancy, which had been weakening and which definitely would be undermined with Home Rule, if not replaced by Catholic supremacy. Those in the Presbyterian or Calvinist tradition were especially fearful of the link between the Home Rule cause and the Catholic Church, as their historical vision was one in which the Catholic Church constituted the embodiment of tyranny and oppression, and, in the eyes of some, the virtual "anti-Christ." Within the province of Ulster Protestant and Catholic populations were about equal in numbers with Protestants decidedly predominant in terms of wealth and position, although there was also a substantial Protestant lower class drawn into severe sectarian rivalry with their Catholic counterparts.

In previous elections the parliamentary contingent from Ulster was generally divided between pro–Home Rule members of the Irish party, supported by the Catholics, and a mixture of Liberals and Conservatives, supported by the Protestants. Henceforth, there would be just two political groupings within Ulster, pro–Home Rule or pro-union (which meant Conservative-Unionist) as it would be the rare Protestant who would approve Home Rule. The same applied to the Protestants in the rest of Ireland. There, however, with the exception of parts of Dublin or the Trinity College representation, anti–Home Rule candidates had a minimal chance of success.

A Conservative government was formed under the Marquis of Salisbury and that party, with a short exception between 1893 and 1895, would exercise control for the next two decades. While ultimately it would bring substantial social and political reform to Ireland, its first approach was to strengthen coercion measures directed by the chief secretary, Arthur Balfour, who was the prime minister's cousin. His stern measures appeared partly in response to a renewed land agitation, called the "Plan of Campaign" that a new agricultural depression had provoked. Many farmers had found it difficult to meet even the rents reduced by the 1881 land act, while landlords found it difficult to grant reductions. While Parnell did not involve himself in it, colleagues in the party, such as John Dillon and William O'Brien, employed the National League in support of the movement, which called on farmers who were denied reductions in their rent to pay no rent but to deposit a reduced rent into a fund to aid those who were evicted. Interestingly, British diplomatic efforts to court the Vatican resulted in a papal condemnation of the Plan of Campaign, but leading Irish bishops, such as William Walsh of Dublin and Thomas Croke of Cashel, were able to draw theological fine points so as to make the condemnation irrelevant to most practicing Irish Catholics. Parnell had, a few years earlier, gained the adherence of the hierarchy in spite of his own Protestantism and even anti-clericalism as the high clerics had agreed to leave the struggle for the advancement of distinctly Catholic education to the Irish party.

In 1887 the *Times* of London published sensationalist allegations linking Parnell with the Phoenix Park murders. Parnell insisted on a public inquiry, which in early 1889 vindicated him when it was discovered that the charges were based on forgeries. The forger admitted as much and shortly afterward committed suicide. Parnell's political position reached a new height with this clearance. The success of Liberals in a number of by-elections, which reduced the Conservative majority, raised expectations of an imminent victory for Home Rule. But at the end of the year, Captain William O'Shea sued his wife, Katherine O'Shea, Parnell's mistress and mother of his children, for divorce, naming Parnell as correspondent. For some years O'Shea had been tolerant of the relationship, even acting as political intermediary for Parnell with British political figures. But anxiety that a legacy might be endangered by his wife's adultery provoked the divorce. Parnell and Mrs. O'Shea did not contest the charges, and the divorce was awarded toward the end of the year with O'Shea even being given custody of the children fathered by Parnell.

Parnell assumed his conduct was that of a complete gentleman in that he had accommodated O'Shea in the course of the affair, including forcing the party to run him as a candidate for Galway. But he did not reckon with the moralist fervor of what had become an important component of the Gladstone Liberal political following—nonconformist or non-Anglican Protestant sentiment, particularly that of its clergy who played a role comparable to that of the Irish Catholic priests in stimulating voting behavior. Although originally given endorsement by the Irish Parliamentary Party, Parnell lost that when the members learned that Gladstone, whose support was essential if Home Rule was to have any chance, insisted that Parnell had to step down for the Liberal–Home Rule alliance to continue. Parnell refused and a majority of his party rejected him. In the following year Parnell used three by-elections in a search for public support against the parliamentary party majority, but his candidates lost in all three. The Catholic bishops were not long in following Gladstone in demanding his resignation and repudiation in the by-elections. In those elections Parnell lapsed into increasing militant nationalist oratory, while churchmen were unrestrained in commenting on his moral failings. In October 1891 his health gave way, and he died at the age of 45.

ACHIEVING INDEPENDENCE

Within four decades of the death of Parnell Ireland became a self-governing dominion within the British Commonwealth, but only after two more efforts at establishing Home Rule, considerable social and political reform from Conservative governments, and a war of independence followed by a civil war. Parnell's Irish Parliamentary Party, after undergoing division and ultimate reunion, then gaining absolute domination over most local government in Ireland, was on the verge of achieving its raison d'être, Home Rule. Then events beyond its control, including a world war, rebellion in Ireland, and oppressive military repression, caused history to pass them by and allow the future of Ireland to be formed by others who were moved by new enthusiasms such as republican separatism and linguistic nationalism. Furthermore, the commitment of the Protestant population in the Northeast to union with Britain remained unshaken, even if the union would be confined to their corner of Ireland.

THE SECOND HOME RULE BILL

The Irish Parliamentary Party was divided when it entered the 1892 general election. The larger anti-Parnell faction, led by Justin McCarthy, and having a new external support organization, the Irish National Federation, formed to replace the Parnellite Irish National League, won 71 seats, while the Parnellites, led by John Redmond, won only seven. The Irish votes enabled Gladstone, aged 83, to form his fourth government. The following year he introduced another Home Rule bill, which differed from the earlier one by continuing Irish representation at Westminster, lowering the Irish portion of the imperial budget from one-fifteenth to one-twentieth, and limiting the veto power of the upper house in the proposed Irish parliament to two years. The bill passed the House of Commons, but failed in the House of Lords. Gladstone's Liberal colleagues dissuaded him from calling for a parliamentary dissolution and going to the electorate to rebuke the Lords. He then resigned and was replaced as prime minister by the earl of Rosebery, who regarded challenging the decision of the House of Lords as inappropriate since there had not been a majority for the rejected Home Rule bill in the House of Commons among the members from England.

Rosebery was a different type of Liberal from Gladstone, whose success had been so dependent on the "Celtic fringe," that is, non-Episcopal Protestants in Wales (largely Methodists) and Scotland (Presbyterians), and Irish Catholics. Rosebery instead championed "Liberal Imperialism," that is, the idea that Liberals should endorse the popular enthusiasm for empire that the Conservatives had helped promote, but direct that enthusiasm toward extending progressive development to other parts of the world; a logic followed even by Fabian Socialists such as George Bernard Shaw. However, Rosebery's aims did not have electoral support, as the Conservative-Unionist alliance triumphed at the next general election in 1895 with an overwhelming majority, which guaranteed that Home Rule would not be considered for some time. In the 1895 election Redmond had been able to increase the Parnellite faction from seven to 11. The anti-Parnellite leader Justin McCarthy stepped down and was replaced by John Dillon.

Within five years the two factions came together under Redmond's leadership, although Tim Healy and William O'Brien would continue to act as independents, and they would continue to have a number of adherents among the Irish parliamentary delegation well into the second decade of the 20th century. O'Brien sought to advance a new land movement through the United Irish League, which aimed to break up and redistribute larger pasture holdings for the benefit of smaller farmers. Redmond and his party argued that such issues constituted distractions from the main goal of Home Rule, the achievement of which became increasingly unlikely. The party continued to proclaim it as an ultimate aim while securing almost monopoly control over local Irish political life. The party's political success was especially facilitated by an 1898 act that ended landlord control over local government by establishing popularly elected councils. This local political success worked to dilute the idealist zeal of the Irish Parliamentary Party as much of its activity fell into the pattern of conventional politics with preoccupation over jobs, contracts, and other aspects of the spoils system. This calming of more ardent nationalist and separatist feelings confirmed the Conservative-Unionist promotion of reform as a means of "killing Home Rule with kindness."

CONSTRUCTIVE UNIONISM

The Conservative governments between 1886 and 1906 passed a number of other measures in addition to electoral reform, which some hoped would make Home Rule irrelevant. They sought to improve the generous Ashbourne Act of 1885, which advanced tenant purchase of land. An 1891 measure failed to attract the interest of many tenants because of complicated financing terms and it annoyed landlords by giving land stock redeemable after 30 years in place of cash as compensation. An 1896 measure improved the terms. Then the 1903 Wyndham Act started the process of making land purchase nearly universal. This act satisfied the landlord by giving a more generous valuation of the land, while giving the tenant purchaser lower interest rates and a longer term of payment. In addition, where more than three-quarters of a landlord's tenants had agreed to terms, the landlord would be compensated for the entire estate while the land commissioners would act as landlords for those tenants reluctant to purchase. Soon tenants had purchased more than 300,000 farms, leaving only 70,000 not purchased. Immediately after independence the Irish Free State made sale of estate land compulsory. This meant that in less than a generation

Ireland had been transformed into a nation of peasant proprietors. Such may well explain the conservative character independent Ireland would assume.

Another reform was the creation of a Congested Districts Board empowered to subsidize the construction of harbors, establishment of fishing, cottage industries, and implementation of improved agricultural methods in areas determined to be poor or destitute according to per capita valuation of land. It also purchased lands and distributed holdings on them. The financing of these projects came from the funds of the disestablished Church of Ireland. There remains some doubt as to the ultimate gains from these well-intentioned efforts, as many of the projects were of a make work, rather than an economically realistic, character. The land purchases expedited the acquisition of land by existing tenants, but few landless laborers gained holdings.

The cooperative movement advanced by the reforming landlord Horace Plunkett, a mixture of private and public action, was another reform. An Irish Agricultural Organization Society encouraged over 800 cooperative organizations to engage in marketing, securing equipment, and obtaining credit. Plunkett later served as head of a public department promoting agricultural and technical instruction.

NEW DIRECTIONS

Superficially, the appearance of constructive unionism, the reforms associated with it, the failure of Home Rule efforts, and the settling of the Irish Parliamentary Party into a more conventional political role made some observers anticipate eventual acquiescence by the Irish to union. The fact that Ireland retained the same number of members in parliament, despite the stagnation in its population numbers, gave its delegation a disproportionate strength that in time might allow Irishmen to assume a greater role in British politics. However, certain cultural movements and a lingering nationalist zeal provided alternative and separatist directions for many ardent younger people turned off by the practical politics of the Irish Parliamentary Party in the post-Parnell era.

One of the earliest was a sporting movement, the Gaelic Athletic Association (GAA), founded in 1884 by Michael Cusack, who formerly ran classes for candidates for police positions, to promote local Irish sports, such as hurling and football, as an alternative to "foreign" and particularly English sports, such as rugby and soccer. Class antagonism served as a partial impetus to the association, as many socially ambitious young white-collar Irish had tended to forsake the games of their peasant ancestors for English sports. Participation in Gaelic sports quickly drew an enthusiastic response from the rural population. Another important promoter was the Catholic Church, particularly Archbishop Thomas Croke of Cashel, who urged avoidance of English games together with English literature and music. Priestly encouragement of youthful involvement in Gaelic athletic activities, which were often conducted on a parish level, was a pastoral device to enhance religious commitment as well as physical development. The fact that Irish was the language employed in playing the games solidified a nationalist mind-set.

As time went on, the GAA specifically forbade its members from attendance at or participation in certain specific "banned" sports like soccer and rugby. A theme was uttered that the Irish games were more "manly," while the others were "effeminate." (Rugby? Soccer?) However, rugby remained the primary game of the better-educated, whether Catholic or Protestant, and most of the private Catholic secondary schools or colleges, particularly those run by the Society of Jesus, had rugby teams. Soccer, on the other hand, remained the popular sport of the urban working class, particularly in Dublin. Gaelic games were predominant in the countryside among the peasantry and the rising middle class. Most important, when the war of independence started, GAA membership served as an almost automatic path to Sinn Féin and IRA involvement.

Another movement, originally apolitical, but which became inseparable from cultural and political separatism, was the Gaelic League,[15] founded by a Protestant, Douglas Hyde, in 1893 to promote the revival of the Irish language. The language had become a minority tongue by the beginning of the 19th century because the natural social leadership of the Irish-speaking population had gone into exile or been confined to second-class status in the penal era. The predominant socioeconomic position of the New English, as well as the need to use the English language in the commercial world to which Catholics turned when land was denied them, weakened the hold of the language on the rising Catholics. When national schooling was started instruction was entirely in English. The Irish-only speaking parents favored this as a way to advance prospects for their children, but, in so doing, the hold of Irish language was weakened for future generations. Possibly the most devastating impact on the language was the high amount of death in and emigration from Irish-speaking areas during the famine of 1845 to 1849. By the beginning of the 20th century probably less than 10 percent of the population spoke Irish regularly, and not many more had even a passing acquaintance with it.

As is often the case, the promoters of a language are people quite distinct culturally and physically from those who regularly use it. In this case the earliest enthusiasts of the language were antiquarians, most likely Protestant and of New English roots. Others of the same background, drawn by the romanticism of Thomas Davis's Young Ireland movement, saw the language as a unifying factor in creating an Irish identity that could overcome the religious divide. At the same time they were not necessarily political separatists. Later, Irish language supporters were romantic conservatives who saw the Irish-speaking peasant world of Ireland as an alternative to the commercial industrial world of 19th-century England. However, very quickly the movement became predominantly identified with and supported by Catholics, particularly younger teachers and priests. It operated culturally in the way the GAA did athletically. Inevitably Gaelic League activists would be drawn into supporting political separatism and even violence. Naturally, the independent Irish government that would emerge from the revolution would remain even to this day, at least nominally, committed to the language cause.

---

[15] *Gaelic League is probably an inappropriate name for an organization to promote the Irish language, which is but one of several Gaelic or Celtic languages, including Scots, Cornish, and Breton.*

A more elitist phenomenon, often linked with these movements, if for no other reason than that it occurred simultaneously with them, was the Irish literary renaissance, whose central event was the opening of the Abbey Theatre in Dublin in 1904. No doubt some wanted a distinct Irish literature that would conform to a separatist ideology that would uncritically idealize things Irish. But the central figures in this movement, including William Butler Yeats, John Millington Synge, and Lady Gregory, were of such literary genius and independence of thought that such an objective would have been inconceivable. The emphasis placed on the Irish people provided the theme for their works. Admittedly, they shared a romantic idealization of the Irish-speaking peasant world as an alternative to the materialist world of urbanism and industry. But they did not make their characters out to be angels and their work had, as does all great literature, a universal message and appeal. Indeed, the fact that some of their work made Irish characters appear less than saintly provoked riots by more militant cultural separatists who saw plays such as Synge's *The Playboy of the Western World* as depreciatory of the Irish.

Distinctly political movements also appeared as alternatives to the Irish Parliamentary Party, even though they would retain a minority position for sometime. One was Sinn Féin, which was started as a political party in 1905, based on the ideas formulated by the journalist Arthur Griffith in his newspaper, *The United Irishman*, beginning in 1898. Griffith called for the members of parliament elected from Ireland to refuse to take their seats in Westminster and form a separate parliament in Ireland—in other words, to proclaim Home Rule without formal parliamentary sanction. He advocated a "Dual Monarchy" arrangement in place of the union, with the same king for the separate nations, Britain and Ireland, much like the Austro-Hungarian emperor was of Austria and Hungary. Griffith also advocated economic protectionism for Ireland as a stimulus to its industrial development. Culturally he believed in Irish distinctness and was critical of some of the plays performed at the Abbey Theatre. His political party ran several candidates unsuccessfully for parliament in the 1906 and 1910 elections, but they achieved some success in local government polls. The movement remained a constitutional one and did not advocate violence.

A message somewhat similar to that of Sinn Féin was the Irish-Ireland of Waterford-born journalist, D. P. Moran. His paper, the *Leader*, championed economic protection, including a buy Irish campaign, cultural distinctiveness, and Irish language revival. He cast slurs on Irish Catholics who were unsympathetic to separatism, whether political or cultural, such as "shoneen," which were comparable in an Afro-American context to "Uncle Tom." Very much an individualist, he was severely critical of many historical and contemporary Irish figures, including those, such as members of Sinn Féin, who ought to be seen as his allies.

Lastly, there remained the Irish Republican Brotherhood, in a semi-somnolent position since the late 1890s with an aged membership dwelling more on past glories or heroics than on future action. However, one former prisoner, Tom Clarke, who had returned from America, began to breath new life into the organization by recruiting a number of younger men. It remained very much underground until 1916 when it was ready to seek Ireland's opportunity while England was at a disadvantage, this time in waging the First World War.

LIBERALS BACK IN POWER

In the January 1906 general election, the Liberals obtained a majority of over 200 seats. Such a majority was almost three times the size of the Irish Parliamentary Party membership in parliament, which meant that the Liberals did not need the Irish votes and could put Home Rule very much on the back burner. The most significant gesture to the Irish was the passage in 1908 of an Irish Universities Act, which ended the old Royal University (a purely examining body), established a new National University that included the old Queens Colleges of Cork and Galway (now to be known as University College Cork and University College Galway) and the Catholic University College Dublin, and transformed Queens College Belfast into Queens University, Belfast. The National University was de facto, if not de jure, Catholic. Another gesture to the Irish, an Irish Councils Bill, which would give some authority to a local council that would be partly elected and partly appointed and would direct some branches of Irish administration, was rejected by the Irish Parliamentary Party as a diversion from the central objective of Home Rule.

The Liberal government committed itself to other significant reforms, including old age pensions and labor exchanges for the unemployed, as well as naval rearmament to match a perceived German threat to British maritime supremacy. All these cost money, which prompted a budget with severely progressive taxation, especially on landed wealth. The Conservative-dominated and hereditary House of Lords rejected the budget. The government, headed by H. H. Asquith, went to the people in calling an election in 1910. The Liberals anticipated an overwhelming victory in casting the election as a battle between the proponents of democracy against the defenders of hereditary privilege and in which a Liberal victory could be followed by legislation restraining the veto power of the upper house.

Amazingly, the results were a virtual tie, with the Liberals getting 275 seats to the 273 for the Conservative-Unionists, which put Redmond and his contingent of 71 in a position to make or break the government. (The new Labour Party held 40 seats.) Rather than accept a situation in which the Irish would determine the government, and using the pretext that the new king (George V had succeeded his father Edward VII in May 1910) should not have to contend with such a constitutional crisis so early in his reign, a series of private meetings were held between the Liberals and Conservatives for almost half a year seeking alternatives, including a national coalition government. However, any potential agreement failed on the issue of what to do about Ireland. It was therefore decided to go to the voters again in December for a clearer mandate one way or the other. This time the two major parties secured exactly the same number of seats, 273, while Labour increased to 42, and the Irish won 83. This meant that the Liberals would need the Irish votes to form a government and to pass legislation limiting the Lords' veto power. But if limitations were placed on the Lords' veto, then the passage of a Home Rule measure would follow in due course.

The overwhelming majority of the upper house resisted the proposed restriction on their veto power, but they yielded when confronted with the threat of the king employing his prerogative to appoint a sufficient number of new peers as to guarantee the measure's passage. Enough lords were concerned enough about the exclusivity of their house so as to "hedge" and accept the reform in contrast to the determined minority wishing to fight to the end in the "ditch" for the full powers of their chamber. The measure stated that any bill passed three years in succession by the House of Commons would become law upon the king's signature regardless of the position of the House of Lords. Subsequently, a Home Rule bill was introduced in 1912, which ought to have been certain of being the law by 1914. The measure called for a two-house Irish parliament, a popularly elected lower house and an appointed upper house, and a reduced Irish representation in the House of Commons at Westminster. The sovereignty of the Irish parliament would be restricted, as the British government would retain control over the police for six years, over defense and foreign policy, and over excise and customs revenues permanently. Nor could the Irish parliament legislate on religious matters.

UNIONIST RESISTANCE

The prospects of Irish Home Rule being achieved spurred furious resistance on the part of unionists in Northern Ireland. In this they were abetted by the leadership of the Conservative Party even to a degree that went beyond parliamentary or constitutional opposition. A new leader had taken over the Conservative Party in the person of Andrew Bonar Law. He reflected a significant change in the party, as his predecessor, Arthur Balfour, had an extraordinary pedigree as a son-in-law of the last Conservative prime minister, Lord Salisbury, a descendant of the Elizabethan favorites, the Cecils. Bonar Law, on the other hand, was a Canadian-born Scot, whose fortune was based on industry. He represented the new influence of business and industry over the Conservative Party, hitherto dominated by hereditary influences and landed wealth. Furthermore, he was a Presbyterian, whereas the party had always been identified with the Church of England. This made him more responsive to the Presbyterian and industrial spirit of Northern Irish unionism and ready to endorse extra-legal action to block Home Rule. At an anti–Home Rule demonstration at Blenheim Palace in July 1912, he suggested that "there are things stronger than parliamentary majorities," as he promised that there was "no length of resistance to which Ulster can go in which I would not be prepared to support them, and in which, in my belief, they would not be supported by the overwhelming majority of the British people."

This clear invitation to turn to extra-constitutional action was taken up by the Ulster Unionists in September of that year when nearly half a million of adult males supporters signed a Solemn League and Covenant to use all necessary means "to defeat the present conspiracy to set up a Home Rule Parliament in Ireland," and should such be forced on them "to refuse to recognize its authority." A few months later, in January 1913, the Ulster Unionist Council, the governing body of the Unionist Party in Ulster, approved the formation of the Ulster Volunteer Force, a paramilitary organization of 100,000 members whose component branches had already been in the process of formation among the various Orange lodges.

A major figure in Ireland in the unionist resistance to Home Rule was Edward Carson, a Dublin-born barrister, member of parliament for Trinity College, and leader of the Unionist Party in Ireland, renowned for his legal competence, including especially his successful and devastating cross-examination of Oscar Wilde in the libel suit that led to his ruination. Carson was generous in his attitudes toward concessions to Catholics on issues short of repeal of the union, but he was ultimately governed by his commitment to the maintenance of the union of the entire island of Ireland with Britain. In other words, Carson was an Irish Unionist, anxious that the whole island of Ireland be united with Britain. The other major figure in the opposition to Home Rule was James Craig, an Ulster Presbyterian from a family that made its fortune from distilling. A member of parliament from County Down, his primary political commitment was to preserve the Ulster he knew, that was, one of Protestant predominance and linked to Britain.

COMPROMISE PROPOSALS

In June 1912 a Liberal MP, T. G. Agar-Robartes, proposed that the most Protestant of the Ulster counties, Antrim, Armagh, Londonderry, and Down, be excluded from the Home Rule act. Carson and the Irish Unionists accepted, but the measure was rejected by a majority of parliament. In 1914, when passage of the measure was inevitable, the prime minister, H. H. Asquith, had received Redmond's approval for the temporary, that is, six years, exclusion from Home Rule of any of the nine counties of Ulster that voted for such from governance by an Irish parliament. This time Carson and associates rejected the measure as being comparable to simply a stay of execution. In fact, the inevitability of a general election within the six years and the possibility of its return of a Conservative-Unionist majority might well have made the exclusion permanent rather than temporary.

TOWARD VIOLENCE

In November 1913, in reaction to the formation of the Ulster Volunteer Force, a nationalist counterpart, the Irish Volunteers, came into being. Prompted by what had happened in Ulster, the medievalist historian Eoin MacNeill, writing in the Gaelic League paper *An Claidheamh Soluis,* in an article titled "The North Began," called for the nationalists to also form a volunteer force to advance their cause. MacNeill headed a provisional committee, which included more militant nationalists with IRB connections, including Bulmer Hobson. The movement grew in numbers within a few months to 75,000. Plans got underway to acquire arms in which the services of such Anglo-Irish sympathizers as the journalist Darrell Figgis, the writer Robert Erskine Childers, the ex-diplomat Roger Casement, and Mary Spring Rice, the niece of the British ambassador to Washington, were drawn. The Irish Parliamentary Party leaders became apprehensive about the movement and Redmond pressured MacNeill into allowing the party to name 25 members to the provisional committee of the Volunteers, which guaranteed the party's ascendancy over the movement in the same way the Ulster Unionists dominated the Ulster Volunteer Force.

Irish unionism, and Ulster unionism in particular, had always a strong presence among the officer corps of the British army. When the prospects of violent resistance to the tentative Home Rule legislation grew closer, a group of officers stationed at the Curragh in Kildare indicated in April 1914 that they would resign rather than have to coerce Ulster. Their commanders were able to exact a concessionary statement from the secretary of war, J. E. B. Seely, that there were no intentions to use the army to crush political opposition to Home Rule. The prime minister forced Seely to resign, along with several generals, but the implication remained that the government might well be confronted with a mutiny should it attempt to coerce Ulster. Soon after, Major Fred Crawford, a zealous Ulster unionist, who had earlier called for Ulstermen to look to another "King Billy" (Kaiser Wilhelm II) to rescue them, arranged successfully and without interference from the authorities the importation into Ulster at Larne and other ports of thousands of rifles, machine guns, and ammunition for the Ulster Volunteer Force and distribute them throughout the province within 24 hours.

At the end of July, when war had started in Europe, but which Britain had not yet entered, Childers and associates were able to land a few hundred rifles at Howth, outside of Dublin. When a crowd in Bachelor's Walk in the city demonstrated in support of the landing the army fired on them, killing three and wounding dozens, a response quite different from the apparent disregard of the earlier importation on behalf of the Ulster Volunteer Force.

Within a week Britain had entered the war against the Central Powers, justifying its entry in opposing the German invasion of Belgium. A Home Rule act was passed, as was another measure suspending the application of the act for the duration of the war. The war spared Britain a potential civil war within Ireland, as well as calmed internal social confrontations in Britain itself, particularly those related to women's suffrage and industrial unionism. Within Ireland, both factions—the Unionist Party and the Irish Parliamentary Party—gave their support to the war and encouraged their members and the members of their respective volunteer forces, the Ulster and the Irish Volunteers, to enlist. Among the nationalists this provoked a split, as the original founders of the movement, including MacNeill and Hobson, opposed Redmond's call to enlist. Redmond then formed a new group, the National Volunteers, which most of the 180,000 members of the Volunteers joined. A minority of about 12,000 remained with MacNeill and retained the name of Irish Volunteers. With this separation from the parliamentary nationalists, MacNeill's movement came more and more under domination by more extreme nationalists, many committed to a violent uprising, although MacNeill adhered to the position that the movement should only turn to force as a defensive action if the authorities were to actually move against the nationalist groups.

During the war, thousands of Irish from both the unionist and the nationalist communities enlisted. The military tended to accept Ulster Volunteer units collectively for incorporation into the army, while the nationalists enlisted only as individuals and were thus scattered among other units. Ironically, this discriminatory treatment probably lessened the number of casualties among nationalist members of the armed forces, although there were many enough, especially incurred during some of the more mindless charges that accompanied several battles along the western front. The loss of life sustained by Ulster at the Battle of the Somme, where 20,000 British lives were lost in a single day in July 1916, stood as a blood sacrifice that worked to intensify loyalty to the British connection on the part of the survivors, who asserted that their compatriots had fallen fighting at its behest.

LABOR ACTIVISM

Irish nationalism, whether of the parliamentary variety or of a more militant character, whether advocates of violence such as the IRB, cultural separatists such as the Gaelic League, or political separatists such as Sinn Féin, had never been preoccupied with the issue of labor. This absence was due partly to the predominantly agrarian character of the Irish economy and partly to the minimal development of industry in most of Ireland outside of Ulster. The strong religious commitment by so many of the Irish population, whether Protestant or Catholic, also inhibited sympathy with the irreligious attitudes of many socialists, still heavily inspired by the writings of Karl Marx. On their part, socialist and labor activists tended to concentrate their efforts in urban and industrial areas and failed to work among the many landless agricultural laborers, probably because of their narrow Marxism, which saw the coming revolution as a consequence of discontent among only the industrial masses.

However, two figures stand out in early 20th-century Ireland as socialist leaders. Both were born abroad of Irish parents. One was James Larkin, born in Liverpool, who first came to Belfast in 1907 attempting to organize dockworkers in line with similar efforts in Britain and in Europe at developing the "New Unionism," based on industrial rather than craft organizations. Sectarian rivalry impeded his efforts in Belfast and he moved to Dublin the next year, where he formed the Irish Transport and General Workers' Union. It continued to grow until 1913 when he attempted to unionize the workers of the United Tramways Company, owned by the wealthy and influential William Martin Murphy, owner also of the *Irish Independent*. Murphy responded to a strike by locking out members of the union. Tensions ran high throughout the fall of that year. There was some rioting and violent police response. The British Trade Unions Council gave financial support to the strike. When the same body refused to undertake sympathy strikes in Britain, Larkin condemned them and cut himself off from their support. Ultimately the strikers capitulated and returned to work on management's terms. Larkin left for America, where he was one of the early members of the American Communist Party, returning to Ireland and to participation in the Irish Labour Party a decade later.

The other figure was James Connolly, born of emigrant parents in Edinburgh. He also came to Ireland as a socialist and labor activist. He even sought to advance the cause in America for seven years. He returned to Ireland in 1910. In 1912 he and Larkin formed the Irish Labour Party and he was assistant to Larkin in the tramway dispute and assumed leadership of the movement upon Larkin's departure. Disappointment at the failure of the strike stirred him to form an Irish Citizens Army, which several hundred joined. Awareness of the inadequacies of the purely socialist appeal in Ireland, and disappointment at workers across Europe having rallied to their respective national causes once the war broke out, despite earlier claims they would fight only for class and not nations, brought about significant changes in his ideology. He sought to reconcile socialism and nationalism and even socialism and Catholicism. This change in thought would bring him into contact with militant separatists, who would include him in their plans to strike violently while Britain was preoccupied with the war.

EASTER 1916

The instrument for insurrection was to be the Irish Volunteers, that is, the minority wing who refused to join John Redmond's National Volunteers in support of the British war effort, remaining instead with Eoin MacNeill under the original label. However, the real movers of insurrection were a smaller group that held a dominant position in the general council of the Volunteers. These were also members of the Irish Republican Brotherhood, that is, the Fenians, committed to the violent achievement of an independent Irish republic. Their agenda for the Volunteers was not the purely defense mood envisioned by Mac-Neill, namely that violence would be used only to resist British attacks on nationalist groups.

Leading IRB figures on the council included the poet and son of a papal knight, Joseph Mary Plunkett; the UCD lecturer and playwright, Thomas Mac-Donagh; and the Gaelic language enthusiast and educational reformer, Patrick (Padraic) Pearse. Éamonn Ceannt, who had worked for the Dublin Corporation, would later join them. They worked closely with Thomas Clarke, the IRB leader, and with the American support group, Clan na Gael, which was dominated by Fenian exile John Devoy and the American jurist Daniel F. Cohalan. The former diplomat turned revolutionary Roger Casement agreed to travel from New York in the still neutral United States to Berlin to facilitate the acquisition of arms from the German government and to recruit volunteers from among any Irishmen in the British forces who had become prisoners of war of the Germans. A military council of the IRB had been set up that included Pearse, McDonagh, Plunkett, Ceannt, Clarke, and Sean McDermott, a County Leitrim native who had become an activist in the IRB and Sinn Féin. In early 1916 James Connolly was drawn into the group and committed his Irish Citizens Army to the proposed uprising.

The ideological and strategic perspectives of some of these central figures in the uprising were various. Clarke obviously started from the traditional Fenian perspective of using violence to achieve an independent republic. Connolly had come to blend socialism with nationalism in his perspective. Plunkett, McDonagh, and Pearse weaved together romantic idealism, Gaelic cultural separatism, and devout Catholicism in constructing their vision for Ireland. Pearse in particular emphasized the notion of a blood sacrifice, parallel to

Christ's death on the cross, in order to reawaken the Irish people to their national mission. In other words, many assumed their effort would be futile, but that in defeat they would sow the seeds that would flourish with Irish independence. Remarkably, and with significant help from an inflexible British military, their goal was realized.

The uprising was scheduled for Easter Sunday, April 23, 1916, when German weapons and volunteers from among the Irish POW's were to arrive. Things went very much awry because of communication difficulties, discoveries by American and British intelligence agencies, and unawareness by the leaders of the Irish Volunteers, specifically MacNeill, Bulmer Hobson, and Michael O'Rahilly, of the full implications of what was under way. They had originally been told that a British operation was in progress against nationalist organizations and, accordingly, they gave their consent to a calling to arms of the more than 10,000 Irish Volunteers. When they discovered it was a deception, MacNeill called off the orders for the Volunteers to assemble on Sunday. In the meantime, Casement had arrived via U-boat on the Kerry shores ahead of time and was captured. There was no one to meet the disguised trawler, the *Aud*, with its cargo of 20,000 rifles. Its captain, Karl Spindler, had no choice but to leave the area, only to be later surrounded by British vessels near Cobh, where he scuttled the ship and its cargo.

Finally, the conspirators issued a counterorder to MacNeill's cancellation orders, this time setting the day for Easter Monday, April 24, when 1,500 assembled in Dublin and seized a number of public positions, including the celebrated General Post Office on Sackville (now O'Connell) Street, where Patrick Pearse, the designated president, proclaimed an Irish republic, which proclamation was signed by the other members of the IRB military council. However, the insurgents failed to make a serious effort to take the lightly defended center of government in Ireland, Dublin Castle, which would have greatly complicated their eventual suppression. The combined forces of the Dublin Metropolitan Police and the reinforced British army brought the uprising under control before the week was over, but not without an extraordinary amount of destruction and casualties. Over 500 were killed, mostly innocent civilians, over a hundred soldiers, and a smaller number of rebels. The 2,500 wounded were also primarily civilians, as well as about 400 soldiers and 120 rebels.

Public sentiment in Dublin was originally overwhelmingly hostile to the rebels for the destruction and suffering their adventure had brought on the city, but also because so many Irishmen were fighting in the war and the action was looked on as a stab in the back. However, the British military commander, Sir John Maxwell, was able to transform the despised into martyrs by conducting a series of court martial trials in which a large number of the leaders were condemned to death. Within 10 days 15 had been executed, including all the signatories to the proclamation of the Irish Republic, before the government, in response to popular and international outrage, stopped the killings. Nearly 3,500 had been apprehended, including, inappropriately since they were not part of the rising, Sinn Féin members, and MacNeill and other nonparticipating Volunteers. But nearly 1,500 were soon released. Besides those executed, 170 others were convicted and sentenced to imprisonment. The remaining 1,800 were interned in England and Wales, although two-thirds of the internees were released within a few months and the remainder before Christmas. Roger Casement was not treated as well. Tried and convicted for treason, he was hung on August 3, 1916.

SINN FÉIN TRIUMPHS

The popular British press had tended to label the Easter Week uprising as a Sinn Féin event, even though Sinn Féin had nothing to do with it, nor was a violent uprising part of the Sinn Féin strategy to achieve an independently governed Ireland. However, many participants in it may have been Sinn Féiners and may have been introduced to separatism through Sinn Féin. The ultimate consequence of the uprising, and the British response to it, worked to transform Sinn Féin into an organization supportive of separatist republicanism rather than self-governance in a dual monarchy. Sinn Féin membership increased significantly in numbers and participants during the uprising. Many who were released from internment came to occupy important positions in the party. Adding momentum to the growth and transformation of the party was the success of three Sinn Féin candidates in three parliamentary by-elections, beginning with the February 5, 1917, victory of George Plunkett, the father of one of those executed, in North Roscommon, followed by the May 9 victory of Joseph P. McGuinness, still a prisoner, in South Longford, and then the July 10 East Clare victory by Eamon de Valera (Éamon de Bhailéarn), whose death sentence after Easter Week had been averted due to his holding American citizenship. Sinn Féin strengthened its uncompromising image by its refusal to join the Parliamentary Party in attending an Irish convention that met futilely at Trinity College from July 1917 through April 1918 in an attempt to resolve the differing goals for the island held by nationalists and unionists.

David Lloyd George, who had replaced Asquith as prime minister the previous December, had called the convention into being. Lloyd George was a modern politician of the democratic age, in contrast to Asquith whose style and roots belonged to the more gentlemanly politics of an era of restricted suffrage. For all his political radicalism, Lloyd George was better able to relate to the military and imperial personnel whose talents were so essential for directing the war. Lloyd George was also sensitive to American opinion on the Irish question, which had become increasingly important with the American entry into the war on April 6, 1917.

In October the convention of Sinn Féin elected Eamon de Valera as its president. The next day he was elected president of the Irish Volunteers, thereby achieving a de facto unification of the two groups, the political arm and the potential military arm of the Irish separatist cause. One group not under de Valera's leadership was the IRB, in which Michael Collins, who had risen to prominence as a organizer of the prisoners interned in Frongoch, Wales, played a major role. The IRB, which called the Easter Rising and which had close contacts with the American support organization, Clan na Gael, and its broader-based affiliate, the Friends of Irish Freedom, regarded itself as the organization bearing the true flame of Irish republicanism and the determiner of republican legitimacy.

In April 1918 Lloyd George, in an effort to appease anti-Irish sentiment in Britain and among unionists, introduced legislation empowering the government to extend military conscription to Ireland, although it was never attempted. This act spelled the death knell for the Irish Parliamentary Party, whose new leader, John Dillon (he replaced John Redmond who had died in March), opposed the measure and was forced to appear as part of an anticonscription coalition with de Valera, which cause also received the endorsement of the Irish Catholic hierarchy. As is always the case, when moderates are forced into a coalition with extreme elements, the extremists gained. The Sinn Féin position, in terms of popular support, was further strengthened when the new lord lieutenant, Field Marshall Lord John French, using powers under the Defence of the Realm Act, began apprehending leading members of nationalist groups, including Sinn Féiners and Volunteers, on the pretext of their involvement in a "German plot."

When a general election was held in December 1918, a month after the end of the war, Sinn Féin swept the board in Ireland, taking 73 seats, leaving the parliamentary party with only six, while the Unionist won 26. This election was the first held under conditions of universal suffrage for males over 21 years of age and suffrage for women who were 30 years of age or over.

In accord with Sinn Féin principles, the Sinn Féin members elected to parliament refused to take their seats in Westminster. All those not still imprisoned because of the "German plot" arrests assembled in Mansion House in

Dublin on January 21 and, calling themselves Dáil Éireann, drafted a provisional constitution for the Irish Republic. The same day at Soloheadbeg, County Tipperary, a group of Irish Volunteers ambushed a cart carrying explosives and killed two policemen, the first violent action in what would be the war of independence.

WAR OF INDEPENDENCE

The war of independence has to be understood in the context of a number of other factors. The general election that had returned so many Sinn Féiners from Ireland constituted a massive triumph for the Conservative-Unionist alliance in Britain as a whole, with the Liberal Party dwindling to a small fraction of its previous size and the new Labour Party still relatively small. The wartime prime minister Lloyd George continued in office, this time leading a coalition consisting of a handful of Liberals still loyal to him and the massive Conservative-Unionist majority. Britain had emerged triumphant from a destructive war and, within months, as a consequence of the peace settlement at Versailles, would be master, admittedly as a trustee for the League of Nations, over vast new areas that had been part of the prewar German and Turkish Empires. While restive noises on behalf of self-rule were being made in India, it was scarcely a moment when Britain would be temperamentally disposed to begin the dismantlement of its empire, as Irish republicans hoped. On the other hand, Britain was committed to the implementation of Home Rule for Ireland if it could get around the dilemma of unionist opposition in the northeast of the island.

It was not as clear from the beginning that either the Sinn Féin mandate or the goal of the Dáil Éireann was to support a violent insurrection. De Valera had escaped from prison in February. The following month the remainder of the Sinn Féin detainees were released. Dáil Éireann was able to meet unimpeded in Dublin, where it elected de Valera as its president on April 1. A significant campaign undertaken by Dáil Éireann was to secure world recognition of its claim that it constituted the government of Ireland. A mission to the Versailles Peace Conference obtained no audience. De Valera himself left Ireland in June for America, where he would remain for a year and a half, seeking financial support from the Irish-American community and recognition from the major American political parties, the U.S. Congress, and the government. He was extremely successful in the first objective, but not in the latter goals, in which he alienated the leading Irish-American supporters, Devoy and Cohalan, who saw his role as distracting and impractical. They suspected him of being likely to compromise on the issue of an independent Irish republic and they disliked his sympathy for the League of Nations, which they feared would be dominated by Britain. They wished to utilize all the resources and energies of the Irish-American community to oppose American membership in the international body.

A very successful move by the Dáil Éireann was its call in June 1919 for the establishment of "arbitration courts" to which the people could turn as an alternative to the existing judicial system in Ireland. In a very short time, these bodies would prevail over most of Ireland, aside from the unionist areas of Ulster, and even opponents of Sein Féin would utilize them for settling legal grievances. In August, to insure the subordination of military factions, the Dáil insisted that all its members and all the Irish Volunteers (whom it considered the Army of the Irish Republic, and later the Irish Republican Army [IRA]) swear allegiance to the republic and the Dáil. By now the authorities became less tolerant of this movement's proclaiming itself an alternative government for Ireland. Repressive proclamations were issued in certain localities outlawing groups such as Sinn Féin, the Gaelic League, and the Irish Volunteers, and, on September 12, the Dáil Éireann itself was declared illegal.

On the military front, the Irish Volunteers began a campaign against the Royal Irish Constabulary, most of whose rank and file were Irish Catholics. It had the expected consequence of causing a substantial numbers of resignations from the force and an abandonment of remote barracks, leaving more and more of the countryside open to Irish Volunteer domination. The resignations were so many that the Royal Irish Constabulary (RIC) was forced to recruit thousands from Britain, especially demobilized soldiers, to fill its ranks. Because of a shortage of regular uniforms, the newcomers were given army tans and black RIC hats, earning them the nickname of "Black and Tans." They would soon gain an unpleasant reputation for brutality in taking retaliatory actions against communities from which Irish Volunteers had come. The Irish Volunteers also began making attacks on the British military itself in Ireland.

Still convinced that Sinn Féin success in the 1918 general election was a freak occurrence and not a true indication of popular sentiment, the government called for local government elections in 1920 in anticipation that the old Parliamentary Party forces, as well as independents and some unionists, would continue to hold the ascendancy. In these elections, held in January for urban bodies. and in June for rural bodies, Sinn Féin enjoyed great success, controlling, with support from nationalists and labour, 172 of 206 urban councils, and being similarly successful in the rural council elections.

One of the most remarkable achievements of the Dáil Éireann government was the ability of its Ministry of Local Government, headed by William T. Cosgrave and assisted by Kevin O'Higgins, to direct the local government bodies in carefully harboring their resources. This was essential after the British designated Local Government Authority began to withhold grants to the local bodies because of their noncompliance with specific orders and after many property owners became reluctant to pay their rates. The local bodies were instructed to use hidden (or laundered) bank accounts to avoid seizure of their funds by either the courts or the government authorities. They also relied to some degree on funds advanced by the Dáil Éireann government itself. The gaining of the allegiance of these local bodies, both the success in the elections to them, and their subsequent acceptance of the Dáil Éireann authority against the official Local Government Authority, was possibly the clearest manifestation to the world that the Dáil Éireann had won the consensus of the Irish people.

Violence on both sides was intensified in 1920. The British passed a Restoration of Order in Ireland Act giving the authorities extraordinary powers of arrest and detention and to conduct military tribunals. Ex-officers of the British army were employed as an auxiliary division to the RIC. Even the military commanders had reservations about the conduct of this group in combating the IRA. Among the most brutal days in that year was November 21, "Bloody Sunday," when members of Michael Collins's (minister of the treasury in the Dáil Éireann government, but also director of intelligence and president of the IRB) elite "squad" killed 14 suspected British agents, for which the Black and Tans retaliated by firing on a crowd at a football match in Croke Park in Dublin, killing a dozen. The following Sunday, an IRA brigade ambushed 18 auxiliaries at Kilmichael in Cork. Two weeks later the Black and Tans and the auxiliaries sacked the city of Cork, destroying City Hall and the Corn Exchange, and causing millions of pounds in damage. In March of the same year the Sinn Féin lord mayor of the city, Tomas MacCurtain, was murdered by the RIC.

But the same year would also see the passage of the Government of Ireland Act, an attempt to cut the Gordian knot of the Home Rule question by separating the island into two components, a six-county Ireland in the North and a twenty-six-county Ireland in the South. Elections were called for Home Rule parliaments for each section. This division of the island also constituted a division of the province of Ulster, as three of its counties—Donegal, Cavan, and Monaghan—were included in southern Ireland. Had they remained in the northern part of Ireland, Catholics would have constituted the majority or near majority in the province, which would have contradicted the very reason for partition: to prevent the Protestants in Northern Ireland from coming under the domination of Catholics. Unfortunately, it meant that a substantial number of Catholics in Northern Ireland found themselves under the domination of Protestants. Elections to both parliaments were held in May 1921. The Unionists received 40 of the seats in the northern body, with Sinn Féin and the nationalists winning six each. All candidates for the southern parliament were returned unopposed: 124 Sein Féiners and four independents who represented Trinity College.

De Valera returned to Ireland from the United States just before Christmas of 1920. His return intensified certain divisions within the Dáil Éireann government as to the proper approach in the struggle with Britain. One wing, headed by Michael Collins and supported by the chief of staff of the IRA, Richard Mulcahy, was deeply involved in the IRB. Their opponents suggested their loyalty was more to the IRB than to the Dáil Éireann. Collins's revolutionary genius had been his ability to direct a guerrilla campaign against the British and their agents, whether local police, civil servants, and even bankers, rather than by direct military confrontation. The other wing, led particularly by Cathal Brugha, the minister for defense, and Austin Stack, the minister for home affairs, were critical of the notoriety Collins had been receiving. Their strategy for waging the struggle would have entailed a traditional manning of barricades, full-fledged assaults on important posts, and carrying the struggle to Britain by high-profile assassinations. De Valera tended to side with them, consenting to a futile attack on the Dublin Custom House on May 25, the virtual eve of the issuance of peace feelers. In the attack nearly 100 of the IRA members were captured and important local government and other public documents were destroyed.

The next month, following a peace overture made by King George V at the opening of the parliament of Northern Ireland, there were meetings with intermediaries such as the South African leader, General Jan Smuts. Finally, on July 11, a truce was agreed to whereby both the British and the IRA ceased military operations and negotiations began as to the agenda for a peace conference. Meetings and exchanges of letters between de Valera and Lloyd George through the summer sought to reconcile their diverse purposes: the Irish aspiration for complete independence and the recognition of the Dáil Éireann as its government and the British wish that Ireland remain a dominion within the Commonwealth. A letter from Lloyd George to de Valera in September inviting him to send an Irish delegation to London to ascertain "how the association of Ireland and the community of nations known as the British Empire may best be reconciled with Irish national aspirations" enabled the conference to convene the following month.

De Valera did not join the delegation, insisting that his position as president required that he not be part of any negotiations that might involve a solution that produced less than an independent Irish republic. Instead, cabinet members Collins, Griffith, and Robert Barton, and attorneys Gavan Duffy and Éamonn Duggan attended. Lloyd George and such senior figures as Winston Churchill, Austen Chamberlain, and Lord Birkenhead represented the British side. Collins and Griffith played the major role for the Irish. The most they were able to obtain in the negotiations was dominion status, which de Valera rejected in a cabinet meeting in Dublin in the first weekend in December, preferring a construct of his own for Anglo-Irish relations that he called "external association." The negotiators were unable to win the British acceptance of de Valera's alternative when they returned to London, and, faced with the prospects of a resumption of hostilities, they signed the treaty on December 6, 1921.

FROM TREATY TO CIVIL WAR

De Valera was outraged at the signing, as were the more zealous republicans in the cabinet, Cathal Brugha and Austin Stack. Some have argued that de Valera opposed the treaty in order to keep the zealots in his camp, hoping at the last moment to gain British acceptance of his external association concept as an alternative to the resumption of war. Even if accepted, it would scarcely have given Ireland the status of an autonomous republic. However, events over the next several months saw de Valera, a sphinx-type figure, become more and more the prisoner rather than the leader of the republican zealots he had tried to keep in line behind a formula that was less than republican.

The major proponents of the treaty were Collins, Griffith, Cosgrave, and, increasingly, Kevin O'Higgins. They argued, in essence, that the negotiators, whose credentials as Irish patriots were unquestioned, could not have gotten anything better. Collins, for instance, acted on the basis of his awareness of the weakened military position of the IRA. What they did get was as great a measure of self-government as Ireland had ever had. The only limitations on sovereignty were a required oath by Irish legislators to the king as head of the association of nations to which Ireland was a member; its legislature was to be summoned and dissolved by the king's agent, the lord lieutenant (but advised by the Irish government); limitations on the Irish military in per capita proportion to that of Britain; continued British maintenance of certain naval facilities in Ireland; and Irish fiscal obligations to its proportionate share of the imperial debt at the time.

The treaty also gave the parliament of Northern Ireland the opportunity to withdraw from the new government of Ireland, which would be called the Irish Free State. However, if it did so, a boundary commission would be formed to adjust the boundary according to popular wishes and economic and geographic considerations.

The debate on the treaty in the Dáil Éireann, which lasted December 14 through January 7, with a lengthy Christmas recess, was an embittered one, featuring degrading personal attacks made on the negotiators. However, the treaty was narrowly approved by a vote of 64 to 57. De Valera then resigned his presidency of the Dáil Éireann and Griffith was elected to replace him.

In keeping with the concept of constitutionality, the British, even in the treaty, never recognized the revolutionary assembly, the Dáil Éireann, and its government. Instead, the treaty required that approval to it be given by the elected parliament of Southern Ireland, that is, the parliament elected the previous June, but nearly all of whose unopposed members had refused to attend the opening session, as they regarded themselves as having been elected to the second Dáil Éireann. To comply with the treaty the parliament of Southern Ireland then met, or at least those who approved of the treaty, which also included the four independents elected from Trinity College. That body approved the treaty and elected, as the treaty required, a Provisional Government of Ireland, under whom the implementation of the treaty and the drafting and acceptance of a constitution for the Irish Free State would take place. The chairman of the Provisional Government was Michael Collins. While the Provisional Government was considered the real governing authority in Ireland, the Dáil Éireann continued as a concession to the scruples of purist Irish republicans.

The cabinet of the Provisional Government included, in addition to Collins, Duggan, O'Higgins, Mulcahy, Cosgrave, Joseph McGrath, Patrick Hogan, and Fionan Lynch. The government had two major strategic objectives: first, to comply with the British expectations of formulating a regime that would conform to the treaty, that is, to establish a dominion government and acknowledge the position of the king, in return for which British forces would be withdrawn from Ireland and the agencies of government would be turned over to dominion bodies of government. Second, to try to secure the acquiescence of the anti-treaty elements within the Sinn Féin Party and the IRA to something short of the ideal of an independent republic. The fact that many full units in the IRA continued to give allegiance only to the Dáil Éireann and not to the Provisional Government made the task all the more difficult.

Within Sinn Féin, at a convention, or *Ard-Fheis*, held in February, the rival factions agreed to postpone a confrontation for three months, at which point an election would be held on the merits of the constitution being prepared for the Free State. It was different with the IRA, as a military convention was held in March against the specific order given by the minister for defense, Mulcahy. Attended primarily by anti-treaty members, it was dominated by the more militant, particularly the likings of Rory O'Connor, Liam Lynch, Liam Mellows, and Ernie O'Malley. O'Connor had even admitted that a military dictatorship might be preferable to an election. De Valera himself had engaged in inflammatory rhetoric about the need to battle other Irish in seeking independence.

A few weeks later, O'Connor and anti-treaty forces of the IRA seized control of the judicial center in Dublin, the Four Courts. The government continued to play for time as Mulcahy began to recruit a national army that would replace

Election propaganda posters for Eamon de Valera, 1923 (*Mary Evans Picture Library*)

the IRA. Its members included pro-treaty IRA members, but also a significant number of Irishmen who had served in the British forces and who had military experience. The IRA itself had increased significantly in numbers during the truce, when membership was less risky and it became fashionable for young men to join.

Many in the British government, especially Winston Churchill, were apprehensive of the true commitment of the Provisional Government to comply with the treaty, especially in view of its tolerance of the open activity of the IRA militants. They became especially cynical when Collins and de Valera entered an electoral pact on May 20 in which both factions agreed not to contest against each other in the forthcoming election, but rather to run exactly the same number of candidates for Dáil seats as each side had in the outgoing Dáil. The election, like the 1921 elections for the northern and southern Irish parliaments, was to be conducted on a single transferable vote (STV) proportional representation system with multiple members elected from each constituency. The outcome, if the electorate complied, would result in a parliament that would duplicate the outgoing second Dáil. The factions would then agree to form a coalition government in which several of the ministers would not be willing to comply with the treaty. A complicating factor was the readiness of other political factions, including the Labour Party, the Farmers Party, and a number of independents, to enter the contest.

Shortly before the election, Provisional Government representatives agreed to substantial revisions in a nearly republican constitution that a committee had drafted for the Free State in order to meet British objections. Collins then urged his electoral supporters to vote as they saw fit when completing their ballots, which was an invitation to disregard the pact suggestion that they vote for both pro-treaty and anti-treaty Sinn Féiners, and cast votes for pro-treaty Sinn Féiners and various others. The results were a significant downgrading of anti-treaty Sinn Féin strength (36 seats) while pro-treaty Sinn Féin proponents secured 58, Labour 17, Farmers 7, and independents 10.

On June 22 the retired field marshall Henry Wilson was assassinated by IRA members, increasing British discomfort at the Provisional Government's continued tolerance of the activities of the IRA. When the anti-treaty group at the Four Courts kidnapped a pro-treaty general on June 27, the Provisional Government attacked the Four Courts the next day, beginning the civil war.

THE CIVIL WAR

While the electorate had indicated overwhelming approval for the treaty, the prospects for the Provisional Government were not so appealing at the onset of the war, as the anti-treaty IRA, or Irregulars as they would be increasingly labeled, held the loyalty of many units throughout the country. However, the government was able to assert its control over Dublin in the first two weeks, capturing significant anti-treaty leaders such as O'Connor and Mellows. Cathal Brugha was fatally wounded when he refused to surrender. Harry Boland also was wounded, captured, and died in prison. By mid-summer the major cities were under government control and the Irregulars were concentrated in the rural areas of the province of Munster, particularly in the counties of Tipperary, Cork, and Kerry. However, the government received two severe blows in August. On August 12 Arthur Griffith, the founder of Sinn Féin and the president of the nominal Dáil Éireann, died of a cerebral hemorrhage. Ten days later, Michael Collins, who had placed the civilian direction of the government in the hands of William T. Cosgrave for the duration of the war while he directed the military operations as commander in chief, was killed in an ambush at Beal na blath, County Cork, not many miles from his birthplace.

Cosgrave became head of the Provisional Government. Significant figures in his government, which was approved by the third Dáil Éireann (the parliament elected in June finally met on September 9), included Kevin O'Higgins, who was vice president and minister for home affairs (later Justice), Ernest Blythe, Desmond FitzGerald, Richard Mulcahy, Joseph McGrath, Patrick Hogan, Fionan Lynch, and Eoin MacNeill. For the most part, the leading figures, with the exception of Mulcahy, were men involved in the civilian rather than the military phase of the struggle, and they would come to regard the treaty as a sacred bond, rather than a tactical concession that could be scrapped should the occasion and the prospects of achieving full republican status permit. Collins, some suggest, was not as temperamentally disposed to the role of constitutionalist.

Because there was no legal basis on which the Provisional Government could arrest and try irregulars, other than British martial law proclamations, the government asked for and received Dáil passage of a resolution calling for an emergency system of military courts with powers of trial, imprisonment, and execution. It could only be a resolution since the constitution of the Free State had not yet been approved and the Dáil did not yet have possess powers. The government's position was further strengthened on October 10 when the Catholic hierarchy of Ireland condemned the violent resistance to the government.

Besides the military campaign against the Irregulars, the government attended to the passage of the constitution of the Irish Free State. The constitution was to be governed by the clauses in the treaty that were restrictive of Irish sovereignty, such as the role of a governor general to summon parliaments and sign legislation, the oath to the king, and so forth. The type of government was to be a parliamentary democracy, elected by STV proportional representation, with stipulated human rights of life, liberty, property, and due process. It included certain then fashionable experiments, such as the initiative and the referendum, and external ministers who were selected and would retain their positions independent of the cabinet. The constitution did not include radical concepts regarding social entitlements, women's rights, or restrictions on war powers advocated by some members, especially those from the Labour Party. The Dáil approved the constitution on October 25. On December 5, legislation adopted by the Westminster parliament approved both the Free State Constitution and the Anglo-Irish Treaty of a year before, satisfying the British insistence that the Free State be based on constitutionalism and legislation rather than violence.

The very day the Irish Free State came into being, December 6, two members of its legislature were shot, one of whom was killed by the Irregulars as part of a retaliatory policy for the military court executions that had started a few weeks earlier in accord with the September 25 Dáil resolution. Before the end of the war those courts would execute 77 people, more than had been executed by British military courts during the war of independence, and among the earlier victims was a leading anti-treaty figure, Robert Erskine Childers. In response to a threat by the republicans to attack any member of the Dáil that had supported the emergency resolution, the Free State cabinet consented to the military's request to take immediate retaliatory action against four prisoners arrested months before at the Four Courts. Even the pro-government press and the archbishop of Dublin condemned the government's action, to which its vice president, Kevin O'Higgins, was the last to concur. One of those executed, Rory O'Connor, had a year before been best man at O'Higgins's wedding. However, there were no further assassination attempts on members of the Dáil, although violence continued, including the burning of the homes of members of the upper house of the legislature, the Seanad, and the killing of O'Higgins's father, a physician in County Laois.

The Seanad, which had delaying powers over legislation, was elected by the lower house, except for a quarter of its members who were nominated by the government. It was designed to give a voice to the unionist and Protestant minority within the 26 counties of the Free State, whose participation was regarded as essential for the successful development of the new state, especially since many of them had played so significant a role in the economy and society of pre-independent Ireland.

For the first four months of 1923, the war consisted primarily of a mopping-up operation by the government. There were substantial casualties and atrocities committed by both sides. The government's employment of hardened Dublin revolutionaries, especially men who had worked under Michael Collins, in the actions in County Kerry met considerable rebuke, even from within the government. However, Mulcahy, the minister for defense, who had to rapidly construct a national army out of a mixture of loyal IRA members, former members of the British army, and raw recruits, understandably defended those under his command.

On April 10 Liam Lynch, the military commander of the irregulars, was killed in action. By April 27 de Valera, president of the revolutionary government that was formed to legitimize the Irregulars, called for the suspension of offensive operations and, a month later, after the government refused to consider suggestions for a treaty with the Irregulars, directed his followers to lay down their arms, ending the civil war. The war had cost hundreds of lives and thousands of casualties, not to mention millions of pounds damage to an economy that was desperately in need of capital for development. The peace began with more than 10,000 prisoners interned, whose acceptance of the legitimacy of the Free State and proclivity to return to violence was still uncertain.

CRISES IN THE FREE STATE

The Free State government had to undertake the task of state building on one hand, while contending with an organized opposition, with ready access to arms, that did not recognize its legitimacy. O'Higgins, as minister for home affairs, assumed the responsibility of securing public safety legislation to allow continued detention without trial after the courts had declared the September 1922 emergency resolution inoperative with the ending of the civil war. He also obtained legislative sanction for an unarmed police force, the Garda Síochána, in formation from the days of the Provisional Government. Even though employing public safety measures to contend with both the presence of an armed opposition to the state and the great deal of lawlessness that had erupted in the wake of the civil war, O'Higgins sought to restore normalcy by using the police and civilian courts, rather than the military, in exercising those powers. What remained of the revolutionary Dáil Courts, some of which had become identified with the Irregulars during the civil war, were discontinued and a new court system, not averse to employing some of the personnel of the old system, was established, which has continued for the most part in Ireland to the present.

In keeping with constitutional requirements that a general election be held within a year after the approval of the constitution, a fourth Dáil Éireann was selected at the end of August 1923 in which the governing party, now calling itself Cumann na nGaedheal, with the hope of drawing support from the large number of Irish who had never been supporters of Sinn Féin, obtained the largest number of seats, 66, but only a plurality in a Dáil enlarged to 153 members. Sinn Féin, which title fell by default to the anti-treaty group, secured 44 seats, Labour won 14, the Farmers Party 15, and independents and others, including a business party, 17. Since Sinn Féin did not recognize the legitimacy of the Dáil to which they had been elected, as they had not recognized the third Dáil, they abstained from attending, which gave Cumann na nGaedheal a majority of those in attendance. Sinn Féin insisted that the second Dáil was the last legitimate Dáil of the Irish Republic. The anti-treaty members of that Dáil continued to meet, adding to their membership any new Sinn Féin victors in the elections to subsequent Dáils, and they elected an alternative government to the Free State.

In spite of the existence of a rival pretender government and the existence of large amounts of unaccounted for arms in the country, the government set about to gradually release many of the 10,000 interned prisoners on an undertaking that they would abide by the law. However, a number of prisoners started a hunger strike protesting the conditions of imprisonment and demanding release. There was a great degree of public sympathy, even from non–Sinn Féin sources, including members of the Catholic hierarchy and others who argued that the detention was unnecessary since the civil war had ended. The government would not yield, and the numbers of strikers dwindled. It was called off when two participants died. The government resumed the policy of release that had been suspended during the strike, as thousands were released before Christmas and every internee was free by the middle of the following summer.

Another major difficulty for the government was the financial need to demobilize large numbers of the National Army, which had grown in numbers to tens of thousands. In the process, professionalism was a major factor in determining who would be retained. Some veterans of the war of independence, especially many closely associated with Michael Collins in various assassinations and assaults by Irregulars, were fearful they would be let go possibly in favor of professionals with British army experience. They organized and called themselves the "Old IRA." The minister for defense and his staff, all members of the IRB, sought to revive the IRB as an alternative to the "Old IRA," and thereby inhibit disaffection within the ranks. This only further antagonized the discontents. They saw the IRB affiliation as the grounds for retention and other favors. In early March a number of the Old IRA officers mutinied, and they based their mutiny in part on what they claimed was the failure of the government to pursue the legacy of Michael Collins. The government responded swiftly with arrests and the mutiny remained very limited. One minister, Joseph McGrath, sympathetic to the mutineers, resigned and threatened to go to the Dáil objecting to the direction of the military. The government inhibited his move by agreeing to an investigation of the military and appointing the police commissioner, Eoin O'Duffy, as commander of the defence forces.

On March 18 the army arrested a number of persons identified with the mutiny, without the approval of O'Duffy and in contradiction to the understanding that mutineers still at large were to be given the opportunity to present themselves. The president of the Executive Council, Cosgrave, was ill at the time, and O'Higgins, as vice president, directed the government. He and his colleagues demanded the resignation of the Army Council because of the action the previous evening. Mulcahy, the minister for defense, thereupon resigned his post. The enquiry committee condemned the mutiny and declared as imprudent the employment of the IRB as an alternative to Old IRA discontent in the ranks. While Mulcahy and associates may have been acting with the best of intentions, the activation of a rival faction would have set a dangerous precedent. O'Higgins's decisiveness in clearing the decks of both groups guaranteed the ascendancy of the civil authority over the Irish military, which has remained a distinguishing feature of independent Ireland.

BOUNDARY COMMISSION

As expected the parliament of Northern Ireland opted not to be included in the Irish Free State immediately after the latter came into being, which meant that the treaty-prescribed boundary commission had to be formed. Earlier, in February and March 1922 short-lived agreements had been made between James Craig, the Northern Ireland prime minister and Michael Collins, the chairman of the Provisional Government, to lessen discriminatory treatment of Catholics in Northern Ireland, particularly in matters of employment and police treatment, in return for cessation of support for the IRA within Northern Ireland and of the boycott in the south of Northern goods. Had either pact survived it was hoped that further cooperation might enable a boundary commission to be avoided. Within Northern Ireland, the RIC was transformed into the Royal Ulster Constabulary and the government also recruited various police auxiliary groups to assist in the maintenance of law and order, especially in view of the IRA continuing its campaign after the truce and the treaty. While it was hoped a proportionate number of Catholics could be recruited for the RUC, the auxiliary forces were uninhibitedly sectarian. That fact, together with the extraordinary special powers given to the minister for home affairs, would remain persistent grievances of Catholics in the north until the 1970s.

Soon after the Free State came into being, and while the civil war was still being fought, requests were made to the British government to call the boundary commission into being. It would be composed of a member for Britain, for Northern Ireland, and for the Free State. A number of factors delayed its formation, including the ongoing civil war and a change in British prime ministers. Lloyd George was eased out by a Conservative backbench revolt in October 1922. His successor, Andrew Bonar Law, resigned in May 1923 when he became aware of his terminal cancer. After a general election in December 1923, his successor, Stanley Baldwin, was compelled to step down, to be replaced by the first Labour Party prime minister, Ramsay MacDonald. But Baldwin and the Conservatives were back in power following the election of October 1924. The British had hoped the need for a boundary commission could be avoided and, to that end, they had arranged in early 1924 for conferences among the concerned parties for a possible unification that would allow some internal Northern Irish autonomy, but the meetings came to naught.

The refusal of the Northern Ireland government to name a representative caused further delay as legislation had to be passed authorizing the British government to name a Northern Ireland representative. The commission finally came into being in November 1924, with Eoin MacNeill, its minister for education, as the Free State representative; the South African jurist, Richard Feetham, the British nominee and chairman; and J. R. Fisher, a barrister, the representative designated by the British for Northern Ireland. MacNeill, a full-time minister and an historian, was no match for the barrister and jurist. He innocently agreed at the beginning to regard the proceedings of the commission as comparable to those of a jury and to accept a unanimous report. He did not seem to take into account the presumption by Feetham that the commission's mandate was not so much to make major boundary changes as to make adjustments that would in no way impair the political viability of Northern Ireland. In fact the nationalists and the Free State had assumed that the commission, on whose formation they had been so insistent, would be governed primarily by the views of the populace, which they expected would result in a substantial loss of territory by Northern Ireland.

A leak of the impending report to the Conservative *Morning Post* on November 7, 1925, intimated that the recommendations would entail a relatively small loss of population and territory by Northern Ireland and even a loss of some territory and population by the Free State. Uproar in the Dáil Éireann prompted MacNeill to resign from both the commission and the ministry. Before the official release of the report, whose publication would make it the rule, several Free State ministers, including Cosgrave and O'Higgins, met with members of the British cabinet, and with Craig, in an effort to avoid the implementation of the report. The British, aware that publication could bring down the Free State government, agreed on December 3 to suspend the report (which was put under wraps for a half century), to maintain the status quo boundary, and, as compensation, to forgive the Free State any obligations it had, which were still to be determined, for its proportion of the imperial debt at the date the treaty was implemented.

The government's defense of the agreement was that even the hoped-for boundary change would have left a substantial number of Catholics in an even-more endangered position in a smaller Northern Ireland. They also argued that the amicable spirit in which the agreement had been reached augured well for better relations with Northern Ireland, which would have to be a prerequisite for any possible political unification of the island.

In October and November of the next year, at the Imperial Conference in London, the dominions of the commonwealth were acknowledged to be autonomous communities equal in status and in no way subordinate one to another. That statement would serve as the basis for the 1932 Statute of Westminster giving the legislatures of the dominions power to overturn any Westminster legislation governing them. At the conference O'Higgins approached both Edward Carson, the former leader of the Irish unionists, and L. S. Amery, the secretary of state for the dominions, with a suggestion similar to Arthur Griffith's "Dual Monarchy" concept. He hoped a separate coronation of the king as "king of Ireland" would make the Northern Ireland government amenable to unification. This willingness to abandon republicanism, even as an aspiration, failed to win British or unionist sympathy, but it did demonstrate an awareness of the inextricable interrelationship between both parts of the island and the other, larger island that, only now, is receiving institutional implementation following the 1998 Good Friday Agreement.

MOVE TOWARD POLITICAL NORMALCY

In November 1925, at the time of the boundary commission crisis, a convention of the IRA withdrew the organization's loyalty to the pretender Dáil Éireann in reaction to fears that some Sinn Féiners elected to the Free State Dáil were softening in their abstentionist position. The fears of the dogmatic IRA were confirmed in March 1926 when de Valera withdrew from the Sinn Féin Party after it narrowly rejected his motion that consideration be given to having members attend Dáil Éireann if the oath to the king was removed. On May 16 he started a new political party, Fianna Fáil, which most of the politically successful members of Sinn Féin joined, leaving only a small rump in the original party.

The Free State felt so confident of the situation that it had already declared amnesty for offenses committed between December 6, 1922, and May 12, 1923, that is, from the conclusion of the treaty to the end of the civil war. It had earlier passed land legislation to complete the land purchase policies started before independence and had undertaken a public works hydroelectric scheme on the Shannon River. Its commitment to a nonpartisan civil service based on talent, including members of the pre-independence civil service, alienated a certain portion of its followers, who assumed public employment would be available for participants in the war of independence and treaty supporters. The presence in the ministry of people such as Patrick Hogan at Agriculture and Patrick McGilligan, who had replaced McGrath at Industry, and their deference to civil servants, especially those at the Department for Finance, where the minister was Ernest Blythe, resulted in a conservative or orthodox fiscal policy likely to alienate rank-and-file members of the electorate. The reduction of publicly provided old age pensions in 1924 epitomized the adherence to fiscal orthodoxy at the price of public favor, but the government justified the same as essential to draw purchasers of public bond issues and capital investors to an economy still being reconstructed from civil war damage.

Another issue in which O'Higgins took particular interest, since it was closely related to public order, was legislation regulating the sale of intoxicating liquor. His overall aim was to curb the excessive number of licensed premises in the country, a phenomenon stemming from the generosity of the judiciary of the old regime to supporters of the Irish Parliamentary Party, generosity extended as part of the "killing Home Rule with kindness" campaign. He also wished to standardize and shorten the hours in which such premises would be open. Vigorous opposition, especially from the vintners, the brewers, and the distillers, some of whom were important supporters of the government, required two separate pieces of legislation, one in 1924 setting set hours out of service and another in 1927, reducing the number of licenses with compensation and making further restrictions on hours of service.

A general election took place in June 1927. Cumann na nGaedheal had to contend with opposition not only from de Valera's new party, Fianna Fáil, which was freshly invigorated with financial support from Irish America, and Sinn Féin, but also from the Farmers Party and the National League (a party led by William Redmond, the son of the late Irish Parliamentary Party leader) on the right and the Labour Party on the left. The failure of Cumann na nGaedheal to form a mass party organization and its tendency to rely on a "politics of deference," that is, endorsement by the professional classes, including the clergy, substantial shopkeepers, and larger farmers, as a stimulus to broader popular support, seriously handicapped it in a contest with the mixed nationalist-populist message of Fianna Fáil. The results gave the government party only 47 seats out of 153, with Fianna Fáil getting 44, Labour 22, the National League 8, Sinn Féin 5, and 16 independents. However, Fianna Fáil's refusal to take the required oath to the king upon entry to the Dáil kept them in their abstentionist position along with Sinn Féin. Accordingly, Cosgrave was again able to form a government, this time with only a plurality of seats.

A month later, on July 10, 1927, Kevin O'Higgins, who had assumed the portfolio of foreign minister as well as justice, was assassinated on his way to Sunday Mass by three IRA members acting on their own accord. They were never apprehended, but their identities were revealed posthumously more than a half century later. The government responded with public safety legislation allowing the suppression of certain periodicals, the outlawing of certain associations, and the use of military tribunals for certain offenses, as well as a constitutional amendment that would compel candidates for the Dáil to declare their willingness to take the required oath.

Rather than abandon the seats to which they had been elected, de Valera and his Fianna Fáil followers signed the required oath on August 11, but only after going through the theatrics of covering the document with a Bible and insisting that they were not taking an oath but only fulfilling a requirement for their signatures. Five days later, a vote of no confidence in the government, supported by Fianna Fáil, Labour, and the National Party, failed to pass by one vote. A National Party member, John Jinks of Sligo, opted to absent himself, after being persuaded in the bar of the Shelbourne Hotel in Dublin that ex-army voters in Sligo would be displeased with his support for bringing de Valera to power. The Dáil was dissolved and, in the subsequent election, Cumann na nGaedheal and Fianna Fáil gained 62 and 57 seats, respectively, with a significant decline in the seats gained by other parties. Enough independents gave Cumann na nGaedheal a majority, giving it another four years in power to continue its work of state-building as well as giving Fianna Fáil four more years to acquaint itself with the rudiments of constitutional politics.

ASSERTING INDEPENDENCE

LAST YEARS OF CUMANN NA NGAEDHEAL

The victory in the second election in 1927 gave the Cumann na nGaedheal government a lease on life for another term. However, its record in that term seemed to be purely defensive, as it appeared to lack the creative energy with which it had taken on state-building amidst and after the civil war. Instead, much of its attention was given to attacking Fianna Fáil, which used the period to master the art of constitutional politics, to strengthen its popular political machinery, and to wean itself from, although probably not completely, irregularism. No doubt the death of O'Higgins was a severe blow to the government as few in it matched his capacity for leadership, articulateness, and energetic authoritativeness. Fianna Fáil, on the other hand, significantly reinforced by monetary contributions from the Irish-American community, developed a broadly based popular organization, which was able to engender a mass following by playing a variety of grievances, which included unemployment, poor returns from the smaller tillage farmers, high rates of emigration, the republican (nationalist) dissatisfaction with the persistence of the oath, dominion status, and partition. Its efforts contrasted with the minimal organization of Cumann na nGaedheal, which relied instead on an outdated politics of deference that expected popular support to ensue from the endorsement of social and community leaders such as clergymen, professionals, businessmen, and strong farmers.

Examples of the purely defensive approach of the government included the passage of a series of constitutional amendments that were designed to work against democracy or the expression of popular will. For the first several years of its existence, the Free State Constitution could be amended simply by the vote of the Dáil and the Seanad. However, it did allow for referendum if and when a specified minority in the Oireachtas (parliament) demanded such. The referendum mechanism was designed to protect a minority against majority tyranny with the authors having in mind the unionist minority in particular. The constitution also allowed initiative, that is, the bringing of a measure to the public, by the petitioning of a substantial number of citizens. The motive behind initiative was to enable a majority to advance a cause to which more conservative institutions were indifferent. The specific cause that was being advanced by initiative was the republican goal of removing the oath to the monarch as a condition for accepting office, an issue that, if put to the electorate, would probably prevail as most Cumann na nGaedheal voters and even elected officials would as soon not have to take the oath. To prevent the crisis arising in which a popular vote could put an end to what was regarded as a treaty-required fixture in the constitution, the government advanced and secured passage by the Dáil and Seanad of an amendment to the constitution that did away with both the referendum and the initiative.

Another amendment, not as clearly designed to inhibit the democratic wishes of the majority, changed the procedure whereby the members of the Seanad were to be elected. One-quarter of the members were up for reelection every three years. In the very first election of senators, most were elected by the Dáil, with a quarter of members being nominated by the executive council, a procedure designed to guarantee a presence in the body of former unionists. For the second trimester, three times as many candidates as there were seats open for reelection (one-quarter of the entire Seanad) were nominated by the Dáil and the Seanad and were voted on by an electorate limited by age. The actual public participation was poor and few knew the great number of candidates who were to be elected by the Single Transferable Voting system, according to which a voter numerically lists his preferential ranking of the candidates. A new amendment ended popular election and resumed the original practice of the Dáil electing the Seanad by proportional voting, which was bound to produce the effect of the upper house eventually duplicating the lower house rather than serve as an independent body of "elders" able to advise and restrain the popular house. On the other hand, it prevented a potentially well organized Fianna Fáil sweep in a popular election.

The government secured a third amendment extending the time period during which the Seanad could delay the passage of a measure it disapproved of, that is, lengthen the suspensive veto power of the upper house. This measure did have the effect of delaying the major constitutional changes that the Fianna Fáil government under Eamon de Valera would introduce when they came to power in 1932, one of which would be the actual abolition of the Seanad itself.

In 1929 the government succeeded in introducing legislation that many people inappropriately came to regard as the essential feature of the Irish Free State era, namely, the establishment of a literary censorship board. The legislation represented the fruit of the recommendations of a commission established in 1925 by O'Higgins to deal with the question of offensive literary works. The idea of controlling salacious and sensational literature was something that met minimal objection in hardly any quarter in the Ireland of that time, or for that matter, in many others nations as well, no more that hate literature or oratory would be regarded as offensive today. However, the actual operation of the censorship board in Ireland became ludicrous. Rather than conducting a systematic rating of literature and determining what ought to be barred from public distribution, the board would respond to individual complaints about single works. In a society with a certain heritage of Puritanism, to which was added the inevitable Puritanism that accompanies revolution and a conviction of the moral superiority of the newly independent nation against its former "oppressor," the censor exercised powers quite broadly, so much so that it almost became an ambition for an Irish author to be censored as a guarantee that his work was worthwhile and likely to succeed outside of Ireland. Paradoxically, the works of James Joyce, although barred for a long time in the United States and elsewhere, were not censored in Ireland. It must also be noted that the censoring authorities continued well after the Cumann na nGaedheal government had ended and were scarcely inconsistent with the spirit of the Fianna Fáil governments that succeeded.

In 1930 and 1931 the worldwide economic depression that followed the Wall Street collapse of October 1929 had taken full hold. Radical political movements of both right and left were appealing to increasing numbers of people, either the lowly paid or the unemployed or those whose relatively comfortable positions had been undermined. Since the Irish economy remained predominantly agricultural and was not especially prosperous to begin with, the depression did not directly effect Ireland. However, that commodity that Ireland continued to export, namely, its young population, who were compelled to emigrate—some to the United States but more increasingly to Britain—found fewer opportunities. Accordingly, those denied the outlet of emigration became another source of discontent.

In such an environment, some of the more subtle figures in Sinn Féin and the IRA, such as Peadar O'Donnell, Seán MacBride, and Frank Ryan, sought to broaden the appeal of their movement away from the exclusively nationalist and republican message to include a social program or dimension. Like many radicals in the world at that time, they looked with tinted lenses at what they perceived as the advancement of equality and development in the Soviet Union, whose planned system seemed to contrast with the misery amidst plentitude in the capitalist world. Few were aware or attentive to the Gulags or the police state over which Stalin presided. In September 1931 Saor Éire was formed to promote republicanism and socialism. However, within a month the Catholic hierarchy, ever vigilant to the danger of communism, condemned the group and a potential popular following quickly dissipated. The government followed through with a proscription of Saor Éire and a number of other named groups, including the IRA, as well as securing a further constitutional amendment allowing military tribunals to try those accused of sedition and membership in named organizations. However, the government overplayed its hand when it sought to ban the new daily newspaper promoting the Fianna Fáil party. Called the *Irish Press*, the paper was founded by Eamon de Valera with funds given to him by Irish-American holders of Dáil Éireann bonds that had been refunded when an American court Solomon-like refused to award the money to either the Irish Free State, Sinn Féin, or similar pretenders to the original Dáil Éireann. The Irish courts refused to uphold the ban, which reinforced the impression of the government losing its act.

Significantly, in December 1931 the British parliament passed the Statute of Westminster, which implemented the recommendations advocated so vigorously by O'Higgins at the Imperial Conference of 1926 that the legislative autonomy of the dominions be acknowledged. The passage of that legislation in essence ought have been seen as allowing the Free State parliament to change those parts of its constitution that had been mandated by the treaty, especially if the treaty was to be seen, as the British claimed, as a piece of British legislation, rather than an international agreement. However, both the British and the Cumann na nGaedheal Party failed to see that point when they would both object to de Valera's ultimately successful undoing of the objectionable treaty requirements after he came to power.

Since a Eucharistic Congress was scheduled to be held in Dublin in June 1932, the government decided to move ahead the date for a general election, which would have to be held within the year as it was almost five years since the previous election. The election was held in February and resulted in Fianna Fáil gaining a plurality, to which were added the seven votes of Labour Party TDs (teachtai Dála [Dáil deputies]), so as to give a clear majority with which to form a government. There was apprehension that some in the government, particularly in the military, might not accept the mandate of the electorate, and some members of Fianna Fáil TDs were reported to have arrived in the Dáil Éireann with weapons in case a counterrevolutionary coup d'état was attempted. Fortunately, the outgoing government accepted the wishes of the people and transferred power to those who, a decade earlier had been their armed enemies. This acceptance, along with the willingness of the new state's civil service and military to work with the new government, marked the final evidence that a democratic and constitutional independent Irish state had been created.

FIANNA FÁIL COMES TO POWER

On becoming president of the Executive Council, de Valera also assumed the post of minister for foreign affairs, which post he would retain until 1948. He named close loyalists to office, for example, Sean T. O'Kelly became vice president of the Executive Council, Frank Aiken became minister for defense, Seán MacEntee became minister for finance, and Seán Lemass became minister for justice. One of the first actions of the new government was to suspend the recent constitutional amendment that authorized the military tribunals for sedition, which suggested a softer attitude toward their old allies in the IRA. In June the undoing of the Anglo-Irish Treaty began with the passage by the Dáil of a constitutional amendment removing the required oath to the king. Seanad opposition delayed its entry into effect until the next year. In the same month, the Irish Free State began to withhold land annuities collected to compensate the British exchequer for its financing of the various land purchase schemes of the late 19th and early 20th centuries. In July the British responded by imposing a 20 percent duty on most exports from the Free State to Britain, which consisted primarily of agricultural produce, especially beef, to which the Irish responded by passing legislation enabling the Executive Council to impose duties on various goods from specific countries, particularly Britain. Thus began what would be called the "Economic War," which would reap great havoc on the Pasteur (pasture) farms in Ireland, but would work hand in glove with the Fianna Fáil ideal of promoting tillage farming and economic self-sufficiency.

The Eucharistic Congress, attending by hundreds of leading churchmen and thousands of laity from abroad, and by hundreds of thousands of Irish, served as a magnificent manifestation of a triumphalist Catholicism celebrating its de facto reestablishment as the religion of the Irish nation after centuries of persecution and social subordination.

James MacNeill, the brother of Eoin MacNeill, who had succeeded Tim Healy as governor general of the Irish Free State, resigned his position after receiving what he considered discourtesies from members of de Valera's government. This gave de Valera the opportunity to further downgrade a position he despised as part of the treaty settlement, since the governor-general was nominally the chief executive of the Irish Free State whose signature, in lieu of the king's, was required for legislation. He appointed a Fianna Fáil stalwart and former TD, Domhanall Ua Buachalla, as MacNeill's replacement, with specific instructions that he was not to live in the vice-regal lodge, nor perform any of the ceremonial or social functions associated with the office, but that he was to reside in his own rural residence and perform the minimal legal duties, such as signing legislation.

In a general election called less than a year after coming to power, de Valera and Fianna Fáil obtained an absolute majority in the Dáil, with Cumann na nGaedheal strength further receding. One of the first steps taken afterward was the dismissal of the police commissioner, General Eoin O'Duffy, who was identified closely with Cumann na nGaedheal. In the spring the constitutional amendment delayed by the Seanad, which abolished the oath, took effect. Later, in November, the Dáil passed constitutional amendments removing the power of the governor general to veto legislation, recommend appropriations, and abolish the right of judicial appeal to the Privy Council.

In the meantime O'Duffy had been elected leader of an organization, the Army Comrades Association, formed primarily of ex–Free State soldiers. The group changed its name to the National Guard, but it soon became more popularly known as the "Blueshirts" in view of its members, like many continental political movements of the time, wearing a blueshirt as a uniform. The organization proposed a march on Dublin to commemorate the deaths of the Free State icons, Griffith, Collins, and O'Higgins. De Valera, aware of possible parallels between Duffy's planned march and Benito Mussolini's actual march on Rome in the previous decade, which brought him to power, prohibited the march and proclaimed the National Guard to be illegal. He had numerous former and/or still active IRA members recruited as police auxiliaries as reinforcements in case of any difficulties. No problems occurred, but the following month the prohibited National Guard reorganized itself as the Young Ireland Association[16] and joined with Cumann na nGaedheal and an independent Centre Party to form a new party, Fine Gael, with O'Duffy as its president.

The Blueshirt movement had some parallels with continental fascism, but more likely it represented an overreaction on the part of former officers of the Free State Army, reinforced by strong farmers severely injured by the economic war, to Fianna Fáil tolerance of IRA attacks on Fine Gael meetings. There was an intellectual component to the movement that drew much of its inspiration from the corporatist thinking in papal social encyclicals, a thinking from which

---

[16] *The Young Ireland Association was subsequently outlawed, but it reformed again under yet another name, the League of Youth.*

Eamon de Valera himself was not far removed. At any rate, the excessive language of O'Duffy, and his actual failure to deliver political power, especially in local government elections, prompted his resignation from the presidency of Fine Gael, whose leadership was assumed by William T. Cosgrave.

Moving from one success to another, de Valera obtained Dáil approval, but expected Seanad delay, of amendments that abolished the Seanad and removed the university seats in the Dáil Éireann, which would eliminate whatever vestiges of unionism might still exist in the Oireachtas. The amendments would not go into effect because of the Seanad delays until the spring of 1936. In September he gained approval of legislation giving pensions to members of the anti-treaty forces in the civil war. In December a cattle and coal agreement was reached with Britain ending some of the more difficult issues in the Economic War.

During the following year, the government began to play a more socially conservative role as it passed legislation requiring the licensing of dance halls on the basis of clergy fear of unregulated countryside dancing undermining youth morality. Other legislation forbade the sale and importation of contraceptives. De Valera had the further satisfaction of acknowledgment by the judicial committee of the British Privy Council itself of the right of the Irish Free State to bar judicial appeals from Ireland to the Privy Council. With the threat from the right, specifically the Blueshirts, dissipated, de Valera turned his attention to bringing his former allies, the IRA, under control. IRA assassination of the son of a land agent in Longford in 1935 and of a retired British admiral in Cork the following year resulted in the group being outlawed, much as the Cumann na nGaedheal government had done.

After King Edward VIII abdicated in December 1936 in order to marry an American divorcée and was succeeded by his brother, George VI, the Dáil Éireann, in an emergency session, passed a constitutional amendment removing any reference to the governor general (and thereby the king) in the constitution and an external relations act that acknowledged the diplomatic representational role of the Crown in acting on behalf of Ireland. The following year, a general election was held on the same day as a referendum for a new constitution for Ireland. Fianna Fáil won the election, but not with an absolute majority, and the constitution, drafted under de Valera's direction, was approved by a vote of 685,105 to 526,943. The government formed under the new constitution was similar in many ways to the one it replaced. It was to be a parliamentary system with the Dáil, elected by the Single Transferable Vote system of proportional representation, continuing as the lower house, selecting the head of the government, who would now be called by the older Gaelic title, Taoiseach. The Seanad was revived with 11 of its members nominated by the Taoiseach, six elected by the universities, and 43 elected from the nominees of five panels, Cultural and Educational, Agricultural, Labor, Industrial and Commercial, and Administrative. The Seanad had very limited delaying power, but it could introduce legislation and could correct or amend measures. It was elected after a general election of the Dáil. Law made the members of the county councils its electors and the panel concept, patterned after the corporatist system of representation nominally adhered to in fascist countries, became largely a legal fiction, as Seanad nominations usually went to defeated

Dáil members or to aspiring future Dáil candidates. Another new feature of the constitution was a popularly elected president who would serve a term of seven years and perform the primarily honorific functions of the governor-general, although he did have the power to refer legislation presented for his signature to the Supreme Court to determine its constitutionality.

Most of the constitution deals, as did the Free State document, with the various powers, duties, and terms of office for branches of government. However, it also contains a number of articles stipulating respect for human rights and advancement of social ideals. Many of these ideals were closely reflective of Catholic social thinking, which would cause some controversy decades later when Ireland would begin to undergo secularizing pressures. Specific issues included the constitution's idealization of a social order in which mothers in families would not feel the economic need to seek employment outside the home and the constitution's prohibition of the dissolution of marriage.[17] Other constitutional features of a more controversial nature included its second and third articles, which made the claim that Ireland consisted of the whole island but restricted the laws of the state tentatively to the 26 counties of the republic. This aspiration succeeded only in strengthening the determination of the majority in Northern Ireland to remain outside a united Irish state.[18] Another clause in the constitution to which few objected at the time, but which was removed in a 1972 referendum, was the recognition of the Catholic Church as the religion of the overwhelming majority of the people and of the existence of various other faiths, but which recognition conferred no official or de jure status. The constitution came into effect in December and Douglas Hyde, the founder of the Gaelic League and a Protestant, was selected as the first president of Ireland, called Eire (the name replacing Irish Free State) the following year.

In April 1938 de Valera successfully negotiated a settlement of the land annuities issue with British prime minister Neville Chamberlain. The issue was resolved with a single lump sum payment by the Irish, which was only a fraction of the total amount expected. The prohibitive mutual tariffs that had been imposed in the Economic War were also ended. In addition the British withdrew from the naval facilities at Berehaven, Cobh, and Lough Swilly allowed to them by the treaty of 1921. With these achievements in hand, de Valera went again to the people in a general election in which Fianna Fáil secured an overwhelming majority in the Dáil.

THE EMERGENCY

The IRA, dominated more by its nationalist than by its socialist wing, issued an ultimatum to Britain to withdraw from Northern Ireland. The organization subsequently undertook a bombing campaign in several British cities, which brought scores of casualties. The Irish government responded to this presumption by an irregular group to act for the Irish people by resorting to the same machinery that the Irish Free State government had employed. Legisla-

---

[17] *Divorce in limited circumstances has since been allowed following a 1995 referendum.*
[18] *These articles were amended as part of the 1998 Good Friday Agreement.*

tion allowed the establishment of military tribunals, internment without trial, and a treason act with a death penalty was passed. When the European war began in September, Ireland, like the other smaller European nations, declared its neutrality unless attacked by either Germany or the Soviet Union. However, the Dáil passed legislation proclaiming a national emergency, enabling the constitutionally stipulated wartime rules, which gave considerable arbitrary power to the state, to apply even though war had not been formally declared.

Ireland would persist in its neutrality throughout the Second World War despite enormous pressures, especially from Great Britain and the United States, to more openly identify with the Allied side. No doubt Irish popular opinion stood on the side of the Allies against the Axis, but de Valera had to contend with the reality of a significant IRA presence in Ireland that would regard any alliance with Britain, considered as "occupying" Northern Ireland, as a betrayal of the nationalist vision of a united Ireland. In addition, the war of independence had occurred less than a generation before and bitterness in many circles was still too close to the surface to be evoked, as would be the case were Ireland to formally join with Britain in the war effort.

On the other hand, the Irish were adamant in rejecting limited overtures by Germany to aid the Axis. Nazi Germany had sought to work with the IRA to foment disturbances behind the lines for the British in Ireland and Northern Ireland. Seán Russell, the leader of the IRA who had made his way to Germany from the United States, and his left-wing opponent, Frank Ryan, who had fallen into German hands after having been captured serving the Republican cause in the Spanish Civil War, were reconciled and placed in a U-boat that headed for Ireland in early 1940. However, the mission was aborted when Russell died. Ryan died a few years later in Germany. There were several other German efforts at parachuting agents into Ireland during the war, which were generally unsuccessful.

Overtures by Winston Churchill, especially upon the American entry into the war in December 1941, for the Irish to join the war effort with a suggested reward of reunification of the island were rejected by de Valera as were all appeals to readmit the British navy to the ports that they had relinquished in the 1938 agreement. The Irish government disapproved of the arrival of American troops in Northern Ireland in 1942 and the establishment of an American naval base in Derry, which inhibited the free movement of American military in Northern Ireland on personal visits to Ireland. However, Irish fire brigades and other relief services readily joined in providing assistance to the people of Belfast when that city became subject to severe German bombing in the spring of 1941. Dublin itself experienced limited and accidental German bombing about the same time. The following year the Irish government disallowed the use of a radio transmitter by the German embassy in Dublin lest it serve to provide intelligence and even weather information to Axis forces. Throughout the war, German airmen who survived crashes or who had to make forced landings in Ireland, usually after missions over Britain or in the Atlantic, were interned for the duration of the war, whereas British personnel in similar circumstances were returned home.

There was much talk that the unavailability of the Irish ports to the British and the Americans inhibited the struggle against the U-boats, which were wrecking havoc on trans-Atlantic shipping. On the other hand, facilities in Northern Ireland gave substantial assistance for conducting the North Atlantic campaign. Furthermore, Irish attachment to the Allied cause would have opened up the generally poorly protected ports and cities to German assault. It is generally conceded that Irish intelligence sources were very cooperative with the Allied effort throughout the war and the British embassy in Dublin was usually unsympathetic to exerting any pressure on the Irish. The American ambassador, David Gray, a cousin of the American first lady, Eleanor Roosevelt, however, was quite undiplomatic in his criticism of the Irish. Probably his outspokenness reflected another agenda, namely, to weaken the political strength of Irish-American opponents of President Franklin Roosevelt, who aspired to secure an unprecedented fourth term. Whatever their effect on American politics, Gray's antics rebounded very much to de Valera's advantage, as Fianna Fáil swept back into power with an absolute majority in the May

Cartoon shows Eamon de Valera holding a sign reading "No Allied Bases in Ireland," as he struggles against a gale labeled "Defeat the Axis." During World War II Ireland remained neutral, despite Allied pressure. *(Library of Congress)*

1944 general election, after having slipped to a mere plurality in an election the previous year.

Toward the end of the European war, de Valera made a gesture, difficult to understand, of calling on the German embassy in Dublin to extend his condolences upon the death of Adolph Hitler, a visit that probably confused even the Germans. Some have argued it was the mathematical and theological side of de Valera prevailing, as it was necessary to the very end to demonstrate the Irish position of neutrality. Others argue it was done to provoke the British so as to enable Fianna Fáil to benefit from the inevitable anti-British backlash in forthcoming by-elections. Provoke it did, as Winston Churchill's victory speech thanked the people of Northern Ireland for their war efforts, which he contrasted with those who benefited by remaining neutral from the sufferings of others. De Valera's rejoinder was an effective, at least to an Irish audience, reminder to the wartime leader that, in his understandable sense of triumph, he had forgotten the legacy of a people who had suffered 800 years of tyranny.

The emergency had brought much discomfort to the Irish, especially shortages of many imports, as British shipping that would have brought such materials had been absorbed in the war effort. There was severe rationing, including restrictions on the use of automobiles, and censoring of the media. Newspapers were inhibited from giving any war news that might reflect sympathy for either side. On the other hand, those Irish who had radio receivers were able to regularly obtain BBC reports and thousands of Irish from both parts of the island were serving in the British forces. Possibly the information isolation of the Irish in the war years gave them a provincialism that would explain their naive expectations in the immediate postwar years that they would have a world audience for their complaint about the partitioning of the island of Ireland.

The shortages of the war years would also have the effect of shaking the populist mandate for Fianna Fáil, especially among its natural constituency, the small farmers, who sensed the benefactors of the regime were increasingly manufacturers of protected, and often inadequate, domestic goods. An example of dissatisfaction was the emergence of a new farmers' party, Clann na Talmhan, whose strength in Dáil Éireann rose to 11 when Fianna Fáil regained its absolute majority in 1944. On the other hand, the major opposition party, Fine Gael, continued in its downspin, as its numbers in Dáil Éireann in the successive elections of 1937, 1938, 1943, and 1944 went from 48 to 45 to 32 to 30. Not surprisingly, its leader, William T. Cosgrave, resigned and was replaced by another stalwart of the Irish Free State, the former minister for defense, Richard Mulcahy, in 1944. Also, the Labour Party experience a split, as a breakaway group, led by William O'Brien of the Irish Transport and General Workers' Union, who objected to the return of James Larkin and his more radical ideology to the party and formed a rival National Labour Party. But a potentially troubling development to Fianna Fáil domination was the formation, in 1946, of a radical republican party called Clann na Poblachta and headed by IRA veteran Seán MacBride, which could present itself as doing what Fianna Fáil had done 20 years earlier: moving beyond the purely nationalist theme and rallying the disinherited and dissatisfied. Its victory in a number of by-elections in late 1947 gave the movement great expectations for the next general election.

COALITIONS AND DE VALERA'S LAST GOVERNMENTS

As expected Fianna Fáil did poorer in the next general election in February 1948. It lost eight seats in a Dáil whose total membership increased by nine (it was curiously argued that a substantial number of Irish emigrants would be returning from England after the end of the war and that the Dáil numbers should reflect a population increase, whereas, in fact, the population was decreasing). Fine Gael gained a single new seat and the combined votes of the two Labour groups gained two seats, the farmers group, Clann na Talmhan lost four seats, the new radical republican group, Clann na Poblachta won 10 seats, which was a disappointment given their expectations and their imprudent decision to contest more seats than they could possibly win, and a variety of other independents won 12 seats. The only conclusion from the election was that Fianna Fáil had lost the confidence of the majority. Accordingly, a coalition of virtually all other groups was formed, with John A. Costello of Fine Gael becoming Taoiseach. The Fine Gael leader, Richard Mulcahy, still provoked too many civil war and postwar memories to be acceptable to some in the coalition. Seán MacBride, the head of Clann na Poblachta, became minister for external affairs, an appointment scarcely conducive to amicable Anglo-Irish relations.

Significantly, it was the Taoiseach, Costello, rather than MacBride, who broke the news that Ireland was going to be proclaimed a republic and would withdraw from the British Commonwealth, which he did in September while visiting Canada. That took place the following Easter Monday, but the British responded by legislating that Northern Ireland would not cease to be part of the United Kingdom without the consent of its parliament and that the Irish were not to be regarded as a foreign nation nor its citizens aliens in Britain. While the Irish had joined the Office of European Economic Development and were to receive American assistance through the postwar reconstruction measure, the Marshall Plan, MacBride made clear that Ireland could not be part of the North Atlantic Alliance or NATO as long as Britain "occupied" Northern Ireland. That same year all of the Irish political parties agreed to a church gate collection in support of an antipartition campaign that had been started by Northern Irish nationalists, but which now received the endorsement and cooperation of the Irish Department of External Affairs. De Valera, soon after losing power in the previous year's election, had gone on an international tour to the United States, Australia, New Zealand, and India, promoting a similar message.

Historically, the other memorable issue during the first coalition government was the "mother and child" scheme of free publicly provided obstetrical and pediatric care proposed in 1951 by Minister for Health Dr. Noel Browne, a colleague of MacBride in Clann na Poblachta. The measure was partly inspired by the more comprehensive system of national health care that had been established by the Labour Government in postwar Britain. Understandably, it was opposed not only by the doctors' organizations in Ireland but also by the hierarchy of the Catholic Church. The ecclesiastical objections were based on a suspicion of state intrusion into private and familial matters that was grounded in earlier papal social teaching and a belief that there should at least be a means test, so that public assistance should go only to the truly indigent. There was also a fear that many of those administering the program, especially if they received their medical training abroad, would be inclined to promote various practices, such as contraception and abortion, that were condemned by Catholic teaching. When his colleagues in the government, including MacBride, deferred to the bishops, Browne resigned his position.

Curiously, in a general election held soon after, Fine Gael gained nine seats in the Dáil Éireann, while a reunited Labour Party lost three and Clann na Poblachta shrank to two. However, Fianna Fáil, which regained only one seat, was able to gain supporting votes from a sufficient number of independents to be able to form another government. That government instituted a system of social insurance for Ireland in 1952. The following year the benefits of the earlier-rejected mother and child scheme were extended to all who qualified for the social insurance system. The attentiveness of the Fianna Fáil government to Catholic anxieties, however, was manifest in the passage of legislation requiring adopting parents to be of the same religion as the child and its natural parents or the mother, if she was unmarried. Then, in another general election in 1954, Fianna Fáil lost a single seat, but Fine Gael gained 10, which, along with the Labour gain of three and the support of other groups and independents, enabled another coalition government to be formed under Costello.

Under this government Ireland finally gained its long sought goal of admission to the United Nations as part of an East-West deal in which Ireland was admitted along with Manchuria. The Soviet Union had earlier objected to Irish membership partly because of its suspicions of Irish softness toward the Axis powers, but primarily because of the ultimately unwarranted suspicion that Ireland would be another Anglo-American pawn in the international body. A census taken at the time also reported that Ireland was experiencing a decline in population, a statistic shared at the time only by the Russian-dominated East Germany (whose fleeing population ultimately was contained only by the construction of the Berlin Wall in 1961) and by communist North Vietnam (many of whose residents, especially Catholics, fled to Western-supported South Vietnam). A great literary debate developed about the "vanishing Irish" and the apparent acceptance by its political authorities of economic and social stagnation under which potential problems were avoided by the outlet of emigration. In such a situation, a few sought an outlet in violent irredentism as the IRA became a violent campaign to "liberate" Northern Ireland in 1956 with a series of attacks across the border on RUC barracks. The campaign would continue, but with greatly reduced activity, until January 1962, when it would be formally called off. The major reason for its failure was the lack of support from within the Northern Irish nationalist or Catholic community, many of whose residents had been benefiting greatly from the economic development of Northern Ireland and from the more generous social welfare and education programs that greatly surpassed those of the Republic of Ireland. Most of the participants in the campaign were from south of the border. One of them, Sean South, from Limerick, even received a virtual hero's funeral after his death in a raid on a police barracks in Fermanagh. No doubt Fianna Fáil gained from a ground swell of nationalist sentiment in a general election that followed soon after, as it gained an absolute majority of seats in Dáil Éireann enabling de Valera to again form a government, which would be his last, in March. Not surprising, that government had no inhibitions about applying the still existing wartime emergency powers against the IRA, especially that of internment, which effectively broke the back of the campaign.

That government would be the last led by de Valera, who in June 1959 would run successfully for the presidency, defeating a Fine Gael and pro-treaty legendary figure, General Seán McEoin. Significantly, a constitutional amendment to replace the Single Transferable Voting system and thereby benefit the largest party, Fianna Fáil, failed, even though its proponents had thought the pro–de Valera vote would carry the amendment along. De Valera, whose age (he was near 77) and declining eyesight made him less able to actively direct government and more suitable for the honorific presidency, was succeeded by his longtime ally in the anti-treaty Sinn Féin and in Fianna Fáil, Seán Lemass.

ABANDONMENT OF ISOLATION AND SELF-SUFFICIENCY

Many of the ministers who had been colleagues of de Valera from the civil war era and the founding of Fianna Fáil were gradually replaced by a new generation of party activists. The new generation included men born just before or after the civil war and some whose families had no record of involvement. New faces included the Cork City TD, Jack Lynch, whose earlier claim to fame was as an outstanding player in the GAA sport of hurling. Another was Lemass's son-in-law, Charles J. Haughey. Another new man, Neil Blaney, from Donegal, was the son of a veteran Fianna Fáil deputy. Kevin Boland was the son of de Valera loyalist and colleague, Gerry Boland. Other stalwarts, such as Frank Aiken and Seán MacEntee, continued in office.

An indication of changing times was the passage, over the objections of the Catholic hierarchy, of legislation extending the Sunday opening of public houses to include rural areas as well as major cities. More important was the government's acceptance of the recommendations of a study titled *Economic Development,* prepared by Dr. T. K. Whittaker, the secretary of the Department of Finance. That report suggested a reversal of the prevailing Irish approach to economic development and government financing, which entailed a mixture of orthodox retrenchment and budget balancing combined with economic protectionism, in favor of a move toward recruiting foreign investment and foreign markets and the belated acceptance of Keynesian use of government finances to stimulate economic development. De Valera had not long moved up to the presidency when his vision of a pastoral Ireland was being abandoned by his own political heirs in the aspiration for industrial and commercial development. Other indices of a new day coming to Ireland was the commencement in 1958 of trans-Atlantic service by the national airline, Aer Lingus, and the establishment in 1960 of an authority to direct a national television service, which began in December 1961.

On the international level, the Irish ambassador to the United Nations, Frederick Boland, was elected president of the United Nations General Assembly and presided at the tumultuous session in 1960 in New York attended by a variety of national leaders, one of whom, Nikita Khrushchev of the Soviet Union, he had to call to order. Ireland also committed troops to the United Nations peacekeeping efforts in the strife-torn newly independent Congo. Ten soldiers were killed in an ambush in December of that year. It was the first of many instances, continuing to this day, of Irish involvement in UN peacekeeping missions. Another instance of less successful diplomacy was the Irish application, made in August 1961, for membership in the European Economic Community or Common Market, which then consisted of six members. Unfortunately, the veto of British membership a year and a half later by President Charles de Gaulle of France also inhibited Irish membership. To offset their mutual exclusion from Europe the British and the Irish signed a free trade agreement two years later in 1965.

In a general election in October 1961, Lemass sought his own mandate from the people. Although Fianna Fáil was able to form a government, gains by both Fine Gael and Labour denied him the absolute majority that de Valera had won in 1957, forcing him to rely on the approval of some independents. But that did not inhibit his ongoing drive for Irish modernization, which even gained him a cover story in *Time* magazine. Further drawing world attention to developments and change in Ireland was the first visit to the country by an incumbent U.S. president. In June 1963, five months before he was assassinated, John F. Kennedy, the first American president of Irish Catholic ancestry, visited. The triumphalism surrounding the visit, which rivaled the 1932 Eucharistic Congress, suggested that the Irish interpreted Kennedy's electoral success in America vicariously as an Irish victory and indeed as a certification that Ireland was truly a nation. Kennedy astutely played into the spirit with his suggestions that had his forebears not left for Ireland, and had de Valera not been sent back to Ireland by his widowed mother in New York, they might have wound up in each other's respective office.

In April 1965 Lemass was able to win two more seats for Fianna Fáil in a general election and thereby secure an absolute majority. Fine Gael, under the leadership of James Dillon, the grandson of the Young Irelander and son of the Parliamentary Party luminary, who had succeeded Richard Mulcahy in 1959, held its own. The traditionally conservative party had accepted in 1964 a program for a "Just Society" advanced by younger members led by Declan Costello, son of the coalition Taoiseach of the 1950s, which introduced a progressive and socially concerned character to the party. Labour also made significant gains, as minor groups and the number of independents declined. That same year legislation passed to correct a long-standing social issue in Ireland, the disinheritance of widows, as they were guaranteed one-half of a husband's estate, or at least one-third where there were children. In the first two months of 1965, an historic exchange of visits by the Northern Irish prime minister, Terence O'Neill, whose succession to power in 1963 suggested a new face for unionism, and Seán Lemass raised expectations for a thawing of the frozen relations and attitudes of the two states toward each other. Lemass appointed a committee that recommended a departure from the prevailing position, which regarded Northern Ireland as somewhat illegitimate and provisional, and to look upon recognition of the validity of unionist identity as the first step toward an accord. On the other hand, the evangelical minister Ian Paisley condemned the visits, which O'Neill had depicted as comparable to chatting with a lovely young lady (the Irish Republic) across the fence, as sinister. He reminded O'Neill that he, a married man, ought not to be chatting across the fence with young ladies!

The next year, which was the golden jubilee of the Easter Rising, the Irish census figures announced for the first time an increase in population, which suggested the success of Lemass's policies. A proposal by the minister for education, Donough O'Malley, for the provision of free secondary school education for all Irish children represented a continuation of the modernization policies. A more ominous note was the murder of a young Catholic by loyalists in Northern Ireland, outraged by a nationalist celebration of Easter Week, and the conviction of Ian Paisley for disturbance of the peace in his protests against nationalist gatherings in the province. Later that year, Lemass resigned as Taoiseach and was succeeded by Jack Lynch, which could be seen as marking the end of the war of independence and civil war generation in Irish political life, aside, of course, from Eamon de Valera, who at 83 years of age was narrowly reelected over Tom Higgins, the nephew of his civil war antagonist, Kevin O'Higgins, to the honorific presidency.

The Lynch government was expected to continue the process of economic and social modernization instituted under Seán Lemass, as well as to continue steps toward rapprochement with Northern Ireland. One significant gesture of modernization was 1967 legislation that removed the ban on all books that had been censored for more than 12 years. In subsequent years the standards for censoring literature would be increasingly liberalized so that, at present, only the most blatantly pornographic material encounters a ban. In fact in society at large, general standards as to acceptable language and/or topics of discussion in a few decades would reverse a prevailing Puritanism and censoriousness to one of almost licentious openness. The government joined with Britain to again apply, in May 1967, for EEC membership, but President de Gaulle again exercised his veto to refuse them entry.

NORTHERN IRELAND

Like his predecessor, Lynch exchanged visits with Northern Ireland prime minister Terence O'Neill in December 1967 and January 1968. Few anticipated that they were on the eve of a societal breakdown in Northern Ireland that would dominate the history and politics of Ireland for the remainder of the century. Ever since the cancellation of the Boundary Commission Report in December 1925 and the acceptance of the status quo boundary, whereby six of the counties of Ulster remained linked to the United Kingdom as the locally governed province of Northern Ireland, Britain and the world seemed to regard the Irish national question as resolved. Even the Irish seemed to give a de facto acceptance to the situation, although formally, as in the second and third articles of their 1937 constitution, they continued to express an aspirational claim to the unification of the island. However, aside from the actions of violent irredentists in the IRA, who waged sporadic campaigns in 1939 and 1940 and again in the 1950s, both of which met with disapproval and severe legal reprobation from the Irish government, little was done to challenge the border. The one exception was the international antipartition campaign started in 1949 by the first coalition government, which soon found that world interest was minimal and was then dropped.

On the other hand, few in Ireland would acknowledge what seemed obvious, namely, that Northern Ireland constituted a separate entity, the majority of whose citizens had a distinct identity from the rest of the inhabitants of the island. Many in the republic felt their pious, but futile, condemnations of partition were sufficient to meet their nationalist obligations, but such expressions did little to meet the numerous and legitimate grievances of the substantial population of nationalists—or Catholics—in Northern Ireland. No doubt those grievances may have appeared relatively minor in a world that had experienced the Second World War, the Holocaust, the imposition of the Iron Curtain across Europe, and the cold war, and they were largely forgotten by a world that was witnessing an end to the colonialist era with the rise of nationalist causes in Asia and Africa from the late 1940s through the 1960s.

This should not been interpreted to mean that the grievances of the nationalist-Catholic minority in Northern Ireland should be trivialized. The grievances had originated with the beginning of Northern Ireland as an entity in 1921, while the war of independence was in its last stages. The Northern Irish government looked on the IRA, then the Army of Dáil Éireann, as its armed enemy, and those in the nationalist community who supported it as subversive. When the Anglo-Irish Treaty was signed and the Irish Provisional Government came into being, the attitude of the Free State toward the Northern Irish government and toward the IRA was murky. To some degree it cooperated with the IRA, even with anti-treaty element in it, against the Northern government, at least up until the outbreak of the civil war, when the IRA became illegitimate throughout Ireland. The Northern government set out to establish both a police force, the Royal Ulster Constabulary, which was essentially the old RIC in Northern Ireland, and a variety of auxiliary forces. The RUC had hoped to recruit a proportionate amount of its members from the Catholic population, an objective that failed largely because of Catholic reluctance to participate in the service of a state they anticipated would not last very long after the boundary commission had finished its work. However, the Auxiliary or "Special" forces, were recruited virtually exclusively from unionist circles, like from the old Ulster Defence Force or the Orange lodges, and became from the start blatantly sectarian. During disorders in 1922, they either participated in or tolerated the murder of and eviction of great numbers of Catholics, especially in sections of Belfast. These forces continued to exist in Northern Ireland up to the 1960s and during times of social confrontation would be called into action "to preserve law and order" usually in a very sectarian manner. In addition, the Northern Ireland minister for home affairs wielded powers under Special Powers legislation to declare states of emergency, which enabled him to employ internment without trial and to suspend the need for a coroner's report in the case of certain deaths. In essence, the police forces of the government, especially its auxiliaries, either indirectly or deliberately regarded the Catholic population as a subject people.

In the matter of politics and elections, Northern Ireland was a democracy, which elected originally 12 members to the Westminster parliament from generally equitably established constituencies. Most of those elected were unionists, but some nationalists of various sort were also elected and, aside from those in Sinn Féin, would take their seats in the House of Commons. The 52-member parliament of Northern Ireland was also elected from equitably drawn constituencies and originally according to the Single Transferable Voting system of proportional representation that the Government of Ireland Act had established in both parts of Ireland. The usual pattern of election results was for between 33 to 39 Unionists to be returned, with the rest divided among nationalists, republicans, northern Irish Labour, or independents. The STV system was abandoned in 1929 and Northern Ireland returned to the British and American first-past-the-post system in single-member constituencies. But this change was implemented not so much to lessen nationalist representation in the house, which remained much the same, but to rein in independent unionists. Nationalists fueled unionist suspicions in the first few years of the state by not taking their seats in what they thought was a body that did not have prospects for a long existence, but, with the 1925 acceptance of the status quo border, they began to attend, although occasionally withdrawing, and they did not formally accept the position of being the formal opposition party until after the first Lemass-O'Neill meetings in 1965.

A crisis with regard to the undemocratic nature of local government arose in 1922, when several local government bodies, whether county councils or other bodies that were under the control of nationalists and/or Sinn Féin, who refused to recognize the Northern Ireland government, were suspended by that government. Then the Single Transferable Vote system, which had allowed nationalists to gain control of these bodies, was ended in Northern Ireland and blatant gerrymandering was applied to facilitate unionist domination of most of the local governments in Northern Ireland, except in areas so overwhelmingly nationalist or Catholic as to make it impossible. Such control subsequently allowed all kinds of discriminatory treatment in hiring for public employment, in the awarding of various public benefits, especially public housing, and in the granting of contracts. A further undemocratic feature of local government elections was the continuance in Northern Ireland, long after it had been dropped in Ireland and in Britain, of a restricted franchise, which was limited to householders and their spouses and which meant that adult children living at home, other relatives living in the house, live-in domestic servants, or roomers could not vote. These restrictions were not based on religion, but, in point of fact, they worked to disenfranchise many more Catholics than Protestants, as did another practice, which allowed owners of businesses to have votes in more than one constituency.

The education system presented another difficulty. The local schools in Northern Ireland, as in the rest of the island, were usually under the direction of a local clergyman, and the religious character of the schools was determined by the religion of that clergyman. With the commencement of the Northern Ireland state, a new education system was established, which sought to bring all schools within state direction and make them nondenominational. The Catholic schools refused to be incorporated in such a system whereby they would lose their identity. Furthermore, many of them at first received direct support from the Free State. Northern Ireland Protestants were also not enthusiastic about a secular educational system. Soon a system was established whereby the state system, which most of the Protestant schools joined, would be 100 percent financed, in terms of capital expenses, regular expenses, and teachers salaries, by the state, but religion could be taught on a voluntary basis. This arrangement satisfied most Protestants, and clergy would often serve on the education boards supervising the schools. An alternative system of voluntary education, which covered the Catholic schools, would also received substantial state support in terms of payment of regular expenses and teachers salaries, but only a fraction of its capital expenses. Over a period of time, the position of the voluntary schools became more equitable, as increasing proportions of expenses were met by the state, until by the 1960s they were virtually entirely supported by the state. Both systems had separate teacher training institutions as well. Many view the existence of the separate systems, regardless of the equitable treatment, as intensifying and reinforcing sectarian distrust within the province.

Much of the difficulty in terms of community relations in Northern Ireland grew out of the stagnant character its economy had developed in the 1920s and 1930s. From having been a jewel in the industrial ascendancy of Britain in the 19th century, standing in striking contrast to the agrarian character of virtually the rest of Ireland, Northern Ireland found itself being bypassed in the wake of industrialization in other parts of the world. Large-scale unemployment became endemic. According to the rationale of the Home Rule established by the Government of Ireland Act of 1920, Northern Ireland was expected to be self-supporting, although most revenues, including income and excise taxes, were collected by the British exchequer. However, after taking the proportionate share of "imperial expenses," those funds were to be returned to the province for use in meeting its expenses, along with locally raised revenues such as real estate taxes and licensing fees. In point of fact, it was soon discovered that the revenue raised could barely meet the expected imperial contribution. A commission was established to make recommendation to deal with the situation and, based on its findings, a formula was devised that called for the imperial contribution to be the last taken after local expenses were met, which eventually resulted in the imperial contribution being negative.

Despite the sufferings brought by the war, especially the bombing of Belfast and the imposition of rationing, hostilities proved to be an economic boon to the province as evidenced by heightened demand for its agricultural produce and increased need for its industrial contributions to the war effort. By the end of the war, the introduction of agricultural machinery and innovation in techniques put the province far ahead of the rest of Ireland. After the war the welfare state introduced by the Labour government guaranteed that the citizenry of Northern Ireland were to receive social welfare benefits on a level with the rest of the United Kingdom, irrespective of the revenue raised in the province. Henceforth, budget making by the government of Northern Ireland became more and more a matter of negotiating for grants from the British exchequer to insure sufficient receipt of funds to enable it to provide comparable levels of public benefits and services for its population. Among the benefits available were universal secondary education and increased opportunities for higher education. In such a situation, the disinterest displayed by the Northern Ireland Catholic community, regardless of professed statements of belief in the ultimate political unity of the island, in the IRA campaign of the 1950s was comprehensible.

But the increasing educational levels attained by Catholics in Northern Ireland raised awareness of the discriminatory treatment they continued to receive in both the public and the private sectors of the economy, not to mention the continuing questionable relationship with law enforcement agencies. However, in the 1960s they were less inclined to raise the national unification issue as much as the question of their rights as citizens. They had become aware of the success of the civil rights campaign by blacks in the United States against discriminatory treatment much worse than that experienced by the Catholics of Northern Ireland. Blacks in the southern United States had to deal with state-imposed segregation in education and in public facilities, including transportation and hospitals, and actual denial of the right to vote for the overwhelming majority, never mind inequities in the private sector. It was believed that with much less ground to cover, a similar campaign of marches, protests, and sit-ins would produce a sympathetic response from a tolerant, open-minded United Kingdom. In such a spirit a Northern Irish Civil Rights Association, with a certain degree of cross community support, was formed in early 1967.

Most among the public and in official circles in the United Kingdom had virtually forgotten about Northern Ireland, assuming that, with the award of self-governance and then outright independence to the rest of Ireland, the Irish problem was solved. The dominant Unionist Party still maintained a formal relationship with the Conservative Party, which governed the United Kingdom for the entire time Northern Ireland had existed, aside from Labour Governments in 1924, 1929 to 1931, and 1945 to 1951. The return to power by Labour in 1964 suggested the prospects of greater response to civil rights protests, especially if couched in civil rights rather than nationalist terms. The presence of a new prime minister in Northern Ireland, Terence O'Neill, prompted hope that civil rights grievances would receive a favorable hearing. In 1963 he had succeed Basil Brooke, who had served in the office since 1943. The first prime minister, James Craig, who had been the leader of Ulster Unionism from the beginning of the crisis surrounding the third Home Rule Bill in 1912, had served until 1940. Both Craig and Brooke were molded by the siege mentality that characterized Unionism in those days, but O'Neill, who had been educated in England and who had served in the British forces during the war, gave indications of approaching matters with a broader perspective. His exchange of visits with Lemass and Lynch, and his reaching out to the Catholic community, were regarded positively.

Unfortunately, events in the next few years would lead to a deterioration in conditions and ultimately to confrontation amounting almost to outright warfare, which would plague the province, the rest of Ireland, and Britain for the remainder of the century. One of the opening episodes involved a sit-in by civil rights protesters at public housing units in Tyrone that were being allocated in a discriminatory manner, mainly for the purpose of preserving the electoral domination of an area by unionists. Within a few months civil rights marches began to take place in various locations in the province, which were soon restricted by the authorities. Refusal to accept restrictions resulted in confrontations with the police and, more especially, with the auxiliary police. Unlike such confrontations in earlier decades, the world was watching closely as international television reports followed events. While many in the unionist community regarded the marchers as troublemakers and a front for the IRA, the general impression was that the police response in preventing marchers from proceeding along designated routes (usually into the center of cities or even near predominantly Protestant areas) was heavy handed and even brutal. So outraged was the nationalist community that their political representatives in the Northern Ireland parliament ceased to act as an official opposition.

O'Neill was aware of the need for reform and he proposed a program to allocate public housing fairly, abolish the gerrymandered Derry municipal council, end the extra vote for owners of businesses in local government elections, establish an ombudsman to hear complaints against the government, and consider revision of the special powers legislation that allowed many of the alleged police abuses. In January 1969 a student group called "People's Democracy," no doubt fueled by the example of the radical student protests on the Continent, especially in Paris, the previous summer that nearly brought down the French government, held a march from Belfast to Derry. The march brought the inevitable counter protests along the way. Then a few miles from the goal, at Burntollet, the marchers were assailed by the auxiliary police and by others, with the regular police looking on, further exacerbating community tensions. In the next month, a Northern Ireland general election was held with Unionists obtaining their usual overwhelming majority, this time 36 of the 52 seats, together with election of three others who called themselves independent unionists. However, 12 of the 36 Unionist Party members were opposed to O'Neill, whose gestures at reform were considered soft and capitulatory. While he held a majority of the votes in the party caucus, he was forced to resign within several months when other figures in the party, one of whom was his own cousin, James Chichester-Clark, challenged him. Chichester-Clark then succeeded as leader of the party and prime minister. In the same month, in a by-election to fill the mid-Ulster seat in the Westminster parliament, Bernadette Devlin, a radical student, who had emerged as the unity candidate of the various nonunionist organizations, ranging from republican through nationalist through civil rights, was elected.

Seemingly unaffected by the troubling developments in Northern Ireland, Lynch's Fianna Fáil government in the Republic won an absolute majority of seats in the Irish general election in June. The number of independents elected continued to decline. The Labour Party did not run as part of an anti–Fianna Fáil coalition, but, inspired by increasing radicalism on the Continent, in anticipation of a popular leftward swing by the electorate and even a potential Labour majority in the near future, ran an independent campaign. However, they were rudely disappointed, receiving fewer votes and so an absolute decline in the number of seats, a defeat some members attributed to "red-baiting" rhetoric and techniques by Fianna Fáil. The Fianna Fáil victory was remarkable in view of the failure the previous year of a constitutional amendment campaign to end proportional representation in Dáil elections, a measure that would have further strengthened the party. This second rejection of such a proposal was a tribute to the independence of the Irish electorate.

That summer saw an intensification of trouble in Northern Ireland during the marching season, the period leading up to the celebration of the anniversary of the Battle of the Boyne on July 12. Tensions mounted further in August at the time of the Apprentice Boys Parade in Derry on August 12. Rioting and disorder in Derry and Belfast resulted in large numbers of Catholics having to flee their homes, which came under assault and were burned down. Other areas erected barricades to protect themselves from marauding loyalist mobs and also to prevent police intrusion. The situation reached a point at which the government in London directed the British military to assume peacekeeping responsibilities in the province.

The rapid issuance of a number of commission reports on the situation, such as the Cameron Commission on the overall disturbances, and the Hunt Commission on the police, both of which acknowledged the legitimacy of grievances and the need for major reforms brought hope for positive change. Some reforms followed quickly, including the abolition of the notoriously sectarian "B Specials," and their replacement by what was hoped could be a nonsectarian Ulster Defense Regiment that would be under the control of the British army. In addition, legislation lowered the franchise age requirement to 18 and ended other restrictions, such as householder requirements, in local government elections, thereby achieving the civil rights aspiration of "one man, one vote."

However, the very presence of the British army in the province, a presence warmly welcomed by most in a beleaguered Catholic community, acted to breath new life into an IRA in Northern Ireland that had been dormant for years and impotent in its response to loyalist assaults. That revitalization would bring about a split within the all Ireland Sinn Féin and IRA the following January, with those, especially from the North, adhering to the more traditional irredentist aspirations and less taken up with the social agenda of the organization's leadership, forming a "Provisional" wing. It was not long before that wing became the major wing in contrast to the "Official" wing. Not insignificant in its emergence was the greater support it received from groups in the Irish-American community, as well as from important figures in the Fianna Fáil Party, who were able to funnel public monies for the purchase of weapons for the movement. It would not be long before world attention would be diverted from the question of civil rights for Catholics in Northern Ireland to that of the presence of British troops in Ireland.

TROUBLESOME THIRTY YEARS

THE END OF STORMONT

In May 1970 Liam Cosgrave, the leader of the opposition Fine Gael Party, brought information to the Taoiseach, Jack Lynch, that members of the cabinet were implicated in supplying weapons to the Provisional IRA. The pretext allowing the arms acquisition was the government's authorization of support during the communal strife of the previous summer for the besieged Catholic nationalists. Support could be interpreted as anything from providing refugee quarters to supplying arms. Two ministers, Charles J. Haughey, for finance, and Neil Blaney, for agriculture and fisheries, were dismissed and charged with illegal purchase of arms using government money. Kevin Boland, minister for Social Welfare, resigned in protest at the dismissal of the others. Charges against Blaney were soon dropped and Haughey and other defendants were acquitted in a celebrated trial despite the contradictory testimony of the defendants. However, Lynch survived a challenge to his leadership by the more nationalist elements in the Fianna Fáil Party. Boland, the last member of a celebrated republican and Fianna Fáil family, formed his own party, Aontacht Éireann, which failed to win electoral support. Blaney, labeling himself Independent Fianna Fáil, continued to win reelection as TD for Donegal North until his death in 1995. Haughey withdrew to the backbenches of the party, biding his time.

The restraint of the more militant elements in Fianna Fáil and the formation of two new political parties in Northern Ireland that same year gave indications of creative political activity other than irredentism. In April, middle-class Protestants and Catholics formed the Alliance Party, which was committed to achieving civil rights for all but not to the ending of the union with Britain. In August, Catholics and some Protestants, such as Gerry Fitt and John Hume, formed the Social Democratic and Labour Party, or SDLP. The next provincial election confirmed the party as the political spokesperson for the Catholic minority of the province, replacing the old Nationalist Party. The SDLP, while not rejecting the nationalist dream of Irish unity, at first de-emphasized that goal and concentrated on addressing issues of civil rights and social justice. The political wing of the IRA, Sinn Féin, did not take part in elections in the province. However, in June 1970 the Conservative Party in Britain returned to power with Edward Heath as prime minister and was inclined to follow the traditional disposition to take its cue on Northern Ireland matters from the Unionist Party.

Unfortunately, early in the following year, the first killing of a British soldier by the IRA occurred. It was not long before the army's role would change from that of a peacekeeper between hostile communities to a combatant against IRA terrorism. The assumption of increased control over security by the British military from local authorities also irritated Unionists. Northern Ireland prime minister James Chichester-Clark resigned and was replaced by Brian Faulkner. The situation worsened further when the SDLP withdrew from the Northern Ireland parliament in July in protest over the lack of an inquiry into the shooting of two men by the army in Derry.

In August Faulkner secured the British government's acceptance of internment without trial to confront increased IRA activism. The device had worked effectively as late as the 1950s in both Northern Ireland and the Republic of Ireland. This time the tactic backfired as considerable rioting developed in protest at the apprehension of hundreds. Furthermore, the lists that were consulted in selecting those to be interned were outdated and inaccurate. As a result, many of the leading IRA figures escaped the net and many innocents were incarcerated and would subsequently become willing applicants to the "recruitment campaigns" of the IRA in the internment camps. Internment scarcely curbed, and probably encouraged, the intensification of the campaign of violence by the IRA, as well as the reprisals by loyalist terrorist groups that were emerging, as the death toll from political violence climbed in 1971 to almost 200 and in the following year to 500.

Civil rights, nationalist, and republican groups, along with the leaders of the SDLP, began to hold marches and meetings protesting internment. The military sought to ban certain of these. In January 1972, restrictions were placed on a

Undated photo shows a member of the Irish Republican Army posing with a weapon. *(Reuters/Landov)*

march in Derry. Organizers complied with the authorities in turning their march away from its intended path, but some disturbances took place, and soon, the military, allegedly coming under fire from one side of the crowd, opened fire. Thirteen civilians were killed, who were all ultimately proved to be innocent. The days that followed saw protests all over Northern Ireland, Ireland, and, even in the United States. The British embassy in Dublin was burned. An official inquiry into the incident by Lord Widgery, which exonerated the military, was generally looked upon as a whitewash.[19]

With the situation in the province continuing to deteriorate, the British government enacted legislation that suspended the parliament of Northern Ireland after more than 50 years in existence and imposed direct rule of the province by a member of the British cabinet, the secretary of state for Northern Ireland, the first of whom was William Whitelaw. The central concern for most in Britain, Northern Ireland, and Ireland ever since has been to find a way to restore provincial government to the area, but in a way that would be satisfactory to both communities.

Even before direct rule, the province-wide government had taken over many of the powers of elected local government bodies in an effort to end the glaring sectarianism that had been practiced by them. However, the people directly elected the provincial government. Now, under direct rule, a British cabinet member had control over all of these government functions, which were originally local. That minister was responsible, not to the Northern Irish electorate, but to a parliament in Westminster of whom only 12 of over 600 members were elected from Northern Ireland. Paradoxically, after most of the far-flung British Empire had attained its independence, six counties on the neighboring island, which had boasted of their "home rule," were now in the position of having become a virtual crown colony.

Despite general public outrage at the "Bloody Sunday" incident, public opinion in the Republic of Ireland was not drawn to the cause of the IRA. Indications of the changed temper of the times included the decision of the Catholic hierarchy in 1970 to withdraw the prohibition on Catholic attendance at the historically Protestant Trinity College Dublin, the simultaneous decision in 1971 of the British and Irish governments to make their interchangeably used currencies decimal, and the January 1972 entry of both states into the European Economic Community. The last decision was endorsed in a May 1972 referendum in Ireland by a vote of 5 to 1. Both Fianna Fáil and Fine Gael favored entry, which Labour opposed. Some interpreted the vote more as one against Sinn Féin, which also opposed entry, rather than for entry. In the same month, the Irish government invoked the 1939 Offences against the State legislation to allow both special categories of accused, primarily IRA members, and charges to be tried in juryless courts before three judges. The following month Secretary of State for Northern Ireland William Whitelaw gave special prisoner status to interned prisoners, which extended opportunities for wearing nonprison

---

[19] *A more recent inquiry, called into being by Prime Minister Tony Blair, and chaired by Lord John Saville, conducted hearings in Northern Ireland and Britain for several years and heard testimony from hundreds, including former prime minister Heath, and has just recently concluded its work, with a report to be forthcoming.*

attire, for holding meetings among themselves, and for socializing. Soon after, the IRA proclaimed a cease-fire and secret talks took place between several IRA leaders and Whitelaw.

COALITION AND EXPERIMENT

The IRA subsequently called off the cease-fire and, within two weeks, planted 22 explosives in Belfast that detonated in close succession and with minimal advance warning, killing 11 and wounding scores of others. In the republic the leader of the Provisional IRA, Sean MacStiofain, was sentenced to six months' imprisonment for IRA membership by one of the special courts authorized in May. The government proposed an amendment to the Offenses against the State Act, which would allow the statement of a police officer to suffice as evidence of an accused person's membership in an unlawful organization, as well as to allow certain types of meetings to be proscribed. The legislation drew considerable opposition in Dáil Éireann from both opposition parties, based on civil liberties concerns. However, bomb explosions in Dublin, which killed two and injured over 100, dissipated much of the opposition and the legislation passed. The next month the president of Provisional Sinn Féin, Ruairi O'Bradaigh, was sentenced to six months' imprisonment for IRA membership by a special court. In March 1973 the Irish authorities seized a vessel, *The Claudia*, off the Waterford coast, which was found to be carrying a large amount of weapons and several IRA members.

The formation in March of a coalition government in Ireland following the February elections enhanced the prospects for a strong attitude against the IRA and possible co-operation with the British government. The new Taoiseach was Liam Cosgrave of Fine Gael, the son of the Irish Free State leader. Garret FitzGerald, the son of another Free State minister, became minister for foreign affairs. Brendan Corish, the Labour Party leader, who had joined with Fine Gael in waging a coalition electoral campaign, became Tánaiste, and the celebrated diplomat-academic Connor Cruise O'Brien, who had already become an outspoken advocate of an anti-irredentist and revisionist approach by the Irish toward Northern Ireland, became minister for posts and telegraphs. The only deviation from the seeming ascendancy of anti-irredentist and revisionist thinking was the failure in May 1973 of Thomas F. O'Higgins, the nephew of the murdered Free State minister for justice, Kevin O'Higgins, to be elected president of Ireland to succeed Eamon de Valera, who in his 91st year, had concluded his second term. He lost narrowly to the Fianna Fáil candidate, Erskine Childers, the son of the war of independence figure who was executed by the Provisional Government during the civil war. Childers died suddenly in November 1974. Cearbhall O'Dalaigh, a member of Fianna Fáil, succeeded him without opposition.

In Northern Ireland, under direct rule, steps were being taken toward a return to devolved government. Elections to local district councils, now shorn of the sectarian gerrymandering that had caused so much difficulty in the past, took place in May. The results, under the Single Transferable Voting system of proportional representation similar to that in use in the Irish republic, gave the Unionists 201 places, the SDLP 76, the Democratic Unionists and Vanguard 74, and the Alliance Party 59. The next month elections to a new Northern Ireland Assembly to replace the prorogued parliament, also under the STV system, returned 23 Ulster Unionist Party candidates and 10 other unionists, 19 SDLP members, eight Alliance members, 17 assorted DUP, Vanguard and loyalist candidates, and one member of the Northern Ireland Labour Party. By November the Ulster Unionists, the SDLP, and the Alliance members of the assembly agreed to form a "power-sharing" coalition executive, to be chaired by Brian Faulkner, with other ministerial posts distributed proportionally to the other parties.

The next month, at a conference in Sunningdale, England, the British and Irish governments and the new Northern Ireland executive confirmed the new system in Northern Ireland, and participants agreed that there would be no change in the status of Northern Ireland in relation to Britain without the consent of the majority of its population. The conference also called for a "Council of Ireland" consisting of ministers and a consultative assembly composed of members from both parts of Ireland to deal with mutual problems. The conference also sought to resolve the dilemma posed by extradition of politically motivated violent criminals to allow them to be tried in the jurisdiction where they were apprehended.

The following May a general strike conducted by the Ulster Workers' Council brought down the Sunningdale Agreement and the coalition executive. Government in the province was paralyzed and the Unionist members of the executive resigned from office. The British government prorogued the assembly and restored direct rule from Westminster. Some believe the general strike succeeded because of a reluctance on the part of the Labour government, formed only after the general elections held in February, to directly confront a workers' strike, no matter who the workers were, especially since electoral success in Britain as a whole had depended so much on labor union support.

A year later the Northern Ireland voters, again according to the STV system, elected a Northern Ireland Convention to formulate a constitutional structure that might allow power to be devolved again to the province. The Ulster Unionists secured 19 places, the more loyalist groups, including the Vanguard Unionists and the DUP 27 places, while the groups that continued to favor power-sharing, the SDLP, Alliance, and a small group of Unionists led by Brian Faulkner, obtained a total of 30 places, which guaranteed that the convention would reject power-sharing and be dissolved the next year.

In the meantime the social turmoil within Northern Ireland began to spill over to the British mainland and to the Irish Republic. In May 1974 car bomb explosions in Dublin and Monaghan killed 31 and injured over 100. In June the Earl and Countess of Donoughmore were kidnapped from their Tipperary home and held for five days by the IRA. In August 19 IRA prisoners escaped from Portlaoise prison. In October 1975 the IRA kidnapped a Dutch businessman in the Irish Republic and held him for a month until a siege by the Garda secured his release. In Britain, bombs in public houses in Guildford in October 1974 and in Birmingham in November killed, respectively, five and 21, and injured 65 and 182. In response, parliament passed a Prevention of Terrorism Act facilitating the deportation from and prohibition of entry into Britain of suspected terrorists.

In July 1976 Christopher Ewart-Biggs, the British ambassador to Ireland, was killed by a land mine near his home in County Wicklow. This killing prompted the Irish government to introduce stronger emergency powers legislation to allow detainees a longer period of detention before being charged. The measure passed the Dáil, and was approved by the Irish Supreme Court, to whom the president had sent the measure for a ruling as to its constitutionality. Minister for Defense Patrick Donegan condemned the president's action as a "thundering disgrace" for having thereby delayed the implementation of the measure. The president resigned in a gesture to protect the dignity of the office. He was succeeded by Patrick Hillery, also of Fianna Fáil and a former minister for foreign affairs, who was also selected unopposed.

In July 1973 the Westminster parliament passed a Northern Ireland Emergency Provisions Act that implemented the December 1972 recommendations of a commission headed by Lord Diplock for dealing with terrorist offenses. The act sought to find a middle ground between the practice of internment without trial and normal trials, which were impossible to conduct in Northern Ireland in view of the threat of terrorist reprisal on jurors and witnesses and because of difficulties in certain areas for law enforcement officials to conduct regular forensic examinations. The legislation resembled that in the Irish republic in making provision for juryless trials. It allowed trials for certain specified offenses to be conducted by a single judge. In addition, the legislation suspended numerous common law restrictions and rules on witnesses and evidence in these cases and allowed prisoners to be detained for several days before being charged. With this legislation in hand, the government ended internment without trial in November 1975.

No doubt many in the nationalist Catholic community regarded the Diplock court system merely as a cover for abuse by authorities, but the courts operated against loyalist terrorists as well. However, a September 1976 ruling by the European Commission on Human Rights that the British were guilty of using torture in the interrogation of republican prisoners reinforced popular nationalist opposition, although that ruling referred to events in the earlier stages of the troubles and not to activity under the Diplock regime. Significantly, the annual number of deaths from political violence in Northern Ireland, which had ranged between 200 and 300 from 1973 through 1976, dropped to slightly over 100 in 1977 and remained at that level or below for the remainder of "the Troubles."

A nonsectarian opposition to the violence sprang up in 1976 when two women, a Protestant, Betty Williams, and a Catholic, Mairead Corrigan, organized peace marches that drew thousands following the death of three children, relations of Corrigan, who were hit by a car fleeing army pursuers. Their efforts drew international attention and earned both women the Nobel Peace Prize for that year.

THE RETURN OF FIANNA FÁIL AND THE HUNGER STRIKE

In 1977 the Fine Gael–Labour coalition government was soundly defeated in a general election in which Fianna Fáil, still led by Jack Lynch, gained an overwhelming absolute majority of 84 of the 148 seats in the Dáil. The coalition regime had exemplified a remarkable effort to blend the traditionally conservative Fine Gael Party, which included a younger socially conscious wing, with a Labour Party just returned to pragmatism after flirtation with unilateral radicalism.[20] Fianna Fáil was able to capitalize on economic problems that included fiscal indebtedness, inflation, and unemployment caused by external factors, such as the OPEC oil embargo, that were beyond the control of the government. Fianna Fáil also offered to end or reduce a number of taxes that annoyed many voters, particularly rural voters, who were not included in the income tax net, such as property rates levied by local government and automobile taxes. In a curiously premature display of supply side economics, the party's financial adviser and later minister for economic planning and development, Martin O'Donoghue, argued that the restraint on taxes would encourage a remarkable economic recovery.

However, the magnitude of the party's victory enabled many backbenchers and newly elected TD's to grow restive and become less amenable to the government's discipline. In late 1979 Jack Lynch announced his resignation. He did so just a few months after the celebratory visit to Ireland in September by Pope John Paul II, which drew audiences in the hundreds of thousands. The pope's message entailed a plea for the rejection of violence in the pursuit of political objectives. But he also warned his Irish audience of the potential for the country to fall prey to irreligion and materialism as modernization and its accompanying consumerism grew. Lynch had expected automatic acceptance of his choice for successor, George Colley, the minister for finance, but, instead, the party selected Charles J. Haughey, the minister for health who had returned from his post–arms trial internal exile.

At first, in view of his identity with the irredentist-minded wing of Fianna Fáil, Haughey as Taoiseach carried ominous implications for Anglo-Irish cooperation in combating terrorism and working toward a resolution of the Northern Ireland imbroglio. In addition, the situation worsened in Northern Ireland with incidents that included the killing of 16 by an IRA bomb in the Le Mons Hotel in Belfast and the ambushing of 18 British soldiers at Warrenpoint, County Down, on the same day that an IRA-planted bomb on a boat killed the Queen's cousin, Earl Mountbatten, off Mullaghmore, County Sligo. A further indication that there would be a cooling of Anglo-Irish relations was the return of the Conservatives to power in Britain and the selection of the first woman prime minister, Margaret Thatcher, in June 1979. Thatcher and Haughey held an exchange of meetings in May and December 1980. Some observers, especially in the Irish Department of Foreign Affairs, began talking of shifting the emphasis on resolv-

---

[20] *Evidence of the contradictory currents at work in the country during the time of the coalition were the Supreme Court ruling in 1973 that legislation prohibiting the importation of contraceptives was unconstitutional, a 1974 vote by Cosgrave and a few others to defeat legislation proposed by his own government to allow the sale of contraceptives, the removal the same year of the Irish language requirement for civil service positions, the celebration of the canonization in 1975 of Oliver Plunkett by Pope Paul VI, another Supreme Court ruling the same year declaring the exemption of women from jury service as unconstitutional, and 1976 legislation removing the requirement that adoptive parents be of the same religion as the natural parents.*

ing the Northern Ireland problem from finding a solution within Northern Ireland toward securing a solution on a London-Dublin axis.

However, another development to be overcome involved the intensification of protest by republican prisoners in Northern Ireland, who balked at not having the special category status allowed to those interned earlier. Those convicted under the Diplock rules were treated as any ordinary prisoner in terms of prison regime and clothing. Those refusing to wear prison garb were confined to their cells. They covered themselves with blankets, a gesture emulated in marches and other protests by sympathizers outside the prison and even outside Northern Ireland, even by some in the St. Patrick's Day Parade in New York City. The protest moved to a new stage when the prisoners began to cover the walls of their cells in which they were confined with their own excrement, which would be periodically hosed down by not too gentle prison staff. By October 1980 a number of the imprisoned protesters went on a hunger strike. The strike was called off after several months with the expectation that their demands would be satisfied. But when the amount of expected concessions were not in fact achieved, a new hunger strike began in March. This time the participants would strike individually in intervals, guaranteeing the continuation of the protest well beyond the death of single strikers. The first striker, Bobby Sands, was also nominated and elected to the House of Commons in a Fermanagh–South Tyrone by-election. Serious disorders and some deaths accompanied his death the following month.

In June a general election in the Republic of Ireland (the membership of the Dáil had increased from 148 to 166 to reflect population growth) resulted in a near dead heat. Fianna Fáil lost both its absolute majority as well as a number of its seats, dropping from 84 to 78, while Fine Gael, led since 1977 by Garret FitzGerald, climbed from 43 to 65 seats. Those 65 votes, the 15 seats gained by Labour, and the votes of three independents, enabled FitzGerald to form a coalition government. Fianna Fáil was hurt especially by the loss of two seats to two of the hunger strikers, whose names had been placed in nomination. The intensity of feeling at the time prompted many hard-line irredentist voters in the republic to turn their animosity toward Haughey, who disappointed them, than to the coalition, from which they had no expectations.

FitzGerald's government sought to soften Thatcher's opposition to concessions, as she regarded the prisoners as criminals and not entitled to such, despite the pleas of many in the Northern Ireland Catholic hierarchy, particularly the cardinal archbishop of Armagh, Tomas O'Fiaich, that the prisoners were young men who in ordinary circumstances would not be criminals. Before the strike was finally called off in September after certain disguised concessions, such as prisoner uniforms that looked increasingly like ordinary clothes, nine others had gone to their deaths and scores were killed in the disturbances that followed the deaths of the strikers. Then, two months later, FitzGerald and Thatcher established the Anglo-Irish Intergovernmental Council, which provided a more regular interchange between the governments rather than the occasional contacts that amounted to ad hoc responses to crises.

However, before much could be done along these lines, the FitzGerald-led coalition government fell from power in February 1982 when some of its independent supporters refused to vote for an increase in VAT taxes on children's shoes. A leading Fianna Fáil figure, Brian Lenihan, made an inappropriate request for President Hillery to not dissolve the Dáil and allow Haughey to form a government. However, the dissolution did take place and another general election was held, at which it Fianna Fáil gained three additional seats. That gain and the votes of several independents, including members of Sinn Féin, the Workers' Party, and an inner-city Dublin community candidate, enabled Haughey to form a government.

COALITION AGAIN AND
HILLSBOROUGH AGREEMENT

Despite Haughey's success, there were ominous signs of dissatisfaction within his own party. In January, while still in opposition, he could not secure the expulsion from the party of Charles McCreevy, a TD for Kildare who was critical of him. In March he confronted a failed attempt by Limerick TD Desmond O'Malley to challenge his leadership of the party. Anglo-Irish relations then soured when the Irish took a neutral stand on resolutions by the European Community and the United Nations supportive of the British in the Falklands War with Argentina during April and May. Also in May, following a Dublin by-election, which the Fine Gael candidate won, Haughey's electoral agent was arrested for personation, that is, voting in more than one place. Another incident involved the resignation in August of Attorney General Patrick Connolly after his apartment mate was arrested for murder. The Taoiseach labeled the episode "grotesque, unprecedented, bizarre, unbelievable," terms that critic Conor Cruise O'Brien turned into the derisive acronym "GUBU," which would plague Haughey for the rest of his career.

In November the Workers' Party and some independents withdrew their support from the government, resulting in a vote of no confidence, a dissolution, and a general election in which Fine Gael gained its greatest number of seats ever, 70, which, when combined with the 16 seats won by Labour, gave the coalition an absolute majority with which to form a government. Dick Spring, the recently elected leader of the Labour Party, became Tánaiste and minister first for the environment and then for energy.

The new government began to pursue a new approach to the Northern Ireland imbroglio, as it hoped to both offset the significant boost in popular support gained by Sinn Féin since the hunger strike and to mollify strained Anglo-Irish relations. In October voters elected another Northern Ireland Assembly in which the Unionists gained 26 seats, the Alliance 10, and the SDLP 14. The capture of five seats by Sinn Féin gained world attention. That party had decided to continue its entry into normal politics that had begun with the Sands's victory in a by-election while on hunger strike. The political approach at this stage served as a complement, not a replacement, to the armed struggle being conducted by the IRA. Then in the June 1983 general election, the leader of Sinn Féin, Gerry Adams, was elected to the House of Commons for West Belfast, although he did not take his seat. He gained 16,000 votes, while two other non-Unionist candidates, the incumbent, Gerry Fitt, who had left the SDLP, and Dr. Joseph Hendron, the SDLP candidate, gained more than 10,000 each.

Nonpolitical actions by the IRA during the period included a breakout of 39 prisoners from the Long Kesh prison in Northern Ireland, of whom 20 were recaptured, in September 1983; the bombing of a hotel in Brighton, England, in October 1984 during the Conservative Party conference in which the prime minister, Margaret Thatcher, narrowly escaped while five others were killed; and the killing of nine by a mortar attack on a RUC barracks in Newry, County Down, in February 1985.

A central gesture by the Irish government in its efforts to wean potential support away from Sinn Féin and to ingratiate non-nationalists in Northern Ireland was the summoning of a New Ireland Forum to which representatives of all constitutional parties in both Northern Ireland and the Republic of Ireland were invited to participate. Naturally the Unionists and the DUP did not come, but some individual unionists did testify at its hearings, as did numerous religious, academic, and business figures from Northern Ireland. Chaired by Dr. Colm O hEocha, the president of University College Galway, the forum, which included representative figures from Fine Gael, Fianna Fáil, and Labour, sought to examine the effect of partition and the contemporary turmoil on Ireland as a whole, and to examine and suggest possible future alternative structures that might be amenable to both communities within Northern Ireland and both parts of Ireland. It issued its final report in May 1984 suggesting various solutions. One was a unification of the island in a unitary state, another was a federal structure, and the third was a mixture of a federal structure and an arrangement to share sovereignty over Northern Ireland by both Britain and Ireland.

The report was issued a month before the visit to Ireland by U.S. president Ronald Reagan, who was given an honorary degree, addressed the Oireachtas, and visited his ancestral roots in Ballyporeen, County Tipperary, while also encountering some protests from Irish critical of aspects of American foreign policy. The government hoped that the close ties of Reagan and Thatcher might rebound to improved Anglo-Irish relations. However, the first reaction of Thatcher to the three alternatives suggested by the New Ireland Forum was dismissive, as she said each of the three was "out." However, the diplomatic corps of both countries began to work earnestly to remedy the problem, as the Irish made the point that the forum had only offered the three suggestions as talking points and was open to any other arrangement that would gain a cross-community consensus.

Diplomatic work bore fruit when an Anglo-Irish Agreement was signed at Hillsborough Castle in November 1985 by Thatcher and FitzGerald precisely along the lines indicating a commitment to institutions for Northern Ireland that would have cross-community support as a prerequisite. The agreement also called for an ongoing Anglo-Irish Intergovernmental Conference to deal with Northern Ireland matters, ranging from nationalist-Catholic grievances to security concerns. An essential element in the agreement was the acceptance of the principle that any change in the constitutional structure of Northern Ireland and its relationship to Britain would require the consent of the majority of the population. However, Unionists were outraged at the agreement, especially since they were not involved in, nor informed about, the developments leading up to it, as were the SDLP. They viewed it as an intrusion by a foreign

government, the Irish republic, in the affairs of the United Kingdom. All Unionists and DUP members of the House of Commons resigned their seats in protest,
necessitating by-elections, which they hoped would show a clear mandate of
popular opposition. Fourteen of the 15 were returned, but the SDLP gained a
seat with the defeat of James Nicholson by Seamus Mallon in the Newry and
Armagh constituency. Unionist protests would continue for a few years afterward. Unionists even protested against the RUC for its restraining Orange
marches through Catholic areas. Not until five years later, in 1990, did they
agree to enter into discussions with other Northern Ireland parties and with the
Irish government on matters related to Northern Ireland.

There was disappointment in some nationalist quarters as well. Sinn Féin
and its various Irish-American support groups labeled the agreement as the
"copper-fastening of partition." Haughey and Fianna Fáil were not supportive.
Remarkably, the future president of Ireland, Mary Robinson, resigned from the
Labour Party in protest at the agreement because it had not included the Unionists in its preparations! In a demonstration of the Irish government's determination to cooperate in resisting violence, Dublin signed the European
Convention on the Suppression of Terrorism in February 1986.

There were two controversial constitutional amendment referenda during
the period of the coalition government. The first, a right to life or antiabortion
amendment, had been proposed by various groups disturbed at the Irish
Supreme Court's liberality in its reading of rights in the wording of the constitution even though not explicitly stated. They had in mind the 1974 ruling
declaring unconstitutional the prohibition on the importation of contraceptives.
They feared the Court might in the future read the right to have an abortion
as implicit in the constitution despite legislation outlawing the same. In the lead
up to the 1982 general election both Fianna Fáil and Fine Gael endorsed the
idea for a referendum, but, once in power, FitzGerald developed reservations.
He and his party did not support the amendment, although individual members of his party did. The Labour Party opposed it. Nonetheless the amendment,
which was vigorously supported by the Catholic hierarchy, carried with 66.9
percent of the votes in September 1983.

Three years later the government proposed an amendment allowing divorce
in limited circumstances, which, if adopted, would alter the existing constitutional stipulation against the dissolution of marriage. Fianna Fáil opposed the
measure, as did the Catholic hierarchy. Troubling to many were the property
implications that would be consequent on a divorce, a matter of special concern
primarily in rural areas where some feared agricultural holdings of a family
would be divided. The amendment was rejected by 63.5 percent of the voters.

In February 1987 the Labour Party's withdrawal of support for the government because of proposed budgetary restraints on social spending resulted in
a general election. The election saw the appearance of a new party, the Progressive Democrats formed in December 1985 primarily by anti-Haughey
members of Fianna Fáil. They were led by Desmond O'Malley and offered a
program of economic conservatism and social liberalism, as well as a spirit of
accommodation toward Northern Ireland and hostility to Sinn Féin and the
IRA. Another player in the election was Sinn Féin, which for the first time indi-

cated a willingness, if elected, to take seats in what it had previously regarded as an illegitimate Dáil. Fourteen Progressive Democrats were elected, surpassing Labour, which obtained 12 seats, while Sinn Féin was unsuccessful. However, Fianna Fáil won 81 seats, 30 more than Fine Gael. With the support of a few independents, Charles Haughey again formed a government.

FIANNA FÁIL IN POWER AND IN COALITION

When in power Charles Haughey reversed his earlier populist appeal and introduced a severe austerity budget to counter inflation and public indebtedness. Alan Dukes, a TD for Kildare South, who had been selected as leader of Fine Gael to replace FitzGerald, followed a strategy of accepting the austerity budget since it was what Fine Gael would have wanted. In a referendum the same year, the public approved by a vote of 69.9 percent Irish acceptance of the Single European Act. The act aimed at establishing a common European external tariff, the free movement of goods, services, persons, and capital within Europe, competition rather than cooperation between companies, and approximation, rather than uniformity, of regulations within and among the member countries.

In an election held in June 1989, Fianna Fáil failed in its ambition to gain an absolute majority and, for the first time in its history, agreed to join a coalition government. Their junior partners were the Progressive Democrats, a group largely composed of former Fianna Fáil members and critics of Haughey, whose own numbers in the Dáil Éireann had fallen from 14 seats to six after the election. Fianna Fáil and Fine Gael both lost two seats in elections to the European Parliament, which places were gained by Labour, the Workers' Party, the Progressive Democrats, and an independent.

The next year Brian Lenihan, the Tánaiste, former minister for foreign affairs, and minister for Defense, was the Fianna Fáil candidate for the presidency to succeed Patrick Hillery, whose second term was ending. Observers expected that the very popular Lenihan would win the election easily. He was not unopposed, however. Fine Gael nominated Austin Currie, a former founding member of the SDLP, who had moved to the republic and was elected as Fine Gael TD for Dublin West. Labour nominated Mary Robinson, the barrister and legal scholar. During the campaign Lenihan denied that he had sought to influence President Hillery in 1982 not to accept Garret FitzGerald's request for dissolution of the Dáil following a vote of no confidence. However, a graduate student produced a taped interview of Lenihan in which he acknowledged to have done such. In the voting in November, Lenihan received 44 percent in the first count, but when the transfers from Currie's votes (which were 17%) were calculated, it gave a majority to Robinson (who had 39% on the first count).

Mary Robinson was the first woman to serve as president of Ireland. To the degree allowed by the office, she played a role that was much more than symbolic. She made many gestures and pronouncements of concern for excluded members of society and created an atmosphere very favorable to the advancement of a feminist agenda in Ireland. After the failure of the Currie candidacy, Dukes stepped down as Fine Gael leader and was replaced by John Bruton, a TD for Meath who had served in various cabinet positions, including as minister for finance and industry and trade, in the 1980s coalition governments. That same month, John Major replaced Margaret Thatcher as prime minister and leader of the Conservative Party in Britain.

In October 1991 an official inquiry began into alleged corruption in the awarding of state assistance to the beef export industry. The following month a group of TD's within Fianna Fáil, including such early supporters as Pádraig Flynn for Mayo West and Albert Reynolds for Longford–West Meath, failed in an effort to oust Haughey as leader. However, early in 1992 Haughey had to resign under threat of a PD withdrawal from the coalition following revelations that he knew of the taping of phone conversations of journalists when he was Taoiseach in 1982. Albert Reynolds replaced him. Within a few months, Desmond O'Malley, the leader of the PD's, increased his demands for public examination of corruption in state support of the beef industry. When Reynolds accused him of dishonesty in levelling his charges, O'Malley demanded that Reynolds withdraw the accusation. Reynolds refused and the PD's withdrew from the coalition, necessitating another general election in November 1992. Fianna Fáil strength in the Dáil fell to 68, its lowest number of seats since 1954 when the Dáil had only 144 members, not 166, and Fine Gael lost 10 seats. Labour, however, more than doubled its membership, winning 33 seats. The PD's made a gain of four seats and a new party, the Democratic Left, which was formed by most of the members of the Workers' Party, who had become disillusioned on discovering that the party had been receiving funds from the Soviet Union, got four seats. In the negotiations following the election, Fianna Fáil and Labour formed a coalition with Reynolds as Taoiseach and Dick Spring, the Labour leader, as Tánaiste and minister for foreign affairs.

On the same day as the general election, the public voted on three referenda, all related to the abortion issue. The stimulus to the introduction of the amendments was a legal case early in the year involving a 14-year-old girl who succeeded in securing the Supreme Court's overturn of an injunction taken by the attorney general to prevent her from going to England to have an abortion. The Court accepted the argument that she would commit suicide unless she had the abortion. The decision allowing her to travel was based on the guarantee in the 1983 antiabortion amendment of the equal right to life of the mother and the child.

One of the amendments allowed for the provision of information about abortion and the other allowed travel abroad to secure an abortion. Both passed with about 60 percent of the vote. The third amendment, which sought to overcome the wording problems in the 1983 amendment by specifically excluding suicide as a health justification for abortion, failed by almost a two-thirds vote. The substantial gains by the Labour Party and the vote on the referenda were seen as indications of the decline in political influence of the Catholic Church. Criticism of the church mounted open following the scandal earlier in the year when Eamon Casey, the bishop of Galway, was forced to resign his position after it was revealed he had fathered a child as bishop of Kerry several years earlier and had been using church funds to support the child. Not unexpected was the passage the next year, 1993, of liberalizing legislation allowing the sale of condoms in Ireland and the legalization of homosexual activity by those over

17 years of age, the later a measure in conformity with a European Court of Human Rights ruling against existing antisodomy legislation in Ireland.

THE PAINFUL PATH TO PEACE

The Hillsborough Agreement required regular meetings of the Anglo-Irish Intergovernmental Conference. However, against the background of intergovernmental cooperation and Sinn Féin political involvement (Adams was reelected for West Belfast in the 1987 British general election in which the Unionists won nine seats, the DUP and the SDLP three each, and one seat by another), there was an intensification of violence. Aware of a planned assault on a police barracks in Loughgall, County Armagh, the British army ambushed the attackers and killed eight IRA members in May 1987. One innocent passerby was also killed. On November 11 an IRA bomb killed 11 at a Remembrance Day service in Enniskillen, County Fermanagh. In November John McMichael, the leader of the loyalist paramilitary group, the Ulster Defence Association, was assassinated. In March 1988 the SAS killed three IRA members in Gibraltar. At their funeral in Belfast a fanatic loyalist gunman killed three mourners. A few days later two British soldiers, out of uniform, turned mistakenly into the route of the funeral procession of those victims and were murdered by mourners.

The following August an IRA bomb in Ballygawley, County Tyrone, killed eight British soldiers. In February 1989, loyalists, possibly in collusion with some in the security services, killed Patrick Finucane, a Catholic solicitor who had acted as a defense attorney for republican defendants. In September of the

Children involved in the rioting in West Belfast, Northern Ireland
(H. Davies/Exile Images)

same year, an IRA bomb killed 10 Royal Marines in Kent in England. In February 1991 an IRA mortar actually hit 10 Downing Street, the residence of the prime minister. Almost a year later, an IRA bomb killed eight workers in a van in Teebane, County Tyrone, who were working for the security forces. The same month loyalists killed five Catholics outside of a bookmaker's shop on the Ormeau Road in Belfast. In March 1993 an IRA bomb killed two children in Warrington, England. The following October another IRA bomb killed 10 on the heavily Protestant Shankill Road in Belfast and a week later a loyalist bomb killed seven in a public house in Greysteel, County Derry.

During this period political and police efforts continued. In December 1987 the Dáil passed legislation allowing extradition in accord with the European Convention on the Suppression of Terrorism, although the Irish attorney general retained the right to determine whether or not IRA suspects should be extradited to the United Kingdom. In January 1988 the Irish Supreme Court ruled that extradition to Northern Ireland should not be refused solely because the defendant claimed political motivation. However, the following December, the Irish attorney general refused to extradite to Northern Ireland an IRA member, already extradited to Ireland from Belgium, because he harbored doubts about the prospects of a fair trial. Along the same lines, the Irish Supreme Court in March 1990 ruled against the extradition to Northern Ireland of escaped IRA prisoners who feared retaliation by prison officials.

As troubling to nationalist and republican circles as the Irish refusal to extradite on certain conditions may have been to unionists, the British government's decision in January 1988 not to prosecute RUC members for allegedly complicity in earlier shoot-to-kill incidents proved as disconcerting. However, the decision of a British court in October 1989 to quash the sentences and to release four prisoners convicted of the 1975 Guildford pub bombing raised hopes of progress. A similar decision in March 1991 resulted in the release and the quashing of the sentences of six who had been convicted of a 1975 bombing in Birmingham. Also significant, the report of the Stevens inquiry that suggested collusion between the Ulster Defence Regiment and loyalist paramilitaries was released in May 1990.

In 1991 the Ulster Unionist Party agreed to participate in a series of three-tiered talks, among the political parties in Northern Ireland, between the British and Irish governments, and between the northern political parties and the Irish government. This was the first departure from the unionist refusal to have anything to do with the Irish Republic following the signing of the Hillsborough Agreement. However, the talks, which began in April and were chaired by an Australian, Sir Ninian Stephens, ended without conclusion in July. The next April, in the British general election, in which the Conservatives under John Major won, Gerry Adams lost his seat for West Belfast to the SDLP candidate, Dr. Joseph Hendron.

The SDLP leader, John Hume, had met with Gerry Adams in January 1988 and had continued a dialogue with him in an effort to bring Sinn Féin in from the cold and into the constitutional democratic process. Some in the SDLP feared that Hume was liable to create a process that would result in the SDLP being overwhelmed by Sinn Féin in the "nationalist-Catholic" community, but

Hume remained convinced that if the talks contributed to peace they were worth the effort. Finally, in April 1993, both men issued a statement calling for the achievement of Irish unification by democratic means and indicating a respect for the unionist identity. The month after, Mary Robinson made the first visit by an Irish head of state to the queen of England, followed the next month by an official visit to Belfast, where she had a brief exchange of words with Gerry Adams. That December the Taoiseach, Albert Reynolds, and the British prime minister, John Major, issued a Downing Street Declaration on Northern Ireland in which the British government asserted it had no strategic or economic interest in the continued connection with Northern Ireland and that the status of the province was to be determined by the wishes of its population, while the Irish government acknowledged that any unification of the island was dependent upon the wishes of the people of Northern Ireland. They called for a meeting of a Forum for Peace and Reconciliation to be established to work toward the democratic and peaceful resolution of the problems of the province. In a sense the ball was placed in Sinn Féin's court to accept constitutional procedures and renounce violence, in which circumstances its case would have a better chance of being heard.

In February 1994 President Bill Clinton of the United States granted, against the advice of the State Department and the CIA, a 48-hour visa to Gerry Adams to participate in a forum on Northern Ireland sponsored by an American foreign affairs group, which had extended invitations to all Northern Ireland political parties. Adams came, as did John Hume and John Alderdice of the Alliance Party. The Unionists and the DUP refused to participate in a conference that included Sinn Féin, even thought participants appeared successively, rather than simultaneously. In doing so, they lost the media advantage to Sinn Féin, as Adams had a field day answering easy questions on American national television. His ability to go to America, which had been encouraged by the American ambassador to Ireland, Jean Kennedy Smith, and her brother, Senator Edward Kennedy, strengthened his hand in persuading the militants in his camp, and the leadership of the IRA, that the time had come to suspend the armed campaign, especially in view of increasing loyalist violence against nationalists and Catholics. The following August the IRA proclaimed a cease-fire. Adams was subsequently given an unrestricted visa to make a triumphal visit to the United States in September. The next month several loyalist groups proclaimed a cease-fire.

RAINBOW COALITION, CEASE-FIRE BREAKDOWN, AND PEACE AGAIN

The Fianna Fáil–Labour coalition government broke up in November 1995 because of Labour displeasure at the appointment of the attorney general, Harry Whelehan, to the Supreme Court. The source of the displeasure was Whelehan's failure to extradite to Northern Ireland a priest accused of pederasty. Following a vote of no confidence, Reynolds resigned as Taoiseach. Bertie Ahern, a TD for Dublin Central and the minister for finance, succeeded him as caretaker Taoiseach until the following month. Subsequently, several of the opposition parties, the more conservative Fine Gael, Labour, and the radical Democratic Left, came together to form a "Rainbow Coalition." John Bruton of Fine Gael became Taoiseach, Dick Spring of Labour served again as Tánaiste and minister for foreign affairs, and Proinsias de Rossa, TD for Dublin Central and leader of the Democratic Left, became minister for social welfare. In February 1995 Bruton and British prime minister John Major issued a Frameworks Document on the future of Northern Ireland, asserting the principle of consent (that is, the wishes of the majority of the province would be required to change its status), the use of exclusively democratic and peaceful methods, and the parity of esteem for both traditions, unionist and nationalist, as guides for any arrangement for the province in forthcoming negotiations. They hoped that negotiations would formulate an agreement to create local institutions with elected officials sharing administrative authority over various matters, North-South institutions to harmonize, consult, and, in some cases, wield executive authority over matters of agreed mutual concern, and East-West structures, including an intergovernmental council in which the Irish government's role with regard to Northern Ireland would be given expression.

In keeping with the optimism following the cease-fire of the previous summer, President Clinton allowed Gerry Adams and other Sinn Féin figures to raise funds in the United States and to attend the celebration of St. Patrick's Day in the White House. In July the RUC forbade an Orange Order march down the Garvaghy Road, Portadown, which adjoins a nationalist neighborhood, but then rescinded the prohibition provided no bands took part in the march. In September David Trimble, whose earlier political roots included membership in the militant Vanguard movement, replaced James Molyneaux as the leader of the Ulster Unionist Party. In November President Clinton visited both Northern Ireland and Dublin and was received in a celebratory fashion in both communities in Northern Ireland as well as in the republic for his commitment to a peaceful resolution of the conflict.

The next month the president's special ambassador for Northern Ireland, former senator George Mitchell, chaired a panel to arrange the preliminaries for negotiations regarding Northern Ireland. Unionists remained reluctant to participate in such talks while Sinn Féin and the IRA had not made a permanent renunciation of the use of force. In January, the Mitchell panel, whose recommendations became known as the Mitchell principles, called for the beginning of all-party talks simultaneous with agreement by all participants to renounce violence together with commencement of the decommissioning of illegally held weapons. The British government, which had retreated from earlier insistence on permanent rejection of violence and on decommissioning as preliminary to negotiations, called for an election of an assembly for Northern Ireland as a framework in which the negotiations for settlement could take place. But the next month, the IRA broke the cease-fire with the bombing of Canary Wharf in London, which produced several fatalities. Later in the year there was a more destructive IRA bombing in Manchester in which casualties were fortunately limited. The Northern Ireland Forum, that is, the assembly called for by the British government, was elected in May. The party breakdown was predictable: the Unionists won 30, the DUP 24, the SDLP 21, Sinn Féin 17,

Alliance 7, independent unionists 7, and 4 others. However, the SDLP withdrew from the forum in July. That month the RUC again reversed itself in first banning and then allowing an Orange Order march down the Garvaghy Road, with subsequent rioting. However, in June, Mitchell began multiparty negotiations with Sinn Féin excluded.

The coalition government in Ireland was united with regard to the prerequisite of full rejection of violence and decommissioning of weapons by paramilitaries as central to a solution on Northern Ireland. But there were inevitable ideological differences among the partners. Fine Gael advanced serious reductions in capital gains taxation, which contributed immensely to the economic boom that would shortly occur in Ireland leading to the republic's designation as the "Celtic Tiger," while Labour and the Democratic Left promoted substantial social benefits, including free university education. Perhaps the most symbolically significant measure was a constitutional amendment narrowly approved in a referendum in November 1995 allowing divorce in Ireland.

In a general election held in May 1997, Fine Gael actually gained nine seats over its earlier total, but Labour representation in the Dáil was cut almost in half, and Fianna Fáil recovered its loses from the previous election. With the support of a number of independents, Ahern formed a coalition government with the Progressive Democrats. The PD leader, Mary Harney, who had succeeded Desmond O'Malley in 1993, became Tánaiste and minister for enterprise and employment. The previous month in Britain, the Labour Party returned to power after 18 years in opposition with a massive victory over the Conservatives. Ten Unionists and two members of DUP were returned for Northern Ireland constituencies as well as three members of the SDLP and two Sinn Féiners (including Gerry Adams, who was returned again for West Belfast).

In June Prime Minister Tony Blair announced his intention to resume the all-party talks in September and he gave the IRA a deadline of five weeks to return to a cease-fire. In July, rioting followed an Orange March down the Garvaghy Road, which was permitted by the RUC. Nevertheless, the IRA did proclaim a cease-fire. By September Sinn Féin was admitted to the all-party talks chaired by Senator Mitchell after Secretary of State for Northern Ireland Mo Mowlam declared the IRA cease-fire to be authentic, and after having accepted the Mitchell principle calling for commitment to nonviolence. However, the unionist parties refuse to participate, as they insisted on decommissioning being settled before negotiations. But by December Ulster unionists dropped that condition. However, an international decommissioning body under Canadian general John de Chastelain was established. In December Adams led the first Sinn Féin delegation to talks at 10 Downing Street. Intensive negotiations at Stormont finally led to the Good Friday Agreement in April 1998, which was accepted by the British and Irish governments, the Unionists, the SDLP, Alliance, and Sinn Féin, but not the DUP.

Central points in the Good Friday Agreement included the establishment of an elected Northern Ireland Assembly and its appointment of a power-sharing executive, formation of cross-border and cross-channel bodies, acceptance of the principle of consent for determining the status of Northern Ireland, Northern Ireland police reform, commencement of the release of prisoners convicted of politically inspired crimes, changing the Irish constitution to remove territorial claims on Northern Ireland, and urging the decommissioning of weapons by paramilitary organizations. The agreement was approved in subsequent referenda in Northern Ireland (by 71.1%) and in the republic (by 94.4%). A Northern Ireland Assembly was elected in June in which the party breakdown was as follows: Unionists 28, SDLP 24, DUP 20, Sinn Féin 18, and 18 among assorted other groups.

PROSPERITY AND PEACE

The Era of Bertie Ahern

Bertie Ahern played a central role in the achievement of the Good Friday Agreement within a year after becoming Taoiseach. He also presided over an extraordinary economic boom as various economic indices catapulted Ireland from having been one of the economic sick men of the European Community to being one of the leaders. The nation set an example for future relatively undeveloped European nations aspiring for membership. Emigration figures, which had assumed high numbers in the mid-1980s, many of whom departing illegally for the United States, were reversed as employment opportunities blossomed for a very well-educated young population. Massive American investment, drawn by the low capital gains tax rates that contrasted with the rest of Europe, played a major part in the boom. The economic good times provided a peace dividend, as the ending of major violence in Northern Ireland created an atmosphere of calm for the whole island.

Unfortunately, the economic prosperity was accompanied by the revelation of a variety of scandals implicating several Irish political figures, especially, but not exclusively, members of Fianna Fáil. The charges prompted the formation of a number of committees of inquiry whose investigations would last several years and give great insight into various forms of corruption, but relatively few actual convictions, although reputations were severely damaged. The most celebrated politician subject to inquiry was the former Taoiseach, Charles J. Haughey, who admitted in July 1998 that he had received enormous gifts prior to and while serving as Taoiseach from wealthy individuals whose interests would be well served by a friend in government. The funds were lodged in offshore accounts, of which he claimed the entire management had been in the hands of his now deceased accountant.

The following October Minister for Foreign Affairs Ray Burke resigned after allegations that he had received gifts in return for influencing local planning decisions in the late 1980s. In January 1999 another Fianna Fáil stalwart, Pádraig Flynn, then a European Union commissioner, was accused of accepting as personal gifts political donations made while he was minister for the environment in 1989. In April 2000 the commission investigating corruption in decision planning in the Dublin County Council heard testimony from Frank Dunlop, a former Fianna Fáil press secretary, that he had given thousands in "brown paper bags" to politicians to influence decisions. In May the commis-

Bank officials work on the Bank of Ireland's trading floor, Dublin, 2004. (*John Cogill/Bloomberg News/Landov*)

sion investigating Haughey heard that the gifts he had received exceeded eight million pounds. The next month a Fianna Fáil TD for Dublin West, Liam Lawlor, resigned from the party for uncooperative behavior before the tribunal examining his receipt of gifts. The same tribunal, headed by Justice Feargal Flood, heard, in the following March, May, and November, of the existence of offshore accounts held by Ray Burke, of his interventions on behalf of construction companies, and of the extraordinary size of the monetary gifts he received while minister for industry and commerce in 1989. In spite of all these scandals involving political figures with whom he was closely associated in the past, Ahern was able to distance himself from them.

The 1997 presidential election were held to select a successor to Mary Robinson, who had resigned a few months before the end of her term in order to assume a position with the United Nations. The Fianna Fáil candidate, Mary McAleese, easily defeated three other women candidates, Adi Roche of Labour, Mary Banotti of Fine Gael, and independent Dana Rosemary Scallion together with one independent male candidate, Derek Nally. McAleese, a barrister and law professor at Queen's University Belfast, was reelected unopposed in 2004.

Other parties attempted to strengthen themselves and position themselves to better challenge Fianna Fáil dominance. In January 1999 the Labour Party and the Democratic Left were amalgamated. The leader of the Labour Party, Dick Spring, had resigned in November 1997 following the very poor showing by the Labour Party candidate for the presidency. Ruairi Quinn, the Labour TD for Dublin Southeast and minister for finance in the Rainbow Coalition, replaced him. In early 2001 a revolt within Fine Gael deposed John Bruton as leader, even though the party had gained strength in the previous general election. Opponents argued that the gregarious and articulate Bruton lacked charisma and he was replaced by Michael Noonan, a TD for West Limerick, who had served in various cabinet positions in coalition governments, including the most recent led by Bruton.

The government narrowly survived a vote of no confidence in November 2001, but, in the general election of June 2002, Fianna Fáil increased its strength by four votes, while Fine Gael's Dail membership was cut almost in half, falling to its lowest figure in half a century. Labour increased its numbers, as did the PD's, the Greens, and Sinn Féin. The later raised the feared specter of a hung Dáil potentially tempting one or another party to consider a coalition or being dependent on Sinn Féin votes to form a government, even though the IRA had not yet disbanded as a private army nor decommissioned its stockpile of weapons and explosives. However, Fianna Fáil strength and the votes of the PD's prevented that from happening as well as the need to rely on a handful of independents, whose agenda was primarily to advance local interests. After the election, Noonan and Quinn resigned their respective leadership posts and were replaced by the Fine Gael TD for Mayo, Enda Kenny, and the Labour and former Democratic Left TD for Dublin Southwest, Pat Rabbitte. In the new government Ahern and Mary Harney continued as Taoiseach and Tánaiste.

Sources of dissatisfaction and concern in Ireland persisted despite obvious widespread prosperity. Grave anxieties existed about the inadequacy of hospital facilities and the belt tightening needed in distributing public welfare benefits. Many were critical of the pro-market and low tax policies of Minister for Finance Charles McCreevy, although others saw these as the reason for prosperity. From another perspective, many sensitive commentators noted the coarsening of Irish society and a growth in materialistic preoccupation with possessions. Disturbing figures appeared about youthful addiction to alcohol and narcotics, less restrained sexuality as indicated by high figures for out-of-wedlock births, and even an increased proclivity to suicide. On the other hand, the influence of the church, the historic promoter of values, had been seriously damaged by a decade or more of revelations of sexual abuse by clergy of young people in their charge or under their influence. The state and the religious orders agreed to provide massive amounts of compensation to claimants of abuse who were residents in state-supported church-run orphanages and industrial schools.

Possible indicators of public unease was the results of June 2004 local and European parliament elections, which saw significant gains by Fine Gael, as well as Sinn Féin, which gained a seat in the European parliament and several places in local governmental bodies. In response, the government sought to put forward the more historic Fianna Fáil pose as a populist party. MacCreevy became a European commissioner, and the foreign minister, Brian Cowan, a TD for Offaly, became minister for finance. He proposed a budget calling for greater generosity, removal of many of the unfortunate and the poorest paid from the tax roles altogether, and lessening of tax credits for the wealthy. One measure that took effect in 2004 and that gained surprising popular adherence and probable emulation in other countries was a ban on smoking in public houses.

THE PEACE PROCESS

The enthusiasm that greeted the Good Friday Agreement dampened not long after, as the implementation of the peace process began to prove difficult. In addition, numerous acts of outrage numbed public sensitivities. In July 1998 a loyalist firebomb killed three young Catholic brothers in their home in Ballymoney, County Antrim. Then, in August, dissident republicans, who had not accepted the cease-fire, set off a bomb in Omagh, County Tyrone, which killed 29. Still, several events kept the momentum of the peace process in motion: In June an independent commission was named to recommend police reforms in Northern Ireland; in July a parades commission forbade the Orange Order from marching down the contested route of the Garvaghy Road in Portadown; in September, President Clinton, who was on the eve of an impeachment inquiry, revisited Ireland and Northern Ireland, including Omagh; in October, John Hume, the SDLP leader, and David Trimble, the Ulster Unionist leader, were named as the Nobel Prize laureates for Peace; and, in November, President McAleese and Queen Elizabeth in November opened a tower in Mesen, Belgium, commemorating the Irish who had died in the First World War.

Later incidents, such as the murder of Rosemary Nelson, a solicitor who defended republicans, in a March 1999 car-bomb explosion, and the admission of responsibility by the IRA for the killing of a number of persons who had been missing since the 1970s, including one whose remains were discovered in May, created an atmosphere of apprehension, as did the ongoing killings, shootings, and evictions within their own communities by republican and loyalists ostensibly to exercise community discipline.

The nonattendance by Unionists in the Northern Ireland Assembly because of the lack of movement by the IRA in decommissioning its stockpile of weapons and explosives resulted in adjournment of the assembly in July 1999. Both governments published in the same month a document titled *The Way Forward*, which laid out the complex mechanism by which the assembly would select its power-sharing ministers as well as a procedure to suspend the assembly if neither a government was established nor weapons were decommissioned by the following May. In September, the independent commission on police reform, which was headed by Conservative politician Christopher Patten, but which also included figures from Northern Ireland, Ireland, and the United States, issued its report that called for significant police reforms emphasizing decentralization of structure, community input, a quota recruitment to insure a large presence of Catholics on the force, the removal of symbols associated with union with Britain, the disbanding of the permanent auxiliary police, and the renaming of the police force so as to drop the "Royal" and the "Ulster" terminology.

Also in September 1999, Senator George Mitchell returned to Northern Ireland to begin a review of the Good Friday Agreement with the various political parties, although the Unionists and Sinn Féin did not meet directly in their participation, and the DUP did not take part other than giving its views to Mitchell. The following month Peter Mandelson, a close political associate of Prime Minister Tony Blair who had replaced Mo Mowlam as the secretary of state for Northern Ireland, together with Mitchell issued a report calling for the reestablishment of the suspended Northern Ireland Assembly because the IRA had indicated a willingness to send a representative to meet with the International Commission on Decommission, headed by General John de Chastelain. The Unionists agreed and the reconvened Northern Ireland Assembly met and elected a 10-member executive council according to the d'Hondt rules of proportional selection.[21] David Trimble served as the first minister and Seamus Mallon of the SDLP as the second minister. Martin McGuinness of Sinn Féin and Peter Robinson of the DUP were also ministers. The next month the powers of devolved government were transferred from the Northern Ireland Office to the Northern Ireland Executive. However, by February 2000 the failure of the IRA to commence decommissioning resulted in the Northern Ireland Executive again being suspended and direct rule from Westminster restored. It was restored yet again in May after the IRA promised to initiate a process to put arms beyond use.

A year later, in July 2001, David Trimble resigned as first minister in protest at the lack of progress on the decommissioning of weapons by the IRA. His associate Reg Empey assumed the role of acting first minister. The following month, the Northern Ireland Assembly was temporarily suspended to allow a delay of six weeks for the parties to resolve differences, particularly with regard to the issue of decommissioning and then to select a permanent first minister. In October, when there had been no progress on decommissioning, the Ulster Unionist and DUP ministers of the executive announced their resignation from the executive, which would have ended the devolved government. However, five days later, the IRA decommissioned some weapons to the satisfaction of the International Commission and the resigned ministers resumed their positions. The next month, Mark Durkan from Derry replaced John Hume as the leader of the SDLP and succeeded Seamus Mallon as deputy first minister.

While the new executive functioned satisfactorily and the ministers from the more extreme parties, the DUP and Sinn Féin, demonstrated an impressive administrative capacity, the continued possession of weapons by the IRA and violent actions and acts of criminality on the part of assorted paramilitaries, including the IRA, caused the Ulster Unionist Council to demand in September that its ministers withdraw from the executive by January if the IRA and Sinn Féin had not demonstrated their commitment to nonviolence and democracy. Earlier in the year, in March, suspicions appeared that the IRA had stolen a document from the Special Branch office of the police, now called the Police Service of Northern Ireland in place of the Royal Ulster Constabulary. In June a database was discovered in the possession of the IRA listing public officials and members of the security forces. Then, in October, the police raided the Sinn Féin offices in Belfast to investigate possible republican intelligence-gathering

---

[21] *The system calls for the first elected to be a member of the largest party. That party's votes are then automatically halved. Then the second member is selected from whatever the largest party is then. That party's votes are subsequently halved to allow another party possibly to be largest. The procedure continues until the 10 members are named. The actual result produced an executive composed of three Ulster Unionists, three members from SDLP, two from the DUP, and two from Sinn Féin.*

and infiltration of the Northern Ireland Office.[22] Subsequently, the Northern Ireland Assembly was suspended until Sinn Féin, as a participant and as a component of the executive, demonstrated that it had ended its links with the IRA.

In April 2003 U.S. president George W. Bush met in Northern Ireland to confer with Prime Minister Blair on the military campaign in Iraq, and he also met with Northern Ireland parties. The following month, the British and Irish governments issued a joint declaration linking the restoration of Northern Ireland institutions to the reduction of security forces and the repeal of antiterrorist legislation. It asked that an International Monitoring Commission be formed to report on violations of the Good Friday Agreement, specifically the continuation of acts of violence, and demanded an end to paramilitary activity, particularly punishment attacks. The commission came into being the following September.

In June Trimble survived a challenge to his leadership of the Ulster Unionist Party when the party council did not accept a proposal disapproving the Anglo-Irish Joint Declaration, but three members of the House of Commons resigned from the Unionist Party in Westminster in opposition to it. In October, Trimble himself regarded an act of decommissioning witnessed by General de Chastelain as insufficiently transparent, and he subsequently stated that he would not share power with Sinn Féin without a full inventory of IRA weapons and a decommissioning timetable. The next month an election to the Northern Ireland Assembly saw a drastic change in the party composition, as the DUP with 30 members surpassed the 27-member Ulster Unionists, and Sinn Féin's 24 members exceeded the SDLP's 18. The Sinn Féin gained seats in the European parliament election the following June, when its candidate won the seat previously occupied by the retiring John Hume.

Alas, the peace process had arrived at the dilemma that had been feared by earlier peace-makers, the ascendancy of the extremes. Originally the advocates of power sharing, from the days of Sunningdale through Hillsborough, and even the Good Friday Agreement, had assumed that the bridge to community reconciliation and peace would be constructed about the middle of the road parties. Now the task was to bring the Democratic Unionist Party, led by Ian Paisley, and Sinn Féin, led by Gerry Adams, to share power. The major obstacle remained decommissioning, or more precisely, the method of verifying the decommissioning. The DUP insisted on the procedure being photographed, which the Irish and British governments approved, but which Sinn Féin regarded as humiliating to the IRA. While a hopeful note was the decrease in paramilitary activity as noted in recent International Monitoring Commission reports, negotiations to restore the power-sharing institutions failed as Sinn Féin and the DUP failed to agree on the method of verification of decommissioning. Soon after there was a £22 million robbery in the Northern Bank in Belfast, which a few weeks later in January 2005, the Police Service of Northern Ireland, with the concurrence of the government of Ireland, claimed was done by the Provisional IRA. Later that month a grisly murder outside a bar in

---

[22] *The case against those arrested was dropped by the prosecution in 2005; subsequently, one of the arrested Sinn Féiners acknowledged he had been acting for years as a double agent for British intelligence.*

Belfast of Robert McCartney was attributed to Provisional IRA members. The sisters and partner of the dead man claimed IRA intimidation inhibited witness cooperation in a police investigation. In February a number of men were apprehended in Cork and more than £2.3 million was found, which was regarded as part of the earlier Belfast heist. The visit by the McCartney family and the bank robbery made Sinn Féin unwelcome in the White House on St. Patrick's Day and incurred general condemnation from leading Irish-American political figures, even some ordinarily sympathetic. Gerry Adams even suggested that the IRA consider decommissioning and ending as a military organization. In the May British general election in Northern Ireland, the trend to strengthen the extremes continued as the Official Unionists delegation at Westminster fell from nine to a single seat, with even the party leader David Trimble losing his seat and subsequently resigning the leadership. The DUP under Ian Paisley climbed from five to nine seats. Sinn Féin gained a seat to five, and the SDLP continued with three seats. After the election, Paul Murphy, the second Roman Catholic in a row to serve in the position, having been preceded by John Reid, a Scottish MP, was replaced as Secretary of State for Northern Ireland by Peter Hain, originally an antiapartheid activist who had come to England from South Africa. He had earlier been a supporter of the troops out of Northern Ireland movement, but had since greatly modified his opinion.

A major breakthrough came in late July, when the Provisional IRA announced that its armed campaign was over and instructed its units to dump arms and members to engage only in peaceful democratic politics. In late September General John de Chastelain, the head of the International Commission on Decommissioning, confirmed that the PIRA had, in fact, put out of use its weaponry, as well as ammunition and explosives, which had been witnessed by a Catholic priest, Alec Reid, and a Methodist minister, Harold Good. In October the International Monitoring Commission reported that criminal and violent activity by the PIRA had virtually ceased during the most recent period of examination. Significant future reductions in the British military presence in Northern Ireland were announced as well as mitigation of security restrictions. Sinn Féin called for Members of Parliament from Northern Ireland to have the right to attend Dáil Eireann, although most TD's were unsympathetic and the nearest that would be considered by some would be permission to speak at special sessions considering Northern Irish questions.

Despite the decommissioning, unionists in general, and the DUP, in particular, remained suspicious and reluctant to consider taking part in a power-sharing regime with Sinn Féin. On the other hand, the Sinn Féin leadership grew in its confidence that its membership in Dáil Eireann would increase in the next Irish general election, which has to be held before mid-2007.

HISTORICAL
DICTIONARY
A–Z

A

Abbey Theatre

The Abbey Theatre was founded in 1904 with the merger of the National Dramatic Company, owned by brothers Frank and William Fay, and the Irish Literary Theatre, founded by W. B. YEATS, Lady GREGORY, and Edward MARTYN. Its patron was Annie E. F. Horniman, whose support enabled the purchase of a converted music hall, formerly the Mechanics Institute in Abbey Street, for productions. The first performance was Yeats *On Baile's Strand.* All of the works of John Millington SYNGE were produced at the Abbey, including his *Playboy of the Western World,* which provoked riots because it drew offense for his depiction of rural Ireland. The Fays withdrew in 1908 and Ms. Horniman ended her annual subsidy in 1910, making the Abbey of necessity self-supporting until 1924, when the IRISH FREE STATE government, through its minister for Finance, Ernest Blythe, extended an annual grant. Most of the hundreds of plays produced by 1951, when it burned down, had been written for the Abbey. The plays of Seán O'CASEY, *The Shadow of a Gunman, Juno and the Paycock,* and *The Plough and the Stars,* were produced for performance at the Abbey. The latter provoked riots in 1926 because of its disparagement of an idealized NATIONALISM. Between 1951 and 1966, the Abbey used the Queen's Royal Theater until returning at its original site to a new theater designed by Michael SCOTT. A smaller theater, the Peacock, was installed in the structure as well. Celebrated actors who have performed at the Abbey include William Shields, Cyril Cusack, and Siobhán McKENNA, and directors have included, in addition to Yeats, Lady Gregory, and Martyn, such luminaries as Ernest BLYTHE, Frank O'CONNOR, Walter MACKEN, Tomas Mac Anna, and Patrick MASON.

absentees

Absentees were nonresident landowners of Ireland. The term usually referred to the many "New English" owners of land acquired as a consequence of conquest and PLANTATION in the 16th and 17th centuries. They were rarely in Ireland and regarded their property solely as a source of rental income, paying little attention to improvements or to the condition of tenants. The phenomenon also occurred in the post-Norman Middle Ages when some of the Norman owners of land in Ireland returned to England during times of distress and disorder, especially in the 14th century.

abstentionism

Abstentionism was the policy advocated by Arthur GRIFFITH, the founder of SINN FÉIN, which called for members elected to the House of Commons from Ireland to abstain from attendance and assemble instead in Ireland to proclaim a separate parliament for the nation. At the time, Griffith hoped the British would acquiesce to a Dual Monarchy arrangement, whereby the British and Irish parliaments would have the same king. No Sinn Féin candidate was elected until 1917, when Sinn Féin had become more clearly republican in objective. The three members elected in by-elections in 1917 and those elected in the general election of 1918 refused to take their seats and the latter formed DÁIL ÉIREANN.

Abstentionism remained the policy of the Sinn Féin Party with regard to Dáil Éireann after the IRISH FREE STATE had come into being, and would remain so until the 1980s. Its members elected from NORTHERN IRELAND continue to refuse to take seats in the House of Commons, although the party members are willing to take seats and occupy ministerial offices in the NORTHERN IRELAND ASSEMBLY and in local government bodies in both Northern Ireland and the Irish Republic.

Act of Union

This act, passed by both the Irish parliament and the British parliament in 1800, united the kingdoms of Great Britain and Ireland, effective January 1, 1801. The act, which ended the parliament of Ireland, gave Ireland 100 seats in the House of Commons, two for each county, two each for Dublin and Cork, and one each for 31 other boroughs and one for TRINITY COLLEGE DUBLIN. Members of what had been the Irish House of Lords would elected 28 of their number as representative peers for life in the House of Lords and the bishops of the CHURCH OF IRELAND would also select four of their number to sit in the same body. The established churches of England and Ireland were united. There was to be free trade between the two countries, except that different duties in both countries on certain home products and foreign imports were to be continued. In addition, duties between both countries on certain manufactured goods, including cotton and woolen products, would continue for 20 years. Separate exchequers were to be kept for the collecting of taxes and the meeting of respective debts, while the Irish were expected to contribute two-seventeenths to meet the expenditure of the United Kingdom, but that in time to come the exchequers could be united. Existing laws in both kingdoms would continue unless changed by legislation passed by parliament. The passage of the act by the Irish parliament was facilitated by generous compensation of place holders and patrons of boroughs. Opponents of the measure included the ORANGE ORDER and the country gentry, while many the Catholic leaders, expecting Catholic emancipation to follow, supported the act.

Adams, Gerry (1948–)
revolutionary politician
Adams became involved in radical republican politics in the 1960s, identifying with the Provisional wing of SINN FÉIN and the IRA. He was interned in 1972, but released to take part in negotiations with the first secretary of state for NORTHERN IRELAND, William WHITELAW. He rose to prominence in Sinn Féin during the HUNGER STRIKES of 1980–81. He was a major figure in steering the party toward electoral politics, in addition to revolutionary agitation and support of the IRA military campaign. Adams became president of the party in 1983 as his ascendancy marked the arrival of members from Northern

Sinn Féin party leader Gerry Adams *(Paul McErlane/ Reuters/Landov)*

Ireland and of younger and less dogmatic figures in the movement. The same year he was elected from West Belfast to the House of Commons, and he has been elected ever since, except for 1992 to 1997. While adhering to the party policy of ABSTENTION from Westminster, Adams did take part both in conversations with SDLP leader John HUME in the early 1990s, which were followed by an IRA cease-fire in 1994, interrupted in 1996 but resumed again in 1997, and in the GOOD FRIDAY AGREEMENT of 1998.

Adventurers

The Adventurers were those who advanced money to support the war against the Irish rebellion in 1642, in return for which an Act of Parliament, signed by Charles I, promised compensation from two-and-a-half million acres of designated Irish land.

Aer Lingus

The national airline, of which the government is the sole shareholder, was started in 1936 with flights to Bristol. Routes were added subsequently to London, Liverpool, and the Isle of Man. The Second World War delayed further development, but afterward service to other British and continental cities began. In 1954 it was the first airline to offer regular service to Lourdes, France. In 1958 trans-Atlantic service was introduced. It encountered difficulties that plagued most of the smaller airlines in the 1980s and 1990s, which prompted some to suggest it selling it off. However, implementation of significant cost-saving measures have recently brought a return to profitability and route expansion.

Agricultural Credit Corporation (ACC)

Founded in 1927, it was the first state-sponsored company. It sought to extend credit to farmers, but for the first four decades its loans were too small in size to significantly foster Irish agricultural development. However, since the mid-1960s and especially since Irish membership in the European Union, agriculture developed enormously. The ACC was empowered to receive deposits from any source and accordingly has become a major banking agency, which makes credit available for agricultural purposes.

Ahern, Bertie (1951–)
politician

Educated by the IRISH CHRISTIAN BROTHERS, and at Rathmines College of Commerce and University College Dublin, Ahern was trained and worked as an accountant. He was elected to the DÁIL ÉIREANN in 1977 as part of FIANNA FÁIL's landslide return to power. A supporter of Charles HAUGHEY in his quest to lead the party, he served as chief whip in 1982. Minister for labor in Haughey's 1987 government, he became minister for finance in 1991. He became Taoiseach upon the resignation of Albert REYNOLDS in 1993, but the withdrawal of the LABOUR PARTY from the governing coalition caused Fianna Fáil to almost immediately fall from power. He returned as Taoiseach following the election of 1997 and again in 2002, both times forming a coalition with the PROGRESSIVE DEMOCRATS. He has been Taoiseach during the negotiations that

Bertie Ahern *(Department of Public Affairs, Dublin)*

resulted in the GOOD FRIDAY AGREEMENT and while Ireland was experiencing the remarkable economic development that led the country to be labeled the Celtic Tiger.

Aiken, Frank (1898–1983)

revolutionary and politician

Born in Armagh and educated by the IRISH CHRISTIAN BROTHERS in Newry, he became active in the IRISH VOLUNTEERS and in the GAELIC LEAGUE in 1913. He was commandant of a Northern Division of the IRA during the WAR OF INDEPENDENCE. He opposed the ANGLO-IRISH TREATY and fought against the PROVISIONAL GOVERNMENT. He was chief of staff of the anti-treaty forces at the time of the proclamation of the cease-fire in May 1923. He was elected as an ABSTENTIONIST *TD* from County Louth in 1923. Aiken was closely associated with Eamon DE VALERA in founding the FIANNA FÁIL party in 1926 and served as minister in every Fianna Fáil government until his own retirement from politics in 1969. He served as minister for defense under de Valera from 1932 to 1939, minister for coordination of defense measures from 1939 to 1945, minister for finance from 1945 to 1948, minister for external affairs from 1951 to 1954 and 1957 to 1968, minister for agriculture for three months in 1957, and TÁNAISTE from 1965 to 1969.

Alderdice, John (1955–)

politician

Born in Antrim in 1955, Alderdice served as leader of the ALLIANCE PARTY from 1987 through 1996, when he was created a life peer. In 1998 he became Speaker of the NORTHERN IRELAND ASSEMBLY created as a consequence of the GOOD FRIDAY AGREEMENT. He presently chairs an international monitoring commission that periodically evaluates the amount of criminality and violence connected to various paramilitary groups in Northern Ireland.

Alliance Party of Northern Ireland

Formed in April 1970 as a middle alternative between the NATIONALISTS and the UNIONISTS in Northern Ireland, it attempted to bridge the sectarian gap by appealing to both Catholics and Protestants, especially those who were middle class and liberal, with a program calling for a commitment to the continuation of union with Britain but also the provision of civil rights to all citizens. Rarely obtaining much more than 10 percent of the vote in any election, whether local of parliamentary, its leader at the time, Oliver NAPIER, served as part of the short-lived power-sharing executive of 1973–74. A subsequent leader, John ALDERDICE, was the speaker of the NORTHERN IRELAND ASSEMBLY created after the GOOD FRIDAY AGREEMENT.

Ancient Order of Hibernians (AOH)

The roots of the AOH are found in 17th and 18th centuries in popular Catholic resistance to persecution and maltreatment by the New English and PROTESTANT ASCENDANCY by means of various secret societies. Formal public organization appeared among Irish immigrants in the United States confronted by anti-Catholic prejudice. Requirements for membership were Irish birth or ancestry and Roman Catholicism. The organization served, as did many friendly societies of the 19th century, to provide insurance and relief assistance to members in the pre–welfare state age. The organization was supportive of the nationalist cause in Ireland, as advanced by either FENIANS or the IRISH PARLIAMENTARY PARTY. Natives of southern Ulster tended to dominate in the earlier phase. In Ireland, the organization was an important force behind parliamentary nationalists in Ulster prior to and in the decades immediately after PARTITION. In the United States, where it remains an active group with membership in the tens of thousands, it became closely identified with St. Patrick's Day celebrations. Increasingly the membership consists of Americans several generations separated from Ireland, although it continues to champion the political unification of Ireland.

Andrews, C. S. (Todd Andrews) (1901–1985)

revolutionary, public servant

Born in Dublin, educated at St. Edna's, the Synge Street Christian Brothers School, and

University College Dublin, Andrews took part in the WAR OF INDEPENDENCE and the CIVIL WAR, the latter on the anti-treaty side. After working for the tourist board and the ESB, he became managing director of the turf development board in 1934. A visit to the Soviet Union convinced him of the potential for developing the peat bogs as a source of electrification. His success was confirmed with his designation as chairman of BORD NA MONA, as the national peat industry organization was titled. In 1958 he became chairman of the CIE, the national transportation authority, where he directed the dismantlement of many railroad lines considered uneconomical. His last post was chairman of the RTE Authority from 1966 to 1970. He wrote two volumes of autobiography: *Dublin Made Me* (1979) and *Men of No Property* (1982).

Andrews, Eamon (1922–1987)
broadcaster

Born in Dublin and educated at the Synge Street Christian Brothers School, Andrews was an amateur middleweight boxing champion who became a sports commentator on Radio Eireann. In 1950 he joined the BBC where he also presented sports programs. Branching into light entertainment programs, he soon became the highest earning performer on British television. Afterward he founded a studio presenting packaged programs and commercials for radio and television. He was the first chairman of the Irish national broadcasting authority (later called RADIO TELEFÍS ÉIREANN) from 1961 to 1966 when television was introduced to Ireland.

Andrews, John Miller (1871–1956)
politician

Born in County Down, Andrews directed his family's linen-bleaching firm and the Belfast Ropeworks. A member of the Northern Ireland PARLIAMENT from 1921 to 1953, he served minister of labor from 1921 to 1937 and of finance from 1937 to 1940, when he became the second prime minister upon the death of Sir James CRAIG. In 1943 he was ousted from

power by members seeking younger faces in government and replaced by Basil BROOKE. However, he remained president of the Ulster Unionist Council, the governing body of the ULSTER UNIONIST PARTY until 1947. An active member of the ORANGE ORDER, he served as grand master of County Down from 1941, of all Ireland between 1948 and 1954, and of the Imperial Grand Council of the World from 1949 to 1954.

Anglo-Irish

The terms refers to the people in Ireland descendant from the New English settlers of the 16th and 17th centuries who made up the PROTESTANT ASCENDANCY that dominated the political, social, and economic life of 18th-century Ireland. Those of the OLD ENGLISH and native Irish who conformed to the established church could also be included. After the passage of the ACT OF UNION they continued their socioeconomic dominance and for the most part opposed the Catholic emancipation campaign, land reform, are efforts to repeal the Act of Union or advance Home Rule. There were significant exceptions. Some Anglo-Irish figures were central to the nationalist cause, such as Charles Stewart PARNELL and Erskine CHILDERS. Others were among the major cultural and literary figures of Ireland; including Oliver GOLDSMITH and Jonathan SWIFT in the 18th century and Douglas HYDE, W. B. YEATS, Lady GREGORY, and Oscar WILDE in the late 19th and early 20th centuries. After independence many of them moved to England. That and the tendency of the children of mixed marriages to become Catholic, if religious at all, worked to lessen their portion of the population of Ireland. However, their numbers have stabilized and they continue to be found in disproportionate numbers in the ranks of the professional classes, and have even become the object of some social emulation by socially upward Irish Catholics.

Anglo-Irish Agreement   See HILLSBOROUGH AGREEMENT; SUNNINGDALE AGREEMENT.

Anglo-Irish Treaty

The treaty signed on December 6, 1921, ending the WAR OF INDEPENDENCE and granting to Ireland, as the IRISH FREE STATE, dominion status equivalent to that of Canada. The Irish signatories were Michael COLLINS, Arthur GRIFFITH, Eamonn DUGGAN, Robert BARTON, and George Gavan DUFFY. British signatories included David Lloyd George, Austen Chamberlain, Lord Birkenhead, and Winston S. Churchill. The president of the revolutionary DÁIL ÉIREANN, Eamon DE VALERA, led the opposition to the treaty on the grounds of its having not achieved republican status for Ireland. Some specific features inhibiting Irish sovereignty included a required oath to be taken by members of the Irish Free State parliament to the king as head of the Commonwealth, the symbolic position of the lord lieutenant in the Irish Free State, such as his power to sign legislation, the retention of naval bases in Ireland by the British navy, the restriction on the size of the Irish military in relation to that of Britain proportionately according to population, continued proportionate Irish fiscal obligations to the public debt of the United Kingdom as of the date of the treaty, and an option to the government of NORTHERN IRELAND to withdraw from the Irish Free State within one month of its entry into being. Opposition to the treaty within Ireland ultimately resulted in the CIVIL WAR (1922–23), which was won by the pro-treaty side.

Anglo-Irish War See WAR OF INDEPENDENCE.

Anglo-Normans

In the 1160s, an Irish king, Dermot McMURROUGH, solicited the services of Norman warriors and vassals of the king of England (their ancestors had arrived in England and Wales consequent to the conquest by William of Normandy in 1066) to assist him in wars with other Irish rulers. The foremost of the Normans was Richard fitz Gilbert, known as Strongbow. They were rewarded with lands for their efforts and went on to conquer further territory. Ultimately, their king, Henry II, apprehensive that they would establish a rival kingship to him in Ireland, came to Ireland to assert his suzerainty over them, as well as to receive acknowledgment as Lord of Ireland from the other Irish kings. Normans from Wales and England continued to settle in Ireland until the mid-14th century. They were regarded as being English in Ireland, and, in the territories they settled—primarily Dublin, Meath and other Leinster areas—that would be called the PALE, political and social institutions paralleling those in England developed. Some Anglo-Normans conquered other territories, especially in Munster, but they tend to intermarry and adapt to the Irish customs.

Annals of the Four Masters

The annals were copies or compilations of Irish texts undertaken by a group of Franciscans led by Micheál Ó'CLEIRIGH in the 1630s. Ó'Cleirigh had been sent back to Ireland from Louvain in the Spanish Netherlands for this mission. They were patronized by a series of Irish gentlemen and aristocrats. They originally sought to compile material related to early Irish saints, but then broadened their work to include genealogies of saints and kings.

annuities

The IRISH FREE STATE government had assumed the responsibility of collecting obligations from Irish farmers who had obtained title to their land through the various Land Purchase acts of the late 19th and early 20th centuries. These "mortgage" payments involved obligations to the British government that had facilitated the original buyout of the landlords. Eamon DE VALERA'S refusal to forward the same to Britain after he came to power in 1932 precipitated the ECONOMIC WAR of the 1930s.

Anti-Partition League

A league organized in 1945 by nationalists in NORTHERN IRELAND, primarily members of the

Nationalist Party, to promote the ending of Irish PARTITION. In 1949 DÁIL ÉIREANN, under the coalition government headed by John A. COSTELLO of FINE GAEL, approved the formation of an All Party Anti-Partition Committee to work with the league to promote, especially through propaganda in the United States and Britain, the cause of Irish unification. The immense human suffering in other parts of Europe and the world as a consequence of the Second World War and the beginning of the cold war inhibited the development of interest in the issue.

Apprentice Boys

An organization that commemorates the role of a group of young apprentices during the siege of Londonderry by the forces of King James II in 1689, in locking the gates of the city and thereby blocking a possible surrender by the governor, Robert LUNDY. The organization, which is vigorously supportive of union with Britain, holds an annual march on August 12. Its militant and sectarian character contributed to the outbreak of violence in 1969. More recent parades have been restrained and are received with some tolerance by the nationalist community.

Aran Islands

Three islands—Inishmore, Inishmaan, and Inisheer—off the coasts of County Clare and County Galway (of which they are part) with areas of 12, $3^1/_2$, and $2^1/_4$ square miles, respectively, and Irish-speaking populations of more than 800 in Inishmore and about 200 in each of the other two islands. The islands are known for the Bronze Age stone forts, especially Dun Aengus on Inishmore at the edge of a cliff, and earlier Christian ruins. The islands are treeless, but stone walls made over the centuries protect the soil from erosion. The soil was formed in part by the laying of seaweed on the bare limestone of which the islands are composed. The population was substantially greater in the early 19th century. The life of the inhabitants had always been identified with brutal weather and material conditions and arduous work. They were the source of inspiration for many writers and artists, particularly John Milington SYNGE, and were the subject of a famous film documentary *Man of Aran* (1934), by the American Robert O'Flaherty. Many natives became celebrated literary figures in Ireland, such as Liam O'FLAHERTY, Máirtín O DIREÁIN, and Breandán O hEITHIR. In more recent times, tourism has become a primary source of income. Airstrips serve all three islands.

Army Comrades Association   See BLUESHIRTS.

Army Mutiny

An ultimatum was issued to the IRISH FREE STATE government in March 1924 by a group of officers, calling themselves the Old IRA, led by Liam Tobin and C. F. Dalton, two close associates of Michael COLLINS, objecting to the government's betrayal of the nationalist objectives of Collins in failing to more vigorously combat PARTITION and in allowing the demobilization then underway in the national army. They had supported the ANGLO-IRISH TREATY tactically rather than in principle. They also feared that veterans of the WAR OF INDEPENDENCE were being overlooked in favor of personnel with British military experience in the process of demobilization. The government's firm resistance prompted the minister for industry and commerce, Joseph MCGRATH, to resign and threaten to expose mismanagement by the military. The government agreed to establish a commission to investigate the same and appointed the police commissioner, General Eoin O'DUFFY, as commander of the armed forces. When the Army Council authorized the arrest of several participants in the mutiny, who had been given a still not expired deadline to return to barracks, the vice president of the Free State government, Kevin O'HIGGINS, who was also minister for justice, acting in lieu of President William T. COSGRAVE, who was ill, had the government demand the resignations of the Army Council, which prompted Richard MULCAHY, the minister for defense, to also resign. Mulcahy and the Army Council were closely identified with the IRISH REPUBLICAN BROTHERHOOD, which they had revived to draw nationalist members of the army away from the Old IRA. The investigating commission ultimately condemned the mutiny and criticized the imprudent use of the IRB to offset the Old IRA. O'Higgins is credited with having effectively removed rival private groups from the military and asserting civilian ascendancy.

Ashbourne Act   See LAND ACTS.

Ashe, Thomas (1885–1917)
revolutionary
Born in Lispole, County Kerry, Ashe was a school principal, a member of the GAELIC LEAGUE and the IRISH VOLUNTEERS. He commanded the Volunteers at Ashbourne, County Meath, at the time of the EASTER RISING. He was sentenced to death for his role, but it was later commuted to life imprisonment, and he was released in 1917. A few months later he was arrested for incitement and sentenced to two years imprisonment. He went on HUNGER STRIKE demanding political status for SINN FÉIN prisoners. He died on September 25, 1917, while being forcibly fed.

Aud
A German cargo vessel disguised as a Norwegian ship that was bringing a cargo of weapons to Tralee harbor for the IRISH VOLUNTEERS simultaneous with Roger CASEMENT's landing via submarine on the eve of the EASTER RISING in 1916. The *Aud* withdrew when it failed to link up with the reception party on shore. The British navy ordered it to sail to Cobh where the captain, Karl Spindler, scuttled the ship before surrendering.

Aughrim, Battle of (July 22, 1691)
The most decisive battle in the war in Ireland between the JACOBITE forces of James II and William III took place not far from Athlone, County Galway. The outcome of the confrontation between the evenly matched armies was uncertain for sometime until the Jacobite commander, the Marquis de Saint Ruth, was killed and his forces demoralized. The Williamite army, under Godard von Ginkel, advanced to a victory in which 7,000 of the Jacobite soldiers were killed while the Williamites incurred only 2,000 casualties. Galway soon surrendered, and the last Jacobite stronghold, Limerick, would fall a several months later.

Auxiliaries
An auxiliary division to the ROYAL IRISH CONSTABULARY, they were formed in 1920 to supplement the police force whose ranks had thinned during the WAR OF INDEPENDENCE. Growing to about 2,000 in number, they were recruited from among demobilized officers of the British Army. They were inadequately prepared for the police auxiliary role for which they had been created. Being outside the discipline of the police, they quickly gained such a reputation for brutality that even their commander, General Frank Crozier, resigned in February 1922. They were distinct from the BLACK AND TANS, who were recruited into the RIC.

B

Bachelor's Walk Incident
(July 26, 1914)

A British regiment was returning from Clontarf, County Dublin, where they had met, but had not interfered with, a group of IRISH VOLUNTEERS bringing arms from the HOWTH GUNRUNNING. They encountered a pro-Volunteer crowd at Bachelor's Walk, who threw stones. Shots were fired at the crowd and three were killed and 38 injured. The incident stood in contrast to the tolerant acquiescence to the gunrunning at the Larne and elsewhere by the ULSTER VOLUNTEERS two months before.

Balbriggan, sack of
(September 20, 1920)

The north County Dublin town was sacked by inebriated members of the BLACK AND TANS in retaliation for the killing of an RIC officer by expanding bullets.

Balfe, Michael William (1808–1870)
composer

Born in Dublin, Balfe went to London in 1823 and subsequently studied in Italy. He wrote thirty operas, including *The Bohemian Girl,* cantatas and songs, and arrangements for Thomas MOORE'S *Irish Melodies.*

Ballingarry, Battle of (July 1848)

A number of YOUNG IRELANDERS were gathering in the south County Tipperary village to consider an armed rebellion. Armed police arrived and took command of the home of a widow farmer, Mrs. McCormick. Some Young Irelanders attacked unsuccessfully, with a few losing their lives in doing so. Police reinforcements arrived and the rebellion ended. Many escaped, but the strongest advocate for rebellion, William Smith O'BRIEN, was arrested.

Ballynahinch, Battle of
(June 12–13, 1798)

A battle in County Down between a primarily Presbyterian force of UNITED IRISHMEN led by Henry MUNRO and the Irish MILITIA and YEOMANRY. The artillery of the government forces, which were smaller in number, overwhelmed the rebel forces, largely armed only with pikes. There were few government casualties, but hundreds of rebels were killed, including the leader, Munro, who was captured, hung, and decapitated. It was the end of the rebellion in Ulster.

Ballyseedy Incident (March 7, 1923)

One of a number of atrocities committed by the IRISH FREE STATE forces in County Kerry against IRREGULAR prisoners who were forced to dismantle a road block that was in fact heavily mined. Eight were killed. Similar incidents occurred near Killarney and Caherciveen in which four and five prisoners, respectively, were killed.

Baltinglass Rebellion (June 1580)

James Eustace, third viscount Baltinglass, raised the papal banner in a call to fight for "faith and fatherland." This was a significant foretaste of the union of OLD ENGLISH and Irish that would form the CONFEDERATION OF KILKENNY more than 60 years later. His move took place simultaneous with the rebellion initiated the previous year in Munster by James Fitzmaurice Fitzgerald. After some success, his revolt dwindled, while the forces in Munster, joined by Spanish troops at SMERWICK, County Kerry, were overwhelmed.

Bantry Bay Expedition
(December 1796)

An invading force of 13,000 French soldiers commanded by General Lazare Hoche left Brest, but almost half were blown off course by storms. The remainder arrived in Bantry Bay on December 22, but prevailing easterly winds deterred them from landing and they ultimately withdrew. Had they landed it might have seriously jeopardized the British position in Ireland.

Banville, John (1945–   )
writer

Novelist, playwright, literary editor (1988–98) and literary critic (since 1998) of the *IRISH TIMES*, Banville wrote such novels as *Nightspawn* (1971), *Doctor Copernicus* (1976), and *Mefisto* (1986), and the plays *The Broken Jug* (1994) and *God's Gift* (2000).

Barington, Jonah (1760–1834)
politician, barrister

A member of the Irish House of Commons from 1790 to 1800, Barington opposed the ACT OF UNION, but he helped bribe others to vote for it. He was knighted in 1807. His financial affairs were extravagant and irregular, which resulted in his going into exile following charges of having misappropriated court funds. He wrote a three-volume *Personal Sketches of His Own Times* (1827–32) and the *Rise and Fall of the Irish Nation* (1833), which feature vigorous commentaries

on many of the central political, social, and cultural figures of the era.

Barnardo, Thomas (1845–1905)
doctor, philanthropist

Born in Dublin, Barnardo went to London as a young man hoping to be a medical missionary. He turned instead to serving the destitute children of London, founding what would be called the Dr. Barnardo Homes. The governing principle was that no child would be refused admission. Thousands of children were served.

Barry, Kevin (1902–1920)
rebel

Educated at BELVEDERE COLLEGE, Barry studied medicine at University College Dublin. A member of the IRA, he took part in a raid on a military vehicle in which six soldiers were killed, one of whom was younger than himself. Captured at the scene with a weapon, he was tried by courts-martial and executed by hanging on November 1, 1920. His execution stirred immense public outrage and grief because of his youth. The episode became the theme of a patriotic ballad.

Barry, Tom (1897–1980)
rebel soldier

Born in West Cork, Barry served in the British army during the First World War. He joined the IRA when he returned to Ireland in 1919. He commanded one of the leading IRA Flying Columns during the WAR OF INDEPENDENCE. One celebrated exploit was the ambush of a number of AUXILIARIES at Kilmichael, County Cork. He opposed the ANGLO-IRISH TREATY, but became a prisoner of the PROVISIONAL GOVERNMENT. His REPUBLICANISM was so strong that it even led to his imprisonment by the government of Eamon DE VALERA in 1934. He opposed the call for Irish Republicans to support the Republican side in the Spanish Civil War. Barry withdrew from IRA activism in 1940 and wrote a memoir titled *Guerilla Days in Ireland* (1949).

Barton, Robert Childers (1881–1975)
republican politician, agriculturalist
Raised in Glendalough, County Wicklow with his cousin, Robert Erskine CHILDERS, Barton attended Rugby and Oxford and was commissioned in the British army during the First World War. He resigned his commission after he was sent to Dublin during Easter Week, where he became a REPUBLICAN. As a Sinn Féiner he was elected from Wicklow to the first and second DÁIL ÉIREANN and served as minister for agriculture. He was imprisoned several times for his republican activism. Barton was one of the delegates to the conference that negotiated the ANGLO-IRISH TREATY, which he signed. However, he took the anti-treaty side afterward. Upon election to the third Dáil, he refused to take his seat. He subsequently withdrew from active politics and concentrated on managing his estates, although he did chair the AGRICULTURAL CREDIT CORPORATION from 1934 to 1954.

Bax, Sir Arnold (1883–1953)
composer
Although born and educated in London at the Royal Academy of Music and having no Irish connections, Bax came to consider himself Irish after reading "The Wanderings of Oisin" by W. B. YEATS. He published poems under the pseudonym, Dermot O'Byrne, some of which were banned by the British as seditious as they commemorated the EASTER RISING. His friends included Padraic COLUM, George RUSSELL, Padraic PEARSE and other Easter Week leaders. The author of several symphonies that reflected Celtic and Irish influences, he also composed for British state occasions and was knighted in 1937.

Béal na mBláth
The site in County Cork where Michael COLLINS was killed in an ambush on August 22, 1922.

Beaufort, Francis (1774–1857)
admiral, hydrographer
Born in Navan, County Meath, Beaufort joined the British navy in 1787, in which he served during the French Revolutionary and Napoleonic Wars, during which he was twice wounded. Appointed hydrographer for the navy in 1829, which post he retained for 26 years, he made nautical surveys in various parts of the world. His work gained universal acceptance for its accuracy and was employed in British Admiralty charts. Beaufort invented the scale of wind velocities, which was named after him.

Beckett, Samuel (1906–1989)
novelist, dramatist, poet
Born in Foxrock, County Dublin, educated at the Portora Royal School, Enniskillen, County Fermanagh, and TRINITY COLLEGE DUBLIN, Beckett taught at Campbell College, Belfast, and then at the École Normale Supérieure in Paris, where he became acquainted with James JOYCE who influenced him to begin writing. He taught at Trinity College from 1931 to 1932, but returned again to the Continent and ultimately to Paris, being uncomfortable with the provincialism and nationalism he found in Ireland. During the Second World War, he was involved with the French Resistance, which earned him a Croix de Guerre. He began to write in French in the 1950s. His most celebrated work was *Waiting for Godot* (1953), an abstract play about people in a nondescript room conversing while waiting for someone who never arrives. His other works, including novels such as *Malloy* (1951) and *The Unnamable* (1953), were similarly abstract and removed from concrete circumstances. He earned the Nobel Prize for literature in 1969.

Bedell, William (1571–1642)
scholar, bishop
Born in Essex, educated at Cambridge, a student of divinity and of languages, Bedell served as Provost of TRINITY COLLEGE DUBLIN from 1617 to 1629. He was appointed Bishop of Kilmore and

Ardagh in 1629, but he resigned from Ardagh in 1633. He favored a more sympathetic apostolic effort on the part of the Church of Ireland rather than a punitive approach to convert the Roman Catholic natives of Ireland to Protestantism. To that end he had catechisms and religious texts printed in Irish, encouraged divinity students to study Irish, and undertook the translation of the Bible into Irish. His manner prompted rebellious Catholics to treat him generously when he was imprisoned in 1641. CONFEDERATION OF KILKENNY military leaders attended his funeral the following year.

Behan, Brendan (1923–1964)
writer

Born in Dublin to a strongly REPUBLICAN family, a nephew of Peadar KEARNEY, Behan left school early and began work as house painter. Involvement with the IRA resulted in his arrest in Liverpool and his sentencing, at 16 years of age, to a Borstal for three years. When he returned to Ireland he was sentenced to 14 years for shooting at a policeman. While in prison, he learned the Irish language from a fellow prisoner. Released as part of a general amnesty in 1946, Behan turned to traveling throughout Ireland and to writing. In 1954 his play, *The Quare Fellow,* appeared, which gained him international celebrity. Similar success attended his next play, *The Hostage* (1958), and his autobiography, *The Borstal Boy* (1958), was a best seller. His subsequent work, including numerous television appearances and travel commentaries, were of less merit. Diabetes and alcoholism brought him a premature death.

Belfast

The principal city of Northern Ireland, a port at the head of Belfast Lough in both Antrim and Down, Belfast in medieval times had been a fortified crossing point on the Lagan River. Arthur Chichester was awarded the land in return for military service to the Crown in 1603. His descendants, the earls and marquises of Donegal, carried out development of the town in the 17th and 18th centuries. The industrialization of the 18th century mushroomed in the 19th, particularly establishment of cotton, then linen, mills and engineering and chemical industries. Later in that century, the shipbuilding firm of HARLAND AND WOLFF was formed, reaching its pinnacle of international renown in 1911 with the launching of the ill-fated RMS *TITANIC.* The capital of Northern Ireland was located at STORMONT, a suburb of the city. Belfast experienced substantial bombing by German aircraft during the Second World War and has been the site of much of the sectarian confrontations that have plagued Ulster and Northern Ireland from the late 18th century on. Many of the more severe atrocities by REPUBLICANS and LOYALISTS have occurred in the city. Distinctly sectarian neighborhoods include the Falls Road and the Shankill. Notable sites and institutions include the City Hall, QUEEN'S UNIVERSITY, and the Botanic Gardens. Its population of 350,000 makes it the second largest city on the island.

Belfast Boycott (1920–1922)

A boycott in the south of Ireland of goods produced in Belfast that occurred in response to anti-Catholic rioting. It received the formal sanction of the revolutionary government of DÁIL ÉIREANN and it was nominally ended when Michael COLLINS and James CRAIG met in early 1922 in an attempt to ease maltreatment of nationalists and Catholics and restrain IRA activism in NORTHERN IRELAND.

Bell, The (1940–1954)
literary magazine

Founded and edited by Sean O'FAOLAIN and then Peadar O'DONNELL, it published many of the major writers of the period. It served as an articulate critic of the predominant Catholic, conservative, and nationalist ethos.

Belvedere College

A secondary-level school for boys run by the Society of Jesus, located on Great Denmark

Street between Parnell Square and Mountjoy Square on Dublin's Northside, its students have included many celebrated figures in modern Irish history, including James JOYCE, Kevin BARRY, and Garret FITZGERALD.

Benburb, Battle of (1646)

In one of the greatest victories in history by Irish forces, Owen Roe O'Neill, nephew of the exiled earl of TYRONE, and his force of 5,000 decisively defeated a Scots army of 6,000 commanded by Robert MUNRO, who lost almost half his forces. However, upon this victory in Armagh, O'Neill moved south to assert supremacy in the CONFEDERATION OF KILKENNY, rather than finishing off Munro's forces, who were allowed to regroup and resume harassment of the Irish in Ulster.

Beresford, Lord John George (1773–1862)

archbishop of Armagh, primate of all Ireland

The Dublin-born, and Eton- and Oxford-educated member of one of Ireland's wealthiest families, Beresford served as bishop in various dioceses of the CHURCH OF IRELAND before coming to Armagh in 1822. He vigorously opposed Catholic emancipation national schools, preferring a more distinctly Protestant system. He restored the cathedral in Armagh, but he also brought immense wealth to himself and his family through his various church offices.

Bergin, Osborn (1872–1950)

linguistics scholar

A native of the city of Cork, Bergin studied at Queens College, Cork, and in Berlin and Freiburg, Germany. Involved with the School of Irish Learning and its journal, *Eriu,* which marked the commencement of the scientific study of Irish, he was the first professor of early and medieval Irish at University College Dublin from 1909 to 1940 and served briefly as the first director of the School of Celtic Studies at the Dublin Institute for Advanced Studies in 1940.

He wrote extensively and completed numerous translations from and into Irish.

Berkeley, George (1685–1753)

philosopher, bishop

Born in Kilkenny and educated at TRINITY COLLEGE DUBLIN, where he served as a tutor and a fellow, Berkeley traveled extensively on the Continent and in America. Ordained in 1709, he returned to Ireland and became bishop of Cloyne beginning in 1734. He remains celebrated as a philosopher. His works include *A Treatise concerning the Principles of Human Knowledge* (1710). Berkeley could be categorized as an idealist in that he regarded the existence of the physical world as dependent on the mind's awareness of it, which awareness is a gift of God. The city in California where the celebrated branch of the University of California is located was named after him.

Bernard, John Henry (1860–1927)

academic, archbishop

Educated at Trinity and ordained in 1886, Bernard served as dean of St. Patricks Cathedral in Dublin from 1902 to 1911. He became bishop of Ossory, Ferns, and Leighlin in 1911 and archbishop of Dublin in 1915. He was provost of Trinity from 1919 to 1927. He advocated stern repression of the Easter Week rebels. He participated in the failed IRISH CONVENTION of 1917. Bernard was one of the southern unionists who negotiated with the PROVISIONAL GOVERNMENT in 1922 regarding the formation of the Irish SEANAD.

Best, George (1946–2005)

athlete

A native of Belfast, Best became one of the foremost players for the Manchester United Football (soccer) team, which he joined in 1963. He scored 136 goals in 361 appearances with the team, and he won the league title in 1965 and 1967 and the European Cup in 1968. Best was named the European Player of the Year in 1968.

He also played for Northern Ireland in European competitions between 1964 and 1977. Unfortunately, a disorderly lifestyle, particularly addiction to alcohol, necessitated his retirement at the age of 26. During the past 30 years, he has been imprisoned for drunk driving and assault, has suffered a marital breakup, and has undergone a liver transplant. On November 25, 2005, Best died due to his alcoholism.

Bianconi, Charles (1785–1875)
businessman
Born in Italy, Bianconi came to Ireland in 1802. A traveling peddler until 1806, he started a shop in Carrick-on-Suir, County Tipperary, and subsequently in Waterford, where Ignatius RICE taught him English. He started to run a coach regularly from Clonmel to Cahir in 1815, which by the 1830s had expanded into a system with over 900 horses and more than 60 cars covering on a scheduled basis more than 4,000 miles a day. With the development of railroads he transformed his system into one that provided service to stations from more remote locations. Bianconi became an Irish citizen in 1831 and was a very strong supporter of Daniel O'CONNELL.

Biggar, Joseph Gillis (1828–1890)
politician
Born in Belfast, a provisions merchant, and a Presbyterian, Biggar joined the IRB. He was elected to parliament from Cavan as a HOME RULE supporter in 1874. He was an advocate of obstructionist tactics in parliament, which were taken up by Charles Stewart PARNELL to advance the cause of home rule. The IRB expelled him in 1877 for his parliamentary involvement. Biggar converted to Catholicism the same year.

Binchy, Maeve (1940–)
writer
Dublin-born, Binchy was a secondary school teacher who turned to journalism with in writing for the *IRISH TIMES* in 1968. She then turned

to writing highly successful novels, beginning with *Light a Penny Candle* (1982) and including *Firefly Summer* (1987) and *Glass Lake* (1994), and collections of short stories, such as *The Copper Beech* (1992). Her works deal with such themes as relationships with family and friends, personal secrets, women's experiences in modern Ireland, small-town narrowness, and the concerns of modern popular Irish culture.

Birmingham, George (1865–1950)
clergyman, writer
The pen name of James Owen Hannay, Birmingham was a Belfast-born Church of Ireland clergyman who was curate in Delgany, County Wicklow, and rector in Westport, County Mayo. He was active in the GAELIC LEAGUE and supported NATIONALISM, arguing that the gentry should lead the Irish cause. His criticism of the Catholic clergy prompted his resignation from the Gaelic League. He served as a British army chaplain in 1916 and after the First World War worked in British parishes. His numerous novels dealt with the condition of Ireland. The titles included *Spanish Gold* (1913), *The Lost Tribes* (1914), and *Up the Rebels* (1919).

Birmingham Six
The nickname given to six Irishmen found guilty of the bombing of two Birmingham public houses in 1974 in which 22 were killed. Considerable public and international agitation asserting their innocence finally resulted in the convictions being overturned and their release in 1991. Their names are Hugh Callaghan, Paddy Hill, Gerry Hunter, Richard McIlkenny, Billy Power, and John Walker.

Birrell, Augustine (1850–1933)
politician
Born in Liverpool, Birrell was a Liberal and served as chief secretary for Ireland from 1906 to 1916. While he held that position, the Irish Universities Act (1908) and another Land Pur-

chase Act (1909) were passed. A failure to foresee the brewing tensions leading up to the EASTER RISING prompted his resignation.

Black, Mary (1955–   )

singer

Born in Dublin, Black made two albums with a group called De Danann in 1983. Holding a strongly traditional musical background, she also includes contemporary songs in her repertoire. Her solo albums, such as *No Frontiers* and *Babes in the Wood,* have enjoyed great success in Ireland and internationally.

Black and Tans

Auxiliaries recruited in Britain in 1920 to reinforce the ranks of the ROYAL IRISH CONSTABULARY whose numbers had seriously declined because of IRA attacks and numerous resignations. The nickname was given because uniform shortages required they wear a mixture of the RIC tunics and the British military trousers. They gained a bad reputation for brutality and reprisals. Estimates of their numbers have been placed at about 7,000. They were joined in the middle of 1920 by another force, the AUXILIARIES, who were better paid and recruited from among discharged army officers, but whose reputation was as, if not more, ominous.

Blackburn, Helen (1842–1903)

suffragist

Born in Valentia Island, County Kerry, the daughter of the manager of the island's slate quarries, Blackburn moved with her family to London in 1859. She became involved in the movement for women's suffrage, editing the journal, *Englishwoman's Review* from 1881 to 1890 and later wrote several books, including *The Condition of Working Women* (1896), *Women and the Factory Acts* (1903), and *Women's Suffrage: A Record of the Movement in the British Isles* (1902).

Blackrock College

A secondary school for males in Blackrock, County Dublin, run by the Holy Ghost Fathers, many of its students have played significant roles in the political and cultural life of modern Ireland. Eamon DE VALERA attended and later taught there.

Blaney, Neil (1922–1995)

politician

A native of County Donegal, in 1948 Blaney succeeded his father who had been a FIANNA FÁIL TD since 1927. He became minister for posts and telegraphs in 1957 and the same year became minister for local government, which he held until 1966, when he became minister for agriculture and fisheries. He was dismissed by the TAOISEACH, Jack LYNCH, in 1970 because of his alleged involvement in importing arms for the Provisional IRA. He was subsequently acquitted when charged for doing such. Afterward, Blaney represented himself as a member of Independent Fianna Fáil. He was always very supportive of a strong REPUBLICAN position on NORTHERN IRELAND. He remained a member of the DÁIL ÉIREANN until 1994. He was also a member of the European parliament for Connacht-Ulster from 1979 to 1984 and from 1989 to 1994.

See also BOLAND, KEVIN; HAUGHEY, CHARLES J.

Blaquière, John (1732–1812)

politician

Born in London of Huguenot descent, Blaquière became chief secretary for Ireland in 1772. He was one of the first to effectively replace the UNDERTAKERS in managing the government's business in the Irish parliament, of which he became a member himself in 1773. He remained in Ireland after leaving his post in 1776.

Blarney Castle

A castle in County Cork that had been the residence of the McCarthys of Muskerry, it is a celebrated tourist attraction. Kissing the "Blarney

Blarney Castle in County Cork *(Library of Congress)*

Stone," a stone on the exterior of one of its higher walls, is reputed to give one a gift of eloquence. The origins of the practice stem from a claim that an earlier occupant of the castle had been so eloquent in evading Queen Elizabeth I's demand that he surrender his estates, which would be regranted to him as her vassal, that she remarked that she had enough of his "blarney."

Blasket Islands

A group of islands off the coast of the Dingle Peninsula, County Kerry, whose population reached nearly 200 in the early 20th century, but which became uninhabited in 1953. The islands had been a major source for students of the Gaelic language revival. Several autobiogra-

phies by natives such as Tomas O Criomhthain, Muiris O'Suilleabhain, and Peig Sayers that depicted the traditional way of life became well known in both Irish and English versions. The former TAOISEACH, Charles J. HAUGHEY, owns one of the islands, Inishvickillane, and has a holiday residence there.

Blood, Thomas (1618–1680)
adventurer

A colonel in the Parliamentary Army in the English Civil War who received land in Ireland, Blood led an unsuccessful plot in 1663 of Cromwellians faced with the loss of lands after the Restoration to seize DUBLIN CASTLE and overthrow the duke of ORMOND, the lord lieutenant under Charles II.

Bloody Friday

On Friday, July 21, 1972, in BELFAST the IRA set off 22 bombs within an hour and a quarter in bus and railway stations and shopping centers. Hoax warnings further confused the security and rescue services. Eleven people were killed and 130 were injured. The savagery of the assault, especially the close-up television news coverage of the removal of remains, countered any sympathy the REPUBLICAN cause had gained from the atrocity of BLOODY SUNDAY in Derry a few months before. The British army was subsequently emboldened to under take "Operation Motorman" in bringing an end to the no-go places in Catholic areas that had been tolerated by the authorities since August 1969.

Bloody Sunday, 1921

Michael COLLINS directed raids on the residences of suspected British agents in Dublin early on the morning of Sunday, November 21, 1920. Fourteen agents were killed and six other were wounded. That afternoon, AUXILIARIES, ostensibly searching for IRA members, but more probably in retaliation, fired on a crowd at a football match in Croke Park. Thirteen were killed and 60 were wounded. The same day three REPUBLICAN prisoners were killed "trying to escape" from DUBLIN CASTLE.

Bloody Sunday, 1972

Civil rights demonstrators staged a march attended by at least 10,000 in Derry on Sunday, January 30, 1972, protesting the policy of INTERNMENT. The authorities had outlawed such marches and were able to confine the area of the march to the REPUBLICAN Bogside area. In the late afternoon, members of the Parachute Regiment were ordered to undertake arrests after some disturbances had occurred. The members of the regiment had in the previous weeks undergone encounters with the IRA and its members were primed for armed confrontation. Claiming they were under fire, the soldiers began to fire on the marchers. Fourteen were killed and 12 were wounded. A government

appointed commission lead by Lord Widgery issued a report on the event, which exonerated the soldiers, but it was condemned by the nationalist community and many independent observers present at the incident as a whitewash. Outrage at the event stirred protests throughout Northern Ireland, Ireland, and the United States. In Dublin a protest march ended in the burning of the British embassy on Merrion Square. In 1998 British prime minister Tony Blair established a new commission headed by Lord Saville to report on the events of Bloody Sunday. The report is awaited.

Blount, Charles, Lord Mountjoy   See
MOUNTJOY, CHARLES BLOUNT, LORD.

Poster depicting the victims of the massacre at Derry known as "Bloody Sunday," 1972 *(Library of Congress)*

Blueshirts

Originally called the Army Comrades Association, and formed in 1932 by IRISH FREE STATE army veterans, the group drew support from the ranks of CUMANN NA NGAEDHEAL supporters after Eamon DE VALERA came to power and especially from strong farmers faced with loss of markets for their cattle when the ECONOMIC WAR set in after de Valera refused to forward ANNUITIES to Britain. When Eoin O'DUFFY was dismissed by de Valera as police commissioner in 1933, he became the head of the movement, which began to assume a fascistic style with the wearing of the same colored shirt, marches, and raised arm salutes. An intellectual foundation was provided by the corporatist social position advanced by a number of Irish academics such as Michael TIERNEY and James J. HOGAN. The movement also presented itself as a protective force for critics of the government who feared attacks by the IRA to whom the de Valera government had granted tolerance. De Valera forbade a contemplated march by the movement on Dublin that O'Duffy had called to commemorate the pro-treaty figures, Arthur GRIFFITH, Michael COLLINS, and Kevin O'HIGGINS on August 12, 1933. That rebuff, which had come after FIANNA FÁIL's overwhelming victory in the January 1933 general election, prompted the Blueshirts to join with Cumann na nGaedheal and the CENTRE PARTY to form a new group called FINE GAEL, which O'Duffy would head. Failure at the local government elections in early 1934 and O'Duffy's extravagant style caused a loss of support and he resigned the party leadership, and subsequently lost even the leadership of the Blueshirts. The movement itself soon faded. However, O'Duffy did lead about 700 of his followers to Spain in support of the Nationalist cause in the Spanish Civil War.

Blythe, Ernest (1889–1975)
politician
Born in Magheragall, County Antrim and a Protestant, Blythe joined the GAELIC LEAGUE and the IRB. He was imprisoned in 1916. He represented Monaghan in the DÁIL ÉIREANN from 1919 to 1933 and was in the SEANAD from 1933 to 1936. He was minister for trade and commerce during the first and second Dail and minister for local government in the PROVISIONAL GOVERNMENT. He became minister for finance in the Executive Council of the IRISH FREE STATE from 1923 until 1932. He was also vice president of the Executive Council from 1927 to 1932. He promoted a policy of fiscal orthodoxy as a means of enhancing the credit of the new state. Toward that end, he secured an unpopular reduction of the old age pension. After he withdrew from politics he became managing director of the ABBEY THEATRE, for which he had earlier secured public assistance. A vigorous champion of the Irish language, Blythe wrote several books, some of which, including two volumes of autobiography, are in Irish.

Boland, Eavan (1944–)
poet
Born in Dublin and educated in London and New York, the daughter of an Irish diplomat, Frederick BOLAND, Eavan Boland was lecturer at TRINITY COLLEGE DUBLIN, a literary journalist for the IRISH TIMES. She has taught at Trinity College, University College, and Bowdoin College, and was a member of the International Writing Program at the University of Iowa and, since 1996, a professor at Stamford University in California. She has published several collections of her poems, including *New Territory* (1967), *The War Horse* (1975), *In Her Own Image* (1980), *Night Feed* (1982), *Outside History* (1990), and *In a Time of Violence* (1994). She has also written a prose memoir, *Object Lessons: The Life of the Woman and the Poet in Our Time* (1995). Her work has dealt with contemporary Irish society in general, but with women's concerns in particular. She holds a position of preeminence especially among female poets, as well as among the many celebrated poets of Ireland in the second half of the 20th century.

Boland, Frederick Henry (1904–1988)
diplomat
Born in Dublin, educated at CLONGOWES WOOD COLLEGE, TRINITY COLLEGE DUBLIN, and the KING'S

INN, Boland joined the Department of External Affairs in 1929. He served as principal officer in the Department of Commerce from 1936 to 1938, but returned to External Affairs where he was secretary of the department until 1950. He became ambassador to the United Kingdom and then Permanent Representative to the United Nations from 1956 to 1964. He was an extraordinary diplomat dealing with such strong willed ministers for foreign affairs as Seán MacBride and Frank Aiken, as well as representing non-aligned Ireland in the beginning and at the height of the cold war. His most celebrated role was in 1961, when, as president of the General Assembly of the United Nations, he gavelled Soviet leader Nikita Khrushchev to order when he was disrupting a speaker.

Boland, Gerald (1885–1973)
politician
Born in Manchester, Boland took part in the EASTER RISING. He represented Roscommon in the Dail from 1919 to 1961, although not attending from 1922 to 1927 as an opponent of the 1921 ANGLO-IRISH TREATY. A founding member of the FIANNA FÁIL Party, he served as minister for posts and telegraph from 1933 to 1936, for lands from 1936 to 1939, and for justice from 1939 to 1948. In the later post, he implemented stringent measures against the IRA, including establishment of military tribunals and institutional internment, and he had to contend with hunger strikes and carry out executions. Boland sat in the SEANAD from 1961 to 1969.

Boland, Harry (1887–1922)
republican revolutionary
Born in Dublin, Boland joined the IRISH REPUBLICAN BROTHERHOOD and was active in the GAELIC ATHLETIC ASSOCIATION. He was a very close friend of Michael COLLINS. Imprisoned for his part in the EASTER RISING, he was involved in the reorganization of the Irish Volunteers and Sinn Féin, while remaining prominent in the IRB. Along with his brother, Gerald BOLAND, he

represented Roscommon in the first and second DÁIL ÉIREANN. He was a member of the Dáil delegation to the United States during the WAR OF INDEPENDENCE, where he was closely associated with Eamon DE VALERA in contending with rival American support groups. Boland opposed the ANGLO-IRISH TREATY and sided with the insurgents in the CIVIL WAR. He was shot in its early stages and died a few days later as a prisoner.

Boland, Kevin (1917–2001)
politician
Son of Gerald BOLAND, Kevin Boland was born in Dublin and was a FIANNA FÁIL member for Dublin South from 1957 to 1970. He served as minister for defense from 1957 to 1961, for social welfare from 1961 to 1966, and for local government from 1966 to 1970. He broke with the government of Jack LYNCH over the dismissal of Neil BLANEY and Charles J. HAUGHEY in 1970 over alleged importation of weapons to REPUBLICANS in NORTHERN IRELAND. Expelled from the parliamentary party, he resigned from Fianna Fail that same year and started his own movement, Aontacht Éireann, which failed to gain any significant following. He continued to attack the Irish government's failure to pursue a more vigorous irredentist policy on Northern Ireland and unsuccessfully challenged the SUNNINGDALE AGREEMENT in the Supreme Court on the grounds that the Irish government ought not to acknowledge British sovereignty over Northern Ireland.

bombing campaigns in Britain
Irish revolutionary nationalists have always been drawn to the concept of taking the war to the enemy, that is, to the British mainland. Efforts to the end have very often backfired in that the casualties were frequently innocent bystanders and popular outrage spurred vigorous opposition to the perpetrators of the deeds. A gunpowder explosion at CLERKENWELL prison in London in 1867 in an attempt to free Fenians failed in its objective, but the incident produced a good number of innocent victims. The IRA

declared war on Britain in early 1939 and planted a number of bombs or explosive devices throughout the country in railroad stations, public lavatories, and postboxes. About half a dozen people were killed and over a hundred were wounded. During the modern troubles, since 1969, there were various bombings in Britain of public figures, the military, public houses, department stores, and major buildings. A car bomb planted by the Official IRA at the Aldershot Military Barracks in February 1972 killed five female employees, a gardener, and a Catholic chaplain. Eleven British soldiers died as a result of explosions at Knightsbridge and Regent's Park, London. Ten bandsmen were killed and more than a score injured from a bomb at the Royal Marines School of Music in Kent. A bomb planted in his car parked at the House of Commons killed the Conservative spokesperson on Northern Ireland, Airey Neave, in March 1979. A bomb explosion in October 1984 at the Grand Hotel in Brighton during the Conservative Party Conference killed five and injured several others, and narrowly missed Prime Minister Margaret Thatcher. Bombings of pubs in Guildford and in Birmingham in October and November 1974 in which a total of more than 20 were killed and more than two hundred injured stirred great outrage and prompted the introduction of severe antiterrorist legislation. Several people were wrongly convicted in both cases, although exonerated many years later. Extensive damage to the London Stock Exchange in 1990, the Baltic Exchange in 1992, and the Nat-West Tower in 1993, which also saw a smaller number of deaths, suggested a new IRA tactic of aiming to inflict substantial material damage as a means of discouraging British commitment to the maintenance of the union with Northern Ireland. The 1994 IRA cease-fire was called off in February 1996 by means of a bomb near the Carnary Wharf building in London at which two were killed and more than a hundred injured. Before the current cease-fire was called in 1997, there was also a massive bombing in the center of Manchester where almost miraculously there were no deaths. Some argue that it was the later bombings more than the earlier ones, which had more personal but less material damage, that made the British government more disposed to deal with the IRA in the hope it would confine its activities to Northern Ireland.

See also BIRMINGHAM SIX; GUILDFORD FOUR.

Bonner, Packie (1960–   )
football player

A native of County Donegal, he played as goalkeeper for the Glasgow Celtic from 1979 until 1994, and with them he made around 500 League appearances and won four League Championship badges, three Scottish Cup winners' medals, and a League Cup winners' medal. He became a regular on the Irish team under the management of Jack Charlton, achieving legendary status during the European Championship campaign in 1988 and in the World Cup competition in 1990 where Ireland reached the quarter-finals and where his skill in a penalty shootout against Romania even received the acknowledgment of Pope John Paul II. He retired in 1994.

Bono   See U2.

Border Campaign

A series of bombings and raids by the IRA in Northern Ireland, especially near the border, that began in late 1956 and was called off in 1962, although it had petered out long before then. The more enthusiastic participants were IRA members from the Republic, two of whom were killed in a foiled raid on a RUC barracks at Brookesborough, County Fermanagh. One of them, Sean South of Garryowen, County Limerick, received an unofficial hero's funeral, and four SINN FÉIN candidates were returned to the DÁIL ÉIREANN in the next general election. However, the authorities in both Northern Ireland and the Irish Republic acted firmly against the campaign, imposing internment in both jurisdictions. The lack of sympathy with the campaign on the part of the Catholic population in Northern Ireland, especially in cities such as DERRY and BELFAST, ultimately convinced the leaders of its futility. Nineteen people died as a result of the campaign.

Bord Fáilte Éireann
(Irish Tourist Board)

A public board established in 1955 to promote tourism to Ireland, it replaced earlier agencies, which had become dormant during the Second World War or had concerned themselves with domestic tourism. The new board sought to draw external visitors to Ireland by carrying out advertising and promotional campaigns overseas by establishing standards by monitoring hotels, guesthouses, and restaurants within Ireland, and by subsidizing local agencies promoting festivals and tourist attractions. Its overseas role was absorbed by Tourism Ireland in 2001, a joint venture by the governments of both Ireland and Northern Ireland. It continues, however, its domestic activities of monitoring and promotion.

Bord Na Mona

Originally established as the Turf Development Board Ltd in 1933, it received its new title in 1946. The agency carries out drainage of substantial bogs in Ireland and harvests the turf or peat extracted from them to fuel electric generating stations, to make peat briquettes for domestic fuel purposes, and to produce horticultural peat moss for a worldwide market. Its director from 1934 to 1958 was C. S. "Todd" ANDREWS.

Boucicault, Dion (1820–1890)
dramatist

A Dublin native, Boucicault was one of the most successful and popular dramatists of the 19th century whose work appeared in Ireland, Britain, France, the United States, and Australia. His numerous plays ranged from comedy to melodrama. Three in particular carried an Irish theme: *The Colleen Bawn* (1860), *Arrah-na-Pogue* (1864), and *The Shaughraun* (1874). His spendthrift life style was unrestrained.

Boundary Commission

Established in accord with the ANGLO-IRISH TREATY of 1921 when NORTHERN IRELAND opted out of inclusion in the IRISH FREE STATE, it sought to revise the boundary between both sections "in accordance with the wishes of the inhabitants, so far as may be compatible with economic and geographic conditions." The commission was not formed until the later part of 1924, with delays occasioned by British efforts to develop alternative compromises to the commission. The members were to be appointed by the governments of Northern Ireland, the Irish Free State, and Great Britain, respectively, with the appointee of the latter serving as chairman. Eoin MACNEIL was the Free State member and Richard FEETHAM, a South Africa justice, was the British appointed chair. A further delay resulted from the Northern Ireland government's refusal to appoint a member to the commission. A ruling by the Privy Council required legislation, passed in both Britain and the Free State, to authorize the British to appoint someone for them. A Northern barrister and a unionist, J. R. Fisher, was named. The commissions' inquiry took several months from late 1924 through early 1925. To avoid the inevitable social disharmony that would ensue from the publication of its report, which would take effect immediately, the commissioners agreed to issue a single report without a minority statement. Unfortunately, the Free State member did not understand until the end that the chair was operating from different premises as to their mandate. Feetham assumed, and Fisher concurred, that they were to make adjustments, rather than substantial revisions, of the boundary so that the integrity of Northern Ireland would not be endangered. This conception clashed with the expectation of the nationalists in both jurisdictions that there would be substantial changes of territory. On November 7, 1925, a Conservative newspaper, the *Morning Post,* leaked the expected report ahead of time and it caused immense consternation in the Free State since it called for relatively minor transfers of territory and population, with part of the transfer involving territory from the Free State, rather than exclusively from Northern Ireland. MacNeill refused to sign the final report and resigned from the commission and from his position as minister for education. A Free State delegation, led by the president of the Executive Council of the Free State, William T. COSGRAVE, and the vice president and minister for justice, Kevin O'HIGGINS, negotiated with members of the British cabinet and with James CRAIG, the Northern Ireland prime minister, from November 28 through December 3. Agreement was reached to maintain the status quo boundary, to suspend and keep secret for almost 40 years the still unpublished commission report, and to relieve the Free State of its treaty obligation to assume liability for its proportionate share of the United Kingdom's public debt at the time of the treaty, which sum had not yet been determined.

Bowen, Elizabeth (1899–1973)
writer

Born and raised in Dublin as well as in the family home in Cork, Bowen's Court, Mitchelstown, Bowen lived at different times in Ireland, England, and the United States. She moved permanently to Kent in 1959 after selling the house that was the subject of her 1942 book, *Bowen's Court,* which gives a picture of ANGLO-IRISH Ireland. The theme of the "Big House" and of ancestors appears in much of her writing such as the novel *The Last September* (1929). She reported on Irish attitudes to the British Ministry of Information during the Second World War. Another novel, *A World of Love* (1955), was set in Ireland. She also wrote *Seven Winters: Memoirs of a Dublin Childhood* (1943). Her many other novels are not Irish in subject or theme, but reflect the same introspective character, such as *The Hotel* (1927), *The House in Paris* (1935), and *Friends and Relations* (1931).

Boycott, Captain Hugh (1832–1897)
land agent

He was the agent on the Earl of Erne's estate at Lough Mask, County Mayo, who was the object of the "moral Coventry" called for by Charles Stewart PARNELL in September 1880 to be employed against the opponents of the LAND LEAGUE. The refusal of locals to work for him necessitated transporting laborers from Ulster; however, the cost of protecting them with troops far outweighed the return from the harvest. His name became the common word in the English language for similar protests of abstaining from dealing with an offending person or enterprise.

Boyle, Henry   See SHANNON, HENRY BOYLE, EARL OF.

Boyle, Richard (1566–1643)
adventurer, politician

Born in Canterbury, England, Boyle came to Ireland in 1588 and soon established a fortune by challenging the title to various properties of the native Irish. He purchased the estate in Munster that Sir Walter Raleigh had acquired as the plantation in the province. He constructed towns, bridges, roads, and ironworks, and was an improving landlord. He was made Earl of Cork in 1620 and a lord justice of Ireland in 1629. He resisted Thomas WENTWORTH's ascendancy in Ireland in the 1630s and was a leading champion of Protestant interests during the wars of the 1640s.

Boyle, Robert (1627–1691)
scientist

The youngest son of Richard BOYLE, the earl of Cork, Robert Boyle was born in Lismore, County Waterford. Educated in England, he spent most of the rest of his life there, although he possessed Irish estates. A classic example of an empiricist and disciple of the scientific method, he devoted his energies to scientific enquiry, although he also wrote on philosophy and theology. Called the "father of chemistry," Boyle contributed to the emergence of the discipline from alchemy to an experimental science. He invented the vacuum pump and developed "Boyle's Law," which deals with the inverse proportion of the pressure and the volume of a gas.

Boyne, Battle of the

The battle between the armies of King WILLIAM III and King JAMES II on July 1, 1690 (July 12 in the newer or Gregorian calendar later adopted in Britain), which turned the tide decisively in favor of the Williamite forces. The armies were quite international in character as William's force of 36,000 included English, Dutch, German, and Ulster Protestants, while James's army of 27,000 included 7,000 French. Louis XIV of France supported James as a means to distract the international alliance that had been created to oppose him. In the battle itself, some of William's forces crossed the Boyne River to the west prompting major portions of James's forces to be drawn toward them, and leaving the eastern front relatively exposed. William then sent the bulk of his army across the river at that point outflanking James, whose forces then retreated in panic. Total casualties were relatively small, 1,000 JACOBITES and 500 Williamites. James fled to France and William gained control of most of the east of Ireland. The final defeat of the Jacobite forces would not be for more than another year, but the annual commemoration of the Battle of the Boyne by Unionists in Northern Ireland has made it the more remembered victory.

Bracken, Brendan (1901–1958)

politician, publisher

Born in Templemore, County Tipperary, Bracken left school at Mungret College, Limerick, and went to Australia, and then to England, where he became involved in publishing, founding the *Banker*, which was later called *Investor's Chronicle*, and later becoming chairman of the *Financial Times* and founder of *History Today*. He worked in Winston Churchill's election campaigns, himself served in parliament from 1929 to 1951, and became parliamentary private secretary to Churchill from 1939 to 1941 and minister of information from 1941 to 1945. Bracken was made a viscount in 1952.

Branagh, Kenneth (1960–)

actor, director

Born in Belfast to a working-class family, Branagh moved with his family to Reading when he was nine years old. He was trained at the Royal Academy of Dramatic Art and began performing with the Royal Shakespeare Company when he was 23, and he secured several leading roles. He performed in television plays; particularly a trilogy entitled *Billy* about Northern Ireland Protestantism. He started his own company, the Renaissance Theatre Company, in 1987 and directed and acted in several of its films. One of the more celebrated, *Henry V,* gained Academy Award nominations for best director and actor. Branagh has continued to both act in and direct a number of other films, most notably Shakespearean plays but also others, such as *Dead Again* (1991), *Peter's Friends* (1992), and *Wild Wild West* (1999).

Breen, Dan (1894–1969)

revolutionary and politician

Born near Soloheadbeg, County Tipperary, this son of a small farmer became involved in the IRB and the IRISH VOLUNTEERS. He took part in the ambush of police escorts for explosives near Soloheadbeg in which two policemen were killed on January 21, 1919, the same day that the first DÁIL ÉIREANN assembled. The incident is regarded as the first armed encounter in the WAR OF INDEPENDENCE. Breen was very active in IRA actions throughout the war in Munster and in Dublin, earning for him the distinction of a formidable price being put on his head by the authorities. He opposed the ANGLO-IRISH TREATY and was an ABSTENTIONIST TD for Tipperary from 1922 until 1927, when he lost running as an independent. In 1932 he was elected for Tipperary for FIANNA FÁIL and served until 1965. Breen wrote about his revolutionary exploits in *My Fight for Irish Freedom* (1924).

Brendan, Saint (500–577)

monk, navigator

Born near Ardfert, County Kerry, Brendan is celebrated for his voyages, described in the early medieval text *Naviagatio Brendani*, which he made with a dozen associates in a currach. The conclusion can be drawn from the account that they sailed as far as Iceland, Greenland, and possibly the east coast of North America. The feasibility of the exploit has been substantiated by a comparable voyage in a leather boat undertaken by 20th-century explorer Tim Severin, who titled his book, the *Brendan Voyage* (1977), after the saint's account.

Brennan, Robert (1881–1964)
revolutionary, diplomat
Born in Wexford, Brennan served as the commander of the IRISH VOLUNTEERS in Wexford during the EASTER RISING, for which he was given a death sentence, later commuted to life imprisonment, and soon after released. He organized a Department for External Affairs for the first DÁIL ÉIREANN government in 1919. He opposed the ANGLO-IRISH TREATY. From 1930 to 1934, Brennan was the director of the *IRISH PRESS* that had been founded by Eamon DE VALERA to advance the fortunes of his party, FIANNA FÁIL. He returned to diplomatic service and was minister to Washington from 1938 to 1947.

Brian Boru (941–1014)
high king of Ireland
Born in Clare, a member of the Dal Cais family, Brian Boru revenged the death of his brother, who had been king of Munster, and assumed the same title himself in 976. By 1002 he had successfully challenged the O'Neills, usually the holders of the title, to the High Kingship of Ireland, and their acquiescence to his claim was acknowledged in the Book of Armagh. A rebellion in Leinster joined by the VIKINGS led to a decisive battle at Clontarf, Dublin, on April 23, 1014, where his forces triumphed, but he was killed. The victory ended the Viking challenge to ascendancy in Ireland, even though the Danes had invaded and conquered England the year before.

Brighton bombing See BOMBING
CAMPAIGNS IN BRITAIN.

Brigid, Saint (450–523)
saint
Foundress of a convent and church in Kildare, Bridget was the subject of biographies that were closely connected with asserting the ascendancy of Armagh in the Irish Church. The devotion to her and the legends that developed as to her miraculous and intercessory powers were often intertwined with and/or drawn from the accounts of a pre-Christian Celtic goddess named Brigantia. Her feast day, February 1, continues to serve as an occasion for practicing traditional folk customs. A St. Brigid's cross, woven from rushes, is common in many households.

Bristol, Frederick Augustus Hervey, fourth earl of (1730–1803)
bishop, patriot
Educated at Cambridge and having taken holy orders, Bristol was made bishop of Cloyne in 1767 and then of Derry in 1768 at a time his brother served as the lord lieutenant of Ireland. He succeeded his brother to the earldom of Bristol in 1774. Despite his background, he was a "Patriot" politically, as he became very involved in the IRISH VOLUNTEERS, sympathized with the American grievances, and championed political rights for Catholics. He spent many of his later years on the Continent, where he was involved in a scandalous affair with the mistress of King William II of Prussia.

Broderick, John See MIDLETON, BRODERICK, ST. JOHN, FIRST EARL.

Brontë, Patrick (1777–1861)
clergyman, poet
Born in County Down, Brontë was educated in Cambridge and ordained in the Church of England. When he arrived in England he changed his name from Prunty. He was a curate in various places in Essex and Shropshire and became permanent vicar in Haworth, Yorkshire, in 1820, where he remained until his death. He wrote

poetry, but Brontë is more renowned as the father of three daughters, Anne, Charlotte, and Emily, famous for their writings. He outlived his wife and all seven of his children.

Brooke, Sir Basil, Viscount Brookeborough See BROOKEBOROUGH, SIR BASIL BROOKE, VISCOUNT.

Brookeborough, Sir Basil Brooke, Viscount (1888–1973)
politician
Born in County Fermanagh, educated at Winchester and Sandhurst, Brooke earned the Military Cross and the Cross de Guerre in the First World War. He resigned from the military in 1920 and was elected to the Northern Ireland Senate in 1921. He resigned from that to head the Ulster Special Constabulary in 1922. Elected to the Northern Ireland PARLIAMENT in 1929 as a UNIONIST, he became minister of agriculture in 1933 and minister of commerce and production in 1941. A leader among those who forced the ouster of John ANDREWS as prime minister to introduce newer and younger figures in government, Brooke succeeded him in 1943 and remained prime minister for 20 years. His period in power coincided with the postwar extension to Northern Ireland of the full benefits of the British welfare state, as all previous fiscal restrictions on the province's receipt of benefits were removed, and with significant economic modernization and improvement. The last factor may well have contributed to the minimal following among the Northern Ireland Catholic community for the IRA's BORDER CAMPAIGN of 1956 to 1962. His attitude toward the Catholic community was narrow and unsympathetic, as he made occasional remarks that were bigoted and dismissed employees from his personal estates because of their religion.

Brosnan, Pierce (1953–)
movie actor
Born in County Meath, Brosnan's first film role was in *The Long Good Friday* (1976). He also was in the television detective series *Remington Steele.* Other films in which he appeared include *Mister Johnson* (1991), *Mrs. Doubtfire* (1993), and *The Thomas Crown Affair* (1999). In 1995 Brosnan succeeded a series of other actors, including Sean Connery, in being cast as James Bond in *GoldenEye* (1995) and continued in the role until 2005.

Brown, Christy (1932–1981)
writer
Born in Crumlin, Dublin, one of 13 children of a bricklayer, Brown suffered from cerebral palsy from birth. Heroic efforts by his mother resulted in his acquiring the ability to read and to write with his foot. He wrote his memories of his childhood in *My Left Foot* (1954) and a fictional work along the same theme, *Down All the Days* (1970), which was translated into many languages. His first work was made into a film by Jim SHERIDAN in 1990 and earned an Oscar. Other novels were less successful, although his first volume of poetry, *Come Softly to My Wake* (1971), was a best-seller.

Browne, Michael (1887–1971)
Dominican friar, cardinal
Born in County Tipperary, educated at Rockwell College and at Rome and Fribourg, Browne was ordained a priest in 1910. He lectured in philosophy at the Angelicum University in Rome from 1919 and served as its rector from 1932 to 1941. Elected as master-general of the Dominican Order in 1955, Browne was made a bishop and cardinal in 1962 and played an important role in the proceedings of the Second Vatican Council.

Browne, Michael (1896–1980)
bishop
Born in Westport, County Mayo, and educated at St. Jarllath's College, Tuam, and Maynooth, where he was professor of theology from 1921 to 1937, Browne became bishop of Galway in

1937. He supervised the construction of numerous schools and churches during his tenure in office, including the opening of a new cathedral in 1966.

Browne, Noel (1915–1997)
physician, politician

Born in Waterford and educated at Beaumont College, London, and at TRINITY COLLEGE DUBLIN, Browne dedicated much of his energies to combating tuberculosis, which had killed his own parents. He was elected to the DÁIL ÉIREANN in 1948 as a member of CLANN NA POBLACHTA and was appointed minister for health in the coalition government formed then. In that post he was successful in combating tuberculosis but was less successful in advancing a MOTHER AND CHILD SCHEME. Plans to establish free universal obstetric and pediatric care programs incurred the opposition of the medical profession, apprehensive about its revenue, and the Roman Catholic hierarchy, fearful that the system would open the door to state sponsorship of medical procedures and practices incompatible with Catholic moral teaching. When the TAOISEACH, John A. COSTELLO of FINE GAEL, and his own party leader, Minister for External Affairs Seán MACBRIDE, acquiesced in the opposition, Browne resigned his office and membership in the party. He was reelected to the Dáil as an independent from 1951 to 1953. In 1957 he was returned as an independent and held office until 1963. He founded the small and short-lived National Progressive Democratic Party in 1958. Then he joined the LABOUR PARTY and was elected in the 1969 general election and was returned as a senator in 1973. In 1977 again an independent, he was returned to the SEANAD, where he served until 1981. He remained an outspoken champion of leftist and anticlerical positions, writing an outspoken autobiography, *Against the Tide*, in 1986.

Browne, Patrick   See DE BRÚN, PÁDRAIG.

Browne, Valentine   See KENMARE, VALENTINE BROWNE, VISCOUNT CASTLEROSSE, SIXTH EARL OF.

Broy, Eamon (1887–1972)
police commissioner

Born in County Kildare, Broy was a civil servant employed in DUBLIN CASTLE and specifically with the secret service arm during the WAR OF INDEPENDENCE. He cooperated with Michael COLLINS in providing him with vital information, even giving him access to the files in the castle. He was ultimately arrested, but released during the truce. He served in senior positions in the DUBLIN METROPOLITAN POLICE in the IRISH FREE STATE. In February 1933 Eamon DE VALERA appointed him police commissioner to succeed Eoin O'DUFFY. He employed reportedly ex-IRA members to serve as an armed police auxiliary to counter the BLUESHIRTS, especially to resist their threatened march on Dublin in August 1933 and any interference with bailiffs seizing cattle from farmers during the ECONOMIC WAR. This group was nicknamed the "Broy Harriers." In 1938 he retired and withdrew from the public arena.

Brugha, Cathal (1874–1922)
revolutionary

Born in Dublin and a student at Belvedere College, Brugha later worked in a church supplies firm and for a candle manufacturer. Active in the GAELIC ATHLETIC ASSOCIATION, the GAELIC LEAGUE, and the IRISH VOLUNTEERS, he was second in command at the South Dublin Union during the EASTER RISING, when he suffered a permanent wound. Elected to the first DÁIL ÉIREANN for County Waterford, he was selected as its president at the opening session on January 21, 1919, pending the escape from jail by Eamon DE VALERA. He was minister for defense during the WAR OF INDEPENDENCE. Regarded along with Austin STACK as the champions of the more militant REPUBLICAN position, Brugha opposed the ANGLO-IRISH TREATY both in the cabinet and in the Dáil debates and fought with the IRREGULARS in the CIVIL WAR. He was fatally wounded in a flamboyant resistance to surrender at the Hamman Hotel on O'Connell Street in Dublin on July 7, 1922, and died two days later.

Brunswick Clubs

Organizations of Protestants formed in opposition to Catholic emancipation in 1827 and 1828, comparable in organizational style, if not numbers, to the CATHOLIC ASSOCIATION. They were a popular movement closely allied politically with the Tory Party in Ireland.

Bruton, John (1947–)

politician

Born in Dublin, educated at CLONGOWES WOOD COLLEGE, University College Dublin, and the KING'S INN, Bruton was a member of DÁIL ÉIREANN for County Meath from 1969 to 2004. He was parliamentary secretary to several ministers in the coalition government of 1973–77 and was minister for finance in the coalition government of 1981–82, and minister for energy, then for trade, commerce, and tourism, and again for finance in the coalition government of 1982–87. He became leader of the FINE GAEL Party in 1990, replacing Alan DUKES, against whom he had contested the leadership position after the resignation of Garret FITZGERALD in 1987. He became TAOISEACH in 1994, following a vote of no confidence when the LABOUR PARTY withdrew from a governing coalition with FIANNA FÁIL. His government was nicknamed the RAINBOW COALITION in view of the contrasting ideology of its members, Fine Gael, Labour, and the Democratic Left. In February 1995 he and British prime minister John Major issued a FRAMEWORKS DOCUMENT based on the earlier DOWNING STREET DECLARATION of 1993. Both documents guided Anglo-Irish relations on the Northern Ireland issue and set the premises on which the ultimate GOOD FRIDAY AGREEMENT of 1998 was based. Bruton staunchly opposed both provocative ORANGE ORDER marches and IRA–SINN FÉIN intransigence. The latter abandoned their 1994

cease-fire in February 1996. The coalition under Bruton oversaw a doubling in the rate of economic growth and a reduction in inflation and unemployment. A constitutional amendment allowing divorce, supported by the government, was narrowly passed. The coalition government ended with electoral defeat in 1997 when Fianna Fail formed a coalition with the PROGRESSIVE DEMOCRATS. Bruton was challenged as party leader in early 2001 and replaced by Michael NOONAN, who was himself replaced following the party's electoral defeat in 2002 by Enda KENNY. Bruton, who continued to serve in the Dáil, was appointed as one of the Irish members of the drafting committee for a constitution for the European Union. In 2004, he became the European Union's ambassador to the United States.

Bryce, James (1838–1922)

historian, politician

Born in Belfast, educated at the University of Glasgow, and at Oxford and Heidelberg, Bryce was Regius Professor of Civil Law at Oxford from 1870 to 1893. He was a Liberal member of parliament and held assorted undersecretarial- and cabinet-level positions, including serving as chief secretary for Ireland from 1905 to 1907, when he became ambassador to the United States. He supported Home Rule and urged Ulster unionists to accept the fact and work out protections for themselves within a united Ireland. Bryce received numerous academic honors and wrote extensively, including *The American Commonwealth* (1888).

B Specials See ULSTER DEFENSE REGIMENT.

Bull, Lucien (1876–1972)

inventor

Born in Dublin, Bull was educated at the University of Paris and became an assistant to Dr. Etienne-Jules Marey in his cinematography laboratory. Specializing in ultrarapid cinematography, he was able to record 500 images per second by 1902. Six years later he invented the electrocardiograph. By 1952 he was able to record one million images per second. Other areas of his research included optical illusions and sound waves.

Burke, Edmund (1729–1797)
politician, political theorist

Born in Dublin, Burke's mother was a Catholic while his father conformed to the CHURCH OF IRELAND to gain admission to the law. Educated at a Quaker school in Kildare, at TRINITY COLLEGE DUBLIN, and at the Middle Temple in London, he abandoned law for literary pursuits. He wrote philosophical works such as *A Vindication of Natural Society* (1756) and *A Philosophical Inquiry into the Origin of Our Ideas of the Sublime and Beautiful* (1757), was editor and contributor to the *Annual Register,* and was a close associate of Samuel Johnson and Oliver Goldsmith. He was the private secretary to William Hamilton, the chief secretary for Ireland from 1759 to 1764, and the following year served in the same post for the Marquis of Rockingham. Burke was elected that year to parliament. As a Whig he wrote *Thoughts on the Cause of Our Present Discontents* (1770), which was critical of court influence on parliament. He was sympathetic to American grievances as evidenced in his celebrated *Speech on American Taxation* (1774) and *Speech on Conciliation with America* (1775), in which he argued that imposing taxes on the colonies or denying the colonists British liberties was impolitic. He identified with the group led by Rockingham and advocated economic reform, that is, the restraining of the use of royal patronage to influence parliament. He served as paymaster of the forces in the 1782 ministry of Rockingham, which was short-lived because of Rockingham's death. He held the same post in the similarly brief Fox-North coalition of 1783. He devoted much of his energies from 1786 to 1788 in advocating the impeachment of Warren Hastings, the governor-general of Bengal, for abuses against the natives by the East India Company. From 1789 on he directed all his energies to combating the French

Revolution, even to the point that he broke with longtime Whig allies such as Charles James Fox. His *Reflections on the Revolution in France* (1790) became the foremost criticism of the premises on which the revolution was based, as he defended adherence to traditional and organically developed social institutions and opposed attempts to reconstruct society according to abstractions. His work provoked the pro-revolutionary *Rights of Man* by Tom Paine. Burke continued in his criticism of the conciliatory attitude of his former Whig associates to the revolution and of any appeasing inclinations in his *Appeal from the New to the Old Whigs* (1791) and his *Letters on a Regicide Peace* (1796). His writings on the revolution remain to this day the leading statement from a conservative political perspective. With regard to his native Ireland, Burke, who had married the daughter of an Irish Catholic doctor, Jane Mary Nugent, in 1759, did not let his conservative hostility to revolution make him unsympathetic to gaining relief for the Catholic majority, who were enduring political, social, and economic impediments under the PROTESTANT ASCENDANCY.

Burke, Thomas Henry (1829–1882)
politician

Born in Galway, Burke was a public servant in the chief secretary for Ireland's office, and became undersecretary in 1869 until 1882 when he and the newly appointed chief secretary, Lord Frederick Cavendish, were murdered by the INVINCIBLES, a splinter wing of the FENIANS, while walking in PHOENIX PARK Dublin, on May 6.

Burntollet Ambush

Burntollet Bridge in County Derry was the scene on January 4, 1969, of an attack by at least 200 loyalists on a civil rights march from Belfast to Derry that had been organized by the radical student group called PEOPLE'S DEMOCRACY. Many of the attackers were members of the B Specials, the police auxiliary, and the police forces protecting the marchers seemed unwilling to seriously protect the marchers. Despite many injuries the march continued on into Derry. The incident was one of the major events that drew world attention to the grievances of the Northern Ireland minority.

Burren

A large area of exposed limestone in the northwest of County Clare extending to the Aran Islands that is rich in geological and archaeological remains. The fissures in the limestone also serve as excellent habitats for great varieties of rare flora.

Butler, Hubert (1900–1991)
essayist

Born in Kilkenny and educated at Oxford, Butler traveled extensively, particularly to the Balkans. He was outspoken in his criticism of the Catholic Church, particularly for its alleged complicity with Nazi atrocities in Croatia, and of Irish Catholic disinterest in the same. He was a champion of nuclear disarmament and religious pluralism, and opposed the antiabortion amendment in 1983. Butler wrote for THE BELL and published collections of his essays, such as *Escape from the Anthill* (1985) and *Grandmother and Wolfe Tone* (1990).

Butler, James   See ORMOND, JAMES BUTLER, 12TH EARL AND FIRST DUKE OF.

Butt, Issac (1813–1879)
politician

Born in County Donegal, the son of a CHURCH OF IRELAND rector, Butt studied at TRINITY COLLEGE DUBLIN where he was a professor of political economy from 1836 to 1841. He became a barrister and was a committed unionist, vigorously opposed to Daniel O'CONNELL. As a barrister he came to defend the YOUNG IRELANDERS and later the FENIANS. By the late 1860s, especially following William Gladstone's disestablishment of the Church of Ireland, he concluded that Ire-

land, including the PROTESTANT ASCENDANCY, would be better served by being more autonomous from Britain. He formed the HOME GOVERNMENT ASSOCIATION in 1870, out of which grew the Home Rule League, which gained 59 of the 103 Irish seats in parliament in the 1874 election. While the movement originally had a substantial Protestant component, it quickly became more decidedly Catholic and nationalist. Members such as Joseph BIGGAR and Charles Stewart PARNELL advocated a tactic of parliamentary obstruction to advance consideration of their goals, but Butt opposed them. In 1877 Butt lost the leadership of the support organization, the Home Rule Confederation of Great Britain, of which Parnell became president, and, in February 1879, he narrowly escaped defeat on a motion of no confidence within his parliamentary group. He died brokenhearted the following May.

Byrne, Edward (1872–1940)
bishop

Born in Dublin and educated at Belvedere College and at the Irish College in Rome, Byrne was ordained a priest in 1895. He served as curate in various Dublin parishes and as rector of the Irish College from 1901 to 1904. He was curate of the Pro-Cathedral in Dublin until 1920 when he became auxiliary bishop and in 1921 succeeded William WALSH as archbishop of Dublin. Byrne tried to foster a peace settlement between the PROVISIONAL GOVERNMENT and the anti-treaty IRREGULARS. Afterward, he maintained cordial relations with both the CUMANN NA NGAEDHEAL government of William T. COSGRAVE and his successor Eamon DE VALERA. He presided over the celebration of the Centenary of Catholic emancipation in 1929 and the EUCHARISTIC CONGRESS in 1932.

Byrne, Gabriel (1950–)
actor

Born in Dublin, Byrne played with the Dublin Shakespeare Society and then at theaters, including the Focus and the ABBEY. He appeared in the Irish television series, *The Riordans,* and in numerous films, including *Defence of the Realm* (1985), *Miller's Crossing* (1990), *Into the West* (1992), and *The Usual Suspects* (1995) and was a co-producer of *In the Name of the Father* (1993).

Byrne, Gay (1934–)
broadcaster

Born in Dublin, Byrne became a broadcaster for Radio Éireann in 1958. He was the presenter for the television program, *The Late Late Show* on Radio Telefís Éireann from its inception in 1962 until his retirement in 1999. For several years he acted as presenter for the televised finals of the festival and competition known as *The Rose of Tralee,* and he did radio work as well. His programs, especially *The Late Late Show* are regarded as having contributed immensely to the increased openness in Irish society in discussing familial, moral, and sexual matters. Gay has won numerous television awards and an honorary doctorate from TRINITY COLLEGE DUBLIN. In 1999 he was awarded the freedom of the city of Dublin. In 1989 he wrote his autobiography titled *The Time of My Life.*

C

Callan, Nicholas (1799–1864)
priest, inventor

Born in Dundalk, County Louth, and educated at the Dundalk Academy by Presbyterian Minister William Neilson, Callan went to MAYNOOTH in 1816 to study for the priesthood, being ordained in 1823. He then obtained his Doctorate of Divinity at Sapienza University in Rome. Returning to Maynooth, he became a professor of natural philosophy and devoted himself to the study of electrical science. Callan invented the induction coil, which led to the modern transformer, and he developed various types of batteries and other electrical apparatuses. He also wrote religious books and acted as a confessor to his students and colleagues.

Canary Wharf bombing   See BOMBING CAMPAIGNS IN BRITAIN.

Cantillon, Richard (1680–1734)
merchant, writer

Born in Ballyheige, County Kerry, Cantillon became a successful merchant in London. He wrote one book, of which only the French translation of the original has survived, titled *Essai sur la nature du commerce en général, traduit de l'Anglais* (1755). The book deals with political economy, currency, and foreign commerce, and it was used as a reference by early giants in the field of economics, such as Adam Smith. Cantillon met a tragic end, being murdered by his cook.

Carelton, William (1794–1869)
novelist

Born in County Tyrone, the son of a peasant family, Carelton was educated at a HEDGE SCHOOL. Originally aspiring for the priesthood, he moved to Dublin and began writing sketches of rural life for anti-Catholic papers. He then wrote a series of novels illustrating the tensions and discords of rural Ireland at the time, which entailed more a critique of the conditions of the peasantry than a derision of them. His books include *The Black Prophet* (1847) and *The Tithe Proctor* (1849).

Carew, George (1559–1629)
soldier

He served in Ireland from 1574 to 1592, attaining the post of privy councilor for Ireland in 1590. Carew served in the duke of Essex's overseas expeditions in the 1590s and was appointed president of Munster in 1600. He succeeded in asserting English authority in the province and was associated with MOUNTJOY in the victory at the Battle of KINSALE. He returned to Ireland in 1610 to undertake survey work for the PLANTATION of Ulster.

Carolan, Turlough (1670–1738)
harpist, composer

Born in County Meath, as a child Carolan and his family went to County Roscommon to work for the MacDermott Roe family, who educated him. When he lost his sight at the age of 18, he was trained to play the harp. He became an itinerant harpist, performing in the big houses of Connacht and Ulster, whether Irish or ANGLO-IRISH, often dedicating his work to the patrons who received him. He composed as well as played, drawing on both traditional folk influences and classical Italian works. His work survives and is frequently played today.

Carrauntuohill

The highest mountain in Ireland situated in the MacGillycuddy Reeks in County Kerry. It is 3,414 feet in height.

Carroll, Paul Vincent (1900–1968)
playwright

Born in Dundalk, educated at St. Patrick's College, Dublin, Carroll taught in Dundalk. In 1921 he immigrated to Glasgow, where he also taught and began writing. His first play, *The Watched Pat* (1930) was produced at the Peacock Theatre, which was followed by the ABBEY THEATRE production of his *Things That Are Caesar's* (1932). His *Shadow and Substance* (1937), which appeared first at the Abbey in 1937 and won the New York Drama Critics Circle Award for the best foreign play in 1938–39, earned him the Casement Award of the Irish Academy of Letters and established him as a dramatist. The play dealt with the tensions within the IRISH FREE STATE between religious orthodoxy and sexual liberalism. He retired from teaching at that point and devoted himself entirely to writing, which included short stories and plays for screen and television, moving to Kent in 1945 to be closer to the British film industry.

Carson, Edward (1854–1935)
politician

Born in Dublin, educated at TRINITY COLLEGE DUBLIN, he was called to the Irish bar in 1877 and was made Irish solicitor general in 1892. Called to the English bar in 1893, his cross examination of Oscar WILDE in his libel action against the marquis of Queensbury led to the writer's disgrace and later conviction. A member of parliament for Dublin University (Trinity College) from 1892 to 1918, he was made English solicitor general in 1900. He served the plaintiff in the libel action taken in 1913 against Cecil

Chesterton in relation to the Marconi scandal. Carson became the leader of the Irish unionists in 1910 and led them in their campaign against what appeared an inevitable HOME RULE Act. He exploited his close contacts with the leaders of the Conservative Party to embolden the unionists of Ulster to consider unconstitutional resistance to Home Rule, beginning with the signing by the overwhelming majority of Protestant adult males of the Ulster Covenant and the formation of the ULSTER VOLUNTEER FORCE. He was a central figure in the negotiations in 1914 on the eve of the measure's passage with Prime Minister H. H. Asquith and the IRISH PARLIAMENTARY PARTY leader, John REDMOND, unsuccessfully seeking to delay the application of Home Rule to Ulster or to give Ulster counties an option to be excluded. Following the outbreak of the First World War, the entire measure was postponed and he became attorney general. Later, under Lloyd George as prime minister, in 1916, Carson accepted office as first lord of the Admiralty with the understanding that six counties of Ulster would be excluded from the ultimate application of Home Rule. However, he was realistic, even though himself a southern unionist committed to the union of all of Ireland with Britain, and he encouraged northern unionists to save as much as they could from inclusion in a home-ruled Ireland. In the 1918 general election, he was returned for the Duncairn constituency of Belfast. In 1921 he resigned as unionist leader and accepted a life peerage.

Casement, Roger (1864–1916)
civil servant, revolutionary

Born in Dublin, but raised in Antrim, Casement was educated at Ballymena Academy. He joined the British colonial service in 1892 and became internationally renowned for his exposure of human rights abuses in the Congo and later in Peru, for which he was honored by a knighthood. Ill heath induced his retirement. He became sympathetic to the Irish NATIONALIST cause, joining the GAELIC LEAGUE and the IRISH VOLUNTEERS. In 1914 he went to America, where

CLAN NA GAEL and the German embassy facilitated his departure for Germany to recruit volunteers from among Irish prisoners of war to follow him back to Ireland to take part in a projected uprising that would be aided by substantial numbers of German arms. He returned to Ireland via U-boat in 1916 actually hoping to discourage the uprising projected for Easter since he believed the German weapons arriving on the vessel the *AUD*, were insufficient. On Good Friday, he was captured soon after landing at Tralee. In England, Casement was tried for treason, convicted, and given the death sentence. His own diaries, which indicated that he was a homosexual, were circulated to counter any public sympathy. He was hung on August 3. His remains were returned to Ireland in 1965, to be reinterned in Glasnevin Cemetery, Dublin.

Casey, Eamonn (1927–)
bishop

Born in County Kerry, educated at MAYNOOTH, and ordained a priest in 1951, after serving in various Limerick parishes, Casey was reassigned to serve the Irish emigrant community in Slough, England, where he became very involved in securing housing for the homeless as national director of the Catholic Housing Aid Society. He was bishop of Kerry from 1969 to 1976 and of Galway from 1976 to 1992, and he became celebrated for his populist manner. Casey was outspoken in his concern for developing nations, serving as chairman of Trocaire, the bishops' relief organization, and he was critical of the role of the United States in the provision of international aid and development assistance, participating in opposition to honoring President Ronald Reagan during his visit to Ireland in 1984. In 1992 revelations that he had fathered the son of an Irish-American woman, Annie Murphy, who was distantly related, led to his resignation. He went to Ecuador to undertake missionary work for almost a decade and then returned to England, where he continued to serve as a priest until returning to a Galway parish in 2006.

Cashel

A modern County Tipperary town that is situated close to a prominent limestone rock that served as the fortification for Munster kings in the Middle Ages as well as the ecclesiastical see of the province of Munster. A chapel on the rock became a Gothic cathedral in the 13th century. It was burned in 1495 and again in 1647. It remains today as a prominent ruin, with the current cathedral being located in the town.

Castle, Richard (1690–1751)
architect

A German-born Huguenot who became the most prominent architect in Ireland in the 18th century, Castle designed Leinster House (now DÁIL ÉIREANN), the rotunda Hospital, and celebrated country homes, including Powerscourt, County Wicklow, and Westport House, County Mayo.

Castlereagh, Robert Stewart, second marquis of Londonderry and Viscount (1760–1822)
politician

Born in Dublin, but raised near Newtownards, County Down, Castlereagh was educated at the Royal School, Armagh, and at St. John's College, Oxford. He was a member of the Irish parliament for County Down from 1790 to 1800 and supported Catholic relief in 1793. Lord Camden, the lord lieutenant, made him Keeper of the Privy Seal and facilitated his elevation to viscount in 1796. He was a close adviser to Camden in his dealings with the UNITED IRISHMEN rising in 1798 and was made chief secretary of Ireland in 1798. He accepted William Pitt's view that the solution to the difficulties in Ireland lay in an ACT OF UNION, and he played a vital role in persuading opponents of the measure in the Irish parliament to accept it by giving numerous sinecures, titles, and compensation. After the union, he sat for County Down in the Westminster parliament and continued as chief secretary for Ireland. Later he served as president of the Board of Control (1802) and secretary of the

War Department (1804–06 and 1807–09). In 1812 he became secretary of foreign affairs and took part in the Vienna Congress (1814–15), which settled the affairs of Europe after the defeat of Napoleon. Suffering from depression, he committed suicide in 1822.

Castletown House

The largest and first of the great country houses of 18th-century Ireland built in Celbridge, County Kildare, for William CONNOLLY, the Speaker of the Irish House of Commons. It influenced the design of both LEINSTER HOUSE in Dublin and the White House in Washington, D.C.

Catalpa Escape   See CLAN NA GAEL.

Catholic Association

Founded by Daniel O'CONNELL in 1823 to advance the cause of Catholic emancipation, the more limited membership group was expanded in 1825 to include associate members whose dues were a shilling a year, a penny a month, and a farthing a week, to transform it into a nonviolent mass movement that millions of Irish Catholics joined. It was a pioneering example that would be emulated elsewhere, such as the Chartists and the Corn Law repeal movements in England and the American civil rights campaign in the 1950s and 1960s. In an era when few had the franchise, the movement was summoned to support and encourage electors ready to vote for pro-emancipation candidates, who won in a number of by-elections in 1826. The association played a major role in O'Connell's own successful candidacy in the by-election in Clare in 1828, which forced the government to capitulate and allow Catholics into parliament. Efforts to proscribe the organization in 1825 were evaded by subtly changing its name.

Catholic Committee

A committee of Catholics formed in 1760 to advance the interests of Catholics in Ireland,

who were still bearing the burdens imposed by the PENAL LAWS. It was originally dominated by landed and aristocratic Catholics such as the earl of KENMARE, who combined requests for redress of grievances with professions of acceptance of the Hanoverian monarchs of England and rejection of the JACOBITE pretensions. In the 1790s the organization came under the leadership of more assertive Catholic middle-class figures, such as Dublin merchant John Keogh, who were more vigorous in demanding removal of political, social, and economic disabilities of Catholics and who even engaged Wolfe TONE as an agent.

Catholic emancipation   See CATHOLIC ASSOCIATION.

Catholic Relief Acts

Legislation passed by the Irish parliament that undid many of the restrictions imposed on Catholics by the PENAL LAWS. Specific measures included: in 1750 Catholics were admitted to the lower ranks of the army; in 1772 they were allowed to take leases of up to 61 years on up to 50 acres of land; Gardiner's Relief Act of 1778 allowed them to take leases for 999 years, but not purchase freeholds outright, and be governed by the same inheritance laws as Protestants rather than have property equally divided among all sons; Gardiner's Relief Act of 1782 allowed Catholics to purchase, hold, or bequeath freeholds on the same terms as Protestants, and Catholics were allowed to serve as school teachers and act as guardians; in 1792 Catholics were permitted to practice as lawyers; and in 1793 Catholics were granted the right to vote in parliamentary elections, to hold civil and military office below specific exceptions, and to obtain university degrees.

Caulfield, James, earl of Charlemont

See CHARLEMONT, JAMES CAULFIELD, EARL OF.

Cavendish, Frederick (1836–1882)
politician

Appointed chief secretary for Ireland in May 1882 to replace W. E. Foster who had resigned over what he considered the appeasement of the Land League in the Kilmainham Treaty, Cavendish was murdered by extreme Fenians called the Invincibles the evening of the day he arrived in Ireland, on May 6, 1882, along with the under-secretary, Thomas H. Burke, while walking in Phoenix Park.

Ceannt, Eamonn (1881–1916)
revolutionary

Born in Galway, educated in Dublin, the son of a member of the Royal Irish Constabulary, Ceannt worked as a clerk in the Treasury Department of the Dublin City Council. He joined the Gaelic League in 1900, Sinn Féin in 1908, the Irish Volunteers and the Irish Republican Brotherhood in 1913, was involved in the Howth gunrunning in 1914, and was one of the seven signatories to the Proclamation of the Irish Republic at the Easter Rising, where he was commander of the South Dublin Union. He was executed on May 8, 1916, by firing squad after a court-martial.

Censorship of Publications Act

An act passed in 1929 based on the recommendations of a government-appointed Committee on Evil Literature formed in 1926. The act established a Censorship Board to ban books and publications deemed to be indecent or obscene. The board interpreted the terms very broadly resulting in the ban of significant works of 20th-century literature, including works by most of the major Irish writers of the era. In a way, it became a mark of distinction for an Irish writer to be banned. In 1967 a new act limited the term of the ban to 12 years, which automatically enabled many of the works to become available. The board continues to function but tends to restrict only works that are clearly pornographic.

Charlemont, James Caulfield, earl of (1728–1799)
politician

A Dublin native who inherited a peerage at the age of six, Caulfield was made an earl for services in defending Belfast against a French threat in 1763. His home, Charlemont House in Rutland (now Parnell) Square in Dublin, presently the Municipal Gallery of Modern Art, is an appropriate choice since Charlemont had founded the Royal Irish Academy in 1785 and his home had served as a center for those interested in the arts and architecture. He involved himself in the Irish Patriot cause and was closely allied with Henry Grattan. He was the commander of the Irish Volunteers in Ulster and was instrumental in attending their 1782 convention at Dungannon, which demanded parliamentary independence.

Charlton, Jack (1935–)
soccer player, manager

Born in Northumberland, Charlton played for Leeds United and for England when it won the World Cup in 1966. He was manager of the Republic of Ireland team from 1986 to 1996, during which Ireland qualified for the European Championship tournament for the first time in 1988, reached the quarter finals of the World Cup in 1990, and found itself in the final 16 in the World Cup in 1994. He was made a "freeman" of Dublin in 1994 and granted honorary Irish citizenship as a consequence. Charlton retired in 1995 and is engaged chiefly today as an afterdinner speaker.

Chartism

A mass political movement in England in the 1830s and 1840s that demanded, through petitions to parliament, universal male suffrage, annual elections, payment of members of parliament, removal of property qualifications for members, equal constituencies, and the secret ballot. Inevitably many Irish immigrants to England were among its primarily working class membership. A leader was Fergus O'Connor. Daniel O'Connell sought to distance his repeal movement from the Chartists, although many among the Irish in England identified with both causes, and later with YOUNG IRELAND. Chartism was feared as a harbinger of revolution, but enthusiasm for it waned as the economic situation improved for the working classes in the 1850s. Significantly, all of the movement's objectives, except annual parliaments, were achieved in the 20th century.

Chichester-Clark, James (1923–2002)
politician

A member of the landed class of Northern Ireland, Chichester-Clark was educated at Eton and served in the British army from 1942 to 1960, retiring as a major to enter the Northern Ireland PARLIAMENT as a Unionist member for South Londonderry. He was linked to the reform-minded prime minister, Terence O'NEILL, under whom he served as chief whip and then minister of agriculture. He resigned from O'Neill's cabinet in April 1969, which helped precipitate O'Neill's own resignation. He then succeeded him, narrowly defeated another contender, Brian FAULKNER. He served as prime minister for two difficult years when civil rights protests were increasingly met with counter protests and then outright rioting. General disorder and intercommunal assaults prompted him, in August 1969, to call on the British army to intervene. In March 1971 he resigned over inability to obtain greater powers to combat the intensifying campaign of the IRA. Faulkner succeeded him.

Chieftains, The
musicians

A traditional music group founded in 1963 by *uilleann* piper Paddy Moloney. Fiddler Martin Fay was among the original group, which was later joined by fiddler Sean Keane, harpist and pianist Derek Bell, and flutist Mark Molloy. Turning professional in 1975, they quickly gained worldwide acclaim. The Chieftains were recognized for their work on the Irish traditional pieces on the soundtrack of the film *Barry Lyn-*

don, and they were named Melody Maker's "Group of the Year" for 1975. They received their first Grammy nomination in 1978 in the Ethnic Recording category. In 1979, at PHOENIX PARK in Dublin, they played before a crowd of 1.35 million people during the visit of Pope John Paul II to Ireland, at which they performed as the opening act. The Chieftains were one of the first groups from the West to visit China, which was chronicled in an album and video, *The Chieftains in China.* In 1983 they became the first group to play in the rotunda of the U.S. Capitol. They received a Grammy nomination in 1989 for best children's recording for *The Tailor of Gloucester,* undertaken with Academy Award–winning actress Meryl Streep. In 1989 the Irish government conferred the title of Ireland's "Musical Ambassador" on them for their contributions to Irish culture. In 1991 they received Grammy nominations in five categories for their work. In the next several years, they were awarded Grammys for *An Irish Evening: Live at the Grand Opera House,* for *Another Country,* and for *Celtic Harp.* The group was honored for contributions to Irish music in receiving a lifetime achievement award at the BBC2 Folk Awards in 2002. Their strength comes from their ability to adhere to traditional Irish music while collaborating with other forms of music—whether classical, popular, or folk—from other cultures.

Childers, Erskine Hamilton (1905–1974)
politician

The eldest son of Robert Erskine CHILDERS, Erskine Childers was born in London and educated at Cambridge. He returned to Ireland after working a few years for an American travel organization and became advertising manager for the *IRISH PRESS* in 1931, and later secretary for the Federation of Irish Manufacturers. Elected to the DÁIL ÉIREANN in 1938 as a member of FIANNA FÁIL, he served in various ministries in Fianna Fáil governments including Local Government, Posts and Telegraphs, Lands, Forestry and Fisheries, Transport and Power, and Health, and was TÁNAISTE as well when in the last post (1969–73). He was elected president of Ireland in 1973, succeeded DE VALERA and defeating Thomas O'Higgins. He died of a heart attack on November 17, 1974.

Childers, Robert Erskine (1870–1922)
politician

Born in England and educated at Cambridge, Robert Childers served as clerk of the House of Commons from 1894 to 1910. His mother was of the Barton family of Glendalough House, County Wicklow. He volunteered to serve in the Boer War and wrote an account of his experiences as well as a novel, *The Riddle of the Sands* (1903), about German preparation for an invasion of England. In 1914 he sailed his yacht, *Asgard,* into Howth with weapons for the IRISH VOLUNTEERS. He earned a DSC for service in the British navy during the First World War. After the war he was elected to the DÁIL ÉIREANN for Wicklow. Childers served as propagandist for the Dáil government and was secretary to the delegation that negotiated the ANGLO-IRISH TREATY of 1921. He opposed the treaty and served as director of publicity for the anti-treaty side during the CIVIL WAR. He was arrested by the Free State authorities at Glendalough House, court-martialed for possession of a weapon under the emergency provision resolution passed by the Dáil, and executed on November 24, 1922.

Church of Ireland

As in England, the Protestant Reformation in Ireland originated in an act of state whereby parliament, at the behest of King Henry VIII, established the church as a national institution independent of the papacy. In Ireland, unlike England, the vast majority of the people and most of the rank-and-file clergy continued to adhere to the Roman Catholic Church, which began to supply rival bishops and clergy to the official religion. The official religion became linked to the New English, that is, the English officialdom and settlers who had come to Ireland beginning in the 16th century who identified with the institutional Anglicization of the country. Being "high" church, the establishment engaged the state in combating both Popery and "low" church Protestantism, both of whom suffered political and social disabilities. There were significant conversions from among some Catholics seeking to avoid the disabilities and penalties of the PENAL LAWS in the 18th century. In the 19th century, liberal attitudes and Catholic activism worked to demonstrate the illogicality of an established church serving only a minority of the population, and, beginning with the Church Temporalities Act in 1833, disestablishment became only a matter of time. It took place in 1869. Since then, the Church of Ireland, whose membership shrank as a proportion of the population following Irish political independence, has continued to play a very constructive moral and social role in its minority position. Immigration into Ireland from the European continent and elsewhere in recent years has even accounted for an increase in membership.

civil rights movement

A movement in Northern Ireland in the 1960s patterned after the campaign by American blacks to end racial segregation and denial of civil liberties. It differed from the longstanding republican and nationalist campaigns by seeking to secure the rights of citizens rather than the goal of Irish unification, although unionist critics predictably regarded the movement as a republican front. It started in 1963 in Dungannon with protests about inequitable public housing allocation. Taking many organizational forms, including the Campaign for Social Justice in Northern Ireland and the creation of the NORTHERN IRELAND CIVIL RIGHTS ASSOCIATION, its participants were not exclusively from the Catholic community. Its goals included equitable allocation of public housing and employment, universal suffrage in local elections, and the repeal of Special Powers Legislation. Police assault on a civil rights march in Derry on October 5, 1968, provoked larger marches and increased police response. In time, Northern Ireland prime minister Terence O'NEILL accepted in principle many of the demands, but before their implementation, community conflict increased, British army intervention took place, and a violent irredentist campaign emerged.

civil war

Dissatisfaction with the ANGLO-IRISH TREATY of December 1921, primarily because it had not brought a republican status to Ireland, persisted during the months that followed its narrow acceptance by the DÁIL ÉIREANN. The majority of the IRA's members did not regarded themselves bound by the treaty or by the PROVISIONAL GOVERNMENT created by it for Ireland, headed by Michael COLLINS. Eamon DE VALERA resigned as president of the Dáil Éireann after its acceptance of the treaty and led the political opposition to it. An attempt at forming a coalition government of pro- and anti-treaty figures by an electoral pact for the scheduled June 1922 election to the Third Dáil fell through. Only 36 anti-treaty deputies were elected to the 128-member body, as the pro-treaty group obtained a plurality. Others elected included LABOUR PARTY members, farmers' representatives, and independents. They also accepted the treaty. The anti-treaty IRA continued to control various posts, most notably the Four Courts building in Dublin. The British government, particularly following the assassination in London of Field Marshall Henry Wilson by IRA members, pressured the Provisional Government to assert its authority, and, after the capture of General J. J. O'Connell by anti-treaty forces and his imprisonment in the Four Courts, the government ordered its bombardment. The siege was successful, but entailed the destruction of countless and priceless public records. Within a few weeks the government had been able to assert its authority over most of Ireland, and celebrated anti-treaty leaders such as Cathal BRUGHA and Harry BOLAND died from wounds in action. However, by resorting to guerrilla warfare the anti-treaty forces were able to continue their campaign in sympathetic rural areas, especially in Munster. Tragic for the Provisional Government was the death on August 12 of Arthur GRIFFITH, who had become president of the by then nominal Dáil Éireann after de Valera's resignation, and the ambushing of Michael Collins in his native County Cork on August 22. The third Dáil Éireann, even before approving a constitution for the IRISH FREE STATE that the treaty called for, passed an emergency resolution allowing internment and military tribunals with powers of capital punishment. The Roman Catholic bishops condemned under pain of excommunication those persisting in the armed opposition to the government. However, the IRA followed through on its death threat to Dáil members who had voted for the resolution under which executions that ultimately would reach 77. One deputy was killed and another wounded on December 7. The government responded with a questionable retaliatory tactic in ordering the execution of four celebrated prisoners, including Rory O'CONNOR and Liam MELLOWS, held since the beginning of the civil war and before the empowering emergency resolution was passed. However, assassinations of Dáil members ceased. Violence and assaults on the property of members of the Irish Free State SEANAD continued, as did atrocities by both sides in the fighting in Munster. Notorious were the killings of republican prisoners forced to work or walk on mined sites in Kerry. Liam LYNCH, the military leader of the republicans, was killed in April. Frank AIKEN, his successor moved toward ending the struggle. The political leader, de Valera unsuccessfully sought to negotiate a settlement with the government, their political leader. He then issued a call on May 24 for his followers to put aside their weapons and continue the goal of securing a republic in other ways. He continued to refuse to recognize the legitimacy of the Irish Free State.

Clancy Brothers and Tommy Makem
singers

An Irish folk group of Tipperary-born brothers, who had been actors in New York, and the

Armagh-born Makem, their repertoire of traditional songs and rebel ballads drew attention from a broader constituency beyond the usual Irish and Irish-American circles, especially after they appeared on American national television. Their success led to a revived interest in traditional song even in Ireland, where pop music had gained ascendancy. Of the three brothers, Paddy, Tommy, and Liam, only Liam survives.

Clannad
musical group
A County Donegal musical group of the same family, the O'Braonains, and near relations, started in the 1970s. They present Irish language songs to traditional tunes. They became internationally popular following a tour of Germany and doing the soundtrack for the British Academy Award–winning film *Robin of Sherwood*. One member, Eithne Ni Bhraonain, known as Enya, left in 1982 and has had great solo success.

Clan na Gael
revolutionary organization
Founded in New York in 1867, the group was a support organization for the IRISH REPUBLICAN BROTHERHOOD or the FENIANS. They assisted and financed various bombing campaigns in Britain and in 1876 rescued escaped Fenian prisoners in Australia with a vessel, the *Catalpa*. They supported Charles PARNELL under the strategy of the "NEW DEPARTURE" in the 1880s. Under the leadership of John DEVOY, they supported the IRB in bringing about the EASTER RISING in 1916. There was a division among the group following the differences between Devoy and Judge Daniel F. COHALAN and Eamon DE VALERA in 1919–20 over fund-raising in America, as Joseph MAC-GARRITY sided with the later. The acceptance of the ANGLO-IRISH TREATY by the former prompted activist Irish-American republicans to follow McGarrity. Although greatly overshadowed by later Irish-American support groups, such as NORAID and FRIENDS OF SINN FÉIN, the Clan na Gael continues as an organization.

Clann na Poblachta
political party
The party was founded in 1946 by a number of republicans and social radicals. Its leader was Seán MACBRIDE, former IRA chief of staff. Its success in several by-elections prompted the group to run many candidates in the 1948 general election, in which it won only 10 seats in contrast to its 13 percent of the vote. However, it did become part of the first coalition government, headed by John A. COSTELLO (FINE GAEL) and including members of LABOUR, NATIONAL LABOUR, and CLANN NA TALMHAN. The party's strength quickly dwindled with MacBride, as foreign minister, failing to support fellow member, Noel BROWNE, minister for health, in his MOTHER AND CHILD SCHEME that had run afoul of the medical profession and the Catholic hierarchy. The party itself was dissolved in 1965 when it held only one seat in the DÁIL ÉIREANN.

Clann na Talmhan
political party
A party founded in 1938 to champion the interests of small farmers. Its greatest electoral success was its winning 14 seats in the 1943 general election. The seven seats it obtained in the 1948 election enabled its leader, Joseph Blowick, to obtain a ministry, Lands and Fisheries, in the coalition government headed by John A. COSTELLO from 1948 to 1951. Afterward the party's strength dwindled. The organization had ceased to exist by 1965.

Clare
A maritime county in the southwestern province of Munster, Clare is bounded on the west by the Atlantic Ocean, on the south by the Shannon Estuary, on the east by the Shannon River including Lough Derg, and on the north by County Galway. It has an area of 1,231 square miles and a population of over 103,000. It is celebrated for its landscape, especially the bared limestone of the Burren with its diverse flora and fauna, underground caves, and turloughs, or shallow lakes, that are dry in the summer. The

The Cliffs of Moher in County Clare *(Library of Congress)*

Cliffs of Moher along its Atlantic Coast are a major tourist attraction. The area south of the cliffs contains many beaches and is a major holidaying location. Clare is celebrated for the strength of its traditional Irish music, hosting major festivals, such as the Willy Clancy festival every summer, and many important figures in the world of traditional music have their origins in the county. Its historical role includes having been the constituency from which Daniel O'CONNELL was elected to parliament in 1828 in defiance of the laws excluding Catholics with the consequence that Catholic emancipation was subsequently granted. It was also the constituency that elected Eamon DE VALERA to parliament as a SINN FÉIN candidate in 1917. Even earlier, BRIAN BORU had been the overlord of Clare before he became high king of Ireland. The county has numerous points of archaeological and historic interest, including the Craggaunowen reconstruction of Bronze Age lake dwellings, the Bunratty folkpark, and Dunguaire Castle. The presence of Shannon Airport and its adjoining industrial park have been a major economic boon to the county. The county town is Ennis and tourism is the major industry. Famous natives have included a GAA founder Michael CUSACK, the nationalist landlord William Smith O'BRIEN, and the submarine inventor John Philip HOLLAND.

Clare, John Fitzgibbon, earl of (1749–1802)
politician

Born in Donnybrook, County Dublin and educated at TRINITY COLLEGE DUBLIN and at Oxford,

Fitzgibbon became a very successful and wealthy barrister. He was a member of the Irish parliament and became attorney general in 1783. He was made lord chancellor of Ireland in 1789 and earl of Clare in 1795. He was a vigorous champion of the ascendancy and the connection with Britain, opposing the unsuccessful efforts of Lord William FITZWILLIAM, a reforming viceroy, to advance concessions to Catholics in 1795. He supported and advanced the ACT OF UNION.

Clarke, Austin (1896–1974)
poet

Clarke replaced his mentor, Thomas MACDON-AGH, as lecturer in English at University College Dublin when he was executed after the EASTER RISING. He first wrote epic poems, including *The Vengeance of Fionn* (1917), but later moved to England where he was a literary journalist and wrote prosody and prose romances. He returned to Ireland where he undertook poetry reviews for the *IRISH TIMES* and broadcasts for Radio Éireann. He wrote verse plays and poetry that satirized church and state. He was a founder of the Dublin Verse-Speaking Society, which evolved into the Lyric Theatre Company that staged verse drama at the ABBEY THEATRE and the Peacock Theatre.

Clarke, Thomas (1857–1916)
revolutionary

Born in the Isle of Wright, but raised in County Tyrone, Clarke went to America and joined CLAN NA GAEL. He was arrested and sentenced to life imprisonment for participation in a bombing camp in England, but was released as part of an amnesty in 1898. He went to America, but returned to Ireland in 1907 and set about revitalizing the IRISH REPUBLICAN BROTHERHOOD. Under the guise of running a news agency, Clarke played a major role in bringing about the EASTER RISING. He was one of the signatories to the Proclamation of Independence issued at the time, but he was also one of those executed after the failure of the rising.

Clerkenwell explosion   See BOMBING CAMPAIGNS IN BRITAIN.

Clifford, Sigerson (1913–1985)
playwright, poet

Sigerson Clifford was born in Cork in 1913 of Kerry parentage. He spent many years of his youth in Caherciveen, County Kerry, with his mother's father Edward Sigerson. The memories of that childhood, that town and area, and his grandfather never left him and were celebrated in his poetry, including titles such as "Where the Old Men Thatched Their Dreams with Adjectives," "The Races at Caherciveen," "The Ballad of the Tinker's Daughter," and "The Boys of Barr na Staide." The latter was his most popular composition and captures beautifully the essence of Caherciveen. He was a civil servant, but also wrote plays. In 1944 he won the Kerry Drama Festival Cup for his first play, *Nano*. His second play, *The Great Pacificator*, was produced by the ABBEY THEATRE in 1947. His other works include *Death Sails the Shannon*, *The Glassy Man*, *The Wild Colonial Boy*, *Travelling Tinkers*, and *Lascar Rock*. He died in 1985.

Cliffs of Moher   See CLARE.

Clongowes Wood College

A secondary educational institution for males run by the Society of Jesus located in County Kildare. Many of its alumni have played significant roles in Irish society, whether in business, law, or politics. It has a socially elitist reputation.

Cobh

The port that had served the city of Cork, known as Queenstown from 1849 to 1922, was the last port of call by the *Titanic* on its fatal voyage in 1912. Thousands of Irish emigrants left here for America. In accord with the ANGLO-IRISH TREATY of 1922, the British were able to maintain a naval facility here until 1938 when Prime Minister Neville Chamberlain agreed to relinquish British ports in Ireland.

Coercion Policy

Refers to various temporary pieces of emergency legislation enacted at various times, especially in the nineteenth century, to deal with disorder in Ireland. It usually entailed imposing curfews and suspending habeas corpus in disturbed areas. It could also refer to suppression of political organizations on the pretext of their being seditious.

Coghlan, Eamonn (1952–)
athlete

A Dublin-born middle-distance runner who studied and trained at Villanova University in Philadelphia, Coghlan set six world indoor records at 1,500 and 2,000 meters and one mile, as well as winning the 5,000 meter race at the 1983 World Championship in Helsinki. Coming in fourth in the 1,500 meters in the 1976 Olympics and in the 5,000 meters in the 1980 Olympics, he won the Wannamaker Mile seven times at the Millrose Games in New York.

Cohalan, Daniel F. (1865–1946)
jurist, nationalist

An American-born son of Irish immigrants, Cohalan became a judge in New York State and became very involved in the politics of the Democratic Party. Cohalan was closely associated with John DEVOY in CLAN NA GAEL, assisting Roger CASEMENT in making his way to Germany in 1914 and in supporting the 1916 EASTER RISING. He founded the American Friends of Irish Freedom, which by the WAR OF INDEPENDENCE had gained support in the Irish-American community from broader circles than the usual Clan na Gael supporters. Cohalan suspected that Eamon DE VALERA would settle for terms less than the establishment of a republic and he and his supporters wished that funds raised for support of the Irish cause be used against American entry into the League of Nations, which they saw as a British instrument. De Valera, who was in America in 1919 and 1920 seeking financial and political support, insisted that he, as president of the DÁIL ÉIREANN, ought to determine where funds should be used in support of the Irish cause. They also clashed over the appeals to be made to American political conventions on behalf of the Irish cause, as the politically well-connected Cohalan believed that de Valera's more absolute requests were certain to alienate Americans. Paradoxically he supported the ANGLO-IRISH TREATY, which infuriated purist republicans, because de Valera opposed it. However, by 1924 he had begun to sour on the IRISH FREE STATE for not using the treaty as a tactic, rather than abiding by it as an international agreement, to further advance republican goals.

Collins, Michael (1890–1922)
revolutionary

Born in County Cork, Michael Collins went to England as a teenager and worked for the postal services and later in financial houses. While in London, he became involved in the GAELIC ATHLETIC ASSOCIATION and in the IRISH REPUBLICAN BROTHERHOOD, and returned to Ireland to participate in the 1916 EASTER RISING. He was among the hundreds interned for several months at Frongoch in Wales, where he assumed a leadership role among his fellows. Upon release, he rose to prominence in both the IRB and SINN FÉIN. When the DÁIL ÉIREANN was established in 1919 he became minister for finance. He was also director of intelligence for the IRA. The absence of DE VALERA during much of the WAR OF INDEPENDENCE enabled Collins to assume de facto control in the struggle. His leadership position in the IRB, which regarded itself as the keeper of the flame of Irish republicanism and many of whose members were also TDs and leading figures in the IRA, and his successful employment of guerrilla and espionage tactics against the British, made him a legendary figure, especially because he remained incognito as a wanted man. He differed

Michael Collins at the funeral of Arthur Griffith in August 1922, days before his own death *(Library of Congress)*

from more classic revolutionary types such as Cathal BRUGHA, minister for defense, and Austin STACK, minister for home affairs, who preferred the more open style uprising like that of 1916. After the truce of July 1921, he was named to the team of negotiators who arrived at the ANGLO-IRISH TREATY. When the Dáil accepted the treaty in January 1922, he was selected as chairman of the PROVISIONAL GOVERNMENT called for by the treaty to implement establishment of the IRISH FREE STATE, a self-governing dominion but not a republic. Having argued that the treaty served as the stepping-stone to greater freedom, he tried to gain the adherence of treaty opponents to the government's position by securing wording in the proposed Free State's constitution as republican as possible (to which the British objected) and entering an electoral pact with his leading opponent Eamon de Valera, which sought to keep the same proportion of pro- and anti-treaty deputies in the next Dáil and to form a coalition government. However, on the eve of the June election

Collins withdrew from the impractical coalition and the electorate returned a Dáil overwhelming supportive or tolerant of the treaty. CIVIL WAR broke out later that month when Collins's government besieged the Four Courts, which was held by IRA units who rejected the treaty. During the war Collins assumed the role of commander-in-chief of the military and relinquished political affairs to William T. COSGRAVE. The government forces had gained ascendancy over most of the country by August, except for the province of Munster. On a visit to his native Cork to boost the morale of government forces and attempt to reach out to old comrades now opposing the government, Collins's convoy came under attack near Béal na mBláth and he was killed on August 22, 1922.

Colm Cille (521–597)
missionary, abbot

Also known by the Latin name, Columba, Colm Cille came from royal stock and was born in Donegal. He studied under St. Finnian of Molville. He founded monasteries in Derry and Durrow, but later became involved in a controversy with Finnian over alleged plagiarism, which dispute led to a military confrontation. He was subsequently banished and departed to found a monastery on Iona in the Hebrides, from where he became the missionary to the Scots.

Colum, Padraic (1881–1972)
playwright, poet

Born in County Longford, Colum was closely associated with the Irish Literary Revival and his early plays were performed at the ABBEY THEATRE. He immigrated to America in 1914. He wrote children's stories for the *New York Sunday Tribune,* lectured at Columbia University, and wrote and compiled folk tales. His earlier plays dealt with the lives of small farmers and his work in America included a mixture of retelling old tales, autobiography, and dramatic lyricism. He published books of children's stories, such as *At the Gateways of the Day* (1924) and *The King of Ireland's Son* (1916), and his *Collected Poems* (1953).

Colwyn Committee

Committee established in 1923 under Lord Colwyn to determine the fiscal relationship between Northern Ireland and the United Kingdom. It suggested that Northern Ireland's contribution to the imperial Exchequer from its revenues should be drawn only from any surplus after local expenditures had been made.

Commonwealth

An association of states comprising the United Kingdom and former dependencies of which Ireland was a member from 1922 to 1949. The ANGLO-IRISH TREATY called for establishment of the IRISH FREE STATE as a dominion comparable to Canada. In an imperial conference in London in 1926 the Irish representatives, particularly Kevin O'HIGGINS, advanced the principle of equality of status for all dominions, and formal legislation, the STATUTE OF WESTMINSTER, confirmed that status, making dominions autonomous of any Westminster parliamentary legislation. The reigning British monarch remains the head of the Commonwealth. Ireland withdrew from the Commonwealth in 1949 when formally proclaimed a republic.

Communist Party of Ireland

Founded in 1921, and led by Roderic Connolly, the son of James CONNOLLY, the small group won the support of radical writers such as Peadar O'DONNELL and Liam O'FLAHERTY, and recognition from Moscow as the Irish sector of the Comintern. It lost that later status and dissolved when James LARKIN, having returned from America, formed the Irish Workers League, which received Moscow's blessing. The Communist Party was reestablished in 1933 and many of its members served as Loyalist volunteers in the Spanish Civil War. In the inhospitable atmosphere of the 1940s and 1950s the party went through several

reorganizations, including a division with adherents in NORTHERN IRELAND. It was always small in number and had electoral insignificance, but members played important roles in the labor union movement. The party was reunited in 1970, but its significance as a left-wing voice diminished as Official SINN FÉIN evolved into the Workers' Party and the Democratic Left in the 1970s and 1980s.

Confederation of Kilkenny

The Confederate Catholics of Ireland, both OLD ENGLISH and Gaelic, nobility and middle class, met in Kilkenny in 1642 to organize a government, which would meet regularly in Kilkenny, to counter the military threat from twin antagonists, the royalists (who controlled the government in Dublin) and the parliamentarians (who would bring a Scottish covenanting army to Ireland) who were combating each other in the English Civil War. The Confederation of Kilkenny committed itself to God, country, and king. A rebellion by Catholics in Ulster the previous year had provoked both the government response as well as the parliament's outrage at the king's suspected softness toward the Catholics. The confederation remained torn by disunity between the Old English and the Gaelic, as the former were more disposed to treat with the royalists and to settle for less than a complete reestablishment of Catholicism as urged by papal representatives to their group. Thomas PRESTON and Owen Roe O'NEILL, the confederation's military leaders, also failed to work harmoniously. Oliver CROMWELL's conquest of Ireland in 1649–50 ended the hopes of the confederation.

Congested Districts Board

A body organized by Chief Secretary Arthur Balfour in 1891 as an example of killing HOME RULE with kindness. It defined certain areas of Ireland as overpopulated and underdeveloped and sought to improve and encourage farming, fishing, and local industry as well as the purchasing of landlord estates for sale to tenants. In 1923 the Irish Free State transferred its functions to a newly created land commission.

Connacht

One of the four historic provinces of Ireland, it covers the west of the island, or, essentially, the area west of the Shannon River, and includes Counties Leitrim, Sligo, Roscommon, Mayo, and Galway. Its name derives from a mythical hero, Conn of the Hundred Battles. The western side of the province is scenically beautiful, but the rocky soil, mountains, and vast areas of bog make agriculture difficult. The eastern side has excellent farming land. Dominant Gaelic families included the O'Flahertys, the O'Rourkes, and especially the O'Connors. After the Normans, they would be joined especially by the de Burghs (Burkes), who would also become Gaelicized. More than any other province, Connacht has retained a distinctly traditional Irish culture, particularly as expressed in music, but also the largest portion of the Gaeltacht. Historical reasons for this are the Composition of Connacht in the 1580s, whereby the traditional Irish and Norman rulers of the area were confirmed in their control of the land in return for their acceptance of the Tudor order and a semifeudal, as opposed to Gaelic, basis for their position. More than a half-century later, the Cromwellian land settlement transported Catholic landowners from other parts of Ireland, further strengthening the Irish flavor of the population. Tragically, Connacht suffered the most during the Great Famine measured by population loss. It was the area where the agitation for land reform, especially the Land League, began in the later 19th century. Contemporary Connacht, even, and perhaps especially, the Connemara sections of Galway and Mayo, which had been linked to poverty, has become a different world, with much-improved new housing and public infrastructure. The area has become a thriving area for vacation homes as well, especially for residents of other areas of Ireland, especially the east.

Connaught Rangers

A regiment of the British army recruited from Ireland. Several of its members mutinied in India in 1920 in protest at the brutality in Ireland of the Black and Tans. Soldiers were killed when the mutineers were besieged. Subsequently 14 of the mutineers were sentenced to death. However, the sentences of all but one, a member of the Irish Republican Brotherhood, were commuted and 61 other were imprisoned. The Rangers were dissolved after the Anglo-Irish Treaty.

Connell, Desmond (1926–   )
philosopher, bishop

Educated at University College Dublin and at the University of Louvain in Belgia, Connell taught philosophy at UCD from 1953 to 1988. He was appointed archbishop of Dublin in 1988 and created a cardinal in 2001. His outspokenness on issues ranging from family planning to participation in non-Catholic religious services has provoked considerable controversy. His coadjutor, Archbishop Diarmud Martin, succeeded him in 2003.

Connolly, James (1868–1916)
revolutionary, labor leader

Born in Edinburgh of Irish parents, Connolly came to Ireland and formed the Irish Socialist Republican Party and a journal, *Worker's Republic.* In 1903 he went to America where he remained for seven years and became involved with other socialist activists. When he returned to Ireland he became the Belfast organizer of the Irish Transport and General Workers' Union, but by 1914 his opposition to the First World War and his nationalist attitudes prompted his move to Dublin. In 1912 he and James Larkin formed the Irish Labour Party in association with the Irish Trades Union Congress. In 1914 he assisted Larkin in the unsuccessful ITGWU strike against a lockout by employers. When Larkin then left for America, he assumed leadership of the labor movement. His originally Marxist philosophy was intertwined with a nationalist perspective that saw the cause of the working class as linked with the cause of national liberation. He formed the Irish Citizen Army and in 1916 linked his force with that of the IRISH VOLUNTEERS dominated by the IRISH REPUBLICAN BROTHERHOOD in the EASTER RISING. He was one of the signatories of the proclamation of an Irish republic and was one of those executed after the failure of the rising.

Connolly, William (?–1729)
politician

Connolly amassed a great fortune selling land confiscated after the defeat of the JACOBITE forces in 1691, becoming one of the richest men in Ireland. He was a member of the Irish parliament and served as its speaker from 1715 to 1729, during which time he undertook construction or his palatial home, Castletown House, in Kildare. His successors as speakers became more closely linked to the government in becoming the UNDERTAKERS, that is, political managers able through patronage to further the executive's wishes in the parliament.

Conway, William (1913–1977)
bishop

Born in the Falls Road area of BELFAST, Conway was educated at QUEEN'S UNIVERSITY BELFAST and MAYNOOTH. After being ordained a priest he studied cannon law at the Gregorian University in Rome and then taught at St. Malachy's College, Belfast, before becoming professor of moral theology as well as canon law at Maynooth. He later became its vice president and edited the *Irish Theological Quarterly.* He was a member of the Income Tax Commission that recommended the introduction of withholding tax or "PAYE," pay-as-you-earn, in Ireland. Appointed auxiliary bishop to John Cardinal D'ALTON in 1958, Conway succeeded him as archbishop of Armagh and primate of all Ireland in 1963. Created a cardinal in 1965, he spoke often at the Second Vatican Council. Instrumental in starting the Irish Catholic relief agency, Trocaire, he was a member of the Pontifical Commission for the Revision of the Canon Law. He endorsed the constitutional revision, which removed reference to the special position of the Roman Catholic Church

in the Irish constitution in 1973. He signed the various pastoral statements issued by Northern Ireland Catholic bishops condemning both paramilitary violence and questionable techniques employed in interrogating interned prisoners.

Cooke, Henry (1788–1868)
Presbyterian minister

Born in County Derry, Cooke was educated Glasgow College and at TRINITY COLLEGE DUBLIN. He was a vigorous proponent of orthodox PRESBYTERIANISM and opposed "New Light" theology and Unitarianism. He was also fearful of Roman Catholicism and vigorously supported the maintenance of the ACT OF UNION. He challenged Daniel O'CONNELL to a debate when he visited BELFAST in 1841, but the Liberator refused. He also opposed the introduction of national schooling in Ireland, which might be secular and/or Catholic, and was able to gain recognition of a distinctly Presbyterian scheme of schools by the authorities. Cooke was professor of rhetoric at a government-endowed theological college and was dean of residence at Queen's College Belfast from 1849 on. Moderator of the Synod of Ulster in 1824, he was also elected moderator of the General Assembly twice, in 1841 and in 1862. His May Street, Belfast, congregation constructed a church for him in 1829, where he remained in active ministry until 1866.

Corish, Brendan (1918–1990)
politician

Born in County Wexford, Corish succeeded his father as one of its TD's in a 1945 by-election. A junior minister in the 1948–51 coalition government and a minister for social welfare in that of 1954–57, he became leader of the LABOUR PARTY in 1960. During the 1960s he opposed the idea of coalition and sought to build Labour into a second or even majority party by recruiting figures from broader sources than just the conventional labor unions. His efforts failed miserably, particularly in the 1969 election, which he had hoped would pave the wave for a glorious socialist future for Ireland. Accordingly, he urged the party's return to coalition politics and waged the 1973 election on those terms with FINE GAEL. The result was another coalition government from 1973 to 1977 in which he served as TÁNAISTE and minister for health and social welfare. Corish resigned as party leader following the coalition's defeat in the 1977 election and did not stand for reelection to the DÁIL ÉIREANN in 1981.

Cork, county and city

Cork is the largest county in Ireland and the city of Cork city is the third largest city on the island. Three eastward flowing rivers, the Lee, the Bandon, and the Blackwater, divide the mountainous ranges that cover the landscape. St. Finbarr founded a monastery on land that later became part of the city, and the VIKINGS and Normans later contributed to its development. The provisions of butter and pickled meat in the 18th century contributed to the city's development and in the 19th and early 20th centuries its port, COBH, or Queenstown, was a last stop for many trans-Atlantic voyages. The county comprised an important part of the territory controlled in the Middle Ages by the McCarthys, one of whom owned BLARNEY CASTLE. Edmund SPENSER, the Elizabethan poet, was a planter there as was in the following century the much more successful Richard Boyle, who became Earl of Cork. The eastern part of the county is especially celebrated for its dairy farming. Industries that have developed in and around the city include distilling, brewing, automobiles and tires (both now closed), oil refining, and, increasingly, chemicals and pharmaceutical products. A constituent part

Blackrock Castle in County Cork *(Library of Congress)*

of the NATIONAL UNIVERSITY OF IRELAND, University College Cork, is in the city. The county has a population of less than half a million, whereas the city and its suburbs total less than 200,000.

Corkerry, Daniel (1878–1964)
writer, teacher

Born in Cork and educated there by the Presentation Brothers and later at St. Patrick's College, Dublin, Corkerry taught in Cork and founded, with Terence MacSWINEY, the Cork Dramatic Society. A supporter of SINN FÉIN and then the anti-treaty side in the CIVIL WAR, he wrote collections of short stories and plays. His most significant work was his study of the culture of Gaelic Ireland in the 18th century, *The Hidden Ireland*. He exerted great influence on writers Sean O'FAOLAIN and Frank O'CONNOR, but they were disheartened by his exclusivist rejection, in *Synge and Anglo-Irish Literature*, as non-Irish of influences that were not Catholic or Gaelic. He was professor of English at University College Cork from 1930 to 1947, and served as a member of the SEANAD from 1951 to 1954.

Cornwallis, Charles, first marquis and second earl (1738–1805)
soldier, administrator

Born in London and educated at Eton, Cornwallis commanded the British forces in the unsuccessful struggle against the Americans in their war of independence. He was appointed commander in chief and lord lieutenant of Ireland in June 1798 after the uprising had started. He pacified Wexford, employing lenient measures, and accepted the surrender of General HUMBERT. After the uprising had been defeated, he worked to advance the ACT OF UNION. Along with the prime minister, William Pitt, he resigned over the king's refusal to accept Catholic emancipation as part of the settlement.

Corrigan-Maguire, Mairead (1944–)
peace activist

A stolen car driven by an IRA member who had been shot by the British army killed Mairead Corrigan-Maguire's sister's three children in August 1976 in BELFAST. Immediately afterward, she and Betty WILLIAMS organized the Peace Movement in Northern Ireland, which brought about massive cross-community demonstrations calling for an end to violence. It was later reformed and reinstituted as the Community of the Peace People. Both women received the Nobel Peace Prize in 1976. She has continued to work with that group, which organizes summer camps as a setting in which young Catholics and Protestants from Northern Ireland can come to know one another and engage in other forms of nonviolence and community outreach. In 1981 she married Jack Maguire, the widower of the sister whose children had been killed. Other recognitions she has received include the Carl Von Ossietzky Medal for courage from the Berlin section of the International League of Human Rights and honorary doctorates from Yale University, the College of New Rochelle, St. Michael's College in Vermont, and others. She also received the 1990 "Pacem in Terris" Peace and Freedom Award in Davenport, Iowa, and the Distinguished Peace Leadership Award from the Nuclear Age Peace Foundation of Santa Barbara, California, in 1992.

Corrs, The See IRISH ROCK MUSICIANS.

Corry, Issac (1755–1813)
politician

MP for Newry, County Down, in the Irish parliament, who had originally been sympathetic to the IRISH VOLUNTEERS, Corry later sided with the government, accepting a series of positions, including chancellor of the exchequer in 1798. He spoke on behalf of the ACT OF UNION. He failed to secure reelection to the House of Commons in 1806.

Cosgrave, Liam (1920–)
politician

Born in Dublin, the son of William T. COSGRAVE, Liam Cosgrave was educated at KING'S INN. Elected to the DÁIL ÉIREANN in 1943, he served as junior minister in the first coalition government (1948–51) and was minister for external affairs in the second (1954–57). In that capacity, he led the first Irish delegation to the United Nations. He succeeded James DILLON as leader of FINE GAEL in 1965. In 1970 he brought information on government arms purchases on behalf of the IRA to the attention of the then TAIOSEACH, Jack LYNCH. When a Fine Gael–LABOUR coalition won the 1973 election, he became Taoiseach. He presided over a ministry of extraordinary talents, including his own party colleagues Garret FITZGERALD and Ritchie RYAN, as well Conor Cruise O'BRIEN from the Labour Party, and exercised effective leadership despite his own social conservatism that differed from the liberalism of some in both the government and the party on issues such as the sale of contraceptives. He led the government's strong opposition to the IRA, especially following incidents such as the assassination of the British ambassador to Ireland, Christopher EWART-BIGGS, in 1976, and sought accommodation with the British in achieving a power-sharing solution for Northern Ireland at the SUNNINGDALE CONFERENCE in 1973. His government significantly expanded social-welfare programs. Inflation caused by external factors, including OPEC restrictions on oil sales and domestic unemployment, contributed to a resounding defeat of the coalition in the 1977 election. Cosgrave resigned as leader of Fine Gael and from the Dáil in 1981.

Cosgrave, William T. (1880–1965)
revolutionary, politician

Born in Dublin, Cosgrave was elected to the Dublin City Council as a SINN FÉIN member in 1909. He took part in the EASTER RISING and was one of those sentenced to death, which was commuted, although he was interned for a while. He represented Carlow-Kilkenny in the First DÁIL ÉIREANN and became minister for local government, in which position he was able to direct most of the local authorities in Ireland to accept the legitimacy of the Dáil Éireann. One of the cabinet who approved the ANGLO-IRISH TREATY, he served as minister for local government in Michael COLLINS'S PROVISIONAL GOVERNMENT, and succeeded him as chairman when he was

ambushed in August 1922. Under the constitution of the IRISH FREE STATE, he became the first president of its Executive Council (or cabinet). He presided over the repression of the republican insurgents in the CIVIL WAR and over the reestablishment of normal constitutional rule in the decade following. His articulate and determined vice president and minister for justice, Kevin O'HIGGINS, often overshadowed him, especially on matters such as the ARMY MUTINY crisis, but he retained a great degree of political flexibility in attempting to mollify more militant nationalist elements in the pro-treaty alliance, which had taken the form of a political party called CUMANN NA NGAEDHEAL. When O'Higgins was assassinated in 1927 he moved decisively to present legislation forcing Eamon DE VALERA and his abstentionist FIANNA FÁIL party to take their seats in the Dáil and become a legitimate constitutional opposition. He risked the loss of power when a no-confidence motion subsequent to Fianna Fáil's entry failed by one vote. In an election immediately after, Cumann na nGaedheal was returned to power for another four and a half years. When the 1932 election resulted in a Fianna Fáil victory, Cosgrave guaranteed that his party accept the democratic mandate of the Irish electorate and give power to men who had been their armed opponents in the civil war of a decade before. He accepted the leadership of Eoin O'DUFFY in the new FINE GAEL party that was formed out of Cumann na nGaedheal, the BLUESHIRTS, and the national center party in 1933, but shortly after he replaced O'Duffy as leader, which position he retained until 1944 when he retired from politics.

Costello, John A. (1891–1976)
politician

Born in Dublin and educated at University College Dublin, a barrister, Costello served as the attorney general for the IRISH FREE STATE government from 1926 to 1932. He was elected to the DÁIL ÉIREANN as a member of CUMANN NA NGAEDHEAL. When a very diverse anti–Fianna Fáil majority sought to form a coalition after the 1948 election, he was selected as a compromise leader and became TAOISEACH from 1948 to 1951 and again from 1954 to 1957, even though he was not a party leader. His first governments withdrew Ireland from the COMMONWEALTH and formally proclaimed Ireland a republic. He presided over the celebrated MOTHER AND CHILD SCHEME controversy. His second government oversaw Ireland's entry into the United Nations and a resumed IRA border campaign of limited extent that lasted well into the 1960s. Costello continued to serve as a TD until 1969.

Coulter, Phil (1942–)

songwriter, producer

Born in Derry, Coulter achieved celebrity writing or arranging Eurovision winning songs, including "All Kinds of Everything" sung by 1970 winner, Dana. In the 1970s he produced albums for folk bands and wrote songs such as "The Town I Loved So Well," about his native Derry, and "Scorn Not Simplicity," about disabled children. He continues as a major figure in the Irish and international entertainment world.

Council of Ireland

A concept that had rarely existed beyond paper, the Council of Ireland was established by the 1920 GOVERNMENT OF IRELAND ACT under which the island was partitioned. It sought to provide a mechanism whereby the governments of both parts of the island could institutionally act together on certain mutual issues, with ultimate aspirations that continued cooperation could lead to political unification. With the establishment of the IRISH FREE STATE in 1922, the authority of the council only applied to NORTHERN IRELAND, even though Free State officials served on it. That anomaly ended as part of the agreement canceling the report of the BOUNDARY COMMISSION in 1925. The concept served as part of the 1973 SUNNINGDALE AGREEMENT, but constituted one of the reasons the Ulster Workers Council staged the general strike in May 1974 that brought down the power-sharing government of the province which the agreement had endorsed. Among the institutions that grew out

of the GOOD FRIDAY AGREEMENT of 1998 is a North-South intergovernmental committee, which meets occasionally on matters of mutual interest and concern and which is similar in functions if not name to the Council of Ireland.

Cousins, Margaret (née Gillespie) (1878–1954)

feminist, educator

Born in Derry, Cousins was imprisoned as a suffragist who threw stones at 10 Downing Street in 1910. Moving to India, she served as the non-Indian faculty member of the Indian Women's University and the cofounder of the Women's Indian Association in 1917. She wrote extensively, taught, and was honored by Pandit Nehru for her contribution to Indian independence.

Cox, Arthur (1891–1965)

attorney

Adviser to the committee drafting the constitution of the IRISH FREE STATE and to the Irish Free State government itself, Cox was a solicitor whose firm still bears his name. He served as president of the Law Society in 1951–52. He married the widow of Kevin O'HIGGINS and, after her death and following his retirement, Cox became a Catholic priest and volunteered to work with Irish Jesuits in Rhodesia, where he was killed in a road accident.

Craig, James, first viscount Craigavon (1871–1940)

politician

Born in Belfast into a millionaire distilling family, Craig began his career in finance, but then served in the Boer War attaining the rank of captain. He was elected MP for East Down in 1906 and emerged as one of the more vigorous young unionist figures. In 1910 he arranged the selection of Edward CARSON, a Dublin unionist, as leader of Irish UNIONISM, while remaining the dominant figure in the Ulster Unionist Council himself. He promoted the Ulster Covenant in 1912, the Larne gunrunning in 1914 in the cause of resisting Irish HOME RULE. During the

First World War he was quartermaster-general in the 36th Ulster Regiment and saw action on the western front. After the war he served as parliamentary secretary successively to the minister for pensions and for the Admiralty. He succeeded Carson as leader of Ulster unionism after, the GOVERNMENT OF IRELAND ACT had created the province of NORTHERN IRELAND, and he became prime minister of the latter in 1921. He took part in two abortive pacts with Michael COLLINS in early 1922 in an attempt to combine lessened maltreatment of Northern Irish Catholics with restraint of the IRA. His primary commitment was to the maintenance of Northern Ireland as a separate entity from the IRISH FREE STATE. He opposed the BOUNDARY COMMISSION, refusing to nominate a member to it, and cooperated with the Irish Free State representatives in achieving the settlement whereby the commission's report was disregarded in order to maintain the status quo boundary. He achieved the abolition of proportional representation in local government elections in Northern Ireland in 1923, which worked to the disadvantage of Catholic nationalists, and in elections to the Northern Ireland PARLIAMENT in 1929, which worked to the disadvantage of independent unionists. He called an election in February 1938 specifically as a reaction to the change in the new constitution of the name Irish Free State to Ireland and to the negotiations between Eamon DE VALERA and Neville Chamberlain in which significant concessions were made to the Irish. He made numerous statements indicating his commitment to the maintenance of the Protestant character of Northern Ireland, such as announcing to the parliament: "We are a Protestant people and a Protestant state." Significant departures were made from the original educational measures for Northern Ireland that were to have advanced nondenominational education so as to allow Protestant instruction in many schools desirous of such. Catholic schools, which had refused to be part of the system, were allowed only partial fiscal support. He was made Viscount Craigavon in 1927. His government was notorious for the retention in office of many who had been ministers from the beginning. In 1940 Craig retired.

Craig, William (1924–)
politician

A UNIONIST member of the Northern Ireland PARLIAMENT for Larne from 1960, Craig served, successively, as government chief whip, minister of home affairs, and minister of health and local government, development, and home affairs again. In that last position in 1968, he ordered the RUC to block a civil rights march in Derry, which helped bring on the modern troubles. He left his office soon after in a dispute over the liberalizing policy of Prime Minister Terence O'NEILL. In 1972 he formed the Ulster VANGUARD Movement to oppose the Westminster prorogation of the Northern Ireland government. He was a major promoter of the general strike that brought down the power-sharing government in May 1974. The same year he was elected for East Belfast to the Westminster parliament as a member of the Vanguard Unionist Party, which he also led in the NORTHERN IRELAND ASSEMBLY (which created the power-sharing executive) and the Northern Ireland Convention (which failed to develop any acceptable alternative to continued direct rule). He lost his seat in the 1979 elections.

Craigavon

A new town created in 1965 between Portadown and Lurgan that was hoped would absorb population overflow from BELFAST. Town planners hoped to attract new industry, which, however, failed to materialize. The town remains a heavily subsidized municipality, consisting primarily of public housing, some of which became derelict and was torn down.

Cranberries, The
music group

See IRISH ROCK MUSICIANS.

Crawford, Frederick Hugh (1861–1952)
soldier

Decorated officer in the Irish Division in the Boer War, Crawford also served in the Royal Army Service Corps in the First World War and was commandant of the Northern Irish Special

Constabulary. His most celebrated role was as the organizer of the gunrunning at the Larne on behalf of the ULSTER VOLUNTEER FORCE in 1914.

Crawford, Robert Lindsay (1868–1945)
journalist
County Antrim–born journalist, Crawford was grand master of the Independent Orange Order, a group of primarily working-class members. He was expelled from that group and dismissed as editor of the *Ulster Guardian* when he supported HOME RULE. He moved to Canada in 1910 and later was trade representative in New York for the IRISH FREE STATE.

Crawford, William Sharman (1781–1861)
politician
Member of parliament for Dundalk, Crawford was a supporter of Catholic emancipation. He differed with Daniel O'CONNELL on REPEAL. He lost his seat in 1837 but was returned for Rochdale in 1841. He advocated federalism rather than repeal. He gave primary attention to legalizing for all of Ireland the Ulster Custom, that is, a practice of fixity of tenure, fair rent, and free sale of tenancy by tenants. To that end he formed an Ulster Tenant Rights Association in 1846, which developed into the Irish Tenant League in 1850.

Crean, Thomas (1877–1938)
explorer
Born the son of a poor farmer in Anascaul, County Kerry, Crean left home at 15 years of age. At 16, he joined the British Navy. His adeptness at seamanship led to his joining Robert Scott's expeditions to the Antarctic in 1901 and 1910, and the subsequent legendary exploration led by Ernest SHACKLETON in 1914. After retirement, Crean returned home and opened a pub, which he called the South Pole Inn.

Croke, Thomas William (1824–1902)
archbishop
Born in County Cork, educated at the Irish Colleges in Paris and Rome, Croke was ordained in 1847. He was president of St. Colman's College, Fermoy, County Cork, from 1858 to 1865, then parish priest of Doneraille, County Cork. He was bishop of Auckland, New Zealand, from 1870 to 1875, when he became archbishop of Cashel. Croke supported the LAND LEAGUE and was able to devise a statement for the Irish hierarchy whereby they could disregard the papal condemnation of the PLAN OF CAMPAIGN. He was a vigorous champion of the GAELIC ATHLETIC ASSOCIATION, whose national stadium in DUBLIN is named after him.

Croker, Thomas Crofton (1798–1854)
antiquarian
Born in Cork, Croker went to London where he was engaged as a clerk for the Admiralty. He frequently returned to southwest Ireland, where he concentrated on collecting poetry and folklore, and published numerous works on the same, such as *Fairy Legends and Traditions in the Southwest of Ireland* (1825–1828), *Legends of the Lakes* (1829), and *The Popular Songs of Ireland* (1839). He was a founder and/or member of various learned societies such as the British Archaeological Association and the Society of Antiquaries.

Cromwell, Oliver (1599–1658)
politician, soldier
Leader of the parliamentary army in the English Civil War and ruler after the execution of Charles I, Oliver Cromwell refused the Crown himself, taking the title of Lord Protector under a written constitution establishing an Instrument of Government in which Ireland and Britain were politically unified under a single parliament. He conquered Ireland for the parliamentary cause, defeating both the Irish supporters of the late king and the CONFEDERATION OF KILKENNY. He landed in Ireland in August 1649 and between then and his return to England in May 1650 wrought destruction in numerous places such as Drogheda, Wexford, Fethard, Kilkenny, and Clonmel, all associated

with brutal massacres reflective of his ideological mission to punish the Catholics of Ireland both for their "superstitious" religion and for their participation in the rising of a decade before. Those he left in command in Ireland finished the conquest and implemented the Cromwellian land settlement whereby anyone who had supported either the royalists or the Confederates, which meant most of the Catholic landowners, were, if not subject to more severe punishment, deprived of their lands and transported to Connacht, ostensibly to be given some land there, which was to be distributed based on a proportion of their earlier holdings. The lands taken from them were to be distributed to Adventurers, that is, those who had given money in support of the parliamentary cause at the outset of the English Civil War, and to the soldiers of the Cromwellian army. In theory, there was to have been a massive colonization of Ireland by new settlers. In fact, much of the land transferred was sold off to the New English, who were the Protestant English whose roots in Ireland were less than a century old. Also, many in the rank and file of the Catholic population did not follow their landlords to Connacht, but remained as tenants under the new owners. The effect of the transfer was to leave only 20 percent of the land of Ireland in the possession of Catholics in contrast to the 60 percent they owned before. The Cromwellian system established a congregational form of Calvinism as the official religion, but allowed some tolerance for other faiths, even allowing Jews to return to England for the first time since the Middle Ages, but not Catholicism, which in Ireland was outlawed with the execution of numerous priests and the forced transportation to the West Indies of numerous laity on assorted grounds. When Cromwell died in 1658, the dominant powers in Ireland quickly followed Britain in accepting the restoration of the monarchy under Charles II, the son of the late king. Both of Cromwell's sons, one of whom, Henry, was then the lord deputy in Ireland, acquiesced in the assertion of power by the old parliament dismissed by the father, which in turn invited the monarchy back.

Cromwellian land settlement See
CROMWELL, OLIVER.

Cullen, Paul (1803–1878)
archbishop

Born in Kildare, Cullen was educated for the priesthood and ordained in Rome, where he served, including being rector of the Irish College, until becoming archbishop of Armagh in 1849. He was transferred to the Dublin archdiocese in 1852 and was made the first Irish cardinal in 1866. He is regarded as the architect of the Counter-Reformation in Ireland as he implemented the reforms 16th-century Council of Trent in disciplinary, devotional, and organizational practices on the Catholic Church in Ireland. He encouraged the building of churches, the establishment of schools, and the promotion of popular devotional practices. A supporter of constitutional political action, he was hostile to revolutionaries and men of violence, including the FENIANS. Cullen's political concerns centered mainly on efforts to assert and advance the position of the Catholic Church in a country where the religion of the minority was the established faith. His anxiety to develop Catholic higher education in Ireland prompted his invitation to John Henry Newman to preside over the first Catholic university, which ultimately would evolve into University College Dublin.

Cumann na mBan
revolutionary organization

A women's organization led by Countess MARKIEVICZ and Kathleen Clarke that became affiliated with the IRISH VOLUNTEERS in 1914, most of its members supported the minority of the Volunteers who refused to support Britain in the First World War. They were supportive of the EASTER RISING and played important roles in the WAR OF INDEPENDENCE as messengers, first aid workers, and publicists. Most of the members opposed the ANGLO-IRISH TREATY and sided with its opponents in the CIVIL WAR during which several hundred adherents were imprisoned. Many continued as supporters of SINN FÉIN and the IRA throughout the 1920s.

Cumann na nGaedheal
political party

The party was founded in early 1923 to support the government of the IRISH FREE STATE. It never gained an absolute majority in Dáil Éireann but was the largest party from 1923 until 1932. The absence of republican Sinn Féin deputies after the 1923 election gave Cumann na nGaedheal a majority of those in attendance. The June 1927 election weakened the party's position, as it only had a plurality rather than majority of the attending deputies. Although it had five seats more than the now attending Fianna Fáil Party after the second 1927 election, the endorsement of the Farmer's Party and other independents were needed to remain in power. The party sought to broaden support for the government from more than the pro-treaty wing of the old Sinn Féin party and to attract following from commercial and propertied elements in society and even former unionists. It relied more on a politics of deference, that is, endorsement by the leading elements in society, including professionals, clergy, and bankers, than on building a mass organization, which may well have contributed to its ultimate demise in the 1932 elections. It also bore the onerous burden of securing public acceptance of the painful and expensive burden of state-building after the destruction of CIVIL WAR in an era when orthodox fiscal attitudes about government indebtedness prevailed. Its insistence on an impartial civil service, rather than patronage, and the assertion of civilian ascendancy over the military at the time of the ARMY MUTINY alienated many of its original supporters. After a very bad performance in the 1933 election, the party merged with the BLUESHIRTS and the National Centre Party into a new political group, FINE GAEL.

Curragh

A military camp in County Kildare since the late 17th century, it was the site of the 1914 "Curragh Mutiny" when Sir Arthur Paget, the commander of the British forces in Ireland, allowed his officers to retire rather than be involved in a potential enforcement of HOME RULE legislation on Ulster. The War Office then reassured the same men that the army would not be employed to coerce Ulster, which worked to further dishearten NATIONALISTS and cause them lose faith in the Liberal government that was advancing the legislation, even though it forced the resignations of the secretary of state for war, J. E. B. Seely, and the commander of the Imperial General Staff, Sir John French. After enactment of the ANGLO-IRISH TREATY, the camp came into the possession of the army of the Irish Free State.

Curran, John Philpot (1750–1817)
barrister

Born in Newmarket, County Cork, Curran became a barrister and king's counsel and was elected to the Irish parliament in 1783. He served as defense counsel for leading UNITED IRISHMEN, including Wolfe TONE. However, in 1803 he refused to defend Robert EMMET, the fiancé of his daughter, Sarah CURRAN. He was Master of the Rolls from 1807 to 1814.

Curran, Sarah (1782–1808)
romantic figure

Daughter of John Philpot CURRAN, Sarah Curran was engaged to Robert EMMET, the leader of the 1803 rising, whom her father refused to defend, and who was executed. Virtually disowned by her family, she moved to Cork and married Captain R. H. Sturgeon of the Royal Marines. She accompanied him when he was stationed in Sicily, but contracted tuberculosis and died in 1808 after they had returned to Hythe, in Kent, England. Her remains lie in the family plot in Cork, and she inspired the Thomas MOORE air, "She is far from the land."

Currie, Austin (1939–)
politician

Born in Coalisland, County Tyrone, Currie was educated at QUEEN'S UNIVERSITY BELFAST. He was elected as a nationalist member in the Northern Ireland PARLIAMENT in 1964, and engaged in protests against discriminatory public housing at Caledon, County Tyrone, in 1968. Active in the NORTHERN IRELAND CIVIL RIGHTS ASSOCIATION, he was a founder of the SDLP, or SOCIAL DEMOCRATIC AND LABOUR PARTY, and was elected to the various failed experiments at substitute legislatures for Northern Ireland in the 1970s and early 1980s. Currie was a member of the short-lived power-sharing executive of 1973–74. Encouraged by Garret FITZGERALD to enter politics in the Irish Republic, he was a FINE GAEL TD for Dublin West from 1989 until 2002. He was the Fine Gael candidate for the Irish presidency in 1990 losing to the LABOUR PARTY candidate, Mary ROBINSON. He served as a minister of state in the Departments of Education, Justice and Health in the "RAINBOW COALITION" led by John BRUTON from 1994 to 1997. Currie was not reelected in the 2002 general election and subsequently withdrew from politics.

Cusack, Cyril (1910–1993)
actor

Born in South Africa, Cusack came to Ireland as a child with his actress mother. He appeared on stage as a child and in the silent film, *Knocknagown* (1918). He was with the ABBEY THEATRE from 1932 to 1945 appearing in more than 60 productions, and then formed his own company, which staged productions in DUBLIN, Paris, and New York. He performed as well for the GATE THEATRE in Dublin and the Royal Shakespeare Company and the English National Theatre. He appeared in more than 50 films, including *Odd Man Out* (1947), *Shake Hands with the Devil* (1959), *Fahrenheit 451* (1966), *Sacco and Vanzetti* (1974), *True Confessions* (1981), and *My Left Foot* (1989). He received honorary degrees from the NATIONAL UNIVERSITY OF IRELAND and TRINITY COLLEGE in recognition of his standing as one of the most prominent Irish actors of the century, whose career spanned 73 years.

Cusack, Margaret Anne (1832–1899)
religious figure

Born in Dublin of Episcopal parents, Margaret Cusack joined an Anglican sisterhood in London, but she converted to Catholicism in 1858. She joined the Irish Poor Clares and took the name of Sister Mary Francis Clare. She went to Kenmare, County Kerry, to undertake relief of the poor at the request of a local clergyman. Although she did much for the poor during the bad harvests of 1879–80, difficulties within her community prompted her to leave. She sought to open a convent at KNOCK, County Mayo, but failed to obtain episcopal approval. In 1884 she founded a new order, St. Joseph's Sisters of Peace, and with papal sanction she went to the United States to serve Irish emigrant working girls. However, after differences with the American Catholic hierarchy, she resigned as mother-general. She wrote numerous biographies of figures such as Daniel O'CONNELL, Father MATTHEW, and saints PATRICK, BRIGID, and Columba (COLM CILLE), as well as an autobiography, *The Nun of Kenmare,* in which she was highly critical of the Catholic clergy. She died in Leamington Spa in England, reportedly having returned to the Anglican Church.

Cusack, Michael (1847–1906)
founder, Gaelic Athletic Association

Born in County Clare, Cusack was a teacher at various schools including BLACKROCK and CLONGOWES WOOD Colleges and then established a school to help students preparing for civil service examinations. He formed a civil service HURLING club, out of which grew the idea of the GAELIC ATHLETIC ASSOCIATION, which he helped found in 1884 with the endorsement of Bishop CROKE, Charles Stewart PARNELL, and Michael DAVITT. He was nicknamed "Citizen Cusack" and served as the model for the character "Citizen" in James JOYCE's *Ulysses.*

D

Dáil Éireann

The lower house of the Irish parliament or legislature, its name comes from the Irish word for assembly. The first Dáil Éireann met on January 21, 1919, and consisted of those SINN FÉIN members elected to the Westminster parliament in the December 1918 election who were neither in prison nor on the run. In accordance with party doctrine, they refused to attend Westminster, forming instead an Irish parliament. Cathal BRUGHA served as the temporary first president pending the escape from prison by Eamon DE VALERA, who then became president or first minister of the Dáil Éireann and who in turn nominated the rest of the ministry. Dáil Éireann in fact was the revolutionary government, under which the WAR OF INDEPENDENCE was conducted and which sought international recognition as the legitimate government of Ireland. The Dáil Éireann interpreted the special elections of 1921 to the parliaments in the northern and southern sections of the island, which had been called for in the 1920 GOVERNMENT OF IRELAND ACT as an election to the second Dáil Éireann. That body also confirmed de Valera as president. However, when the Dail narrowly approved the ANGLO-IRISH TREATY in January 1922, he resigned and Arthur GRIFFITH took his place. The Dail then became a symbolic body as real authority for receiving power from the British was with the then PROVISIONAL GOVERNMENT headed by Michael COLLINS. The Provisional Government was selected in accord with the treaty by the members of the parliament of Southern Ireland, essentially the same people who made up the Dail, but with the addition of the unionist or

independent members elected from TRINITY COLLEGE (anti-treaty Sinn Féiners refused to attend), and with the exception of those Dáil members elected to the parliament of Northern Ireland, also established by the 1920 legislation. Then, in June 1922, an election for a third Dáil Éireann was held in which the pro-treaty wing of Sinn Féin secured a plurality, which, when combined with the seats won by the Irish LABOUR PARTY, farmers representatives, and independents, gave pro-treaty members an overwhelming majority over the anti-treaty Sinn Féiners, who refused to take their seats. That body acted as the constituent assembly that would approve a constitution for the IRISH FREE STATE. In accord with the constitution, another Dáil had to be elected within a year of the constitution's approval. Since 1921, members of the Dáil have been elected by universal adult suffrage (over 18 years of age since 1974) by a system of single transferable proportional representation. The constituencies presently elect from three to five members, depending on the population of the constituency. Constituency boundaries and number of members can change based on changes in population, as can the total number of members of the Dáil. The Dáil can be dissolved by the president upon a vote of no confidence or at the request of the TAOISEACH (the title given to the head of ministry by the 1937 constitution), but an election has to be held at least every five years. The Dáil nominates the Taoiseach, who names his colleagues in the ministry. The 1922 Irish Free State constitution established an upper house, the SEANAD, selected by differing electorates, which holds only a suspensive veto on legislation. When de Valera held power in the 1930s, he had the Seanad abolished by constitutional amendment, but then reestablished a comparable body in the new constitution for Ireland that he successfully submitted to the electorate in 1937, which also held a purely suspensive veto and a membership that was indirectly elected or nominated.

D'Alton, John (1883–1963)
archbishop

Born in Claremorris, County Mayo, D'Alton received his doctorate in divinity in Rome, but also studied at Oxford and Cambridge. He taught as a professor of classics at MAYNOOTH from 1912 to 1936 when he became its president. He was made bishop of Meath in 1943 and then archbishop of Armagh and primate of all Ireland in 1946, being made a cardinal in 1953.

Daly, Cahal (1917–)
archbishop

Born in Loughguile, County Antrim, Daly was educated at St. Malachy's College, Belfast, QUEEN'S UNIVERSITY BELFAST, MAYNOOTH, and, after becoming a priest, at the Institut Catholique in Paris. He lectured at Queens in scholastic philosophy. He became bishop of Ardagh and Clonmacnoise in 1967, bishop of Down and Conor (Belfast) in 1982, and archbishop of Armagh and primate of all Ireland in 1990. He was made a cardinal in 1991 and retired in 1996. His position as bishop coincided with much of the modern Northern Ireland troubles, and he was especially outspoken in his ecumenical appeals for community reconciliation, his uninhibited condemnations of paramilitary violence, and his noting the side effects of the same on community and family life. He is regarded as having contributed greatly to the remarks made at Drogheda by Pope John Paul II on his 1979 visit when he earnestly pleaded for the renouncement of violence. On matters of Catholic doctrine and teaching, he was uninhibitedly orthodox, opposing efforts at legalizing abortion and divorce within the Irish Republic, but at the same time insisting on hierarchical opposition to any effort at imperiling the rights of the Protestants of Northern Ireland should political unity be achieved. Clerical sexual scandals, many involving paedophilia, which severely damaged public confidence in the church in Ireland, began to appear while he was primate.

Davis, Thomas (1814–1845)
publicist, cultural nationalist

Born in Mallow, County Cork, the son of a British army surgeon, Davis studied at TRINITY COLLEGE DUBLIN and became a barrister, although never practicing. With John Blake DILLON and Charles Gavan DUFFY, he cofounded the *NATION*, a paper stressing cultural NATIONALISM and featuring essays on the distinct history, culture, and language of Ireland. Davis wrote many romantic poems and ballads celebrating Irish history and culture, among them *A Nation Once Again* and *The West's Asleep.* It paralleled similar movements in other European nations that were either not unified or part of larger political entities. The circle about the paper became known as YOUNG IRELAND and supported Daniel O'CONNELL in the REPEAL campaign of 1843. He split with O'Connell on the Irish Universities legislation advanced by Prime Minister Robert PEEL in 1845. Davis supported nonsectarian colleges as a means of achieving cultural and national unity among Irish Catholics and Protestants, while O'Connell preferred that there be distinct denominational religious courses in any institutions established as alternatives to Trinity with its CHURCH OF IRELAND character. He died a few months after.

Davitt, Michael (1846–1906)
nationalist revolutionary, agrarian radical

Born in Straide, County Mayo, Davitt went to England after his family was evicted. He lost his right arm in 1856 in an industrial accident as a child laborer. He joined the IRISH REPUBLICAN

BROTHERHOOD in 1865. In 1870 he was convicted and sentenced to 15 years imprisonment for purchasing arms for the FENIANS. After serving seven harsh years in Dartmoor Prison, he was released in 1877. Afterward, he traveled to America, meeting John DEVOY, before returning to his native Mayo, where he organized the mass meetings that resulted in the formation in 1879 of the LAND LEAGUE with Charles PARNELL as its president. Davitt was instrumental in achieving the strategy of the NEW DEPARTURE whereby the IRB and its American supporters, the Land League, and the IRISH PARLIAMENTARY PARTY subordinated their differences and collaborated to advance Irish self-government and peasant proprietorship of the land. He later broke with Parnell for being too moderate on the land issue, and he came to accept Henry George's notions of land nationalization. He was in the forefront of those who opposed Parnell's leadership of the parliamentary party after the divorce scandal. He was elected several times to parliament, but lost his seat on one occasion for having been imprisoned and on other for having been bankrupt. Davitt was returned other times, however, representing Mayo and Kerry, and he joined with William O'BRIEN in founding an independent Irish party. He opposed the Boer War, retiring from parliament in protest, and wrote several books, including *The Fall of Feudalism in Ireland* (1904).

Day-Lewis, Cecil (1904–1972)
poet

Born in County Laois, but raised in England and educated at Oxford, Day-Lewis joined a circle of left-wing poets that included W. H. Auden, Stephen Spender, and Louis MacNEICE. He lectured at Cambridge, Oxford, and Harvard, and was made poet laureate in 1968. He also wrote mystery fiction under a pseudonym, Nicholas Blake.

Day-Lewis, Daniel (1957–)
actor

Son of poet Cecil DAY-LEWIS, Daniel Day-Lewis has appeared in numerous films, including *My Beautiful Launderette* and *A Room with a View* (both 1986) and *My Left Foot* (1989), for which he received an Academy Award. The latter film, based on the life of an Irishman afflicted with cerebral palsy, sparked Day-Lewis's interest in his Irish roots and led to his becoming an Irish citizen. He has more recently appeared in *Gangs of New York* (2002), based on Irish Americans in New York in the 19th century.

de Brún, Pádraig (1889–1960)
priest, scholar

Born in Grangemockler, County Tipperary, and educated at Rockwell College, University College Dublin, the Sorbonne, and Göttingen, de Brún was ordained a priest in 1913 and taught mathematics at MAYNOOTH from 1914 to 1945. He translated Greek and Latin classics such as *Antigone* (1926) and *Oedipus Rex* (1928) into Irish, as well as modern French and Italian works. His translation of Dante's *Inferno* into Irish was published posthumously. He wrote poetry in Irish and English and was the coauthor of a life of Christ, *Beatha Íosa Críost* (1929), in Irish. He was made president of University College Galway in 1945, made a monsignor in 1950, and director of the Arts Council in 1959. His brother was the Dominican superior and cardinal Michael BROWNE.

De Clare, Richard Fitz Gilbert (Strongbow) (1153–1176)
warrior, feudal lord

Also known as Strongbow, De Clare was a vassal of Henry II who was recruited by Dermot MacMurrough to assist him in a dispute with the king of Breifne and with Rory O'Connor, overlord of Ireland. Arriving in Ireland in 1170 with a force of over a thousand, he quickly conquered much of eastern Ireland. Married to Dermot's daughter, Aoife, he succeeded him as king of Leinster in 1171. Fear that his vassal might establish a separate kingdom prompted Henry II to come to Ireland that same year and assert his own kingship over the entire island.

Defenders

A secret society that sprang up among the Catholics of Armagh in the late 18th century as a counter to assaults from the Protestant PEEP O'DAY BOYS. A noteworthy confrontation was at Loughall, County Armagh, in September 1795 called the Battle of the Diamond, which was won by the Protestants and following which the ORANGE ORDER came into being. The Defenders combined Freemasonic secrecy and organization and romantic Catholic conservative idealization of a lost Gaelic Catholic order, which it was hoped could be restored by relief from abroad. The movement spread rapidly outside of Ulster and became curiously allied with the UNITED IRISHMEN during the 1798 rising. Afterward it declined and was replaced by a populist agrarian vigilantism known as RIBBONISM.

Delaney, Ronnie (1935–   )
athlete

Born in Arklow, County Wicklow, Delaney studied and ran track at Villanova University in Pennsylvania. In 1956 he was the fourth person to run the mile in under four minutes. In the same year at the Olympics running for Ireland, he set a new Olympic 1,500-meter record. He was undefeated in 40 indoor races in the United States, setting three indoor world records for the mile.

Democratic Unionist Party (DUP)

Familiarly referred to as the DUP, this party was formed in 1971 by the Reverend Ian PAISLEY, who has been its leader ever since. Its membership is much larger and remains distinct from his Free Presbyterian Church. The party was designed to provide a populist and uncompromising alternative to traditional UNIONISM. It opposed the Anglo-Irish agreements seeking to resolve Northern Ireland difficulties such as the SUNNINGDALE AGREEMENT of 1973, the HILLSBOROUGH AGREEMENT of 1985, and the GOOD FRIDAY AGREEMENT of 1998. However, the party took its proportionate seats in the power-sharing executive formed by the NORTHERN IRELAND ASSEMBLY called for by the last agreement. Until 2003 it remained second in

strength to the official unionists, although it had gained significant strength represented by success in European and Westminster parliamentary elections and local elections within Northern Ireland. In the fall of 2003, it surpassed the Ulster Unionist Party in elections to the Northern Ireland Assembly and, since then, several leading figures from the Ulster Unionists, including Jeffrey Donaldson, have switched to it. Other leading figures in the party include Peter Robinson and Nigel Dodds. In the May 2005 general election, the DUP won nine of the 10 seats for Northern Ireland held by Unionists at Westminster.

Derrig, Thomas (1897–1956)
politician

Born in Westport, County Mayo, Derrig served in the IRISH VOLUNTEERS and SINN FÉIN and was arrested several times during the WAR OF INDEPENDENCE. A member of the DÁIL ÉIREANN, he opposed the ANGLO-IRISH TREATY and refused to take his seat when elected for Carlow-Kilkenny in 1923. A founding member of the FIANNA FÁIL Party, he was minister for education in the DE VALERA governments from 1932 to 1948 other than for a nine-month period in 1939–40. He served as minister for lands in the 1951–54 de Valera government. He advocated making the study of Irish compulsory in schools.

Derry (Londonderry)

Derry is the name of both a county and a city in Northern Ireland. The county was formed by the amalgamation of the county of Coleraine with parts of Antrim, Donegal, and Tyrone at the time of the Ulster Plantation. It is a scenic area of fertile lowlands and ranges of hills. The city sits on the site of a monastery founded in the sixth century by COLM CILLE. In the Middle Ages it served as a diocesan center and the site of abbeys and friaries, but it declined and was virtually abandoned during the 16th-century conquests. It was revitalized as part of the plantation and became a great historical symbol for Ulster Protestants by reason of its valiant resistance to the JACOBITE armies when besieged in 1689. In the 18th and

19th centuries, its boundaries expanded beyond its historical walls and across the river Foyle. Eventually the textile industry came to predominate. The city has been a flashpoint in the modern Northern Ireland troubles because of its proximity to the border, which separated it from its natural hinterland to the west in County Donegal. Also, the city was de facto segregated, with many of its Catholics living in the Bogside, an area near the old city but identified with unemployment, poor conditions, and industrialization in its worst form, and one in which blatant sectarian gerrymandering of local government elections took place. Many of the early clashes in the 1960s grew from police and police auxiliary assaults on the Bogside following Catholic-NATIONALIST protests against the triumphalist spirit of the Protestant and UNIONIST APPRENTICE BOYS parades celebrating the 1689 defense of the city. Derry was one of the sites where authorities attacked civil rights marchers when they ignored proscriptions on their parades. BLOODY SUNDAY 1972 was one of the most unforgettable incidents in that sad history. There have been great advances recently in community reconciliation and significant economic rejuvenation. It remains the second largest city in Northern Ireland with a population of approximately 100,000.

Despard, Charlotte (1844–1939)
suffragist, revolutionary

Born in Edinburgh, after being widowed Despard became active in the Independent Labour Party and the women's suffrage movement. She moved to Ireland in 1910 and joined SINN FÉIN during the WAR OF INDEPENDENCE even though her own brother, Lord French, was the lord lieutenant for a period of the time. She opposed the ANGLO-IRISH TREATY and remained linked with others of its opponents, including Maud GONNE and Peader O'DONNELL, and she joined the Communist Party.

de Valera, Eamon (Edward George De Valera, Éamon de Bhailéara) (1882–1975)
revolutionary, politician

Born in New York, Eamon de Valera was sent back to Ireland as an infant by his mother after the death of his father, who was of Spanish extraction, to be raised by her brother in Bruree, County Limerick. He was educated at BLACKROCK and University College Dublin. He was gifted in mathematics and afterward taught at several Dublin schools, including Blackrock. He joined the GAELIC LEAGUE in 1908, where he met his future wife, Sinead Ni Fhlanagain. He joined the IRISH VOLUNTEERS and was commandant of the seized Boland's Mills during the EASTER RISING. Although sentenced to death by martial court, his sentence was commuted to life imprisonment. He was released the following year, 1917, and shortly afterward was elected as a SINN FÉIN candidate to parliament for East Clare in a by-election. In October he became the president of Sinn Féin and in November of the Irish Volunteers. One of the Irish activists imprisoned under the "German plot" allegations in 1918, he was nonetheless reelected in the 1918 general election. He escaped from Lincoln Prison in England on February 3, 1919, and returned to Ireland, where he was selected as president of the first DÁIL ÉIREANN that had been formed by the abstentionist Sinn Féin MP's. A few months later he went to the United States to promote an external loan for Dáil Éireann and to advance the prospects of international recognition. While in the United States he clashed with the leaders of the Irish-American support organization, the Friends of Irish Freedom, Justice Daniel COHALAN, and John DEVOY on the issues of authority over funds raised in the United States, the primacy of support for the cause in Ireland versus opposition to American entry to the League of Nations, and tactics in dealing with American political parties. The controversy ultimately inducing the formation of a rival group, the American Association for the Recognition of the Irish Republic.

He returned to Ireland at the end of 1920 and was the major figure in negotiating a truce with the British on July 11, 1921. After personal meetings and extended correspondence with Prime Minister David Lloyd George, was reached a formula to permit negotiations as to the relationship between the aspirations of the Irish

Eamon de Valera addresses the crowd in Cork, 1922. *(Library of Congress)*

people and the British COMMONWEALTH. He was not one of the plenipotentiaries sent to negotiate in October and opposed the ANGLO-IRISH TREATY that they ultimately accepted on December 6, primarily because of the dominion status it conferred on Ireland, as he preferred a concept of "external association" between Ireland and the empire, which he himself had formulated. When Dáil Éireann approved the treaty, he resigned as president of the Dáil Éireann and was the leader of the anti-treaty wing of Sinn Féin, which refused to accept the PROVISIONAL GOVERNMENT called for by the treaty. He refused later to attend the third Dáil Éireann elected in June 1922 in which the majority accepted the treaty. While he did not call for violent resistance to the government, de Valera's rhetoric encouraged many in Sinn Féin to side with the anti-treaty wing of the IRA in occupying places and disregarding the authority of the government. After the CIVIL WAR started, he became the president of a rival government to that of the elected third Dáil Éireann. In May of 1922 he issued the call to the anti-treaty forces to put aside their weapons when their armed struggle had proved fruitless. He was arrested and interned for over a year by the Irish Free State authorities while campaigning in the August 1923 general election to the fourth Dáil Éireann to which he was reelected. His elected anti-treaty colleagues continued to abstain from attendance.

In 1926 he sought to secure Sinn Féin approval to attend the Dáil Éireann if the oath of recognition to the king as head of the association of nations was removed, but he was unsuccessful, whereupon he formed a new political party, which most of his elected Sinn Féin colleagues joined. Called FIANNA FÁIL, it was willing to take its seats if the required oath was removed. Although 44 Fianna Fáil deputies were elected in the June 1927 election, their refusal to take the required oath barred them from taking their seats. The following month after the minister for justice, Kevin O'HIGGINS, was assassinated, the threat by the Irish Free State government to advance legislation that would unseat abstentionist deputies forced de Valera and associates to rationalize their signing the oath under the pretext that they had not read it and were only complying a requirement for their signature. Soon after they took their places, a no-confidence motion in the government failed after the Speaker cast a tie-breaking vote in opposition. A subsequent election strengthened both the government party, CUMANN NA NGAEDHEAL, and Fianna Fáil, at the expense of other groups.

Fianna Fáil obtained a plurality in the general election of 1932 and, together with the votes of the LABOUR PARTY, Eamon de Valera became president of the Executive Council and formed the first Fianna Fáil government. His major concern was to remove all elements from the Irish Free State constitution that related to the imperial connection, including the oath and the right of judicial appeal to the Privy Council. He set out to minimize and ultimately end the office of governor-general and abolish the SEANAD. This required constitutional amendments, which could be and were delayed by the Seanad. He also ceased forwarding the land annuity payments arising from the land purchase legislation to the British government. The latter retaliated with a high tariff requirement on imports from Ireland, but coincided with de Valera's commitment to a protectionist policy. A major challenge in his early years in power was the development of the BLUESHIRTS, a group that some feared might attempt a putsch against the government, but he decisively inhibited their activities. A few years later he acted as decisively against the IRA, members of whom he had earlier released from Irish Free State restrictions, by again subjecting adherents to special tribunals and internment,

even employing constitutional amendments granting wartime emergency powers after the outbreak of the Second World War in which some in the IRA sought to collaborate with a prospective German invasion of the British Isles.

De Valera's most permanent achievements include the drafting of a new constitution in 1937 and its electoral acceptance, which removed all reference to the British connection while at the same time not formally withdrawing from the COMMONWEALTH and allowing via an External Relations Act certain diplomatic functions to be performed for Ireland by the king. He ultimately reached a very favorable accord with Prime Minister Neville Chamberlain in 1938 in which a small lump-sum payment settled the land annuities issue, severe tariffs restrictions on Irish goods entering Britain were removed, and the British surrendered naval bases they had been allowed to keep in Ireland by the 1921 treaty. While leading the Irish delegation at the League of Nations (he occupied the post of minister for external Affairs while also heading the government from 1932 to 1948), he was outspoken in condemning aggression, specifically that of Italy against Ethiopia in 1935 and in supporting the application of sanctions. However, during the Second World War he persisted in asserting Irish neutrality against appeals, primarily from the British and the Americans, and less from the Germans, in emphasizing the impossibility of Ireland participating in an alliance while a part of the nation, Northern Ireland, was controlled by another country. However, Irish sympathy de facto was with the British and the Americans as evidenced by sharing of intelligence information, release of airmen who crashed in Ireland, and restrictions imposed on communications from the German legation. However, de Valera's symbolic sympathy call to the German legation in Dublin on Hitler's death alienated many.

De Valera served as president of the Executive Council and then TAOISEACH (as the head of government was called in the 1937 constitution) until 1948, when a coalition of all other parties replaced his government for three years. He returned to power again in 1951 until 1954, and then again in 1957 after an electoral victory in which his party secured the largest majority in the Dáil Éireann until that date. Finally, in 1959, he was elected president of Ireland and reelected again in 1966. He died two years after the end of his second term, at which time he was the oldest head of state in the world.

Although a revolutionary both in the war of independence and in the civil war, de Valera's own personal social philosophy was decidedly conservative and very Catholic, as he idealized a traditional and rural Ireland. A primary but unrealized goal was the restoration of the Irish language. Significantly and ironically, his immediate and personally nominated successor, Seán LEMASS, began the process whereby de Valera's protectionist and self-sufficient vision of Ireland was dismantled.

Devereux, Robert, second earl of Essex

See ESSEX, ROBERT DEVEREUX, SECOND EARL OF.

Devlin, Joseph (1871–1934)
politician

Of West Belfast working-class origins, Devlin first worked as a barman and then as a journalist. He was elected to Westminster in 1902 for Kilkenny as a member of the IRISH PARLIAMENTARY PARTY, and then served for West Belfast from 1906 to 1922. He supported John REDMOND in his call for the IRISH VOLUNTEERS (as National Volunteers) to support the British war effort in 1914, took part in the failed 1917–18 IRISH CONVENTION, declined to succeed Redmond as leader of the parliamentary nationalists, but led the NATIONALISTS in Ulster and even defeated SINN FÉIN candidate Eamon DE VALERA in the 1918 general election. He opposed partition and was a leader of the Irish nationalists elected to the Northern Ireland Parliament in 1921, who did not take their seats until 1925. He also represented Fermanagh-Tyrone in Westminster from 1929 to 1934. Devlin was highly committed to working-class issues, but he was also a champion of Catholic causes and played a large role in the revivification in 1905 of the Ancient Order of Hibernians as an activist social organization.

Devon Commission

A commission appointed by Prime Minister Robert Peel under Lord Devon in 1843 that inquired into the Irish agrarian system, including the relations between tenants and landlords, methods of cultivation, and ways of agricultural improvement. The Irish Great FAMINE made most of its recommendations academic.

Devoy, John (1842–1928)
revolutionary, journalist

Born in Kildare, Devoy joined the IRISH REPUBLICAN BROTHERHOOD in 1861, then served for a while in the French Foreign Legion to gain military experience. He was a major IRB organizer but was imprisoned in 1866 for 15 years. He was released in 1871 on terms that he leave the British Isles. He went to the United States where he became active in CLAN NA GAEL, the IRB support organization. He organized the *Catalpa* expedition that brought escaped Fenian prisoners in Australia to the United States. He went on to be a major figure in formulating the NEW DEPARTURE in which American supporters joined with the IRB, the LAND LEAGUE, and the IRISH PARLIAMENTARY PARTY in advancing Irish self-government and land reform. He supported the revived IRB under Tom CLARKE, helping arrange Roger CASEMENT's expedition to Germany in 1914 and supported the EASTER RISING. He was a central figure in the American Friends of Irish Freedom and split with Eamon DE VALERA on the mission of the latter to America during the WAR OF INDEPENDENCE. His newspaper, *Gaelic America,* supported the pro-treaty position in the Irish CIVIL WAR, possibly because of his suspicions of the authenticity of de Valera's REPUBLICANISM. He visited Ireland for the last time in 1924 and died and was buried in America in 1928.

Diamond, The   See PEEP O'DAY BOYS.

Dillon, James (1902–1986)
politician

The son of John DILLON and grandson of John Blake DILLON, James Dillon was elected as an independent TD for West Donegal in 1932. Although he had cast a vote for the formation of the first government of Eamon DE VALERA, he soon after founded a party, the NATIONAL CENTRE PARTY, which soon merged with CUMANN NA NGAEDHEAL and the BLUESHIRTS to form FINE GAEL, of which he became a vice president. From 1937 until 1969 he was TD for County Monaghan. Dillon represented the older parliamentary nationalist perspective in contrast to the SINN FÉIN origins of many in Fine Gael and was also a remarkable parliamentary orator. In 1942 he withdrew from the party when his appeal for support for the anti-Axis allies in the second World War was rejected and he remained an independent until 1951. However, Dillon did serve as minister for agriculture in the 1948–51 coalition government and rejoined Fine Gael in 1951, serving in the same position in the 1954–57 government, and then becoming leader of the party from 1959 until 1965.

Dillon, John (1851–1927)
politician

Son of John Blake DILLON, Dillon studied medicine but turned to politics and land agitation. A leading figure in the LAND LEAGUE, he was also IRISH PARLIAMENTARY PARTY member of parliament for Tipperary (1880–85) and East Mayo (1885–1918). He was imprisoned several times in the 1880s for his land activism. He had accompanied Charles Stewart PARNELL on his American fund-raising tour, but in the later 1880s he disregarded his opposition by serving as a leading figure in the PLAN OF CAMPAIGN, a more militant continuation of land agitation. He helped Archbishop CROKE in devising a formula enabling Irish Catholics to bypass apparent papal condemnation of the plan. Although in America at the time of the divorce scandal, he broke with Parnell and supported his ouster from leadership. When the party was reunited in 1900, he became deputy leader under the Parnellite John REDMOND. He was skeptical of the terms of land purchase legislation, disapproved of making Irish compulsory in the National University of Ireland, and feared the militancy of the IRISH REPUBLICAN BROTHERHOOD as likely to jeopardize the prospects of HOME RULE. He succeeded Redmond as leader of the Irish Parliamentary Party and presided over its demise and replacement by SINN FÉIN in the 1918 election.

Dillon, John Blake (1816–1866)
politician

Born in Ballaghaderreen, County Mayo, Dillon studied at MAYNOOTH and at TRINITY COLLEGE, becoming a barrister. He was a founder of YOUNG IRELAND, serving as a cofounder along with Thomas DAVIS and Charles Gavan DUFFY of the

John Dillon *(Library of Congress)*

NATION. He took part in the 1848 rising, but escaped arrest and made his way to America, where he practiced law until returning to Ireland in 1855. He was elected to parliament for Tipperary in 1865 and, while supporting repeal of union with Britain, opposed the FENIANS.

direct rule

When the Northern Ireland PARLIAMENT was suspended on March 24, 1972, following the refusal of its prime minister, Brian Faulkner, to surrender security powers and end INTERNMENT, responsibility for the governance of the province and authority over its officials and public services was given to a secretary of state for Northern Ireland, who was also a member of the British cabinet. Rule by a secretary of state continued until December 1999, when a Northern Ireland Executive was selected by the NORTHERN IRELAND ASSEMBLY in accord with the GOOD FRIDAY AGREEMENT, although at this writing the same has again been suspended pending a willingness of the major Northern parties to agree to serve together in a power-sharing government.

Disestablishment

The CHURCH OF IRELAND was disestablished by legislation in 1869 under which the church became a voluntary body. Aside from the church buildings and yards, all of its properties were disendowed, with about half being given to a Church Temporalities Commission for the purpose of supporting the clergy and other church officials, and the rest made available for the relief of the poor, to endow higher education, and to encourage agriculture and fisheries. The annual grant to MAYNOOTH College and the *REGIUM DONUM*, or regular grant to Presbyterian ministers, were also ended at the time.

Document No. 2

Eamon DE VALERA proposed an alternative to the ANGLO-IRISH TREATY of 1921 to his cabinet. He was reluctant to make it public during the DÁIL ÉIREANN debates on the treaty itself, but the document was ultimately included as an amendment to the treaty. It did not differ significantly from the treaty other than its insistence that Ireland was to be associated with the British COMMONWEALTH, of which association the king was head, but that Ireland was not a dominion and an oath to the king as head of the association was not to be required. It allowed British control of naval facilities in Ireland and granted Northern Ireland the same options available in the treaty.

Doheny, Michael (1805–1863)

poet, nationalist revolutionary

Son of a small farmer near Fethard, County Tipperary, Doheny became a barrister. He was a member of the Repeal Association and wrote poetry for the *NATION*. He took part in the 1848 uprising and afterward went to the United States, continuing to practice law and becoming one of the founders of the FENIANS in 1858.

Donegal

The most northwestern county in Ireland as well as the fourth largest in area, it has a population of over 137,000 and an area of 1,864 square miles. It is bounded on the north, the west, and the south by the Atlantic Ocean, except for a brief stretch about 10 miles long where it adjoins Leitrim. The eastern boundary of the county is Northern Ireland. Malin Head on the Inishowen Peninsula is the northernmost point on the whole island. St. COLM CILLE was associated with Donegal. It was the center for the O'Donnells and was called Tir Chonaill. Most of its chieftains fled to the Continent after the failure of the great uprising by O'Neill and O'Donnell in the late 16th and early 17th centuries. The landscape of mountains and beaches is breathtaking, but provides generally poor agricultural land. It has also made much of the county inaccessible and unattractive to planters. Much poverty was associated with the county in the 18th, 19th, and early 20th centuries, as many of its male population were compelled to seek seasonal work in Scotland. All of that is past history nowadays. Scenic attractions include the step cliffs at Slieve League, which are the highest in Europe, Mount Errigal, and the fifth-century B.C. fortress, the Grianan of Aileach. The largest town is Letterkenny, which has thrived because of the border, in the absence of which it would have been simply a suburb of Derry. Other towns include the county town Lifford, Ballybofey, the resort town of Bunoran, and the fishing town of Killybegs. Celebrated natives have included the home government advocate Issac BUTT, Cardinal Michael LOGUE, the Franciscan scholar Michael O'CLEARY, and the writer and revolutionary Peadar O'DONNELL.

Donegan, Patrick (1923–2000)
politician

A FINE GAEL TD for County Louth from 1954 to 1957 and 1961 to 1981, Donegan served as minister for defense from 1973 to 1976. In a speech at a military base in October, he referred to then president Cearbhall O'DALAIGH's referral of an Emergency Powers measure to the Supreme Court as a "thundering disgrace." The president resigned over the failure of the TAOISEACH, Liam COSGRAVE, not to have immediately insisted on the resignation of the minister for undermining the independence and dignity of the presidency. Donegan himself subsequently resigned as minister for defense. He became minister for lands and briefly minister for fisheries in 1977. Donegan retired from politics in 1981.

Dowden, Edward (1834–1913)
critic

Born in Cork and educated at Queen's College, Cork, and at TRINITY COLLEGE DUBLIN, Dowden was appointed to the chair of English literature at Trinity in 1867. He became well known for his critical works, including *Shakespeare: His Mind and Art* (1875) and studies of Shelley and George Eliot. An urbane critic, Dowden was a unionist in political sentiment, but tolerant of other views.

Down

Located on the northeast coast of the island, Down is situated in Northern Ireland. It is bounded on the north by County Antrim and on the west by County Armagh, but most of it is bounded by the Irish Sea. Belfast Lough, which enters the city's port, is on the north, and Carlingford Lough is on its south, separating it from the Republic of Ireland except for a narrow strip of land where Warrenpoint is located. The same area contains the celebrated Mountains of Mourne. The county has a population of over 63,000 and an area of 953 square miles. St. PATRICK reputedly lived in Down when first brought to Ireland as a slave and it is claimed he is buried there. New English and Scottish settlers were there before the Ulster Plantation, as Hugh Montgomery and James Hamilton acquired the lands of the imprudent O'Neills, which gave a greater authenticity to the Protestant and unionist identity of many in the county. The presence of BELFAST in the county explains its highly industrial character, as many of its major towns have become suburbs of the city, such as Bangor, Holywood, and Newtownards. The Ards Peninsula in the northeast is virtually cut off from the rest of the county by the picturesque Strangford Lough. Celebrated natives of the county have included the nationalist Bulmer HOBSON, the painter Sir Joshua REYNOLDS, the writer George "AE" RUSSELL, and the economist civil servant T. K. WHITAKER.

Downing Street Declaration

A joint statement issued on December 15, 1993, by Prime Minister John Major and TAOISEACH Albert REYNOLDS in which Britain declared it had no selfish strategic or economic interest in Northern Ireland and the Irish government declared its acceptance of the principle of consent whereby the constitutional status of Northern Ireland could not be changed without the approval of its people. The declaration was a response to the private conversations being conducted by SOCIAL DEMOCRATIC AND LABOUR PARTY leader John HUME and SINN FÉIN president, Gerry ADAMS, in the hope of securing Sinn Féin's renunciation of violence and thus bringing it into the constitutional process. The IRA proclaimed a cease-fire the following August.

Doyle, Roddy (1958–)
writer

A schoolteacher in North Dublin, Doyle wrote the trilogy *The Commitments* (1987), *The Snapper* (1990), and *The Van* (1991), based on modern working-class life. His books were made into films and a later book, *Paddy Clarke Ha Ha Ha* (1993), won the Booker Prize. The latter book and *The Woman Who Walked into Doors* (1996) deal with the frailty of family life.

Drennan, William (1754–1820)
poet, radical activist

Drennan was born in Belfast and was the son of a Presbyterian minister. Educated at Glasgow and at Edinburgh, he became a doctor and practiced in BELFAST, Newry, and, from 1789 on, in DUBLIN. There he became one of the founders of the UNITED IRISHMEN. He was acquitted on a charge of sedition in 1794 and afterward withdrew from active participation in the movement, although he remained committed to radical reforms such as Catholic emancipation. He wrote poems celebrating United Irishmen, such as "The Wake of William Orr," in memory of an executed United Irishman. Drennan was the first to coin the term *Emerald Isle* as a name for Ireland. He came into wealth and returned to Belfast in 1807 where he published a literary magazine and founded the Royal Belfast Academical Institution.

Drogheda

This town in County Louth is located near the mouth of the Boyne River and was founded by the Normans in medieval times. It was the site of the more celebrated of Oliver CROMWELL'S massacres in Ireland. The head of St. Oliver PLUNKETT is preserved in St. Peter's Church. In the 19th century, milling and brewing were its foremost industries. With a contemporary population of about 30,000 it is increasingly home for many commuters to DUBLIN.

Drummond, Thomas (1797–1840)
engineer, public administrator

Born in Scotland, Drummond served in the Royal Engineers and worked on the Ordinance Survey of Ireland. He was undersecretary for Ireland from 1835 to 1840 during the Whig ministry with which Daniel O'CONNELL was allied. He was responsible for implementing significant reforms, especially the recruitment of Catholics for public service. Among the reforms were the establishment of the ROYAL IRISH CONSTABULARY, the appointment of independent Stipendiary Magistrates, and the conversion of tithes into a fixed rent, all of which lessened public disorder. He annoyed many landlords by his insistence that property "had its duties as well as its rights." Drummond died while in office.

Dublin

Dublin is the largest city on the island and the capital of the Republic of Ireland. Its population, including its suburbs, is just short of one million, and it is located in County Dublin at the mouth of the river Liffey. The city started as a VIKING settlement in 841 and later in the medieval period was the center of Anglo-Norman power in Ireland. Dublin came into its glory in the 18th century, when it was regarded as the second city in the empire, as the nobility, gentry, and professionals of the PROTESTANT ASCENDANCY constructed fine mansions, broad squares, and substantial public buildings and the city spread eastward from its walled medieval location. But with the ACT OF UNION, the glory of the city declined and it became known for its poverty, a situation that continued well into the 20th century. This situation existed despite the growth of the city as a hub of a communications network featuring railroads extending throughout the country and two canals that extended west. The city expanded beyond the canals both northward to Drumcondra and Clontarf and southward to Rathmines and Rathgar. Dublin served as the scene for many of the major modern historical developments in Ireland. The old Irish parliament from before the Act of Union met there and Dublin was the site of the EASTER RISING of 1916 as well of many violent encounters during the WAR OF INDEPENDENCE and the opening stages of the CIVIL WAR. Dublin's population grew enormously during the latter part of the 20th century, prompting the government to aim at relocating many of its agencies throughout the country to counter the complications of overpopulation, commuter sprawl, suburbanization, and rural depopulation. It is a city noted for the youthful age of its population and for being the center of the economic rejuvenation

of the 1990s, by which Ireland has become known as the "Celtic Tiger."

Dublin Castle

The original building was constructed on the orders of King John in 1204. It served as the center of British authority in Ireland, especially from the 16th through the early 20th centuries. The lord deputies and lord lieutenants resided there until the construction of the Vice Regal Lodge in PHOENIX PARK in the late 18th century. During the period of the ACT OF UNION it served as the administrative center for the governance of Ireland. It was the objective of various insurrections ranging from the rebellion by Silken Thomas (Thomas FitzGerald, tenth earl of KIL-

St. Patrick's Cathedral in Dublin *(Library of Congress)*

DARE) in 1534 to the EASTER RISING in 1916. After the ANGLO-IRISH TREATY the castle was surrendered to the PROVISIONAL GOVERNMENT on January 16, 1922. It is presently used for public functions, especially diplomatic receptions.

Dubliners, The

A popular folk group started in 1962, their repertoire stressed Dublin street songs, sung in a decidedly Dublin accent. Ronnie Drew, Ciaran Bourke, and Luke Kelly were among the original members. The group has undergone several personnel changes over the years. Ronnie Drew left the group for a time in the 1970s and was replaced by Jim McCann. Ciaran Bourke collapsed on stage in 1974 and never recovered (he eventually died in 1988). Luke Kelly died in 1984. They were replaced by Sean Cannon and Eamonn Campbell. After 34 years, Drew left the band for good and was replaced by Paddy Reilly. They even ranked high in the British charts in the 1960s. They were comparable to the CLANCY BROTHERS and Tommy Makem in the Irish ballad revival of that decade. They have have recorded dozens of albums over the years, and have released albums commemorating their 15th, 25th, 30th and 40th anniversaries together. Though many different musicians have at one time or another been members of The Dubliners, one physical feature they have all had in common is their sporting of large, bushy beards. Paddy Reilly, the newest member, is the sole exception.

Dublin Metropolitan Police

A police force whose responsibility was limited to the city and county of Dublin and County Wicklow that was distinguished from the ROYAL IRISH CONSTABULARY. Its intelligence wing worked to counter the FENIANS and the force was employed in disturbances in 1913 against a lockout of unionized tramway workers, which made it unpopular. However, it was not engaged against insurgents in the WAR OF INDEPENDENCE, which allowed its continuance after the establishment of the Irish Free State, unlike the RIC. However, in 1925 it was amalgamated into the GARDA SÍOCHÁNA, the national police force.

Duffy, Charles Gavan (1816–1903)
politician, journalist
Born in County Monaghan, Duffy was self-educated and became a journalist, as well as being called to the bar. He was one of the founding editors of the *NATION* in association with Thomas DAVIS and John Blake DILLON, who also were leaders in the YOUNG IRELAND movement. He was imprisoned along with Daniel O'CONNELL in 1844 after the cancellation of the Clontarf monster meeting in support of repeal of the ACT OF UNION. Along with other Young Irelanders he broke with O'Connell in 1846 on the abstract question of the legitimacy of using violence. He actually took part in the abortive 1848 rising, but he was acquitted after four attempts at conviction. Duffy revived the *Nation*, became a leader of the IRISH TENANT LEAGUE, and was elected to parliament for New Ross in 1852. However, he became disillusioned with the Independent Irish Party group in parliament and emigrated to Australia in 1855, where he achieved success in politics in becoming the prime minister of Victoria in 1871 and being knighted in 1873. In 1880 he retired to the south of France and wrote extensively, especially memoirs and biographies about the Young Ireland movement. His writings were particularly critical of O'Connell.

Duffy, George Gavin (1882–1951)
lawyer, politician
Son of Charles Gavan DUFFY, born in England and educated in France and at Stonyhurst, Duffy practiced as a solicitor in England. He served as part of the defense team for Roger CASEMENT and soon after moved to Ireland where he was called to the Irish bar. He was a SINN FÉIN TD for South Dublin in the first, second, and third DÁIL ÉIREANN. Along with Sean T. O'Kelly, he sought to present the case for the Dáil Éireann at the Versailles Peace Conference. He also represented

the Dáil Éireann at Rome in 1920. Duffy was one of the plenipotentiaries that negotiated the ANGLO-IRISH TREATY in 1921, although was a reluctant signatory to it. He did vote for it in the Dáil Éireann and accepted the post of minister for external affairs in the PROVISIONAL GOVERNMENT, but resigned in August 1922 in protest at the suspension of the Dáil Éireann courts. He resigned his seat in the Dáil Éireann in 1923 over the failure to treat republican prisoners as prisoners of war and returned to legal practice. He was appointed to the High Court in 1937 and appointed its president in 1946. Duffy was an adviser to the drafting of the 1937 constitution, especially its statement of fundamental rights.

Duggan, Eamonn (1874–1936)
lawyer, politician

Born in County Meath, Duggan was a solicitor who took part in the EASTER RISING. He represented the family of hunger striker Thomas ASHE at the inquest following his death. He was elected for Meath to the DÁIL ÉIREANN from 1918 to 1933. He was arrested during the WAR OF INDEPENDENCE and was one of the plenipotentiaries at the negotiations for the ANGLO-IRISH TREATY in 1921 and served as minister for home affairs in the PROVISIONAL GOVERNMENT until September 1922. He was a parliamentary secretary to the minister for defense and the Executive Council in the CUMANN NA NGAEDHEAL government. Duggan was elected to the SEANAD in 1933, being the last elected official to have to take the controversial oath to the king upon taking his place.

Dukes, Alan (1945–)
politician

Educated at University College Dublin, Dukes was an economist who worked for the Irish Farmer's Association, ultimately directing their office at EC headquarters in Brussels. From 1976 to 1980 he served on the staff of EEC commissioner Richard Burke. In 1981 he was elected to the DÁIL ÉIREANN for County Kildare as a member of FINE GAEL and became minister for agri-

culture in the short-lived government headed by Garret FITZGERALD. In the second of his ministries, he became minister for finance until 1986 when he was made minister for justice. When Fine Gael and its coalition partner, LABOUR, lost power in 1987, he replaced Fitzgerald as the leader. During his leadership in opposition he adhered to the "Tallaght Strategy" of approving the economizing measures of TAOISEACH Charles HAUGHEY that many saw as contrary to Haughey's own electoral message but closer to Fine Gael thinking. Following a poor performance by Fine Gael in the 1990 presidential election he was ousted as party leader and replaced by John BRUTON. In February 1994 Dukes became involved in a failed attempt to oust Bruton as leader, and he resigned from the front bench. In December 1994 Bruton became Taoiseach and Dukes failed to secure a ministerial position. Two years later, in December 1996, Dukes returned as minister for transport, energy and communications. In 1997 Dukes became chairman of the Irish Council of the European Movement. In 2001 he backed Michael Noonan in a successful bid to become leader of Fine Gael. He retired from politics after losing his seat in the general election of 2002 and was recently appointed director general of the Institute of European Affairs.

Dungannon Clubs

Bulmer Hobson and Denis McCullough founded this organization of Ulster nationalists in 1905 in commemoration of the DUNGANNON CONVENTION of 1782. Its objectives were to propagandize for Irish separatism, economic self-sufficiency, Irish language restoration, and establishment of a republic. The group was eventually absorbed into SINN FÉIN between 1906 and 1908. Its founders were also members of the IRISH REPUBLICAN BROTHERHOOD.

Dungannon Convention

A convention of the IRISH VOLUNTEERS, meeting in Dungannon, County Tyrone, on February 15, 1782, passed resolutions demanding parliamentary and judicial independence for Ireland and the mitigation of the PENAL LAWS. The publicity it received contributed to the passage of a measure demanding parliamentary independence, introduced by Henry GRATTAN, by the Irish parliament the following April and the ultimate acceptance of such by the parliament at Westminster later the same year.

Dunlop, John Boyd (1840–1921)

inventor, industrialist

Born in Scotland, Dunlop went to BELFAST and practiced as a veterinarian. In 1887 he redeveloped a pneumatic rubber tire that had been earlier invented in 1845. His design, using a rubber inner tube, began to be mass produced in 1890 by the Dunlop Company. He sold the patent shortly afterward for a considerable sum and went on to develop further innovations in line with the development of the automobile industry.

Dunraven, Windham Thomas Wyndham Quin, fourth earl of (1841–1926)

landowner, politician

Born at Adare, County Limerick, educated at Christ Church, Oxford, where he did not take a degree, Dunraven was a correspondent for the *London Daily Telegraph* and covered Abyssinia (Ethiopia) in 1867 and the Franco-Prussian War in 1870–71. He traveled in the United States and wrote about Yellowstone National Park and was a competitor as a yachtsman in the Americas Cup races in 1893 and 1895. A Conservative member of parliament, he served as undersecretary of state for the colonies in 1885–86 and 1886–87, and chairman of the commission on sweated labor from 1888 to 1890. He is best remembered as a constructive UNIONIST who promoted alternative solutions to the HOME RULE issue and the land question. He chaired a land conference in 1902–03 and through the Irish Reform Association, of which he was president, championed a scheme of devolution through local government in 1904, but it met with disapproval from both the Ulster unionists and the southern NATIONALISTS. He was a member of the first Seanad of the IRISH FREE STATE. He was regarded as a model landlord on his 39,000-acre estate at Adare.

Dwyer, Michael (1771–1815)

revolutionary

A UNITED IRISHMAN who took to the Wicklow Mountains following the failure of the rising, Dwyer had a bounty on his head for five years. He was supposed to join Robert EMMET in the 1803 rising but never received the signal to do so. Afterward, he surrendered and was transported to Botany Bay and ultimately to Tasmania. But in 1808 he returned to Sydney and even became high constable.

E

Eames, Robert (1937–)
archbishop

Educated at Methodist College, Belfast, QUEEN'S UNIVERSITY BELFAST, and TRINITY COLLEGE DUBLIN, Eames served as a curate in Bangor, County Down, and then as rector in Belfast before becoming bishop of Derry and Raphoe in the CHURCH OF IRELAND in 1975 and then bishop of Down and Connor in 1980. In 1986 he became archbishop of Armagh, and was created a life peer in 1995. A celebrated advocate of peace and understanding, he advised the Irish government about Protestant concerns prior to the issuance of statements regarding Northern Ireland. He plays a significant role within the general Anglican Communion. He is the recipient of honorary degrees from both of his alma maters as well as the Universities of Lancaster and Cambridge. In 2003 he was appointed chairman of the Lambeth Commission on Communion to examine challenges to Anglican unity arising from the ordination of homosexual bishops in the United States, which issued a report in October 2004 that called for avoidance of actions that inhibit unity.

Earls, Flight of the

Hugh O'NEILL, the earl of Tyrone, and Rory O'DONNELL, the earl of Tyrconnell, fled Ireland with a group of their followers from Rathmullen, County Donegal, on September 4, 1607. They had been defeated in the extended war between 1594 and 1603 and had arrived at a peace settlement with Lord MOUNTJOY under which they were permitted to keep their positions, but under English law with their titles derived from the king rather than based on the Gaelic system of succession. Historians still debate whether their flight was prompted by apprehension that their position in their territories was liable to be further weakened by the New English authorities or whether they were already plotting with potential continental allies and their plans had become known to the authorities. At any rate their departure, which turned out to be permanent, enabled the English to commence the PLANTATION of Ulster, that is, the settlement of the lands that they were interpreted to have abandoned.

Easter Rising

The rising took place in Dublin between April 24 and May 1, 1916. It was planned by the military council of the IRISH REPUBLICAN BROTHERHOOD (IRB), which held sway over the IRISH VOLUNTEERS. Originally planned for Easter Sunday, it was delayed when Eoin MACNEILL, the head of the Irish Volunteers, called off the orders for the Volunteers to mobilize throughout the nation. He did so when he discovered that a rising had been called to contest the policy that military action should be taken only for defensive purposes and that an expected arrival in Kerry of German weapons and volunteers from among Irish prisoners of war in Germany, arranged by Roger CASEMENT, had fallen through. The IRB leaders then went ahead with an operation generally limited to Dublin on Easter Monday as about 1,000 volunteers and 200 members of James CONNOLLY'S IRISH CITIZEN ARMY seized a number of public positions within Dublin and made the

GENERAL POST OFFICE on Sackville (now O'Connell) Street their headquarters. Padraic PEARSE read a proclamation announcing the establishment of a provisional government of the Irish Republic. Other places in the city where they established positions included the Four Courts, Jacob's Biscuit Factory, St. Stephen's Green, and the Royal College of Surgeons. Over the next four days, the British forces, reinforced with 2,500 men from the CURRAGH, began attacking the various rebel positions. By Saturday most had been overtaken, at a cost of 500 dead and 2,500 wounded (many civilians caught in crossfire), and millions in damage. Pearse at the General Post Office agreed to surrender unconditionally.

Toward the end of the week, General Sir John MAXWELL arrived to take command of the situation. Martial law was proclaimed and martial courts began trials of leaders of the rising, of whom fifteen were executed between May 3 and May 12, included Pearse, Connolly, and Thomas CLARKE. Ninety-seven others were sentenced to death, but outrage on the part of a public that had opposed the rising as well as pleas from churchmen and Irish parliamentary party leaders prompted a halt to the executions. But the executions served as a trigger, which achieved the objective of the rebels, most of whom, in knowing that their military plan was futile, believed their blood sacrifice would waken

Irish prisoners being marched along a Dublin quay under British guard, during the Irish insurrection that began on Easter Monday, 1916 *(Library of Congress)*

Irish public outrage and engender general sympathy with their objectives. The 97, along with more than 120 others, were sentenced to various terms of imprisonment and nearly 2,000 other suspected rebels were interned in camps in Britain. The latter were released before the year was out and all were released by July 1917.

Economic War

Soon after forming his government in 1932, Eamon DE VALERA announced the suspension of payment of land annuity sums to the British government. The monies were payments made in return for government financing of land purchase by tenants from landlords under the various Land Purchase acts of the late 19th and early 20th centuries. The British retaliated by imposing tariffs on cattle and agricultural imports from Ireland. The Irish government in turn imposed tariffs on such British goods as coal, cement, machinery, and electrical goods entering Ireland. Obviously, the war was more damaging to Ireland, 96 percent of whose exports went to Britain, but it did coincide with de Valera's policy to make Ireland economically self-sufficient. The Irish cattle trade was devastated, as many outraged farmers were drawn to the appeal of the anti–de Valera BLUESHIRT movement, but there was some increment in tillage, especially of grains, and a boost in employment in protected and subsidized industries, such as cement and sugar beet cultivation. A gradual softening of attitudes began following a 1935 pact dealing with cattle and coal and ending with a 1938 agreement between de Valera and Prime Minister Neville Chamberlain, which terminated the tariffs in return for a final lump-sum payment of 10 million pounds in lieu of the annuities.

Edgeworth, Henry Essex (1745–1807)

A cousin of Maria EDGEWORTH, Henry Edgeworth's father had converted to Catholicism and he was educated by the Jesuits and at the Sorbonne. He became a priest and served the poor of Paris and later the English and Irish in the city.

He took the surname "de Firmont" because of the difficulty the French had in pronouncing Edgeworth. He became spiritual director to the sister of King Louis XVI in 1791 and was the confessor for the king prior to his death as the guillotine in 1793. Edgeworth escaped to England, but declined positions in Ireland, becoming instead chaplain to the exiled king Louis XVIII in Saxony. When the exiled court went to Russia he accompanied it. He died there from fever contracted while ministering to French prisoners of war.

Edgeworth, Maria (1767–1849)
writer

One of 22 children of Richard Lovell EDGEWORTH, Maria Edgeworth helped raise her siblings as well as acting as agent for the estate her father brought his family to in Edgeworthstown, County Longford. She also wrote various works ranging from educational books and children's tales to novels, which earned her an international reputation. *Castle Rackrent* (1800) and others with an Irish setting such as *The Absentee* (1812) and *Ormond* (1817) deal with much of then contemporary Irish society, especially relations between the Protestant Ascendancy and the general population, and landlords and the peasantry. Her work drew the admiration of Sir Walter Scott, with whom she exchanged visits. She also wrote novels, including *Belinda* (1806), with an English setting. She used her own resources and raised assistance from abroad to provide relief for victims of the Great FAMINE in the last years of her life.

Edgeworth, Richard Lovell (1744–1817)
landlord, inventor

Born in Bath, England, and educated at Oxford and TRINITY COLLEGE DUBLIN, Richard Edgeworth settled in his vast estate at Edgeworthstown, County Longford, in 1782. Married four times and the father of 22 children, including the writer, Maria EDGEWORTH, he was a landlord who undertook measures for reclaiming bogs and improving roads and sought to alleviate conditions for his tenantry. He also invented a pedalless bicycle, a pedometer, and a system of telegraphy between Galway and Dublin, and wrote about education in collaboration with his daughter. A member of the Irish parliament for Johnstown, County Longford, he supported Catholic emancipation and parliamentary reform. He opposed the ACT OF UNION.

Electricity Supply Board

Legislation passed by the IRISH FREE STATE established the Electricity Supply Board (ESB) as a public corporation for providing electricity through a national network of generating stations. The first such was the Shannon Scheme at Ardnacrusha, County Clare, while other rivers were utilized in later decades. Many peat-fired generators were also employed in connection with BORD NA MONA. Naturally oil, gas, and coal are the other major sources of power for contemporary stations. Priority was given to industry, then to urban areas, and finally by the mid-1970s virtually all of rural Ireland was electrified.

Emergency, the

The period of the Second World War from September 1939 through May 1945 when Ireland (or Eire, as then designated) maintained its neutrality despite pressures from Britain and later the United States to enter the war against the Axis and to a lesser degree from the Germans to side with them. Eamon DE VALERA, as TAOISEACH and as minister for external affairs, remained committed to neutrality, a position objected to by few in Ireland. Strict censorship was imposed on the Irish media to inhibit public sympathy being drawn to either side in the war. Strict rationing was also required because few goods were available for import from Britain due to war-induced demands and restricted availability of shipping. The government employed EMERGENCY POWERS LEGISLATION to intern hundreds of IRA members, as well as imprison hun-

dreds more, and even execute six, because the IRA's declaration of war on Britain and readiness to collaborate with Germany could have jeopardized Ireland's neutrality.

Emergency Powers legislation

From the beginning of the Irish state, as well as Northern Ireland, legislation has been enacted empowering the state to employ extraordinary powers to deal with internal challenges to its authority. The instruments the authorities have employed have included military tribunals, internment, juryless trials, and various deviations from standard common law procedural rules. Northern Ireland employed a series of Special Powers Acts, which later became permanent, evoked by the minister for home affairs in emergencies, which over a period of time gained a reputation for being employed in a sectarian manner. The IRISH FREE STATE passed during the CIVIL WAR an Emergency Resolution giving extraordinary powers to military tribunals. After the civil war, various temporary public safety measures were passed to deal with the continued existence of IRA and SINN FÉIN movements that had not accepted the legitimacy of the state. Similar legislation was passed after the assassination in 1927 of Kevin O'HIGGINS, minister for justice, and again in the early 1930s. Eamon DE VALERA, although having campaigned against such measures while in opposition and having released interned IRA members upon coming to power, invoked the same type measures against the challenge posed by the BLUESHIRTS in 1933 and 1934. But he also used it against the IRA a few years later following the killing of a landlord and of a retired British naval officer. With the outset of the Second World War, an Emergency Powers Act was passed giving powers of internment to the minister for justice, in addition to existing Treason and Offences against the State acts. In 1976, following the assassination of Christopher EWART-BIGGS, the British ambassador, another Emergency Powers Act was passed to facilitate the implementation of the existing Offences against the State Act.

Similarly in Northern Ireland, after the suspension of its parliament and the imposition of DIRECT RULE, the old Special Powers Legislation was replaced by a Prevention of Terrorism Act and by the employment of juryless courts, with restrictions on standard procedural and evidence rules, to combat the activities of the IRA and of assorted loyalist groups.

Emmet, Robert (1778–1803)
revolutionary

Robert Emmet was the younger brother of Thomas Addis EMMET. He was born in Dublin of a Protestant family of Kerry and Tipperary origins. He was forced to withdraw from TRINITY COLLEGE in 1798 because of his UNITED IRISHMEN involvement. After the failure of the 1798 uprising he went to the Continent, making contact with exiled Irish activists and with Napoleon. Returning to Ireland, Emmet began to organize for another rising that might coincide with an expected resumption of war between France and Britain. An explosion in an arms depot necessitated that he act prematurely, calling the rebellion into action on July 23, 1803. There was inadequate coordination with expected allies, including Michael DWYER in Wicklow, and, as a result, only about 100 took part in a futile effort to storm DUBLIN CASTLE. On the way, the group murdered the Lord Chief Justice, Lord Kilwarden. Emmet escaped, but was apprehended a month later, tried, and executed on September 20. He became an icon in Irish nationalist martyrology because of his romance with Sarah Philpot CURRAN and his speech from the dock in which he asked no man "to write his epitaph" until "my country takes her place among the nations of the earth."

Emmet, Thomas Addis (1764–1827)
revolutionary, barrister

Born in Cork, Thomas Emmet was the elder brother of Robert EMMET, and studied medicine at the University of Edinburgh and law at the Inns of the Court, London. A prominent barris-ter, he was a useful defender of the UNITED IRISH-MEN, with whom he was associated. He was among a number of leaders in the group arrested in March 1798 who, after confessing, were given the option of exile. Emmet was first interned in Inverness Shire and then moved to Amsterdam in 1802 and New York in 1804, where he became politically prominent.

Encumbered Estates Act

Legislation passed by parliament in 1849 during the Great FAMINE, which sought to facilitate the change of ownership of Irish land with the expectation that an inefficient landlord class could be replaced by an improving ownership comparable to that of England. The legislation enabled land straddled with debts and other "encumbrances," such as wills that restricted transfer of land other than to eldest sons, nonetheless to be sold. The act resulted in the sale of almost a quarter of the land in the country, but most of the purchasers were Irishmen and many were speculators rather than improvers.

Enniskillen bombing

Eleven people, all of whom were civilians, were killed by an IRA bomb at the Remembrance Day Ceremony on November 8, 1987, at the cenotaph in Enniskillen, County Fermanagh. It was a major terrorist deed that proved counterproductive for the IRA.

Essex, Robert Devereux, second earl of (1566–1601)

A favorite of Queen Elizabeth I, as had been his father who had campaigned to colonize east Ulster in the 1570s, where he was responsible for the massacre of the population of Rathlin Island. The earl of Essex had failed to achieve success in actions against Spain, which greatly disappointed the queen. Accordingly, he sought to regain her confidence by accepting the Lord Lieutenancy of Ireland in 1599 and undertaking a war against the Irish forces led by Hugh

O'NEILL. Despite an enormous force, his efforts failed and he negotiated a truce with O'Neill and then returned of his own volition to England to explain his position. The queen was unconvinced and he was arrested. In 1601 he was beheaded.

Eucharistic Congress

Ireland was host to the 31st Eucharistic Congress, an international assembly of Catholics designed to promote understanding of and devotion to the Eucharist, that is, the presence of Christ in the consecrated bread and wine, in June 1932. The event was timed to coincide with celebration of the approximate 1,500th anniversary of St. PATRICK's mission to Ireland. It also provided an occasion to manifest the linkage of nationalism and religion with the implication that Catholicism, the religion of the vast majority of the Irish people, was again the de facto religion of Ireland now that the country had achieved political independence. The highlight of the congress occurred with attendance by a million people at a Mass in PHOENIX PARK at which John MCCORMICK sang "Panis Angelicus." The presence of over 100 bishops, nine cardinals, and thousands of overseas pilgrims made it one of the first occasions on which the recently formed first FIANNA FÁIL government could assert its international legitimacy.

European Union

The organization of European states that began with the six-member Common Market created in March 1957. Ireland unsuccessfully applied for membership in 1961, but was turned down along with Great Britain because of Charles de Gaulle's apprehension that the expansion would serve as a wedge for American domination of Europe. After de Gaulle resigned the French presidency in 1970, both countries quickly reapplied and were accepted. A plebiscite was held in Ireland in 1972 in which more than 80 percent of the voters approved joining. Formal entrance took place in January 1973. Since then the organization has

expanded in membership as well as changed in character, developing from an exclusively economic partnership to a political entity as reflected in the name change from Common Market to European Community to European Union. The European Parliament was formed with, within a few years, membership directly elected from the voters of the member states. Increasingly, member states have been required to conform to European Union standards on a variety of issues ranging from human rights to economic rules to environmental standards. The Irish electorate has accepted by referenda in 1987 and again in 1992 European legislation and agreements to finalize creation of a single European market and a common European currency that, in January 2001, replaced the former national currencies of most members. Membership has brought substantial benefits to the Irish economy, as Ireland, which on joining had been the poorest member, has been a net beneficiary when grants received are matched against Irish contributions. That factor has played a major part in the phenomenal economic growth of the country in the latter part of the 20th century, so much so that Ireland is expected in the future to be a net contributor rather than beneficiary, especially with the expansion in membership and the inclusion of less developed nations. Union insistence on conformity to certain standards has also affected Ireland socially, most decidedly in the area of women's right, as the Irish government was forced in the 1970s to abandon its practice of dismissing female civil servants upon marriage. In 2001, the Irish electorate at first rejected the Treaty of Nice that would have allowed further expansion of the union, but a year later accepted the same after a formal declaration acknowledging Irish neutrality in exempting the country from military policy of the union. On May 1, 2004, the union grew to 25 members with the admission of former satellites of the Soviet Union, including Poland, Hungary, Latvia, Estonia, Lithuania, the Czech Republic, and Slovakia, as well as Slovenia, formerly part of Yugoslavia, the Greek portion of Cyprus, and Malta. A major current concern is the rejection by some European electorates of ratification of a fundamental constitution that had been drafted for the European Union.

Ewart-Biggs, Christopher (1922–1976)

diplomat

British ambassador to Ireland, Ewart-Biggs had been a soldier in the Second World War and lost his right eye in the Battle of El Alamein in 1942. He served as British consul in Algiers in 1961, where hard-line French *colons,* who opposed concessions to Algerian nationalism, made him an object for assassination. In 1976 the Provisional IRA detonated a land mine destroying his car as he was driven from his residence in County Wicklow to the British embassy in Dublin. His death prompted the passage of EMERGENCY POWERS LEGISLATION and the establishment of an annual memorial prize in his honor awarded to recipients judged to have contributed to improved Anglo-Irish relations.

External Relations Act

Legislation introduced by Eamon DE VALERA on the occasion of the abdication of King Edward VIII, it allowed the king to act on the advice of the Irish Executive Council in naming consuls and signing treaties so long as Ireland was associated with the COMMONWEALTH of Nations of which he was the symbol. At the same time, de Valera introduced legislation for a new constitution for Ireland, which eliminated all reference to the Crown. It was his way of achieving the proposals of his famous DOCUMENT NO. 2, put forward during the debate on the ANGLO-IRISH TREATY of 1921.

F

Famine, the Great

Historically, Ireland has experienced famine numerous times, including several outbreaks in the 18th century. However, that of 1845 to 1849 was the most monumental in terms of both human casualties and socioeconomic transformation. The famine occurred because of a fungus that hit the potato crop. The landholding system in Ireland that had developed in the 17th and 18th centuries created a situation in which a small number of landlords owned most of the land, much of which was worked by tenants holding very small portions and with very short and insecure leases. Indeed, especially in the western sections of the island, several layers of tenants developed between the owners, many of whom were absentees living in Britain who regarded their holdings only as sources of rental revenue, and the actual occupants, who might hold only enough land to grow a crop of potatoes with which to feed the family in return for laboring for a larger tenant. While some owners were improving landlords who sought to enhance drainage and improve cultivation, the system worked against such individuals as the ample production of potatoes stimulated intensive employment of inexpensive labor and uneconomical subdivision of land. Furthermore, there was an absence of industry to absorb a population that had grown phenomenally in a century.

Such a land system and economic structure made Irish society extremely vulnerable when a fungus hit the potato crop in 1845 and in 1846, leaving too few seed potatoes for planting in 1847 when things might have improved, and the blight resumed in 1848 and 1849. The original response by the government under Conservative prime minister Robert PEEL was to provide public works projects so that earned income could purchase alternative food as well as to order large amounts of Indian corn for relief. However, Peel fell from power after he had broken with his own party by advancing successfully the repeal of the protective tariffs known as the Corn Laws. The new government formed by the Whigs, headed by Lord John Russell, who on matters of religious tolerance and democratizing reforms were more sympathetic to the Irish and to Irish Catholics especially, approached the famine from the perspective of 19th-century liberalism, which stressed the preeminence of an unfettered free market and distrust of governmental action. Public works were to be instituted only for projects that would not compete with the market. Poor relief was punitive and limited. The costs of relief were expected to be borne by the heavily indebted landowning class of Ireland. Many officials, such as Sir Charles Trevelyan of the Treasury Office, took a heartless attitude toward the tragedy which they regarded in Malthusian terms as an appropriate corrective to imprudent and wastrel social organization and behavior. Some even saw it as divine retribution.

Such attitudes, along with the actual exportation of food from Ireland (more was imported, and the starving could scarcely afford to buy that which was exported), created a heritage of bitterness, leading many in later years to interpret the Great Famine as deliberate genocidal policy of Britain toward the Irish. No doubt, there was a large element of bias and dislike of the Irish

This 1880 engraving by Thomas Nast depicts a woman on the shore of Ireland, holding up a sign for help to American ships while a starving family huddles behind her. *(Library of Congress)*

that inhibited the response that might have developed had the event taken place in Britain itself, and it did seem to be in retrospect an astonishing failing on the part of the then wealthiest nation in the world toward an island to which it was politically united. But deliberate genocide seems too strong a word in view of such 20th century phenomena as the Holocaust.

The scope of the tragedy can be measured by the decrease in the Irish population from 1841 to 1851 from over 8 million to 6.5 million and to 5.5 million 10 years later. Probably up to a million deaths directly resulted from the famine, either through starvation or through disease as a consequence of malnutrition. The rest of the population decline was attributable to emigra-

tion, primarily to North America but also to Britain. Within Ireland the famine was followed by a decline in smallholdings of only a few or a fraction of acres and an increase in middle-sized holdings of more than 20 acres. The generations after the famine witnessed an extremely prudent determination by landholders to maintain and increase their holdings rather than subdivide them, with the consequent expectation that most children in the relatively large Irish rural families could expect to have to emigrate or accept life as an unmarried worker on the family farm. Also the expected heir was inhibited from marrying too soon as his parents were unenthusiastic about a daughter-in-law entering the household while they were still active. The results produced continued, astonishing decline in the Irish population up until the 1960s, when it amounted to less than half of what it had been 120 years before.

Farmer's Party

Owners of larger farms had their interests championed in the first decade of Irish self-governance by the Farmer's Party, which elected 11 members to the DÁIL ÉIREANN in the June 1922 election. They were supportive of the treaty and their numbers increased in the 1923 election to 15. They were generally supportive of the CUMANN NA NGAEDHEAL government. Their numbers declined in the 1927 elections to 11 and then six. Following the decline in the party's representation to four in 1932, those remaining members joined the NATIONAL CENTRE PARTY, which, soon after, amalgamated with Cumann na nGaedheal to form FINE GAEL.

Farquhar, George (1677–1707)
playwright
Born in Derry, Farquhar studied at TRINITY COLLEGE DUBLIN, but left after penning what was considered to be irreverent writing. He became an actor in Dublin, but abandoned that profession after he had accidentally stabbed a colleague onstage. Going to London, he wrote plays, pri-

marily comedies that were well received. They included *Love and a Bottle* (1698), *The Constant Couple* (1699), and *The Inconstant* (1699). He became an army recruiter in Ireland and later wrote *The Recruiting Officer* (1706).

Faul, Denis (1932–)
priest

Born in County Louth, Faul was president of St. Patrick's Academy in Dungannon, County Tyrone. He was also a chaplain in the Maze Prison. He was outspoken in his criticism of the judicial system of Northern Ireland and abuses by the police and the British military in the 1970s and early 1980s. In the 1990s he was outspoken in his criticism of the IRA, which he depicted as engaged in criminality, and was defensive of the police, which incensed some Catholics and NATIONALISTS. He served as parish priest of Carrickmore, County Tyrone.

Faulkner, Brian (1921–1977)
politician

Born in County Down to a business family and educated in Dublin, Faulkner was elected to the Northern Ireland parliament in 1949 as a UNIONIST. He served as minister for home affairs from 1959 to 1963 and had to deal with the IRA campaign of that period. He was later minister of commerce (1963 to 1969) and minister of development (1969 to 1971). He opposed the liberalizing reforms promoted by Prime Minister Terence O'NEILL and helped bring about the latter's resignation in 1969. He became prime minister himself in 1971 and introduced INTERNMENT that same year, which many believe backfired in promoting rather than discouraging IRA recruitment. The increasing disorder in Northern Ireland, including the BLOODY SUNDAY incident of January 1972, caused the British government to ask Faulkner to surrender control over security matters to Westminster. He refused to do so, whereupon the British suspended the Northern Ireland parliament and ministry, to be replaced by DIRECT RULE. In an about-face, Faulkner formed a power-sharing executive that included members of the SOCIAL DEMOCRATIC AND LABOUR PARTY (SDLP) and the ALLIANCE PARTY in 1973 and he accepted the HILLSBOROUGH AGREEMENT the same year, which included creation of the unionist bogeyman, a Council of Ireland. The general strike the following May by the Ulster Workers Council brought that experiment to an end. Faulkner, isolated from many unionists, formed a separate Unionist Party of Northern Ireland, but it fared badly. He was honored with a peerage in 1976 but died the following year in a horse-riding accident.

Faulkner, George (1678–1707)
printer

Born in Dublin, Faulkner went to London to practice his trade, but he returned to Dublin and opened his own business in 1726. He printed two newspapers, the *Dublin Journal* and the *Dublin Post Boy,* and his business became a center of Dublin literary life. He reprinted a number of English titles and was the first to publish a collected version of Jonathan SWIFT's works.

Feetham, Richard (1874–1965)
jurist

Born in South Africa and educated at Oxford, Feetham became a judge of the Supreme Court of South Africa in 1923. In 1924 the British government named him chairman of the BOUNDARY COMMISSION. His narrow interpretation of the mandate of the commission brought about a report that proved unsatisfactory to nationalist opinion. The report's conclusions were not implemented, allowing the status quo boundary between NORTHERN IRELAND and the IRISH FREE STATE to continue.

Fenians

The Fenians were a revolutionary nationalist movement of the second half of the 19th century founded by veterans of the 1848 Rising and YOUNG IRELAND. The name is derived from the

Fianna, the legendary soldiers of Finn McCool, an ancient Celtic hero. The name is applied to all Irish nationalist revolutionaries of the time (and by some, even to contemporary republicans), but ought specifically to be applied only to the American support organization, founded in 1858 in New York by John O'MAHONY, for the specific revolutionary organization formed at the same time in Ireland by James STEPHENS, which would come to be called the IRISH REPUBLICAN BROTHERHOOD. The Fenians split into factions, with one group continuing to support O'Mahony as leader while others supported W. R. Roberts and formed a "Senate" to overrule the executive. Others grounds for division included the desire of some Fenians, especially those with military experience from the American Civil War, to launch an invasion of Canada with the hope it would stir an Anglo-American conflict from which Irish separatism would benefit. Three unsuccessful efforts were made, one across the border from Maine attacking the island of Campobello in the Bay of Fundy in April 1866, another two months later across the Canadian border along the Niagara Falls River, and a third four years later. When John Stephens arrived from Ireland in 1866 fleeing arrest, discontent arose from those impatient at his failure to call a rising in Ireland. The dissatisfaction resulted in his replacement by a Colonel Thomas Kelly, who the next year sailed for Ireland to take place in the rising of March that failed because of infiltration, overwhelming British military force, and bad climate. These failures prompted the formation of a new organization, CLAN NA GAEL, which endured as an effective Irish-American support organization for revolutionary Irish NATIONALISM into the 20th century.

Ferguson, Harry George (1884–1960)
inventor

Born in Hillsborough, County Down, in 1909, Ferguson built the first airplane constructed entirely in Ireland. He developed an apparatus in mounting a plough on a tractor as part of the effort to increase food production during the Second World War, which ultimately became the Ferguson tractor and that originally was to be produced by Ford following a verbal agreement between Ferguson and Ford, an agreement that the Ford Company later repudiated. As a result of a successful lawsuit, Ferguson was financially able to launch his own company. He later concerned himself with automatic transmission. In 1914 he participated in gunrunning by the ULSTER VOLUNTEER FORCE at the Larne.

Ferguson, Samuel (1810–1886)
antiquary, poet

Born in Belfast and called to the bar, Ferguson became deputy keeper of public records and was involved in the Royal Irish Academy. While opposed to violence, he was friendly to many in the YOUNG IRELAND movement. He was a champion of the Gaelic revival, wrote poetry for various publications, including *Dublin University Magazine,* and made significant antiquarian contributions, including *Ogham Inscriptions in Ireland, Scotland and Wales* (1887), which was published posthumously.

Fermanagh

An inland county in the northwest of Ireland, it is one of the counties of Northern Ireland. It is crossed by the river Erne, serving almost as a catchment area for the river and its lakes. The county has a population of 52,000 and an area of 648 square miles. It was planted by English Anglicans more than Scottish Presbyterians, having been the kingdom of the Maguires. It suffered greatly during the Great FAMINE and its population was primarily Catholic and nationalist, even though included in Northern Ireland with partition, which, compounded by the area's economic stagnation (except for sport fishing and tourism), explain the intensity of bitterness that occurred during the troubles, particularly the more recent ones. Famous natives have included the Northern Ireland prime minister Basil BROOKE and Second World War field marshall Alan Alanbrook. Its county town is Enniskillen.

Fianna Fáil

The name of this political party means "Soldiers of Destiny." It is the largest political party in the Irish Republic and has been in power since 1932 for all but the following ministries, none of which were reelected: 1948–51, 1954–57, 1973–77, 1981, 1982–87, and 1994–97. Furthermore, Fianna Fáil had always ruled by itself, until 1989. In any government it has formed since then, it has been the senior partner in coalitions with either the PROGRESSIVE DEMOCRATS or the LABOUR PARTY. Eamon DE VALERA formed the party in 1926 when SINN FÉIN refused to accept his motion that they consider entering the DÁIL ÉIREANN of the IRISH FREE STATE if the oath to the monarch was removed as obligatory. He brought most of the politically astute members of Sinn Féin and colleagues in the anti-treaty cause, including Seán LEMASS, Frank AIKEN, Sean MACENTEE, and Sean T. O'Kelly, along with him. By broadening their appeal beyond simply opposing the treaty and/or championing irredentism, but also raising the populist issues of the concerns of small tillage farmers, emigration, and unemployment, they gained a vast following, many from among the more nationalist elements within the CUMANN NA NGAEDHEAL following. Party growth was facilitated by financial support from America and by astute local organization, in contrast to the Cumann na nGaedheal tendency to seek support by means of endorsement by social leaders from among the clergy, bankers, professionals, strong farmers, and businessmen. De Valera was able to form his first government in 1932 when his party gained a plurality in the Dáil and Labour gave its consent to a government led by him. He kept power in elections in 1933, 1937, 1938, 1943, and 1944. He returned to power after elections in 1951 and 1957, and his successor, Seán Lemass, kept the party in power in 1961 and 1965, as did his successor, Jack LYNCH in 1969. Lynch regained power in 1977. His successor, Charles J. HAUGHEY lost power in 1981, regained it the following February, lost it again that November, but returned to office in 1987. The party retained power in a coalition in 1989,

as it did under Haughey's successor, Albert REYNOLDS, in 1992. A coalition government of all but Fianna Fáil ruled for less than three years from 1994 to 1997, but since then, with Bertie AHERN as TAOISEACH, the party has been in power, again as part of a coalition with the Progressive Democrats. All of the presidents of Ireland, with the exception of the apolitical first president, Douglas HYDE, and the first women president, Mary ROBINSON of the Labour Party, have been members of Fianna Fáil.

The party delights in its label, the "Republican Party," to the great annoyance of Sinn Féin, who see it as having sold out the cause, beginning with de Valera's employment of emergency powers against the IRA. However, Fianna Fáil under de Valera did dismantle most of the monarchical features attached to the Irish Free State, leaving only the withdrawal from the COMMONWEALTH and the formal proclamation of republican status to the coalition that had replaced him in 1948. There was discontent within the party during the 1970 arms trial, when some were disappointed in Jack Lynch's dismissal of several members of his government for alleged supplying of weapons to the Provisional IRA in the early stages of the modern Northern Ireland conflict. However, despite occasional nationalist and Anglophobic gestures at times by Charles Haughey, he and other Fianna Fáil leaders moved constantly throughout the 1980s and 1990s to acquiescence in a solution for Northern Ireland based on consent by the majority of its people.

The party in its origins was regarded as the party of the poor. Even before the end of the 1930s, its protectionist policy of national self-sufficiency inevitably made it attractive to those business interests that would gain by protection. At the same time, it retained its mass support by provision of small grants (often noneconomic) to small holders and pensions to anti-treaty CIVIL WAR veterans.

By the 1960s, when de Valera had retired from active partisanship and had moved up to the national presidency, the economic policies were largely reversed as international trade and foreign investors were sought. The new generation of party leaders proved astute in entrepreneurial skills and financial wizardry. One commentator suggested the men who wore cloth caps and rode in horse and carts gave way to the wearers of mohair coats and drivers of Mercedes.

While accepting modernization, the party's record in government in the 1970s and early 1980s tended to be fiscally irresponsible in bringing public debt to astonishing levels. Remarkably, when he returned to power in 1989, Haughey reversed his earlier record and applied a policy of austerity, as expected by the European Community, and helped set the stage for the economic boom of the closing years of the 20th century. Many, but not necessarily all, elements in the party are vocally Catholic and oppose many of the changes in the social mores of modern Ireland. The party was overwhelmingly hostile to allowing divorce in Ireland and favored continuing restriction on abortion.

Field, John (1782–1837)
composer, pianist

Born in Dublin, Field was engaged by piano manufacturer Muzio Clementi to travel throughout Europe demonstrating his instruments. Field himself settled in Russia in 1803 and there composed most of his work. He developed "Nocturnes" for solo performance, which influenced the work of Chopin. Field also composed piano concertos and a quintet.

Fine Gael

The name of this political party means "Family (or Tribe) of the Gaels." Founded in 1933 out of a union of such opponents of the new government of Eamon DE VALERA as CUMANN NA NGAEDHEAL, the National Centre Party, and the BLUESHIRTS, its first leader was Eoin O'DUFFY. However, his eccentric rhetoric and political ineptness resulted in his replacement by William T. COSGRAVE. The party represented more conservative elements in Irish society such as larger farmers, business interests, and the professional classes, but it was

unable to seriously challenge the populist and nationalist appeal of de Valera, and its numbers in the DÁIL ÉIREANN fell to about a quarter of that body's total membership. However, it has remained until the present the second largest party in the nation. Although small in absolute number of TD's, the party did lead two coalitions of all the other parties opposed to FIANNA FÁIL in two governments from 1948 to 1951 and from

Poster for the Fine Gael party *(Library of Congress)*

1954 to 1957. Its leader from 1944 to 1959 was Richard MULCAHY, however his serving as TAOISEACH would have been incompatible with a government that included the more radically nationalist CLANN NA POBLACHTA Party because of his role in the CIVIL WAR. Instead John A. COSTELLO served as Taoiseach. James DILLON replaced Mulcahy as party leader in 1959. In the 1960s younger members of the party advanced programs with a more socially conscious character, much like the left wing of the European Christian Democratic Party. Important theorists of this school were Garret FITZGERALD and Declan Costello. Liam COSGRAVE succeeded Dillon in 1965 and was Taoiseach in a coalition government from 1973 to 1977. Garret Fitzgerald replaced him as leader after the coalition was defeated in the 1977 election and led the party to new heights in strength in the Dáil in the election of 1981, forming another coalition, again with the LABOUR PARTY. The coalition was ousted early the following year, but was returned before the year was out and remained in power until 1987. In the Fine Gael–led coalitions of the 1970s and 1980s, a major revolution in national attitudes regarding Northern Ireland took place as the Irish government came to accept the notion that political unification of the island required prior consent by the majority of the Northern Ireland population. After the coalition lost power in the 1987 election, FitzGerald stepped down as leader and Alan DUKES replaced him. Three years later Dukes was ousted from leadership and replaced by John BRUTON. After a vote of no confidence in a Fianna Fáil government in 1994, Bruton formed a "RAINBOW COALITION" government consisting of Fine Gael, Labour, and Democratic Left, which lasted until 1997. In early 2002 John NOONAN replaced Bruton as leader and led the party to a crushing defeat in a general election in which many of its senior TD's lost their seats. Subsequently, Enda Kenny replaced Noonan. One of the party's selling points, particularly with regard to elections to the European Parliament, is its affiliation with the European People's Party (the Christian Democrats), one of the largest groups in that body.

Fisher, Joseph R. (1855–1939)
journalist

A County Down native, Fisher was a journalist who had been foreign editor of the *Daily Chronicle*, and editor of the *Northern Whig*, as well as author of works on law and the press. He was nominated by the British government in 1924 to act as the member for Northern Ireland on the BOUNDARY COMMISSION when the Northern Ireland government refused to name a member.

Fitt, Gerry (1926–2005)
politician

Born into working-class West Belfast family, a merchant seaman for several years, Fitt was elected to the Belfast City Council in 1958, then to the Northern Ireland PARLIAMENT at Stormont in 1962, and to the Westminster parliament in 1966, he was a member of the Republican Labour Party. While in the House of Commons he interested a number of Labour Party members in the plight of Northern Ireland Catholics, and some of them were with him during a DERRY civil rights march in October 1968 when he was injured by police. He was one of the founding members of the SOCIAL DEMOCRATIC AND LABOUR PARTY (SDLP) in 1970, becoming its first leader. He served as the deputy chief executive in the short-lived power-sharing executive in 1973–74. His criticism of the violent campaign by the IRA caused militants to attack his home in 1976. Disappointed at the British Labour government's policy in Northern Ireland, he abstained on a vote of no confidence, which brought down the government in 1979. The same year he resigned from the SDLP because he believed the party overemphasized a nationalist agenda at the expense of civil rights and social questions. He opposed the HUNGER STRIKE by IRA prisoners in 1980–81, which further irritated many of his more militant West Belfast constituents. He failed to win reelection in 1983, when he was opposed by an SDLP candidate and by Gerry ADAMS of SINN FÉIN who was elected. Soon after he was named a life peer. He died in 2005.

Fitzgerald, Barry (1888–1961)
actor

Barry Fitzgerald was the stage name of William Shields, a Dublin-born civil servant. He used the stage name since he remained a civil servant until 1929, working only as a part-time actor until then, even though he performed at the ABBEY THEATRE. He was a member of an Abbey group that toured the United States in the 1930s. Fitzgerald arrived in Hollywood and appeared in a John Ford film of Seán O'CASEY's *The Plough and the Stars* (1936). He went on to appear in a number of films, such as *How Green Was My Valley* (1942) and *The Quiet Man* (1952), and won an Academy Award for *Going My Way* (1944). He also acted on Broadway, where he received a New York critics' award for his role in Casey's *Juno and the Paycock.*

FitzGerald, Garret (1926–)
politician

A son of Desmond FitzGerald, a CUMANN NA NGAEDHEAL minister in the Free State government, FitzGerald's mother, although an ardent nationalist, came from a Protestant and unionist background, and his maternal relatives made him aware, in contrast to most Irish public figures, at a youthful age of the reality of the distinctive Northern Ireland and unionist identity. He was educated at BELVEDERE COLLEGE and at University College Dublin. He worked for a number of years for AER LINGUS, before becoming a lecturer in economics at University College Dublin in 1959. He wrote extensively on economical and political topics for Irish and foreign newspapers. He was elected as a FINE GAEL member of the Irish SEANAD in 1965 and then to the DÁIL ÉIREANN in 1969 for Dublin Southeast. He was identified with the progressive or liberalizing wing of the party and wrote a significant collection of essays titled *Toward a New Ireland* (1972), which argued that Irish unity could result more from internal modernization, liberalization, and ecumenicalism than from an uncompromising irredentist approach. FitzGerald served as foreign minister in the coalition government of 1973 to 1977 and played a central role in developing a more flexible and accommodating policy with regard to Northern Ireland reflected in the SUNNINGDALE AGREEMENT of 1973. He was a vigorous proponent of EEC membership and was Foreign Minister during Ireland's first presidency of that body. His ability in languages and overall intellectuality made a remarkable impression throughout Europe. After the coalition was defeated in the 1977 election, he succeeded Liam COSGRAVE as leader of Fine Gael and led the party to unprecedented strength in Dáil membership in the following decade. He became TAOISEACH of a short-lived coalition government in July 1981 at the height of the HUNGER STRIKE by IRA prisoners in Northern Ireland. He again became Taoiseach in late 1982 leading a coalition government that lasted until 1987. In the later government he called the NEW IRELAND FORUM that advanced, on a multiparty basis, tentative alternatives for a solution to the Northern Ireland question and successfully negotiated the HILLSBOROUGH AGREEMENT with Prime Minister Margaret Thatcher in 1985, which gave the Irish government an unprecedented role as a regular consultant with the British government in considering matters affecting the nationalist minority in Northern Ireland as well as on cross-border security matters, and which also asserted the necessity of securing cross-community consensus toward any new governing structures or a constitutional status for Northern Ireland. During his ministry two controversial constitutional amendments were put to the Irish electorate. The first, which he had originally endorsed but later opposed, was an amendment against abortion, even though abortion was illegal in Ireland. The amendment passed overwhelmingly in 1983. The second, in 1985, was an amendment allowing, on very restricted conditions, divorce in Ireland. He supported the same but the voters rejected it in the same proportions as they had approved the amendment on abortion. LABOUR PARTY dissatisfaction with fiscal restraints that FitzGerald thought necessary caused the government to resign, and when FIANNA FÁIL won the subsequent election he stepped down as party leader. He remained in the Dáil until 1992 when he retired completely from politics. He continues to write a weekly column in the IRISH TIMES, has published an autobiography, All in a Life (1991), and other historicopolitical essays, and lectures at home and abroad. He lectures widely at home and abroad on public affairs. He did come out of political retirement to campaign for a yes vote in the second Nice referendum held in 2002. Since 1997 he has served as chancellor of the NATIONAL UNIVERSITY OF IRELAND.

Fitzgerald, George Francis (1851–1901)
physicist
Born in Dublin and educated at TRINITY COLLEGE DUBLIN, he became a professor of natural philosophy there and developed the electromagnetic theory of radiation. His further research in electric waves was an important contribution to Einstein's theory of relativity.

Fitzgerald, Gerald (Garret Mor), eighth earl of Kildare See KILDARE, GERALD (GARRET MOR), EIGHTH EARL OF.

Fitzgerald, Gerald (Garret Og), ninth earl of Kildare See KILDARE, GERALD (GARRET OG), NINTH EARL OF.

Fitzgerald, Thomas (Silken Thomas), 10th earl of Kildare See KILDARE, THOMAS (SILKEN THOMAS), 10TH EARL OF.

Fitzgibbon, John, earl of Clare See CLARE, JOHN FITZGIBBON, EARL OF.

Fitzmaurice, George (1878–1963)
playwright
Born in County Kerry, Fitzmaurice was the son of a CHURCH OF IRELAND clergyman. He joined the civil service where he remained until his retirement in 1943, with the exception of army service during the First World War. He wrote several plays with a peasant theme, some of which were produced at the ABBEY THEATRE: They included The Country Dressmaker (1907), The Pie Dish (1908), and The Magic Glasses (1913), and which drew the acclaim of William Butler YEATS. But Yeats did not care for some subsequent plays, such as The Dandy Dolls (1913) and Twixt the Giltinans and the Carmodys (1923). However, he continued to write, and works by him were produced at the Abbey between 1945 and 1953.

Fitzmaurice, James Christopher (1898–1965)
aviator
Born in Dublin, Fitzmaurice joined the British army at the outset of the first World War, but was discharged for being underage. He later reenlisted, served in the infantry, was wounded, and commissioned. He transferred to the Royal Flying Corps, which later became the Royal Air Force. He served until 1922, when he resigned his commission and returned to Ireland after the signing of the ANGLO-IRISH TREATY. He was one of the first members of the Irish Air Corps, serving various missions for the government during the CIVIL WAR. By 1926 he had become the commanding officer of the Air Corps. In 1927 he was the copilot in an unsuccessful attempt to fly across the Atlantic from east to west, as the plane was forced to land at a beach in County Kerry. The next year, along with two Germans, Captain Herman Kohl and Baron Gunther von Hunefeld, he was successful flying from Baldonnel airfield in Dublin to Greenly Island, Labrador, in completing the first east-west trans-Atlantic flight in history. He resigned from the Air Corps after government disinterest in his proposal to launch air services between Ireland and Britain. In 1934 he sought to fly in an Australian Air Race on behalf of the Sweepstakes benefiting Irish hospitals, but technical difficulties disqualified his

plane from entering. Afterward, he lived in America and in England, but he returned to Ireland in 1951.

Fitzwilliam, William Wentworth, second earl Fitzwilliam (1748–1833)

politician

An English Whig, Fitzwilliam was appointed lord lieutenant in January 1795. His wife was Irish and he had Irish ancestry and an Irish estate. He was sympathetic to relief legislation on behalf of Irish Catholics, but his views and appointments irritated the dominant PROTESTANT ASCENDANCY, which forced his dismissal two months later, contributing to the subsequent rise in sympathy for the UNITED IRISHMEN.

Flannery, Michael (1902–1994)

IRA fund-raiser

Born in Nenagh, County Tipperary, Flannery was a youthful participant in the WAR OF INDEPENDENCE and on the anti-treaty side in the CIVIL WAR. He was among the thousands of republican prisoners interned during the year after the civil war. Immigrating to America during the era of the IRISH FREE STATE, he lived for over half a century in Jackson Heights, a quiet residential section of New York City, working for a large insurance company and serving as an active and faithful member of his local Catholic parish. At the same time he remained involved in all kinds of Irish social activities, including the GAELIC ATHLETIC ASSOCIATION. More significantly, he remained very active in CLAN NA GAEL. After the Northern Ireland troubles began in the late 1960s, he was one of the founders and the president of NORAID, a support organization for the Provisional IRA and SINN FÉIN in the United States. The group raised considerable amounts of money, but insisted the money was to benefit only families of imprisoned republicans. In 1981 he and several others were indicted for purchasing arms on behalf of the IRA, but they were acquitted as their defense argued that since the person from whom they had purchased the weapons was an occasional supplier for CIA mis-

sions, they assumed what they were doing was in accord with the wishes of the American government. In 1983 he was named grand marshall of the New York St. Patrick's Day Parade, which prompted the archbishop of New York, Senator Daniel Patrick Moynihan, the Irish consulate in New York, and various federal agencies, to protest by nonparticipation or other gestures of objection. In later years he broke with Provisional Sinn Féin when it announced a willingness, if elected, to accept seats in the DÁIL ÉIREANN. He supported the purist Republican Sinn Féin that prefers the armed struggle to the political approach taken since the mid 1990s. Flannery died in the fall of 1994, after the cease-fire proclaimed the previous summer by the Provisional IRA.

Flight of the Earls See EARLS, FLIGHT OF THE.

Flood, Henry (1732–1791)

politician

Born in Dublin and educated at TRINITY COLLEGE DUBLIN and at Oxford, Flood was elected to the Irish parliament for Kilkenny in 1759. A gifted orator, he became a leading figure among the "Patriots" or opposition; however, he lost support when he accepted a position as vice treasurer in 1775 under the impression that he could advance his beliefs better in office. He was dismissed from the post in 1781, but remained distrusted by the Patriots. However, in 1782 and after, he outflanked Henry GRATTAN by taking a more demanding position, insisting on more irrevocable terminology for the act proclaiming Irish legislative independence. He also championed more radical parliamentary reform in terms of broader franchise and more equal constituencies, although he opposed extending the right to vote for members of parliament to Catholics, and earned a great amount of support from the more general public.

Flood, William Henry Grattan (1857–1928)

musician, historian

Born in Lismore, County Waterford, educated at Mt. Melleray and at the Catholic University, which became University College Dublin, Flood was the organist at Enniscorthy Cathedral. He wrote several works on the history of Irish music, including *Story of the Harp* (1905), *History of Irish Music* (1905), and *Story of the Bagpipes* (1911). He also wrote *Diocese of Ferns* (1916) and *History of Enniscorthy* (1920), was the Irish correspondent for *The Tablet,* and was made a Knight of St. Gregory in 1922.

Ford, Patrick (1837–1913)

journalist

Born in Galway, Ford emigrated as a child with his parents to the United States in 1841. He became an editor of a Boston newspaper in 1855, served in the Union army in the American Civil War, and founded *The Irish World* in 1870, which he edited until his death. He was a supporter of the FENIANS and the LAND LEAGUE, insisting on the social dimension to the national cause. Ford was instrumental in promoting the collaboration of various Irish personalities such as John DEVOY, Michael DAVITT, and Charles Stewart PARNELL in the NEW DEPARTURE in 1879. Later he supported John REDMOND and the HOME RULE cause in 1912.

Forster, William Edward (1818–1886)

politician

A Liberal English politician identified with such Gladstonian reforms as the secret ballot and broader popular education, Forster became chief secretary for Ireland during the agitation by the LAND LEAGUE. While defending the Land Act of 1881, which was unsatisfactory to the Land Leaguers, he employed coercion powers of internment against opposition, and even had Charles Stewart PARNELL and Michael DAVITT imprisoned. He resigned his post in protest at the KILMAINHAM TREATY, whereby they were released in return for softening their opposition to the land legislation, which was also modified to their wishes. His immediate successor, Lord Frederick CAVENDISH, was assassinated upon arrival in Ireland.

Foster, John, Baron Oriel
(1740–1828)

politician

Born in Collon, County Louth, and educated at TRINITY COLLEGE DUBLIN, Foster served as a member of the Irish parliament from 1761 until the ACT OF UNION and of the British House of Commons from 1769 until 1821, when he was raised to a peerage. As chancellor of the Exchequer in Ireland he secured passage of a Corn Law that protected and encouraged tillage in Irish agriculture. He was a vigorous champion of the PROTESTANT ASCENDANCY, especially in his post as Speaker of the House of Commons in the Irish parliament, a post he held from 1785 until the parliament was ended with the Act of Union. He opposed Catholic emancipation and the Act of Union, personally keeping the Speaker's mace after the last meeting in 1800.

Four Courts, the

The central building in the Irish judicial system that houses both the Supreme Court and the High Court, it was built in the late 18th century. This landmark example of Georgian architecture was designed by Thomas Cooley and James GANDON. Under the Act of Union it housed the traditional four courts of the time: Chancery, King's Bench, Exchequer, and Common Pleas. The opening shot of the Irish CIVIL WAR occurred here as the provisional government sought to dislodge a group of anti-treaty members of the IRA from their occupancy of the building. The successful assault resulted in major destruction, including fires, which destroyed priceless and irreplaceable public records.

Fowke, Francis (1823–1865)

architect

Born near BELFAST, Fowke served in the Royal Engineers. He designed the Museum of Science and Engineering in Edinburgh, the National Gallery in Dublin, and the Royal Albert Hall in London.

Frameworks Document

A joint statement issued by Prime Minister John Major and TAOISEACH John BRUTON in February 1995 about the future relations between Northern Ireland and Ireland in which the principle of consent is central to any change in status and the formation of political institutions with popular consensus. The document evolved from the earlier DOWNING STREET DECLARATION and served as a foundation upon which would be built the GOOD FRIDAY AGREEMENT. It was issued six months after the proclamation of a cease-fire by the Provisional IRA, but before any formal negotiations about political structures had begun.

Freeman's Journal

A newspaper founded in DUBLIN in 1763 to support the popular radical Charles LUCAS. In the early part of the 19th century it supported the government, but in the second decade the paper became more independent, and, under a series of proprietors and editors that included Michael Staunton, Sir John Grey Dwyer, and his son Edward Dwyer, it became the champion of rising middle-class and Catholic NATIONALISM, supporting O'CONNELL, Catholic emancipation, REPEAL of the ACT OF UNION, the LAND LEAGUE, and HOME RULE. It supported Dillon in the split in the IRISH PARLIAMENTARY PARTY following Charles Stewart PARNELL's divorce scandal. It continued to support the party until its demise after the 1918 elections. It supported the ANGLO-IRISH TREATY and was the victim of IRA destruction of its printing presses and building after it published an account of the IRA Army Convention of March 1922 that was dominated by anti-treaty elements. Soon after the paper was absorbed by the IRISH INDEPENDENT.

Free Presbyterian Church

The church is a religious denomination with about 100 congregations, mainly in Northern Ireland, some in the Irish Republic, and others around the world. Rev. Ian PAISLEY founded the church in 1951. He came from a conservative and independent evangelical background and the theology of the church reflects his position. He and his church take a very strong position against Roman Catholicism, which they see as a Satanic corruption of Christianity, although they deny personal hostility toward individual Catholics whom they hope can be saved. The church is inevitably identified with the DEMOCRATIC UNIONIST PARTY, which Paisley founded, but the following and membership of the latter is much greater. The central congregation is at the Martyrs Memorial Church on Ravenhill Road in Belfast.

French, William Percy (1854–1920)
songwriter

Born in County Roscommon in a landowning family, French was educated at TRINITY COLLEGE DUBLIN and became an engineer for the Department of Public Works. He turned to journalism and then song writing. Collaborating with Houston Collisson, who composed the music, he wrote a number of songs, many drawn from his experiences with Public Works, which became a musical comedy, but some of the later works identified with particular places in Ireland and became among the more cherished songs. They include "The Mountains of Mourne," "Come Back Paddy Reilly to Ballyjamesduff," and "The Darling Girl from Clare." Others remain entertaining and amusing, such as "The West Clare Railway" and "Phil the Fluther's Ball."

Friel, Brian (1929–)
playwright, short-story writer

Born in County Tyrone and educated at St. Columb's College, DERRY, MAYNOOTH, and St. Joseph's Teacher Training College in BELFAST, Friel's early short stories and plays appeared in the *New Yorker* and on the BBC. His great breakthrough was the play *Philadelphia Here I Come* (1964), which enjoyed international success. It was about the emotional conflict between an emigrating Donegal son and his widower father who are unable to communicate with each other.

Another play was *The Loves of Cass McGuire* (1966) about an Irish women returned from years in the United States. In the 1970s he began to work with the ABBEY THEATRE, where his plays, including *The Freedom of the City* (1973), about the tragic events in Derry between 1969 and 1972, and *Faith Healer* (1980), about a faith healer, religious belief, and national identity. Later plays included *Translations* (1980), which was produced by the Field Day Theatre Company in Derry that he had helped form to cut across political and sectarian divisions. It dealt with the complications arising from efforts by British Ordinance Survey mapmakers in dealing with Irish-speaking locals in their efforts to obtain the names of localities. Another play well received internationally was *Dancing at Lughnasa* (1990), in which the return from Africa of an Irish missionary priest to stay with his sisters provides the occasion to express pent-up resentments at Irish Puritanism and celebration of a less inhibited pre-Christian sexuality.

Friends of Ireland

A private caucus of American senators and congressmen that was formed in the late 1970s in response to the appeal of the "Four Horsemen" (Senator Daniel Patrick Moynihan [D-N.Y.] and Senator Edward Kennedy [D-Mass.], Congressman Tip O'Neill [D-Mass.], and Governor Hugh Carey [D-N.Y.]) to Irish Americans to stop supporting the IRA. It was an alternative to another congressional caucus headed by Congressman Mario Biaggi [D-N.J.] that was uninhibited in echoing the SINN FÉIN line. The formation of the caucus was partly inspired by Irish diplomats Sean Donlon and Michael Lillis and played a major role in marginalizing the supporters of the IRA in Irish America.

Friends of Sinn Féin

After the Provisional IRA cease-fire in 1994 and the emphasis on the political approach by SINN FÉIN, U.S. authorities became increasingly tolerant of visits to the United States by Sinn Féin leaders hitherto barred. This enabled their American supporters to move in higher circles in their fund-raising efforts. Whereas earlier major fund-raising had been done by NORAID and involved collections in bars and dancehalls as well as less expensive annual dinners, the newly formed Friends of Sinn Féin, whose leaders included a number of professionals, especially attorneys, began to hold expensive fund-raising dinners in major hotels where hundreds of guests paid hundreds of dollars for individual tickets. Sinn Féin as a consequence drew several millions of dollars in support, which they were able to employ in political campaigns in Ireland and Northern Ireland, where, until 2004, an exception was made allowing the use of foreign-collected funds for domestic political purposes. The money Sinn Féin garnered in America vastly exceeded the combined collections gathered for all other political groups in Ireland and Northern Ireland.

G

Gaelic Athletic Association (GAA)

This organization was founded in the fall of 1884 following an appeal by Michael CUSACK to promote national sports. It was designed to give a prominence and prestige to popular games like hurling and football that could rival "English" sports like rugby and soccer that drew support from the PROTESTANT ASCENDANCY and the urban population. Maurice Davin was the first president and important patrons included Archbishop Thomas CROKE of Cashel, Charles Stewart PARNELL, and Michael DAVITT. The primary support for the organization came from the rural population or the recently urbanized, still in contact with their rural roots. Branches of the organization sprang up throughout the country and soon competitions between local teams expanded to included competitions between county-wide teams, the ultimate winners becoming All-Ireland champions. Formal and uniform rules were drawn up for games, which had varied from region to region. The organization inevitably became intertwined with the politics of the time, as there existed a strong influence by the IRISH REPUBLICAN BROTHERHOOD. The GAA took punitive steps to inhibit its members from being drawn to the influence of "English" sports, as a "ban" with a penalty of expulsion was placed on attending or participating in foreign games, including rugby or soccer. The GAA served as a ready recruiting ground for IRISH VOLUNTEERS and, later, members of the IRA at the time of the EASTER RISING and the WAR OF INDEPENDENCE. The organization retains its strong nationalist spirit, although such attitudes have become more flexible as the celebrated "ban"

was ended in 1971. Even more recently the disqualification from membership of members of "foreign" forces, specifically the ROYAL ULSTER CONSTABULARY and the British army, has been lifted. In 2005 the GAA agreed to allow soccer and rugby to be played in Croke Park. Live television coverage of the games and acceptance of commercial sponsorship have enabled the organization of an amateur sport to assume a highly sophisticated and professional character as the historic Dublin playground, Croke Park, has been transformed into a modern stadium able to hold up to 80,000. An interesting aspect of the organization has been the continued participation by "exile" organizations in the United States and Britain, whose teams compete with Ireland-based teams. In the United States a common practice has been sponsorship of Ireland-based players to visit and play a number of games for American teams in return for their transportation and employment (usually in construction work). It has been suggested that it was the GAA more than anything else that created the very strong county loyalties of the Irish, especially since the counties themselves were largely the product of Anglo-Norman and English influence.

The major games sponsored by the GAA are hurling and football. Hurling, which has an ancient history and is referred to in Celtic folklore, is comparable to field hockey. It is played with a hard ball, called the *sliotar*, and the players carry a wooden stick called the hurley. Scoring is by hitting the ball over the goal post for one point or under for three points. There are 15 players on a side. Gaelic football has the same system of scoring and the same number on a team and consists of a curious mixture of soccer and rugby, with participants able to use their hands in picking up, passing, and even making short runs with a round ball, which they primarily must advance by kicking. Women's versions of both sports also exist with similar local, county, and national championships. The rules are slightly different. Women's hurling is called *camogie*. Enthusiasm for the women's games has grown considerable in more recent years.

Gaelic League

Founded in 1893 by Douglas HYDE, who became its first president, Eoin MacNEILL, and Father Eugene O'Growney, it sought to revive Irish as the popular language of the island. It grew rapidly, especially through distribution of its newspaper, *An Claideamh Solus,* and soon had hundreds of branches throughout the country. The league encouraged those who sought to learn the language to visit remote areas, usually in western Ireland, where the language was still spoken. In 1908 the organization successfully secured establishment Irish as a compulsory subject in the NATIONAL UNIVERSITY OF IRELAND, which had just been established. When the organization became more closely linked with the struggle for political independence, Hyde resigned as president. Since independence, the organization has been successful in making Irish a compulsory subject in all schools and as a qualification for civil service positions. In more recent years there has been a relaxation of the requirements. Although it is no longer compulsory, those who demonstrate competence in Irish are given bonuses. Statistics as to the actual success of the language revival remain the subject of much controversy, but there is no doubt that, even though Irish is the first official language of the state, English remains the spoken tongue of at least 95 percent of the population. On the other hand, schools that teach all subjects in Irish have thrived in non-Irish-speaking areas such as the city of DUBLIN, and both militant nationalists and many others have studied the Irish language in Northern Ireland during the troubles of the 1970s and continuing today.

Gaeltacht

The term describes areas of Ireland in which Irish is the vernacular tongue, although the term originally applied to areas in Scotland where Gaelic was spoken. With the establishment of the Irish Free State a committee was created to determine which districts of the country were *fíor-Ghaeltacht* (fully Irish), where Irish was spoken daily by more than 80 percent of the population, and *Breac-Ghaeltacht* (partially Irish), where between 25 and 79 percent spoke Irish. Gaeltacht areas were determined to exist in 12 counties. Various public benefits were made available to residents of those areas who qualified as Irish speakers. In the 1950s a further study resulted in a revision of the Gaeltacht boundaries, which resulted in a substantial shrinkage of area. Extraordinary efforts to develop those areas have been made, including the establishment in 1957 of a public agency, Gaeltarra Éireann, to stimulate economic development and investment. In 1980 a public board, Udaras na Gaeltachta, which would be elected by Gaeltacht residents, was established to direct development in the areas. In 1996 a public television station was established to broadcast in the Irish language. Nonetheless, census returns from the areas indicate a further decrease in the proportion of the resident population who speak Irish on a daily basis. The population of the entire Gaeltacht in 1996 was less than 90,000 and only slighty more than 20,000 spoke Irish daily. The influx of non-Irish speakers, partly as a consequence of development, has hastened the decline.

Gageby, Douglas (1918–2004)
editor

Born in Dublin, educated at the Belfast Royal Academy and at TRINITY COLLEGE DUBLIN, Gageby worked for the *IRISH PRESS,* then became editor of the *Sunday Press,* and later of the *Evening Press.* He became managing director of the *IRISH TIMES* in 1959 and served as its editor from 1963 to 1974 and again from 1977 to 1986. He was able to complete the process whereby the paper was transformed from serving as a voice for southern Irish Protestant and unionist opinion into becoming more broad-based in its readership. It gave increased attention to social issues and employed increasing numbers of women writers. Its circulation as well as its international prestige steadily increased.

Gallagher, Patrick ("Paddy the Cope") (1873–1966)

cooperative activist

Having left school at the age of nine, Gallagher worked as a day laborer in Strabane and then went on to do the same in England and Scotland. He returned to Donegal with the hope of establishing a cooperative enterprise, influenced by and supported by George RUSSELL ("AE"). His enterprise, which dealt in fertilizer and foodstuffs, encountered opposition from many middlemen and business competitors. Nonetheless, from its very small beginnings it thrived. Gallagher wrote a biography in 1939 titled *My Story*. His nickname comes from the mispronunciation of the concept he advocated.

Galway

Galway is the second-largest county in Ireland. It is divided east and west by Lough Corrib. The west contains part of the very scenic, but historically poor, area of Connemara. It includes such sights as the Twelve Bens mountain range and retains one of the larger concentrations of Irish speakers. Just south are the Irish-speaking Aran Islands. East Galway has a limestone basis for very fertile grassland and has successful market towns, such as Tuam and Ballinasloe. The city of Galway, located near the mouth of the Corrib, traces its formal foundation to the late medieval period. It is situated in what had been the territory of the O'Flahertys and later the de Burgos, who became the Burkes. Leading figures after formal award of borough status were the primarily Anglo-Norman merchant families who were nicknamed the twelve tribes. The city prospered in large part because of considerable trade

Fishermen's cottages in Claddagh, a suburb of Galway, 1900 *(Library of Congress)*

with the Continent. It fell on bad times from the Great FAMINE on, but there has been a remarkable recovery in the last quarter of the 20th century. Galway includes extensive suburban development, which ironically threatens the Irish-speaking character in nearby areas. University College Galway (now National University of Ireland, Galway) is thriving and Galway, with its annual Arts Festival, has become one of Ireland's cultural centers. It holds eminently successful horse races annually, which draw thousands. A center for traditional music, the site of historic landmarks and buildings, and its status as gateway to Connemara and the Aran Islands make it one of Ireland's major tourist spots.

Galway, James (1939–)

flutist

Born in Belfast, Galway studied at the Royal College of Music in London and the Conservatory in Paris, and played with the London Symphony Orchestra and the Royal Philharmonic Orchestra in the late 1960s and then with the Berlin Philharmonic Orchestra until 1975, before beginning a solo career. He has performed internationally, including appearances at both the White House and Buckingham Palace. Galway performed in the Academy Award–winning ensemble that recorded the soundtracks for the film trilogy *Lord of the Rings*. His repertoire includes classical work, jazz, and contemporary songs. He received the Order of the British Empire in 1979 and was knighted by Queen Elizabeth II in 2001.

Gandon, James (1743–1823)
architect

Born in London, Gandon completed his apprenticeship in the firm of William Chambers while the Casino at Marino, DUBLIN, was being planned for Lord Charlemont. After successfully establishing his own business, he later moved to Ireland in 1781. There he designed such major buildings as the Customs House, the FOUR COURTS, an extension to the parliament building, and what is now called O'Connell Bridge, which together contributed to the neoclassical character of Georgian Dublin.

Garda Síochána

The police force of the Irish state, the Garda Síochána was formed in the spring of 1922 by the PROVISIONAL GOVERNMENT to replace the demobilized ROYAL IRISH CONSTABULARY. After some disturbances in the ranks, especially after the appointment of RIC veterans to senior positions, the original commissioner, Michael Staines, was replaced by General Eoin O'DUFFY, who was eminently successful in transforming the new body into a successful and disciplined, as well as unarmed, police force for a nation enduring a CIVIL WAR and subsequent widespread disorder. The body received formal legislative establishment by the DÁIL ÉIREANN in 1923 at which point an amendment by a LABOUR PARTY TD, Cathal O'Shannon, changed the organization's name from "Civic Guard" to "Garda Síochána," which means "Guardians of the Peace." Within two years the force absorbed the DUBLIN METROPOLI-

TAN POLICE, a force dating from before independence. The original plans called for a force of 4,000, but today it numbers more than 11,000. A major crisis occurred in 1933 when Eamon DE VALERA dismissed Commissioner O'Duffy and allowed ex-IRA members to be recruited as auxiliaries in an effort to restrain feared violence by O'Duffy's followers who had joined the new movement he had started, the BLUESHIRTS. But civilian authority remained predominant and the police were later employed in apprehending IRA members when de Valera turned on them. The contemporary Garda is like any modern police force, employing all the techniques of evidence gathering, communications, and mobility that are necessary to deal with such matters as political violence, drug dealing, and organized crime—a far cry from the earlier days of a lone officer patrolling country roads on a bicycle. It remains unarmed, other than employing weapons in limited numbers on special occasions.

Gate Theatre

Founded in 1928 by Michael Mac Liammoir and Hilton Edwards, the Gate Theatre sought to provide a complimentary alternative to the ABBEY THEATRE as it offered international and nonpeasant contemporary Irish drama. It used the Abbey for its productions at first until it established its own theatre in the Rotunda Hospital complex in 1930. Plays by Ibsen, Chekhov, O'Neill, SHAW, and Cocteau are some of those performed there, and actors such as James Mason and Orson Welles have appeared. In the late 1970s and early 1980s the theater floundered somewhat, especially after the deaths of its founders, but it has undergone a rejuvenation under a new director, Michael Colgan, who took over in 1983.

Geldof, Bob (1954–)
singer

Born in Dublin and educated at BLACKROCK COLLEGE, Geldof founded the popular music group, the Boomtown Rats, in 1975, which enjoyed enormous success. In 1985 Geldof organized a great number of popular musicians to participate in an internationally televised charity concert called "Live Aid," which raised millions in support of relief for famine in Ethiopia. In 1986 Queen Elizabeth II knighted him for his humanitarian work. In March 2005 Geldof announced plans for a series of concerts on July 2 to raise money and awareness of issues facing the African continent.

General Post Office

Built between 1814 and 1819, the building dominated Sackville (now O'Connell) Street with its six-column Portland stone Greek Revival Ionic portico. It was seized to serve as headquarters for the EASTER RISING in 1916 and it was from here that Padraic PEARSE proclaimed the Irish Republic. Firing from British vessels in the nearby Liffey River gutted the building in suppressing the rising. A sculpture, *The Death of Cuchulain,* installed in 1935, is a memorial to the 1916 dead. The building continues to serve as the General Post Office.

Geraldine League

An alliance of primarily Irish chieftains in the late 1530s that was led by Manus O'Donnell, the husband of Eleanor Fitzgerald, the aunt of the exiled and youthful KILDARE heir after the execution of Thomas ("Silken Thomas") Fitzgerald and his uncles. The alliance gave signs of a national consciousness and a religious solidarity against the Anglicizing policies and religious reformation being furthered by King Henry VIII and his deputy for Ireland, Lord Grey. It sought to align itself with an international and Catholic effort against Henry VIII, but after Grey defeated its forces in 1539, the alliance dissipated.

Giant's Causeway

Spectacular columns near Portrush, County Antrim, on the northern coast of Ireland that give the impression of steps composed of basalt that geologists assume were caused by the cool-

ing of lava that had poured out of fractures as the earth's crust cooled millions of years ago. Myth has held that it was a causeway build by giants as a passageway to Scotland.

Gilbert, John Thomas (1829–1898)
historian
Born in Dublin, Gilbert served as librarian for the Royal Irish Academy for 34 years and was cofounder of the Irish Celtic and Archaeological Society. He also helped to establish the Public Records Office and served as its secretary from 1867 to 1875. He wrote *History of the City of Dublin* (1861) and *History of the Viceroys of Ireland (down to 1500)* (1865).

Gogarty, Oliver St. John (1878–1957)
surgeon, writer
Born in Dublin, educated at Mungret, Stonyhurst, and Clongowes Colleges, TRINITY COLLEGE DUBLIN, and Oxford, Gogarty was a nose and throat surgeon. He was a student friend of James JOYCE and inspired the character "Buck Mulligan" in *Ulysses*. He wrote poetry, *Collected Poems* (1951), and plays, three of which appeared at the ABBEY THEATRE, as well autobiographical memoirs and reminiscences such as *As I Was Going Down Sackville Street* (1937), and *It Isn't This Time of Year at All!* (1954). He supported the ANGLO-IRISH TREATY and was a member of the SEANAD of the IRISH FREE STATE (1922–36). Antitreaty forces captured him, but he escaped by swimming the Liffey in mid-January, in return for which he presented two swans in thanks. However, republicans subsequently burned his house in Renvyle in Connemara. Disheartened by the atmosphere of Ireland in the DE VALERA era, he went to the United States in 1939. There he continued to write until his death.

Goldsmith, Oliver (1728–1774)
writer
Born in County Longford the son of a CHURCH OF IRELAND clergyman, Goldsmith studied at

TRINITY COLLEGE DUBLIN and at Edinburgh, before settling in London where he worked at various positions including apothecary, physician, musician, and editor. He wrote hack histories and encyclopedia contributions, before commencing his more serious work, such as the novel *The Vicar of Wakefield* (1764), his poems "The Traveller" (1764) and "The Deserted Village" (1770), and the play *She Stoops to Conquer* (1773). He was part of Samuel Johnson's circle and was a close friend of Edmund BURKE, both of whom share the distinction of having commemorative statues erected by the main entrance to Trinity College.

Gonne MacBride, Maud (1866–1953)

revolutionary

Born in England, Maud Gonne's father was a British army officer and her mother had inherited wealth. She was educated privately in France, but came to Ireland in 1882 to act as hostess for her widowed father, who had been stationed there. She returned to France to recuperate from tuberculosis and fell in love with a nationalist journalist named Lucien Millevoye, with whom she had two children, a son who died and a daughter Iseult, who survived and married the novelist Francis Stuart. However, their relationship broke up and she returned to Ireland, where she resumed nationalist activism. She had earlier agitated among tenant farmers in Donegal and had campaigned for the release of Fenian prisoners. She was sympathetic toward the IRISH REPUBLICAN BROTHERHOOD and the Boers in South Africa, and visited England, Scotland, and the United States campaigning on behalf of Irish and French nationalist causes as well as that of the Boers. She was the object of William Butler YEATS's unsuccessful proposals of marriage, but did act the lead role in his play *Cathleen ni Houlihan.* Gonne also organized a republican suffragist society in 1900 called *Inghinidhe na hEireann* (Daughters of Ireland). In 1903, having converted to Catholicism, she married a Boer War veteran, John MacBride, with whom she bore a son, Seán MACBRIDE, later Irish

foreign minister and Nobel laureate. However, the marriage ended in divorce and MacBride returned to Ireland. He was one of those executed after the EASTER RISING. She then returned to Ireland and resumed her militancy there, using the surname of MacBride. One of the many nationalist-activists arrested in 1918 on the basis of a so-called German plot, she opposed the ANGLO-IRISH TREATY and was imprisoned during the CIVIL WAR, but was release after she went on hunger strike. Continuing to agitate on behalf of republican prisoners and the republican cause in general after the Civil War, Gonne became involved in controversy in 1926 with Seán O'CASEY over his play *The Plough and the Stars.*

Good Friday Agreement

This agreement was reached on April 10, 1998, after months of intensive and difficult negotiations involving the British and Irish governments, and most of the political parties of Northern Ireland, with the significant exception of the DEMOCRATIC UNIONIST PARTY. The negotiations began in September 1997, following the proclamation of a second cease-fire by the IRA after the newly elected British prime minister Tony Blair had invited Sinn Féin to join in talks without conditions. Former U.S. senator George Mitchell chaired the proceedings. The American president, Bill Clinton, who maintained a close interest in the proceedings and intervened frequently to promote progress, had earlier named Mitchell as his special envoy on Northern Ireland. At times, both SINN FÉIN and the Ulster Democratic Party (the political wing of a loyalist paramilitary group, the ULSTER DEFENCE ASSOCIATION) were expelled because of instances of political violence. Blair and the Irish TAOISEACH, Bertie AHERN, were ultimately able to persuade UNIONIST leader, David TRIMBLE, and Sinn Féin leader, Gerry ADAMS, to accept the agreement to which the SOCIAL DEMOCRATIC AND LABOUR PARTY and the ALLIANCE PARTY were more easily amenable. The agreement built upon the foundations of the earlier HILLSBOROUGH AGREEMENT (1985), as well as the DOWNING STREET

DECLARATION (1993) and the FRAMEWORKS DOC-UMENT (1995), as it called for a power-sharing provincial government within Northern Ireland and ongoing consultation between the British and Irish governments on matters relating to Northern Ireland. The domestic institutions called for within Northern Ireland including an assembly proportionately elected, out of which, again by a intricate proportionate mechanism, a multiparty ministry was to be formed and measures would require cross-community consent, that is, a majority within each community. New North-South ministerial councils were to meet regularly and as well as a British-Irish Council. Articles two and three of the Irish constitution, with their claims to the whole of the island, were to be repealed. Within Northern Ireland, an independent commission was to make suggestions as to how the police force ought to be reformed, prisoners who had been convicted of paramilitary crimes and whose affiliate paramilitary groups had declared cease-fire were to be released within two years, and the agreement was expected to lead to the ultimate decommissioning of paramilitary weapons. A specific promise by Blair to Trimble that such would come about, even though the language was not as precise in the formal agreement itself, led him to accept. Elections in both jurisdictions, the Irish Republic and Northern Ireland, resulted in approval by overwhelming majorities of, respectively, 94 and 71 percent. Trimble and John HUME, the SDLP leader, were awarded the Nobel Peace Prize the following fall. At this writing the NORTHERN IRE-LAND ASSEMBLY has been suspended because of the refusal of the largest political party following the 2003 elections, the Democratic Unionist Party, to share power with Sinn Féin.

Government of Ireland Act, 1920

Legislation passed by the government of Prime Minister David Lloyd George that sought to overcome the dilemma of Northern Ireland UNIONIST resistance to the still to be implemented HOME RULE legislation and actual revolutionary proclamation of independence by the DÁIL ÉIRE-ANN. The measure partitioned Ireland into two sections: a six-county NORTHERN IRELAND and a 26-county SOUTHERN IRELAND, each of which was to elect a "home ruling" parliament by proportional representation. The institutions created by the legislation, to which an election was held in 1921, became the government for Northern Ireland until suspended in 1972. However, in the rest of Ireland, the Dáil Éireann interpreted the election to a southern parliament that year as an election to a second Dáil. SINN FÉIN won unopposed 128 of the 132 seats. Only the four non–Sinn Féiners, independents or unionists representing TRINITY COLLEGE DUBLIN, regarded themselves as members of the southern parliament. However, in accord with the ANGLO-IRISH TREATY, the pro-treaty majority in the Dáil met with those four, and as the sitting southern parliament, gave their consent to the treaty and chose the PROVISIONAL GOVERNMENT of Ireland that would implement the treaty and receive the handover of power from the British.

governor-general

The ANGLO-IRISH TREATY of 1921 called for the appointment of a governor general to act for the Crown in the IRISH FREE STATE in such matters as would be stipulated in its constitution, specifically such matters as signing legislation, meeting foreign representations, and summoning or dissolving the legislature. The Free State government very quickly asserted its de facto authority to nominate the governor-general and to make clear that his actions would be done on the advice of the government, rather than that of the Crown or the British government. The first governor-general was the Irish parliamentary party figure Tim HEALY, who was succeeded in 1928 by James MacNeill. In 1932 MacNeill resigned over slights he perceived directed at his office by members of Eamon DE VALERA's government. Domhnall Ua Buachalla, who was a loyal de Valera follower, replaced him. Under his tenure the ceremonial and social features of the office, particular entertainment at the vice regal lodge in PHOENIX PARK, were discontinued and he performed only the legally required functions of appointments and signings. The External Relations Act of 1936 ended the office. The governor-general's residence became the residence of the Irish president, an office established by the 1937 constitution of Ireland.

Graces, the

The Graces were promises made by King Charles II in 1627 to representatives of both Irish nobility and members of the Irish House of Commons in return for the award to him of substantial funds to maintain his army in Ireland. The promises consisted of 51 sections, and they ranged from reductions in court fees to the lessening of export fees and the ending of monopolies to guarantees of land titles from royal challenges and the easing of penalties for nonattendance at the established church. However, even though the Irish parliament granted the requested subsidies in the spring of 1628, a parliament was not summoned to meet later that year to pass the legislation, which would make the Graces effective. Six years later the king's new lord deputy, Thomas Wentworth, gained another subsidy only after indicating that Graces could be expected. However, only a few were actually passed. The government's ability to play on the rival fears of Protestants and Catholics that one or the other would benefit unduly from the Graces accounted, in part, for success in stopping their passage.

Grand Canal

One of two canals systems proposed by the Irish parliament in 1756. The Grand Canal constituted the southern route and was laid out to run between the south bank of the river Liffey in Dublin to the river Shannon. The first section, from Dublin to Sallins, County Kildare, opened in 1779, and the last stop on the Shannon opened in 1805. Branches were constructed to other terminals, such as Ballinasloe in 1828 and Kilbeggan in 1835. However, it was not long after the canals were completed that the railroad era began, which led to the canals' ultimate demise. Commercial traffic on the waterways ended in 1954, although they are increasingly used for pleasure craft.

Grattan, Henry (1746–1820)
politician

Born in Dublin, Grattan was educated at TRINITY COLLEGE DUBLIN and studied law at the Middle Temple, being called to the bar in 1772. He became a member of the Irish parliament in 1775 and quickly rose to prominence as one of the more articulate Patriots who were challenging the government on issues such as free trade, an independent judiciary, and especially Irish legislative independence. The achievement of the latter in 1782 marked his most glorious accomplishment and the Irish parliament rewarded him with a grant of 50,000 pounds for his leadership in the cause. The grant gave him the independence to continue his political career. He continued to oppose those in the PROTESTANT ASCENDANCY who readily supported the government's interest, although he did not identify with others in the patriot camp who advocated more radical reforms such as a broader franchise and an equalization of constituencies. He championed relief of Catholics from penal disabilities and opposed the ACT OF UNION. Following enactment of the latter, he stood for and was elected to the Westminster parliament. He served as MP for Dublin from 1806 until 1820, and frequently advanced legislation for Catholic emancipation.

Grattan's Parliament

The term refers to the Irish parliament after the achievement of legislative independence in 1782 and until the ACT OF UNION. In reality, while the parliament had obtained legislative independence, the executive was not responsible to that parliament, but rather was led by a member of the British cabinet. This factor made the era less glorious than later oratory would suggest. Henry GRATTAN's name was given to the parliament because of his leading role in the agitation to obtain legislative independence.

Gray, David (1870–1968)
American ambassador

The U.S. ambassador to Ireland from 1940 through 1947, during and after the Second

World War, Gray was unusually unsympathetic to the Irish people. He was persistently critical of Irish neutrality in the war and sent depreciatory reports to Washington. His memories of the period reflect not just disagreement with Irish policy but a general patronizing attitude toward the Irish. It has been suggested that his feelings were prompted by dislike of opposition by significant numbers of Irish Americans to President Franklin D. Roosevelt, whose wife, Eleanor, was a cousin of Gray's.

Green, Alice Stopford (1847–1929)

historian

Born in Kells, County Meath, Green married English historian J. R. Green in 1877. When he died seven years later, she completed and revised his works. Her home became a meeting place for writers, scholars, and politicians. Roger CASEMENT was a friend. She became increasingly sympathetic to the call for Irish HOME RULE and wrote books in its support, such as *The Making of Ireland and Its Undoing* (1908) and *Irish Nationality* (1911). After the EASTER RISING, she moved to Dublin, where her home on 90 St. Stephen's Green became a intellectual gathering place comparable to her home in London. Green wrote a pamphlet critical of UNIONISM entitled *Ourselves Alone and Ulster* (1918). She supported the ANGLO-IRISH TREATY and was named to the first SEANAD of the IRISH FREE STATE by William T. COSGRAVE in 1922. She wrote a last book, *A History of the Irish State to 1014.*

Greenwood, Sir Hamar (1870–1948)

politician

Born and educated in Canada, Greenwood became a member of parliament in 1906. He was made chief secretary for Ireland in 1920 during the height of the WAR OF INDEPENDENCE. He also was a member of the British party that negotiated the ANGLO-IRISH TREATY.

Gregg, John Robert (1867–1948)

inventor

Born in County Monaghan and educated in Glasgow, Gregg studied systems of stenography. He developed his own system of shorthand and published it in a short pamphlet. He then moved to the United States in 1893. There he published a revised version and established his own publishing company. Having written many books on commercial education, he began to edit *American Shorthand Teacher* in 1920, which later became the *American Business World.* His system of shorthand became the most widely used in North America.

Gregory, Lady Isabella Augusta (née Persse) (1852–1932)

playwright, folklorist

Lady Gregory was born in Roxborough, County Galway, was educated privately, and in 1880 married Sir William Gregory, a widower who owned an estate, Coole Park, also in County Galway. A few years after his death in 1892, she met William Butler YEATS through their mutual friend Edward MARTYN. From the following year on, 1897, Yeats regularly holidayed at her home in Coole Park, where both she and he gathered folklore information, particularly from the area known as Kiltartan. She was able to capture the idiom of a peasantry that thought in Irish but spoke in English. She, Yeats, and Martyn were involved in the Irish Literary Theatre and she, Yeats, and John Milington SYNGE were directors of the ABBEY THEATRE. She remained involved with it for the rest of her life and her home at Coole Park became a gathering spot for major figures in the Irish literary world, including Yeats, Synge, George RUSSELL ("AE"), George MOORE, and Seán O'CASEY. She wrote more than a score of plays herself, as well as translations of Irish heroic sagas and works on folklore.

Gregory Clause

The clause constituted an amendment to the Poor Relief Act for Ireland passed during the

Great FAMINE. William Gregory of Coole Park, County Galway (whose second wife was Lady Isabella Augusta GREGORY), was a Conservative MP for Dublin at the time. The clause excluded any tenants whose holding exceeded one-quarter of an acre from receiving outdoor poor relief. The clause in effect expedited considerable clearances of tenants by landlords as many with more than a quarter of an acre were still too impoverished to continue as tenants if they could not get poor relief.

Griffin, Gerald (1803–1840)

writer

Born in LIMERICK, Griffin was the ninth son of a brewer and was educated at a HEDGE SCHOOL. He worked for local newspapers until he went to London in 1823 where he began writing for *The Literary Gazette.* In 1826 he published a collection of stories *Holland Tides and Other Tales* and then returned to Ireland where he published *Tales of the Munster Festivals* (1827). He next wrote a novel, *The Collegians* (1829), which was published anonymously. It was based on a celebrated murder case and inspired the play *The Colleen Bawn* (1860) by Dion BOUCICAULT. Other stories by him appeared in the mid-1830s. Griffin entered the IRISH CHRISTIAN BROTHERS in 1838 and spent the last years of his life teaching in Cork.

Griffith, Arthur (1871–1922)

nationalist leader, politician

Born in Dublin and educated at the IRISH CHRISTIAN BROTHERS' School, Strand Street, Griffith left school early to apprentice as a printer, joined the GAELIC LEAGUE, and worked in South Africa for several years before returning to Ireland to found the newspaper *United Irishman,* in which he advocated cultural and political NATIONALISM. He formed a political organization called CUMANN NA NGAEDHEAL (which name the governing party in the IRISH FREE STATE also gave itself). His ideas were explicitly stated in his book *The Resurrection of Hungary* (1904). Griffith advocated

the repeal of the ACT OF UNION, but he did not want to wait for the British parliament to do so. Rather, he urged that Irish members elected to parliament not attend, but instead assembly separately and proclaim themselves the parliament of Ireland. The monarch would be retained, but with the distinct title of "king of Ireland" in the same manner as, in the dual monarchy of Austria-Hungary, the ruler held the titles emperor of Austria and king of Hungary. In 1907 his organization together with like-minded groups merged to form a party called SINN FÉIN, the name adopted from a policy he had advocated in his writings. The party ran several unsuccessful candidates in national elections and by-election. He sympathized with the IRISH VOLUNTEERS, but he was not a participant in the EASTER RISING, although he was interned under suspicion of participation. He accepted Eamon DE VALERA's assumption of the presidency of Sinn Féin in 1917. Imprisoned again in 1918 along with many other nationalist activists on suspicion of being part of the alleged German plot, Griffith was returned to parliament for Cavan in the December 1918 general election in which Sinn Féin virtually swept the board in Ireland. After release from prison, he entered DÁIL ÉIREANN and became acting president while de Valera was fund raising in America (1919–20). He was one of the plenipotentiaries who negotiated the ANGLO-IRISH TREATY. His reassurance to David Lloyd George that he would not break off negotiations on the Ulster issue if other Irish demands were met gave the British prime minister the strong hand he needed to achieve Irish acceptance of the treaty, which mandated establishment of a BOUNDARY COMMISSION to adjust the partitioned territory. When de Valera resigned as president of the Dáil Éireann after a majority had accepted the treaty, Griffith was selected as his successor, although real authority in the transfer of power was held by the PROVISIONAL GOVERNMENT headed by Michael COLLINS. When Griffith died on August 12, 1922, of a cerebral hemorrhage, he was still president of the Dáil Éireann, as the third Dáil, newly elected in June 1922 with a pro-treaty majority, had not yet assembled because the CIVIL WAR had broken out between anti-treaty forces and the government.

GUBU

An acronym coined by Conor Cruise O'BRIEN from the terms used by then TAOISEACH, Charles HAUGHEY, in August 1982 in responding to the arrest of a house guest of the attorney general for murder. The terms were "grotesque, unbelievable, bizarre, and unprecedented." O'Brien suggested that the terms could be applied to much of the government's policy and not just the one incident.

Guildford Four

The name given to four individuals, Patrick Armstrong, Gerald Conlon, and Paul Hill, all Belfast natives, and Carole Richardson, an Englishwoman, imprisoned for 15 years after having been convicted of bombing a public house in Guildford, Surrey, in which five people were killed. In 1989 they were released and deemed wrongfully convicted. The conviction had been based on forced confessions, even though the actual perpetrators had acknowledged responsibility.

See also BIRMINGHAM SIX; BOMBING CAMPAIGNS IN BRITAIN.

An advertisement for the Irish beer Guinness sits atop the entrance to a pub in Dublin, 1995. *(Giovambattista Bartoletta/Landov)*

Guinness Brewery   See GUINNESS FAMILY.

Guinness Family

brewers, philanthropists

Arthur Guinness (1725–1803) founded the brewery in Dublin in 1759. Its product, dark stout, would come to be regarded by some almost as the Irish national drink, although there are other brewers of stout. A threat of popular boycott of his product because of his opposition to the Rising of 1798 prompted him to develop an export trade to England. His grandson, Sir Benjamin Lee Guinness, sole owner of the business from 1855 to 1868, built up a large export trade and expanded the home market. In the 19th and 20th centuries, the company's formidable plant at St. James Gate in Dublin was expanded, and an extensive export business to Britain, Europe, the British Empire, and the United States was cultivated. Sir Benjamin was elected lord mayor of DUBLIN, and paid for and supervised the restoration of St. Patrick's Cathedral. He served as a Conservative MP for Dublin, 1865–68. His son, Sir Arthur Edward Guinness, baron Ardilaun (1840–1915), succeeded him as head of the business until 1877, but was more celebrated for his philanthropy, including the restoration of Marsh's Library, the extension of the Coombe Hospital, and the purchase and laying out of a park, St. Stephen's Green, which he presented to the city. He was also Conservative MP for Dublin from 1874 to 1880, when he became a peer. His brother, Edward Cecil Guinness, first earl of Iveagh (1847–1927) established the Guinness Brewery as a public corporation in 1886 of which he became chairman. He was also a generous contributor of funds to hospitals and housing for the poor. His son, Rupert Edward Cecil Lee Guinness, second lord Iveagh (1874–1967), was educated at Eton and Trinity College, Cambridge, served in the Boer War, and was a unionist MP from 1908 to 1910 and from 1912 to 1927. He succeeded his father as chairman of the business in 1927 and paid careful attention to its expansion, including establishment of breweries in London and Africa. He was a generous benefactor to Dublin hospitals and, in 1939, donated his Dublin house, Iveagh house, to the Irish Department of External (now Foreign) Affairs. Family interest in the business declined to a very small percentage by the 1980s and the business is today part of an international conglomerate, Diageo.

Gwynn, Stephen (1864–1950)
author, politician

The grandson of William Smith O'BRIEN, YOUNG IRELAND leader, Gwynn was born in Dublin and educated at St. Columba's College, Dublin, and Brasenose College, Oxford. He was a school teacher for a while, but then turned to journalism in London. He was elected MP for the city of Galway from 1906 to 1918 as a member of the IRISH PARLIAMENTARY PARTY and, following an appeal from the party leader, John REDMOND, he served with the Connaught Rangers in the First World War. Gwynn wrote numerous biographies, including *Robert Emmet* (1909), *Henry Grattan and His Times* (1904), *John Redmond's Last Years* (1919), *Sir Walter Scott* (1930), and *Dean Swift* (1933), and also wrote poetry, which appeared in his *Collected Poems* (1923).

H

Halpin, Robert Charles (1836–1894)
merchant seaman

Born in Wicklow, Halpin went to work at sea at the age of 10. He survived a shipwreck when he was 15, became a third mate at 17, served on regular trans-Atlantic voyages, and then became a second mate on a ship serving the Australian wool trade. In 1855 he began working on steamships, advancing to the rank of captain at the age of 22. Before he was 30 he commanded the *Great Eastern,* the largest ship at the time which laid trans-Atlantic cables from Valentia to Newfoundland in 1866. He continued captaining that and other ships in cable laying.

Hamilton, Hugh Douglas (1739–1808)
portrait painter

Born in Dublin, Hamilton became a successful portrait painter in ovals ($9^1/_2$ by $7^1/_2$ inches) using pastels. He went to London in 1764 where his clients included King George III and the Prince of Wales. In the 1780s he was in Rome where he began doing portraits in oils, including those of many individuals doing their Grand Tour. Hamilton returned to Ireland in 1791, continuing to paint portraits in oils of leading figures of the period.

Hamilton, James Archibald (1747–1815)
astronomer

Born in Athlone and educated at TRINITY COLLEGE DUBLIN, Hamilton took holy orders in the CHURCH OF IRELAND. While rector, he built an observatory at Cookstown, County Tyrone, and studied the planet Mercury and various meteors. His papers deal with the determination of longitude and the distances to the stars.

Hamilton, William Rowan (1805–1865)
mathematician

Born in Dublin, Hamilton learned several modern and ancient languages as a child, and while still a student at TRINITY COLLEGE DUBLIN his mathematical knowledge and intellectual powers were such that he was appointed professor of astronomy and director of Dunsink Observatory while still an undergraduate. His mathematical writings, particularly on quaternions, earned him international regard. He was knighted in 1835, twice honored by the Royal Society, and made an honorary member of most European scientific academies. Hamilton wrote poetry and was a friend of Samuel Taylor Coleridge, William Wordsworth, and Maria EDGEWORTH. His personal life was unhappy.

Harland and Wolff

Edward Harland (1831–95), a native of Yorkshire, was manager of the shipbuilding firm in BELFAST that had opened in 1791. He bought the firm in 1858 and was joined in ownership by Gustav Wilhelm Wolff (1834–1913), a native of Hamburg who had come to Belfast in 1857. The company earned renown after it began building liners for the White Star company, including such vessels as the *Oceanic,* the *Olympic,* the *Titanic,* and the *Britannic.* The company thrived during the First and Second World Wars, although its production halved between the wars and declined sharply after 1961. Harland reduced his role in the company in the 1880s, becoming active in unionist politics, serving as lord mayor of Belfast in 1885 and a MP for North Belfast in 1889. Wolff also withdrew from involvement, turning to other businesses and to Conservative politics, being elected a Conservative MP for East Belfast in 1892 and 1910. Their junior partner, William Pirrie (1847–1924), directed the firm following their withdrawal and became chairman in 1895. He became a Liberal in politics in 1905, but found his workforce unsympathetic to HOME RULE. The hiring practices of the company earned a reputation of being highly sectarian.

Harney, Mary (1953–)
politician

Born in Ballinasloe, County Galway, Harney was educated at TRINITY COLLEGE DUBLIN. Unsuccessful as a FIANNA FÁIL candidate for Dublin South East in the 1977 election, she was nominated to the SEANAD the same year by TAOISEACH Jack LYNCH. She was elected to the Dáil in 1981 for Dublin South West and has served ever since. In 1985 she broke with her party and its leader, Charles J. HAUGHEY, by supporting the HILLSBOROUGH AGREEMENT. The same year she left the party and joined the PROGRESSIVE DEMOCRATS. When that party joined in coalition with Fianna Fáil in 1989 she became minister of state for the Department of the Environment. Four years later she replaced Desmond O'MALLEY as leader of that party, becoming the first female leader of a party in Irish history. When that party again entered into coalition with Fianna Fáil in 1997 she became TÁNAISTE, which position she still retains, as well as being minister for health and children. She is identified with a commitment to market economics and has suggested that Ireland pattern its economic policies more in the American than the European manner.

Harris, Richard (1930–2002)
actor

Born in Limerick and educated at Crescent College, Limerick, and at the London Academy of Music and Art, Harris made his acting debut in 1956 in the production of Brendan BEHAN's *The Quare Fellow*. In his film roles he moved beyond playing stock Irish characters to earn an Oscar nomination for his role as a Rugby player in *The Sporting Life* (1963). He played King Arthur in the stage version of *Camelot* in 1980 and sold five million copies of a record titled *MacArthur Park*. He appeared in many other movies, the most impressive performance being Bull McCabe in *The Field* (1990) for which he also received an Oscar nomination.

Harty, Herbert Hamilton (1879–1941)
composer, conductor, pianist

Born in Hillsborough, County Down, Harty went to London where he established a reputation as a composer and an accompanist. From 1920 to 1933 he was the conductor of the Manchester Halle Orchestra, which earned him a knighthood in 1925 and numerous honorary doctorates, as well as a remarkable reputation for the orchestra itself. He introduced the works of Sibelius, Berlioz, Strauss, Shostakovitch, and Mahler to English audiences. His own creations included *Comedy Overture* (1907), *Violin Concerto* (1909), and *Irish Symphony* (1910), and a tone poem *With the Wild Geese* (1910).

Harvey, Beauchamp Bagenal (1762–1798)
United Irishman

Born in Wexford and educated at TRINITY COLLEGE DUBLIN, Harvey was called to the bar in 1782, where he pursued a successful career in law. He championed Catholic emancipation and parliamentary reform and became active in the UNITED IRISHMEN. He inherited estates from his father that carried a substantial annual income. Harvey accepted a request by the Wexford rebels in 1798 that he serve as their commander. After their defeat at New Ross, he was captured, court-martialed, and hung.

Haughey, Charles J. (1925–)
politician

Born in Castlebar, County Mayo, and educated at University College Dublin where Haughey studied commerce, he served in the DÁIL ÉIRE-ANN from 1957 to 1992. He was the son-in-law of Seán LEMASS, TAOISEACH from 1959 to 1966, and served as minister of several important departments, including Justice from 1961 to 1964, Agriculture from 1964 to 1966, and Finance in 1966 when Jack LYNCH succeeded. In 1970 he was dismissed from the government because of his alleged involvement in the provision of weapons to Northern Ireland militants, although he was acquitted in a subsequent trial. He remained in the backbenches of the party for several years. Then two years after the return of FIANNA FÁIL to power in the 1977 election, he gained majority support to become leader and Taoiseach after the resignation of Lynch in 1979, even though Lynch had expected another figure, George Colley to succeed him. Haughey had a reputation for leniency toward the Provisional IRA, yet he attempted to deal with the very anti-IRA new British prime minister, Margaret Thatcher. During the "dirty protest" and later hunger strike by REPUBLICAN prisoners in Northern Ireland jails, who demanded special prisoner status, Haughey, for all his republican tendencies, failed to satisfy the more militant among the protestors. He lost power in a close election in mid-1981, but was back again early the next year when the FINE GAEL–LABOUR coalition lost votes on a controversial tax measure. However, numerous scandals and distrust of him from within the Fianna Fáil Party led to the coalition's return to power in November of the same year. Haughey became Taoiseach again after the 1987 general election. Astonishingly, he introduced policies calling for economic restraint that contradicted those he had earlier advocated, but which received the acquiescence of the Fine Gael leadership, especially Alan DUKES. Distrust of Haughey lingered and, in an election called in 1989, Fianna Fáil found itself compelled, for the first time in its history, to form a coalition with another party, the PROGRESSIVE DEMOCRATS, whose membership consisted largely of ex–Fianna Fáil members. In 1992 he had to resign as Taoiseach over allegations of corruption in order to ensure the continuance of the coalition. Several years later, public tribunals revealed that he had received enormous private gifts from wealthy figures and institutions who did considerable business with the government or could benefit from the government's tolerance. Haughey faced payment of an enormous tax bill and fine for this unreported income, which vastly exceeded his public salary. Haughey's conduct confirmed the suspicions of many that his princely lifestyle and substantial property holdings were of questionable origin. On the other hand, even critics acknowledge that the fiscal discipline he introduced, in contrast to his own earlier rhetoric, paved the way for the phenomenal Irish economic performance toward the end of the 20th century.

Hayes, Michael (1889–1976)
politician, academician
Born in Dublin and educated at Synge Street Christian Brothers School and University College Dublin, Hayes was a lecturer in French at UCD. A member of the IRISH VOLUNTEERS, he fought at Jacob's Biscuit Factory during the EASTER RISING, but he escaped capture. He was interned during the WAR OF INDEPENDENCE and organized classes in history, Irish, English, French, and Spanish for other prisoners. He was elected to the second DÁIL ÉIREANN and took his seat after being released from prison. A supporter of the ANGLO-IRISH TREATY, he served as minister for education from January to September 1922 as well as minister for external affairs in the summer of that year. He was elected Speaker, or *Ceann Comhairle*, of the third Dáil and remained in that post until 1932. He lost his seat in the 1933 general election. Hayes was elected to the SEANAD in 1938, was FINE GAEL leader in that body, and retained his seat until 1965. He taught Irish at UCD from 1933 to 1960, being named professor in 1951.

Hayes, Michael Angelo (1820–1877)
painter
Born in Waterford, Hayes specialized in painting horses, particularly prints of Charles BIANCONI's

traveling cars. He served as military painter to the lord lieutenant and exhibited at the Royal Academy in London. He was also a member and later officer of the Royal Hibernian Academy.

Healy, Cahir (1877–1970)
nationalist politician

Born in County Donegal, Healy moved to Enniskillen as a young man and worked in a solicitor's office, as a land agent, and as a journalist. He was a member of SINN FÉIN and was interned in 1922, the same year he was elected as an MP for Fermanagh-Tyrone. He was not released until 1924. He did not run for the seat again until 1931 when he was elected again in a by-election, holding the seat until 1935. He sat again for Fermanagh–South Tyrone from 1950 to 1955, and also was elected to the Northern Ireland PARLIAMENT in 1925 and again from 1929 to 1965, although he was again interned for two years from 1941 to 1943.

Healy, Timothy (1855–1931)
lawyer and politician

Born in Bantry, County Cork, Healy immigrated to England where he became a journalist, particularly for the *NATION*. He worked for Charles Stewart PARNELL and was elected to parliament himself in 1880 for Wexford. He was a major figure in Parnell's tactics of obstruction in parliament to advance Irish issues, noted for articulateness and severe sarcasm. He was called to the bar in 1884. Healy began to distance himself from Parnell's promotion of the candidacy of his mistress's husband, Captain William O'Shea, for the IRISH PARLIAMENTARY PARTY seat for Galway. He also differed with Parnell in supporting the PLAN OF CAMPAIGN, a continuation of the land agitation in the later part of the 1880s. He sat for different Irish constituencies in his parliamentary career, including South Londonderry (1885–86), North Longford (1886–92) North Louth (1892–1910), and Northeast Cork (1910–18). He was a leading figure in the ouster of Parnell as leader of the party following his refusal to step down, as urged by the Lib-

eral leader and ally of the Irish William Gladstone. Healy was part of a group named the "Bantry Band," which included his relatives A. M. and T. D. SULLIVAN. In the first two decades of the 20th century he served as an independent MP being critical of the Irish Parliamentary Party. In the 1918 general election, sensing the trend in developments, he withdrew his candidacy to allow a SINN FÉIN victory. In 1922, after the formal establishment of the IRISH FREE STATE, he was named its first GOVERNOR-GENERAL.

Healy-Hutchinson, John (1724–1794)
politician

Born in Gortroe, County Cork, Healy-Hutchinson was educated at TRINITY COLLEGE DUBLIN and called to the Irish bar. He adopted the last name of an heiress whom he married. Serving for Lanesborough in 1759 and for the city of Cork from 1760 to 1790, he was a skilled parliamentarian and one of the dominant figures in the Irish House of Commons. A leading supporter of the government, he received regular patronage in return, the most startling of which was appointment as provost of Trinity College, which he sought to use as a private patronage source for his family. On the other hand, he was sympathetic to free trade, political independence, and liberty for Catholics.

Heaney, Seamus (1939–)
poet

Born near Castledawson, County Derry, and educated at St. Columb's College and at QUEEN'S UNIVERSITY BELFAST, Heaney taught at secondary level schools before joining the staff at Queens in 1966, the same year in which his first collection of poems, *Death of a Naturalist,* was published. His poetry reflected the hard routines of the rural life in which he was born and raised. In 1970–71 he was a guest lecturer at the University of California, Berkeley, and in 1972 moved to Glanmore, County Wicklow, becoming the head of the English Department in Carysfort College, County Dublin, from 1975 to

1981. His collection, *North* (1975), deals with the horrors of the situation of Northern Ireland by linking it to past antecedents. He began to receive numerous prizes for his work, including the Somerset Maugham Award (1967), the Duff Cooper Prize (1975), the Whitbread Award (1987 and 2000), and the Nobel Prize in literature (1995). Heaney joined the faculty of Harvard University in 1984, although subsequently being poet in residence and then professor of poetry at Oxford from 1989 to 1994. His publications continued, including *Station Island* (1984), which features encounters with past literary figures, victims of sectarian violence, and challenges to allegiances, *The Haw Latern* (1987), *Seeing Things* (1991), *The Spirit Level* (1996), and *Electric Light* (2001). He was a founding director of the Derry theater company, Field Day, and his play *The Cure at Troy* was performed there in 1990. He published several collections of essays, including *The Government of the Tongue* (1988) and *The Redress of Poetry* (1995). His later work has deviated from specifically Irish themes to reflect interest in eastern European poetry.

Hearts of Oak

A secret group of Protestant peasants in Armagh, Tyrone, and Londonderry who, in the 1760, protested violent collection of tithes by the established clergy and judicial requirement for householders to provide personal labor in road construction. They wore sprigs of oak in their hats as an identifying badge. Their violence was short-lived as the law requiring road work was modified.

Hearts of Steel

Protestant tenants who, between 1770 and 1773, attacked the cattle and property of others who had taken over their holdings when they refused to pay the heavy charge for renewal of their leases demanded by Lord Donegall. Public sympathy was critical of Donegall and the activism of the "Steelboys" helped to guarantee the Ulster Custom whereby tenants were sure of

renewal of lease. Many of the participants soon after went to America where they became strongly Anglophobic in the period of the American Revolution and after.

Hedge Schools

These were schools run privately and irregularly in the eighteenth century and the early nineteenth century as a means whereby Catholics could circumvent the PENAL LAW restrictions on both Catholic educational institutions and on Catholics going abroad for education. The teachers were often itinerant educators who offered a mixed curriculum of classics, math, geography, and history, often dependent on whatever books might be available. Although some were notorious in their personal lives, most were deservedly regarded with the respect accorded the clergy and were called upon to perform paralegal services like drafting wills and letters. Many were renowned as educators and as poets. Typical was the County Kerry poet, Eoghan Rua Ó SUILLEABHÁIN. Figures of eminence in Irish society, such as Daniel O'CONNELL, received their earlier education in the hedge schools. The schools discontinued with the establishment of national schools in the 1830's.

Hennessy, Richard (1720–1800)

soldier, distiller

Born in Ballymoy, County Cork, Hennessy joined the WILD GEESE by going to France in 1740 and enlisting in the French army. An officer in an Irish regiment, he fought in various battles of the War of the Austrian Succession, including Fontenoy. After being wounded he retired from military service and married a widowed cousin, who was also related to Edmund BURKE. In 1765 he moved to Cognac and started the distillery, which continues to this day.

Henry, Paul (1876–1958)

painter

Born in Belfast, the son of a Baptist minister, Henry was educated at the Royal Belfast Academic Institute and the Belfast School of Art. He went to Paris in 1900, studying at the Académie Julien and under Whistler. He did landscapes in charcoal, but also came under the influence of the postimpressionists. He stayed in London for about a decade where he further developed his interest in landscape painting. In 1912 he visited County Mayo remaining in Achill Island for seven years, where he flourished as a landscape painter, employing the techniques of Whistler and the postimpressionists in capturing in his landscapes the wild scenery of the west of Ireland. Henry returned to Dublin where he held many exhibits, helped found the Society of Dublin Painters, and became a member of the Royal Hibernian Academy in 1929. He was also employed to design travel posters for the Irish Tourist Board.

Hervey, Frederick Augustus, fourth earl of Bristol   See BRISTOL, FREDERICK AUGUSTUS HERVEY, FOURTH EARL OF.

Higgins, Francis (1746–1802)
social climber
A poor man who left Downpatrick, County Down, for Dublin, where, having become an attorney's clerk, he converted to Protestantism, Higgins posed as a landlord, and successfully courted a wealthy lady. He became an attorney, ran gaming houses, and took over the FREEMAN'S JOURNAL, which he used to attack the political opposition, especially the UNITED IRISHMEN. A paid political informer, he was rewarded for the information that led to the capture of Lord Edward FITZGERALD.

Hillsborough Agreement
This Anglo-Irish agreement was signed on November 15, 1985, by Prime Minister Margaret Thatcher and Taoiseach Garret FITZGERALD. It grew out of efforts by the diplomats of both nations to strengthen the moderate forces in Northern Ireland, especially given the increasing electoral strength of SINN FÉIN, the political wing of the Provisional IRA that had emerged following the HUNGER STRIKE. It also sought to avoid the difficulties that caused the failure of the overly ambitious SUNNINGDALE AGREEMENT of 1973. The most significant components of the agreement were the statement that the constitutional status of Northern Ireland could be altered only with the approval of the majority of its population, that the development of provincial governing institutions would have to receive the consent of both communities—Protestant UNIONIST and Catholic NATIONALIST—and that regular conferences between both governments would take place to consider problems affecting the Northern Ireland minority (the Catholics) and cross-border security. Lastly, a secretariate, which would include Irish civil servants, would be established in Northern Ireland to service these conferences. Unionists of all stripes were critical of the agreement, which they claimed was reached without consulting them, unlike the moderate Catholic SOCIAL DEMOCRATIC LABOUR PARTY, whose leaders were in regular consultation with the Irish diplomatic corps during the negotiations. This was a point expressed even in the Republic of Ireland, as Mary ROBINSON, the future president of Ireland, resigned from the LABOUR PARTY in protest at its complicity in reaching the agreement. All unionist MP's resigned their seats to force a by-election with which to register popular outrage. All but one was returned. Sinn Féin, its supporters, and the FIANNA FÁIL opposition in the republic also criticized the agreement for "copper-fastening" the partition of the island. However, the secret to the success of the agreement was its placing negatives as to what could not be done rather than set up institutions that could be torn down. Eventually, moderate unionists moved toward discussions, and even the IRA called a cease-fire nearly nine years later. The GOOD FRIDAY AGREEMENT of 1998 can be viewed as having been built on the foundations of the Anglo-Irish Hillsborough Agreement.

Hoban, James (1762–1831)
architect

Born in Callan, County Kilkenny, Hoban studied architecture in DUBLIN under Thomas Ivory and probably worked on the City Hall and the Customs House. He went to the United States in 1785, settling in Charleston, South Carolina. He won the contest to design the White House, the presidential mansion in Washington, D.C., in 1792. His work demonstrated parallels with Leinster House in Dublin. He designed various hotels in Washington, the State and War Offices, and contributed to the rebuilding of the White House after it had been burnt down in the War of 1812.

Hobson, Bulmer (1883–1969)
revolutionary

Born in Holywood, County Down, of Quaker background and educated at the Friends' School in Lisburn, Hobson was drawn to various NATIONALIST and Gaelic causes, such as the GAELIC LEAGUE, the GAELIC ATHLETIC ASSOCIATION, and the DUNGANNON CLUBS, which merged in 1907 with CUMANN NA NGAEDHEAL to form SINN FÉIN. He started a number of short-lived papers, such as *The Republic* (1906) and *Irish Freedom* (1911–14). He broke with Sinn Féin in 1910 because of what he perceived to be its inactivity and, instead, turned his efforts to the cause of the IRISH REPUBLICAN BROTHERHOOD. Hobson broke with its Supreme Council when it condemned his acceptance of John REDMOND's request to nominate half the Provisional Committee members of the IRISH VOLUNTEERS in 1914. He opposed the EASTER RISING and it was Hobson who alerted Eoin MACNEILL to the fact an actual rising was being planned. He withdrew from the revolutionary movement after the rising and turned his energies to such matters as the theater, social credit, and afforestation. Hobson was appointed chief of the stamp sector of the Revenue Commissioners upon the formation of the IRISH FREE STATE.

Hogan, James (1898–1963)
soldier, academic

Born in Kilrickle, County Galway, educated at CLONGOWES WOOD COLLEGE and University College Dublin, and brother of Patrick Hogan, the minister for agriculture in the IRISH FREE STATE, James Hogan was a member of the IRISH VOLUNTEERS at the time of the EASTER RISING. He served in County Clare during the WAR OF INDEPENDENCE. Although appointed professor of history at University College Cork in 1920, he did not take up his post until 1923 as, a supporter of the ANGLO-IRISH TREATY, he took a post in the national army, serving particularly in military intelligence. He was one of the academic and intellectual supporters of the FINE GAEL Party when it was founded, although he was critical of Eoin O'DUFFY, the first leader of the party. Hogan wrote extensively for journals such as *Studies* and the *Proceedings* of the ROYAL IRISH ACADEMY. Hostility to communism, including fears of its possible inroads in Ireland, was a major concern of his in the 1930s. He remained on the faculty of UCC for 40 years.

Holland, John Philip (1841–1914)
inventor

Born in Liscannor, County Clare, Holland was, for a while, a member of the IRISH CHRISTIAN BROTHERS, and taught in several of their schools. He withdrew from the order and went to the United States in 1872, settling in Paterson, New Jersey. He sought to interest the United States navy in his notion of a submarine, but without success. However, CLAN NA GAEL gave him $60,000 to develop his vessel, which he constructed between 1879 and 1881 and called the *Fenian Ram*. It was hoped it could be used against British vessels in the eventuality of another FENIAN rising. In 1895 Holland formed his own private company to continue his experiments, and then secured a contract from the United States navy to build a vessel. Later, the British navy ordered several of his vessels.

Holt, Joseph (1756–1826)
United Irishman

Holt emerged as a leading commander of the UNITED IRISHMEN during the Rising of 1798. His surrender in November of that year signaled that the revolt was over. He was transported to New

South Wales, where he prospered. He left Australia to return to Ireland in 1812, but a series of adventures, including shipwreck on the Falklands, capture by the British while then traveling on an American vessel (the Anglo-American War of 1812 was occurring at the time), delayed his return to Ireland until 1814.

Home Government Association

Founded in 1870 by Issac BUTT, the Home Government Association sought to promote a federal arrangement within the United Kingdom whereby Ireland would be given its own parliament for domestic matters. The movement drew a curious mixture of followers, including unionists apprehensive about the policies of the Liberal government of William Gladstone toward Ireland, former YOUNG IRELANDERS who remembered Issac Butt as one of their legal defenders, and FENIANS who sought an independent Irish republic. The movement was replaced by the HOME RULE League in 1873.

Home Rule bills

There were three serious considerations given by the Westminster parliament to establishing a local parliament for Ireland in the late 19th and early 20th centuries. The first was in 1886 when William Gladstone's acceptance of the Irish Parliamentary Party objective of Home Rule enabled him to form a government and soon after introduce a Home Rule bill. The bill failed in the House of Commons on June 8 because of significant dissent by many members of Gladstone's own Liberal Party, led by Joseph Chamberlain. The measure proposed establishment of a two-house Irish legislature, the upper house of which would consist of 28 peers and 75 members elected for 10-year terms by a restricted electorate, the lower house of 204 members would be elected for a five-year term by those then currently eligible to vote for members of parliament. Ireland would have no representation in the Westminster parliament and its own parliament would have no power to legislate on matters concerning the monarchy, foreign policy, defense,

foreign trade, excise or customs, nor establish or endow a religion. The lord lieutenant would act for the monarch as the Irish executive. The Irish parliament would control its own taxes in Ireland and Irish revenue would consist of domestic Irish taxes and Westminster taxation in Ireland less a predetermined Irish contribution to the imperial exchequer up to a maximum that could not be exceeded and which would be subject to revision in 30 years. Judges were appointed by the Irish government but the DUBLIN METROPOLITAN POLICE would remain under British control for two years and the ROYAL IRISH CONSTABULARY would be permanently under British control. A second Home Rule bill was also introduced by Gladstone when he was again prime minister for the fourth time in 1893. The measure passed the House of Commons, but was rejected by the House of Lords. This bill would have made the upper house of the proposed Irish legislature a body of 48 members elected for eight years by a restricted electorate, and the lower house a body of 103 members elected by the existing parliamentary franchise for five years. The Irish legislature would have the same restrictions on its sovereignty as in the 1886 measure, with an additional reservation to the Westminster Parliament of matters relating to landlord-tenant relations and the purchase and letting of land. The lord lieutenant's term was restricted to six years. The revenue system would be the same, except that there would be an imperial grant to meet one-third of the cost of the police, and the Irish imperial contribution was to be one-third of the total revenue raised in Ireland, which system would be subject to revision in six years. The Irish would appoint their own judges other than the members of the Irish Supreme Court who for the first six years were to be appointed by the Westminster parliament. Gladstone resigned office following the failure of the measure in the House of Lords and his Liberal successor, Lord Rosebery, refused to go to the electorate on the issue as he reasoned that since a majority of the members of the House of Commons from England had opposed the measure it would be inappropriate to attempt to appeal over the heads of the Lords to the electorate.

A third Home Rule bill was introduced by Prime Minister H. H. Asquith in 1912. This measure stemmed from support given by the Irish to the House of Lords Reform Act of 1911, which stipulated that any legislation vetoed by the Lords would become law if passed by the Commons a third time and signed by the king. Vehement opposition by the Conservatives and more especially the UNIONISTS, who threatened violent resistance to its implementation, did not prevent its passage in 1914. However, because of the outbreak of the First World War, both the Irish Parliamentary Party and the Unionists agreed to the suspension of its implementation for the duration of the war. This measure created a two-house Irish parliament: The upper house, a Senate, would have 40 members originally named by the lord lieutenant for five years, but afterward to be elected by the same electorate as would elect the 164 member, five-year term, popular assembly or House of Commons. As in the earlier bills, differences between the two houses were to be settled by the majority of both combined. There were the same restrictions on the Irish legislature's power as in the earlier bills as well as reserving to the Westminster parliament control over the new social welfare instrument such as old age pensions and national insurance for a minimum of 10 years. The Westminster parliament would retain control over collection of taxes and land purchase matters, although the Irish could levy varying taxes and impose additional duties on matters already subject to excise taxes. Irish revenue would consist of those revenues raised in Ireland plus a fixed imperial grant that would gradually be reduced. Ireland would be exempt from imperial expenses for a period of time until an equitable contribution could be determined. The RIC would be controlled by Westminster for the first six years.

Hone, Evie (1894–1955)
artist

A Dublin native handicapped by infantile paralysis, Hone studied art in London and Paris, where she mastered the principles of cubism. She held her first exhibits in Dublin in 1924. Her work was abstract, but interest in Georges Rouault and his religious subjects prompted her to turn to stained-glass work, for which she soon received many commissions. In 1937 she converted to Catholicism. Her works include windows in the Farm Street Jesuit Church in London and in the chapel at Eton College.

Horan, James (1912–1986)
priest

Born in Partry, County Mayo, educated at St. Jarlath's College, Tuam, and at MAYNOOTH, Horan was a curate for a number of years in Glasgow before returning to the west of Ireland. He became a curate at KNOCK, County Mayo, the celebrated Marian shrine and site of apparitions in 1879, and its pastor in 1967. He developed the site into a modern pilgrimage center and petitioned successfully for the development of an airport, which for a time, received public assistance, and which was finally open in 1986. He had a modern basilica constructed as well. The high point of his direction of the Knock Shrine came in 1979 with the visit by Pope John Paul II on his Irish pilgrimage.

Hothouse Flowers   See IRISH ROCK MUSICIANS.

Howth gunrunning

On July 26, 1914, 900 rifles and 29,000 rounds of ammunition were landed at Howth for the benefit of the IRISH VOLUNTEERS. The weapons and ammunition were purchased in Germany and delivered to Howth in his yacht the *Asgard,* by Erskine CHILDERS. Among those planning the enterprise were Eoin MACNEILL, Mary Spring Rice, and Roger CASEMENT. A detachment of soldiers were unsuccessful in intercepting the delivery, but on returning to Dublin, they fired on a hostile crowd at BACHELOR'S WALK, killing four and wounding 37. The gunrunning constituted the NATIONALIST response to the UNIONIST gunrunning in April that year at the Larne.

Humbert, Jean-Joseph (1755–1823)

general

Born in Meuse, France, of humble parentage and orphaned at an early age, Humbert organized a company of volunteers to support revolutionary France against invasion. In two years he rose in rank to general of brigade and was an activist Jacobin in Paris. He played a leading role in the merciless pacification of the province of the Vendée that had supported the counterrevolution. He commanded a French force of over 1,000 that landed in Killala, County Mayo, on August 23, 1798, in support of the revolt of the UNITED IRISHMEN. They were joined by about 1,500 Irish peasants and won a number of victories, especially at Castlebar, County Mayo, but were ultimately defeated at Ballinamuck, County Longford. After surrendering he and the French forces were treated civilly and allowed to return to France. Their Irish allies were savagely repressed. He was wounded near Zurich in 1799. He took part in the expedition to Santo Domingo that captured the leader of the black revolt Toussaint Louverture. Incurring Napoleon's displeasure, he was exiled in Brittany. Later he went to the United States, arriving in New Orleans in 1814. He participated with the American forces in the Battle of New Orleans on January 8, 1815, the last battle of the War of 1812, where he commanded the mounted scouts and was commended by General Andrew Jackson for his bravery. He spent the rest of his days in New Orleans.

Hume, John (1937–   )

politician

Born in Derry and educated at St. Columb's College and at MAYNOOTH, Hume was a young secondary school teacher when he became involved in the movement for civil rights for the Northern Ireland Catholic minority. He rejected the rival appeals to Northern Catholics made by the old Nationalist Party, which, although constitutional, placed national unification as its essential goal, as well as of SINN FÉIN, which rejected constitutional politics and was open to

violence. Instead, he turned toward civil rights with the hope that the resolution of injustice would eliminate sectarian distinction and break the barriers between individuals more than between states. He was active in the Derry Citizens Action Committee, which grew out of the disturbances of 1968, and in the Northern Irish Civil Rights Association the following year. In 1970 he was one of the founding members of the SOCIAL DEMOCRATIC AND LABOUR PARTY, after having defeated Eddie McAteer, the leading NATIONALIST, for the Foyle seat in the Northern Ireland PARLIAMENT in 1969. He was one of the members of the short-lived power-sharing government that had been set up in 1973. In 1979 he was elected to the European Parliament and in 1983 to the House of Commons, in addition to being regularly elected to a series of experimental assemblies in the 1970s and early 1980s that the British government had called in an effort to achieve consensus on devolved government for Northern Ireland and replace the direct rule that had commenced after the prorogation of the Northern Ireland government in 1972. In 1979 he also replaced Gerry FITT, who had resigned as leader of the SDLP in the belief that it turned too "green" or nationalist. Hume worked closely with the Irish government in seeking to offset the appeal of Sinn Féin among Irish Americans, especially during the hectic time of the HUNGER STRIKE and in opposing local American efforts to inhibit investment in Northern Ireland through the imposition of the MacBride Principles. He contributed to the NEW IRELAND FORUM that the Irish government had called to hear constitutional alternatives to the existing Northern Ireland status and he contributed ideas reflected in the HILLSBOROUGH AGREEMENT. In 1992 he undertook a series of private conferences with Sinn Féin leader Gerry ADAMS in an effort to bring that movement out of the cold and into the regular political process. He was successful as the Provisional IRA declared a cease-fire in 1994, which it broke in 1996, but resumed in 1997. Then, in 1998, Sinn Féin joined the SDLP, the UNIONISTS, and the ALLIANCE PARTY, in accepting the GOOD FRIDAY

AGREEMENT. For his efforts in bringing it about, Hume shared the 1998 Nobel Peace Prize with Unionist leader David TRIMBLE. Hume did not take a place as the deputy first minister in the new Northern Ireland government that subsequently came into being, deferring to his deputy in the SDLP, Seamus MALLON. In 2001 Hume resigned as leader of the SDLP and did not run for reelection to the European Parliament in 2004. While the institutions of that agreement are temporarily in suspension, political violence has ceased. On the other hand, the last province-wide election in 2003 has seen the replacement of the SDLP by Sinn Féin as the leading party among the nationalist community (Hume's seat in the European Parliament was won by a Sinn Féin candidate) and the replacement of the unionists by the DEMOCRATIC UNIONIST PARTY led by Rev. Ian PAISLEY as the leading voice of UNIONISM. In short, rather than strengthen the middle ground, the extremes have gained.

hunger strike

A hunger strike is a tactic used historically by Irish prisoners with a political agenda. Its roots go back to ancient times when aggrieved parties would fast outside the property of their antagonist in an effort to shame them into concession. Two hunger strikers during the struggle for political independence who carried their protest to its fatal end were Thomas ASHE, who sought political status when convicted and imprisoned for incitement in 1917 and who died while being forcibly fed, and Terence MACSWINEY, the lord mayor of Cork who died in August 1920 after 74 days on hunger strike protesting his imprisonment under the Defense of the Realm Act. Republican prisoners of the Irish Free State staged a hunger strike some months after the end of the CIVIL WAR, protesting both the conditions of their imprisonment and their actual internment. It was called off after two men had died. When many IRA members were interned by the DE VALERA government during the period of the Second World War, three of them went the full course in a futile effort to gain political status.

The most celebrated recent hunger strike was that undertaken in 1981 by republican prisoners in Northern Ireland. Their objective was to obtain political status with all the benefits of internal organization and absence of prisoner uniforms that had been denied to all prisoners convicted, in contrast to the earlier award of such to those interned without trial. The protest had started with refusal to wear the uniforms, prisoners wrapping themselves in blankets instead, for which they were confined to their cells. The protest escalated to a "dirty protest," whereby they smeared their cell walls with their own excrement. Finally, in late 1980, several of them went on hunger strike. When they had assumed they had gained concessions they went

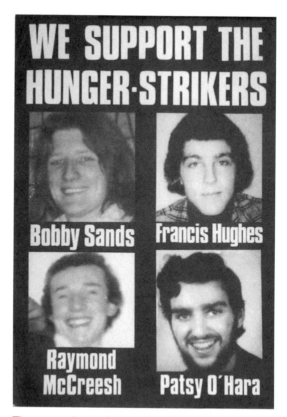

The poster shows photographs of the first four people to join the 1981 hunger strike, and the first four to die. (CAIN)

off the strike. However, the concessions were not what they had expected. Accordingly, a new strike was begun in March, but this time a strategy was adopted by which participants began the strike, not on the same date, but rather on a staggered basis, so as to ensure that the public effect of any deaths would persist for some time. The first striker, Bobby Sands, was even elected to parliament for Fermanagh–South Tyrone while on strike. His death in May on the 66th day of the strike provoked considerable civic disturbance and a number of deaths, many of innocent bypassers. Nine more strikers died during the next four months, not to mention several score of deaths consequent upon violence during the period. Although originally apprehensive about the strike, the leadership of SINN FÉIN witnessed enormous international interest and some support for the movement. The publicity helped galvanize Sinn Féin's move into electoral politics in winning a number of seats in subsequent elections to a temporary Northern Ireland Assembly the following year while at the same time still not renouncing the use of violence in pursuit of their goals. The strike itself was called off, partly through the intervention of Father Denis FAUL, partly by a disguised awarding of some concessions by British authorities.

hurling

One of the major sports promoted by the GAELIC ATHLETIC ASSOCIATION, its origins go back to remote times in Irish history. Interestingly, the medieval Statutes of Kilkenny, which sought to exclude Gaelic or Irish influences from within the Anglo-Norman Pale region of Ireland, banned the game. With the formation of the GAA, its rules were codified. It resembles Irish football in its system of scoring (three points for a goal hit under the goal posts or one point for it being hit over the posts), the size of its field, the number of players on a team (15 per side), and the duration of a game. However, it is similar to field hockey in that the ball is small and hard and it is played with a wooden stick (a hurley or *sliotar*). Counties Cork, Kilkenny, and Tipperary

have been historically the most successful winners of intercounty championships.

Hussey, Thomas (1746–1803)
bishop

Born in County Meath and educated in Seville, after ordination Hussey was assigned to the Spanish court and, as chaplain to the Spanish ambassador in London, was asked by George II to seek the detachment of Spain from the pro-American alliance that continental European states had formed during the American Revolution. A correspondent with Edmund Burke, he became the first president of the college at MAYNOOTH on its foundation in 1795. He served as the Catholic chaplain-general to the army in Ireland where some unrest had developed about Catholic soldiers. Later, he was bishop of Waterford and Lismore. Hussey's diplomatic skills were reportedly put to use in negotiating a concordat between Napoleon and Pope Pius VII in 1802.

Hyde, Douglas (1860–1949)
scholar, first president of Ireland

Born near Castlerea, County Roscommon, Hyde was the son of a CHURCH OF IRELAND rector. He was educated at TRINITY COLLEGE DUBLIN, where he earned an LL.D. He was a brilliant linguist, knowledgeable in Latin, Greek, Hebrew, French, German, and Irish. He taught for a year at the University of New Brunswick in Canada before returning to Roscommon, where he devoted himself to literary pursuits, especially the collection of poetry and folklore in Irish. He published such collections as *Beside the Fire* (1889) and *Love Songs of Connacht* (1893). In 1893 he was one of the founders of the GAELIC LEAGUE, becoming its first president. The movement thrived for the next two decades, as he went on fund-raising tours on its behalf to the United States. He became the first professor of Irish at University College Dublin in 1909 and remained there until 1932. The Gaelic League had been instrumental in achieving in 1908 the goal of making Irish a required subject for entrance to the NATIONAL UNIVERSITY OF IRELAND. Nonpolitical, Hyde became disheartened by the close links that had developed between the Gaelic League and political, and possibly violent, separatism, and he resigned in 1911. He served as a member of the SEANAD of the IRISH FREE STATE from 1925 to 1926, and in 1938 he was selected unopposed as the first president of Ireland following the terms of the 1937 constitution, serving a full term until 1945.

I

Inchiquinn, Murrough O'Brien, first earl of (1614–1674)
soldier and politician
Although from a leading Gaelic family, he had become a Protestant when made a royal ward. He was governor of Munster at the onset of the wars of the 1640s and soon sided with the parliamentary side. Later he moved to the royalist side. In exile after the Cromwellian conquest, he was involved with the Irish regiments in France. He converted to Catholicism while in exile and, after the restoration, recovered his lands in Munster in 1663. Marriages between his Protestant children and those of the earl of Orrery (Roger Boyle, the son of Richard BOYLE, the earl of Cork) further secured his social and landed position.

Independent Irish Party   See IRISH TENANT LEAGUE.

Industrial Development Agency
Originally entitled the Industrial Development Authority, this government body was formed in 1949 to encourage and stimulate industrial development in a highly protectionist Irish economy. By the 1970s it concentrated on attracting foreign investment. By the 1990s the agency was divided into two separate entities, one promoting domestic industrial development, and the other, recruiting foreign investment in Ireland. The former ultimately became Enterprise Ireland while the latter was titled the Industrial Development Agency. It has succeeded in attracting over 1,000 foreign companies, nearly half from the United States, drawn by its provision of generous grants and Ireland's relatively low capital gains tax regime.

Instrument of Government
This was the written constitution that governed the British Isles under Oliver CROMWELL. Proclaimed in December 1653, the document decreed political unification of the islands with a single parliament in which Ireland had 30 members, many of whom were officers in the Cromwellian army. However, the ideal of Ireland's separate political identity did not disappear, even among the New English, who had applauded Cromwell's conquest of Ireland.

internment
This term refers to government detention or imprisonment of individuals without trial. It was employed regularity in both NORTHERN IRELAND and Ireland during times of turmoil. In Northern Ireland it was primarily directed against alleged REPUBLICANS when the Ministry of Home Affairs would employ the Special Powers Legislation allowing such. The IRISH FREE STATE had legislative sanction in its earlier years to utilize internment against irreconcilable opponents of the ANGLO-IRISH TREATY. It was also employed by the government of Eamon DE VALERA in the late 1930s and during the Second World War against the IRA. Its most successful use in both sections of the island was against the IRA campaign of 1955–63. It was employed again by the Northern Ireland government in August 1971 against the invigo-

rated IRA. However, many of those interned were simply civil rights activists, purely political republicans, or innocents, while many of the major figures in the Provisional IRA escaped the roundup. Accordingly, the tactic could be seen as having backfired, as it worked to encourage recruitment into the IRA among those interned or among their friends outside. The process allowed the interned to be given a special political category and to organize among themselves within the detention camps, which facilitated use of the prisons as a training ground for the IRA. Internment was discontinued in December 1975. In its place a system of juryless trials, in which certain common law principles regarding witnesses and testimony were dispensed, was employed to contend with the difficulty of getting impartial jurors or conducting routine criminal and forensic examinations. The system was employed against both republican and LOYALIST terrorists, in contrast to the tendency to use internment almost exclusively against republicans.

Invincibles

The Invicibles were a secret society of more extreme FENIANS, some of whose members assassinated the newly appointed chief secretary for Ireland, Lord Frederick CAVENDISH, and the undersecretary, Thomas H. Burke, in PHOENIX PARK on May 6, 1882, soon after Cavendish's arrival in Ireland. He had replaced William FOSTER, who had resigned over what he considered concessions to Charles Stewart PARNELL and the LAND LEAGUE. Parnell and his associates quickly denounced the assassinations so as not to risk the loss of improving relations with the government of William Gladstone.

IRA   See IRISH REPUBLICAN ARMY.

Irish (language)

Irish is a Celtic language akin to Scots Gaelic, Manx, Cornish, and Breton. It was the predominant language in Ireland from pre-Christian times through the late 17th century. ANGLO-NORMAN domination of parts of Ireland in the later medieval period caused its decline in those areas. The political, cultural, and religious Anglicization of Ireland in the 16th and 17th centuries, particularly the defeat of the Gaelic aristocracy that had sided with the JACOBITE cause between 1688 and 1691, resulted in growing identification of the language with the lower classes and with economic stagnation. This was especially the case during the era of the PENAL LAWS. In the 19th century the language issue was never central to many who espoused either repeal of the ACT OF UNION, Catholic emancipation, or even outright political separatism. The massive decline in population in the primarily Irish-speaking western areas at the time of the Great FAMINE and in the generations after, through starvation or emigration, and the development of popular publicly financed education in English furthered the process of the language's decline. Only toward the end of the 19th century with the development of the GAELIC LEAGUE did language revival become intricately linked with the NATIONALIST cause. Even by then, probably less than a few thousand of the population was exclusively Irish speaking. With political independence the state encouraged the revival of the language, requiring it as a subject in schools and for qualification for the civil service, as well as subsidizing certain areas, designated GAELTACHT, where Irish was the prevailing tongue. However, the popular revival never took off, partly because of a degree of cynicism that was associated with the use of the language by some politicians who made symbolic evocations rather than significant use of the language. Other factors included the spread throughout Ireland of the modern media, with made the whole island part of the North Atlantic Anglophone community. On the other hand, almost as a consequence of the removal of many of the requirements for Irish in completing education or obtaining public positions, there has been a significant increase, especially outside of the declining Gaeltacht regions, in interest in the language among a committed minority, many of whom can be seen as converts to Irish, rather than natural speakers.

This is reflected in the growth of Irish-only schools, which approximately 30,000 Irish children attend. The Irish-speaking Gaeltacht population is presently less than 30,000, although the number of Irish speakers or at least those able to converse in Irish, is significantly larger. Nonetheless, even though constitutionally regarded as the national language, it remains decidedly the tongue of a small minority.

Irish Brigade

A group of Irish MP's who combined in the 1851 session of parliament to oppose the anti-Catholic Ecclesiastical Titles Bill. They later established the Catholic Defense Association, which worked with the IRISH TENANT LEAGUE to support the Independent Irish Party that achieved success in the 1852 election, but which began to crumble following the acceptance of positions in the ministry of Lord Aberdeen by two of its members, William KEOGH and John SADLEIR, despite a pledge not to take office.

Irish Brigades   See WILD GEESE.

Irish Christian Brothers

A religious order founded in 1802 in Waterford by Edmund RICE for the education of poor boys. The order played a major role in the rejuvenation of Irish Catholicism in the 19th century, as they provided education, and particularly secondary education, which allowed the advance of thousands of Irish peasant children into the lower middle class, especially into clerical and civil service positions. Their central role in the formation of Irish youth continued well into the late 20th century. Their system of education was characterized by emphasis on Catholic orthodoxy, Irish NATIONALISM, and Gaelic revivalism. The brothers were particularly adept at pragmatic and disciplined instruction with which to qualify their charges for examinations, especially examinations for positions in both public and private service. The decline in religious vocations

in the last third of the 20th century has seen the numbers in the order decline substantially, as very few are still teaching. The Irish Christian Brothers order does have branches in several other countries. The order has been embarrassed by the revelations of pedophilic abuses by some members in the mid-20th century.

Irish Citizen Army

A group formed in November 1913 by James CONNOLLY from members of the IRISH TRANSPORT AND GENERAL WORKERS' UNION to defend labor rallies at the time of the Dublin lockout. The numbers in the force were never more than 400. After the failure of the protest against the lockout and after the union's leader James Larkin had gone to America, Connolly's position evolved more and more into a combination of socialism and NATIONALISM and he turned the group, now down to a little more than 200, into a potential revolutionary force for insurrection against England. Associated with him in this was Countess MARKIEVICZ. In early 1916 he was drawn into the confidence of the IRISH REPUBLICAN BROTHERHOOD leadership and linked his group with their plans for the EASTER RISING. His detachment of over 200 was deployed in St. Stephen's Green and the Royal College of Surgeons during Easter Week. After the collapse of the revolt, Connolly and a colleague, Michael Mallon, were among those executed. The group remained in existence during the WAR OF INDEPENDENCE, working with the IRA. At the outbreak of the CIVIL WAR, most of the members went along with Markievicz in opposing the ANGLO-IRISH TREATY and were among the many arrested after the fall of the FOUR COURTS and other places held by irregulars in Dublin.

Irish colleges

Numerous seminaries were established on the Continent as part of the Counter-Reformation effort to confront the Protestant Reformation. With the imposition of a Protestant religious establishment in Ireland, the need for such colleges to train a Catholic clergy for Ireland became essential. Philip II of Spain was one of the early patrons of such institutions, beginning with establishment of a college at Salamanca in 1592. Within a century there were 30 such colleges throughout Europe, especially in Spain, the Netherlands, and France. With the declining power of Spain and the loss of its position in the Netherlands, France became the primary center for this exile education for Irish Catholics, especially as a large exile community had settled in France, many in the service of the French armies. With the revolution in France at the end of the 18th century, these schools were suppressed, and a seminary was established at MAYNOOTH to facilitate the education of Irish priests at home, where the more severe of the penal restrictions on the church were being removed. The government even agreed to subsidize the institution.

Irish Congress of Trade Unions (ICTU)

The umbrella national organization of the various Irish unions, the ICTU was formed in 1959. It plays a major role as the labor participant in the social partnership whereby certain formulae among rates of compensation increments are negotiated among labor, business, and government to minimize industrial confrontation. The formula has played a significant role in the recent economic growth of Ireland. An Irish Trades Union Congress (ITUC) had been formed in 1894, which helped to found the Irish LABOUR PARTY in 1914. However, the organization split in 1930 into two bodies, the ITUC and the Congress of Irish Trade Unions, until reunited in 1959 as the ICTU. Membership is over three-quarters of a million, including a quarter of a million in Northern Ireland, where the organization has effectively pursued a neutral course in the sectarian and constitutional troubles.

Irish Convention

Prime Minister David Lloyd George summoned a convention in July 1917 in an effort to arrive at an agreement over a formula for Irish self-government. He sought to arrive at some kind of HOME RULE without having to wait for the implementation of the 1914 Home Rule Act that had been postponed for the duration of the First World War. He was also anxious to appease pro-Irish sentiment in the United States, which had just recently entered the war as an ally. Attendees included UNIONISTS, members of the IRISH PARLIAMENTARY PARTY, and a number of independents, including Horace PLUNKETT. SINN FÉIN did not attend. The convention issued a report the following April calling for self-government, but it was rejected by the Unionists.

Irish Examiner

A daily newspaper, originally called the *Cork Examiner,* that was founded in 1841 by John Francis Maguire, but taken over after his death in 1872 by Thomas Crosbie, whose family continue to control it. Although covering more than local news, it retained a provincial character with a very loyal readership until 2000, when it changed the name and the general appearance of the paper. It still trails the other daily morning papers—the IRISH TIMES and the IRISH INDEPENDENT—in circulation.

Irish Free State

The name of the Irish state called for by the ANGLO-IRISH TREATY of 1921. It was formally established in December 1922 when the British government accepted the constitution approved by DÁIL ÉIREANN. A self-governing dominion of the British Commonwealth, its name was replaced in 1937 by Eire, or Ireland, with the approval by the Irish electorate of a new Irish constitution. The new document did not include references to the monarchy or to the dominion status, although Ireland remained a member until 1949.

Irish Independent

Originally titled the *Irish Daily Independent* when founded in 1891 as a paper for supporters of the recently deceased Charles Stewart PARNELL, it employed members of the IRISH REPUBLICAN BROTHERHOOD. In the beginning of the 20th century, William Martin MURPHY, the successful entrepreneur, took over the paper and gave it its present name in 1905. It was a supporter of the ANGLO-IRISH TREATY and continued to support CUMANN NA NGAEDHEAL and subsequently FINE GAEL until recently, being regarded as the voice of the Catholic middle class. A Sunday paper, the *Sunday Independent,* and an evening paper, the *Evening Herald,* were also affiliated with it. In 1973 the newspaper group was acquired by international businessman Anthony O'REILLY, who added a number of other papers, including many Irish local papers, to his control. Its tone is less socially conservative, although relatively conservative on economic issues and expressing disapproval of strong irredentist NATIONALISM with regard to the Northern Ireland question.

Irish National Liberation Army

This was the military wing of the Irish Republican Socialist Party, a small faction within OFFICIAL SINN FÉIN, that disapproved of the latter's abandonment of the armed struggle in the early 1970s. It also attracted more radical members of the Provisional IRA. It tactics have been characterized by ruthlessness and brutality, including shooting worshipers at a Pentecostalist church in Armagh in 1983. Internal feuds probably drew as many casualties and public attention to the organization than its campaign for national liberation.

Irish Parliamentary Party

This party grew out of the HOME GOVERNMENT ASSOCIATION. It consisted of many members of parliament elected in 1874 who favored a local parliament for Ireland. Issac BUTT was the original leader. Some members challenged his opposition to the use of obstructionist tactics in parliament to gain attention to their issues, and turned to Charles Stewart PARNELL as their leader. Butt died in 1879 and Parnell was selected as leader after the 1880 election. Under him, strict discipline was imposed on the members, who were dependent on the party for campaign funds and for their living while at Westminster in the era before members of parliament were paid and when it was assumed that only independently comfortable

"gentlemen" should serve. Parnell was able to secure finances for the party in part by his involvement in the new dimension in Irish politics whereby his party, the IRISH REPUBLICAN BROTHERHOOD, their Irish American supporters, and the LAND LEAGUE, agreed to work together to advance the HOME RULE cause. The party gained virtually all seats from Ireland other than the seats won by unionists, primarily, but not exclusively, in ULSTER. A split in the party developed when Parnell was ousted as leader after his involvement in a divorce scandal. By the beginning of the 20th century the split had been resolved with the pro-Parnellite, John REDMOND, leading the party until his own death in March 1918. After local government reform in the 1890s the party dominated most of the Irish county councils, urban district councils, and other elected bodies, again with the exception of UNIONIST dominated areas of Ulster. Redmond's successor, John DILLON, witnessed the ending of the party with the SINN FÉIN landslide in the 1918 general election, although the Northern Ireland wing of the party continued up until the 1970s under the name NATIONALIST.

Irish People

James STEPHENS, the founder of the IRISH REPUBLICAN BROTHERHOOD, started this paper as the official organ of the movement in 1863. John O'LEARY was editor, Charles J. KICKHAM and Thomas Clarke LUBY were contributors, and Jeremiah O'DONOVAN ROSSA was business manager. It was suppressed in 1865. William O'BRIEN, who led the United Irish League, a secessionist movement from the IRISH PARLIAMENTARY PARTY, started a paper by the same name that lasted from 1899 to 1908. NORAID, the Irish Northern Aid Committee that was an American support organization for the provisional SINN FÉIN and the IRA, published a weekly paper of the same name in the United States from the 1970s through the 1990s.

Irish Press, The

Eamon DE VALERA founded the *Irish Press* in 1931 as a daily newspaper and as a voice for the FIANNA FÁIL Party. He raised about $500,000 in the United States to help finance the paper.

Much of the funds came from purchasers of bonds supporting the DÁIL ÉIREANN during the WAR OF INDEPENDENCE who had had their contributions returned by an American judge who refused to decide whether the IRISH FREE STATE or the pretender Dáil Éireann, recognized by opponents of the ANGLO-IRISH TREATY, should have the funds. De Valera induced many of these to give the money to him as more representative of the Ireland they desired. The paper quickly drew a vast audience, particularly from the lower middle class, small farmers, and laborers. Its celebrated editors included Frank Gallagher and Tim Pat Coogan, both very ardent NATIONALISTS although the later would in retirement write a severely depreciatory biography of de Valera, who had originally controlled the editorial policy of the paper, until his son, Vivion, succeeded. The *Irish Press* started a Sunday edition in 1949, the *Sunday Press,* and an evening edition, the *Evening Press,* in 1954. By the late 1980s the character of the paper, which had much appeal to an earlier audience, had changed and readership declined. An American publisher purchased controlling interests, but subsequent legal battles about the new arrangement further weakened the appeal of the paper and it ceased publication in 1995.

Irish Republican Army (IRA)

The IRA constituted the Army of the Irish Republic, that is, of the DÁIL ÉIREANN, during the WAR OF INDEPENDENCE. Its membership consisted of the IRISH VOLUNTEERS, that is, the remnant of that group who had not followed John REDMOND's 1914 call to join the NATIONAL VOLUNTEERS and support the British effort in the First World War. An additional minority of the Volunteers accepted the call of the IRISH REPUBLICAN BROTHERHOOD and took part in the EASTER RISING of 1916. Members of the Irish Volunteers took the first military action against the ROYAL IRISH CONSTABULARY simultaneous with the formation of the Dáil Éireann in January 1919. The Dáil insisted that the military group consider itself the Army of the Irish Republic under the authority of Minister for Defense Cathal BRUGHA. Simultaneously, the Irish Republican Brotherhood, dominated by Michael COLLINS, the minis-

ter for finance and also the director of intelligence, and including the chief of staff of the army, Richard MULCAHY, held overlapping jurisdictions in both directing the IRA and pursuing its own tactics. Throughout the war of independence tension persisted between Collins and Brugha over Collins's more advanced guerrilla warfare strategy and Brugha's romantic idea of revolution by siege. The rivalry persisted after the ANGLO-IRISH TREATY was concluded in December 1921, when Brugha and his allies desired to continue the fight until a full republican status was gained for Ireland while the more realistic Collins accepted dominion status as a step toward the full goal. Most of the units of the IRA remained opposed to the treaty and Mulcahy, as minister for defense in the PROVISIONAL GOVERNMENT called for by the treaty, set about organizing a new National Army, drawing from loyal IRA units and new recruits. Although Eamon DE VALERA, the president of the rival government during the CIVIL WAR, and Frank AIKEN, the chief of staff of the IRA, called for an end to the armed struggle in the spring of 1923, the organization continued. However, by late 1925 the IRA, fearful that many in the SINN FÉIN Party were ready to enter the Dáil éireann if the oath to the king was removed as an obligation of its members, asserted that it would henceforth be governed by its own internal officialdom. De Valera came to power in 1932 constitutionally. He and his followers entered the Dáil Éireann in 1927 when faced with the prospects of losing their unused seats if that they not take them. Among his first steps was to remove various types of punitive legislation that had allowed many IRA members to be imprisoned. Further steps he took to win them to the FIANNA FÁIL approach of achieving REPUBLICANISM by political rather than military means included awarded them with pensions for their service in the antigovernment side during the civil war and giving public employment to them, even as police auxiliaries. However, even de Valera turned on them when violent actions were taken in the mid 1930s against a retired British naval officer and a landlord. He invoked similar legislation as that employed by the CUMANN NA NGAEDHEAL government against the IRA in the

1920s. When the IRA commenced a campaign against Britain on the British mainland in 1939, de Valera's government employed the full energies of the state against them, convicting many, some of whom were executed, and interning many more, for the duration of the Second World War.

The IRA always had right and left wings, with the former more concerned with the military and national struggle and the later more attuned to social questions. Typical of the former was Seán RUSSELL, who launched the bombing campaign in London, and who was in Germany during the Second World War trying to facilitate support for the IRA. Left-wing IRA figures include the writer, Peadar O'DONNELL, who sought to set up a left-wing party, SAOR ÉIRE, in the 1930s, and Seán MACBRIDE, who later would emerge as minister for external affairs in a coalition government from 1948 to 1951. Although continuing organizationally, the IRA was relatively inactive until the mid-1950s when it commenced a campaign against the continued partition of Ireland. The participants were predominantly from the Irish Republic and their various assaults on ROYAL ULSTER CONSTABULARY barracks and other public facilities in NORTHERN IRELAND received minimal support from Northern Catholics and nationalists who were reaping the benefits of the extension to the province of the full benefits of the British welfare state and expanded educational opportunities. The vigorous implementation of a policy of INTERNMENT in both jurisdictions of Ireland furthered weakened the effort, although not until after there had been a massive funeral for one IRA member from Limerick who had been killed in action and after some Sinn Féin members were elected to the Dáil Éireann, but did not take their seats. After the border campaign was called off in 1962 more left-wing types dominated the IRA and Sinn Féin, who sought again to emphasize social issues and forge international links. However, after the 1969 social confrontations in Northern Ireland, when there were savage assaults on Catholic sectors, especially in Belfast, more nationalist-minded members of the organization, especially those from Northern Ireland, challenged the passive intellectuals controlling the movement. A split developed between the

challengers, who became known as Provisional IRA (and Sinn Féin), the organization, who were called OFFICIAL IRA and Sinn Féin. The former had a much larger following, both in Ireland, Northern Ireland, and in the United States, while the latter, a few years later, gave up the armed struggle and would ultimate call itself the Workers' Party. As the Northern Ireland troubles intensified in the 1970s and 1980s Northern members assumed control of the Provisional IRA and Sinn Féin. In the 1980s, especially after the HUNGER STRIKES of 1981, Sinn Féin–IRA began to combine politics with armed struggle, or as one leader, Martin McGUINNESS put it, "the ballot and the armalite." Sinn Féin stood for electoral office, although they did not take seats in Westminster. However, their willingness to take seats in the Dáil Éireann led to secession by the more doctrinaire, primarily southern Irish, who formed a rival Republican Sinn Féin party and a Conti-

A Republican poster in support of the Provisional Irish Republican Army, 1974 *(CAIN)*

nuity IRA. In the 1990s, when the IRA proclaimed a cease-fire in 1994 and renewed it again in 1997, other militants seceded to form the 32 County Sovereignty Movement and the Real IRA. However, aside from some pockets of territory, the secessionists remain minorities, although the Real IRA did inflict the horrendous bombing in Omagh in 1998. Although virtually all of those convicted and imprisoned in Northern Ireland during the troubles, whether republican or loyalist, have been freed, the IRA itself continued its unwillingness to surrender or decommission its substantial store of weapons and explosives, much smuggled into Ireland from abroad in the 1980s. Finally, in 2005, the IRA agreed to dump its arms and to engage only in democratic politics. The decommissioning was confirmed by the International Commission on Disarmament. However, unionists, especially the DUP, remained skeptical of complete IRA abandonment of criminality and some weapons.

Irish Republican Brotherhood (IRB)

This secret organization was formed in 1858 by James STEPHENS, a veteran of the YOUNG IRELAND cause who had returned to Ireland after a number of years in exile on the Continent. The movement emphasized in its oath a commitment to the achievement of an Irish republic. The organizational structure resembled a pyramid, with the commander dealing with captains, who in turn dealt with sergeants, who dealt with individual members, and no one dealing with anyone outside of his own subgroup other than the immediate superior to whom he would report. The organization drew a substantial number of members, especially among first-generation town residents, the sons of peasant farmers. Naturally a great amount of support developed among Irish who had gone to the United States, especially those who were refugees from the Great FAMINE. The support organization that developed there was CLAN NA GAEL. Both the American wing and the IRB itself were commonly referred to as FENIANS. The IRB met with the displeasure of authorities who suppressed its newspaper, the *IRISH PEOPLE*, in 1865. The Catholic Church was also condemnatory, especially of the

secret character of the movement, as Cardinal Paul CULLEN saw in it a spirit similar to the anticlerical movements then growing in strength on the Continent. In fact, virtually all the members were Catholics. The ideology of the movement centered on the national struggle with minimal attention given to social or economic questions. Stephens was ousted from leadership under Irish-American pressure because of his tardiness in starting an actual uprising, which did take place in several places in Ireland in early 1867. The rising was quickly suppressed, partly because police intelligence learned of the plans. The leader who had replaced Stephens was a Colonel Thomas J. Kelly, who was himself arrested. An effort to rescue him from imprisonment in England resulting in the killing of a police sergeant with a subsequent execution of three members. Execution transformed them into the Manchester Martyrs. An effort to free other Fenian prisoners later the same year by blowing up a prison wall actually killed a number of bystanders. However, out of the commotion there developed a new attention to Ireland in British political circles, especially on the part of William Gladstone, who became prime minister the following year determined to bring peace to Ireland. The IRB remained relative quiescent during the 1870s as some of its members even joined the HOME RULE movement, although those who were elected to parliament, Joseph BIGGAR and Thomas Power O'CONNOR, were forced to resign from the organization. The exiled activist, John DEVOY, helped bring the movement to the NEW DEPARTURE whereby the Fenians and the LAND LEAGUE and the IRISH PARLIAMENTARY PARTY combined their energies to advance the land cause and maximum strength in parliament. On the other hand, in the 1880s, exile supporters, such as Jeremiah O'DONOVAN ROSSA, gave their support to a bombing campaign on the British mainland. From the late 1880s to the early 20th century, the organization again was dormant, seemingly more intent on celebrating past glories or lamenting past defeats, than on advancing a program or a strategy. Then, the return from New York to Dublin by Thomas CLARKE, a former prisoner, and the interest of younger Northern activists such as Bulmer

HOBSON, Sean MacDermott (Seán MACDIAR-MADA), and Denis McCULLOUGH, and the encouragement of John Devoy in New York, brought new life to the movement. It quickly gained an important hand in the IRISH VOLUNTEERS that had formed in 1913. When most of the membership had withdrawn from the Volunteers to follow John REDMOND into the NATIONAL VOLUNTEERS, the IRB gained the governing hand in the ruling councils of the Volunteers. In such a position they were able to call the EASTER RISING. During the WAR OF INDEPENDENCE, the IRB operated almost separately from the DÁIL ÉIREANN and the IRISH REPUBLICAN ARMY, which the Volunteers had been renamed, although its members served in both. Michael COLLINS was the leading figure in the organization, which regarded itself as the determiner of what would be the ultimately legitimate Irish Republic. Collins was able to call upon the IRB loyalties of many in the Dáil Éireann to win their acceptance to the ANGLO-IRISH TREATY, which scarcely met the republican ideal because he pictured the agreement as a step along the way toward establishment of a republic. Before and during the CIVIL WAR, the minister of defense of the IRISH FREE STATE, Richard MULCAHY sought to revitalize the IRB within the National Army, whose general staff were all members, as a means of counteracting some disgruntled members of the army, who called themselves the "Old IRA." A brief ARMY MUTINY in 1924 by the latter collapsed, but the government, especially Vice President and Minister for Justice Kevin O'HIGGINS, used the occasion as grounds for ridding the army of both groups, which he saw as a threat to the concept of civilian supremacy over the military. The IRB was formally disbanded in 1924.

Irish rock musicians

In the wake of U2 several other Irish groups have attained international prominence combining rock, soul, and traditional music. They include the Corrs, the Cranberries, and the Hothouse Flowers. The Corrs are a folk rock band from Dundalk, County Louth, consisting of three sisters, Sharon, Andrea, and Caroline, and one brother, Jim, from the Corr family, who rose to prominence in the late 1990s. They combine folk, pop, and traditional Irish music in their presentations. They were formed to audition for the 1991 film *The Commitments*. Their great success in several albums in the late 1990s had its origins in their being spotted in a Dublin club by the American ambassador to Ireland, Jean Kennedy Smith. Their first album, *Forgiven, Not Forgotten*, was successful in Australia, France, and Britain, as well as in Ireland, while their 1998 album *Talk on Corners* gained worldwide success. Both albums were certified as gold in the United States. In 2004, they released *Borrowed Heaven* (2004), an international favorite, and a new Irish-themed album titled *Home* is scheduled to be released in September 2005. The Cranberries were a rock-and-roll group formed in Limerick in 1990. They achieved widespread and mainstream international popularity with a series of very popular albums, including *Everybody Else Is Doing It, So Why Can't We* (1993), *No Need to Argue* (1994), *To the Faithful Departed* (1996), *Bury the Hatchet* (1999), and *Wake Up and Smell the Coffee* (2001). Although a "best of" compilation titled *Stars* was released in 2002, the group disbanded in 2003 and the following year announced they were taking some time to pursue individual careers. The members were Mike Hogan, the bass guitar player; Noel Anthony Hogan, Mike's brother, the guitarist; Fergal Patrick Lawler, drummer; and Dolores O'Riordan, an Irish singer, and the vocalist, keyboardist, and backing guitarist for the band. The Hothouse Flowers combine both rock and soulful rhythm and blues with an Irish flavor. They first came to international prominence when they performed in the interval between contestant performances and scoring during the 1988 Eurovision Song Contest. Their albums include *People* (1988), *Home* (1990), *Songs from the Rain* (1993), *Born* (1998), and *Into Your Heart* (2004). Leading figures in the group are Liam O'Maonlai and Fiachra O'Braonain.

Irish Tenant League

A group that grew out of a tenant-right conference called in Dublin by John Grey, the editor of the *FREEMAN'S JOURNAL*, Charles Gavan DUFFY, of YOUNG IRELAND and editor of the *NATION*, and Frederick LUCAS, editor of the

Tablet, an English Catholic weekly, which sought to make the Ulster Custom, which gave tenants security of occupancy or right of compensation for eviction, formal legislation applicable to all of Ireland. They put the issue to candidates at the forthcoming general election and 40 of the members elected agreed with the cause. Those members would form part of the Whig, radical, and Peelite alliance that forced the ministry of Lord Derby from power in December 1852. Also know as the Independent Irish Party, the willingness of two of them to take office in the succeeding coalition government under Lord Aberdeen led to their demise as a group.

Irish Times, The

This daily newspaper was founded in 1859 and reflected Conservative and UNIONIST opinion. The industrialist, John Arnott, took over the paper in 1873 and his family retained control until the mid-20th century. In 1974 a public trust was established to guarantee the continuance of the paper's independence. From 1922 on, its readership numbers were quickly surpassed by the IRISH INDEPENDENT and later by the IRISH PRESS, as the unionist and Protestant population of independent Ireland dwindled significantly. The paper continued to champion the British Empire, although obviously accepting and supporting the Irish Free State as part of that empire. From the 1960s on the character of the paper changed, in large part under the direction of editor Douglas GAGEBY, who was sympathetic to the political unification of Ireland and whose tenure gave the paper a decidedly liberal flavor that appealed increasingly to the Irish intellectual class. Its international coverage greatly surpassed that of other Irish dailies and it became undoubtedly the Irish paper of record. Its circulation numbers also thrived. In 1985 Conor Brady became its first Roman Catholic editor and Geraldine Kennedy succeeded him in 2002 as the first female editor.

Irish Trades Union Congress (ITUC)

A national organization of Irish labor unions formed in 1894 that in 1912 it helped found the Irish LABOUR PARTY. Rivalry between William O'BRIEN and James LARKIN was followed by Larkin's creation of a rival organization, the Workers' Union of Ireland in 1924. When Larkin's group was readmitted to the Irish Trades Union Congress in 1945, O'Brien led a secession of the IRISH TRANSPORT AND GENERAL WORKERS' UNION, which then formed a Congress of Irish Trade Unions. Both groups were reunited in 1959 as the IRISH CONGRESS OF TRADE UNIONS.

Irish Transport and General Workers' Union (ITGWU)

This union was founded in 1909 by James LARKIN and in 1910 it affiliated with the IRISH TRADES UNION CONGRESS (ITUC). Its organizational efforts provoked the lockout by employer William Martin MURPHY in 1913–14. The union's failure in that instance prompted Larkin to leave for the United States, as James CONNOLLY succeeded him. After Connolly was executed following the EASTER RISING, Thomas Foran, P. T. Daly, and William O'BRIEN held the leadership and successfully expanded the organization, which included 100,000 members by 1919. When Larkin returned from America in 1923, he failed in an attempt to resume control and organized a rival Workers Union of Ireland, which reflected his radical syndicalist perspective. Rivalry between the two groups persisted through the 1930s and early 1940s, until Larkin and his group reaffiliated with the ITUC and the LABOUR PARTY, which provoked O'Brien and the ITGWU to withdraw and form a rival Congress of Irish Trade Unions and several Labour TD's formed an allied National Labour Party. The break was not resolved until 1959 when both umbrella groups came together as the IRISH CONGRESS OF TRADE UNIONS. In 1990 the ITGWU joined with the Federated Workers' Union of Ireland to form the SERVICES, INDUSTRIAL, PROFESSIONAL AND TECHNICAL UNION (SIPTU), which has played a major role in negotiating the national social partnership.

Irish Unionist Alliance

This group of southern UNIONISTS grew out an earlier organization, the Irish Loyal and Patriotic Union that had unsuccessfully tried (aside from Trinity College) to promote anti–HOME RULE candidates in the 1885 general election. Its members were small in number but extremely important in terms of business and land ownership, including Lord Midleton and the Marquis of Lansdowne. They played a significant role in negotiations over a third Home Rule bill. After the bill's passage many of them formed a Unionist Anti-Partition League under Lord Midleton. They opposed Home Rule, but entered into negotiations with Eamon DE VALERA toward the end of the WAR OF INDEPENDENCE, and after conclusion of the ANGLO-IRISH TREATY with representatives of the PROVISIONAL GOVERNMENT in working out conditions, including representation in the Irish SEANAD, which enabled them to play a constructive role in the new independent Ireland.

Irish Volunteers

The Irish Volunteers were two distinct groups. One was the group formed in the 18th century at the time of the American Revolution. They were a volunteer force recruited to provide a substitute defense force for Ireland after significant numbers of the British army had been withdrawn to serve in the war in America. Their numbers grew to 80,000 and they became allied with those in the Irish parliament campaigning for legislative independence. Their gatherings and conventions were means of applying public pressure to force the issue.

The second group was formed in response to the November 1913 editorial appeal by Eoin MAC-NEILL in *An Claidheamh Soluis*, the GAELIC LEAGUE publication, for a militia force to be organized among Irish NATIONALISTS in emulating what the UNIONISTS had done in Ulster as a threat to forcefully resist HOME RULE. The IRISH REPUBLICAN BROTHERHOOD quickly occupied important positions in its governing council until John REDMOND was allowed to nominate half of the governing council. The group grew to 200,000 members. When the First World War started, and after the Home Rule Act was passed but postponed, Redmond asked the members to support the British war effort. Most joined with him in forming a new group called the NATIONAL VOLUNTEERS. However, 11,000 refused and continued as Irish Volunteers. Their president, Eoin MacNeill, took the position that they would not support England's war, but would not take offensive action unless the authorities moved against nationalist groups. However, a minority in the governing council, led by the IRB members, planned, without MacNeill's approval, the EASTER RISING in which more than 1,000 participated. The organization continued after Easter Week, but with the release of those interned by 1917, the direction of the organization, as with SINN FÉIN, moved in a more militant direction with Eamon DE VALERA becoming president of both groups. When the WAR OF INDEPENDENCE started in January 1919, the Irish Volunteers became the Army of the Irish Republic, later the IRISH REPUBLICAN ARMY, of the government of the DÁIL ÉIREANN.

Irregulars

Those who took up arms against the ANGLO-IRISH TREATY in the CIVIL WAR were called the Irregulars by the PROVISIONAL GOVERNMENT and later the IRISH FREE STATE as a means of suggesting the illegitimacy of their claim to be acting on behalf of the people of Ireland, whose votes in the June 1922 election had confirmed the pro-treaty proponents in power.

J

Jackson, William (1737–1795)
United Irishman

Born in Dublin, Jackson took holy orders in London where he served as a curate and then secretary to the Duchess of Kingston. He was also a radical journalist and supported the American Revolution. He went to France in 1792 to evaluate the chances of a successful French invasion of England. Back in Dublin, an associate informed on him and he was found guilty of high treason, but he poisoned himself while in the dock.

Jacobitism

The term refers to the cause of the deposed king James II, as well as to the claims by his son, James III, and grandson, Charles Edward, to the throne of England and is taken from the Latin for James, *Jacobus.* Support for the Jacobite cause in Ireland was strongest in James II's time, when he came to Ireland, was accepted by a parliament, and fought a war unsuccessfully against the forces of King William. Although he fled to the Continent after defeat at the Battle of the BOYNE, his followers among the OLD ENGLISH and Gaelic Catholics of Ireland continued the struggle until the conclusion of Treaty of Limerick. Many Irish exiles afterward served in continental armies and they were sympathetic to the later Jacobite landings in Scotland in 1715 and again in 1745, both of which ultimately failed. Their numbers were continually replenished by recruits from an Ireland in which the PENAL LAWS were in force against Catholics. However, the general disinterest among the Catholics of Ireland in the Jacobite cause at the time of these respective landings by the Pretenders lessened distrust of Catholics on the part of the Protestant establishment and led to a softening of the enforcement of the penal laws and then of their gradual repeal.

Jameson, Andrew (1855–1941)
distiller

Born in Scotland and educated at Cambridge, Jameson became chairman of the distillery founded by his family in 1905. He was also a director of the Bank of Ireland for 54 years and high sheriff for Sligo in 1898 and Dublin in 1902. He took part in the IRISH CONVENTION of 1917 and was a leading spokesperson for southern unionist opinion. Jameson took part in negotiations with the PROVISIONAL GOVERNMENT that facilitated participation in the new state by willing unionists. He himself was a member of the SEANAD from 1922 to 1936.

Jellett, Mainie (1897–1944)
artist

Born in Dublin, Jellett studied at the National College of Art. Subsequently she studied in London and Paris, where she joined Evie HONE in studying under Albert Gleizes in developing the technique of cubism. She returned to Ireland in the 1930s after successful exhibitions of her work in Paris and Dublin. Her work, which was among the first displays of abstract art in Ireland, met with some criticism at first, even from George RUSSELL, but she eventually gained acceptance.

She completed murals for the British Empire Exhibition in Glasgow (1938) and the Irish Pavilion at the New York World's Fair (1939). Jellett was a founding member of the Irish Exhibition of Living Art.

Johnson, Thomas (1872–1963)
politician, trade unionist
Born in Liverpool, Johnson left school at the age of 12, worked first as a messenger boy, and moved to Ireland in 1892 where he worked for a fish importer and then as a commercial traveler. He became involved with the developing Irish labor movement, becoming vice president of the IRISH CONGRESS OF TRADE UNIONS in 1918, as well as having been a founding member of the Irish LABOUR PARTY in 1912, of which he was a vice chairman. He called a strike in opposition to conscription in Ireland in 1918 and won the approval of the Labour Party to abstain in the 1918 election in which SINN FÉIN prevailed over the IRISH PARLIAMENTARY PARTY. He was one of a committee that drafted the idealistic Democratic Program for the first DÁIL ÉIREANN. He accepted the ANGLO-IRISH TREATY and was elected to the third Dáil Éireann in 1922. Since Sinn Féin members abstained from sitting in the Dáil, he became the leader of the largest opposition group as leader of the Labour Party parliamentary delegation and played a major role in criticizing some of the more severe provisions of the CUMANN NA NGAEDHEAL government's EMERGENCY POWERS legislation. He was reelected in the June 1927 election and secured the votes of the Labour Party that, with those of FIANNA FÁIL, led to a no-confidence vote against the government of William T. COSGRAVE, which, however, failed because of the tie-breaking pro-government vote by the Speaker. He was not reelected in the general election called immediately afterward. Johnson was a Labour Party member of the SEANAD from 1928 to 1936, was a founding member of the Labour Court from 1946 to 1956, and was general secretary of the International Congress of Trade Unions until 1945.

Johnston, Denis (1901–1984)
playwright
Born in Dublin and educated at Cambridge and Harvard, Johnston's first play *The Lady Says "No!"* was rejected by the ABBEY THEATRE, but produced in 1929 at the GATE THEATRE. The title came from the note Lady GREGORY sent rejecting it. He joined the staff of the Gate subsequently and his play *The Moon in the Yellow River* was produced there in 1931. He went to London in the mid-1930s to work for the BBC, where he became a war correspondent during the Second World War. Afterward he lectured at several American universities. Other plays include *A Bride for the Unicorn* (1933), *Storm Song* (1934), *The Golden Cuckoo* (1939), *The Dreaming Dust* (1940), *A Fourth for Bridge* (1948), *Strange Occurrence on Ireland's Eye* (1956), and *The Scythe and the Sunset* (1958). He also wrote autobiographical works, including *Nine Rivers from Jordan* (1953).

Johnston, Francis (1760–1839)
architect
Born in Armagh, Johnston was the architect who designed St. George's Church, Temple Street, the conversion of the Parliament of Ireland building into the Bank of Ireland, the alteration of the Vice-Regal Lodge (now Aras on Uachtarain), the GENERAL POST OFFICE, and the Chapel Royal in DUBLIN CASTLE. He served as adviser on construction of Nelson's Pillar.

Johnston, William (1829–1902)
politician
Born in County Down, Johnston was a prominent member of the ORANGE ORDER and was imprisoned under an act dealing with party processions. He was ousted from a post as fisheries inspector because of the violence of his oratory against the LAND LEAGUE. He was elected an MP for South Belfast in 1885 and held the seat until his death in 1902. In parliament he vigorously opposed HOME RULE.

Joly, John (1857–1933)
inventor

Born in County Offaly of continental European parents, Joly was educated at Trinity College Dublin. His inventions led to his appointment there as professor of geology and mineralogy. Joly's scientific work included invention of a process for color photography, estimation of the age of the Earth by measuring the salinity of the sea, use of radioactive dating methods in geology, and development of new methods of radiotherapy.

Jones, Thomas Alfred (1823–1893)
painter

Of unknown parentage, Jones was raised by the Archdale family of Kildare Place, Dublin. Educated at the Royal Dublin Society and Trinity College Dublin, he did not complete his degree but traveled on the Continent for three years before returning to Dublin to practice as a portrait painter and as an exhibitor at the Royal Hibernian Academy, to which he was elected in 1860 and became its president in 1869. He was knighted in 1880.

Jordan, Neil (1950–   )
writer, film director

Born in Sligo, Jordan was raised in Dublin and educated at St. Paul's, Raheny, and at University College Dublin. He published a collection of short stories, *Night in Tunisia* (1978), and novels, *The Past* (1980) and *The Dream of a Beast* (1983). He then turned to directing films, such as *Angel* (1982) and *The Company of Wolves* (1984). Two of his films, *The Crying Game* (1992), which won him an Oscar for the best screen play, and *Michael Collins* (1996), are directly related to Irish politics and history. Other films he directed have included *The Butcher Boy* (1997), *In Dreams* (2000), and *The Honest Thief* (2002).

Joyce, James (1882–1941)
writer

The oldest son of a very large middle-class Dublin family whose fortunes had declined to virtual poverty because of the father's spendthrift inclinations, Joyce was given an excellent education at Jesuit schools like Clongowes Wood and then Belvedere. He studied at University College Dublin, where his academic performance was unimpressive as he opted for the role of intellectual independence and literary astuteness. He went to Paris after his studies, but came near to destitution. He returned to Dublin in 1903 shortly before the death of his mother. He worked occasionally as a teacher, but in 1904 he left for Zurich with a Galway girl, Nora Barnacle. They later moved to Trieste where they taught English at a Berlitz school. He returned briefly to Dublin in 1909 when he unsuccessfully attempted to run a cinema. Joyce went back to Trieste, although he returned to Dublin in 1912 where he arranged for the publication

James Joyce *(Library of Congress)*

of his collection of short stories titled *Dubliners* (1914), which gave great insights into the Dublin of the time. He then returned to Trieste and never came back to Ireland. In 1916 he published an autobiographical novel *Portrait of the Artist as a Young Man,* which was a recasting of an earlier work, *Stephen Hero.* In 1915 he and Nora and their two children moved to neutral Zurich where he wrote a play *Exiles* (1918), which was an autobiographical explanation of why he could not return to Ireland, and began working on *Ulysses.* He received financial support from the Royal Literary Fund and in 1917 began to receive support, which he would get for the rest of his life, from a patron, Harriet Shaw Weaver. In 1920, at the behest of Ezra Pound, who had published *The Portrait of an Artist* in serial form in his magazine *The Egoist,* he and his family moved to Paris. They remained there until the beginning of the Second World War when they returned to Zurich. In 1922 *Ulysses* was published. This account of a single day in Dublin, June 16, 1904, the same day he met Nora Barnacle, constituted a stream-of-consciousness novel that is regarded as one of the outstanding examples of 20th-century writing. The work was censored in numerous countries, including Britain and the United States, but remarkably not in Ireland. Over the next 17 years, he worked on *Finnegan's Wake* (1939), selections from which had appeared in various small journals. It met with a mixed response, partly because of the extraordinary difficulty in reading it, as he employs remarkable linguistic tricks and uses various languages. At the time he was suffering from visual ailments that resulted in occasional blindness together with family afflictions that included a mentally ill daughter and an unhappily married son. He died in Zurich in 1941. In the eyes of many, he was the greatest writer of the 20th century and a following amounting to a Joyce cult exists, as evidenced by the fantastic price the sale of his erotic letters to Nora Barnacle received at a recent auction and by the exploitation of the centennial of "Bloomsday," the day on which *Ulysses* took place, by the Irish tourist industry.

K

Kane, Robert John (1809–1890)
scientist

Born in Dublin and educated at TRINITY COLLEGE DUBLIN, Kane published the *Elements of Practical Pharmacy* in 1831 and the next year founded the *Dublin Journal of Medical Science*. He was a member of the commission appointed by Robert PEEL to investigate the potato blight, which caused the Great FAMINE. His lectures on the development of industry in Ireland, which were published as *Industrial Resources in Ireland* (1844), led to the government's establishment, at his suggestion, of a Museum of Irish Industry in 1846, of which he became director. He was made president of Queen's College, Cork (later University College Cork), which he held until 1873. In 1877 he was made president of the Royal Irish Academy and in 1880 vice chancellor of the Royal University of Ireland, the examining body created to allow degrees to be given to students at the Catholic University of Ireland (which would later become University College Dublin).

Kavanagh, Patrick (1904–1967)
poet

Born in Inniskeen, County Monaghan, Kavanagh worked as a farm laborer and cobbler. He wrote for local journals until his writing was discovered by George RUSSELL ("AE"), who published three poems of his in the *Irish Statesman* in 1929. In 1936 his first collection was published as *Ploughman and Other Poems*. He went to England and wrote an autobiography *The Green Fool* (1938). Kavanagh returned to Dublin where he remained the rest of his life. In 1942 he published *The Great Hunger*, a lengthy poem that presents a bitter picture of rural life in Ireland as one of poverty, disheartenment, and sexual frustration. Later he published a novel, *Tarry Flynn* (1948), which was banned in Ireland but which carried much the same message. Kavanagh underwent surgery for lung cancer in 1955. However, he continued his work, writing as an occasional journalist, editing with his brother Peter a journal, *Kavanagh's Weekly*, 13 issues of which appeared, and additional poetry, which were collected in *Come Dance with Me Kitty* (1960) and *Collected Poems* (1964). His influence on Irish poets of the late 20th century was immense.

Keane, John B. (1928–2002)
writer

Born in Listowel, County Kerry, where he owned a public house, Keane wrote articles, plays, short stories, and novels that combined humor and tragedy in reflecting the rural and small town atmosphere of his own area and the tensions between modernizing elements and local traditions and prejudices. Although he had written plays, beginning in 1959 with *Sive*, his work did not appear in the ABBEY THEATRE until the 1980s when it became a regular part of the repertoire. One of his plays, *The Field* (1965), was made into a film by Jim SHERIDAN in 1990. Other well-received plays include *Many Young Men of Twenty* (1963), *Big Maggie* (1969), and *Moll* (1972). He also published collections of short columns and humorous letters, such as *The Gentle Art of Matchmaking and Other Important Things* (1973) and *Unlawful Sex* (1978).

Keane, Molly (1905–1996)

novelist, playwright

Born in County Kildare, Keane wrote a number of successful novels and plays under a pseudonym, M. J. Farrell. Then in 1981 she published *Good Behavior* under her own name, which was followed by other works, including *Time after Time* (1983) and *Conversation Piece* (1991). Her works deal with declining Anglo-Irish families who cover familial disorder with a veneer of cultivation, an atmosphere in which she came of age.

Keane, Roy (1971–   )

soccer player

Born in Cork, Keane played for a local team, the Cobh Ramblers, before being signed to play for Nottingham Forest in 1990. Three years later he was signed by Manchester United for a then record sum of money. He captained his team to European Champions League, Premiership, and Football Association Cup titles. He was part of the Republic of Ireland team in the 1994 and 1998 World Cup competitions, but he had difficulties with the coach over what he perceived as inadequate training facilities and withdrew before the first match in the 2002 competition.

Kearney, Peadar (1883–1942)

songwriter

Born in Dublin and educated at the Christian Brothers School Marino, Kearney left school at 14 and worked at various odd jobs, although eventually turning to housepainting. He was a member of the Gaelic League and the Irish Republican Brotherhood, and took part in the Howth gunrunning and the Easter Rising. His most famous song, which became the national anthem, was "The Soldier's Song." Other songs he wrote included "Down by the Glenside" and "Whack Fol De Diddle." Kearney returned to house painting after his revolutionary involvement and his song writing. He was the uncle of the playwright Brendan Behan.

Keating, Geoffrey (Seathrún Céitinn) (c. 1580–c. 1644)

theologian, historian

Born near Caher, County Tipperary into an Anglo-Norman family, Keating was educated for the priesthood at Reims and Bordeaux. He returned to Ireland as a parish priest in the diocese of Lismore and Waterford in 1610. Keating was regarded as a remarkable preacher. One of his works was *The Three Shafts of Death,* a devotional tract in scholarly Irish that served as a model for Irish clergy in preparing their sermons for several of centuries afterward. He also wrote a theological defense of the Mass, reflective of a Counter-Reformation perspective. He also wrote an historical work, *Foras Feasa ar Eirinn,* a narrative history of Ireland from the earliest of times to the coming of the Normans, that contrast with its contemporary, the Annals of the Four Masters, in that it is a narration rather than a record of events and dates.

Kells, Book of

This book is an illuminated manuscript of the four Gospels in Latin. It dates from about 800 and probably originally came from Iona, the monastic settlement in Scotland founded by the Irish missionary monk Colm Cille. It is one of the best examples of earlier medieval northern European works of its kind. It was brought to Kells, County Meath, probably to protect it from Viking raiders. In the 17th century it came into the possession of Trinity College Dublin, in whose possession it remains. Its illustrations of Christ, the Virgin and Child, and other religious images drawn from the scriptures, its decorative initials, and its elaborate ornamentation reflect Celtic, Germanic, and Mediterranean influences.

Kelly, Eamon (1914–2001)

actor

Born in County Kerry, Kelly was a technical school teacher who took to acting, eventually becoming a regular performer at the Abbey The-

ATRE. His performance as the father in the tortuous father-son relationship in Brian FRIEL's play *Philadelphia Here I Come* gained him an international reputation in the 1960s. He gained immense popularity by his one-man performances as a *seanchai*, or storyteller, in the fashion common in peasant houses in rural Ireland up until the mid-20th century prior to the easy accessibility of mass media like radio and television.

Kelly, John (1931–1991)
politician
Born in Dublin and educated at Glenstal Abbey, University College Dublin, Oxford, Heidelberg (from where he obtained a doctorate in jurisprudence), and the KING'S INN, Kelly was a professor of jurisprudence at UCD from 1965. He wrote two important texts, *Fundamental Rights under the Irish Constitution* (1961) and *The Irish Constitution* (1967). He also edited the *Irish Jurist*. He was called to the bar in 1957. He was a FINE GAEL member of DÁIL ÉIREANN for Dublin South from 1969 to 1991 when he died. Briefly appointed attorney general in 1977, he was minister for foreign affairs and minister for industry and commerce in the short-lived coalition government of 1981. He was not in the coalition government from 1982 to 1987, as he was hostile to serving in a coalition with the LABOUR PARTY. However, he supported the government in preference to a Charles HAUGHEY–led FIANNA FÁIL government. Appointed to the NEW IRELAND FORUM, he did not sign its final report, which he regarded as unrealistically nationalist in its proposals. One of the more articulate and outspoken members of the Dáil, he was severe in attacking stupidity and simplistic positions. Among the objects of his scorn were the advocacy of a diplomatic policy of neutrality and socialism. His conservative attitudes were balanced with a willingness to entertain certain liberal concessions like the sale of contraceptives, as he regarded certain matters as beyond the competence of state authority. Another theme he raised was a reconciliation of the two wings of the old SINN FÉIN party, Fine Gael and Fianna Fáil, in a grand conservative coalition. On the other hand, he was severely critical of modern irredentist NATIONALISM as championed by PROVISIONAL SINN FÉIN and the Provisional IRA.

Kenmare, Valentine Browne, Viscount Castlerosse, sixth earl of (1891–1943)
columnist
Born in Killarney and educated at Downside and at TRINITY COLLEGE DUBLIN, he served in the Irish Guards in the First World War and was wounded in action. He was a columnist for Lord Beaverbrook's *Sunday Express* from 1926 to 1941. He also had a beautiful golf course laid out on the family estate near Killarney.

Kennelly, Brendan (1936–   )
poet
Born in Ballylongford, County Kerry, and educated at TRINITY COLLEGE DUBLIN, Kennelly was a professor there from 1973 until his retirement in 2004. He has published more than 20 books of poetry, novels, translations, and has edited anthologies, including *The Penguin Book of Irish Verse* (1970). His poetry and translations deal with his ancestral roots in Kerry, personal difficulties including his failed marriage and his alcoholism, and his cardiac surgery. His work also gives ear to the marginalized and the outcast. His books include *Cromwell* (1983), *The Book of Judas* (1991), and *The Man Made of Rain* (1998).

Keogh, William Nicholas (1817–1878)
politician, judge
Born in Galway and educated at TRINITY COLLEGE DUBLIN, Keogh was called to the bar and practiced successfully on the Connacht circuit. He was a member of Parliament for Athlone from 1847 to 1856, originally as a Conservative, the only Roman Catholic Conservative MP. Later,

after working to found the Catholic Defense Association, he became one of the members of the Independent Irish Party whose votes helped bring down the government of Lord Derby in 1852. However, he and a colleague, John SADLEIR, broke ranks with the party and accepted office in the subsequent coalition government headed by Lord Aberdeen. The position he accepted was that of solicitor general. Later he became Attorney General and in 1857 a judge of the Court of Common Pleas. His rulings and commentary was particularly severe in subsequent trials of FENIANS. Keogh also ruled in favor of a Conservative candidate in a disputed election for the MP for Galway County in 1872, unseating the HOME RULE candidate. His ruling was very unpopular and he was burnt in effigy. In 1878, while traveling in Germany he committed suicide.

Kerry

One of the larger counties in terms of area, Kerry is situated in the southwest of Ireland, having several lengthy rocky and mountainous peninsulas, Dingle, Iveragh, and Brera, that jut out into the Atlantic Ocean. Seven miles out from the Iveragh Peninsula are the Skelligs Rocks, the largest of which rises over 700 feet from the sea, that housed for several centuries an early Christian monastery until raided by the Vikings. Kerry's scenery, both in those peninsulas and around the Lakes of Killarney and the area east, particularly the Derrynasaggart Mountains, is striking and explains why tourism is one of the leading sources of employment in the areas. The farmland in the north is fine, but the rest of the county, because of its mountains and bogs, is more appropriate for sheep farming. The highest mountain in Ire-

Lakes from Kenmare Road, Killarney in County Kerry *(Library of Congress)*

land, CARRAUNTUOHILL (3,414 feet), forms part of the McGillyduddy Reeks southwest of the Lakes of Killarney. The population stands at over 132,000 and there are several major towns, including Tralee, Killarney, Castleisland, Listowel, Kenmare, and Killorglin, many of which have attracted industries, especially following the development of an airport between Tralee and Killarney, which services flights to other parts of Ireland, Britain, and the Continent. The leading political figure in 19th century Ireland, Daniel O'CONNELL, was a native of the county and his home at Derrynane is presently a museum and the estate has become a national park. Kerry was the scene for some of the more brutal defeats of the Geraldine opponents of Queen Elizabeth I in the late 16th century and some of the more bitter encounters during the Irish CIVIL WAR in the 20th century. The county has also provided numerous literary figures for Ireland ranging from 17th- and 18th-century Irish poets such as Aodhagan O'Rathaille and Eoghan Rua O'Suilleabhan to 20th-century figures such as John B. KEANE and Brendan KENNELLY. The remarkable record of the county's team in Gaelic Football, where it has won the greatest number of All-Ireland Championships, is another source of local pride.

Kettle, Thomas M. (1880–1916)
politician, poet

Born in Dublin and educated at CLONGOWES WOOD COLLEGE and University College Dublin, Kettle was the son of a LAND LEAGUE founder and married Mary Sheehy, one of daughters of David Sheehy, an anti-PARNELL member of the IRISH PARLIAMENTARY PARTY. He served as Irish party MP for East Tyrone from 1906 to 1910 and lectured on economics at University College Dublin. He was in the IRISH VOLUNTEERS and helped purchase the weapons that were brought in at the HOWTH GUNRUNNING. When the First World War broke out he joined the Royal Dublin Fusiliers and worked to draw recruits. He opposed the EASTER RISING, although he was a close friend of some of the leaders who were

executed. Kettle subsequently volunteered for serve on the front in France and was killed in action in September 1916 at the Somme.

Kickham, Charles (1828–1882)
writer, revolutionary activist

Born in Mullinahone, County Tipperary, an accident severely impaired Kickham's hearing and his eyesight as a teenager. Nonetheless he was active in the YOUNG IRELAND movement and later in the IRISH REPUBLICAN BROTHERHOOD (IRB), as he was coeditor of the movement's newspaper, the *IRISH PEOPLE*. The later involvement resulted in his being imprisoned for 14 years after trial before Justice William KEOGH in 1865. He was released in poor health in 1869, returning home where he resumed his activism, running successfully for parliament for Tipperary and becoming a member of the Supreme Council of the IRB in 1872. In this period he wrote a series of very popular novels, such as *Sally Kavanagh* (1869) and *Knocknagow* (1873), and ballads, including "Patrick Sheehan" and "Rory of the Hill."

Kiely, Benedict (1919–)
writer

Born in Dromore, County Tyrone, Kiely was educated at University College Dublin and worked as a journalist in Dublin from 1940 to 1965. He has published several novels, including *Land without Stars* (1946), *The Captain with the Whiskers* (1960), *Proxopera* (1977), and *Nothing Happens in Carrickmacross* (1985), and several collections of short stories, including his *Collected Stories* (2001). He is an effective user of comedy and irony and often deals with matters related to the Northern Ireland troubles.

Kildare

A county in the eastern province of Leinster, its name comes from Cill Dara, the church of the oak tree, reputedly a monastery founded by Saint BRIGID. It was established as a county by the Anglo-Normans in the 13th century and its earls were the Fitzgeralds. It was a central area of the Pale, the Anglo-Norman reserved area of medieval Ireland. It is celebrated for its fine land, which services the needs of the nearby Dublin market, and for estates. A remarkable natural feature is the Curragh, which in addition to being an army base, has a plain of over a thousand acres and has hosted horse races for centuries. Another important racing venue in the county is Punchestown in the north. The county is celebrated for horse breeding. Two important educational institutions in the county are the Jesuit secondary school, Clongowes Wood College, and Maynooth College, which is part of the National University of Ireland, but which also includes a Catholic seminary. The county has a population of over 150,000 and is increasingly an area from which many employed in Dublin commute. Growing towns include Leixlip, Celbridge, Maynooth, and Kildare.

Kildare, Gerald (Garret Mor), eighth earl of (1456–1513)

lord deputy

Kildare was the dominant political figure in Ireland in the late 15th and early 16th centuries, able to skillfully assert his own dominant position over both English and Gaelic lords as well as serve the interests of the kings of England, several of whom appointed him as their lord deputy in Ireland, even though he was linked with failed efforts by pretenders to the Crown. He became earl of Kildare upon the death in 1478 of his father. Although he was lord deputy he supported the pretender efforts of Lambert Simnel against King Henry VII, the first Tudor king of England, in a campaign that received the endorsement of the parliament of Ireland. He was also sympathetic to a similar campaign of Perkin Warbeck in 1490s. Henry replaced him as lord deputy with Edward Poynings under whom legislation was passed subordinating the agenda of the Irish parliament to the king's privy council. However, realizing that he needed him to maintain any claim over Ireland, the king reap-

pointed him as deputy. Subsequently, he married the king's cousin Elizabeth St. John. His son Gerald (Garret Og) Fitzgerald was raised as a royal hostage and married Elizabeth Zouche, a royal ward. Henry VII had given though to invading Ireland in 1506, but reconsidered and invested Fitzgerald with greater powers. In 1513 during a battle with a local lord, Garret Mor incurred wounds from which he died.

Kildare, Gerald (Garret Og), ninth earl of (1587–1534)

lord deputy

Educated in England while a hostage to King Henry VII to guarantee the faithfulness of his father Gerald Fitzgerald, and married to Elizabeth St. John, a royal ward, Kildare was appointed lord high treasurer when he was allowed to return to Ireland in 1504. He succeeded his father as lord deputy and as earl of Kildare in 1513. He clashed with the Butlers, the earls of Ormond. King Henry VIII increasingly came to distrust him and several times summoned him to London to account for himself. In 1519 he replaced him with a series of others as lord deputy. However, in 1532 he again reappointed him. But two years later, the distrust of the Ormonds and of Thomas Cromwell, who sought to lessen royal dependence on feudal vassals like Kildare and replace them with public servants, prompted Henry to again summon him and imprison him in the Tower of London, where he died less than three months after incarceration.

Kildare, Thomas (Silken Thomas), 10th earl of (1513–1537)

rebellious vassal

Educated in England, Kildare was named vice deputy by his father, Gerald Fitzgerald, who was then lord deputy, in 1534 when summoned to London by Henry VIII. On the father's instructions, he dramatically repudiated allegiance to the king at a meeting of the royal council in Dublin. A total of 140 horsemen, whose helmets had silken fringes (hence the nickname), accompanied him. When the father, who was imprisoned in the Tower, died in September, Thomas succeeded him as earl. He was unsuccessful in attacking Dublin, failed to get support from possible continental allies such as the pope and the Holy Roman Emperor in what he sought to characterize as a rebellion on behalf of the Catholic Church against the Protestant Henry VIII. An English force under Sir William Skeffington overwhelmed Kildare's Castle at Maynooth while he was away and slaughtered the defenders in March 1535. The following August he surrendered to Lord Leonard Grey, who as lord deputy would implement the Reformation in Ireland. Although promised his life for surrendering, Silken Thomas was taken to London, placed in the Tower, and, in February 1537, executed along with his five uncles on the basis of an act of attainder.

Kilkenny

A county in southern Leinster, through which three rivers, the Nore, the Barrow, and the Suir flow, partly forming the boundaries with neighboring counties. The ANGLO-NORMAN medieval parliament of Ireland, while meeting in the town of Kilkenny, passed the famous Statute of Kilkenny (1366) that sought to exclude Gaelic culture from the PALE. The county was dominated by the Anglo-Norman Butler family, who controlled Kilkenny Castle in the town. It was the center of the Catholic Condeferation during the wars of the 1640s. Craft workshops established in 1963 in Kilkenny Castle became a center for design in ceramics, textiles, and furniture. Important natives of Kilkenny include the philosopher George BERKELEY, the founder of the IRISH CHRISTIAN BROTHERS, Edmund RICE, and the architect who designed the White House, James HOBAN. The population of the county is over 80,000.

Kilkenny, Statute of

Legislation passed in 1366 by the ANGLO-NORMAN medieval parliament of Ireland that sought to maintain the distinct culture of the PALE at a time when many were moving to England and the population was declining because of the Black Death, a plague that afflicted Europe in that century. The Anglo-Normans were required to maintain the English language, names, and laws and were not to intermarry with the native Irish, emulate their style of dress, nor patronize their poets. Native Irish were excluded from important ecclesiastical posts within the Pale as well.

Killala (landing)

A French force of about 1,000 led by General Jean-Joseph HUMBERT landed on the north coast of County Mayo on August 23, 1798, in support of the rising of that year. Within a few days, joined by hundreds of native Irish, they defeated British forces at Castlebar. However, within another fortnight, they were forced to surrender. The French were allowed safe passage back to France, but hundreds of the Irish participants were executed.

Kilmainham, Treaty of

The term refers to the agreement between Charles Stewart PARNELL and the government of William Gladstone in May 1882 whereby land agitation was to be discouraged in return for the release from prison of Parnell and extension of the benefits of recent land legislation, which sought to fix rents and to give tenants an interest in the holding, to farmers who were in arrears on their rent.

Kilmainham Gaol (Jail)

A prison built in 1796 that served as the place of incarceration for many Irish revolutionaries and political activists from the Rising of 1798 through the Irish CIVIL WAR. Those incarcerated and executed there include Robert EMMET, the leaders of the EASTER RISING of 1916, and Erskine CHILDERS. Prisoners have included Thomas Addis EMMET, Charles Steward PARNELL, and Michael DAVITT. It was closed in 1924 and is presently a museum.

Kilmichael

Kilmichael is located in County Cork near the town of Macroom, which was the scene of one of the more celebrated IRA exploits in the WAR OF INDEPENDENCE. A column led by Tom Barry ambushed a BLACK AND TANS force in November 1920. The incident occurred a week after BLOODY SUNDAY in Dublin when innocents at an afternoon football match were killed by the British forces after the morning executions of British agents by Michael COLLINS's hit squad. Controversy continues as to whether those ambushed had surrendered and were killed in cold blood or whether some faked surrender hoping to resume fire when the captors' guard had been let down.

King, William (1650–1729)

archbishop, politician

Born in County Antrim, King was educated at TRINITY COLLEGE DUBLIN, and became a priest of the CHURCH OF IRELAND, although his parents were Scottish Presbyterians. He became dean of St. Patrick's Cathedral in Dublin. A champion of King William, as well as having long been a critic of both Presbyterianism and Catholicism, he was briefly imprisoned until released after the Battle of the Boyne. Then he became the bishop of Derry. He wrote a defense of the Williamite cause titled *State of the Protestants under the Late King James's Government.* In 1703 he became the archbishop of Dublin. He displayed a Protestant Irish patriotism in his opposition to the appointment of Englishmen to important church positions, in defending the independence of the Irish parliament, and in supporting Jonathan SWIFT in his agitation against the minting contract given to a friend of the mistress of King George I. He was a lord justice as well during the period of his archbishopric.

King's Inn

Would-be barristers are trained at this institution that was chartered in 1792 and is presently managed by senior barristers and judges. After passing highly competitive entrance examines,

the students must, if they have not already received a law degree, study for the same and take courses for two more years that involve attending court, sitting for a variety of examinations, and dining at the King's Inn on 10 occasions in each of those two years, after which they are "called to the bar."

Kinsale, Battle of

The Cork coastal town of Kinsale was the site of the decisive battle in December 1601 when the forces of Hugh O'NEILL and Hugh O'DONNELL and their Spanish allies were decisively defeated by English armies. Their failure can be attributed to both their exhaustion following their long march from ULSTER and their not having properly coordinated with the Spanish forces that had occupied the town. The Irish armies, forced to retreat northward after suffering many casualties, met with harassment, often from fellow Irish Catholics, on the way. Within a year and a half O'Donnell had gone into exile and O'Neill surrendered at Mellifont, County Louth, to the lord lieutenant, accepting his title and lands from Queen Elizabeth (whom he did not know had just died) and abandoning his claim to the same based on Gaelic tradition and law.

Kinsella, Thomas (1928–   )

poet

Born in Dublin and educated at University College Dublin, Kinsella worked for years as a civil servant in the Department of Finance. But in 1965 he became a writer-in-residence at the University of Southern Illinois and then a professor of English at Temple University in Philadelphia. His collections of poems, beginning with *Poems* (1956) and continuing through *Nightwalker and Other Poems* (1968), began to establish him as a significant poet of the social and cultural changes in Ireland since independence and a poet with an important international reputation. Later works include *Butcher's Dozen* (1972) relating to the BLOODY SUNDAY massacre of that year, his own translation of Irish poetry such as *The*

Tain (1969), and the editing of *The New Oxford Book of Irish Verse* (1986). His poetry has been assembled in *Thomas Kinsella: Collected Poems, 1956–2001* (2001).

Kirby, Michael (1906–2005)
fisherman, storyteller

Born and residing in Ballinskelligs, County Kerry, except for a short stay in the United States simultaneous with the Great Depression, Kirby was a small farmer and fisherman most of his life. He developed a great interest in the folklore, legends, and history of his native area and was articulate in the local Irish language in a period when its use was nearly extinct. He put his memories and knowledge to pen and authored eight books on the subject in Irish and two in English, specifically *Skelligside* (1990) and *Skelligs Calling* (2003).

Knock

The County Mayo village is the site of an apparition in 1879 of the Blessed Virgin, St. Joseph, and St. John the Evangelist at the gable of a church. The apparition and the start of pilgrimages to the site occurred at about the same time agitation that would lead to the formation of the LAND LEAGUE had begun, also in County Mayo. It remains a center of pilgrimage that draws more than a million visitors a year. Under the direction of Monsignor James HORAN, the site benefited from the construction of a basilica and an airport as well as a visit in 1979 by Pope John Paul II.

L

Labour Party

The party was formed in 1912 by James CON-NOLLY and James LARKIN. It was closely associated with the Irish Trade Union Congress. The party, at the behest of its leader, Thomas JOHNSON, did not contest any seats in the 1918 general election in which SINN FÉIN overwhelmed the IRISH PARLIAMENTARY PARTY, or in the 1921 election in which Sinn Féin candidates to the second DÁIL ÉIREANN ran uncontested. Johnson, however, did play a role in authoring the Democratic Program of the newly founded first Dáil. The party did run candidates for the third Dáil and, by its members taking their seats (unlike Sinn Féin victors), it accepted the ANGLO-IRISH TREATY. With the absence of the Sinn Féin members, Labour became the largest participating opposition party to CUMANN NA NGAEDHEAL. However, it was then and remains today a third party in a political scene in which the two main factions are the institutional descendants of the rivals wings of Sinn Féin who differed on the Anglo-Irish Treaty. Labour joined with FIANNA FÁIL in an unsuccessful motion of no confidence in the government in 1927. In 1932 Labour voted to enable Eamon DE VALERA to form a Fianna Fáil government. It moved away from supporting him in the later 1930s, although itself experiencing a significant reduction in its membership in the Dáil to usually less than 10 members. It had a brief recovery in the 1943 election, but fell again in the 1944 election in both Dáil seats and absolute votes. The party, like the labor movement, experienced a split between left-wing elements and conservatives, with the later calling themselves the National Labour Party. It took its place in gov-

ernment for the first time while in the throes of that split, as the coalition government headed (1948–51) by John A. COSTELLO of FINE GAEL included members of both wings of Labour. The party was reunited in 1950 and would take part in the second coalition government from 1954 to 1957. After Johnson lost his seat in the second 1927 election, the party was led by T. J. O'CONNELL to 1932, William NORTON to 1960, and Brendan CORISH to 1977. In the late 1960s the party attracted members a number of academic and decidedly left-wing figures such as David Thornton and Conor Cruise O'BRIEN with the hope that such an appeal would transform Irish politics in moving Labour from the status it had occupied from the beginning of the state as being the third party to becoming one of the two major parties in the republic. However, the 1969 election proved disastrous, and the party moved toward working with Fine Gael in a coalition, which came to power from 1973 to 1977, again in 1981 and from 1982 to 1987. Frank Cluskey assumed the leadership after the coalition defeat in the 1977 election, succeeded by Michael O'LEARY from 1981 to 1982. Dick SPRING was leader from 1982 to 1997, during which period Labour served in three coalition governments, with Fine Gael from 1982 to 1987, with Fianna Fáil from 1992, when Labour got its highest ever vote in a general election, through 1994, when Labour broke with the coalition by voting a no-confidence motion in the government, and then joined with Fine Gael and with the Democratic Left (which the Workers' Party had become) to form a RAINBOW COALITION that ruled until the 1997 general election. Another achievement for the party was the election in 1990 of its candidate Mary ROBINSON as president of Ireland. After the 1997 election Ruairi QUINN succeeded Spring as party leader. The Democratic Left also amalgamated with the party. When the party performed poorly in the 2002 election, Quinn stepped down and was succeeded by Pat Rabbitte, whose political roots lay in the Official Sinn Féin–Workers' Party tradition. The party is identified with the European Social Democrats in the European parliament. A significant rural membership has historically acted as a restraining influence on its political radicalism. However, changing social and cultural mores in Ireland have enabled the party to be a leading champion for feminist, reproductive, and other social issues.

Lake, Gerard (1744–1808)
general

Lake became the British military commander in Ulster in December 1796 and for the following year and a half led a brutal operation against the UNITED IRISHMEN and their supporters. Even though concern was expressed about the severity of his methods he was made commander in chief of all the military in Ireland in April 1798 as wider repression was extended and when the rising of that year ensued. He was replaced the following June by Lord CORNWALLIS.

Lalor, James Fintan (1807–1849)
land reform agitator

Born in Tinakill, County Laois, and educated at Carlow College, the son of a strong farmer, Lalor suffered from bad health owing to a spinal disorder. He developed an interest in the land question and differed with his own father who followed the position of Daniel O'CONNELL that the land issue could be dealt with after repeal of the ACT OF UNION had been achieved. He supported the YOUNG IRELAND members who broke with O'Connell and argued that land reform must be linked with repeal. His writings in the NATION insisted that the land should belong to those who worked it, a position that was not accepted by its editors,

James Fintan Lalor *(Library of Congress)*

Charles Gavan DUFFY and William Smith O'BRIEN, although it won attention from more zealous Young Irelanders such as John MITCHELL, who espoused the same perspective in his journal the *United Irishman*. He advocated rent strikes to counter eviction, and started a successor paper to the *United Irishman* after Mitchell's arrest and transportation, which was called the *Irish Felon*. He was arrested after the Rebellion of 1848, but was released because of his poor health. Lalor was involved in futile efforts to stage another rising the following year, but his health deteriorated further and he died. His writing about the land question, particularly the notion that the land belonged to those who worked it or to the nation as a whole, had much greater impact in later years on activists Michael DAVITT, James CONNOLLY, Padraic PEARSE, and Arthur GRIFFITH than they had in his own lifetime.

Land acts

Land acts were numerous pieces of legislation passed by the British parliament in the latter part of the 19th century and in the early part of the 20th century that sought to give what were called the Three F's, namely, fixity of tenure, which meant no eviction if rent was paid; fair rent, which meant rent was to be below market value; and free sale, which meant a tenant could sell his interest in the holding, that is, the improvements he had made, to an incoming tenant. These were the objectives sought by the IRISH TENANT LEAGUE. They were based on what was common practice, although not a legal requirement, in Ulster—the Ulster Custom— since the 18th century. Ultimately the legislation would benefit more than half a million tenants on Irish agrarian land, most of which was owned by a few thousand landlords, about a third of whom lived outside the country and a few hundred of whom owned estates exceeding 10,000 acres in size. Passage of the acts achieved the outright transfer of most of the land to the tenants through government facilitated purchase schemes. Some of the legislation was particularly important. The 1870 Landlord and Tenant Act sought to give legal definition to the Ulster Custom, that is, the notion that tenants had a right to fair rent, fixity of tenure, and a right to sell the tenancy to another, as well as to be compensated if evicted and for having made improvements on the holding. The 1881 Land Law Act more effectively established the Ulster Custom by establishing a LAND COMMISSION and Land Court to which tenants could protest excessive rents. The first of a series of land purchase acts was passed in 1885 (Ashbourne Act), which allowed £5,000,000 to be made available to enable tenants to borrow the full purchase price, to be repaid at 4 percent over a period of 49 years. An 1891 land act provided £33,000,000 for land purchase, but an amendment to it in 1896 was necessary to make it attractive. A 1903 land act (the Wyndham Act), which sought to induce landlords to sell by requiring all of their estate, not just individual tenancies, to be sold, in return for payment of a bonus in addition to the agreed price, and the right to buy back on the same terms the demesne land. The act, whose terms were set at $3^1/_4$ percent over $68^1/_2$ years, resulted in the transfer of about 7,000,000 acres. Later legislation by the IRISH FREE STATE government in 1923, 1927, and 1933 made the sale of all land not yet transferred compulsory, reduced rates of payment, and reduced arrears.

Land Commission

This was a quasi-judicial body set up under the 1881 Land Law Act to determine fair rents. It also was authorized to facilitate tenant purchase. Later legislation gave it authority to compel sale of land to those who had none.

Land League

The National Land League of Mayo was founded in August 1879 by Michael DAVITT and later expanded into the Irish National Land League by Davitt and Charles Stewart PARNELL. The league developed in response to an agrarian depression that had provoked increased rents and evictions. The league partly drew on a heritage of violent agrarianism dating back to the previous century in the form of secret groups like the Ribbonmen (see RIBBONISM) and the WHITEBOYS, but it was also influenced by the writings of James Finan LALOR about the land being the property of those who worked it and of the nation. Its tactics included rent strikes and boycotts of any landlord who would evict or any tenant who would take the place of another evicted tenant. The organization became part of the NEW DEPARTURE in Irish politics whereby it, CLAN NA GAEL, and the IRISH PARLIAMENTARY PARTY coalesced in pushing for land reform and self-government. The authorities were suspicious of the league's potential for violence, the heritage it drew upon, and its associates, as well as the implications of "land communism" that some read in its manifestoes. When the 1881 Land Act failed to address the problem posed by many tenants in arrears and the league continued its agitation, the government imprisoned Parnell and Davitt. They were subsequently released under terms of the Treaty of KILMAINHAM by which the government agreed to amend the legislation in return for efforts by Parnell and Davitt to urge a cessation of land disturbances.

Land Purchase acts   See LAND ACTS.

Land War

The term refers to the various campaigns to advance land reform in Ireland between the late 1870s and the early 20th century. The usual tactic to achieve tenant security, fair rents, and ultimate tenant acquisition of the land, was rent strike, although there were many incidents of violence. The major phases between 1879 and 1882 were connected with the LAND LEAGUE and from 1886 to 1891 with the PLAN OF CAMPAIGN.

Lane, Sir Hugh (1875–1915)
art collector

Born in Douglas, County Cork, Lane established a successful art dealership in London and begun collecting an impressive collection of modern works beginning with a trip to Paris in 1905. A nephew of Lady GREGORY, he was introduced by her to literary and artistic circles in Ireland. He helped establish a Municipal Gallery of Modern Art in Dublin in 1908 and indicated a desire to transfer his modern holdings to a more permanent structure for that gallery that he envisioned would cross the river Liffey. The lack of response to his offer prompted him to withdraw it, although he was made director of the National Gallery of Ireland in 1914. Lane was lost as one of the passengers on the *Lusitania* that was sunk by a German U-boat off Cork in 1915. Prior to departure, he had added a note to his will, but did not have it witnessed, giving the collection to the city of Dublin. Legal struggle over its control has resulted in the paintings being shared by the Dublin Municipal Gallery of Modern Art, now called the Hugh Lane Gallery, and the National Gallery, London.

Langrishe, Sir Hercules (1731–1811)
politician

Born in Knocktopher, County Kilkenny, and educated at TRINITY COLLEGE DUBLIN, Langrishe was the member of the Irish parliament for the borough of Knocktopher, of which he was sole proprietor, from 1761 to the ACT OF UNION in 1800, which he supported and for which he received generous compensation for the borough seat that was ended with the legislation. He was a friend of Edmund BURKE and championed relief of Catholics from the PENAL LAWS. One of Burke's works is titled *Letter to Sir Hercules Langrishe* (1792).

Lansdowne, William Petty-Fitzmaurice, third marquis of (1780–1863)
politician, landlord

Born in London and educated at the Westminster School, Edinburgh University, and Trinity College Cambridge, Lansdowne served as a member of the House of Commons from 1803 to 1807, but he lost his seat when he supported Catholic emancipation. He succeeded his half brother in the House of Lords and became identified with reformist causes, but not Catholic emancipation or REPEAL of the ACT OF UNION. He was president of the Council under the Whig governments of Lords Grey and Melbourne (1830 and 1835 to 1841). He championed relief for the Great FAMINE victims in the House of Lords and had a reputation as an improving and benevolent landlord on his vast estates in Kerry and Limerick. He also befriended the poet and songwriter Thomas MOORE.

Laois

This is a midland county in the province of Leinster that has excellent agricultural land especially suitable for cereals and grazing and a population of nearly 60,000 on 664 square miles. It has several towns, including Portlaoise, noted for its prison; Portarlington, which had been a settlement for Huguenots, the 18th-century French

Protestant exiles; Mountmellick, originally a Quaker settlement; and Abbeyleix, an estate town designed in the 18th century. Laois was one of the first counties in Ireland established in the sixteenth century. Challenges to New English authority by the native O'Moore's, along with the native O'Connors in neighboring OFFALY, resulted in both counties being the first areas in Ireland subject to PLANTATION and renamed as Queens and Kings Counties, respectively, in honor of Queen Mary and her husband, King Philip of Spain, in 1556. A striking natural feature is the rock of Dunamase on which is a castle that had been a fortress of Dermot McMurrough, king of Leinster, who invited the Normans to come to Ireland. Queens and Kings Counties were given back their Irish names, Laois and Offaly, after political independence. See also MACMUIRCHADA, DIARMAIT.

Laois-Offaly Plantation   See LAOIS; OFFALY; PLANTATION.

Lardner, Dionysisus (1793–1859)
scientific writer
Born in Dublin and educated at TRINITY COLLEGE DUBLIN, Lardner became a professor of natural philosophy at the University of London in 1827. His major work was in initiating and editing encyclopedias of scientific knowledge, beginning with the *Cabinet Cyclopedia,* which consisted of 133 volumes published between 1829 and 1849, as well as the nine-volume *Dr. Lardner's Cabinet Library* (1830–32) and the 38-volume *Edinburgh Cabinet Library* (1830–44). His affair with the wife of a cavalry officer resulted in dissolution of the couple's marriage by an act of parliament and the award of £8,000 to the aggrieved husband. Lardner's lecture tours in the United States in the 1840s were very remunerative. Afterward, he settled in Paris.

Larkin, James (1876–1947)
labor organizer
Born in Liverpool of Irish parents, Larkin was a laborer and seaman. He went to Belfast in 1907

and Dublin in 1908 as a dock union organizer, where he displayed remarkable ability as an agitator and speaker. He formed the IRISH TRANSPORT AND GENERAL WORKERS' UNION (ITGWU) in 1909. It was an example of the "New Unionism" whereby general and unskilled workers were being organized on an industrywide rather than craft basis. He was involved in the formation of the Irish LABOUR PARTY in 1912. His organizing efforts prompted Dublin employers, led by William Martin MURPHY to apply a lockout against members of Larkin's union in 1913. A massive strike, including sympathetic strikes by other unions, ensued, but the confrontation ended in a victory for the employers. Disillusioned, Larkin went to the United States where he quickly became involved in radical activism, including association with the nascent American Communist Party. He was imprisoned, but released by Governor Alfred E. Smith of New York in 1923. Larkin returned to Ireland, but the leadership of the Labour Party and of the ITGWU regarded him as too radical for their liking. He formed a separate Workers Union of Ireland, which did not affiliate with the Irish Trade Unions Congress (ITUC) until the early 1940s, at which point he had also returned to the Labour Party. In the meantime, he had twice been elected to the DÁIL ÉIREANN, from 1927 to 1932 and from 1937 to 1938, as well as having been elected to the Dublin Corporation. His return with that of his group to the Labour Party and the ITUC and his election to the Dáil as a member of the Labour Party, resulted in secession by more conservative members, who formed a National Labour Party and a Congress of Irish Trade Unions. He lost his seat in the 1944 general election, but remained active in the union until his death.

Lavelle, Patrick (1825–1886)
priest, social activist
Born at Mullagh, near Louisburg, County Mayo, Lavelle was educated at MAYNOOTH and at the Irish College, Paris. He had to leave a position at the later institution following a dispute with the

rector. He returned to Mayo, where he became the parish priest at Mt. Paltry. While there he led a public campaign demanding better treatment of tenants on the estate of Thomas Plunkett, the CHURCH OF IRELAND bishop of Tuam. He also combated evangelical proslytizers. In 1861 he incurred the displeasure of Cardinal Paul CULLEN, archbishop of Dublin, when he preached at the funeral of Terence Bellew MacMANUS, the YOUNG IRELAND exile whose burial was transformed into a major show of support for the FENIANS. However, Lavelle's own bishop, John MacHALE of Tuam, supported him. He was later the parish priest of Cong, County Mayo. In 1862 Lavelle gave a celebrated lecture on "The Catholic Doctrine of the Right of Revolution." His activism in the 1872 election enabled Judge William KEOGH to overturn the election of a HOME RULE candidate.

Lavery, Hazel (1880–1935)
society hostess

Born in Chicago to a family of some wealth (Martyn), Lavery met her second husband, John LAVERY, when traveling in Europe to study art. She became friendly with significant literary and political figures ranging from George Bernard SHAW through Lord Birkenhead to Winston Churchill. She was particularly sympathetic and useful to the Irish nationalist cause, and she hosted representatives of the DÁIL ÉIREANN government, especially the plenipotentiaries negotiating the ANGLO-IRISH TREATY, and subsequently the PROVISIONAL GOVERNMENT and then Free State representatives at social functions and gave them contacts and an opportunity to have their case heard in what otherwise would have been an unsympathetic London. The many paintings by her artist husband include pictures of the Irish leaders. His painting of her, as the symbolic *Hibernia*, served as the watermark on Irish currency until 2001. She was especially close to Michael COLLINS and Kevin O'HIGGINS, as some insist the attachment was romantic. O'Higgins advocated the appointment of Sir John Lavery as GOVERNOR-GENERAL of Ireland in view of her capabilities as social hostess, but the suggestion came to naught after O'Higgins's assassination.

Lavery, Sir John (1856–1941)
artist

Born in Belfast, Lavery was sent to relatives after both parents had died while he was still a child. He studied at the Glasgow School of Art and subsequently in London and Paris and had established a reputation by the mid-1880s when he was commissioned to paint the visit of Queen Victoria to the Glasgow Exhibition. Great demand for his services as a social painter developed in fashionable circles. In 1910 he married a young American widow, Hazel Martyn (Hazel LAVERY). During the First World War he served as the official war artist of the British government. His work includes numerous portraits of significant people, including Terence MacSWINEY, Michael COLLINS at his burial, and Roger CASEMENT at his trial. Lavery was knighted in 1918 and elected a member of the Royal Academy in 1921. The painting of his wife Hazel as *Hibernia* became the watermark for Irish currency until recently.

Lavin, Mary (1912–1996)
writer

Born in Massachusetts, but brought to Ireland as a young girl, Lavin was educated at University College Dublin. She wrote several novels and numerous short stories for which she is more acclaimed. Her work deals with the lives and difficulties of the ordinary Irish middle class and notes especially the stoicism displayed amidst intense pressures from family and friends. Her works include were *Tales from the Bective Bridge* (1942), *The House in Clewe Street* (1945), *Mary O'Grady* (1950), and *A Single Lady* (1956). She has won numerous prizes, including the Katherine Masefield Prize (1961) and the Eire Society (Boston) Gold Medal.

Lawless, Emily (1845–1913)
writer

Born in Kildare, the daughter of the third Lord Cloncurry, Lawless was educated privately. She wrote numerous works of history, travel, poetry, and especially novels. Although from a UNIONIST background, she had spent much time in the west of Ireland, especially Galway, where her mother's people lived and could write empathetically of the Irish situation, especially of the difficulties of emigration and defeat. Her works include *Hurrish* (1886), a novel dealing with the LAND LEAGUE; *Grainne: The Story of an Island* (1892); *Maria Edgeworth* (1904), the study of a writer with whom she had much in common; *With the Wild Geese* (1902), poetry; and *The Races of Castlebar* (1913). Ill health induced her move to Surrey in England, where she died.

Lawless, Matthew James (1837–1864)

artist

The Dublin-born son of a wealthy solicitor, Lawless studied art at the Langham School in London and under the Irish artist Henry O'Neill. He was very successful as an illustrator for periodicals and his work was exhibited at the Royal Academy. One painting of his, *The Sick Call* (1863) is on exhibit in the National Gallery of Ireland. Ill health ended his career and life prematurely.

Lawless, William (1772–1824)

soldier

Born in Dublin and qualified as a surgeon, Lawless was a member of the UNITED IRISHMEN and a friend of Lord Edward Fitzgerald. He fled to France when subject to arrest and entered the French army. He became a captain in the Irish Legion in 1803 and was personally decorated by Napoleon for bravery. Lawless had become a lieutenant colonel when he lost a leg in the Battle of Lowenburg in 1813. He was promoted to general of the brigade and retired.

League of Nations, Ireland in the

Ireland became a member of the League of Nations in 1923 against the wishes of Great Britain, which sought to act in the League for members of the British COMMONWEALTH and, paradoxically, Irish-American nationalists such

as Daniel COHALAN, who regarded the League of Nations as an instrument of British wishes. Ireland was elected to the Council of the League in 1930. Eamon DE VALERA, who served as minister for external affairs as well as president of the Executive Council (later TAOISEACH), was president of the Council in 1932 and president of the Assembly of the League in 1938–39. An Irish diplomat, Seán LESTER, was the last secretary-general of the League of Nations from 1940 to 1946.

Le Brocquy, Louis (1916–)

artist

Born in Dublin and educated at TRINITY COLLEGE DUBLIN, Le Brocquy had studied chemistry and worked at the family business before self-educating himself in art in England and on the Continent. Together with Evie HONE and Mainie JELLETT, he helped to set up the annual Irish Exhibition of Living Art in 1943 as a means of encouraging public awareness of contemporary patterns in art. His work reflects cubist influences and later Polynesian and Celtic head cults. Along the later lines he has completed a series of ancestral heads, as well as images of writers such as W. B. YEATS, James JOYCE, and Samuel BECKETT. He has also completed watercolors and landscapes, as well as tapestries and book illustrations, such as Thomas KINSELLA's translation of *The Tain* (1969). Le Brocquy was made director of the Irish Museum of Modern Art in 1989, has received honorary degrees from Trinity College Dublin, University College Dublin, and is a Saoi of Aosdana (the Irish academy of arts and letters or honorary society of creative figures in Ireland whose 200 members co-opt vacancies). His work is on exhibit in numerous international fixtures, such as *Girl in White* in the Ulster Museum, *Tinkers Resting and Woman* in the Tate, London, *A Family* in the National Gallery of Ireland, *Head of an Irish Martyr* in the Smithsonian, Washington, D.C., and *Image of Shakespeare* in the Guggenheim in New York. He is regarded by some as Ireland's most distinguished living painter.

Lecky, William Edward Hartpole
(1838–1903)
historian

Born in Dublin and educated at TRINITY COLLEGE DUBLIN, Lecky was one of the foremost historians in the later half of the 19th century, particularly because of his *History of England in the Eighteenth Century,* eight volumes (1878–90) and his *History of Ireland in the Eighteenth Century,* five volumes (1892). He also wrote *Leaders of Public Opinion in Ireland* (1861). Other important works of his include *The History of the Rise and Influence of the Spirit of Rationalism in Europe* (1865) and *Democracy and Liberty* (1896). He was a member of parliament for Dublin University (Trinity College) from 1895 to 1902. Lecky was a Liberal UNIONIST and opposed HOME RULE, but his writings on Irish history demonstrated sympathy and understanding, distinctly in contrast to popular, almost racist, views of the Victorian era.

Le Fanu, Sheridan (1814–1873)
journalist, writer

Born in Dublin, educated at TRINITY COLLEGE DUBLIN, Le Fanu was a grand-nephew of Richard Brinsley SHERIDAN. He also had Huguenot ancestry. His father was a clergyman. He was called to the bar, but turned instead to journalism, as he bought three Dublin newspapers and amalgamated them into the *Dublin Evening Mail* in 1839. After the death of his wife in 1858, Le Fanu withdrew from active society and turned to writing novels and short stories, many of a ghost-story character. They included *The House by the Churchyard* (1863), *Uncle Silas* (1864), and *In a Glass Darkly.* From 1869 to 1872 he was editor of the *Dublin University Magazine.*

legislative independence

The term applies to the goal of the PATRIOT Party in the Irish parliament in the 1770s and early 1780s. It sought the repeal of the Declaratory Act passed by the British parliament in 1720 that proclaimed the right to legislate for Ireland and the authority to amend POYNINGS' LAW, which in 1494 required all legislation under consideration in the Irish parliament to obtain prior approval by the king and council. Both goals were attained in 1782, but they were made academic by 1800 when the ACT OF UNION ended the Irish parliament.

Leinster

One of the four provinces of Ireland, Leinster is located in eastern Ireland and includes the counties of Carlow, Dublin, Kildare, Kilkenny, Laois, Longford, Louth, Meath, Offaly, Westmeath, Wexford, and Wicklow. The name comes from *Laighan,* which refers to a powerful family or clan in eastern Ireland in pre-Christian times who sought to emphasize their difference from the other people of Ireland. In medieval times, Leinster contained the PALE, seat of the ANGLO-NORMAN settlers.

Leinster House

Presently the meeting place of the DÁIL ÉIREANN and SEANAD ÉIREANN, Leinster House was originally the townhouse constructed for James FitzGerald, the earl of Kildare, in 1745 and whose design inspired Thomas HOBAN in planning the White House in Washington, D.C. It became the property of the Royal Dublin Society in 1815 and in 1924 the government of the Irish Free State purchased it for its present use.

Leitrim

Leitrim has the smallest population of all the counties with slightly over 25,000. Its scenery is unspoiled. A land of plateau and drumlins, it is poorly drained. Some beef cattle and sheep are produced and there are angling opportunities in the lakes that form the border with Fermanagh, Cavan, and Roscommon. The county has a three-mile coastline between Sligo and Donegal. Carrick-on-Shannon is the county town.

Lemass, Seán (1899–1971)
revolutionary activist, politician

Born in Dublin and educated at the IRISH CHRISTIAN BROTHERS' schools, Lemass joined the IRISH

VOLUNTEERS and took part in the EASTER RISING. He was an officer in the IRA during the WAR OF INDEPENDENCE, but was imprisoned from December 1920 until after the truce. He took the anti-treaty side and was one of those who occupied the FOUR COURTS. He was also elected to the DÁIL ÉIREANN in the June 1922 election, but abstained from taking his seat until the FIANNA FÁIL Party that he helped Eamon DE VALERA found entered in 1927. He was interned by the provisional GOVERNMENT and then the Irish Free State government from December 1922 to December 1923. He served as minister for commerce and industry in all of the de Valera governments, with a brief exception between 1939 and 1941 when he occupied the important post of minister of supplies created because of the shortages caused by the outbreak of the Second World War and which he retained when he returned as minister of commerce and industry. He also became TÁNAISTE when Sean T. O'KELLY became president of Ireland in 1945. He was the main director of the policy of economic protectionism that characterized Ireland from the 1930s to the late 1950s, and in the early stages of which there had been significant industrial development, house construction, and road building, although losses in agricultural employment occurred. However, protection was cited as a major reason for Irish economic stagnation after the Second World War. Always a pragmatist rather than an ideologue, Lemass became more favorable to encouraging foreign investment and trade, and was sympathetic to the Program for Economic Expansion formulated by T. K. WHITAKER, which program he set out to implement when he succeeded de Valera as TAOISEACH in 1959. In short order tax concessions were formulated for foreign investors, free trade was negotiated with Britain, and an application filed Common Market membership. Employment numbers increased, emigration numbers declined, and economic output increased substantially. Lemass sought to encourage amicable relations with the government of NORTHERN IRELAND and end the virtual and mutual nonrecognition that had existed for decades by formally visiting Northern Ireland prime minister Terence O'NEILL

in 1965. He led the Fianna Fáil Party to success in two general elections: In 1961 they ruled with a plurality, and in 1965 they retained power by having as many seats as all other parties combined. He retired from office the following year.

Lenihan, Brian (1930–1995)
politician
Born in Dundalk, County Louth, Lenihan was educated at University College Dublin and at the KING'S INN. He was elected to the SEANAD in 1957 and to the DÁIL ÉIREANN in 1961 as a FIANNA FÁIL member for Roscommon. He held numerous ministerial positions in Fianna Fáil governments, including minister for education 1968–69, transport and power 1969–73, forestry and fisheries 1977–79, agriculture 1982, and foreign affairs 1973, 1979–81, and 1987–89. He lost his seat in the 1973 general election, but served as leader of Fianna Fáil in the Seanad, until he returned to the Dáil in the 1977 election. In 1989 he successfully underwent a liver transplant operation in the United States. In the subsequent general election Lenihan garnered an early victory in part because of overwhelming sympathy, and he was appointed minister for defense. That year he was the losing Fianna Fáil candidate for the Irish presidency in an election won by the LABOUR PARTY candidate, Mary ROBINSON. It was the only time Fianna Fáil has ever lost a presidential election and the defeat may be partly attributable to his denial, which he had elsewhere acknowledged, that he had tried in 1982 to influence then-president Patrick HILLERY not to call a general election but instead ask Charles HAUGHEY to form a government upon the collapse of the coalition government of Garret FITZGERALD. Lenihan was subsequently dismissed as minister for defense by Taoiseach Charles Haughey but he was reelected to the Dáil in 1992. He died in 1995.

Lester, Seán (1888–1959)
diplomat
Born in Carrickfergus, County Antrim and educated at Methodist College, Belfast, Lester joined the Gaelic League and the IRISH REPUBLICAN

BROTHERHOOD, although he was a Protestant. He served as news editor of the *Freeman's Journal* when he joined the newly formed Department of External Affairs in 1923. He was appointed Irish representative at the LEAGUE OF NATIONS in 1929. In 1933 the League appointed him its high commissioner for the Free City of Danzig. He encountered continual criticism from the German press for his protests against maltreatment of the Jews. He served as secretary general of the League of Nations from 1940 to 1946, by which time the international organization had become increasingly irrelevant during the Second World War, and he presided at its closing session in 1946. It was replaced by the United Nations after war's end.

Lever, Charles James (1806–1872)
physician, author, diplomat

Born in Dublin and educated at TRINITY COLLEGE DUBLIN, Lever was a dispensary doctor in various posts in Ireland, including during a cholera epidemic in 1832. In the 1840s he became acquainted with William Makepeace Thackeray, who acknowledged Lever's assistance in his writings on Ireland. Lever himself turned to writing full time, editing the *Dublin University Magazine* from 1842 to 1845 and settling on the Continent in 1847 where he served as British consul in various places, including Spezia and Trieste. He wrote numerous novels about army life and about Irish subjects, which prompted many to label his work as "stage-Irish." His books include: *Charles O'Malley* (1841), *Tom Burke of Ours* (1844), *The Knight of Gwynne* (1847), and *Barrington* (1862).

Lewis, C. S. (Clive Staples Lewis) (1898–1963)
writer

Born in Belfast, Lewis was educated at Oxford where he held a fellowship at Magdalen College until 1954 when he was appointed to the chair of medieval and Renaissance English at Cambridge. He wrote the scholarly *The Allegory of Love* (1936) but is more generally know for his several works of popular Christian apologetics, such as *The Screwtape Letters* (1940), and his children's fantasy tales, the seven-volume *Chronicles of Narnia* (1950–56).

Lichfield House Compact

An understanding reached in 1835 between Daniel O'CONNELL and the Whigs headed by Lord David Melbourne whereby O'Connell and his followers in parliament would support Melbourne in forming a government. In return various reforms would be advanced in Ireland such as Municipal and Poor Law Reform, and there would be appointments of Catholics to public positions. While these were being achieved O'Connell suspended agitation for repeal of the ACT OF UNION.

Limerick

The county, which is in the province of Munster and whose northwest boundary is the Shannon River, has a population of over 175,000 and its eastern area is part of the agriculturally rich Golden Vale extending through Tipperary to north Cork. The city of Limerick, with a population of over 50,000, was founded by the VIKINGS in the 10th century, later becoming the seat of the O'Briens, until taken by the ANGLO-NORMANS in the 13th century. The 1691 Treaty of Limerick marked the final capitulation by the supporters of the JACOBITE cause of King James II, and its terms of generous treatment to the Catholics of Ireland were soon ignored with the advent of the PENAL LAWS. The town prospered as the port for the Shannon and subsequently by its proximity to Shannon Airport. The county has many late medieval castles and major sights in the city include, from the 13th century, King John's Castle and St. Mary's Cathedral (Protestant), as well as the contemporary St. John's Cathedral (Catholic). Other important features include the University of Limerick, or NATIONAL UNIVERSITY OF IRELAND Limerick, noted for its strong emphasis on technology and commerce, and the Hunt Museum,

A view of the rapids on the Shannon in County Limerick *(Library of Congress)*

which contains one of the finer collections of art in Ireland. Literary figures who originated in Limerick include Gerald GRIFFIN and Frank McCOURT.

Literary Revival

The term refers to the literary outpouring between 1880 and 1920 that was largely inspired by ancient tales, especially those that had been translated into English. Romanticism, idealism, and mythology fired the works of people such as William Butler YEATS, John Millington SYNGE, and Lady GREGORY, who saw in their romantic view of ancient Ireland and its mythology an ideal alternative to much of modernity and particularly what they saw as a disheartened Ireland after the fall of Charles Stewart PARNELL.

The Irish language and the way in which Irish speakers spoke English provided ample materials for these writers. The works, deliberately or not, helped fuel the zeal that emboldened the EASTER RISING.

Loftus, Adam (c. 1533–1605)
archbishop

Born in Yorkshire, educated at Cambridge and ordained a Catholic priest, Loftus accepted the religious system of Queen Elizabeth for a comprehensive national church with relative tolerance for different shades of theological thought, but not for the authority of the papacy. He held Calvinist inclinations. He was chaplain to the Earl of Sussex when the latter assumed the Lord Lieutenancy of Ireland in 1560. He became archbishop of Armagh in 1563 and of Dublin from 1567 to 1605. He helped found TRINITY COLLEGE DUBLIN (originally a seminary for the CHURCH OF IRELAND) and served as a member of a royal commission that sought to advance the Reformation in Ireland. He was also lord chancellor of Ireland from 1581 to 1605.

Logue, Michael (1840–1924)
cardinal

Born in Carrigart, County Donegal, Logue was educated at MAYNOOTH College and was professor of dogmatic theology at the Irish College in Paris from 1866 to 1874 when he became curate of Glenswilly. From 1876 until 1879 he taught at Maynooth and then became bishop of Raphoe, where he assisted in distributing relief to famine victims from sums he collected on a visit to the United States, in encouraging afforestation and temperance, and in discouraging illicit distilling. In 1887 he became archbishop of Armagh and primate of all-Ireland. He criticized the PLAN OF CAMPAIGN as imprudent, opposed Charles Stewart PARNELL after his divorce, supported the GAELIC LEAGUE, opposed the tentative extension of conscription to Ireland in 1918, but opposed both the violent campaign of the DÁIL ÉIREANN and the reprisal policy of the British authorities during the WAR OF INDEPENDENCE. An appeal from Logue helped end a HUNGER STRIKE by republican prisoners of the Irish Free State government in 1923.

Lombard, Peter (c. 1555–1625)
archbishop

Born in Waterford and educated at Oxford and at the University of Louvain, Lombard became the Catholic archbishop of Armagh in 1601 and supported Hugh O'NEILL in his nine-year war (1594–1603). After the defeat of O'Neill, he began to reconsider the appropriate approach of Irish Catholics toward the monarchy of James I, whom he believed they should recognize as the lawful king in return for tolerance.

Londonderry   See DERRY.

Long, Walter (1854–1921)
politician

Born in Bath, Long became a member of parliament in 1880 and served as president of the Board of Agriculture from 1895 to 1900. He was chief secretary for Ireland from March to December 1905. When he lost his seat in South Bristol in the 1906 general election, he was returned as the member in parliament for South County Dublin and was selected to lead the UNIONIST Party, which he held until succeeded by Sir Edward CARSON in 1910. Long aspired to lead the Conservative Party in 1910, but deferred to Andrew Bonar Law.

Longford

This midland county in the province of Leinster is bordered on the west by the Shannon River and Lough Ree and has a population of over 30,000. The Royal Canal runs through the rich grasslands in its southern areas. The county was created in the 16th century and settled by planters in the 1620s, one of whose descendants in Edgesworthtown was Maria EDGEWORTH. The O'Farrells were the earlier masters of the territory. The force led by the French who landed in KILLALA in 1798 was defeated by Lord CORNWALLIS at Ballinamuck.

Longford, Edward Pakenham, sixth earl of (1902–1961)
theatrical producer

Educated at Eton and at Oxford, Longford succeeded to his title when his father was killed at Gallipoli during the First World War. In 1931 he rescued the GATE THEATRE from bankruptcy, but, in 1936, disagreements with its founders, Michael McLiammoir and Hilton Edwards, led to the formation of a separate company, Longford Players, which used the Gate for six months a year and at other times performed around the country, playing an important role in the development of amateur theater in rural Ireland. Its repertoire included his translations of classic plays and plays he had written himself. He translated Brian Merriman's *Midnight Court* from Irish. From 1946 to 1948 Longford served as a member of the SEANAD on the nomination of Eamon DE VALERA. He received honorary degrees from TRINITY COLLEGE DUBLIN and from the NATIONAL UNIVERSITY OF IRELAND.

Longley, Michael (1939–)
poet
Born in Belfast and educated at TRINITY COLLEGE DUBLIN, Longley was associated with the Northern Group workshop of poets. His poetry deals with life amidst the strife that beleaguered the province in the later part of the 20th century. His books include *No Continuing City* (1969), *An Exploded View* (1973), *Man Lying on a Wall* (1976), and *Echo Gate* (1979). Longley served on the Arts Council of Northern Ireland from 1970 to 1991. Later poetry has drawn on the classics, rural life in Mayo, and universal themes for inspiration. One book, *The Weather in Japan* (2000), won the Whitbread Prize.

lord lieutenant
Also referred to as the viceroy, the lord lieutenant was the nominal chief executive in Ireland and representative of the sovereign. The title was used regularly since 1696, whereas the title lord deputy was used earlier. During most of the 18th century, the lord lieutenant was only occasionally present in Ireland and used the UNDERTAKERS to move the government's program through the Irish parliament. But during his term of office from 1767 to 1782, George TOWNSEND took a more direct role in managing affairs, maintaining a full-time residence in Ireland, and dispensing with the need for the Undertakers. After the ACT OF UNION and throughout the 19th and early 20th centuries, more and more of the political management and administration of Ireland fell to the chief secretary. The lord lieutenant's role was largely ceremonial and social. The post of GOVERNOR-GENERAL in the IRISH FREE STATE was similar.

Louth
The smallest county in Ireland in terms of area (317 square miles), Louth is in the province of Leinster, but its northern half abuts into Ulster, where it is surrounded by Monaghan, Armagh, and Down. Its population is large (over 101,000) as it contains two cities, Dundalk and Drogheda. The former is an industrial town, celebrated for brewing, and had been located on the northern edge of the PALE during the Middle Ages. Drogheda, historically renowned for the massacre there by the forces of Oliver CROMWELL in 1649, was famous for brewing and industry, but it is increasingly a suburb for people commuting to Dublin. The head of St. Oliver PLUNKETT is preserved in its Church of St. Peter. Much barley and oats are harvested in the rich agricultural lands in the south of the county. The southern border is the Boyne River. Other historic sites include the early Christian monastic ruin MONASTERBOICE and the medieval MELLIFONT Abbey.

loyalism
The term refers to the militant UNIONISTS, usually from working-class areas, who are allied with or members of paramilitary groups such as the ULSTER DEFENCE ASSOCIATION (UDA) and the ULSTER VOLUNTEER FORCE (UVF). Both groups acceded to the cease-fire and the GOOD FRIDAY AGREEMENT and had political organizations that contested for seats in the NORTHERN IRELAND ASSEMBLY established in accord with that agreement, but the political wing of the UDA, the Ulster Democratic Party, was unsuccessful, while the UVF allied group, the Progressive Unionist Party, did elect two members. They continue to possess weapons and persist in using violence, including engaging in criminal activity such as dealing in drugs, smuggling, and protection, thus giving grounds for unease about the settlement.

Luby, Thomas Clarke (1822–1901)
nationalist revolutionary

Born in Dublin and educated at Trinity College Dublin, Luby joined Young Ireland and contributed to the *Nation*. He followed the movement after the break with Daniel O'Connell. After the failure of the 1848 uprising he tried to organize another revolutionary group but was unsuccessful. He was a founding member of the Irish Republican Brotherhood and edited its paper, the *Irish People*. He was imprisoned for such involvement in 1865. Released from his 20-year sentence after six years, he left Ireland and came ultimately to the United States where he was active in Clan na Gael. Luby was suspicious of the Irish Parliamentary Party and the New Departure and supported a violent dynamiting campaign in the 1880s.

Lucas, Charles (1713–1771)
radical politician

Born in County Clare, Lucas practiced as an apothecary in Dublin. He agitated against municipal corruption and ran for the parliament of Ireland in 1749 on "patriot" issues such as free trade and Irish constitutional autonomy. However, before the election he went into exile for fear of being arrested after the parliament had declared him an enemy of the country because of his radical pamphleteering. While in Leiden, the Netherlands, he qualified as a doctor. He returned to Dublin in 1761 and was elected to parliament for the city of Dublin and became a leading figure among the Patriots in parliament campaigning for various issues such as the Octennial Act, passed in 1768 limiting the life of parliaments to eight years. He was regarded as the John Wilkes of Ireland, in being compared to the contemporary London radical who also incurred parliamentary displeasure.

Lucas, Frederick (1812–1855)
journalist, politician

Born in England a Quaker, Lucas converted to Catholicism in 1839 and founded the Catholic paper, *The Tablet,* in 1840. He came to Ireland in 1849 and joined with Charles Gavan Duffy in founding the Irish Tenant League to champion tenant rights. That group linked with the Irish Brigade, which opposed the anti-Catholicism of the tentative Ecclesiastical Titles Bill, to form the Independent Irish Party, a short-lived group of MPs that helped bring down Lord Derby's government in 1852. Within several years Lucas differed with Cardinal Paul Cullen over political strategy, even securing a hearing to explain his position to Pope Pius IX, thanks to the intervention of his friend, Archbishop John MacHale of Tuam. He died soon after his appeal to Rome.

Lundy, Robert (?–c. 1717)
soldier

A Scottish Presbyterian, Lundy was a lieutenant colonel in the Williamite army. He was given command of the forces in the city of Derry, soon to be besieged by the Jacobite Army. A defeat at a battle near Clady and Lifford made him skeptical of his continued ability to defend the city and he urged surrender. Local opposition, largely from the Apprentice Boys, forced his ouster and he fled in disguise. Although arrested in Scotland, Lundy was rehabilitated and served as an English-paid adjutant in the Portuguese army. His name became synonymous with defeatism, and it is a term of opprobrium among Unionists and Loyalists for anyone demonstrating a willingness to compromise or abandon the cause of Northern Ireland separateness from the rest of Ireland.

Luttrell, Henry (1655–1717)
soldier

Born in Dublin, Luttrell commanded a regiment serving under Patrick Sarsfield in the Jacobite army in Connacht. After the Treaty of Limerick, he brought his regiment over to the Williamite army, leaving bad feelings and suggestions of betrayal. Later he commanded Irish Catholics serving the Venetians against the Turks and then served in the Dutch army. He was assassinated in Dublin.

Lynch, Jack (1917–1999)

politician

Born in the city of Cork, Lynch was educated at University College Cork and at the KING'S INN, qualifying as a barrister. He was an outstanding athlete, playing HURLING for Cork in the early 1940s when the county won numerous GAELIC ATHLETIC ASSOCIATION championships. He was elected to the DÁIL ÉIREANN for the city of Cork as a member of FIANNA FÁIL, and he retained his seat until retiring in 1981. He served as minister for education from 1957 to 1959, for industry and commerce from 1959 to 1965, and for finance from 1965 to 1966, when he became party leader and TAOISEACH upon the retirement of Seán LEMASS. The choice of Lynch marked a compromise between the rival candidacies of George Colley and Charles J. HAUGHEY. His selection reflected a new era for the party as he had neither personal nor ancestral republican roots. Besides having an amicable personality and an ability to compromise, Lynch continued the program of pragmatic modernization begun by Lemass, including accommodation with Northern Ireland. He led the party to an easy electoral victory in 1969. The same year the modern Northern Ireland crisis broke out, and, in the following year, he was forced to remove two cabinet members, Haughey and Neil Blaney, on implications of importing weapons to the Provisional IRA. Two other members, Gerry BOLAND and Michael O'Morain, resigned in sympathy with those ousted. Haughey was acquitted in a controversial trial, but Lynch nonetheless retained majority support from the party and persisted in his position that resolution of the difficulties in Northern Ireland could be solved only constitutionally. Lynch presided over considerable educational reform in Ireland, particularly the extension of free secondary education and transportation to schools. He also successfully applied for Irish membership in the European Common Market. He had strong EMERGENCY POWERS LEGISLATION passed in late 1972 against the activities of the IRA. In 1973 his party lost the election to the FINE GAEL–LABOUR coalition, but they returned to power following an overwhelming victory in 1977. The size of the Fianna Fáil majority enabled his antagonists within the party to strengthen their position, and when he decided to resign in 1979, expecting George Colley to be selected as his successor, Charles Haughey was selected, drawing particularly upon the votes of newly elected members of the Dáil.

Lynch, Liam (1890–1923)

revolutionary soldier

Born in Ballylanders, County Limerick, Lynch was a brigade commander of the IRA during the WAR OF INDEPENDENCE. He opposed the ANGLO-IRISH TREATY and was made chief of staff of the IRA at an army convention held over the opposition of the PROVISIONAL GOVERNMENT in March 1922. However, he resigned as a member of the executive of the IRA because of difference in tactics over its challenge to the authority of the government and its Ministry of Defense. He opposed the IRA takeover of the FOUR COURTS, although he did join in just before it was attacked by the government. He escaped and became commander of the southern division of the IRREGULARS as well as serving as IRA chief of staff. In November 1922 he issued the orders for the IRA to shoot DÁIL ÉIREANN members who had approved the emergency powers resolution authorizing military tribunals and executions of irregulars. Even though the Irregular campaign had been driven back to guerrilla operations in parts of the province of Munster, he rejected suggestions by some to surrender unconditionally. On the way to a conference of the IRA executive to consider suggestions of both Eamon DE VALERA and Frank AIKEN that negotiations with the government be undertaken he was killed in an attack by government forces in the Knockmealdown Mountains straddling the Cork-Tipperary border on April 10, 1923.

Lyons, Francis Stewart Leland (1923–1983)

historian

Born in Derry and educated at TRINITY COLLEGE DUBLIN, Lyons lectured in history at Hull University and at Trinity. He became professor of modern history at the University of Kent in 1964 and then became Provost of Trinity College Dublin from 1974 to 1981. He wrote authoritative biographies of John DILLON (1968) and Charles Stewart PARNELL (1977) and a definitive and general history, *Ireland since the Famine* (1971), as well as reflective lectures *Culture and Anarchy in Ireland* (1979) a classic statement of what some would call the position of REVISIONISM on modern Irish history.

M

McAleese, Mary (1951–)
barrister, president of Ireland

Born in Belfast and educated at QUEEN'S UNIVERSITY BELFAST, McAleese was called to the Northern Ireland bar. She was appointed a professor of criminal law at TRINITY COLLEGE DUBLIN in 1975 and worked for RADIO TELEFÍS ÉIREANN from 1979 to 1981. She advised the Roman Catholic hierarchical delegation testifying to the NEW IRELAND FORUM in 1984. She became vice chancellor of Queen's University Belfast in 1994 and in 1997 as a candidate for FIANNA FÁIL. McAleese was elected president of Ireland and was reelected without opposition in 2004.

Mary McAleese *(Department of Foreign Affairs, Dublin)*

McAliskey, Bernadette Devlin (1947–)
radical activist

Born in Cookstown, County Tyrone, McAliskey was educated at St. Patrick's Girls Academy, Dungannon, and at QUEEN'S UNIVERSITY BELFAST. She was active in the civil rights movement in Northern Ireland in the late 1960s, especially the more radical and predominantly student group called People's Democracy. She was elected as a compromise anti-UNIONIST candidate in a by-election to the Westminster Parliament for mid-Ulster in 1969, the youngest ever women MP as she took her seat on her 22nd birthday. She was imprisoned for six months for her involvement in setting up barricades in DERRY during the disturbances of 1969 and she physically assaulted Reginald Maulding, a member of the cabinet, in the House of Commons when he tried to explain what had happened in Derry on BLOODY SUNDAY in 1972. Her parliamentary career ended in 1974, and she remained identified with the more radical and socialist elements of the republican movement. She had alienated many Irish-American supporters of the NATIONALIST and/or REPUBLICAN position in 1969 when, on a fundraising tour, she gave the keys of the city of New York that she had received as a honor to the radical Black Panthers. She was seriously wounded by LOYALIST terrorists who attacked her home in 1981. That did not deter her continued activism, especially on behalf of republican prisoners, especially during the HUNGER STRIKE of that year, and she has continued to remain active, although she has lost the central position she had occupied in the early years of the troubles.

MacArdle, Dorothy (1899–1958)
writer, republican activist

Born in Dundalk to a prominent brewing family, she was educated at University College Dublin and taught English at Alexandra College, Dublin, which she had attended. She became active in the GAELIC LEAGUE and in SINN FÉIN. She opposed the ANGLO-IRISH TREATY and became a strong supporter of Eamon DE VALERA. At his behest, she wrote *The Irish Republic* (1937), which became the classic account of the republican and anti-treaty position. She also wrote *Tragedies of Kerry* (1946) about atrocities committed by the Irish Free State soldiers during the CIVIL WAR. She was the drama critic for the *IRISH PRESS* in its early years and wrote a number of novels, short stories, and plays such as *Atonement* (1918), *Earthbound* (1924), and *Fantastic Summer* (1946).

McAteer, Edward (1914–1986)
politician

Born in Britain, McAteer's Donegal-born father brought the family to DERRY when he was two years of age. He was educated by the IRISH CHRISTIAN BROTHERS and worked as a tax officer and then as an accountant. He was elected to the Northern Ireland PARLIAMENT for mid-Londonderry in 1949 and then for the Foyle in 1953, when he became leader of the Nationalist Party. Although he had been supportive of the Anti-Partition campaign that the Irish government had advanced in the late 1940s and early 1950s, by 1965, after the meeting between Seán LEMASS and Terence O'NEILL in 1965, he led his party into accepting for the first time the role as the official opposition in the Northern Ireland Parliament. His political perspective was as a traditional nationalist and conservative, one bypassed with the emergence of the CIVIL RIGHTS MOVEMENT. John HUME defeated him as the Foyle representative in 1969 and the emergence of the SOCIAL DEMOCRATIC AND LABOUR PARTY eliminated the old Nationalist Party as the champion of the Northern Ireland Catholic minority.

McAuley, Catherine (1778–1841)
founder of religious order

Born in Dublin, McAuley inherited money from the husband of a lady whom she served as a companion. She studied educational methods in France and set up a school and orphanage in 1827. McAuley established a religious order, the Sisters of Mercy, which received papal approbation in 1835. The Sisters of Mercy have as their special mission the care of the underprivileged, and the order has expanded to five continents.

MacBride, John (1865–1916)
republican activist

Born in Westport, County Mayo, MacBride was a member of the IRISH REPUBLICAN BROTHERHOOD. He found them to be out of date and inactive and emigrated to South Africa, where he supported the Boer's cause in their war with Britain. He became a close friend of Arthur GRIFFITH and met Maud GONNE, whom he married in 1903 and with whom had a son, Seán MACBRIDE. MacBride returned to Ireland and took part in the EASTER RISING. He was one of those executed afterward.

MacBride, Seán (1904–1988)
republican politician

Born in Paris, the son of Maud GONNE and John MACBRIDE, Seán MacBride was educated in Paris and in Ireland before attending University College Dublin and the KING'S INN. A qualified barrister, his politics were strongly REPUBLICAN, including even serving for a while as chief of staff for the IRISH REPUBLICAN ARMY. After the end of the Second World War, he founded a new political party, CLANN NA POBLACHTA, which sought to give a constitutional voice to republicans and to those suffering the prospects of unemployment and emigration in the stagnant Irish economy of the time. After some success in by-elections, the party's achievements in the 1948 general election were disappointing, possibly because it ran more candidates than it should have in view of its minority position. However, the party served as part of the first coalition government from 1948 to 1951, and he served as minister for external affairs, during which time he promoted the futile anti-partition campaign and presided over Ireland's withdrawal from the British COMMON-WEALTH. His differences with his party colleague Dr. Noel BROWNE over proposals to provide free obstetrical and pediatric services led to the party's decline and to the government's fall from power. Afterward, he involved himself in international human rights issues, working for UNESCO and serving as one of the founders of Amnesty International. He won the Nobel and Lenin Peace Prizes in successive years, 1976 and 1977. He formulated the MacBride Principles to guide potential foreign investors in Northern Ireland that were designed to discourage discriminatory hiring and sectarian hostility in the workplace, principles that many American states required managers of public employee retirement funds to follow in making investments. Some argued that the principles worked more to discourage investment and employment than to promote equity, and that they contributed to the province's instability. Political figures from across the board in Northern Ireland, with the exception of SINN FÉIN, argued against them. In 1985 MacBride campaigned against an unsuccessful proposed amendment to the Irish constitution that would have allowed divorce in limited circumstances.

MacBride Principles See MACBRIDE, SEÁN.

McCabe, Edward (1816–1885)
archbishop
Born in Dublin and educated at MAYNOOTH, McCabe was ordained in 1838, was a curate in Clontarf, then parish priest of St. Nicholas Without from 1853 until 1865 when he became parish priest of Kingstown (Dun Laoghaire). In 1877 he became an auxiliary bishop to Cardinal Paul CULLEN, whom he succeeded as archbishop of Dublin in 1879, and was created a cardinal in 1882, the second Irishman so honored. He was a political and theological conservative as he was unsympathetic to the LAND LEAGUE.

McCarthy, Justin (1830–1912)
journalist, politician
Born near the city of Cork, family poverty inhibited McCarthy's ambition to be a barrister. He turned to journalism as a young man, covering the trials of leaders of YOUNG IRELAND for the *Cork Examiner* before moving to England where he started working for the *Northern Daily Times* in Liverpool in 1854 and then in 1859 for the *Morning Star* in London, of which he became editor in 1864. In 1870 he became lead writer for *The Daily News*. He began to write popular history, such as *History of Our Times*, which appeared serially from 1877 to 1905, and supported the IRISH PARLIAMENTARY PARTY under Charles Stewart PARNELL, who encouraged his running for parliament. He was returned for County Longford in 1879 and became vice chairman of the party. He became its chairman after the deposition of Parnell, with whom he broke after the divorce scandal. Failing eyesight prompted him to step down in 1896. He continued to dictate books. Among the titles he published were lives of several English kings, Sir Robert PEEL, and Pope Leo XIII, *Irish Recollections* (1911), and several novels, including *Dear Lady Disdain* (1875) and *Miss Misanthrope* (1879).

M'Clure, Robert John Le Mesurier (1807–1873)
explorer
Born in Wexford, M'Clure was adopted by a General Le Mesurier, who had him educated at Eton and Sandhurst. Entering the navy in 1824, he served on an Arctic expedition in 1836 and in 1848 was first lieutenant to Sir John Ross in the search for Sir John Franklin and his crew who had set out to find a Northwest Passage. On another expedition in search of Franklin in 1850, his own ship, the *Investigator*, became ice-bound. After being released he discovered Baring's Island, the Barrow's Straits, and then the Northwest Passage. Ice-bound again, M'Clure did not return to England until 1854, when he was knighted and later made an admiral.

McCormick, John (1884–1945)
tenor

Born in Athlone and educated by the Marist Brothers and at Summerhill College, Sligo, McCormick won a tenor competition at a *Feis Ceoil* in Dublin in 1902 and afterward studied in Italy. He made his operatic debut in London in 1907 at Covent Garden and appeared in 1909 in New York at the Manhattan Opera House. He was a member of the Boston Opera Company (1910–11) and the Chicago Opera Company (1912–14) and then made appearances at the Metropolitan Opera. McCormick then turned to popular concerts offering both classical and Irish songs, and he made numerous recordings. He was made a papal count in 1928 and retired in 1938. Although he had become an American citizen, McCormick died in his home in Booterstown, Dublin.

McCourt, Frank (1931–)
writer

Born in New York, McCourt returned to Limerick with his Irish parents and grew up there. He came back to the United States in 1949 and eventually qualified as a teacher of English at the prestigious Stuyvesant High School. After retiring he published memoirs of his difficult childhood. Entitled *Angela's Ashes* (1996), named after his mother, the book enjoyed phenomenal success and earned him a Pulitzer Prize. A film version appeared in 2000. A continuation of his memoirs, titled *'Tis: A Memoir* (1999), which dealt with his coming to New York, did not enjoy the same success.

McCracken, Henry Joy (1767–1798)
revolutionary

Born in Belfast to a wealthy Presbyterian merchant family, McCracken managed the family cotton factory. He joined the UNITED IRISHMEN and in 1796 was imprisoned for over a year in KILMAINHAM GAOL, Dublin. When the local leader, Robert Simms, hesitated in leading a planned attack on Antrim Town during the Rising of 1798, he assumed the leadership, but the group he led was defeated. He was recognized when he tried to escape to America. Refusing a reprieve if he would name other leaders, McCracken was hung in Belfast.

McCullough, Denis (1883–1968)
revolutionary

Born in Belfast, McCullough joined the IRISH REPUBLICAN BROTHERHOOD (IRB), but he was disappointed at the organization's moribund condition at the beginning of the 20th century. He joined with Bulmer HOBSON in developing the Dungannon Clubs to draw the interest of younger men in revolutionary activism. He was later brought into the leadership of the reactivated IRB in 1906. Imprisoned for his actions in 1915, he was out in time, as president of the Supreme Council of the IRB, to support the EASTER RISING. Timing and organizational confusion prevented his bringing a delegation of Belfast IRISH VOLUNTEERS to join in the rising, although he was interned at Frongoch in Wales afterward. McCullough later became involved in developing a domestic Irish insurance company, the New Ireland Assurance Company.

MacCurtain, Tomas (1884–1920)
republican politician

Born in Ballyknockane, County Cork, MacCurtain was educated by the IRISH CHRISTIAN BROTHERS and became a clerk. He was active in the GAELIC LEAGUE and joined SINN FÉIN and the IRISH REPUBLICAN BROTHERHOOD. He was a commandant of the city of Cork IRISH VOLUNTEERS and opposed the appeal by John REDMOND to support the British war effort in 1914. Although he did not order his group into action during the EASTER RISING, he was imprisoned afterward. During the WAR OF INDEPENDENCE he organized an efficient communications system between the county and city brigades of the Volunteers, who by now were the IRA. He was the first Sinn Féin member to be elected lord mayor of Cork in January 1920, but, two months later, members of the ROYAL IRISH CONSTABULARY killed him as was formally reported in the coroner's court record.

McDermott, Frank (1886–1975)

politician

Born in Sligo and one of the 12 children of a counsellor to the King, McDermott was educated at Downside and at Queen's College, Oxford. He served in the British army during the First World War rising to the rank of major. He then became a banker in New York, moved to France in 1927, and then back to Ireland in 1929. Elected to the DÁIL ÉIREANN as an independent for Roscommon, he and James DILLON founded a new political party, the National Centre Party, which gained 11 seats in the 1933 election. The group merged with CUMANN NA NGAEDHEAL to form the United Ireland Party under the leadership at first of Eoin O'DUFFY. The party later called itself FINE GAEL. McDermott became disillusioned with O'Duffy and, after O'Duffy left, with the party itself for its criticism of Eamon DE VALERA's support for LEAGUE OF NATIONS sanctions against the Italian invasion of Ethiopia. In 1937 de Valera appointed him to the Irish SEANAD, which had been created by the new constitution of that year. Subsequently, MacDermott was correspondent for the *Sunday Times* from Dublin from 1938, from New York from 1942, and from Paris from 1945 to 1950. He wrote a *Life of Wolfe Tone* (1939).

MacDiarmada, Seán (1884–1916)

revolutionary

Born in Kiltyclogher, County Leitrim, and having received little formal education, MacDiarmada worked as a youth in Glasgow and returned to Belfast, where he was employed as a bartender. There he became friends with Bulmer HOBSON and Denis MCCULLOUGH and helped to revitalize the IRISH REPUBLICAN BROTHERHOOD (IRB). A crippling attack of polio in 1912 did not inhibit his continued activism, especially in trying to control the IRISH VOLUNTEERS for the IRB. He broke with Hobson over the latter's acceptance of John REDMOND's demand to bring the Volunteers under the aegis of the IRISH PARLIAMENTARY PARTY. He was briefly imprisoned in 1915. He was part of the military council of the IRB that organized the EASTER RISING and forged the document that temporarily convinced Volunteer commander Eoin MACNEILL that a government offensive was going to be undertaken against nationalists and that a rising was appropriate. While MacNeill realized he had been fooled and called off the Easter Sunday mobilization, MacDiarmada and others went ahead with the rising the next day. He was one of the seven signatories to the proclamation of an Irish Republic, fought at the GENERAL POST OFFICE during the rising, and was one of those executed by the British the next month.

MacDonagh, Thomas (1878–1912)

poet, revolutionary

Born in Clouhjourdan, County Tipperary, and educated at Rockwell College, he taught secondary school until moving to Dublin in 1908 where he went to University College Dublin, where, after receiving his B.A. and M.A., he became a lecturer in English. He had become a close friend of Padraic PEARSE, whom he helped in setting up St. Enda's College. He was active in the IRISH VOLUNTEERS and organized the march to collect the guns brought into HOWTH in 1914. He joined the IRISH REPUBLICAN BROTHERHOOD and became a member of the secret military council that planned the EASTER RISING. A signatory to the proclamation of an Irish Republic and a commander of a force at Jacob's Biscuit Factory, he was one of those executed. Several of his books of poems were published, including *Through the Ivory Gate* (1902), *The Golden Joy* (1906), and *Lyrical Poems* (1913), and a play, *When Dawn Is Come* (1908), which was produced by the ABBEY THEATRE.

MacDonnell, Antony (1844–1925)

public administrator

Born in Shragh, County Mayo, and educated at Summerhill College, County Sligo, and Queen's College, Galway, MacDonnell joined the Indian Civil Service. He was responsible for significant reforms protective of tenant farmers and became the lieutenant governor of a large area with a population of 40 million. Ill health forced his retirement in 1901 and he was given the post of undersecretary for Ireland, where he provided considerable assistance to George WYNDHAM, the chief secretary who advanced the celebrated LAND ACT of 1903. McDonnell was a Catholic who believed in eventual HOME RULE, but who thought Ireland was not yet ready for it. His approach irritated both NATIONALISTS who saw him working to delay their goal and UNIONISTS who believed he was softening in his attitude toward union. He worked on the legislation that established the NATIONAL UNIVERSITY OF IRELAND and QUEEN'S UNIVERSITY BELFAST in 1908. In 1908 he was made a baron. He also served on the futile Irish Convention of 1917 to 1918 that failed to arrive at an amicable settlement of the delayed Home Rule question.

McDyer, James (1911–1987)

priest, social activist

Born in Glenties, County Donegal, educated at St. Eunan's College, Letterkenny, and at MAYNOOTH, McDyer worked for years in London ministering to Irish workers before returning to Donegal. In 1951 he became a curate at Glencolumbkille and its parish priest in 1971. He organized numerous cooperative enterprises in the economically and technically backward community in bringing public water supply, electricity, and paved roads, and later a factory and a tourist center to the town.

McElligott, James J. (1893–1974)

civil servant

Born in Tralee, County Kerry, and educated at University College Dublin, McElligott joined the Local Government Board in 1913. He also joined the IRISH VOLUNTEERS and took part in the EASTER RISING. He was interned afterward, at one point imprisoned in the cell next to that of Michael COLLINS. Released in 1917, he became a freelance journalist and then the editor of the *Statist,* a London financial weekly. In 1923 he returned to Ireland and helped form the Depart-

ment of Finance, serving as its secretary from 1927 to 1953, when he became governor of the Central Bank, which he held until 1960. His views on financial and economic questions were very traditional in placing emphasis on free markets, trade, and government fiscal prudence.

MacEntee, Seán (1889–1984)

politician

Born in Belfast and educated at St. Malachy's College and the Belfast Municipal Institute of Technology, MacEntee qualified as an engineer. He took part in the EASTER RISING, for which he was condemned to death, but the sentence was commuted to life imprisonment and he was released as part of the 1917 amnesty. While again imprisoned he was elected as a SINN FÉIN MP for South Monaghan in the 1918 general election and, upon release, took his seat in the DÁIL ÉIREANN. He lost his seat in 1923 when he ran as an abstentionist and anti-ANGLO-IRISH TREATY candidate. He had supported Eamon DE VALERA in founding the FIANNA FÁIL Party, was elected for Dublin County in 1927, and took his seat along with other elected members of that party in 1927. MacEntee was a minister in all Fianna Fáil governments until going to the backbench in 1965, serving in the following ministries: Finance, 1932–39; Industry and Commerce, 1939–41; Local Government and Health, 1941–48; Finance, 1951–54; and Health, 1957–65. Although initially a radical on the national question, he developed into one of the more conservative figures in the Fianna Fáil Party on social and economic issues. His wife, Margaret Browne, was a lecturer at University College Dublin and the sister of Cardinal Michael BROWNE and priest-scholar Pádraig DE BRÚN. Their daughter is the poet Máire MHAC AN TSAOI.

McEoin, Seán (1884–1973)

soldier-politician

Born in Bunhaly near Granard, County Longford, McEoin was a farmer and blacksmith who joined the IRISH VOLUNTEERS in 1914. He played a major role in the WAR OF INDEPENDENCE rising in rank from commandant to general. Nicknamed "The Blacksmith of Ballinalee" for his successful rout of a BLACK AND TANS raid on that town in March 1921, he was arrested and sentenced to death. An escape effort organized by Michael COLLINS failed, but his life was spared by Eamon DE VALERA who insisted on his release as one of the preconditions for the July 1921 truce. MacEoin supported the ANGLO-IRISH TREATY, having been elected to the DÁIL ÉIREANN in May 1921 while in prison. He was in charge of the Western Command of the National Army during the CIVIL WAR. He withdrew from politics and remained an officer in the army of the IRISH FREE STATE, rising to chief of staff in 1928. The next year he resigned from the military, returning to politics as a deputy for Sligo/Leitrim and, from 1932 to 1965, for Longford/Westmeath. A member of FINE GAEL, McEoin was minister for justice from 1948 to 1951 and minister for defense from 1954 to 1957, as well the party's unsuccessful candidate for the presidency of Ireland in 1945 and in 1959.

McGahern, John (1935–   )

writer

Born in Dublin but raised in Cootehall, County Roscommon, McGahern was educated at St. Patrick's College, Dublin, and at University College Dublin. He was the son of a sergeant in the GARDA SÍOCHÁNA. McGahern was a teacher in a national school in Clontarf, Dublin. His first novel, *The Barracks* (1963), was patterned after his own childhood experiences. His second novel, *The Dark* (1965), was banned in Ireland under the existing censorship legislation and he was dismissed from his teaching post. He moved to England and later the United States, but came back to Ireland in 1974. He has continued to write novels and short stories, all dealing with exile, sex, and personal relationships. Other novels have included *The Leavetaking* (1975, rev. 1984), *The Pornographer* (1979), and *Amongst Women* (1990), which was shortlisted for the Booker Prize, and earlier volumes of short stories have been reissued as *Collected Stories* (1992). He

has received an honorary D.Litt. from TRINITY COLLEGE DUBLIN among numerous other awards.

MacGarrity, Joseph (1874–1940)

republican activist

Born in Carrickmoe, County Tyrone, MacGarrity emigrated to Philadelphia in 1892 where he became a successful tavern owner. He was very active in CLAN NA GAEL, becoming a member of its executive in 1912. He was closely involved with support efforts for the IRISH REPUBLICAN BROTHERHOOD led by Daniel COHALAN and John DEVOY and for the WAR OF INDEPENDENCE through the Friends of Irish Freedom (FOIF). He organized the fund-raising tour by Eamon DE VALERA in 1919 and 1920 and sided with him in his dispute with Cohalan and Devoy as he successfully ran the American Association for the Recognition of the Irish Republic as an alternative to the FOIF. He opposed the ANGLO-IRISH TREATY and then opposed de Valera's leading FIANNA FÁIL into the DÁIL ÉIREANN in 1927. They were briefly reconciled, especially when de Valera, after assuming power mitigated the pressures the CUMANN NA NGAEDHEAL government had put on the IRA. However, when de Valera began to move against them in 1936, McGarrity broke completely as he continued to support SINN FÉIN and the IRA, including their bombing campaign in 1939 and their approach to Nazi Germany for assistance.

McGee, Thomas D'Arcy (1825–1868)

journalist, politician

Born in Carlingford, County Louth, McGee was active in YOUNG IRELAND and wrote for the *NATION*. Active in the 1848 rising, he fled to America where he founded a paper in New York in which he denounced the clergy for their inactivity at the time of the rising. He then moved to Boston where he founded another paper that was originally militant, but became more conservative and constitutional. In 1857 he moved to Canada and became politically active in efforts to achieve dominion home rule, serving as president of the Council of the Legislative Assembly and then minister for agriculture and emigration. He denounced the FENIAN raid on Canada and was assassinated in Ottawa by Irish NATIONALISTS. He wrote several books of history, such as *History of the Irish Settlers in North America* (1852) and *A Popular History of Ireland* (3 vols., 1862–69), and poetry.

McGilligan, Patrick (1889–1979)
politician

Born in Coleraine, County Derry, McGilligan was educated at St. Columb's College, Derry, CLONGOWES WOOD COLLEGE, and at University College Dublin. He was called to the bar in 1921. He was a member of SINN FÉIN and unsuccessfully contested a seat for Derry in the 1918 election. McGilligan was a CUMANN NA NGAEDHEAL and later a FINE GAEL member of the DÁIL ÉIREANN for the NATIONAL UNIVERSITY OF IRELAND from 1923 to 1937 and then for Dublin Northwest and Dublin Central until 1965. He served as minister for industry and commerce from 1924 to 1932 as well as minister for external affairs from 1927 to 1932. He was part of the Irish delegation to COMMONWEALTH Conferences that led to the drafting of the STATUTE OF WESTMINSTER, giving maximum autonomy to Commonwealth members. McGilligan promoted the Shannon Electric Power Scheme. From 1934 to 1959 he was a professor of law at University College Dublin where he influenced a generation of future attorneys and judges. During the coalition governments of the 1950s, he served as minister for finance from 1948 to 1951, where he began the budgetary distinction between capital and current spending, and attorney general from 1954 to 1957.

McGrath, Joseph (1888–1966)
politician

Born in Dublin and educated by the IRISH CHRISTIAN BROTHERS, McGrath served in the IRISH VOLUNTEERS and took part in the EASTER RISING. He was elected as a SINN FÉIN candidate for Dublin in the 1918 general election. He became minister for labour in the DÁIL ÉIREANN government in 1920. A supporter of the ANGLO-IRISH TREATY, he was minister for commerce and industry in the PROVISIONAL GOVERNMENT and in the Irish Free State government. He resigned in protest after the ARMY MUTINY during which he had been sympathetic to the rebellious officers. The secession by some party members in the Dáil from CUMANN NA NGAEDHEAL, who sympathized with his more nationalist perspective on both the mutiny and on relations with Britain, failed to make much headway in a number of by-elections in 1925. In 1925 the government appointed him labor director at the Shannon hydroelectric power project. In the 1930s he was one of the organizers of the Irish Sweepstakes that succeeded in raising vast sums for Irish hospitals. McGrath also turned his energies to promoting Waterford crystal and Donegal carpets, as well as to horse breeding.

McGuckian, Medbh (1950–   )
poet

Born in Belfast and educated at QUEEN'S UNIVERSITY BELFAST, McGuckian's poetry has won numerous prizes such as an Eric Gregory Award in 1980 and a Cheltenham prize in 1989. She was made writer-in-residence at Queen's University Belfast and TRINITY COLLEGE DUBLIN and a visiting professor at the University of California, Berkeley. Her work deals with privates themes, as well as comments on the Northern Ireland conflict and gender concerns. Published books of poems include *The Flower Master* (1982) *The Greenhouse* (1983), *Venus and the Rain* (1984), *On Ballycastle Beach* (1988), *Marconi's Cottage* (1991), *Shelmalier* (1998), and *Drawing Ballerinas* (2001).

McGuigan, Barry (1961–   )
boxer

Born in Clones, County Monaghan, as an amateur McGuigan won a gold medal as a featherweight in the 1978 Commonwealth Games and the Irish senior bantamweight title the same year. As a professional he won the British featherweight title and the European championship in 1983 and became the World Boxing Authority featherweight champion in 1985. At matches, as a gesture toward community reconciliation in Northern Ireland, he had *Danny Boy* or *The Londonderry Air* played instead of *The Soldier's Song*. After a couple of successful defenses of his WBA title, he lost in 1986 in Las Vegas. McGuigan was inactive the following year, but returned to the ring in 1988 and took part in four fights, losing the last in four rounds, which was only the third loss in his career of 35 fights.

McGuinness, Martin (1950–)
revolutionary politician

Born in the Bogside, Derry, McGuinness became involved with SINN FÉIN and the IRA in 1969, and was imprisoned several times. He rose to such a significant position in the Provisional IRA that he served as a member of a delegation sent to negotiate in England with then secretary of state for Northern Ireland William Whitelaw, in 1972, and in recent years has acknowledged his leadership position in the IRA at the time of BLOODY SUNDAY in Derry in 1972. At the time of the HUNGER STRIKE in 1981, he and Gerry ADAMS were able to assume command of the republican movement from its Dublin leadership and turn toward a combination of political and military action. He was one of the Sinn Féin candidates elected to a NORTHERN IRELAND ASSEMBLY in 1982 from which they abstained. He was one of the negotiators with the British and Irish governments and other political leaders in the extensive discussions and maneuvering that ensued from the 1994 IRA cease-fire, interrupted from 1996 to 1997, that culminated in the 1998 GOOD FRIDAY AGREEMENT (GFA). McGuinness was elected to the Westminster parliament for Mid-Ulster in 1997, to which seat he was reelected in 2001 and in 2005 although he does not attend, refusing to swear allegiance to the queen. In 1998 he was elected to the Northern Ireland Assembly created in accord with the GFA. He served as minister for education in the power-sharing government created by that

assembly in 1999. He was reelected to that assembly in 2003, although it has not yet met.

MacHale, John (1791–1881)
archbishop

Born in Tobbernavine, Tiraweley, County Mayo, MacHale was educated at MAYNOOTH, ordained a priest in 1814, and served as professor of dogmatic theology in Maynooth from 1820 to 1825, when he became adjutor bishop of Killala, County Mayo, the first Irish bishop since the Reformation era to have been entirely educated in Ireland. In 1834 he became archbishop of Tuam, where he served until his death in 1881. He vigorously opposed proselytizing efforts by the Kildare Place Society, which the government subsidized in its efforts to promote education in Ireland. He supported Daniel O'CONNELL in the Catholic emancipation struggle. He opposed the system of national education and QUEEN'S COLLEGES being promoted by Robert PEEL as "Godless colleges." MacHale often clashed with Archbishop Paul CULLEN on issues, as he opposed John Henry Newman as rector of the Catholic University, and gave support to the pro-Fenian priest Patrick LAVELLE. His vigorous defense of Catholicism did not inhibit him from opposing the proclamation of the doctrine of papal infallibility at the First Vatican Council. His NATIONALISM and sympathy for the Catholic peasantry of Ireland also did not prevent him from opposing the LAND LEAGUE.

Macken, Walter (1915–1967)
writer

Born in Galway, Macken became an actor in An Taibhdhearc in Galway and later performed at the ABBEY THEATRE and in New York, as well in a movie version of a play he had written, *Home Is the Hero* (1953). Besides writing a number of plays, he wrote several novels, many of them with a historical setting, such as *Seek the Fair Land* (1959), about the Cromwellian period, and *The Silent People* (1962), about the Great FAMINE, and pictures of Galway life in the first half of the 20th century, such as *Rain on the Wind* (1950) and *The Scorching Wind* (1964). Macken was appointed artistic director of the Abbey Theatre in 1966, a year before he died.

McKenna, Siobhán (1923–1986)
actor

Born in Belfast and educated at St. Louis Convent, Monaghan, and at University College Galway, her acting career began with An Taibhdhearc in Galway. In 1944 she was performing at the ABBEY THEATRE. From there she went on to phenomenal success internationally in the theater, the cinema, and on television. Her significant roles included Pegeen Mike in John Milington SYNGE's *Playboy of the Western World* and St. Joan in George Bernard SHAW's *St. Joan.* She appeared in films such as *Dr. Zhivago* and *Of Human Bondage.*

McKenna, Stephen (1872–1934)
journalist, scholar

Born in Liverpool, McKenna was a journalist who joined the Greek side in the 1897 Turkish-Greek War. He then became a European correspondent for the *New York World.* He came to Dublin in 1907 and began to write for the *FREEMAN'S JOURNAL.* He was friendly to many of the leaders of the EASTER RISING, but they forbade him from participating due to his ill health. After the establishment of the IRISH FREE STATE, he returned to England where he continued working on a five-volume translation of the *Enneads of Plotinus* (1917–30), which earned him a gold medal from the Royal Irish Academy that he refused to accept because of the word *Royal.*

MacManus, Terence Bellew (1811–1861)
Young Irelander, Fenian

Born in Temo, County Fermanagh, MacManus went to Liverpool, where he ran a successful business. He returned to Ireland to join the YOUNG IRELAND rising of that year. He was captured, tried, and sentenced to death, but the latter was commuted to transportation to Tasmania. He escaped from there and came in 1852 to the United States,

where he died impoverished in 1860. However, his remains were brought back to Ireland, and he was given a highly publicized funeral in 1861 that enhanced the renown of the IRISH REPUBLICAN BROTHERHOOD, even though, if not because, Cardinal Paul CULLEN forbade his lying-in-state in the Pro-Cathedral. Father Patrick LAVELLE, in defiance of the cardinal, spoke at the funeral.

Mac Muirchada, Diarmait (Diarmuid mac Murchada, Dermot McMurrough) (1110–1171)
medieval Irish king

The king of Leinster, Mac Muirchada was befriended by the Ui Neill O'Neill king of Ulster, but was disliked by O'Conchobhair (O'Connor), the high king of Ireland, who allied with O'Ruairic (O'Rourke), the king of Brefni. Mac Muirchada had a long standing dispute with the later whose wife he had abducted. When Ui Neill was killed in battle in 1166, O'Conchobhair expelled Mac Muirchada from his kingdom. In turn he fled to Britain seeking the intervention of Henry II on his behalf. He got instead the support of Normans in Wales, led by Richard FitzGilbert (Strongbow), who, in return, received Mac Muirchada's daughter, Aoife, in marriage. Mac Muirchada died in battle in 1171. FitzGilbert inherited his domain, beginning the Norman settlement in Ireland.

MacNamara, Brinsley (John Weldon) (1890–1963)
actor, writer

Born near Delvin, County Westmeath, MacNamara (his pen name) became an actor in the ABBEY THEATRE in 1910. In 1918 he wrote a celebrated novel, *The Valley of the Squinting Windows,* which took the provincialism and hypocrisy of small-town life in early 20th-century Ireland. The book made him famous, but also incurred considerable hostility. He wrote another novel, *The Clanking of Chains* (1920), which similarly took on frailties of Irish life, as did several plays he wrote for the Abbey between 1919 and 1945.

MacNeice, Louis (1907–1963)

poet

Born in Belfast and raised in Carrigfergus, County Antrim, MacNeice, the son of a clergyman in the CHURCH OF IRELAND, attended school in England from the age of 10, including Oxford University. His contemporaries there, with whom he became closely associated in the 1930s, including W. H. Auden, Stephen Spender, and Cecil DAY-LEWIS, were left-wing poets whose concerns ranged from the Spanish Civil War to domestic social injustice to sympathy with revolutionary causes elsewhere. He lectured at the University of London until becoming a BBC writer and producer in 1940. His poetry of that era included *Blind Fireworks* (1929) and *Autumn Journal* (1939). Later work included *Holes in the Sky* (1948) and *Solstices* (1961).

MacNeill, Eoin (1867–1945)

historian, politician

Born in Glenarm, County Antrim, and educated at St. Malachy's College, Belfast, and at the Royal University of Ireland, MacNeill was a professor of early medieval history at University College Dublin from 1909 to 1941. A founding member of the GAELIC LEAGUE, he edited the group's paper *An Claidheamh Soluis*. In its issue of November 1, 1913, he wrote an article entitled "The North Began," which was a call for the formation of the IRISH VOLUNTEERS in emulation of the ULSTER VOLUNTEER FORCE that the UNIONISTS had formed to oppose HOME RULE. The group was established and he served as its chief of staff. He opposed John REDMOND when he gained half of the seats on the ruling committee of the Volunteers for his own nominees from the IRISH PARLIAMENTARY PARTY. He also opposed Redmond's call for the Volunteers to join the British forces in the First World War. He continued to lead the rump of the organization, which retained the name of Irish Volunteers, after most had followed Redmond in forming the NATIONAL VOLUNTEERS. However, he took a position that the Volunteers should take military action only if British authorities took the offensive against NATIONALIST groups, which differed from the plans for an armed uprising being prepared by other leaders such as Padraic PEARSE, who also served on the military council of the IRISH REPUBLICAN BROTHERHOOD. Learning of their plans, he called off a mobilization for Easter Sunday, 1916, but the others went ahead with a reduced force the next day in staging the EASTER RISING. As a member of SINN FÉIN, he was elected to parliament for Derry in the 1918 general election and entered the DÁIL ÉIREANN. He was minister for industries in the Dáil Éireann government from 1919 to 1921 and was Speaker or *Ceann Comhairle* of the Dáil during the debates on the ANGLO-IRISH TREATY, which he supported. He became minister for education in the PROVISIONAL GOVERNMENT and remained in that post in the Irish Free State, although his own son, Brian, was killed in action as an anti-treaty republican. He was named as the Free State nominee to the BOUNDARY COMMISSION, but resigned the post (as well as his ministerial position) immediately prior to the expected release of the commission's report when a news leak indicated an award would be unsatisfactory to nationalists because the amount of territory transferred to the Free State would be much smaller than expected and some Free State territory would be transferred to NORTHERN IRELAND. He had not expected the commission to make territorial awards based on the narrower mandate of economic and geographic considerations rather than popular wish, but he kept silent until just before the report was due to be released because he believed naively that he held a juridical rather than a political position. He lost his Dáil seat in the 1927 general election and turned primarily to academic pursuits, which included founding the Irish Manuscripts Commission. He published books on Irish history, such as *Phases of Irish History* (1919) and *Celtic Ireland* (1921).

MacNeill, James (1869–1938)

civil servant, governor-general

Born in Glenarm, County Antrim, and educated at BELVEDERE COLLEGE and BLACKROCK COLLEGE and at Cambridge University, MacNeill served in the Indian Civil Service from 1890 to 1914, when he returned to Ireland. He joined SINN FÉIN and served on the committee which drafted the constitution of the Irish Free State and served as high commissioner in London for the Free State from 1922 to 1928, when he was named to succeed Timothy HEALY as governor-general of the Free State. In 1932, in protest over what he believed to be a depreciation of his position by the government of Eamon DE VALERA, he published letters critical of the government and was forced to resign. He was the brother of Eoin MACNEILL.

MacNevin, William (1763–1841)
physician, United Irishman

Born in Ballynahowma, Augrim, County Galway, MacNevin was brought to the Holy Roman Empire by his uncle, who was physician to the Empress Maria Theresa, and there received a medical education. He returned to Ireland and practiced in Dublin. He supported the CATHOLIC COMMITTEE and then joined the UNITED IRISHMEN. MacNevin was arrested in 1798 and imprisoned in Scotland until 1802. After release he served in the French army, but in 1805 he went to New York where he held major medical posts, including that of founder of the Duane Street Medical School.

McQuaid, John Charles (1895–1973)
archbishop

Born in Cootehill, County Cavan, McQuaid was educated at St. Patrick's College, Cavan, BLACK-ROCK COLLEGE, CLONGOWES WOOD COLLEGE, and at University College Dublin. A member of the Holy Ghost Fathers, he was ordained a priest in 1924 and became dean of studies at Blackrock College in 1925 and its president in 1931. He was close to Eamon DE VALERA, who consulted him on the drafting of the 1937 constitution, especially its clauses on religious and social matters. He was made archbishop of Dublin in 1940, the only Irish bishop who was a member of a religious order. His surprise appointment was attributed variably to the influence of de Valera and to the papal nuncio in Dublin. As archbishop he energetically pro-

moted church involvement in social problems, especially family welfare, undertook extensive church and school construction, and presided over an almost doubling of clergy and religious in his diocese. His social thought reflected that of papal thinking in the 1930s, which looked with suspicion on the overweaning position of the state in familial matters such as education and health, and he led the hierarchical opposition to the MOTHER AND CHILD SCHEME of free obstetrical and pediatric care promoted by Minister of Health Noel BROWNE in 1951. He was an unapologetic defendant of Catholic doctrine and orthodoxy, as he believed the colleges of the NATIONAL UNIVERSITY OF IRE-LAND failed to meet his ideal of a Catholic university, although he did not object to attendance by Catholics, in contrast to TRINITY COLLEGE DUBLIN, which he forbade Catholics from attending without express permission from their bishops, a ban that was lifted by the Irish hierarchy in 1970 and which he acquiesced to. MacQuaid was among the conservative minority of the hierarchy who had reservations about much that was done at the Second Vatican Council in 1963 to 1965 and reluctantly implemented some of the recommended liturgical, disciplinary, and organizational changes it promoted. He is regarded as having been one of the most powerful figures in the nation during his episcopate. His firm position on doctrine and moral questions was matched with an extraordinary amount of private generosity and charity. He retired as archbishop in 1972, a year before his death.

MacRory, Joseph (1861–1945)
archbishop

Born in Ballygawley, County Tyrone, MacRory was educated at St. Patrick's Seminary, Armagh, and at MAYNOOTH. He was ordained a priest in 1885 and founded Dungannon Academy the same year. He became a professor of sacred scripture and Hebrew at Maynooth in 1889, and the school's vice president in 1912. While there he helped found the *Irish Theological Quarterly* in 1906. He became bishop of Down and Conor in 1915 and archbishop of Armagh in 1928. Elevated to the cardinalate in 1929, MacRory was an outspoken champion of the grievances of the Catholic minority in NORTHERN IRELAND.

MacSwiney, Mary (1872–1942)
republican activist

Born in London, but raised in Cork and educated at Queen's College Cork, MacSwiney lost her position as a teacher in 1916 because of her NATIONALIST activities. She championed the SINN FÉIN cause in 1920 in America, where she testified to a commission on conditions in Ireland. The next year she succeeded her brother, Terence MACSWINEY, as a member of the DÁIL ÉIREANN. He had died on HUNGER STRIKE after being imprisoned soon after having been elected lord mayor of Cork. Opposed to the ANGLO-IRISH TREATY, she was imprisoned during the CIVIL WAR. She broke with Eamon DE VALERA when he entered the Dáil in 1927, as she continued to regard it as an illegitimate institution until her death.

MacSwiney, Terence (1879–1920)
republican, hunger striker

Born in the city of Cork and educated at the North Monastery and at the Royal University of Ireland, MacSwiney helped found the Cork Celtic Literary Society and the Cork Dramatic Society, and was active in the GAELIC LEAGUE and the IRISH VOLUNTEERS. He was elected to parliament for Mid-Cork in the 1918 general election and instead became a member of the DÁIL ÉIREANN. He was elected lord mayor of Cork in March 1920, succeeding Tomas MACCURTAIN, who had been murdered by members of the ROYAL IRISH CONSTABULARY. He was himself arrested and sentenced to two years imprisonment in England, but went on HUNGER STRIKE in protest. He died after 74 days of fasting, despite attempts to forcibly feed him. MacSwiney was the author of a number of plays, such as *The Revolutionist* and *The Warriors of Coole.*

Madden, R. R. (Richard Robert Madden) (1798–1888)
physician, historian

Born in Dublin, Madden was educated to practice medicine in London. He traveled and practiced medicine there, on the Continent, and in the Middle East before going to Jamaica as a magistrate supervising the abolition of slavery in 1833. He took similar positions in Cuba and in Africa from 1836 through 1843. He lived in Lisbon for three years and was a correspondent for the *Morning Chronicle* before taking a position as an inspector of the condition of aborigines in Western Australia in 1846. When he returned to Dublin he became secretary to the Charitable Dublin Fund Board from 1850 to 1880. He also wrote numerous historical works, such as *The United Irishmen, Their Lives and Times,* (1843–46), *The Life and Times of Robert Emmet* (1847), and an *Historical Notice of the Penal Laws against Roman Catholics* (1863).

Mahon, Charles James Patrick ("The O'Gorman Mahon") (1800–1891)
politician, adventurer

Born in Ennis, County Clare, on March 17, 1800, Mahon was educated at TRINITY COLLEGE DUBLIN. A member of the CATHOLIC ASSOCIATION, he supported Daniel O'CONNELL and was himself elected as a member of parliament for Clare in 1830. He was unseated on a charge of bribery and O'Connell supported his victorious opponent in the next election. Although called to the Irish bar in 1834, he never practiced and instead traveled throughout the world. He became a friend of both Louis Philippe and Talleyrand. Returning to Ireland, he was elected to parliament for Clare in 1847. When defeated narrowly in 1852, Mahon set out traveling again, this time being appointed a lieutenant in the international bodyguard of the czar. He subsequently served as a high-ranking officer in the Uruguayan and Chilean militaries, in the Union army during the American Civil War, and later in the army of Napoleon III. Afterward, he moved to Berlin where he became acquainted with Otto von Bismarck. Returning to Ireland, he supported the HOME RULE movement and was an IRISH PARLIAMENTARY PARTY MP for Clare from 1879 to 1885 and for Carlow from 1887 to his death. He opposed Charles Stewart PARNELL after the divorce scandal. Ironically, he was reported to have been the one who introduced Parnell to Captain William O'SHEA, whose wife became Parnell's mistress.

Mallon, Seamus (1936–   )
politician

Born in Markethill, County Armagh, and educated at St. Joseph's College, Belfast, Mallon turned to education, becoming headmaster of St. James' Primary School in Markethill. He also involved himself in the civil rights movement in the 1960s and then in the SOCIAL DEMOCRATIC AND LABOUR PARTY (SDLP), whose vice chairman he became in 1979. As a member of the party he was elected both to the power-sharing assembly of 1973–74 that collapsed after the failure of the SUNNINGDALE AGREEMENT and to the unsuccessful 1975 Northern Ireland Convention. He was appointed by nomination of the TAOISEACH, Charles HAUGHEY, to the Irish SEANAD, for a short term in 1982, but which appointment barred him for taking a position in a NORTHERN IRELAND ASSEMBLY to which he had been elected in 1982. He was a outspoken critic of both police abuses and the violence of the IRA. In 1986 he was elected to parliament for Newry and Armagh in a by-election following the resignation of UNIONIST MP's in protest at the HILLSBOROUGH AGREEMENT. A supporter of talks between SDLP leader John HUME and SINN FÉIN leader Gerry ADAMS in the early 1990s, he was a major negotiator for the SDLP in the talks leading up to the GOOD FRIDAY AGREEMENT of 1998. Subsequently he became deputy first minister in the devolved government of Northern Ireland called for by the agreement. In 2001 he did not accept reappointment as first minister nor as successor to John Hume as SDLP leader. He did not run for reelection to the Northern Ireland Assembly in 2003 nor for Westminster in the 2005 general election.

Manchester Martyrs

The Manchester Martyrs were three FENIANS, William Philip Allen, Michael Larkin, and Michael O'Brien, who were publicly hung in Manchester on November 23, 1867, for the killing of a police sergeant while they were res-cuing Fenian prisoners. Their executions served as a catalyst for the development of pro-Fenian sympathy in Ireland.

Mangan, James Clarence (1803–1849)
poet

Born in Dublin to a poor family, Mangan worked as a clerk but taught himself other languages and began writing for various Dublin journals, often under pseudonyms. He worked for the Ordinance Survey from 1833 to 1839, during which period he became acquainted with learned and scholarly types he ordinarily would not have encountered. In the 1840s he became associated with YOUNG IRELAND and wrote for the movement's paper the *NATION*. His poetry reflected alienation and personal introspection and in many ways prefigured many later writers ranging from Rimbaud through Edgar Allan Poe to James JOYCE. His most celebrated poem was "Dark Rosaleen," which served as a source of inspiration to many Irish patriots. He led an eccentric personal life, as he abused alcohol, was addicted to opium, dressed unusually, and suffered from generally bad health, which explained his early death during a cholera epidemic coincidental to the Great FAMINE.

Markievicz, Constance, Countess (1868–1927)
republican activist

Born in the Gore-Booth family of Lissadel, County Sligo, Markievicz studied art at the Slade School in London and in Paris. She married the Polish count Casimir Markievicz, who was a painter. They had one daughter, but the marriage broke up. She returned to Ireland and became involved in SINN FÉIN and in the women's group *Inghinidhe na hEireann,* writing pamphlets and pieces for movement papers, taking part in suffragist protests, and working in soup kitchens for strikers' families during the 1913 lockout dispute. She served as an officer in James Connolly's IRISH CITIZEN ARMY and took part in the EASTER RISING. Her death sentence afterward was commuted. She also converted to Catholicism. Markievicz was the first women ever elected to the House of Commons when she stood as a Sinn Féin candidate for Dublin in the 1918 general election. She took a seat instead in the DÁIL ÉIREANN and served as minister for labor from 1919 to 1921. She opposed the ANGLO-IRISH TREATY, was imprisoned by the IRISH FREE STATE from 1923 to 1924 for her support for the IRREGULARS during the CIVIL WAR, and was returned as an abstentionist Sinn Féin TD for Dublin City South in 1923 and again in 1927, but she died shortly after the last election.

Martyn, Edward (1859–1923)
playwright
Born in a Catholic landed family, Martyn was educated at Beaumont College and at Oxford. He was a founder in 1899 with William Butler YEATS and Lady GREGORY of the Irish Literary Theatre, for which wrote the play *The Heather Field* (1899). He withdrew from the group when subsequent work of his was rewritten. He was more comfortable with Thomas MACDONAGH and Joseph Mary PLUNKETT and founded with them the Theatre of Ireland in 1906. Martyn was a member of SINN FÉIN and was a founder of a choir at the Catholic procathedral in Dublin.

Mathew, Theobold (1790–1856)
priest, temperance advocate
Born in Thomastown, County Tipperary, Mathew was ordained a priest in 1814. A member of the Capuchin order, he worked in Cork for 20 years, ministering primarily to the poor and founding schools. In 1838, encouraged by Protestant philanthropists, he started a temperance crusade to take on the serious drinking problem in his area. His success prompted him to make it a national effort. Thousands came to hear him preach temperance in various locations and large numbers took a pledge to abstain from intoxicating drink. Between 1839 and 1845 an estimated 5 million individuals were reported to have done so, which figures are substantiated by the remarkable reduction in revenue from drink and by the number of publicans who went out of business. Daniel O'CONNELL regarded the movement as having greatly assisted in the mobilization of thousands for the monster meetings he held as part of his repeal of the ACT OF UNION campaign in 1843. Mathew took his temperance cause to the United States, originally aiming his efforts at Irish Americans, but also working closely with many Protestant temperance advocates, many of whom were not well regarded by Irish Americans.

Maxwell, John (1859–1929)
soldier
Born in Liverpool, Maxwell was a career officer in the British army, who had served in the Sudan and in the Boer War, as well as having been chief staff officer in Ireland (1902 to 1904), and commander of the forces in Egypt (1909–12) before retiring. Recalled to duty during the First World War, he served in France and in Egypt, before taking command of the forces in Ireland during the EASTER RISING, which he crushed within two days after arriving. He ordered military tribunals, which tried and executed 15 of the leaders of the rising (97 others sentenced to be executed had their penalties reduced to life imprisonment), more than 120 others were sentenced to terms of imprisonment, and hundreds more were interned without trial. However, all those imprisoned or interned were released within a year. Maxwell became commander in chief in northern England in November 1917, and later served again in Egypt before retiring in 1922.

Maynooth
Maynooth is the popular name for the institution of higher education in the town of the same name in County Kildare. It was founded in 1795 by an act of the Irish parliament, encouraged by William Pitt the Younger, the prime minister, who gave a grant of £9,000 to establish a seminary for Roman Catholic clergy for students whose education on the Continent had been inhibited by the revolution in France. The seminary was called St. Patrick's College. When seminaries began to be established in the various

dioceses in the 19th century, St. Patrick's College became the center for further study for those locally educated. In 1845 Robert PEEL had the endowment multiplied threefold as an annual grant. When the CHURCH OF IRELAND was disestablished in 1869, the endowment for Maynooth was discontinued. However, there was a last capital grant of £369,000. In 1899 St. Patrick's College, Maynooth, became a Pontifical University and in 1910 part of the NATIONAL UNIVERSITY OF IRELAND. A separate lay college was established at Maynooth in 1966 and today greatly exceeds the seminary in numbers of faculty and students.

Mayo

The third-largest county in Ireland, Mayo has a population of nearly 120,000. Located in the western province of Connacht, it juts out into the Atlantic, bound on the east by Sligo and Roscommon and on the south by Galway. The center of the county contains fine agricultural land. The county capital, Westport, is situated in the center and was the site of the foundation of the LAND LEAGUE. Dairy cattle are important in the area near Ballinrobe. The east and the west tend to be barren, with the Nephin Beg range of mountains in the northeast and the Sheefry Hills and Mweelrea and Patry Mountains to the south and east. The northeast barony of Erris contains the largest blanket bog in Ireland, and Achill is the largest offshore island in Ireland. Croagh Patrick, a mountain near the town of Westport, has been traditionally regarded as a site where St. PATRICK prayed and fasted. Thousands of religious pilgrims climb the mount annually on the last Sunday of July. The village of KNOCK, the site of an apparition by the Blessed Virgin, contains a major basil-

Achill Head in County Mayo *(Library of Congress)*

ica and is similarly visited by thousands of pilgrims. An ultimately unsuccessful French expedition landed in Killala in August 1798.

Meagher, Thomas Francis (1822–1867)
Young Irelander

Born in Waterford and son of a wealthy merchant, Meagher was educated at CLONGOWES WOOD COLLEGE and Stonyhurst. He was one of those in YOUNG IRELAND who broke with Daniel O'CONNELL on the nonviolence pledge. His use of the word sword so many times in a speech attacking O'Connell for "stigmatizing the sword," earned him the nickname "Meagher of the Sword." He took part in the rising of 1848 and was transported to Tasmania, from where he escaped to the United States in 1852. He became a brigadier general in the Union army in the American Civil War in commanding the "Irish Brigade," which consisted of several New York regiments of Irish rank and file and which fought heroically in several major battles, including Bull Run and Gettysburg. After the war, Meagher retired as lieutenant general and became acting governor of the then territory of Montana. In 1866 he died in a drowning accident.

Meath

A county in the province of Leinster, with a population of over 130,000, that touches the Irish Sea on the east and borders Louth and Cavan on the north, Westmeath and Offaly on the west, and Kildare and Dublin on the south. The Boyne River runs through the county and its rich limestone makes it the primary grassland in the country for fattening cattle. The county has important archaeological and historical sites, such as Neolithic burial sites at Newgrange, Dowth and Knowth, the hill of Tara, where the high kings were crowned, and the site of the Battle of the Boyne, the determining battle in the failed JACOBITE cause. Navan, the county town, has an important lead-zinc mine. Trim was originally an ANGLO-NORMAN fortification that guarded the western edge of the PALE.

Mellifont

A ruined abbey in County Louth was the first Cistercian monastery founded in Ireland (1142) at the behest of St. Malachy. It was part of the movement toward reform of the Irish church in bringing it into conformity, in discipline and practice, with the rest of the church in medieval western Europe.

Mellows, Liam (1892–1922)
republican, socialist revolutionary

Born near Manchester, Mellows was raised by grandparents near Inch, County Wexford. Working as a clerk in Dublin, he joined the IRISH REPUBLICAN BROTHERHOOD in 1912 and was associated with the NATIONALIST youth movement formed by Countess MARKIEVICZ, *Na Fianna Eireann*. He was also influenced by the socialist ideas of James CONNOLLY. In 1913 he became a member of the provisional committee of the IRISH VOLUNTEERS, but was deported to England after arrest for his organizational efforts. He returned to Ireland to take part in some actions in Galway as part of the EASTER RISING. He escaped arrest and went to America. In 1920 Mellows acted as an advance man for Eamon DE VALERA on his fund-raising trip and clashed with Irish-American figures such as Daniel F. COHALAN, and John DEVOY. Elected to the DÁIL ÉIREANN for Galway, he returned to Ireland and acted as a purchase agent for the IRA during the WAR OF INDEPENDENCE. He opposed the ANGLO-IRISH TREATY and was a member of the anti-treaty IRA that had seized the FOUR COURTS. He was arrested after the PROVISIONAL GOVERNMENT had besieged the forces at the beginning of the CIVIL WAR. Mellows was executed along with Rory O'CONNOR, Joseph McKelvey, and Richard Barrett by the government both to retaliate for the IRA assassination of one member of the Dáil and the wounding of another and to inhibit their persisting in further assassination of legislators who had voted in favor of the EMERGENCY POWERS LEGISLATION authorizing military tribunals and executions of IRREGULARS.

Mhac an tSaoi, Máire (1922–)

poet

Born in Dublin, the daughter of Seán MACENTEE, Mhac an tSaoi spent the summers of her youth in the West Kerry GAELTACHT, the roots of her mother's family. Her uncle was Pádraig DE BRÚN, the renowned priest and scholar of Irish. She was educated at University College Dublin and at the Sorbonne. She worked at the School of Celtic Studies and on the *English-Irish Dictionary* (1958) edited by Tomas de Bhaldraithe. She qualified as a barrister and worked for the Department of External or Foreign Affairs from 1947 to 1962. She is married to Conor Cruise O'BRIEN and collaborated with him in writing *A Concise History of Ireland* (1972). She is the preeminent female poet in Irish, as her works reflect technical sophistication in its drawing on both classical Irish poetry and popular Gaeltacht traditional verse. She has inspired the work of many other poets and has earned numerous awards. Her titles include *Coldadh an Ghaiscigh* (1973), *An Galar Dubhach* (1980), and *An Cion go dti Seo* (1987), and she has recently published her autobiography.

Midleton, Broderick, St. John, first earl (1856–1942)

politician, landlord

Born in County Fermanagh, educated at Eton and at Balliol College, Oxford, and a leading landlord, Lord Midleton served as a Conservative MP from 1885 through 1906. Prominent in the Conservative Party as well as being a UNIONIST opposing HOME RULE, he held several undersecretaryships in Conservative-Unionist governments and was secretary of state for war from 1900 to 1903. He was a member of the IRISH CONVENTION from 1917 to 1918.

Militia

The term describes a military reserve recruited from among civilians during an emergency. A Militia Act of 1715 required local authorities to organize such among Protestants. The IRISH VOLUNTEERS, which were formed to take the place of British forces sent to combat the American Revolution, made the Militia redundant. However, in the 1790s a new Militia was raised that could include Catholics within the rank and file. More than 30,000 were recruited and used in suppressing the UNITED IRISHMEN insurrection of 1798. Fear of disaffection among the ranks prompted the practice of assigning members to different units. Some were executed for having joined the United Irishmen.

mission

A practice particularly associated with the Irish Catholic Church beginning in the mid-19th century as part of the devotional revolution encouraged by Cardinal Paul CULLEN. It consisted of a visit to a parish by a number of priests who were members of a specific religious order, very often Redemptorists, for several weeks during which nightly services would be held in which doctrinal and moral teachings would be emphasized and opportunities for confession would be made available.

missionaries

Apostolic endeavors to foreign lands have long been associated with Irish Christianity dating back to the early monks like COLM CILLE and Columbanus. With the rejuvenation of the Catholic Church in Ireland in the 19th century, especially following Catholic emancipation, the church began to encourage sending priests and religious abroad to serve the many Irish emigrant communities in Britain, America, and Australia, as well as to serve as missionaries to non-Christian lands, particularly those that were part of the expanding British Empire. In addition to orders already existing in Europe that had a missionary apostolate, such as the Holy Ghost Fathers and the Mill Hill Missionaries, new orders were founded in Ireland, including the St. Patrick's Missionary Society, the Columban Sisters, and the Medical Missionaries of Mary. Their impact, both religiously and socially, on the developing world has been immense. Their numbers reached a peak in the 1960s, but, with the decline in religious vocations, the ranks have dwindled, although many young Irish act as volunteers in aid missions, both secular and religious, to developing nations.

Mitchel, John (1815–1875)
Young Irelander

Born in Dungiver, County Derry, and the son of a Unitarian minister, Mitchel was educated at TRINITY COLLEGE DUBLIN. He became associated with YOUNG IRELAND and wrote regularly for the *NATION*. He was among those who broke with O'Connell. He was influenced by the ideas of James Fintan LALOR and championed the rights of tenants and the tactic of rent strike. He started his own paper the *United Irishman* to advance these ideas, which did not find favor with more socially conservative Young Irelanders. His publication earned him arrest in May 1848 under a

John Mitchel. Lithograph by N. Currier, 1848 *(Library of Congress)*

treason law, conviction, and transportation to Tasmania. He escaped and made his way to New York, where he worked as a journalist, and then to Tennessee, where he farmed. He supported the Confederacy during the American Civil War, even defending the institution of slavery. He returned to Ireland and ran successfully for parliament for North Tipperary in 1875, but he was unseated because of his earlier conviction. He died almost immediately upon his being elected a second time. Mitchel published his memoirs of transportation, *Jail Journal* (1854), and other works on Irish history.

Mitchell, George John (1933–   )
politician

Former United States senator from the state of Maine, who had been the leader of the Democratic Party in that body, Mitchell was made special ambassador for President Bill Clinton in efforts to reach a settlement of Northern Ireland controversy. After the Provisional IRA had declared a cease-fire in August 1994, he was named chairman of an international body to consider the breakdown in negotiations for a political settlement posed by the continued possession of weapons by paramilitary groups. In January 1996 the body put forward the so-called Mitchell principles, which called for a commitment to peaceful activity and to disarmament. The IRA's resumption of a bombing campaign shortly after the proclamation of the principles excluded SINN FÉIN from taking part in negotiations that began later that year. However, when they again called a cease-fire in July 1997, they did enter negotiations, presided over by Mitchell, which ultimately concluded in the GOOD FRIDAY AGREEMENT. He was later called back to chair deliberations in attempting to resolve the reluctance of some parties to agree to participate in the power-sharing government called for by the agreement before the process of decommissioning of weapons by paramilitary groups had taken place. His efforts to mediate in the Northern Ireland peace process were recognized in his being named chancellor of the QUEEN'S UNIVERSITY BELFAST. He also received the Presidential Medal of Freedom on March 17, 1999. From 2000 to 2001 he served chairman of the Sharm el-Sheikh International Fact-Finding Committee to examine the Middle East crisis.

Moloney, Paddy   See CHIEFTAINS, THE.

Molyneaux, James (1920–   )
politician

Born in Crumlin, County Antrim, Molyneaux served in the Royal Air Force during the Second World War and was wounded. He was elected a UNIONIST PARTY member of parliament for South Antrim from 1970 to 1983 and for Lagan Valley from 1983 to 1997. He opposed the SUNNINGDALE AGREEMENT and took over as leader of the Unionist Party in 1979, succeeding Harry West. Although he had earlier been part of a broader Ulster Unionist Coalition, along with Ian PAISLEY, against the idea of power sharing, he distanced himself from the DEMOCRATIC UNIONIST PARTY leader when the latter turned to a LOYALIST strike in 1977. He succeeded in preventing the DUP from overcoming the ascendancy of the Unionist Party. More inclined to advance integration with Britain than achieve Northern Ireland devolution, he suggested reforms on a local government rather than a provincial level. Molyneaux opposed the HILLSBOROUGH AGREEMENT. After the Provisional IRA cease-fire and the DOWNING STREET DECLARATION had greatly changed the province's political atmosphere, he resigned the leadership of his party in 1995. He was made a life peer in 1997.

Molyneux, William (1656–1698)
philosopher, scientist

Born in Dublin and educated at TRINITY COLLEGE DUBLIN, a close friend of philosopher John Locke, Molyneux became acquainted with him when living in England during the JACOBITE Wars in Ireland. He translated Decartes's *Meditations,* wrote and studied on optics (prompted in part by his late wife having gone blind) and astronomy, was a surveyor engineer for the King's Buildings, a founding member of the Dublin Philosophical Society, and a member of the Irish parliament for Trinity College Dublin. His most celebrated book was *The Case of Ireland's Being Bound by Acts of Parliament in England Stated* (1698), which called for the political autonomy of the Irish parliament and challenged the claims of the English parliament to legislate for Ireland. The book was condemned by the English House of Commons. His ideas were greatly influenced by those of John Locke and would serve as one of the first statements of the Irish PATRIOT position by members of the PROTESTANT ASCENDANCY. Their assertion of an Irish NATIONALISM against British economical and political interference would rarely be extended to include the overwhelming majority of the population who were Catholic.

Monaghan

One of the three Ulster counties that was not partitioned from the rest of Ireland in 1920 by the GOVERNMENT OF IRELAND ACT, Monaghan is characterized by a drumlin topography of rolling hills. It is bounded on the west, north, and east by the Northern Ireland counties of Fermanagh, Tyrone, and Armagh, and on the south by Cavan, Meath, and Louth. The MacMahon family dominated the territory until 1590, when Elizabethan authorities suppressed the family and replaced them with other native chieftains and a few English settlers. This PLANTATION by natives spared Monaghan from the Ulster Plantation of the early 17th century. As a consequence, its population remained predominantly Catholic, but with a significant Protestant minority. Its current population stands at over 52,000 and its principal towns are Monaghan, the county town and site of the cathedral for the Catholic diocese of Clogher, Clones, Castleblaney, and Carrickmacross. The county is primarily rural, but with some linen and lace making, as well the production of cereal products and wood furniture, in addition to cattle rearing. Celebrated historical and cultural figures include Charles Gavan DUFFY and Patrick KAVANAGH.

Monasterboice

A monastic ruin in County Louth, it was founded in the sixth century. It contains two sandstone high crosses dating from the ninth or 10th centuries with impressive Old and New Testament subjects sculpted on them. There is also an early medieval round tower.

Montague, John (1929–)

poet

Born in New York, Montague was sent back to County Tyrone as a youngster and raised by relatives. He was educated at University College Dublin and at Yale University. His poetry reflects resentment at separation, family and marital troubles, and Northern Ireland troubles. Important works include *The Rough Field* (1972), *A Slow Dance* (1975), *The Great Cloak* (1978), and *The Dead Kingdom* (1984). He held an academic post at University College Cork, from which he retired and in 1998, and he has also held the Ireland Chair of Poetry.

Montgomery, Henry (1788–1865)

Presbyterian clergyman

Born in Killead, County Antrim, Montgomery was educated at Glasgow College and held a living at Dunmurray, County Antrim, from his ordination in 1809 until his death. He was also headmaster of the English School in the Royal Belfast Academical Institution, in which position his theological positions and the institution itself were denounced by the Rev. Henry COOKE for "Arianism," that is, an unorthodox understanding of the Blessed Trinity. He refuted the challenge and led a secession from the Presbyterian Synod of Ulster that was called the Remonstrant Synod and consisted of 17 congregations. He supported Catholic emancipation and national education, although he opposed REPEAL of the ACT OF UNION.

Moore, Brian (1921–1999)

novelist

Born in Belfast and educated at St. Malachy's College, Moore served as an air raid warden in the early years of the Second World War and from 1943 to 1945 worked for the British Ministry of Transport in Algiers and Naples. After working for a United Nations Relief Agency in Warsaw in 1946 and 1947, he emigrated to Canada in 1948, becoming a journalist and turning to writing. His first novel, *Judith Hearne* (later re-titled *The Lonely Passion of Judith Hearne*) (1955), was widely acclaimed and ultimately led to a film version, as would three other of his novels. His books deal with displacement, family ties, and the search for identity, and take place in a wide-ranging selection of localities and historical periods, from wartime Belfast in *The Emperor of Ice Cream* (1965), through New York literary life in *An Answer from Limbo* (1962), a thriller set in a Mediterranean resort and in California called *Cold Heaven* (1983), the experiences of Jesuit missionaries in 17th-century Canada in *Black Robe* (1987), and collaborationists in wartime France in *The Statement* (1995). He came to the United States in 1959 and received a Guggenheim fellowship and moved permanently to California in 1965. He received many literary prizes in Britain and Canada, where he twice received the Governor-General's Award.

Moore, Christy (1945–)

singer, songwriter

Born in Newbridge, County Kildare, Moore abandoned work in a bank to start a musical career. His first album was *Prosperous* (1972), which led to the formation of a musical group called Planxty that combined American folk and traditional Irish in employing guitar and bodhran. He has mainly worked solo, performing traditional and comic songs as well as original songs filled with humorous and sarcastic political and social commentary.

Moore, Colonel Maurice (1854–1939)

soldier, politician

Born in Moore Hall, Ballyglass, County Mayo, son of George Henry MOORE and younger brother of George Moore, educated at St. Mary's College, Birmingham and at Sandhurst, Maurice Moore was commissioned in the Connaught Rangers in 1875. He fought in the Kaffir and Zulu Wars and commanded a battalion in the Boer War. When he retired to Ireland he supported John Redmond and the Irish Parliamentary Party and joined the Irish Volunteers. He was an independent critic of the Irish Free State government and ultimately came to support the Fianna Fáil party and served in the Seanad.

Moore, George (1852–1933)
writer

Born in Moore Hall, Ballyglass, County Mayo, the son of George Henry Moore, a Catholic landlord and member of parliament whose 50,000-acre estate he inherited, he left his estate in 1870 to study painting in Paris. He failed and turned to writing, originally poetry. Returning to Ireland, he arranged for an agent to handle his estate during the agitation by the Land League. He then went to London to write novels, many of which were banned because of their scandalous, for the times, content. In 1894 his work, *Esther Waters,* enjoyed high critical acclaim. William Butler Yeats influenced his return to Ireland to join the Irish Literary Theatre, where he edited and collaborated on several plays. He also published short stories, novels, and an autobiographical trilogy *Hail and Fairwell* (1911–14), dealing with the defeat of landlordism and with triumphant Catholicism. He then returned to London, where he had his only child by Lady Maud Cunard and continued writing.

Moore, George Henry (1811–1870)
politician, landlord

Born in Moore Hall, Ballyglass, County Mayo, Moore was educated at Oscott Hall, Birmingham, and at Christ Church College, Cambridge. He was a well-regarded landlord who supported tenant rights. He was elected to the House of Commons for County Mayo in 1847 and later was a founder of the Catholic Defence Association formed to combat the Ecclesiastical Titles Bill of Lord John Russell. He was a leader of the Irish Brigade that became the Independent Irish Party that helped bring down the government of Lord Derby in 1852. He lost his seat in 1857, but regained it again in 1868 until his death. Moore was the father of George Moore and Maurice Moore.

Moore, Thomas (1779–1852)
lyricist, poet

Born in Dublin, the son of a grocer, Moore was one of the first Catholics to attend Trinity College Dublin. He was a friend of Robert Emmet, but was not involved in the United Irishmen. His translation of the classical Greek *Odes of Anacreon* (1800) gained him admission to fashionable circles in London, even gaining him an Admiralty post for a brief while in Bermuda during which his deputy absconded with a large sum of money for which Moore was held responsible. He was saved by the generosity of Lord Lansdowne and his publisher. From 1808 to 1834 he produced 10 editions of *Irish Melodies,* which were set to music from traditional Irish airs. Although dealing with Irish tragedy, suffering, and defeat, they were received well in England and throughout Europe, giving a dignity to Irish culture, and for which he was regarded as Ireland's national bard. His fame paralleled that of other romanticists, including Sir Walter Scott and Lord Byron. A close friend of the latter, he burned his memoirs at the request of his widow. Moore wrote biographies of Byron, Richard Brinsley Sheridan, and Edward Fitzgerald. He was married to actress Elizabeth Dyke and, tragically, all five of their children died.

Moran, D. P. (Denis Patrick Moran) (1872–1936)
journalist

Born in Waterford, Moran worked in London as a journalist for a while and was an active member of the Gaelic League. He returned to Ireland in 1898 and, in 1900, started a paper the *Leader,* in which he expounded his philosophy of an Irish Ireland that would assert its own language, customs, and manners, and be economically self-sufficient. He was skeptical of many other NATIONALIST movements ranging from the IRISH PARLIAMENTARY PARTY through SINN FÉIN to the IRISH REPUBLICAN BROTHERHOOD, and was particularly hostile toward much of the LITERARY REVIVAL, especially John Millington SYNGE's *The Playboy of the Western World.* He coined terms like *West Briton* and *shoneen* to describe any Irish who did not meet his standards of distinctness from and hostility toward British influence.

Morrison, Van (George Ivan Morrison) (1945–)

musician

Born in Belfast, Morrison left school at 16 to join a showband that was starting to include rhythm and blues and rock in its repertoire. In 1966 he went on his own. His first single, "Brown Eyed Girl," made the top 10 in the United States. He followed with an album *Astral Weeks* (1968), which enjoyed phenomenal success and is still regarded by some as his best. Numerous albums of comparable quality and success followed, such as *Moondance* (1970), *Tupelo Honey* (1971), *St. Dominic's Preview* (1972), *Hardnose the Highway* (1973), *It's Too Late to Stop Now* (1974), *Wavelength* (1978), *Common One* (1980), *Inarticulate Speech of the Heart* (1983), and *Irish Heartbeat* (1988; with The CHIEFTAINS). The last reflected a tendency of later years for him to collaborate with other artists, including Bob Dylan and Cliff Richard. In 1992 he received an honorary DL from the National University of Ulster, in 1993 he was inducted into the Rock and Roll Hall of Fame, and in 1996 he received an MBE (member of the Order of the British Empire).

Mother and Child Scheme

The term refers to legislation proposed by Dr. Noel BROWNE, minister for health in the coalition government of 1948 to 1951 that sought to extend free gynecological and pediatric care to pregnant Irish women and young children. It met the expected opposition of the medical profession, but also the hierarchy of the Catholic Church in Ire-

land who remained suspicious of the expansion of the role of the state beyond providing welfare to those qualifying by a means test. The hierarchy was also suspicious that such a program could serve as a wedge through which contraception and abortion would be encouraged in Ireland. The government deferred to the apprehensions of the bishops and Browne resigned.

Mountjoy, Charles Blount, Lord (1563–1606)

soldier and administrator

Appointed lord lieutenant of Ireland, Blount secured the English conquest of Ireland in 1603 by preventing the consolidation of the forces of the future earl of TYRONE, Hugh O'Neill, and Hugh O'DONNELL with the Spanish forces at the Battle of KINSALE, thereby enabling him to rout the Irish and prompt the Spanish withdrawal in December 1601. Within two years he induced O'Neill, whose forces were on the verge of submission, to enter into the Treaty of Mellifont, whereby he accepted both an earldom in lieu of his Gaelic title and the new order of law and public institutions. He did not inform O'Neill of the imminent, and then actual, death of Queen Elizabeth until after the treaty lest it embolden him to continue his resistance. He continued as lord lieutenant and sought to inhibit any inclinations by the administration to persecute the defeated.

Moynihan, Maurice (1902–1999)

civil servant

Born in Tralee, County Kerry and educated at University College Cork, Moynihan joined the Department of Finance in 1925, became private secretary to Eamon DE VALERA when he became TAOISEACH in 1932, and became secretary of the Department of the Taoiseach in 1937. He held that post until 1961 as he also worked with John A. COSTELLO when he led two coalition governments from 1948 to 1951 and 1954 to 1957 and de Valera's FIANNA FÁIL successor, Seán LEMASS, between 1959 and 1961. After he resigned he became governor of the Central Bank until

1969. Subsequently, Moynihan published two books: *Currency and Central Banking in Ireland* (1975) and *Speeches and Statements by Eamon de Valera* (1980).

Mulcahy, Richard (1886–1971)
revolutionary soldier, politician

Born in Waterford and educated by the IRISH CHRISTIAN BROTHERS, Mulcahy worked in the postal services. He joined the IRISH VOLUNTEERS in 1913 and was second in command of the Volunteers under Thomas ASHE in an encounter with the ROYAL IRISH CONSTABULARY at Ashbourne, County Dublin, during the EASTER RISING. Interned at Frongoch, Wales, until 1917, he rejoined the Volunteers upon return to Ireland. He was elected as a SINN FÉIN candidate for parliament for Clontarf, County Dublin, in the 1918 general election, but chose to join the DÁIL ÉIREANN. He was the chief of staff of the army of the Irish Republic (the IRA) during the WAR OF INDEPENDENCE. A supporter of the ANGLO-IRISH TREATY, he was minister for defense in the PROVISIONAL GOVERNMENT and then the IRISH FREE STATE government until 1924. He was also a member of the IRISH REPUBLICAN BROTHERHOOD. Identified with a harsh policy toward the IRREGULARS during the CIVIL WAR, he was able to assemble a substantial national army made up of pro-treaty IRA members, especially members closely identified with Michael COLLINS, men who had served in the British army and new recruits. He resigned following the ARMY MUTINY of 1924 when colleagues in the cabinet, especially Minister for Justice Kevin O'HIGGINS, objected to the army's unauthorized arrests after the mutiny had been called off. O'Higgins also disapproved of Mulcahy's employment of the unofficial IRB as a means of countering the private group within the army that had staged the mutiny. Mulcahy remained loyal to the CUMANN NA NGAEDHEAL Party and returned to government as minister for local government in 1927. He was one of the founding members of the FINE GAEL Party that emerged to replace Cumann na nGaedheal. He was the leader of the party from 1944 to 1959, but deferred to John A. COSTELLO as TAOISEACH during the coalition governments from 1948 to 1951 and 1954 to 1957, serving instead as minister for education. He was elected continually to the Dáil for Dublin constituencies from 1918 until his resignation in 1959, except for 1937 to 1938 and 1943 to 1944.

Munro, Henry (died 1798)
United Irishman

Born in Lisburn, County Antrim, a linen draper, Munro became the military commander of United Irishmen of County Down, replacing an arrested commander, William Steel Dickson. He was selected because of his popularity and his previous experience in the IRISH VOLUNTEERS. He commanded his forces in their defeat at the Battle of BALLYNAHINCH, staying in the field to the end. While hiding after the battle, he was betrayed, court-martialed in Lisburn, and sentenced to be hung and beheaded before his own door.

Munster

One of the four historic provinces of Ireland, Munster is the largest. It occupies the southwestern portion of the island and includes Counties Clare, Limerick, Kerry, Cork, Waterford, and Tipperary, of which only the latter is landlocked. The name comes from an ancient goddess named Mumha. Gaelic rulers who dominated in medieval times included the McCarthys and the O'Briens (including BRIAN BORU), and Cashel in present-day Tipperary was an important political and ecclesiastical center. With the arrival of the Normans, the FitzGeralds (earls of Desmond) and the Butlers (earls of Ormond) dominated, although many of them became Gaelic in culture themselves. Munster resistance to the 16th-century Tudor attempt to impose a new order failed and plantation ensued. Significant planters included Richard BOYLE, later earl of Cork, and William PETTY, whose descendants became the Marquises of LANSDOWNE. The plantations did not involve the removal of the rank and file of the native population. Furthermore, the establishment of shires, or counties, had begun to develop with the arrival of the Normans.

Murphy, Dervla (1931–)

Dervla Murphy was born in Lismore, County Waterford, and educated at the Ursuline Convent, Waterford. After the death of her invalid mother she took to travelling and writing. She traveled by bicycle to often exotic and distant places, including Ethiopia, Madagascar, Cameroon, Peru, Central America, and Rwanda, and often took her young daughter with her. Excellent books have resulted from her journeys. Her first book *Full Tilt* (1965) recorded her travels from Ireland to India by bicycle. A book about her visit to Northern Ireland, *A Place Apart* (1978), won the Ewart-Biggs Memorial Prize (named after the British ambassador assassinated in Ireland in 1976). She also examined race relations in England in her book *Tales from Two Cities* (1987).

Murphy, William Martin (1844–1919)

businessman, newspaper proprietor

Murphy was born in Bantry, County Cork, and educated at BELVEDERE COLLEGE, Dublin. He took over the family contracting business and expanded it from constructing churches, schools, and bridges in Ireland to building railroads in England and Africa, and he became the director of the Dublin Tramways Company. He also owned Clery's Department Store and the Imperial Hotel. As an IRISH PARLIAMENTARY PARTY member of parliament from 1885 to 1892, he sided with Tim HEALY in forcing the ouster of Charles Stewart PARNELL from leadership. He purchased the *Irish Catholic* and the Parnellite

Irish Daily Independent, which he turned into the *Irish Independent.* Possibly he is most remembered for his hostility to the unionizing effort in 1913 by James LARKIN and his IRISH TRANSPORT AND GENERAL WORKERS' UNION. He successfully broke the union's effort by a lockout, which he encouraged other employers to support. The confrontation entailed massive demonstrations, rioting, and police assaults, as well as international gestures of sympathy with the strikers.

Murray, Daniel (1768–1852)

archbishop

Born in Arklow, County Wicklow, Murray was educated at the Irish College in Salamanca, Spain, returning to Ireland after his ordination in 1792 to serve as a curate in Dublin and in Arklow. The Rising of 1798 made him apprehensive of violent movements and influenced his relationship with the existing political authorities. He was made coadjutor bishop of Dublin in 1809, was president of MAYNOOTH from 1812 to 1813, and succeeded John Troy as archbishop of Dublin in 1823. He had visited Rome in 1814 and 1815 to indicate to the papacy the Irish opposition to the proposed allowance of a veto over Episcopal appointments to the British government in return for allowing Catholic emancipation. He supported Daniel O'CONNELL in his campaign for the same and in other efforts to achieve equity for Catholics in Ireland. Willing to work with the government, he accepted the system of national education as well as the proposed QUEEN'S COLLEGES, both vigorously opposed by other bishops, especially Archbishop John MACHALE of Tuam, as "Godless colleges." He also opposed O'Connell's repeal campaign. He was offered, but refused, an appointment to the Privy Council.

N

Nagle, Nano (Honoria Nagle) (1728–1784)
educator, founder of a religious order
Born at Balgfirrin, near Mallow, County Cork, in a comfortable family, Nagle was educated in Paris. Although it was illegal at the time, she started a number of schools for Catholic children in Cork in the 1750s, devoting an inheritance to the effort. In 1771 she brought the Ursuline nuns to join in the effort, but their approach was primarily to educate the well-to-do. Accordingly she founded a new order, called the "Order of the Presentation of the Blessed Virgin Mary," which would concentrate on working with the poor. She paid for the construction of a convent and school that opened in 1777. She died in 1784 and the order received papal approval in 1791. Its work expanded beyond Ireland to England, America, Australia, and India.

Nathan, Mathew (1852–1937)
public official
Born in England, Nathan was an officer in the Royal Engineers. He served in Africa and in the colonies and then in the War Office. He was made undersecretary for Ireland in 1914. Nathan dismissed the likelihood of an imminent nationalist uprising in early April 1916, even taking no precautionary action after the arrest of Roger CASEMENT. He was himself trapped in DUBLIN CASTLE during the EASTER RISING and resigned his position on May 3. Nathan was subsequently criticized by a Royal Commission for not having alerted Chief Secretary Augustine BIRRELL of the danger of a rising.

Nation, The
A weekly newspaper founded in 1842 by Charles Gavan DUFFY, Thomas DAVIS, and John Blake DILLON, it became the voice of popular nationalism and of the YOUNG IRELAND movement. The paper helped generate a national consciousness with its articles, poetry, and stories and was an Irish parallel to similar ethnic and cultural efforts by nationalists on the European continent at the time, whether those seeking unification of politically divided "nations" like Germany and Italy or those seeking independence, such as Poles, Czechs, and Hungarians, who were part of larger empires. The paper supported Daniel O'CONNELL in the repeal campaign, but broke with him in 1846 when he insisted on a repudiation of the concept of physical force as a means of advancing the Irish cause. The paper also disagreed with the Catholic hierarchy, especially Archbishop John MACHALE, on the issue of the QUEEN'S COLLEGES, which the bishops regarded as irreligious, but which Young Ireland saw as an instrument by which to engender a nonsectarian national consciousness. John MITCHEL became a major contributor to the paper after the death of Davis, but he broke with it over Duffy's moderation on the land issue. Duffy resumed editing the paper after its suppression at the time of the rising of 1848. It supported the IRISH TENANT LEAGUE and the Independent Irish Party in 1852. When Duffy moved to Australia in 1855, A. M. SULLIVAN took over. While the paper criticized the FENIANS, it supported Issac BUTT as well as Charles Stewart PARNELL and the LAND LEAGUE. However, it

broke with Parnell after the divorce issue and ceased publication in 1891.

nationalism

The term *nationalism* has been applied to a variety of groups differing in tactics and even in ideals. Nationalism usually means a desire to promote a separate and sovereign state for a particular nation that would encompass all of the claimed national territory and all of the people of the nation. Nationalism in that sense began in Ireland with the UNITED IRISHMEN of the late 18th century who sought an Irish republic that would include all Irishmen regardless of religious belief or lack of such and would be separate from Britain. However, earlier Irish leaders, the Ulster earls who lost to MOUNTJOY at the Battle of Kinsale, the leaders of the CONFEDERATION OF KILKENNY, and the JACOBITE forces who were defeated in 1690, were not as clearly insistent on absolute separatism from Britain, as the motto of the Confederation was "Pro Deo, pro patria, et pro regnum," and the Jacobites were fighting for James II as king of Ireland. Many in the PROTESTANT ASCENDANCY in the 18th century asserted Irish national rights, having in mind the claim of the Irish parliament to autonomy from the British parliament, but they were scarcely separatists and were well aware that their position of ascendancy over the Catholic majority was closely connected to the British connection. After 1798 nationalism followed two courses, revolutionary and constitutional, although many individuals were linked with both dispositions. The central figures in the constitutional form of nationalism were Daniel O'CONNELL, Issac BUTT, Charles Stewart PARNELL, and John REDMOND. They sought to achieve Irish self-governance, equitable treatment for the Catholic majority, and land and other social reforms through constitutional means and never called for outright separatism from Britain. Examples of the revolutionary tradition in nationalism include the United Irishmen, those of YOUNG IRELAND who took part in the rising of 1848, the FENIANS and the IRISH REPUBLICAN BROTHER-HOOD, and SINN FÉIN (after 1917), and the IRA. They regarded the use of physical force as appropriate in the pursuit of a separate Irish republic.

National University of Ireland

Legislation in 1908 sought to satisfy the lingering dissatisfaction of the Irish Catholic Church with the existing higher educational system. The church disapproved of the non-sectarian QUEEN'S COLLEGES of Cork, Galway, and Belfast, and had to contend with the necessity of students of the Catholic University in Dublin having to take examinations from a distinct public body, which was empowered to award degrees. The legislation made the colleges in Cork and Galway and the existing University College Dublin constituent members of a national university, and MAYNOOTH was recognized as a college, but not a fully constituent college until 1967. Nominally nondenominational, the schools were de facto Catholic up until the last third of the 20th century.

National Volunteers

When a minority of the IRISH VOLUNTEERS, about 10,000, refused to heed the call of John REDMOND to support the British war effort in 1914 and retained the Irish Volunteer title for themselves, the majority who supported him became known as the National Volunteers. Many of their 170,000 members served on the western front. Unlike the ULSTER VOLUNTEERS, they were not absorbed as a single group into the forces. This discriminatory treatment by the British military might, ironically, have spared the National Volunteers from the high number casualties suffered by many of the Ulster Volunteer units in many of the brutal encounters of the first World War, notably at the Somme.

Neeson, Liam (1953–)
actor

Born in Ballymena, County Antrim, Neeson worked in the Lyric Players' Theatre in BELFAST and in the ABBEY THEATRE, DUBLIN, before being cast in the film *Excalibur* (1981). He received a Tony Award for his appearance on Broadway in *Anna Christie* in 1993. The same year he received an Oscar nomination for playing the leading role in *Schindler's List* (1993). He has also appeared in such films as *Suspect* (1987), *Rob Roy* (1995), the epic biography *Michael Collins* (1996), and *Kinsey* (2004).

Neilson, Samuel (1761–1803)
United Irishman

Born in Ballyroney, County Down, the son of a Presbyterian minister, Neilson became a draper and made a fortune. By 1790 he abandoned business and turned to politics. He was one of the founders of the UNITED IRISHMEN in 1792, especially its promotion of the ideal of the unity of all Irishmen in spite of religious creed. He founded and edited the society's paper, the NORTHERN STAR, in 1792. He was arrested in 1796 in Dublin but released in 1798 because of ill health. In 1798 he was again arrested and wounded in a failed attempt to rescue the arrested Lord Edward Fitzgerald. Neilson was among the United Irishmen who were detained in Fort George, Scotland, for four years, and then released. He left for the Netherlands and ultimately made his way to the United States in 1802, where he died the following year.

New Departure

The term refers to the cooperation of FENIANS, land activists, and parliamentarians in promoting land reform, and ultimately Irish self-governance, that came about in late 1878 and early 1879. Leading figures in the movement include Michael DAVITT, John DEVOY, and Charles Stewart PARNELL.

Newgrange

A prehistoric monument built in the Boyne Valley, County Meath, about 3000 B.C., it consists of a 36-foot high mound that is 280 feet in diameter, in which there is a 60-foot passage leading to a chamber that is lit by the rays of the rising sun at the winter solstice. The passage and chamber feature stones decorated with megalithic art.

New Ireland Forum

A forum called by TAOISEACH Garret FITZGERALD in May 1983 to which all constitutional parties in Ireland and Northern Ireland were invited. The UNIONIST and the DEMOCRATIC UNIONIST PARTY did not attend, but the ALLIANCE PARTY and the SOCIAL DEMOCRATIC AND LABOUR PARTY (SDLP) from Northern Ireland did come, and some Unionist members gave individual testimony at its hearings. SINN FÉIN, because of the IRA connection, was not invited. After scores of meetings, the forum issued a report the following May signed by FINE GAEL, FIANNA FÁIL, the LABOUR PARTY, and SDLP participants that recommended three solutions for the Northern Ireland impasse: a unitary state for Ireland, a federal organization of the island, or the sharing of joint responsibility by Britain and Ireland for Northern Ireland. The report also affirmed that any other arrangement which would receive the consent of the majority of the people in both communities in Northern Ireland was satisfactory. Margaret Thatcher, the British prime minister, bluntly rejected all three suggestions, stating that each was "out." But soon after, intensive negotiations between both governments began that resulted in the 1985 HILLSBOROUGH AGREEMENT between the two governments.

Newman, John Henry (1801–1890)
churchman

Born in London, Newman was educated at Trinity College, Oxford, and was a fellow of Oriel College. He was ordained a priest in the Church of England in 1824. He was made the Vicar of St. Mary's Oxford in 1826. Newman was a leading figure in the Tractarian Movement that espoused a high church perspective and was critical of Erastianism that is, any effort by the state to inhibit or alter the character of the church. Tractarians feared Catholic emancipation as well as legislation that effected the organization of the CHURCH OF IRELAND. Ironically, Newman's religious orthodoxy led him ultimately to accept Catholicism, which he joined in 1845. He was ordained a Catholic priest in Rome in 1847 and returned to England, where he founded the Oratorian Order at Edgbaston near Birmingham. He was appointed rector of the projected Catholic University in Dublin in 1851 and his lectures the following year to the Irish hierarchy formed the basis of his *The Idea of a University* (1873). However, he only held the position from 1854 to 1858 as his tenure was beset with restraints on his autonomy, especially from more nationalist-minded bishops such as John MACHALE, the institution's financial difficulties, and its inability to award degrees. He returned to England to work with his order, continuing to write major theological works, including his autobiography *Apologia pro Vita Sua* (1864). Newman was made a cardinal in 1879.

Ní Chonaill, Eibhlin Dhubh (c. 1743–1800)
poet

One of 22 children of Domhnail Mor O'Conail and the aunt of Daniel O'CONNELL, Ní Chonaill was widowed after a youthful marriage. In 1767 she fell in love with Art O'Laoghaire, a veteran officer in the Hungarian Hussars of Empress Maria Theresa. Despite the disapproval of her politically more prudent family, she married the hot-tempered soldier. O'Laoghaire quarreled with Abraham Morris, the high sheriff of Cork, who had earlier had him arrested and unsuccessfully prosecuted. The same Morris demanded the right to purchase the race-horse of O'Laoghaire, in accord with the PENAL LAW inhibiting Catholics from owning horses worth more than £5. When O'Laoghaire refused, he was again outlawed. He met Morris, who was escorted by soldiers, and was killed. When his wife, pregnant with their third child, discovered his death, she composed her lament, *"Caoineadh Airt Uí Laoghaire"* (Lament for Art O'Leary), that is considered one of the greatest poems in the Irish language. It condemns Protestantism and the English rule of law.

Ní Dhomhnaill, Nuala (1952–   )
poet

Born in Lancashire to Irish-speaking parents, Ní Dhomhnaill was raised in Tipperary, but spent much time in her youth in the West Kerry GAELTACHT. Educated at University College Cork, she lived on the Continent and in Turkey for a number of years. All of her poetry is composed in the Irish language. Her books include *An Dealg Drighin* (1981), *Fear Suaithinseach* (1984), *Feis* (1991), and *Cead Aighnis* (1998). Her poetry reflects a feminist perspective and traditional folk symbolism.

NORAID

The acronym for the Irish Northern Committee founded in the United States in 1970 by Michael FLANNERY, John McGowan, and Jack McCarthy ostensibly to raise money for the families of imprisoned Irish republicans. In fact, it was regarded as the major fund-raiser for the Provisional IRA, securing its funds through dinners and collections in bars and at athletic events. The organization also published a weekly newspaper the *IRISH PEOPLE*, most of whose copy came from *An Poblacht*, the SINN FÉIN paper in Ireland, although strongly anti-American or socialist messages were excluded. Its leader, Michael Flannery, was unsuccessfully prosecuted for trying to purchase arms for the IRA in 1982, as the jury accepted the defense argument that since the source of the weapons was someone with whom the CIA had earlier dealt, it was assumed that the purchase of weapons for the IRA had the sanction of the American government. The following year Flannery was the Grand Marshal of the New York St. Patrick's Day Parade, to which the archbishop of New York, the Irish consul general in New York, and several leading Irish-American political figures, including Senator Daniel Patrick Moynihan (D-N.Y.) objected. Flannery and others in NORAID objected to the willingness of Sinn Féin to accept seats in the DÁIL ÉIREANN, and transferred their allegiance to the fringe Republican Sinn Féin and the Continuity IRA. Since the cease-fire in 1994 most Sinn Féin fund-raising in the United States has been done by the Friends of Sinn Féin, which draws from an increasingly professional following and hosts upscale dinners in downtown hotels to which tickets cost in the $500 and up range.

Norbury, John Toler, first earl of
(1745–1831)
judge

Born in Beechwood, County Tipperary, and educated at TRINITY COLLEGE DUBLIN, Toler became a member of the Irish parliament for Tralee in 1776. His loyal support of the government earned him appointment as a solicitor-general in 1789 and attorney general in 1798. He voted for the ACT OF UNION in 1800 and in return was created Baron Norbury and made chief justice of the Court of Common Pleas. His lack of legal knowledge and superficial disposition and cruelty on the bench outraged Daniel O'CONNELL, who petitioned parliament to have him removed from office. He was ultimately induced to resign in return for a generous pension and an earldom.

Normans   See ANGLO-NORMANS.

Northern Ireland

A province that came into being with passage of the GOVERNMENT OF IRELAND ACT of 1920, which sought to resolve the dilemma posed by the opposition of the unionist Protestant majority in the historic province of Ulster to inclusion in a united Ireland as called for by the 1914 Home Rule Act, whose implementation had been postponed for the duration of the First World War. The development of a revolutionary regime in Dublin, calling itself the Republic of Ireland, establishment of the DÁIL ÉIREANN and support

for a war of insurrection hardened animosities. The act divided the island by taking six of the nine Ulster counties, which together had a clear unionist majority, and giving it its own government and parliament with the same degree of autonomy as was granted to a government of southern Ireland, which would rule the remaining 26 counties. The latter never came into being, as the members elected to it considered themselves the Dáil Éireann government. Later, the majority of the same members, having accepted the 1921 ANGLO-IRISH TREATY, agreed to act as the PROVISIONAL GOVERNMENT of Ireland in implementing the treaty and establish the Irish Free State as a dominion. The parliament of Northern Ireland took the option offered in that treaty to exclude itself from the Free State. A BOUNDARY COMMISSION, called for by the treaty to adjust the boundary "in accordance with the wishes of the inhabitants, as far as may be compatible with economic and geographic conditions," made relatively minor recommendations of territorial transfer. The report it had drawn up drew opposition in the Irish Free State and the British and Free State governments agreed to suspend the findings and maintain the status quo.

Because it had come into being during the Irish WAR OF INDEPENDENCE, the government of Northern Ireland tended to regard its Catholic and NATIONALIST minority as inherently subversive. The continuation of IRA action lent strength to this feeling, as did the refusal of nationalist majorities in local elected bodies to give recognition to the Northern Ireland government, as they anticipated a boundary commission ruling that would seriously dismember the province. The government then began to end proportional representation, first at the local government level, and later province wide for election to its parliament. Gerrymandering techniques were employed as well at the local level to ensure maximum strength for the unionists. Furthermore, the franchise in local government elections was limited to householders and their spouses, and extra franchises were granted for ownership of businesses in other constituencies, all of which tended to work in favor of unionists. The refusal of the nationalist politicians to take their seats in the parliament in the early years and, at the same time, their refusal until the 1960s to act as a formal opposition party added to the problem.

Police tended to be exclusively unionist, although this stemmed in part to Catholic reluctance to serve. Auxiliary police forces were more blatantly sectarian. Special Powers Legislation enabled the Ministry for Home Affairs to be dismissive of civil liberties, particularly of Catholics, in times of social turmoil. An educational system that began initially as nonsectarian quickly evolved into a segregated one whereby the state schools were de facto Protestant and the Catholics attended their own schools. Over time, the state increased its support for the Catholic system, so that by the last third of the 20th century Catholic schools were financed on a comparable basis. In such a society, communal suspicions prompted discriminatory hiring and renting practices, a situation made worse by the shrinking economic position of the province. The irredentist aspirations of Irish nationalists, especially the professions in articles 2 and 3 of the 1937 Irish constitution, fueled the siege mentality of the Northern Ireland government.

The province was expected to be self-sufficient financially, drawing on the transferred revenues it could levy, such as property rates, licence fees and so forth, and what was left over from the reserved revenues—income, corporate, and excise taxes—that were applied and administered by Westminster, after a proportionate amount was taken for imperial expenses such as foreign policy, defense, and national debt. In fact, it was soon determined that imperial contributions should be significantly reduced and then applied as a last charge. Ultimately, Northern Ireland was to receive a subsidy to guarantee that its social welfare benefits would be on a par with the rest of the United Kingdom.

The experience of the Second World War, where Northern Ireland industry and farming contributed vitally to the British war effort and the province served as a base for Americans employed in the drive to liberate Europe, had a bountiful effect on the economy of Northern Ireland. That and the extension to the province of the postwar welfare state produced a startling disparity between its economic position and the stagnant conditions existing in the rest of the island. At the same time, IRA figures, based primarily in the South, launched a terrorist campaign the mid-1950s. But it was called off in the early 1960s largely in view of the disinterest on the part of the supposed beneficiaries, Northern nationalists.

Meetings in the mid-1960s between a new Northern Ireland prime minister, Terence O'Neill, and the Irish TAOISEACH, Seán LEMASS and his successor, Jack LYNCH, created optimism for improved relations between both parts of the island and within Northern communities. On the other hand, many Catholics in the North, having benefited from the educational opportunities that were nonexistent in the Republic Ireland, acquired a broader perspective and changed their demands for political unification to demands for full rights of citizenship. Taking a cue from what the African-American population had done in pursuit of redress of even more severe grievances, they began to engage in protest marches and sit-ins. The majority community began to interpret these events as the beginning of a new IRA campaign and the police, especially the AUXILIARIES, responded in a very heavy-handed manner. In the summer of 1969, disorder in both Belfast and Derry and the British military was sent in to maintain peace. Originally received amicably by the Catholics, they soon became the objects of a renewed IRA campaign to unite Ireland.

The situation went from bad to worse when the British acceded to implementation of the Northern Ireland government's tactic of internment without trial of suspected IRA figures in August 1971. Protests at this measure mounted and in January 1972, in Derry, several innocents were shot by soldiers who claimed they were responding to firing from the crowd. Within several months, the British suspended the Northern Ireland government that had been in operation

A British soldier takes cover in West Belfast, Northern Ireland, 1989. *(H. Davies/Exile Images)*

both a right of the Republic to act on behalf of the nationalist community of Northern Ireland and a recognition that any change in the constitutional status of the province would require the consent of the majority of its people. When an IRA cease-fire in 1994, interrupted from 1996 to 1997, was followed by all-party discussions, a GOOD FRIDAY AGREEMENT emerged in 1998, which opened the door for the devolution of power to the province through a proportionally elected Northern Ireland Assembly and a power-sharing Northern Ireland Executive. It also called for extensive social and police reforms, release of prisoners, and a commitment to non-violence. Disagreement about the decommissioning of weapons in the possession of paramilitary groups and the unwillingness of unionists to serve with SINN FÉIN until such is achieved has resulted in suspension of the government and continued to direct rule.

Northern Ireland has an area of 5,241 square miles and a population of 1,685,257. It consists of Counties Antrim, Down, Armagh, Fermanagh, Tyrone, and Derry. The majority of the population is Protestant, but not by the large proportion at the time of the founding of the province. Major industries include aerospace, shipbuilding, agriculture, textiles, information technology, and tourism. An unusually high proportion of the workforce is employed by the state.

Northern Ireland Assembly

Soon after the abolition of the PARLIAMENT OF NORTHERN IRELAND an effort was made to return to devolved institutions in Northern Ireland, rather than have the province ruled directly by the government in Westminster. The first attempt was an election of a Northern Ireland Assembly in June 1973. The assembly had 78 members elected by the single transferable vote system of proportional representation that had been followed in the earlier elections to the Parliament of Northern Ireland and which was the method followed by elections in the Republic of Ireland. About two-thirds of the members were various sorts of

since 1921. Significantly, important powers had already been taken away from local governments by the provincial government in an effort to curb discriminatory practices. The effect then was to centralize the administration of the province in a single British department, the Northern Ireland Office.

These matters remained for nearly 30 years, despite brief efforts at creation of Northern Ireland Assemblies, notably one in 1973–74, that encompassed the concept of power sharing, that is, distribution of executive authority proportionate to all parties, rather than a continuation of control by the permanent unionist majority. In 1985 the HILLSBOROUGH AGREEMENT between the British and Irish governments acknowledged unionists. The assembly selected a power-sharing coalition executive with members from both communities. However, the experiment failed after a general strike by loyalist workers in the spring of 1974 and the assembly was dissolved. The following year a Northern Ireland Constitutional Convention was elected, also with 78 members and by single transferable voting. Again, about two-thirds of those elected were unionist. A broad coalition of unionist groups, calling itself the United Ulster Unionist Coalition, and including the Unionist Party, opposed any power sharing, and the convention was unsuccessful. Another attempt at gaining cross-community consensus for devolved institution was an election in October 1982 of another Northern Ireland Assembly, also of 78 members and elected by single transferable vote. This election was significant since it was the occasion of the first serious effort by SINN FÉIN to run candidates for office. They gained five seats, but they and the 14 members of the SOCIAL DEMOCRATIC AND LABOUR PARTY (SDLP), the constitutionalist nationalist party, refused to take part guaranteeing that the assembly would fail of its purpose. The next Northern Ireland Assembly was elected in June 1998 following the GOOD FRIDAY AGREEMENT of that year. It had 108 members, also elected by single transferable voting, among whom the ULSTER UNIONIST PARTY and the SDLP were the largest. The assembly and the power-sharing executive it elected, however, were subject to numerous suspensions, primarily related to failure of the IRA to advance with the decommissioning of its arsenal. A second election to the new assembly was held in November 2003 and resulted in the DEMOCRATIC UNIONIST PARTY and Sinn Féin becoming the respective largest parties in the two communities. Their failure to agree on the formation of an executive has meant the continuation of direct rule and the assembly has not met.

Northern Ireland Civil Rights Association

A broad-based association of civil libertarians, left-wing activists, nationalists, and others sought to draw attention to civil rights as opposed to irredentist grievances in Northern Ireland in the 1960s. It was patterned after the civil rights movement by and on behalf of African Americans. Basic demands included an end to political gerrymandering, implementation of the principle of one man, one vote, a prohibition on discrimination, and reform of police procedures and organization. The protests were often met by excessive police action and popular unionist fears that the association served as a front for the IRA.

Northern Star

The newspaper of the UNITED IRISHMEN that first appeared in 1792, the *Northern Star* championed the ideal of an Irish nation indifferent to religious rivalries. The paper ceased publication after its printing presses were destroyed in 1797 by the Monaghan militia that General Gerald LAKE, the military commander in Ulster, employed in the repression of the United Irishmen.

Norton, William (1900–1963)
politician

Born in County Kildare, Norton worked as a post office clerk and became a member of the national executive of the Post Office Workers' Union. He was elected to the DÁIL ÉIREANN from Dublin in 1926, but he lost his seat the next year. He served as president of the Executive Council of the Postal, Telegraph and Telephone International from 1926 to 1932. In 1932, he was returned to the Dáil Éireann for Kildare and became leader of the LABOUR PARTY, which helped to vote Eamon DE VALERA into his first ministry. He achieved the removal of the words "Workers' Republic" from the Labour Party constitution in 1937 in an effort to appease the Roman Catholic hierarchy, but, in 1943, Norton supported the return to the party of the more radical James LARKIN. Larkin's inclusion, however, led to the secession from the party by the IRISH TRANSPORT AND GENERAL WORKERS' UNION and its affiliated TD's. He served as Tánaiste and minister for social welfare in the first coalition government from 1948 to 1951 and Tánaiste and minister for industry and commerce in the second coalition government from 1954 to 1957.

The split in the party was resolved in 1950 and it won 19 seats in 1954, but fell back to 12 in 1957. He resigned as leader in 1960.

O

O'Brien, Conor Cruise (1917–)

writer, politician

Born in Dublin and educated at Trinity College Dublin, O'Brien worked in the Department for External Affairs from 1944 to 1961. He also wrote literary criticism under the pseudonym of Donat O'Donnell. He served as a member of the Irish delegation to the United Nations from 1956 to 1961, when he was seconded to serve in the UN mission to the strife-torn newly independent Congo. He resigned that post and his position with the Irish diplomatic corps in the same year in protest at the deference shown to Western interests in the Congo. From 1962 to 1965 he served as chancellor of the University of Ghana and, from 1965 to 1969, he held a chair at New York University, where he was an outspoken critic of American policy in Vietnam. In 1969 he was elected as Labour Party TD for Dublin Northeast and served as minister for posts and telegraphs in the coalition government from 1973 to 1977. He was the Labour spokesperson on Northern Ireland and became increasingly critical of the irredendist objectives of Irish nationalists, especially in his book *States of Ireland* (1972). He lost his Dáil seat in 1977 but was elected to the Seanad for Trinity College and served until 1981. O'Brien was editor of the *Observer* from 1978 to 1981, wrote regular columns for the *Irish Times* until 1986 and then for the *Irish Independent,* and he continued to write books, including *Siege: The Saga of Israel and Zionism* (1986); *The Great Melody* (1992), a sympathetic study of Edmund Burke; and *The Long Affair* (1996) a critical examination of Thomas Jefferson's enthusiasm for the French Revolution. In 1996 he joined the U.K. Unionist Party and secured a seat in the elections of May 1996 to a Northern Ireland Assembly designed to advance peace talks. He resigned from the party in 1998 when some of its members objected to his suggestion that unionists might be better off accepting a United Ireland in contrast to feared appeasement of Sinn Féin/IRA by the British government. He is married to the poet Máire Mhac an tSaoi.

O'Brien, Edna (1936–)

novelist, short-story writer

Born in Tuamgransy, County Clare, O'Brien went to London in 1959. She wrote three novels, *The Country Girls* (1960), *The Girl with Green Eyes* (1962, 1964), and *Girls in Their Married Bliss* (1964), that had strong autobiographical undercurrents and dealt with female sexual awakening and paternal domination in Ireland. The books were banned by the Censorship Board in Ireland ensuring her literary success with a number of other novels, such as *August Is a Wicked Month* (1965) and *A Pagan Place* (1970), as well as collections of short stories, including *The Love Object* (1968) and *Returning* (1982), most of which relate to Ireland and her County Clare background although she lived in England. Later works have gone beyond the earlier themes to deal with incest and the IRA, such as *House of Splendid Isolation* (1994) and *Down by the River* (1996).

O'Brien, Vincent (1917–)

horse trainer

Born in Churchtown, County Cork, O'Brien became an amateur jockey and then moved to

Ballydoyle Hose in County Tipperary, where he began training horses. Horses he trained went on to win all the principal national hunt races, including the Grand Nationals in 1953, 1954, and 1955. Other horses trained by him have won a record number of British and Irish classic flat races. Individual horses have won the Champion Hurdle three times, the British Triple Crown, and the Prix de l'Arc de Triomphe, making him one of the best trainers in the world.

O'Brien, William (1852–1928)
agrarian activist, journalist, politician

Born in Mallow, County Cork, O'Brien studied law at QUEEN'S COLLEGE Cork, but he did not complete his studies because of ill health. He wrote for a number of papers, including the *FREEMAN'S JOURNAL,* and then became editor of the Parnellite paper *United Ireland,* from 1881 to 1890. He became a member of parliament for Mallow in 1883 and became a leading figure in the IRISH PARLIAMENTARY PARTY. He was associated with Tim HEALY and John DILLON in organizing the PLAN OF CAMPAIGN rent strike on behalf of tenants from 1886 to 1891 during which he was arrested several times. In 1887 he was returned to parliament for Cork Northeast and for the city of Cork in 1892. He opposed Charles Stewart Parnell after the divorce scandal. However, the UNITED IRISH LEAGUE that he founded in 1898 served as a vehicle that prompted the reunification of the parliamentary party under a Parnellite, John REDMOND, in 1900. O'Brien launched a new paper, *The Irish People,* that called for the unification of UNIONISTS and NATIONALISTS, and landlords and tenants, which helped prompt a land conference out of which emerged the Wyndham Land Purchase Act. He split with his party when it refused to employ a similar conference to advance Irish self-government, but he rejoined in 1908. He resigned his seat for the city of Cork City in 1909, but returned to politics the next year, regaining his seat and starting a new party, the All for Ireland League. He did not contest the election of 1918 as he anticipated SINN FÉIN vic-tory, and later refused to be serve as a member of the SEANAD of the IRISH FREE STATE as well as to accept a FIANNA FÁIL nomination offered shortly before his death.

O'Brien, William (1881–1961)
trade unionist

Born in Clonakility, County Cork, O'Brien grew up in Dublin, where he became a tailor. He was a founder member of the IRISH TRANSPORT AND GENERAL WORKERS' UNION (ITGWU), and he was involved in the 1913 strike against the lockout. Because of his close association with James Connolly O'Brien was interned after the EASTER RISING even though he had taken no part in it. He became general secretary to the LABOUR PARTY and helped Thomas JOHNSON draft the Democratic Programme of the First DÁIL ÉIRE-ANN. He was interned again in 1920 for having assisted the IRA. O'Brien served two short terms in the Dáil, 1922–23, for Dublin South, and 1927 (June–September) for Tipperary, and he was general secretary for the Labour Party from 1931 to 1939 and chairman of its administrative council from 1939 to 1941. His primary interest lay with his position as general secretary of the ITGWU and he resisted efforts by James LARKIN to regain control of the union after his return from the United States. When Larkin, who had formed a rival Workers' Union of Ireland that had cut into the size of the ITGWU, was read-mitted to the Labour Party in 1943, O'Brien led the ITGWU in disaffiliating with the Labour Party and in founding a rival Congress of Unions. A breakaway National Labour Party was also formed. He retired as general secretary after serving 22 years in the position in 1946.

O'Brien, William Smith (1803–1864)
politician

Born in Dromoland Castle, County Clare, into a Protestant landowning family, O'Brien was educated at Harrow and at Cambridge and entered parliament as a Tory for Ennis in 1828. He was a supporter of Catholic emancipation, but remained independent of Daniel O'CONNELL. He was returned to parliament for Limerick from 1835 to 1848. He became a supporter of the Repeal Movement after O'Connell had been imprisoned in 1843 and became closely linked to the YOUNG IRELAND movement. He split with O'Connell in 1846 over issues such as the "Godless" QUEEN'S COLLEGES and over O'Connell's attempt to develop an alliance with the Whigs. Although he was unsupportive of the more extreme views on land and on the use of violence espoused by James Fintan LALOR, Thomas Francis MEAGHER, and John MITCHELL, he was placed on trial under the Treason Felony Act in 1848. The charges against him failed. However, he was converted to the idea of insurrection a few months later and took part in the unsuccessful Young Ireland rising in Ballingarry, County Tipperary. O'Brien was sentenced to death for his participation, which was later reduced to transportation to Tasmania, from where he was released and pardoned in 1854. He returned to Ireland and remained out of politics for the remainder of his life.

Ó Cadhain, Máirtín (1906–1970)
writer in Irish

Ó Cadhain was born in Cois Fharraige in the Connamarra GAELTACHT in Galway. He became a schoolteacher as well as a member of the IRA. In 1936 he was dismissed as principal of a national school because of his politics. He was elected to the Army Council of the IRA in 1938 and interned in 1939 and again from 1940 to 1944. He moved away from the IRA because of its lack of a social and economic program. As early as 1939 he had published a volume of short stories in Irish entitled *Idir Shúgradh agus Dáirire.* Another, called *An Braon Broghach,* appeared in 1948 and a third collection in 1953, *Cois Caoláire,* was set, like the others, in the Galway Gaeltacht but had a more existential examination of the individual than the community. From 1953 to 1956 he wrote a weekly column in Irish for *The Irish Times* and two novels, *Cré na Cille* (1949) and *Athnuachan* (1951, published 1995). His

writing reflected a Marxist analysis of the language question, as he viewed English cultural hegemony as reflective of the economic power structure, which had to be broken to change English cultural dominance. He worked in the translation department of the Dáil until he became a lecturer in Irish at Trinity College Dublin in 1956. He became an associate professor in 1967 and professor of Irish in 1969. He was supportive of the Irish language and the rights of the Irish speakers through groups such as Muintir na Gaeltachta, Misneach, and the Gaeltacht Civil Rights Movement, as well as the Gaelic socialist newspaper *An tEireannach.* He was friendly to the Communist Party of Ireland and translated the Communist Manifesto and the International into Irish. He died in 1970.

O'Casey, Seán (1880–1964)
playwright

Born in a working-class Protestant family in Dublin, O'Casey became involved early in socialist, labour, language, and NATIONALIST movements. He was particularly supportive of James LARKIN and James CONNOLLY, although he disapproved of the latter's leading the IRISH CITIZEN ARMY into the EASTER RISING. A few years later he began to write plays about recent Dublin history, and their performances gave a tremendous financial boost to the ABBEY THEATRE. They included *The Shadow of a Gunman* (1923), which deals with the WAR OF INDEPENDENCE, *Juno and the Paycock* (1924, about the Irish CIVIL WAR, and *The Plough and the Stars* (1926), about the Easter Rising. Their revisionist perspective created much controversy and resulted in O'Casey's involvement in a public debate with Hanna SHEEHY SKEFFINGTON. He subsequently moved permanently to England where he continued to write plays reflective of his socialist perspective, although not as clearly antinationalist. They included *The Silver Tastle* (1929), *Red Roses for Me* (1943), and *Purple Dust* (1945). The censoring of a dramatization of James JOYCE's *Ulysses* at a Dublin Theatre Festival prompted him to withdraw his own plays in protest and to embargo his plays from Ireland for five years. He also wrote six volumes of autobiography.

Ó Ceallaigh, Seán T. (1882–1966)

revolutionary, politician, president of Ireland

Born in Dublin and educated at the O'Connell Schools, Ó Ceallaigh spent much of his youth in Galway. He joined the GAELIC LEAGUE in 1898 and was manager of its paper *An Claidheamh Soluis*. He was also a founding member of SINN FÉIN and was elected to the Dublin City Council for that party in 1906. A participant in the EASTER RISING, he was subsequently interned. He was returned for Dublin to the first DÁIL ÉIREANN and was a member of the Irish delegation that was unsuccessful in seeking a hearing at the Paris Peace Conference in 1919. He sat for Dublin constituencies continuously until 1945. He opposed the ANGLO-IRISH TREATY and supported the IRREGULARS in the CIVIL WAR. He abstained from attendance at the Dáil Éireann until 1927, when he, as a founding member of the FIANNA FÁIL Party, followed Eamon DE VALERA, in signing the oath and taking a seat in the body. Ó Ceallaigh served as minister for local government from 1932 to 1939, Tánaiste from 1937 to 1945, and minister for finance from 1939 to 1945. In 1945 he was elected the second president of Ireland, defeating Seán McEOIN of FINE GAEL and Patrick McCartan, Independent, on the second count. He was returned unopposed in 1952.

Ó Cleirigh, Micheál (c. 1590–1643)

historian

Born in Kilbarron, County Donegal, Ó Cleirigh was a trained historian in the Gaelic tradition. He joined the Irish Franciscans as a brother in Louvain in the Spanish Netherlands in 1623. From 1626 to 1637 he worked in Ireland transcribing manuscripts on Irish history and hagiography. His most famous work is the *ANNALS OF THE FOUR MASTERS*.

Ó Connaill, Seán (1853–1931)

storyteller, small-time farmer, fisherman

Born in Cill Rialaig, Ballinskelligs, County Kerry, and unschooled, Ó Connaill's stories provided the impetus to Seamus Duilearga to begin his lifelong systematic collection for the Irish Folklore Institute and the Irish Folklore Commission and to publish his great work *Leabhar Sheain I Chonaill* (1948).

Ó Connaire, Pádraig (1882–1928)

writer in the Irish language

Born in Galway, at school Ó Connaire developed a love for the Irish language and a desire to write in it. He won Oireachtas prizes for his writing in 1904 and 1908, although he had gone to London to work as a civil servant. While there he wrote several stories, such as *Nora Mharcius Bhig agus Sgealta Eile* (1909) and a novel *Deoraiocht* (1910), which marked him as the pioneer in modern prose in Irish. Alcoholism prompted him to leave his wife and family and return to Ireland in 1914, where he survived by writing for assorted journals and newspapers.

O'Connell, Daniel (1775–1847)

political leader

Born in Cahren, near Cahirciveen, County Kerry, to a family that was part of the Catholic gentry that had maintained its position despite the PENAL LAWS, Daniel O'Connell was educated by hedge schoolmasters, at St. Omer and Douai in France, and then studied for the bar in London. He spoke Irish before he spoke English and was congenitally disposed to the Gaelic and Catholic society that had been suppressed for the previous few centuries. The frightful experience of the violent revolution in France that required he and his brother to flee to England from their schools also profoundly influenced him. In England he became sympathetic to radical utilitarianism of a Benthamite and Godwin variety, which emphasized individual independence, was distrustful of tradition for its own sake, and was skeptical of religion and committed to its disestablishment. He was one of the first Catholics admitted to the bar after the repeal of penal legislation excluding them. He was sympathetic to the reform goals of the UNITED IRISHMEN, but disapproved of the 1798 uprising. Unlike many of the more conservative and accommodating Catholic gentry, he opposed the ACT OF UNION. He quickly made a name and fortune for himself as a barrister and was particularly outspoken in defending Catholic tenants. O'Connell possessed extraordinary oratorical abilities, sometimes even demagogic, which he was well able to employ as a barrister, as a political agitator, and as a member of parliament. When a case seemed certain of defeat he was not reluctant to use it as a means to assail the very system itself, including judges and prosecutors. Such tactics even got him involved in a duel in which his opponent was killed. He took up the cause of Catholic emancipation, which was suggested by Prime Minister William Pitt as something that should accompany union. However, he rhetorically argued that he would prefer repeal of the Act of Union and restoration of the Irish parliament even if it that were to be accompanied by the Penal Laws. He gained ascendancy in the CATHOLIC ASSOCIATION and was able to turn possible hierarchical sympathy away from a suggested combination of Catholic emancipation with a right of veto by the government over hierarchical appointments. By this time he had returned to his Catholic faith, although he never shed the liberal views on church-state relations he had earlier developed. In the 1820s he expanded organized activity on behalf of Catholic emancipation beyond a limited upper- and middle-class enterprise and created one of the first mass democratic political movements, enrolling hundreds of thousands of hitherto apolitical peasants in the movement by receiving from them a minimal weekly contribution of a farthing a week or a penny a month, usually collected at Sunday Mass. Some of the funds were used to replace the kind of income he would have received as a barrister, but which he forsook to pursue the Catholic emancipation cause. His organization backed candidates supportive of Catholic emancipation and used the mass following to embolden those Catholics who did have the vote to act against the wishes of the landlords. In 1828 O'Connell ran himself in a Clare parliamentary by-election and won. The government ultimately

Daniel O'Connell *(Library of Congress)*

capitulated and passed legislation permitting Catholics to take seats in parliament without having to take an oath contrary to their faith. However, O'Connell had to stand again for the seat before he could be admitted. In the 1830s he secured a following among a minority of the members elected from Ireland and used his position in parliament to advance equitable treatment for the Catholics of Ireland. When he was unlikely to get satisfaction, he resorted to raising the issue of REPEAL of the Act of Union, but the one time he moved for it in parliament, he was overwhelmingly defeated. His greatest success after Catholic emancipation was negotiating the Lichfield House Compact with the Whigs in 1835, as their subsequent government extended numerous significant improvements in Ireland ranging from employment and appointment of Catholics to public positions to the beginning of a state sponsored elementary education system. In the 1840s when the Whigs fell from power and the Tories, or Conservatives, formed the government under

Robert PEEL, he turned again to the issue of repeal. He was joined by members of the middle class, young people, and intellectuals in the Young Ireland movement in a campaign that featured monster meetings of hundreds of thousands in historically symbolic sites of Ireland. However, the government proscribed the concluding meeting, scheduled for Clontarf. O'Connell acquiesced rather than incur a violent confrontation. He spent the greater part of the next year in jail upon conviction of sedition, although the conditions of his incarceration were comfortable and the conviction was overturned by the House of Lords. Subsequently, he began to quarrel with the Young Ireland movement, particularly over members' support of Peel's Universities bill, which would have created nonsectarian universities in Ireland. O'Connell sided with the Catholic bishops who argued for a Catholic university in view of the existing Protestant Trinity College. He later sought to have Young Ireland formally repudiate the idea of employing violence to achieve its political ends. Its members broke with his movement and formed their own organization. O'Connell, broken in health, made his last appearance in parliament in 1847, pleading for more assistance for his Great FAMINE–afflicted land. He died a few months later on his way to Rome. O'Connell's success in mobilizing of the previously silent Catholic masses marked his greatest achievement. Some see him as the great tutor of the Irish in the art of democratic politics. His utilitarian pragmatism made him unsympathetic to violent revolutionary causes and he demonstrated unconcern about the decline of his native Irish language and the spread of English through popular education and economic modernization. Both attitudes have made generations of nationalists and language revivalists critical of him. However, those who celebrate Ireland's heritage of constitutional democracy and religious tolerance cherish his memory.

O'Connell, J. J. "Ginger" (1887–1944)
soldier

Born in County Mayo and educated at CLONGOWES WOOD COLLEGE and at University College

Dublin, O'Connell served in the U.S. Army from 1912 to 1914. When he returned to Ireland, he joined the IRISH VOLUNTEERS. He was interned after the EASTER RISING. During the WAR OF INDEPENDENCE he served as assistant to the chief of staff of the IRA, Richard MULCAHY. He supported the ANGLO-IRISH TREATY and became deputy chief of staff of the national army that Mulcahy, as minister for defense, was organizing for the PROVISIONAL GOVERNMENT. He was kidnapped by the anti-treaty republicans and imprisoned in the FOUR COURTS, which they had controlled for some weeks. His kidnapping served as the spark that lit the CIVIL WAR as the Provisional Government then began to lay siege to the Four Courts. He continued to serve in the Irish army, holding posts as quartermaster-general from 1932 to 1934 and director of military archives from 1934 to 1944.

O'Connell, Michael (Mick O'Connell) (1937–)
soccer player

Born in Valentia Island, County Kerry, O'Connell played for the Kerry GAA team from 1956 through 1972, when it won four All-Ireland Championships. He was renowned for his stylish and superb fielding and kicking and was regarded as one of the greatest players of his generation. He was awarded an honorary doctorate from University College Cork in 2004.

O'Connell, Thomas J. (1882–1969)
trade unionist, politician

Born near Knock, County Mayo, O'Connell was educated at St. Patrick's College, Drumcondra, Dublin, and qualified as a teacher. He served the general secretary of the Irish National Teachers' Organization from 1916 to 1948. He was a LABOUR PARTY TD for Galway from 1922 to 1927 and for Mayo from 1927 to 1932. He succeeded Thomas Johnson as leader of the parliamentary Labour Party in 1927 and cooperated with the FIANNA FÁIL Party in opposing the government of William T. COSGRAVE. O'Connell lost his own seat in the 1932 election that brought Eamon DE

VALERA and Fianna Fáil to power. He was a member of the SEANAD from 1941 to 1944, from 1948 to 1951, and from 1954 to 1957.

O'Connor, Arthur (1763–1852)
United Irishman

Born in Mitchelstown, County Cork, O'Connor was a barrister and was a member of parliament for Philipstown from 1791 to 1796. He was closely associated with Lord Edward Fitzgerald in his UNITED IRISHMEN activism. He was arrested in England in February 1798 when fleeing to France. O'Connor was imprisoned in the Tower of London and later in Fort George in Scotland. Released he went to France in 1802 and served as a general in the French army.

O'Connor, Charles Andrew (1854–1928)
lawyer

Born in Roscommon and educated at St. Stanislaus's College, Tullabeg, County Offaly, and at TRINITY COLLEGE DUBLIN, O'Connor was called to the bar in 1878, made a Queen's Counsel in 1894, served as solicitor general for Ireland from 1909 to 1911 and attorney general for Ireland from 1911 to 1912, and Master of the Rolls in Ireland from 1912 to 1924, upon which appointment he was knighted. He served as a judge of the Supreme Court of the IRISH FREE STATE from 1924 to 1925.

O'Connor, Christy (1924–)
golfer

Born in Knocknacarragh, County Galway, O'Connor came to professional golf in his late twenties, but he was regarded as the best Irish player of his times. He finished in the top five seven times in the British Open, was Irish professional champion 10 times, won, along with Harry Bradshaw, the World Cup for Ireland in 1958, and played in 10 Ryder Cup matches between 1955 and 1973.

O'Connor, Feargus Edward (1794–1855)
radical leader

Born in Connorville, County Cork, the nephew of Arthur O'CONNOR, Feargus O'Connor was educated at TRINITY COLLEGE DUBLIN and was called to the bar. He was elected a member of parliament for the city of Cork in 1832 as one of Daniel O'CONNELL's supporters. However, he fell out with O'Connell and was not returned in the 1835 election. He remained in England, becoming involved in radical and pro–working-class agitation that developed into the Chartist Movement. He edited a weekly paper called the *Northern Star*, and, after a period of arrest, he emerged as the leader of Chartism. However, he quarreled with other leaders and was unwilling to cooperate with middle-class radicals. He championed a scheme to settle urban workers on rural smallholdings, but it came to naught. He presided over the great meeting in 1848 that accompanied the massive Chartist petition for immediate democratization of British politics. But it failed to secure a hearing and improved economic conditions subsequently dampened Chartist enthusiasm. His increasing eccentricity led to his being declared insane. He was committed to an asylum in 1852 and died three years later.

O'Connor, Frank (1903–1966)
writer

Frank O'Connor was the pseudonym of Michael O'Donovan, who was born in the city of Cork, and drawn to writing and to an interest in Irish tradition by his teacher, Daniel CORKERRY. He fought in the WAR OF INDEPENDENCE and on the anti-treaty side in the CIVIL WAR, for which he was interned. He was working as a librarian when he embarked on a literary career, as he became associated with the circle about George RUSSELL's *Irish Statesman*. Moving to Dublin he became acquainted with William Butler YEATS. He is most renowned for his short stories, the first collection of which was *Guests of the Nation* (1931) based on his war of independence experiences, followed by others such as *Bones of Con-*

tention (1936), *Crab Apple Jelly* (1944), *The Common Chord* (1947), *Domestic Relations* (1957) and various collections of his stories, including *Collected Stories* (1981). His stories often deal with the life of lower-middle-class Catholics in Cork during his youth and during the Irish Free State era. He served on the board of the ABBEY THEATRE during the 1930s and in the 1940s was poetry editor of Sean O'FAOLAIN's publication, *The Bell*. In the 1950s he taught at various American universities, but returned to Ireland in 1961 and lectured for two years at TRINITY COLLEGE DUBLIN, where he was awarded an honorary degree. O'Connor wrote acclaimed autobiographical works, *An Only Child* (1961) and *My Father's Son* (1968), translations of early Irish poetry, literary criticism, and literary history.

O'Connor, Rory (1883–1922)
republican revolutionary
Born in Dublin, O'Connor was educated at CLONGOWES WOOD COLLEGE and at University College Dublin, from where he received a degree in engineering. He worked as an engineer in Canada for four years from 1911 to 1915 before returning to Ireland. He took part in the EASTER RISING and was wounded and interned afterward. He split with the IRISH REPUBLICAN BROTHERHOOD over the issue of its retaining its secrecy even though the DÁIL ÉIREANN had proclaimed itself publicly as the Irish Republic. He served as director of engineering for the IRA during the WAR OF INDEPENDENCE, and he directed jail escapes in Manchester, burnings in Liverpool, and an escape from Mountjoy Jail. He also assisted the civilian side of the government in local administration, working with Kevin O'HIGGINS. O'Connor opposed the ANGLO-IRISH TREATY and became chairman of the Military Council of the IRA, which rejected the authority of the PROVISIONAL GOVERNMENT. He was among the leaders establishing republican control of the FOUR COURTS, but was captured at the beginning of the CIVIL WAR when the Provisional Government besieged the garrison. On December 8 he was one of four republican prisoners executed with the approval of the Irish Free State cabinet in retaliation for the IRA's assassination of a member of the DÁIL ÉIREANN and its threats to other members. Kevin O'Higgins, the minister for home affairs, at whose wedding the year before O'Connor had been best man, reluctantly acquiesced in the cabinet decision.

O'Connor, Sinéad (1966–)
singer
This Dublin-born singer achieved success with her first album *The Lion and the Cobra* (1987), but reached celebrity status with her *Nothing Compares 2 U* (1990) that topped the charts in 17 countries. Later albums, such as *Am I Not Your Girl* (1993), *Universal Mother* (1994), and *Faith and Courage* (2000), have not been as acclaimed. Her troubled childhood and difficulties in her adult private life may well have prompted her controversial gestures, which included tearing up a picture of Pope John Paul II on an American television appearance and refusing to appear on stage if the American national anthem was played. A more recent provocative action involved her ordination as a priest by a dissenting Catholic priest who himself had been made a bishop by a schismatic Tridentine rite bishop.

O'Connor, Thomas Power (1848–1929)
journalist, politician
Born in Athlone, County Westmeath, O'Connor was educated at QUEEN'S COLLEGE Galway. He wrote in Dublin for *Saunders Newsletter* and joined the *London Daily Telegraph*. When he moved to England (1870) he became a strong supporter of the Home Rule Confederation of Great Britain, a support organization for the HOME RULE campaign in Ireland. From 1880 to 1885, he served as an IRISH PARLIAMENTARY PARTY member of parliament for Galway, and from 1885 to 1929 he continued as an Irish nationalist MP for Liverpool. He opposed Charles Stewart PARNELL in the split within the parliamentary party. He founded and edited several newspapers, including the *Star* in 1887, the *Sun* in 1893, and *T.P.'s Weekly* in

1902 (he was nicknamed "Tay Pay"). He was the first president of the British Board of Film Censors in 1917 and in his later years was known the "father of the House of Commons" in terms of longevity of service. He wrote several books, including *Life of Lord Beaconsfield* (1876), *Gladstone's House of Commons* (1885), *The Parnell Movement* (1886), and *Memoirs of an Old Parliamentarian* (1929).

O'Conor, Charles Owen (The O'Conor Don) (1838–1906)
politician, author

Born in Dublin, O'Conor was the eldest son of the O'Conors of Belanagare and Clonalis, County Roscommon. He was educated at Downside Abbey and at London University. He served as a Liberal member of parliament for Roscom-

Charles O'Conor *(Library of Congress)*

mon from 1860 to 1880. In parliament he championed Catholic causes, especially on education issues, and supported Issa BUTT's HOME RULE campaign. He served on various commissions relating to reform in penal servitude and in factory conditions and supported reform in the land tenure system. O'Conor served as president of the ROYAL IRISH ACADEMY and of the Society for the Preservation of the Irish Language. His writings included *The O'Conors of Connaught* (1891).

O'Conor, Roderic (1860–1940)
painter

Born in Milton, County Roscommon, O'Conor studied at the Metropolitan School of Art and the Royal Hibernian Academy in Dublin and at the Académie des Beaux-Arts in Antwerp, Belgium. He left Ireland in 1886 and began studying and painting in Paris. From 1891 to 1904 he lived in Brittany and was part of the Paul Gauguin circle of artists. O'Conor was also influenced by the work of van Gogh. His subjects included Breton peasants and seascapes, but when he returned to Paris in 1904 he turned to painting still lifes, nudes, and portraits. He moved permanently to Maine-et-Loire, France, where he is buried.

Ó Criomhthainn, Tomás (1856–1937)
fisherman, stonemason, writer

Ó Criomhthainn was a native of the BLASKET ISLANDS off County Kerry, which were a great source for scholars such as Robin Flower seeking the purest version of traditional Irish. As an adult he taught himself how to read and write the language that was his natural tongue, and when he left the Blaskets he began to write accounts of his own life there that were published as *Allagar na h-Inise* (1928). His autobiography came next, *An t-Oileanach* (1929), which was translated as *The Islandman* (1934) by Robin Flower. Flower later transcribed and published stories dictated by Ó Criomhthainn that were published as *Seanchas on Oileain Thiar* (1956). Other Blasket Island natives, including Peig Sayers and Muiris Ó Suileabhain, followed him in writing about their birthplace.

O'Curry, Eugene (1796–1862)
translator, archaeologist

Born in Doonaha, County Clare, O'Curry had no formal education. He was employed by the Ordinance Survey between 1835 and 1842 where he worked with John O'DONOVAN, his brother-in-law. He moved on to become a cataloguer in the ROYAL IRISH ACADEMY, TRINITY COLLEGE DUBLIN, and the British Museum. He later became a collaborator in translating Irish manuscripts such as the ANNALS OF THE FOUR MASTERS (1848–51) and *The Ancient Music of Ireland* (1855). He served as the first professor of history and archaeology at the Catholic University of Ireland. Three volumes of his lectures were published: *Lectures on the Manuscript Materials of Ancient Irish History* (1861), *On the Manners and Customs of Ancient Ireland* (1873), and (posthumously) *Ancient Laws of Ireland*.

Ó Dálaigh, Cearbhall (1911–1978)
lawyer, president of Ireland

Born in Bray, County Wicklow, and educated at University College Dublin, where he graduated in Celtic studies, and at the KING'S INN, Ó Dálaigh was called to the bar in 1934. He served as Gaelic editor of the IRISH PRESS from 1931 to 1942. He was an unsuccessful FIANNA FÁIL candidate for the DÁIL ÉIREANN in two elections, but he served as attorney general twice, from 1946 to 1948 and from 1951 to 1953. Ó Dálaigh was appointed to the Supreme Court in 1953 and became chief justice in 1961 and a member of the Europe Court of Justice in 1972. On the Supreme Court he was known for his liberal exercise of judicial review power in ruling certain rights as implicit in the constitution, even if not explicitly stated. When incumbent president Erskine CHILDERS died in office in 1974, he was selected unopposed as president. In 1976 he resigned in protest at the government's failure to rebuke the minister for defense, Patrick DONEGAN, for having labeled the

president "a thundering disgrace" because he had referred, as was his constitutional option, EMERGENCY POWERS LEGISLATION to the Supreme Court to rule on its constitutionality.

O'Dea, James Augustine (Jimmy Augustine O'Dean) (1899–1965)
comedian

Born in Dublin, O'Dea qualified as an optician in Edinburgh. However, he turned instead to the stage as a comedian, playing Dublin characters, especially a "Biddy Mulligan, the pride of the Coombe." He appeared on stage, such as at Dublin's Royal Theatre and the Gaiety Theatre, on the BBC, and in film, including *Penny Paradise* (1938) and *Darby O'Gill and the Little People* (1959), a Disney production in which he played the king of the leprechauns.

Ó Direáin, Máirtín (1910–1988)
poet

Born in Inishmore, one of the Aran Islands, Ó Direáin left the island at the age of 18 to work as a clerk for the Department of Posts and Telegraphs. Ten years later he moved to Dublin to become a civil servant in the Department of Education. While in Galway he had become involved in the Irish language movement and acted with Taibhdhearc na Gaillimhe. In Dublin he broadened his literary contacts and began writing poetry for various journals, including the IRISH PRESS. He published at his own expense several collections of his work, *Coinnlea Geala* (1942) and *Dainta Aniar* (1943). His work marked a break with traditional forms and meters and Ó Direáin has been called the first modern Irish poet. Later work, such as *Rogha Dainta* (1949), *O Morna agus Danta Eile* (1957), *Cloch Choirneil* (1966), and *Craobhog Dan* (1986), established his reputation. His poems reflect nostalgia for life on the Aran Islands and the alienation induced by modern urban life. He received an honorary doctorate from the National University of Ireland in 1977 and numerous other literary prizes, including the Ossian-Preis in Paris, also in 1977.

O'Doherty, Cahir (1587–1608)
lord of Inishowen

Favorably treated at the court of Elizabeth I and confirmed in his lands, O'Doherty was married to a daughter of Lord Gormanstown and appointed a justice of the peace and an alderman in Derry. He was foreman of the jury that regarded the Flight of the Earls as treasonous. However, Sir George Paulet, the governor of Derry, viewed him as a traitor also and required his posting sureties. When Paulet struck him in a dispute about the sale of land, he raised a rebellion that sacked the city and killed Paulet. However, he himself was killed shortly after in a skirmish near Kilmacrenan, County Donegal.

O'Donnell, Daniel (Danny O'Donnell) (1961–)
singer

Born in Kincaslough, County Donegal, O'Donnell began his singing career in the 1980s accompanying his sister Margo, a popular showband singer. Beginning in 1983 with a self-produced single, he has since eclipsed her. He is very well received in Britain and Ireland as well as among Irish-American audiences, and has 20 top-40 albums in Great Britain, and 15 top-40 singles. He appeals primarily to middle-aged audiences as his repertoire consists of a mix of popular traditional and religious music.

O'Donnell, Frank Hugh (F. H. O'Donnell) (1848–1916)
politician, journalist

Born in County Donegal and educated at QUEEN'S COLLEGE Galway, O'Donnell had a brief association with the IRISH REPUBLICAN BROTHERHOOD. He became a journalist, writing for *The Morning Post*. In 1874 he was elected to parliament for the city of Galway, but his election was disallowed on grounds of clerical intimidation on his behalf and on his libelling his opponent. He was elected for Dungarvin, County Waterford, three years later and held the seat until 1885. O'Donnell was an obstructionist, together with others such as Joseph BIGGAR and Charles Stewart PARNELL among the HOME RULE party. He was disappointed that he, rather than Parnell, had not succeeded Issac BUTT as leader and never worked well with Parnell or the LAND LEAGUE movement. Other members of the IRISH PARLIAMENTARY PARTY, including Tim HEALY, regarded him as a crank. He sued the *London Times* over its articles on "Parnellism and Crime." The tribunal held to rule on the lawsuit determined the articles to be forgeries and Parnell was vindicated. He wrote a number of books, including *How Home Rule Was Wrecked* (1895) and *History of the Parliamentary Party* (2 vols., 1910).

O'Donnell, Manus (1490–1564)
lord of Tyrconnell

He succeeded his father as Lord of Tyrconnell in 1537. In 1539 he joined Conn O'Neill, the lord of Tyrone, in an unsuccessful attempt to restore the earldom of Kildare to the nephew of his wife, Eleanor FitzGerald, but in the following year submitted to Henry VIII, in allowing his position to be regarded as coming from the king. He wrote bardic poetry.

O'Donnell, Peadar (1893–1986)
writer, revolutionary

Born in Meenmore, County Donegal, O'Donnell was educated at St. Patrick's College in Dublin. He was a teacher on Arranmore Island off the west coast of Donegal, but he also became a social activist as he traveled to Scotland to agitate on behalf of Donegal laborers who had emigrated there. He fought with the IRA in the WAR OF INDEPENDENCE, opposed the ANGLO-IRISH TREATY, and was imprisoned when the PROVISIONAL GOVERNMENT forces attacked the FOUR COURTS at the beginning of the CIVIL WAR. While in prison he was elected to the DÁIL ÉIREANN for Donegal in 1923 as a member of SINN FÉIN, but he did not take his seat. He was a member of the Executive and the Army Council of the IRA until 1924 and opposed those in Sinn Féin who switched to FIANNA FÁIL. He sought to turn Irish REPUBLICANISM in a more socialist direction in the late 1920s, serving as one of the founders of SAOR ÉIRE in 1931. He predated Fianna Fáil in demanding the end to payment of land annuities. In the 1930s he recruited volunteers for the Republican side in the Spanish Civil War and continued to try to move Irish republicanism in a socialist direction, founding the Republican Congress with George Gilmore and Frank RYAN. O'Donnell served as editor of *The Bell* from 1946 to 1954 and wrote several novels, usually depictions of rural life, such as *Islanders* (1928), *On the Edge of the Stream* (1934), *The Big Window* (1955), and *Proud Island* (1975), along with autobiographical works such as *The Gates Flew Open* (1932) and *There Will Be Another Day* (1963).

O'Donnell, "Red" Hugh (1571–1602)
lord, military leader

"Red" Hugh O'Donnell was the son of Hugh O'Donnell, the lord of Tir Connaill. He was kidnapped in 1587 on the orders of Sir John Perrott, the lord deputy, who sought a hostage because of his fear that the O'Donnell family posed a threat to British authority. He was imprisoned in DUBLIN CASTLE, but successfully escaped on Christmas night 1591. He became the chief of the O'Donnells in May 1592 and soon joined in the rebellion against English authority that became known as the Nine Years' War (1594–1603). A leader in the celebrated Irish victory at the Battle of the Yellow Ford in August 1598, he was successful in Sligo and elsewhere in Connacht. O'Donnell was an ally of Hugh O'Neill, the earl of TYRONE, who was also the lord of the O'Neills and the leading figure in Gaelic resistance to the Anglicization policy of the government. After the truce that O'Donnell and O'Neill forced on Robert Devereux, the earl of ESSEX, expired and an English offensive commenced under Charles Blount, lord MOUNT-JOY, their forces marched south to relieve a Spanish army under siege from Mountjoy. They were defeated in the Battle of KINSALE on Christmas Eve, 1601. Some suggest that O'Donnell's impetuosity outweighed O'Neill's policy to avoid direct confrontation and indirectly wear down the enemy. Soon after, O'Donnell went to

Spain seeking further assistance from King Philip III, who received him favorably, but he became ill and died the following September.

O'Donoghue, David James (1866–1917)
man of letters

Born in Chelsea and, having acquired only a local elementary school education, O'Donoghue was self-taught by reading in the British Museum. He began to write for various periodicals, including the *Dublin Evening Post*, and published an encyclopedia, *Poets of Ireland* (1892–93). Moving to Ireland, he operated his brother's bookselling and publishing business, and published further titles of his own, including a *Life of Emmet* (1907). He was made librarian at University College Dublin in 1909.

O'Donoghue, Martin (1933–)
economist, politician

Born in Dublin and educated at University College Dublin and at TRINITY COLLEGE DUBLIN, O'Donoghue was an economic consultant for the Department of Education and the Department of Finance and became the economic adviser to TAOISEACH Jack LYNCH from 1970 to 1973. Elected to the DÁIL ÉIREANN for Dun Laoghaire in 1977, he was the architect of the "supply side" economic manifesto that contributed to the FIANNA FÁIL party's massive victory in that election. He served as minister for economic planning and development, but the post was abolished when Charles J. HAUGHEY succeeded Lynch as Taoiseach in 1979. O'Donoghue served as minister for education in Haughey's second government in 1982, but he resigned his post as part of the anti-Haughey rebellion within the party. Not returned to the Dáil in the general election of that year, he was elected to the SEANAD, where he served until 1987.

O'Donovan, John (1809–1861)
scholar

Born in Attateemore, County Kilkenny, O'Donovan worked for the ORDINANCE SURVEY from 1830 to 1842. His travels all over Ireland investigating local place names and manuscripts prompted his writing a series of *Letters,* later published in 50 volumes (1924–32), that constitute an invaluable source of antiquarian information. He founded, along with his brother-in-law Eugene O'CURRY, the Irish Archaeological Society in 1840. He published a *Grammar of the Irish Language* (1845), and a translation of the ANNALS OF THE FOUR MASTERS in seven volumes (1848–51). He cataloged Irish manuscripts for TRINITY COLLEGE library, was called to the bar in 1847, and appointed professor of Celtic Studies at QUEEN'S COLLEGE Belfast, in 1852. He and O'Curry were translators of old Irish legal texts, but both died before publication of their work, *Ancient Laws of Ireland.*

O'Donovan Rossa, Jeremiah (1831–1915)

nationalist revolutionary

Born in Rosscarbery, County Cork, O'Donovan was an early member of the IRISH REPUBLICAN BROTHERHOOD. After a brief stay in the United States, he returned to manage the Fenian paper the *IRISH PEOPLE* in 1863. He was arrested and sentenced to life imprisonment in 1865, but he was released in 1871 along with other Fenians after an investigation determined that they had been maltreated. He accompanied John DEVOY to New York, where he remained very active in the IRB support organization, CLAN NA GAEL. He organized a "skirmishing fund," to support a violent campaign in Britain, which was opposed by Devoy, and he subsequently broke with Clan na Gael. O'Donovan visited Ireland twice in subsequent years, but lived the rest of his life in New York. When he died his remains were brought to Ireland. At his funeral in 1915 Patrick PEARSE gave his famous oration with the message that while she held the graves of her Fenian dead, "Ireland unfree shall never be at peace."

O'Duffy, Eoin (1892–1944)

soldier, police commissioner, politician

Born in Castleblayney, County Monaghan, O'Duffy was an assistant county surveyor. A member of the IRISH VOLUNTEERS, he commanded the Monaghan Brigade of the IRA during the WAR OF INDEPENDENCE. He became deputy chief of staff in the IRA and supported the ANGLO-IRISH TREATY. When Richard MULCAHY became minister for defense, he succeeded him as chief of staff in 1922. He had been elected to the DÁIL ÉIREANN for County Monaghan in 1921 and remained in office until appointed commissioner of police by Kevin O'HIGGINS later that year. O'Duffy played a significant role in developing a new unarmed police force at a time of CIVIL WAR and after. In 1924 he was given an additional post of inspector general of the defense forces following the ARMY MUTINY crisis and contributed to the subordination of the military to civilian authority. He continued as police commissioner, placing much emphasis on police participation in sports and in stimulating idealism and pride in the force. He was dismissed as police commissioner by Eamon DE VALERA in 1933 after the FIANNA FÁIL party advanced to an absolute majority after the second election in a year. O'Duffy subsequently headed an organization of former army officers, which was called the Army Comrades Association. He renamed it the National Guard. It joined with CUMANN NA GAEDHEAL and the NATIONAL CENTRE PARTY to form a new opposition group to Fianna Fáil, which was called FINE GAEL. O'Duffy became the first president of the new party. Under his leadership the movement began to manifest signs of the "shirted" politics common on the Continent at the time, including members of the National Guard wearing BLUESHIRTS, from which the nickname of the movement came. He tried to stage a march on Dublin in commemoration of the deaths of Arthur GRIFFITH, Michael COLLINS, and Kevin O'Higgins, but the de Valera government impeded its taking place as they feared marchers would seek to stage a coup d'état. The Fine Gael Party itself tired of O'Duffy's extravagance and political ineptitude, as evidenced by their very poor showing in 1934 local elections, and he resigned as leader. Several years later he recruited Irish volunteers in support of the Nationalist side in the Spanish Civil War, and several hundred spent six months with him there. When he died in 1944 he was given a state funeral.

O'Dwyer, Micheál (Mick O'Dwyer) (1936–)
Gaelic soccer player, coach
Born in Waterville, County Kerry, O'Dwyer first played for the county team in 1952 and played regularly for them between 1958 and 1974, when four All-Irelands were won. In 1975 he became manager of the team and in 15 years guided it to eight All-Irelands, including four years in succession from 1978 to 1981. In later years he became manager first of the Kildare team and later Laois. Under his tutelage both teams improved immensely from a previously long record of poor to average performance.

Ó Faich, Tomás (1923–1990)
cardinal, scholar
Born in Crossmaglen, County Armagh, Ó Faich was educated at St. Patrick's College, Armagh, MAYNOOTH, University College Dublin, and Louvain. He was ordained a priest in 1948 and taught history at Maynooth from 1953 to 1974 when he became the institution's president. He was a fluent Irish speaker and his academic specialization was the early Irish missionaries to the Continent in the sixth and seventh centuries. He became archbishop of Armagh and primate of Ireland in 1977 and was made a cardinal in 1979. His period as primate included the first and only visit to Ireland by a pope, John Paul II in 1979, and some of the more difficult episodes of the Northern Ireland conflict, especially the 1981 HUNGER STRIKES. He had the monumental task of reconciling ecumenical and peaceful goals with his own personal roots in fiercely republican south Armagh and his sensitivity to maltreatment of prisoners by the authorities. The Catholic Church continued to wield sufficient influence in Ireland in his time to successfully promote an antiabortion constitutional amendment (1983) and discourage an amendment allowing divorce (1985). He died en route to Lourdes, France.

O'Faolain, Seán (1900–1991)
writer
Born in the city of Cork, Daniel CORKERRY was an early mentor. O'Faolain was educated at University College Cork and later at Harvard. He took part in the WAR OF INDEPENDENCE and on the anti-treaty side in the CIVIL WAR. Both experiences provided the background for many of his short stories. His first collection was *Midsummer Night's Madness* (1932). He also wrote novels, one of which, *Bird Alone* (1936), was banned by the Irish censors. He wrote biographies, including one about Daniel O'CONNELL, *King of Beggars* (1938), and Hugh O'NEILL, *The Great O'Neill* (1942), collections of essays, such as *The Irish* (1947), and an autobiography, *Vive Moi!* (1965). In 1941 he founded the *Bell*, a literary journal that challenged the autocratic and theocratic atmosphere of independent Ireland, and continued to edit it until 1946. He developed a theory of the short story, influenced by Maupassant and Chekhov, which appeared as *The Short Story* (1948), and he continued to write many of them himself, one collection of which was *I Remember! I Remember!* (1962) that has as its recurring theme the Catholic middle class of independent Ireland, which he depicts as repressed.

Offaly
A midlands county in Leinster, Offaly is south of County Westmeath. The Slieve Bloom Mountains separate it from County Laois to the south. On the west the Shannon River runs between it and the neighboring counties of Roscommon and Galway. Tipperary is to its southwest, and Meath and Kildare are to its east. Together with Laois, Offaly was part of the first plantation under Queen Mary, and was established as Kings County in honor of King Philip II of Spain, Mary's husband. The name Offaly was restored after independence. In the east of the county are raised bog lands known as the Bog of Allen and to the west are the grasslands that become the floodplain of the Shannon River. The county town is Tullamore with a population of 10,260, while Birr is the major town in the southwest of

the county. A major industry is peat production, as well as grazing and the growth of cereals. The total population is 63,702 and the area is 772 square miles.

Offences against the State Act   See
EMERGENCY POWERS LEGISLATION.

Official IRA
When the Northern Ireland troubles began in the summer of 1969, many NATIONALISTS and REPUBLICANS in the North were disappointed at the inability of the IRA to give them protection against LOYALIST mobs and the B Specials. They blamed the primarily Dublin-based leadership of the IRA and SINN FÉIN for the state of unpreparedness as the primary emphasis of the leadership since the end of the campaign of the late 1950s and early 1960s had been on pursuing a left-wing social agenda rather than the national struggle. A split resulted in the following winter when those who held a more nationalist rather than socialist temperament formed a separate organization that was given the temporary name of Provisional IRA and PROVISIONAL SINN FÉIN. The breakaway group won the support of most Irish nationalist activists in the United States. Those who remained loyal to the existing leadership called themselves the OFFICIAL IRA and OFFICIAL SINN FÉIN. Their socialism at first did not inhibit their talking part in violent actions, including a futile bombing of a British army base in England, Aldermaston, in which many of the victims were Catholic working women. But by 1972 they suspended their military operations and regarded the irredentist struggle as inherently sectarian. Members who would not go along with this approach separated into another group that called itself the IRISH NATIONAL LIBERATION ARMY, which never had a very large following, but which committed some of the more atrocious deeds during the troubles. The political wing of Official SINN FÉIN a number of years later called itself Sinn Féin—the Workers' Party, and later just the Workers' Party. A further split

developed after the discovery in the 1990s that the group had received subsidies from the Soviet Union, and most members formed a new organization, the Democratic Left, that several years later amalgamated with the LABOUR PARTY.

Official Sinn Féin
Majors portions of the membership of both SINN FÉIN and the IRA broke with the movement's leadership in early 1970 because of dissatisfaction over its being unprepared for the violent confrontations of the previous summer in Northern Ireland, as well as with its internationalist and socialist agenda. The supporters of the leadership were called OFFICIAL SINN FÉIN in contrast to those breaking away who were labeled PROVISIONAL SINN FÉIN. The challengers drew the support of most of the members and over a period of time would be considered Sinn Féin without the possibly pejorative adjective. At first Official Sinn Féin did not reject violence, but was not as adept at employing it, and ultimately abandoned it, renaming itself Sinn Féin the Worker's Party and then just the WORKERS' PARTY.

O'Flaherty, Hugh (1898–1963)
priest
Born in Cahirciveen, County Kerry, O'Flaherty studied theology in the Killarney seminary and in Rome. He was ordained in 1925 and worked in the Vatican. He served as a diplomat for the Holy See in Egypt, Haiti, Santo Domingo, and Czechoslovakia, and in 1934 was named a monsignor. During the Second World War he visited prisoner-of-war camps in Italy and used Vatican Radio to get word to the families of prisoners if their loved ones were alive. When Italy withdrew from the Axis and released thousands of prisoners, O'Flaherty recruited other priests and even communists in the Resistance in facilitating the concealment of several thousand escaped Allied soldiers and Jews from the German forces who still controlled much of Italy. Although he often wore disguises, the Germans discovered

his involvement. Afterward, he stayed within the diplomatically immune Vatican to meet his contacts. After the liberation of Italy, he was as solicitous for aiding Germans who had become prisoners, including the SS chief in Rome, who had sought to have him arrested. After the war he received a CBE and the U.S. Medal of Freedom. He retired to Ireland after suffering a stroke in 1960 and settled in Cahirciveen to live with his sister and died there in 1963. He was portrayed by Gregory Peck in the film *The Scarlet and the Black* (1983), which dealt with his activities in Rome during the war.

O'Flaherty, Liam (1896–1984)
writer

Born on Inishmore, the largest of the Aran Islands, O'Flaherty studied at Rockwell College in Tipperary. He entered the Holy Ghost Fathers aspiring for the priesthood and studied at BLACK-ROCK COLLEGE and University College Dublin. Abandoning his vocation he joined the Irish Guards and was wounded on active duty on the western front during the First World War. After the war he traveled throughout Europe and the Americas. Returning to Ireland, he was a founding member of the Communist Party. He was one of a group that took over the Rotunda in Dublin in January 1922 to draw attention to social problems. He sympathized with the anti-treaty forces in the CIVIL WAR, but went to London to avoid arrest by the PROVISIONAL GOVERNMENT. O'Flaherty then began writing novels and short stories, beginning with *Thy Neighbour's Wife* (1923), which was followed by *Spring Sowing* (1923) and *The Black Soul* (1924). His next work, *The Informer* (1925) won the James Tait Black Memorial Prize and was adapted into a successful motion picture produced by John Ford. He visited the Soviet Union and Hollywood and continued producing a great number of novels and short stories, including *Civil War* (1925), *The Assassin* (1928), *The Mountain Tower and Other Stories* (1929), *Skerrett* (1932), *Shame the Devil* (1934), *Famine* (1937), and *Insurrection* (1950). Later publications, such as *Dull* (1953), were collections of his short sto-

ries. His works entailed a mixture of historical fiction, autobiographical experience, and psychological insight.

O'Flaherty, Roderic (1629–1718)
landlord, scholar

Born at Moycullen Castle, County Galway, O'Flaherty studied at St. Nicholas' College, Galway. He was deprived of most of his family estate after the wars of the 1640s, although he secured a partial restoration in the 1670s. Although impoverished, he wrote a history of Ireland in Latin, *Ogygia, seu Rerum Hibernicarum Chronologia* (1685), which was published in England, and a description and local history of his own area of Ireland in English, *Chronological Description of West or h-Iar Connaught* (1684), which was not published until 1846 by the Irish Archaeological Society.

O'Grady, Standish James (1846–1928)
writer

Born in Castletown, Berehaven, County Cork, and educated at TRINITY COLLEGE DUBLIN, O'Grady was called to Irish bar, but, under the influence of John O'DONOVAN and Eugene O'CURRY, he turned to popularizing the work of antiquarians and other scholars about ancient Irish history. His books included *History of Ireland-Heroic Period* (2 vols., 1878–91), *Early Bardic Literature of Ireland* (1879), *Finn and His Companions* (1892), and the *Coming of Cuchulain* (1894). His worked helped inspire both the LITERARY REVIVAL and the GAELIC LEAGUE. Many of his books exhibited the character of adventure stories designed to inspire young readers with an interest in Gaelic myth and tradition. He personally held an aristocratic and UNIONIST perspective, as he opposed HOME RULE, and expressed a romantic vision that looked to the Anglo-Irish landlords to accept Gaelic identity, resist NATIONALISM and democracy, and become the natural leaders of an Ireland where differences between Protestants and Catholics would be healed. Disillusionment following the advance of nationalism, especially revolutionary nationalism, prompted his permanent departure from Ireland in 1918.

O'Growney, Eugene (1863–1899)

clergyman, Irish language revivalist

Born in Ballyfallon, County Meath, and educated at St. Finian's College, Navan, and at MAYNOOTH, O'Growney developed an interest in the Irish language as a youth and spent his holidays in various Irish-speaking areas, including Kerry, Donegal, and the Aran Islands. He was ordained a priest in 1889 and became curate at Ballynacargy, County Westmeath. He contributed articles in Irish to the *Gaelic Journal,* whose editor he became in 1891. He became professor of Irish at Maynooth in 1891 and was made vice president of the GAELIC LEAGUE in 1893. He wrote weekly lessons in Irish for the *Gaelic Journal* and for the *Weekly Freeman,* which were published in book form as *Simple Lessons in Irish* (1894). Ill health required that he move to the dry climate of Arizona in 1894 and his failure to recover necessitated his resigning from Maynooth, although he continued to write for the *Weekly Freeman.* He died in 1899 in Los Angeles, but Americans contributed funds to have his remains reinterned at Maynooth in 1901.

O'Hanlon, Redmond, Count (d. 1681)

outlawed chieftain

O'Hanlon was a Gaelic chieftain whose estates in Ulster were seized after the Cromwellian conquest. During the 1670s he led an outlaw band, nicknamed "Tories," who were able to gain tribute in Armagh and Tyrone. DUBLIN CASTLE put a price on his head and, in 1681, his foster brother killed him at Eightmilebridge, County Down, and his head was placed on a spike over Downpatrick Jail.

O'Hara, Maureen (1920–   )

film actress

Born in Dublin, Maureen O'Hara appeared on the radio as a child and in the ABBEY THEATRE as a teenager. After her appearance in an Irish film *My Irish Molly* (1938), she began a Hollywood career in *The Hunchback of Notre Dame* (1939). She appeared in 50 films and her most famous performances were in playing the female lead roles in *How Green Was My Valley* (1941) and *The Quiet Man* (1952), both made by John Ford.

O'Hegarty, Patrick Sarsfield (1879–1955)

civil servant, writer

Born in Carrignavar, County Cork, O'Hegarty was educated at the IRISH CHRISTIAN BROTHERS' School North Monastery, Cork. He worked for the Post Office in both Cork and London. During the First World War he was transferred back to England, but in 1918 he resigned rather than comply with a required oath of allegiance. Already active in various Irish organizations, including the IRISH REPUBLICAN BROTHERHOOD, he opened a bookstore in Dublin. He was a regular contributor to the *Irish Book Lover* and to *Irish Freedom,* which he edited from 1911 to 1914. As a member of the Supreme Council of the IRB, he accepted the ANGLO-IRISH TREATY. In 1922 he became secretary to the Department of Posts and Telegraphs and remained in that position until his retirement in 1944. He wrote numerous books, including *John Mitchell* (1917), *Sinn Féin, an Illumination* (1919), *Ulster: A Brief Statement of Fact* (1919), *A Short Memory of Terence MacSweeney* (1922), *The Victory of Sinn Féin* (1924), and *A History of Ireland under the Union* (1952). He also published bibliographies of numerous figures in modern Irish history, including Patrick PEARSE, Arthur GRIFFITH, Michael COLLINS, Kevin O'HIGGINS, and Roger CASEMENT. He edited a short-lived journal *The Separatist,* which sought to reconcile CIVIL WAR antagonists.

Ó Hehir, Micheál (1920–1997)

sports broadcaster

Born in Dublin, Ó Hehir made his first public broadcast in announcing the 1938 All Ireland semi-final. He went on to broadcast Gaelic matches for almost 50 years, and continued doing telecasts of the same. His broadcasts were relayed to distant Irish communities in the South Pacific and in Africa, as well as the United States. He had a capability to capture and transfer the excitement of the match to his listeners in the radio audience and possibly make the event even more exciting than it was. He covered other sporting events, including horse races, and was the commentator for the radio and television coverage of the visit in 1963 to Ireland by President John F. Kennedy and the coverage in Ireland of Kennedy's funeral in Washington, D.C., several months later. He was a racing correspondent for the IRISH INDEPENDENT, head of sports for RADIO TELEFÍS ÉIREANN, and a columnist for the Sunday Press. A stroke in August 1985 ended his broadcasting career.

O'Higgins, Ambrose (1720–1801)
viceroy of Peru

Born in Dangan Castle, County Meath, O'Higgins was sent to Cadiz with expectations of entering the priesthood. Instead, he went to Peru, where, after several unsuccessful attempts in business, he entered the army engineer corps and gained rapid promotion as Count of Bellenar, then Marquis of Osmorno, and the governor general, or viceroy, of Peru from 1796 to 1801.

O'Higgins, Bernardo (1778–1842)
father of Chilean independence

Born in Chile, the son of Ambrose O'HIGGINS, Bernardo O'Higgins was educated in England and Spain, and returned to Chile in 1802. After his father's death he became active in the cause of Chilean independence from Spain. He joined the revolution in 1810 and was commander of the Chilean army in 1813. When the rising was defeated, he fled to Argentina, but returned to lead a successful revolt in 1817–18. He became the supreme director and virtual dictator until 1823. He instituted reforms in education and land tenure and sought to curb bull fighting and

gambling. Conservative elements opposed to such reforms forced him from power and he lived the rest of his life in Peru.

O'Higgins, Kevin (1892–1927)
politician

Born in Stradbally, County Laois, educated at CLONGOWES WOOD COLLEGE, Knockbeg College, County Carlow, MAYNOOTH, the Catholic Seminary in Carlow, and University College Dublin (UCD), his grandfather was T. D. SULLIVAN, a leading figure in the IRISH PARLIAMENTARY PARTY. He had aspired to the priesthood, but abandoned that pursuit after disciplinary and academic difficulties in seminaries, and turned to law, studying first at UCD. He joined the IRISH VOLUNTEERS and SINN FÉIN. He was imprisoned for several months in 1918 for seditious agitation in speaking against conscription. He was a successful SINN FÉIN candidate for Laois in the 1918 general election and sat in the first DÁIL ÉIREANN. He was elected to the second and third Dáils for the combined Laois-Offaly constituency. He was appointed an assistant to William T. COSGRAVE in the Ministry of Local Government and played a major role in directing local elected bodies to transfer their allegiance to the Dáil government. O'Higgins was asked by Eamon DE VALERA to take part in cabinet meetings, even though he was not a minister. De Valera sought to nominate him as part of the negotiating team for the ANGLO-IRISH TREATY, but he declined in view of his impending marriage. He broke with de Valera in becoming one of the foremost champions of the treaty. He served as economics minister in the PROVISIONAL GOVERNMENT, and was one of the central negotiators with the British in transferring authority and winning acceptance of the constitution for the IRISH FREE STATE. When the CIVIL WAR started he was assigned to the military as an assistant adjutant-general. After the deaths of Arthur GRIFFITH and Michael COLLINS, he became minister for home affairs (later renamed justice) and vice president of the Executive Council in the government led by William T. Cosgrave. O'Higgins directed Dáil consideration and approval of the Irish Free State constitution. During and after the civil war, he was identified with those taking a very hard line against the anti-treaty forces. He even acceded reluctantly to the retaliatory executions of four republican prisoners (including his own best man (Rory O'CONNOR), in retaliation for the launching by the IRISH REPUBLICAN ARMY (IRA) of an assassination campaign against members of the Dáil. His own father was subsequently killed in an IRA raid on his home. In the 1923 general election after the civil war, he was returned to the Dáil for County Dublin, and again in the 1927 election. In both cases he served as a member of the CUMANN NA NGAEDHEAL Party, which had been formed to support the government and to draw support from the many in Ireland who had not identified with Sinn Féin. For two years after the civil war, he had various forms of EMERGENCY POWERS legislation enacted until finally he was satisfied that standard public safety legislation could restrain armed opponents of the state. On the other hand, he directed, even during the civil war, the development of an unarmed police force and moved to restore a normal judiciary, replacing both military courts and the revolutionary Dáil Éireann courts. He was also very insistent on employment of civil service principles in the recruitment of a public service for the government and not to regard service in the revolution as a guarantee of employment. After the ARMY MUTINY in 1924 and during the illness of Cosgrave, he acted against both the mutinous Old IRA and the IRISH REPUBLICAN BROTHERHOOD, which the minister for defense, Richard MULCAHY, and the Military Council had hoped to employ against the former, as he insisted on the ascendancy of civilian authority over the military and any private organizations within the military. When the BOUNDARY COMMISSION report proved so disappointing to nationalist aspirations, he took part in the negotiations that resulted in the status quo being retained in return for the Free State being excused of its treaty obligation to contribute to the imperial debt at the time it attained self-government. He secured legislation curbing the hours of sale of intoxicating liquor and limiting the number of licensed premises. During the Imperial Confer-

ence in 1926 he was a leading figure advancing the autonomy of the Irish Free State and other dominions, which received legislative acknowledgment with passage of the STATUTE OF WESTMINSTER in 1932. At the same conference he broached the concept of a dual monarchy solution as a means to unite Ireland under a joint monarch who would also be the king of Britain. It reflected his increasing sensitivity to Northern Ireland UNIONIST identity as a prerequisite to any ultimate reunification. On July 10, 1927, three IRA gunmen, probably acting on their own initiative and impulsively upon seeing him, shot him while he was walking to Mass not far from his home. His dying words struck notes of forgiveness and a plea for the end of violence in Ireland. Legislation proposed after his assassination forced Eamon de Valera and his FIANNA FÁIL Party to take their seats in the Dáil and to become a constitutional rather than an abstentionist opposition.

O'Higgins, Thomas (1916–2003)
politician, jurist

Born in County Cork, O'Higgins was the son of Dr. T. F. O'Higgins, a leading figure in the Army Comrades Association and in the FINE GAEL Party, and the nephew of Kevin O'HIGGINS. He was educated at CLONGOWES WOOD COLLEGE, University College Dublin, and the King's Inn, and called to the bar in 1938. He was a Fine Gael TD for Laois-Offaly from 1948 to 1973 and was Minister for Health in the second coalition government from, 1954 to 1957, when he started the state-run Voluntary Health Insurance system. He was twice the Fine Gael candidate for the Irish presidency, narrowly losing to Eamon DE VALERA in 1966 by only 11,000 votes, and losing by almost 50,000 to Erskine CHILDERS in 1973. He was of the Irish Supreme Court from 1974 to 1985 and was a judge on the European Union Court of Justice from 1985 to 1991.

Ó hUiginn, Tadhg Dall (1550–1591)
poet

Born in Sligo and raised in Donegal, Ó hUiginn was trained as a bardic poet. About 40 of his poems survive, and they consist of tributes addressed to various local lords, such as the O'Neills, the Maguires, and his patron, the O'Connor Sligo. His work constitutes an excellent manifestation of bardic style. It gives a good impression of the life of the Gaelic aristocracy.

Old English

The term refers to those in the 16th and 17th centuries whose antecedents had come to Ireland as part of the ANGLO-NORMAN settlements of several centuries before. They had resisted the centralization of government in hands of newly appointed officials, recently from England, the "New English," during the reign of the Tudors and the Stuarts, especially to the subordination of the Old English quasi-feudal authority to political officers and to the imposition of the Protestant Reformation on the church in Ireland. At the same time the Old English did not naturally ally with the Gaelic society, in spite of common opposition to the New English and to the Reformation, as their collaboration in the CONFEDERATION OF KILKENNY in the 1640s was beset by distrust and disparity of objectives and strategies.

O'Leary, John (1830–1907)

Fenian

Born in Tipperary and educated at TRINITY COLLEGE DUBLIN, O'Leary abandoned legal studies when he realized that being a barrister required taking an oath of allegiance to the British crown. He tried studying medicine at both QUEEN'S COLLEGE Cork and Queen's College Galway, but was unsuccessful. He was imprisoned for a short while after involvement in NATIONALIST skirmishes in Tipperary in 1848. He was editor of the *Irish People,* the Fenian paper, from 1863 to 1865 when he was arrested and sentenced to 20 years imprisonment. He was released after nine years on the condition that he stay out of Ireland for the rest of the term. O'Leary spent his exile in Paris and returned to Ireland in 1885. He wrote his *Recollections of Fenians and Fenianism* (1896) and had a remarkable influence on W. B. YEATS and his interest in Irish history.

Omagh

The county town of TYRONE, population about 20,000, and the location of the Ulster-American Folk Park, which was the scene of the deadliest bombing of the modern Northern Ireland troubles on August 15, 1998, several months afer the GOOD FRIDAY AGREEMENT. Dissident republicans, specifically the Real IRA, whose political wing is the 32 County Sovereignty Movement, and who had not accepted the cease-fire, gave inaccurate warning messages that sent crowds in the direction of a bomb that had been planted in a car. There were 29 deaths, including two unborn twins, and 310 injuries.

O'Mahony, Eoin ("Pope" O'Mahony) (1904–1970)

raconteur

Born in Cork and educated at Presentation College, Cork, CLONGOWES WOOD COLLEGE, University College Dublin, TRINITY COLLEGE DUBLIN, and the KING'S INN, he qualified and practiced for a few years as a barrister. He made several unsuccessful efforts to run for the DÁIL ÉIREANN as a FIANNA FÁIL candidate. Later he turned to genealogy, and became renowned as an authority on Irish families and great houses, as he appeared regularly on the radio and traveled and lectured extensively in Europe and in the United States, where he was a visiting professor at the University of Southern Illinois. He was also made a Knight of Malta, which might have a partial reason for his nickname.

O'Mahony, John (1815–1877)

Fenian leader

Born in Kilbeheny, County Limerick, O'Mahony was educated at TRINITY COLLEGE DUBLIN. He took part in the 1848 YOUNG IRELAND uprising, after which he fled to Paris. There he became acquainted with James STEPHENS. Although he went to New York, where he translated Geoffrey Keating's *History of Ireland* (1857), he remained involved in the Irish NATIONALIST cause and joined with Stephens in forming the IRISH REPUBLICAN BROTHERHOOD and its American counterpart, the FENIANS, among whom he was the Head Centre. He also served as an officer in the Union army in the American Civil War. Both he and Stephens lost their leadership positions in 1867 over their failure to expedite a rising in Ireland and an invasion of Canada, although he later attempted an unsuccessful effort to carry out the latter. His remains were brought back to Ireland and he was buried in a Fenian-type funeral reminiscent of that of Terence Bellew MACMANUS, which he had attended in 1861, and followed in 1915 by that of Jeremiah O'DONOVAN ROSSA.

O'Malley, Desmond (1939–)

politician

Born in Limerick, educated at Crescent College, Limerick, University College Dublin, and the incorporated Law Society, O'Malley was the nephew of Donogh O'MALLEY, and succeeded him as a FIANNA FÁIL member of the DÁIL ÉIREANN for Limerick East in 1968. He held that seat until his retirement in 2002. He was a parliamentary secretary for TAOISEACH Jack LYNCH in 1969 and was minister for justice from 1970 to 1973. He was strongly opposed to the IRA and promoted legislation for nonjury trials for certain types of cases. He was minister for industry, commerce, and energy in Lynch's ministry from 1977 to 1979. Although he supported George Colley in the party vote to select a successor to the retiring Lynch in 1979, the successive Charles HAUGHEY appointed him minister for industry, commerce, and tourism from 1979 to 1981 and again in his short ministry in 1982. However, he resigned after refusing to support Haughey in a challenge to his leadership in October. In 1985 he was expelled from the party and formed a new party, the PROGRESSIVE DEMOCRATS, whose program was for social liberalism, market economics, and flexibility with regard to NORTHERN IRELAND. When failing to secure an absolute majority in the 1989 election, Charles Haughey agreed to lead Fianna Fáil in its first coalition in history with O'Malley's Progressive Democrats. O'Mal-

ley served again as minister for industry and commerce. In 1992 O'Malley and the Progressive Democrats forced Haughey to resign over allegations that he was aware of earlier wiretapping of journalists by threatening to withdraw from the coalition. Later that year O'Malley and his party withdrew from the coalition following a dispute with Haughey's successor, Albert REYNOLDS, over allegations regarding government favoritism in its subsidization of the beef export industry. A subsequent election resulted in a short-lived Fianna Fáil–LABOUR coalition government. O'Malley subsequently resigned as leader of the Progressive Democrats, being succeeded by Mary HARNEY, the first-ever female party leader. He was unsuccessful in an election to the European Parliament in 1994. He stepped down from the Dáil in 2002.

O'Malley, Donogh (1921–1968)

politician

Born in Limerick, educated at Crescent College, Limerick, CLONGOWES WOOD COLLEGE, and University College Galway, and qualified as an engineer, O'Malley was elected as a FIANNA FÁIL member of the DÁIL ÉIREANN for Limerick East in 1961 and in 1965. He was minister for health from 1965 to 1966 and minister for education from 1966 to his death. He established free education in secondary education, closed many small rural elementary schools, provided transportation to more centralized schools and to secondary schools, began leaving certificates in vocational schools, and tried unsuccessfully to merge TRINITY COLLEGE DUBLIN and University College Dublin.

O'Malley, Ernie (1898–1957)

revolutionary republican

Born in Castlebar, County Mayo, O'Malley was educated at the O'Connell Schools and University College Dublin, where he studied medicine. He joined the IRISH VOLUNTEERS during the EASTER RISING. He was interned afterward.

During the WAR OF INDEPENDENCE, he traveled throughout Ireland organizing the IRISH REVOLUTIONARY ARMY (IRA). He was captured and tortured in 1920, but escaped in 1921 to become commander of the Second Southern Division of the IRA. He opposed the ANGLO-IRISH TREATY and was a leading figure in the occupation of the FOUR COURTS. He escaped capture during its siege by the PROVISIONAL GOVERNMENT forces, but continued as a member of the Army Council of the anti-treaty IRA until his capture in November 1922. He remained imprisoned until July 1924, taking part in a HUNGER STRIKE in the fall of 1923 and being returned as SINN FÉIN member of the DÁIL ÉIREANN for Dublin North in the 1923 election. After release he traveled in Spain, then the United States and Mexico. He raised money for the formation of the IRISH PRESS, studied art, and wrote. He married an American sculptor, Helen Hooker, and returned to Ireland in the mid 1930s. The first volume of his memoirs of the war of independence, *Another Man's Wound* (1936) brought him literary fame. In 1947 he was elected to the Irish Academy of Letters. A sequel to his autobiography, *The Singing Flame,* was published posthumously in 1978. It deals with the CIVIL WAR period.

O'Malley, Grace (c. 1530–c. 1600)

sea captain, tribal leader

Born in County Mayo, O'Malley came from a seafaring family. Much of the account of her life is based on legend. Her nickname "Grainne Mhaol," is alleged to have derived from her having cropped her hair closely to look like a boy when accompanying her father on voyages. Her first husband was Donall O'Flaherty from West Galway. After he died, leaving her with three children, she married Richard Burke of the prominent Mayo family. Her capability as a sea captain made her a source of concern to the English authorities. She was imprisoned at times in Limerick and in DUBLIN CASTLE after conflict with the British forces. Later she was threatened with execution, but obtained release by a pledge from her son-in-law. At another time she took refuge in Ulster, but obtained pardon from Queen Eliz-

abeth, allowing her to return to Connacht. She is reported to have traveled to London where she met with the queen in 1593 and obtained certain property concessions. However, she later supported the northern earls in their rebellion.

Ó Móráin, Donál (1923–2001)

Gaelic language revivalist

Born in Waterville, County Kerry, educated at Colaiste Mhuire, University College Dublin, and the KING'S INN, Ó Móráin was called to the bar in 1946. He became the chairman of Gael-Linn, an organization promoting the use of Irish and economic development of the Irish-speaking areas in 1963. From 1970 to 1972, he was chairman of the RADIO TELEFÍS ÉIREANN Authority, but the government dismissed the members of the body when a directive against carrying material supportive of violent organizations was breached following an interview of the chief of staff of the IRA. However, he was reappointed to the authority by the coalition government from 1973 to 1976, and he continued on the board of Gael Linn.

O'More, Rory (c. 1592–c. 1666)

descendant of Gaelic chieftain

Rory O'More was the grandson of the O'More chieftain who had been deposed with the PLANTATION of Laois and Offaly. Owner of a castle in Kildare and married to a member of a prominent OLD ENGLISH Catholic family, he was one of the participants in the failed plot to seize DUBLIN CASTLE in October 1641. O'More was a minor figure in the Catholic Confederation and escaped imprisonment after the conquest of Ireland by the forces of Oliver CROMWELL by hiding.

See also TYRONE, CONN O'NEILL, FIRST EARL OF.

O'Neill, Hugh, second earl of Tyrone

See TYRONE, HUGH O'NEILL, SECOND EARL OF.

O'Neill, Owen Roe (1590–1649)

military commander

The nephew of Hugh O'Neill, the second earl of TYRONE, he served in the Spanish army until he came to Ireland in 1642 to take part in the rebellion that had started as part of the CONFEDERATION OF KILKENNY in which the Gaelic and OLD ENGLISH Catholics had joined to fight for the king, for Ireland, and for Catholicism. He led his forces to a major victory against the Scottish army under Robert Monro at the Battle of BENBURB. However, rather than extending his control over Ulster, he moved south and became embroiled in the internal disputes of the confederation. O'Neill died in 1649 on his way to join a futile new alliance of royalists and Gaelic forces against the soon-to-be-successful forces of Oliver CROMWELL.

O'Neill, Shane (1530–1567)
O'Neill chieftain

Son of Conn O'Neill, first earl of TYRONE, he challenged the claim of his half-brother, Matthew, to succeed the father as Baron Dungannon and as earl of Tyrone, and had him killed. He fought with other clans in Ulster, including the O'Donnells of Tir Chonaill and the Scot McDonnells in Antrim, leaving hundreds dead. He unsuccessfully sought to gain recognition from Queen Elizabeth as the earl of Tyrone. When defeated in battle by the O'Donnells, he sought refuge from the McDonnells in Cushendum, but they murdered him in 1567.

O'Neill, Sir Phelim (1605–1653)
military leader

Although brought up in the PALE, educated at Lincoln's Inn, made a justice of the peace, elected a member of the Irish parliament for Dungannon, and socially associated with the Protestant planter class, he was one of the leaders of the uprising in Ulster in 1641. He insisted he had taken up arms in defense of the king against the parliamentary forces, but the uprising turned very sectarian with numerous atrocities being committed against the Protestants. Owen Roe O'NEILL surpassed him in importance in the CONFEDERATION OF KILKENNY. After the triumph of the Cromwellian army he was betrayed and executed in 1653.

O'Neill, Terence, Lord O'Neill of the Maine (1914–1990)
politician

Born in London, educated at Eton College, Terence O'Neill served as a captain in the Irish Guards from 1939 to 1945. He was elected a UNIONIST MP for Bannside, County Antrim, in the Northern Ireland PARLIAMENT in 1946 and served as parliamentary secretary to the minister for health (1948–52), Deputy Speaker of the House (1953–56), minister for home affairs (1956), and minister for finance (1956–63). In the last post he successfully attracted foreign investment and industry. He succeeded Sir Basil Brooke, Lord BROOKEBOROUGH, as leader of the Unionists and as prime minister in 1963. He brought a broader, less provincial or defensive vision to NORTHERN IRELAND, as he opened contacts with the Catholic minority community, although not without a patronizing tone, and with the government of Ireland. He held an exchange of visits with the TAOISEACH, Seán LEMASS. These gestures irritated elements in the unionist population, especially independent Evangelical minister Ian PAISLEY. At the same time they emboldened many in the Catholic population to call for civil liberties as opposed to irredentist demands. Demonstrations, sit-ins, and marches were met by counterdemonstrations and violence, often tolerated by the police, and participated in by the police auxiliaries. In November 1968 he announced a program of reforms. Opposition within his cabinet led to the dismissal of William Craig, the minister for home affairs. In a general election in February 1969, O'Neill narrowly retained his own seat in Bannside against Paisley, while the majority in the parliamentary party continued to support him. But in April things turned against him and he resigned as prime minister and party leader, being replaced by Major James CHICHESTER-CLARK, his own cousin, whose resignation as minister for agriculture had precipitated the crisis.

O'Neill, Turlough (1530–1595)
Ulster chieftain

The successor to Shane O'NEILL as the leader of the O'Neills, he was married to Lady Agnes

Campbell, the daughter of the earl of Argyll, which gave him access to the support of thousands of Scottish mercenaries. He played a role as protector of the Gaelic Irish in Ulster, although also bargaining with the British administrators in Dublin, including Lord Deputy, Sir Henry Sidney and Lord Deputy Sir John Perrot. He remained on amicable terms with the authorities when Hugh O'Neill second earl of TYRONE, began to challenge them. Hugh O'Neill succeeded him as the leader of the O'Neills.

O'Nolan, Brian (1911–1966)
novelist, columnist

Born in Strabane, County Tyrone, O'Nolan was educated at BLACKROCK COLLEGE and at University College Dublin. He worked as civil servant until he retired in 1952 owing to ill health. He wrote a number of novels and plays under the pen name of Flann O'Brien, such as *At-swim-two-birds* (1939), *An Beal Bocht* (in Irish) (1941), *The Hard Life* (1961), and *Faustus Kelly* (1943). He is possibly better remembered for his satirical column in the IRISH TIMES titled *An Cruiskeen Lawn*, written under the pen name, Myles na Gopaleen. Objects of his scorn were pompous, but hypocritical and ill-informed, champions of Irish culture. His works often interwove elements of Celtic mythology with modern life.

O'Rahilly, Alfred (1884–1969)
academic, clergyman

Born in Listowel, County Kerry, O'Rahilly was educated at BLACKROCK COLLEGE and at University College Dublin. He had entered the Society of Jesus, but did not continue to ordination to priesthood. Holding a M.A. and Ph.D. in mathematics, he joined the faculty of University College Cork. He was also active in SINN FÉIN, and as a member of the Cork Corporation he proposed both Tomas MACCURTAIN and Terence MACSWINEY for lord mayor. The former was murdered by the BLACK AND TANS and the latter died on HUNGER STRIKE. He supported the ANGLO-IRISH TREATY and was on the committee

drafting the constitution of the IRISH FREE STATE. He was a member of the DÁIL ÉIREANN for the city of Cork from 1923 to 1924. He served on the Banking Commission from 1934 to 1938 and on the Commission on Vocational Organization from 1939 to 1943, and was president of University College Cork from 1943 to 1954. As president he started Cork University Press and expanded the library tenfold. His interests and publications were varied, ranging from mathematics through social science through electromagnetism. A contributor to academic journals and the popular press, he was often outspoken and controversial. He was firmly committed to papal social teaching. After the death of his wife and his retirement, he was ordained a priest and later made a monsignor.

O'Rahilly, Michael Joseph ("The O'Rahilly") (1875–1916)
nationalist

Born in Ballylongford, County Kerry, O'Rahilly was educated at CLONGOWES WOOD COLLEGE and at University College Dublin. Ill health prompted him to move to the United States from 1898 to 1909. When he returned to Ireland he became involved in SINN FÉIN and the GAELIC LEAGUE, as he was managing editor of *An Claideamh Soluis* to which he invited encouraged Eoin MACNEILL to write the article "The North Began," which led to the formation of the IRISH VOLUNTEERS. He was allied with MacNeill in opposing the EASTER RISING, but when it began he joined the garrison at the GENERAL POST OFFICE. He was killed leading a charge out of the building on Friday, April 29, 1916.

O'Rahilly, Thomas Francis (1883–1953)
scholar

Born in Listowel, County Kerry, and educated at the School of Irish Learning and at the Royal University of Ireland, O'Rahilly was a professor of Irish at TRINITY COLLEGE DUBLIN (1919), research professor at University College Cork

(1922–35) and afterward at University College Dublin. He was the first director of the School of Celtic Studies at the Dublin Institute for Advanced Studies in 1940. O'Rahilly was a major contributor to studies in the Irish language. His works include *Danta Gradha: An Anthology of Irish Love Poetry (1350–1750)* (1926), *Irish Dialects, Past and Present* (1932), *The Two Patricks: A Lecture on the History of Christianity* (1942), and *Early Irish History and Mythology* (1946).

Orange Order

The Orange Order came into being during the sectarian clashes in County Armagh in 1795 between Protestant PEEP O'DAY BOYS and Catholic DEFENDERS. It consisted of an association of lodges patterned after the Masonic Order and was committed to defend the king so long as he defended the PROTESTANT ASCENDANCY. The organization, whose rank and file were weaver-farmers, enjoyed the patronage of the landlords. Many of its members filled the ranks of the YEO-MANRY in the suppression of the UNITED IRISHMEN rebellion of 1798. Originally opposed to the ACT OF UNION, which it feared would enhance the position of Catholics, the order quickly came to accept and support it, and the king's brother, the duke of Cumberland, served as its Grand Master. In 1836 the order was dissolved because of its link to violence, but individual lodges continued with landlord support. By the 1870s, legislation against party processions was repealed, which allowed the order to revitalize itself. It became closely identified with the UNIONIST Party in the struggle against HOME RULE and remains an important component of unionist opinion, both within the official Unionist Party and the Democratic Unionist Party. Although a certain amount of its activities are social and purely commemorative, the numerous annual marches by various branches of the order every July near or on the anniversary of the Battle of the BOYNE have often provoked sectarian clashes. In recent times the political authorities under the Northern Ireland Office have moved through a Parades Commission to bar or reroute certain marches

Protestant Orangemen march by a mainly Catholic area in West Belfast, 2002.

through Catholic areas, which has often provoked counterprotests, especially those associated with Drumcree Church in Portadown, County Down.

Ó Rathaille, Aogán (1670–1729)

Irish poet

Born in the Sliabh Luachra district of County Kerry, Ó Rathaille's poetry dealt with the fortunes of the Gaelic landholding families of the area, particularly the MacCarthys, who were being dispossessed after the failure of the JACO-BITE cause in 1689 to 1690. They had been the patrons on whose estates he held land and were being replaced by Nicholas Browne, Viscount Kenmare. Browne's son, Valentine, became the particular object of his outrage. In one of his poems, Ó Rathaille depicted Valentine as a nonnative upstart unappreciative of the culture he was deposing as demonstrated by his failure to reestablish the poet on the land. His work became the foremost example of what would be called the *aisling* poetry that lamented the loss of position and dreamed of the return of the Jacobites, a prospect not unimaginable in the early part of the 18th century.

Ordinance Survey

An official British government department, part military and part civilian, that produced a topographical map of Britain in 1791 was commissioned to do the same in Ireland in 1824. It was headed by Colonel Thomas Colby and Lieutenant Thomas Larcom, who engaged individuals such as Eugene O'CURRY and John O'DONOVAN in a parish by parish examination of natural topography, including hills, woods, bogs, climate, and harvesting times; ancient topography, including churches, graveyards, prehistoric monuments, and accounts of folklore and tradition; modern topography, including towns, dwellings, and machinery, the state of roads, and the general scenic appearance; and social topography, including habits, types of nourishment, amusements, dress, and obstructions to improvement. The map was published by counties between 1833 and 1846 at six inches to the statute mile and was used both for valuation and for planning roads. The work of mapping Ireland and Northern Ireland continues to this day by Departments of Cartography in Dublin and Belfast.

O'Reilly, Sir Anthony (Tony O'Reilly) (1936–   )

entrepreneur

Born in Dublin and educated at BELVEDERE COLLEGE and University College Dublin, O'Reilly qualified as a solicitor. He played rugby for 16 years, from 1955 to 1970, winning 29 caps for Ireland in international competition, and also playing for the British Lions with whom he set records. He worked for the H. J. Heinz Corporation from 1973 to 2000, becoming president and chief executive in 1987. He has invested extensively in media interests and is chairman of the Independent News and Media Group, which owns the *IRISH INDEPENDENT* and other newspapers. O'Reilly was one of the founders of the Ireland Fund, which promotes cultural activities in Ireland, and which contributed to his earning a knighthood from Queen Elizabeth in 2001.

Ó Riada, Seán (1931–1971)

composer, musician

Born in Adare, County Limerick, Ó Riada was educated at University College Cork. He served as assistant music director at Radio Éireann from 1953 to 1955. Subsequently he made arrangements for the Radio Eireann Singers and Light Orchestra, and was music director of the ABBEY THEATRE. In 1960 he was commissioned to compose the music score for *Mise Eire* and *Saoirse,* film documentaries about the history of the Irish state, and for the film version of *The PLAYBOY OF THE WESTERN WORLD* (1962). He also launched a traditional Irish music group, *Ceoltoiri Cualann,* that began in evening gatherings in his own home. Many of the group later formed the CHIEFTAINS. He was made an assistant lecturer in music at University College Cork in 1963 and moved to Coolea in the County Cork GAELTACHT. He composed three Masses: *Cuil Aodha* (1965), *Glenstal* (1968), and *A Requiem* (1969). The later, intended for eventual use at state funerals, has never been publicly performed.

Ormond, James Butler, 12th earl and first duke of (1610–1688)

soldier, statesman

Born in London, Butler became a royal ward after the death of his father and was therefore raised as a Protestant. He succeeded his grandfather as earl in 1633 and was made commander in chief in Ireland in 1640. He supported the king during the 1641 rebellion and led the royalist forces against the parliamentary forces in Ireland. He was involved in negotiations that sought to ally the royalists with the CONFEDERATION OF KILKENNY; however, in 1646 the Papal Nuncio, Giovanni Batista RINUCCINI, condemned an agreed-upon pact for its failure to promise reestablishment of

Catholicism. Butler later transferred Dublin to the parliamentary side and departed for England. He returned and arranged another alliance with the confederation in 1649, but the successful invasion of Cromwell required him to leave for France, where he identified with the court in exile. Following the restoration, at the beginning of the reign of Charles II he was made a duke and again lord lieutenant of Ireland. He was dismissed in 1669, but reappointed in 1677. Butler withdrew from public life in 1685 after the succession of James II.

Orr, William (1766–1797)
United Irishman
Born in Farranshane, County Antrim, Orr was a Presbyterian and the owner of a large farm. Active in the United Irishmen, he held moderate views. However, he was charged with administering a treasonable oath to two soldiers, and, although defended by John Philpot Curran, he was convicted and hanged at Carrickfergus on October 14, 1797. The assumption of his innocence inspired public outrage for some time with the slogan "Remember Orr."

O'Shea, Captain William H. (1840–1905)
adventurer
Born in Dublin and educated at Trinity College Dublin, his wealthy solicitor father bought him a commission in the army. He married Katharine Wood (O'Shea) in 1867, sold his commission when his father ceased to support an expensive lifestyle, tried banking in Spain where he quarreled with his uncle, and then went bankrupt running a stud farm in England. He became dependent on the companion's income his wife received from her wealthy aunt, although he did not live very often with her. He joined the Irish Parliamentary Party in 1880 and was returned as a member of parliament for Clare that year. O'Shea was one of those who had facilitated the negotiations with William Henry Gladstone that led to the Treaty of Kilmainham. In 1885 he

stood for Liverpool as a Liberal, but failed. Charles Stewart Parnell secured his nomination (and election) for Galway in a 1886 by-election against the wishes of other leading figures in the party. In 1889 O'Shea sued his wife (with Parnell named as co-respondent) for divorce, which went uncontested, and which was granted. He left public life afterward.

O'Shea, Katharine (née Wood) (1845–1921)
mistress and later wife of Charles Parnell
Born in Essex, O'Shea married Captain William H. O'Shea in 1867. In 1875 she became the companion to her wealthy aunt, Mrs. Benjamin Wood, at Eltham, Kent, where O'Shea occasionally visited. After Charles Steward Parnell's selection as leader of the Irish Parliamentary Party in 1880 she made his acquaintance and a mutual attraction developed. As his mistress she bore him two children. The general assumption was that O'Shea was aware of the affair, as he was rewarded with a seat with the Parliamentary Party in 1886 over the opposition of many members. When the wealthy aunt died, leaving a fortune to Katharine and removing the need to avoid a scandal that would inhibit the regular livelihood and the inheritance, O'Shea sued for divorce on grounds of adultery with Parnell named as co-respondent. The suit was not contested and O'Shea was given custody of the children. Following the divorce granted in November 1890, she and Parnell married in June 1891. Parnell died the following October with his health broken and his political career destroyed. She survived amid periods of mental breakdown until 1921.

Ó Siochfhradha, Pádraig ("An Seabhac") (1883–1964)
educator, civil servant, author
Born in Dingle, County Kerry, ÓSiochfhradha was a Gaelic League activist and an Irish Volunteers organizer. He was imprisoned three times as a Volunteer. He was a civil servant from

1922 until 1932, and then headed the Educational Company of Ireland and Talbot Press. He published modern versions of old texts, such as *An Ceithearnach Caolriabhach* (1910), and a collection of short stories about rural life, *An Baile Seo 'Gainn.'* He also wrote a humorous book for children, *Jimin Mhaire Thaidhg* (1921). He used the pen name "An Seabhac" (The hawk). He served in the SEANAD from 1946 to 1954.

Ó Suilleabháin, Eoghan Rua (1748–1784)
poet in Irish

Born in the Sliabh Luachra area near Killarney, County Kerry, Ó Suilleabháin was a poet taught at a bardic school and maintained his own school. However, the era of special social status for poets had passed and he was forced to wander as an occasional teacher and as a laborer. At one point he served in the British navy and composed a poem, *In Rodney's Glory,* celebrating a victory of his commander, Admiral Rodney, over the French fleet. His poems were celebrated throughout Munster and many of them, having been written to traditional airs, survived popularly, especially his *aisling* poems, which expressed a hope for the restoration of the former Gaelic society. Much of his work also dealt with ordinary life and his own misadventures. Others were celebrations of women. He died of a fever resulting from a wound incurred in a brawl. His poems were collected and published in 1901 by Patrick Dineen and again in 1937 by Risteard O Foghludha.

Ó Suilleabháin, Muiris (1904–1950)
author

Born on the Great BLASKET ISLAND off the coast of County Kerry, Ó Suilleabháin spent his early years in Dingle on the mainland after his mother had died and only returned to the island when he was seven. He remained and learned to speak Irish as did all the islanders. In 1927 he went to Dublin and joined the police. He was stationed in the Galway GAELTACHT. While there he wrote an autobiography in Irish *Fiche Blian ag Fas*

(1933), which was translated by George Thomson and Moya Llewelyn Davies and published in London as *Twenty Years A-Growing.* The book presented a sentimental picture of life on the island. He retired from the police in 1934, married, and settled in Connemara, where he drowned while swimming in 1950.

O'Sullivan, John Marcus (1881–1948)
academic, politician

Born in Killarney, County Kerry, and educated at St. Brendan's College, Killarney, CLONGOWES WOOD COLLEGE, and University College Dublin, O'Sullivan was awarded a Ph.D. at the University of Heidelberg in 1906 and became professor of modern history at University College Cork in 1910. He was a CUMANN NA NGAEDHEAL member of the DÁIL ÉIREANN for Kerry from 1924 until 1937 and for North Kerry from 1937 to 1943 (as a member of FINE GAEL). O'Sullivan served as parliamentary secretary to the minister for finance from 1924 to 1926 and was minister for education from 1926 to 1932, as well as member of the Irish delegation to the LEAGUE OF NATIONS in 1924 and from 1928 to 1930.

O'Sullivan, Maureen (1911–1998)
actress

Born in Boyle, County Roscommon, O'Sullivan appeared with the tenor John MCCORMICK in the film *Song o my Heart* (1930). She played Jane, the female lead, in the series of *Tarzan* films with Johnny Weismuller in the 1930s. She performed on Broadway and in television programs, and later in her life returned to film, appearing in *Hannah and Her Sisters* (1986), *Peggy Sue Got Married* (1986), and *Stranded* (1987). She married the director John Farrow, and one of their children is the actress Mia Farrow.

O'Sullivan, Sonia (1969–)
athlete

Born in Cobh, County Cork, this middle- and long-distance runner is one of Ireland's foremost female athletes. O'Sullivan won the 1,500- and 2,000-meter championship in the World Student Games in 1991, a silver medal in the 1,500-meter World Championship in 1993, a gold medal in the European Championship of 1994, both the long and short course events in the World Cross-County Championships in 1998, and a silver medal in the 5,000-meter race in the Olympics in Sydney in 2000.

O'Sullivan Beare, Donall (1560–1618)
chieftain
The chieftain of the O'Sullivan clan at Beare, County Cork, O'Sullivan took part in the Battle of KINSALE. Afterward, he and his forces hid in the Cork and Kerry mountains in anticipation of further aid from King Philip III of Spain. When it was not forthcoming he left Glengariff on December 31, 1602, with 400 soldiers and 600 women and children seeking refuge in Ulster.

During the march north they were continually harassed by English and local chieftains. Only 35 had survived when they reached the shelter of the O'Rourke's in Breffni in Leitrim. The next year, he and his wife and children sailed to Spain, where the king conferred a knighthood, a pension, and the title of the earl of Berehaven. He was killed in Madrid by an Anglo-Irish refugee.

Owen, Nora (née O'Mahony) (1945–   )
politician
Born in Dublin and educated at University College Dublin, and qualified as an industrial chemist, Owen was a FINE GAEL member of the DÁIL ÉIREANN for Dublin North from 1981 to 1987 and from 1989 to 2002. She was the party's deputy leader in 1993 and served as minister for justice from 1994 to 1996. She lost her seat in the 2002 general election. Owen is a grand-niece of Michael COLLINS.

P

Paget, Arthur (1851–1928)

soldier

Paget entered the Scots Guards in 1869, served in the Ashanti Wars, in the Sudan, and in South Africa, and became a major general in 1900. He was commander in chief of the British army in Ireland from 1914 to 1917. He related the information to those under his command that any officer who was a native of Ulster would be exempt from duty in protecting the military's arms depots in Ulster, which, it was feared, might be taken by the ULSTER VOLUNTEER FORCE, but that other officers were not exempt. However, in what became known as the mutiny at the CURRAGH, a subordinate, Major-General Sir Hubert Gough, and 57 officers not entitled to exemption indicated a willingness to risk dismissal rather than serve in action against Ulster. At the time of the EASTER RISING, General John Maxwell superseded him in authority and he resigned the next year.

Paisley, Ian Richard Kyle (1926–   )

clergyman, politician

Born in County Armagh, Paisley was educated at the Ballymena Model School and at the South Wales Bible College. His father, a Baptist minister, ordained him to the ministry in 1946. In 1951 he founded and became moderator of the Free Presbyterian Church. Always an opponent of liberalism within the Protestant churches and of ecumenicism, he led a protest against the lowering of the flag on the Belfast City Hall on the occasion of the death of Pope John XXIII in 1963. He was outspoken in his criticism of the meetings of Northern Ireland prime minister Terence O'NEILL

with TAOISEACH Seán LEMASS in 1965. His protests resulted in his being imprisoned for several weeks in 1966. The fundamentalist American school, Bob Jones University, awarded him an honorary doctorate. He took part in counterprotests and harassment of civil rights protests, for which he was imprisoned in 1969. He challenged O'Neill for his seat in the Northern Ireland PARLIAMENT in the 1969 general election, but lost narrowly. When O'Neill resigned a few months later, Paisley was returned to the Stormont parliament as a member for Bannside. Shortly after he was released from prison as part of a general amnesty. The following June, in the British general election, Paisley was returned to the Westminster parliament for North Antrim and has held the seat since. In 1971 he founded a rival DEMOCRATIC UNIONIST PARTY, which vigorously sought for the return of majority rule government in Northern Ireland. He was a major opponent of the power-sharing experiment in 1973 and 1974 that was brought down by the Ulster Workers Council general strike. Besides his seat at Westminster, he topped the poll from Antrim North to the NORTHERN IRELAND ASSEMBLY elected in 1973, out of which was formed the short-lived power-sharing government brought down by the Ulster Workers Council general strike the following spring. He also topped the poll from Antrim North in the 1975 election to a Northern Ireland Constitutional Convention and in a 1982 election to a Northern Ireland Assembly, both of which failed to arrive at a consensus on a devolved form of government for the province. He and his party continually opposed the concept of power sharing and championed the restoration of majority rule for the province. In 1979 in the first popular election of members of the European Parliament, he was one of the three members elected from Northern Ireland, and he continued to be reelected until 2004, when he stepped down, and another member of his party was elected in his place. He opposed the Anglo-Irish Agreement of 1985 and opposed the GOOD FRIDAY AGREEMENT of 1998, although he was elected to the Northern Ireland Assembly called for by that agreement and members of his party served as ministers in the power-sharing government it elected. In the 2003 elections to that assembly, his party became the largest party in Northern Ireland, surpassing the UNIONIST Party. In the 2005 British general election he was reelected and his party won 11 of the 12 seats held by Unionists at Westminster. He and his party remain unconvinced that the IRA has abandoned violence and criminality despite its professions of decommissioning in 2005 and therefore still refuse to share power with Sinn Féin, the largest nationalist party in Northern Ireland. Some commentators are hopeful that the electoral success of his party, the prospects of its becoming the largest party in a government, his advancing age, and the pragmatic temper of other leading figures in the party who are not necessarily co-religionists of his, will contribute to a growing cooperative approach in politics.

Palatines

Protestant refugees from the Palatine region in the German Rhineland settled in Ireland in 1709. But by 1720 only 185 of the original 821 families remained. Their ranks were further diminished when most left for America in the 1760s. Their Protestant beliefs were reinforced by the development of Methodism. The Palatines settled primarily in the counties of Kerry, Tipperary, Wexford, and Limerick, particularly in the Limerick town of Rathkeale.

Pale

The term applies to the constantly changing area in Leinster surrounding DUBLIN that was considered to be occupied and ruled by the English, or the ANGLO-NORMANS, and distinct from the rest of Gaelic Ireland in medieval and early modern Ireland, where even the Normans had become Gaelicized. English law, institutions, and language prevailed there, even though a substantial portion of the population was native Irish. By the end of the Tudor reign the advent of the New English and the political centralization imposed on Ireland made the term antiquated. The actual term was first used in 1495.

Parker, Dehra (née Kerr-Fisher, Dame Dehra S. Parker) (1882–1963)
politician

Parker was first married to Lieutenant-Colonel Robert Spenser Chichester and organized nursing units in support of the ULSTER VOLUNTEER FORCE during the HOME RULE crisis of 1912–14. She was vice chairwoman of the Ulster Women's Unionist Council from 1918 to 1930 and UNIONIST member of the Northern Ireland PARLIAMENT for Londonderry from 1921 to 1929, as well as a justice of the peace and a member of a local rural district council and a board of guardians. Her first husband died in 1921. In 1929 she married Rear Admiral Henry Parker, and gave up her parliamentary seat. She returned to politics in 1933 when her successor, and son-in-law, James CHICHESTER-CLARK died, and held the seat for Londonderry until 1960. Parker served as parliamentary secretary to the minister for education from 1937 to 1944 and minister for health from 1949 to 1957.

Parliament of Northern Ireland

The parliament was created by the GOVERNMENT OF IRELAND ACT, 1920, which established separate parliaments for the six northern counties and the 26 southern counties. The first election took place in May 1921. That election and those of 1922 and 1925 were held according to the single transferable vote system of proportional representation, whereby the voters rank candidates in multiseat constituencies according to preference and victors are declared when candidates receive, either through first preferences or subsequent preferences, sufficient votes to meet a quota based on the size of the electorate and the number of seats available. This system was changed, beginning with the 1929 election, to the first past-the-post system of single-member constituency representation. The franchise for electors was similar to that of the rest of the United Kingdom, except that birth in Northern Ireland or residence for seven years in the United Kingdom was required and plural voting in other constituencies was permitted. Also, until 1969 four of the seats were for Queen's University Belfast. In addition there was a House of Lords with limited amending and delaying powers. It had 26 members, two of whom, the lord mayors of Belfast and Londonderry, were ex-officio, and the others were elected for eight-year terms by the lower house by proportional voting, half to be elected every four years after the initial election. The executive consisted of a cabinet responsible to the parliament, although nominally the executive power was vested in the monarch through the governor-general.

Of the 52 seats, the Unionists always held a decided majority that only three times went below 36. Nationalists rarely elected more than a dozen members, and many absented themselves from participation in the early years of the parliament and only assumed the role of official opposition in 1965.

The parliament had the power to legislate for Northern Ireland other than for certain "excepted" services that concerned the United Kingdom as a whole, such as the Crown; the armed forces;, foreign relations; external trade; naturalization; coinage; weights and measure; patent rights; reserved services such as certain taxation, banking, postage, deeds and land purchase registration; and the Supreme Court of Northern Ireland. The act assumed that Northern Ireland would be able to pay for its own services as well as make a contribution to the expenses of the government of the United Kingdom. Part of its revenue was expected to come from transferred revenues, such as motor vehicle taxes, stamp duties, and limited excise duties. Another portion would come from reserved revenues, such as income tax, capital gain tax, and customs and excise duties, for which taxes Northern Ireland and Great Britain were part of a single fiscal unit. The United Kingdom government would determine the amount to be given to Northern Ireland after a deduction to cover the expenses of reserved services performed in Northern Ireland and after the calculation of an imperial contribution for defense, foreign relations, and national debt expenses. Very soon it became apparent that Northern Ireland, especially with the development of the welfare state, was unable to make an appropriate imperial contribution or pay for reserved services and, in fact, would eventually need actual subsidy from the United Kingdom exchequer to meet its own expenses.

The parliament was suspended on March 30, 1972, and abolished by the Northern Ireland Constitution Act of July 18, 1973. Since then there have been various elections to a NORTHERN IRELAND ASSEMBLY, as well as a Northern Ireland Constitutional Convention, in an attempt to form province-wide institutions that would receive consensus across communities. The efforts remain a work in progress.

Parnell, Anna (Anna Catherine Marie Parnell) (1852–1911)

political activist

Born in Rathdrum, County Wicklow, and educated by governesses and at the Royal Hibernian Academy of Art, Parnell was the sister of Charles Stewart PARNELL. She worked to raise funds for the LAND LEAGUE in the United States and formed the Ladies Land League in 1881. When the latter group became indebted, her brother paid off its obligations with the understanding that the organization be dissolved. She lived from then on in England. She lost her mental stability after her brother's death, and she died in a drowning accident.

Parnell, Charles Stewart (1846–1891)
politician

Born at Avondale, County Wicklow, Charles Stewart Parnell's paternal family were Protestant landlords while his mother was the daughter of an American admiral. He studied at Magdalen College, Cambridge, but did not finish. In 1875 he was elected to parliament for County Meath as a member of the HOME RULE Party. Soon he became one of the leader practitioners of the obstructionist parliamentary tactics that were disapproved of by the party leader, Issac BUTT. In 1879 he became the president of the LAND LEAGUE. Earlier that year he had met with Michael DAVITT, the Land League founder, and John DEVOY, the CLAN NA GAEL leader, in forming the NEW DEPARTURE in Irish politics whereby the FENIAN and constitutional forces would collaborate to promote land reform. Butt died in 1879 and Parnell, who had visited the United States and spoke before a joint session of Congress, was selected as the leader of the IRISH PARLIAMENTARY PARTY. In 1881 Parnell was linked to Land League agitation in opposition to land legislation passed by the government of William Gladstone and he was imprisoned, along with Davitt, for sedition. The following spring both were released in a deal called the Treaty of KILMAINHAM, in which agitation was suspended in return for further modifications of the legislation. When the new chief secretary for Ireland and his deputy were assassinated almost immediately afterward in PHOENIX PARK, Parnell instantly condemned the killings. In 1885, his party reached its apex of power as it won 86 seats in parliament. Its strength stemmed from the firm discipline exercised over the members by the leadership, as most were not independently wealthy and needed support from the funds the party had raised, partly in America, to campaign and to maintain themselves in London while parliament was in session. Since the Irish seats were equal in number to the difference between the Conservative plurality and the seats held by the Liberals, the decision by Gladstone to support the Irish goal of Home Rule brought the Irish to support him, thus enabling

Charles Stewart Parnell *(Library of Congress)*

him to form a Liberal government in 1886. However, when he introduced a Home Rule bill, there was sufficient secession from the Liberal Party to defeat the measure. In the succeeding election the Conservatives were returned decisively to power and would remain in power for 17 of the next 20 years. In 1887 a charge was made in *The London Times* that Parnell had approved of the Phoenix Park murders. In 1889 a public inquiry later vindicated him as the charges were based on documents that were forgeries. Later that year Parnell was named as a co-respondent in a divorce suit filed by Captain William O'SHEA against his wife, Katherine O'SHEA, who was Parnell's mistress. The suit was not contested. The next year, Gladstone, the leader of the Liberal Party, which was very dependent on nonconformist Protestant clerical support, told the Irish party that the alliance between the two parties could not continue if an admitted adulterer remained their leader. The parliamentary party voted overwhelming to oust Parnell. For the next several months, he challenged the party leadership by running allies in a series of by-elections, but he was defeated in all of them. The Catholic hierarchy in Ireland, which had always been suspicious of Parnell's anticlericalism and his secularism, but which had collaborated with the party, jumped at the opportunity raised by the nonconformist clergy in England to turn on Parnell, guaranteeing his political destruction. In October 1891, broken politically and in ill health, he died. Nonetheless, he remains historically, along with Daniel O'CONNELL, one of the two great figures of Irish NATIONALISM in the nineteenth century.

partition

The division of the island of Ireland into two distinct political entities that resulted from the GOVERNMENT OF IRELAND ACT passed in 1920. Six counties in the province of ULSTER became NORTHERN IRELAND and the other 26 became SOUTHERN IRELAND, both of which received HOME RULE with separate devolved parliaments and governments. Nearly all of those elected to the parliament in the South considered themselves to have been elected to the second DÁIL ÉIREANN and continued the WAR OF INDEPENDENCE that ended in the ANGLO-IRISH TREATY of 1921 which transformed Southern Ireland into the Irish Free State, a dominion within the British COMMONWEALTH. Northern Ireland exercised its option of remaining apart from the Free State to continue as a self-governing province within the United Kingdom. The recommendations of a BOUNDARY COMMISSION called for by the treaty to make minor territorial transfers from both sides of the boundary were not implemented, as a disappointed Free State government preferred the status quo in return for other fiscal concessions. The Northern Ireland government had never accepted the idea of the commission and similarly accepted the status quo. The constitution of Ireland passed in 1937 made claim to the entire island, but limited the effect

of its governance in the meantime to the 26 counties. All agreements between the British and Irish governments since the Anglo-Irish Agreement at HILLSBOROUGH and through the GOOD FRIDAY AGREEMENT assert the principle that the status of Northern Ireland and its linkage to Britain will not be changed without the consent of its population.

Paterson, Frank (1938–2000)
tenor

Born in Clonmel, County Tipperary, Paterson was a prizewinner at a Dublin Feis Choil and then studied singing in London, the Netherlands, and Paris. He performed as a classical soloist with major orchestras in Europe and the United States. He then turned to more popular ballads and inspirational songs, making 36 recordings, and giving concerts widely in the United States and Ireland. Paterson sang in Phoenix Park on the occasion of the visit of Pope John Paul II to Ireland and also in the filmed version of *The Dead* by James Joyce and in the film *Michael Collins.*

Patrick (c. 389–c. 461)
patron saint and apostle of Ireland

Patrick was born in southwestern Britain, probably in a Roman gentry family. As a teenager he was kidnapped by Irish raiders and sold into slavery in what is now County Antrim. After six years, inspired by visions, he escaped and returned home. He studied for the priesthood and was ordained in Gaul and appointed bishop to the Irish by the pope. He then set out to fulfill a call in a dream and returned to Ireland in 432. Most of his mission was concentrated in the north, and the diocese of Armagh has historically based its claim to primacy on the view that it served as the base for his mission. Much understanding of him comes from his own writings, especially his *Confession* and his *Epistola,* as well as from writings of a few centuries after his death by champions of the primacy of Armagh and which are based on legends and oral tradition. He was not the first Christian missionary to Ireland and there were probably some Christians among the Irish before him. However, the extent of his efforts and the general collective vision of his role make his position as apostle of the Irish indisputable. His feast day, March 17, remains, even where secularized, the feast day for Irish everywhere in the world.

Patriot Parliament

The session of the Irish parliament summoned by James II in 1689 that recognized him as the king of Ireland as opposed to the challenge by his son-in-law and daughter, William and Mary. The members were overwhelmingly Catholic and they voted to end POYNINGS' LAW and to undo the land settlement that had followed CROMWELL'S conquest. The defeat of the JACOBITE cause made the effect of their actions short-lived.

Patriots

The term applies to those in Irish politics in the 18th century anxious to assert the autonomy of the Irish parliament from that of Britain, especially from the implications of POYNINGS' LAW, the 15th-century measure that made the agenda of the Irish parliament subject to the king's Privy Council, and the Declaratory Act of 1719 which asserted the right of the British parliament to legislate for Ireland. The Patriots were Protestants whose own antecedents in Ireland were quite recent, and their patriotism sometimes did not involve inclusion of the overwhelming majority of Irish Catholics. Important Patriots included Jonathan SWIFT, William MOLYNEUX, Charles LUCAS, and Henry GRATTAN.

Pearse, Patrick (Padraic Pearse) (1879–1916)

revolutionary, educator

Born in Dublin, Pearse's father, a monument sculptor, was English. He was educated at the Royal University of Ireland and was called to the bar, but not practice. As a youngster he acquired an interest in the Irish language, and he became very active in the GAELIC LEAGUE, editing its journal, *An Claidheamh Soluis,* from 1903 to 1909. He also became active in SINN FÉIN and contributed articles to its paper the *United Irishman.* To put his language, nationalist, and educational ideas into practice, he founded an Irish language school for boys, St. Edna's, in 1908, located first in Ranelagh and then in Rathfarnham, Dublin. To reinforce his love for the Irish language he spent his summers in Rosmuc, County Galway, where he had built a cottage. Pearse solicited funds for the school in America, where he received the approval and encouragement of John DEVOY and Joseph MacGARRITY of CLAN NA GAEL. He wrote numerous plays, essays, and short stories in Irish and English, a critique of the Irish educational system, *The Murder Machine* (1912), and a number of political pamphlets. Although he had earlier supported the HOME RULE movement, he grew disillusioned as to its successful achievement. An early member of the IRISH VOLUNTEERS, he stood with the minority who refused to support John REDMOND'S call to support the British in the First World War. His celebrated oration at the graveside of Jeremiah O'DONOVAN ROSSA in August 1915 was one of the more dramatic suggestions of an imminent turning to arms by Irish NATIONALISTS. His efforts to link the Gaelic League with the cause alienated its founder, Douglas HYDE. In 1913 Pearse joined the IRISH REPUBLIC BROTHERHOOD and served on the military council that planned the EASTER RISING. As president he signed and read the Proclamation of the Irish Republic at the GENERAL POST OFFICE on Monday, April 24, 1916, and as commander in chief surrendered on Saturday, April 29. He was executed by firing squad on May 3.

Peel, Sir Robert (1788–1850)

politician

Born in Lancashire and educated at Christ Church, Oxford, Peel first sat in parliament as a Tory for Cashel, County Tipperary, in 1809, although afterward he represented an English constituency. He was chief secretary for Ireland from 1812 to 1818 in which position he developed a permanent antagonism to Daniel O'CONNELL, who employed some of his most bitter vitriolic speech against him. A scheduled duel between them was prevented by the arrest of O'Connell. He had employed coercion legislation in Ireland and had restrained the Catholic Board, which was championing Catholic emancipation. On the other hand he began the Peace Preservation Police, the first public police force as opposed to the posse-type law enforcement used by the landlord-dominated grand juries of the time. The force and its successors were nicknamed the "Peelers." He also arranged for the provision of relief at the time of a less well known famine in 1817. From 1822 to 1830 he served as home secretary and was leader in the House of Commons from 1828 to 1830 while Arthur Wellesley, the duke of WELLINGTON, was prime minister, and in that capacity, in 1829, he was compelled to yield and introduce the legislation granting Catholic emancipation after O'Connell's electoral success in Clare. He was briefly prime minister in 1834 and 1835 and longer from 1841 to 1846. Between those terms O'Connell and his followers gave their support to the Whig government of Lord John Russell in return for substantial reforms within Ireland, especially with regard to the employment of Catholics in public positions. O'Connell shifted his emphasis back to the cause of the REPEAL of the ACT OF UNION when Peel was in power as he anticipated no interest in further reform in Ireland. Peel had the last monster meeting O'Connell had called for Clontarf prohibited and O'Connell tried and convicted for sedition (the conviction was subsequently reversed by the House of Lords). However, Peel also sought to outflank the repealers by promoting nonsectarian colleges in Ireland and by expanding the subsidy to the Catholic seminary at MAYNOOTH. The former legislation passed, but was opposed by O'Connell and the Catholic hierarchy who had advocated formal Catholic education as an alternative to Protestant TRINITY COLLEGE DUBLIN. When the Great FAMINE struck in 1845, Peel was quick to respond with relief and public works, which contrasted with the laissez-faire

approach of the Whigs who replaced him in 1846, even though they had the support of O'Connell who assumed the Whigs were better disposed toward the Irish than the Conservative-Tories. He fell from power when he supported the Whig and radical cause of repeal of the Corn Laws that his own party had authored and defended.

Peep o'Day Boys

Secret and sectarian group of Protestant weaver-farmers who fought with Catholic groups in County Armagh in the 1790s, the most celebrated encounter being the Battle of the Diamond near Loughgall, County Armagh, on September 21, 1795. Their victory contributed to the popular mood that facilitated the formation of the ORANGE ORDER, which many of the participants joined.

Penal Laws

Legislation passed by the parliament of Ireland after the defeat of the JACOBITE cause that sought to inhibit any Catholic political and social revival in Ireland and to guarantee the land settlement of the mid-16th century. The laws violated the spirit and the letter of the Treaty of Limerick in which the Catholics who had accepted the rule of William and Mary were guaranteed the rights they had held under Charles II. The pragmatic William did not approve the legislation, but accepted it in view of the determination of the PROTESTANT ASCENDANCY that dominated the parliament and government in Ireland to guarantee their position. The laws, which were passed over a number of years, included the following: prohibitions on Catholics sending their children abroad for education, and on the establishment of Catholic schools; banishment from Ireland of all Catholic bishops and priests who were members of religious orders, and the required registration of any remaining priests; prohibition of religious intermarriage; prohibition of Catholics purchasing or inheriting land from Protestants, or taking leases longer than 31 years; the requirement that the land of a Catholic be divided equally among his sons unless the eldest had converted to Protestantism; and exclusion of Catholics from public office, serving as officers in the military or as barristers, and barred from the right to vote if otherwise qualified. The aim of the legislation was to exclude Catholics from the public life of the country and to reduce those with wealth over a number of generations so as to confine Catholicism to the lower classes with the expectation of its eventual disappearance. After the failure of the Jacobite attempts to return to the throne of England in 1715 and especially again in 1745 and the minimal interest of Irish Catholics in the cause, many in the Irish Protestant Ascendancy lessened their apprehension of Catholics. Reduced fears of Catholicism combined with growing Protestant tolerance derived from both their acceptance of the notions of the Enlightenment and their own diminished religious enthusiasm to mitigate the enforcement of the Penal Laws. Between 1778 and 1793 most of the penal legislation was repealed.

Penn, William (1644–1718)

founder of the colony of Pennsylvania

Educated at Oxford, Penn was expelled in 1661 for failure to conform to the Church of England. He settled on his father's estate at Shanaquary, County Cork, where he was a victualler for the British navy at Kinsale. He became a Quaker and in 1681 was governor of the colony of Pennsylvania, which became celebrated for its religious tolerance.

People's Democracy

A student movement formed in Northern Ireland in late 1968. In January 1969 it organized a civil rights march from Belfast to Derry that encountered a particularly savage assault by LOYALISTS aided and abetted by the Police Auxiliaries at BURNTOLLET outside of Derry. The radicalism of the group led to its demise as more prudent and moderate figures assumed the leadership of the civil rights cause.

Perrot, John (c. 1527–1592)

Elizabethan courtier

Perrot served as the president of Munster from 1570 to 1573 at the time of the Desmond Rebellion, which he effectively suppressed. He returned as lord deputy in Ireland from 1584 to 1588 when he was successful in implementing the policy of composition in Connacht, whereby the Gaelic chieftains were allowed to retain their holdings by pledging loyalty to the new order. He achieved some success seeking similar accommodations in Ulster. However, he was less successful in Munster. That fact together with unpopularity within the PALE resulted in his recall and ultimate trial for treason.

Petrie, George (1790–1866)

antiquarian, musician, painter

Born in Dublin, Petrie was attached to the ORDINANCE SURVEY. He had earlier written numerous articles on antiquarian and travel subjects and had painted numerous landscapes that were exhibited at the Royal Hibernian Academy. He received gold medals from the ROYAL IRISH ACADEMY for his *Essay on the Round Towers of Ireland* (1845) and his studies that made up *Ecclesiastical Architecture of Ireland*. He also published *The Ancient Music of Ireland* (1855) and his collection of nearly 1,600 tunes were later published as *The Complete Collection of Irish Music as Noted by George Petrie* (1902–05).

Petty, William (1623–1687)

surveyor

Born in Hampshire and having studied at various continental universities and at Oxford, he became a fellow of Basenose College, Oxford, in 1649 and professor of anatomy in 1651. The next year he was made physician-general to the army in Ireland and was given the task of mapping the lands that would be effected by the Cromwellian land settlement. The work was called the "Down Survey." He himself was rewarded with large estates in County Limerick and County Kerry. His work was later published as the first atlas of

Ireland (1685). He was a founding member of the Royal Society and was awarded a knighthood by Charles II. He also published a *Treatise on Taxes and Contributions* (1662) and *The Political Anatomy of Ireland* (1672). His wife was made Baroness Shelburne after his death, as he had refused a peerage. His descendants inherited the title, to which was later added the Marquis of Lansdowne. Many of them were members of the British cabinet. Their record as landlords was considered generally to have been a good one, having taken steps to improve conditions.

Petty-Fitzmaurice, William, third marquis of Lansdowne See LANSDOWNE, WILLIAM PETTY-FITZMAURICE, THIRD MARQUIS OF.

Phoenix Park

One of the largest enclosed parks in an urban area, it contains 1,762 acres on the north bank of the river Liffey in Dublin. Originally seized by the Crown at the time of the confiscation of the monasteries in the century, Charles II turned it into a deer park, and the lord lieutenant, Lord Chesterfield, made it a public park in 1747. The park contains the residence of the Irish president, Aras an Uachtarain (which had earlier been the Vice Regal Lodge), the residence of the American ambassador to Dublin, had been the site of the EUCHARISTIC CONGRESS of 1932, and was where more than a million people assembled for the visit of Pope John Paul II in 1979. Phoenix Park was the scene of the murder of a newly appointed chief secretary and his deputy in 1882 by an extreme group, the INVINCIBLES.

Pigott, Richard (1828–1889)
journalist, forger
Born in County Meath, Pigott owned nationalist newspapers, the *Irishman,* the *Flag of Ireland,* and the *Shamrock.* He sold them to the IRISH PARLIAMENTARY PARTY in 1881, which used the papers to develop *United Ireland,* a paper controlled by Charles Stewart PARNELL. He possessed a copy of Parnell's signature from the transaction and from it was able to compose forgeries implicating Parnell in the PHOENIX PARK murders in 1882. He sold the forgeries to the *London Times* for funds with which to meet debts and they were published in a series of articles in March 1887. The cross examination of Pigott in February 1889 at a special commission established by the House of Commons demonstrated that the documents were forgeries. Exposed, he went to Madrid and committed suicide. The commission's report vindicated Parnell.

Pioneer Total Abstinence Association

A society founded by Rev. James Cullen, S.J., in 1898 in which people pledged to abstain from alcoholic drink for life. The movement grew immensely with a half-million members by the 1950s and attendance of 90,000 at a jubilee gathering in 1949. In more recent times membership has declined significantly as younger people are less inclined to pledge themselves to total abstinence, but a significant number remain faithful in a time when alcohol and abuse of other substances have become a source of major concern in Ireland.

Plan of Campaign

A tactic employed in the late 1880s on behalf of tenants aggrieved at their landlords. It was conceived by such leading members of the IRISH PARLIAMENTARY PARTY as Tim HEALY, William O'BRIEN, and John DILLON, and consisted of a rent strike in which the rent money was placed in a trust fund to help tenants confronted with eviction. Charles Stewart PARNELL did not approve the measure and was able to persuade its organizers to limit action to 116 estates. There was division among the Catholic hierarchy about the plan, which was supported by William WALSH, the archbishop of Dublin, and Thomas CROKE, the archbishop of Cashel. However, the papacy issued a statement condemning the plan that was generally ignored by supportive clergy. The chief secretary, Arthur BALFOUR, employed coercion legislation against the plan. His refusal to condemn a magistrate, who instructed the police not to hesitate to shoot, earned for him the nickname of "Bloody Balfour." The campaign petered out in the early 1890s as its funds declined and as the party became occupied with the issue of the split over leadership engendered by Parnell's disgrace. Settlements were made with the landlords in 84 of the 116 estates while tenants reneged on the landlords' terms in 15 others, and there was no settlement in the rest.

plantation

The term refers to the policy of the English monarchy in the 16th and early 17th centuries to replace rebellious or disloyal subjects in Ireland, primarily the Gaelic chieftains, with outside colonizers or planters. Plantation could only be avoided by accepting the policy of SURRENDER AND REGRANT, whereby a Gaelic ruler would give up his ancient title and accept a title from the sovereign, with all of the restrictions that followed, including the introduction of English law and property concepts. The first plantations were those in LAOIS and OFFALY, followed by those in Munster after the failure of the Desmond rebellions. Lastly there was the Ulster plantation, which followed the Flight of the Earls in 1607. The last plantation was the most enduring since it entailed the settlement in the designated areas of Ulster of a substantial number of settlers from Scotland and England, who replaced the native population that had been moved to less attractive areas in the province. In the other plantations, it was only the leaders of the old society that were replaced, with the existing rank and file of the population remaining as the workforce and as the tenants.

Playboy of the Western World, The

A play by John Millington SYNGE that appeared in Dublin at the ABBEY THEATRE in 1907 and caused rioting. The play tells the tale of a young man who flees his native area after he thinks he has killed his father and goes to a remote rural pub. His boasts about committing the deed to impress the locals, especially the publican's daughter. They regard him as a hero. However, when the father arrives and the son, in all docility, follows his command to come home, their illusions, especially those of the young lady, are destroyed. Opposition to the play came from NATIONALISTS, especially members of SINN FÉIN, who saw the play as a mockery of the native Catholic Irish peasantry.

Plunkett, George, Count (1851–1948)
politician

Born in Dublin and educated at CLONGOWES WOOD COLLEGE and at TRINITY COLLEGE DUBLIN, Plunkett served as president of the Society for the Preservation of the Irish Language, vice president of the Irish National Literary Society, vice president of the Royal Irish Academy (1908–09 and 1911–14), president of the Royal Society of Antiquaries of Ireland, and was granted a title as an award by the papacy. His son, Joseph Mary PLUNKETT, was executed after the EASTER RISING, and Plunkett was subsequently dismissed as director of the National Museum of Ireland, where he had served since 1907. In 1917 he was elected as a SINN FÉIN member of parliament for North Roscommon. He abstained from attending parliament. He was reelected and entered the first DÁIL ÉIREANN and was appointed minister for foreign affairs. Elected to the second Dáil he served as a non-cabinet minister for fine arts from August 1921 to January 1922. He opposed the ANGLO-IRISH TREATY, but was reelected to the third Dáil as an abstentionist member of Sinn Féin. Plunkett did not follow Eamon DE VALERA into the FIANNA FÁIL party, and was defeated in the June 1927 election while still running as a Sinn Féiner. He wrote books such as *The Architecture of Dublin* (1908) and *Introduction to Church Symbolism* (1932), as well as poetry, including *Arrows* (1921) and *Echoes* (1928).

Plunkett, James (James Plunkett Kelly) (1920–2003)
novelist, short-story writer

Born in Dublin from a working-class background, Plunkett worked for the Dublin Gas

Company and was a labor union official. He wrote stories for the *Bell* and plays, including one about James LARKIN. He worked as a producer for radio and later for television. He is best remembered for his historical novels about Dublin life in the first half of the 20th century, including *Strumpet City* (1969) and *Fairwell Companions* (1977).

Plunkett, Joseph Mary (1887–1916)
poet, revolutionary

Born in Dublin, the son of Count George PLUNKETT, Joseph Plunkett was educated at BELVEDERE COLLEGE, Stonyhurst College, Lancashire, and University College Dublin. He published a collection of poetry *The Circle and the Sword* (1911), and, with Thomas MACDONAGH and Edward MARTYN, he founded the Irish Theatre in 1914, and, with MacDonough and Padraic COLUM, founded the *Irish Review.* He was also a member of the IRISH VOLUNTEERS and the IRISH REPUBLICAN BROTHERHOOD, of which he was a member of the military council that planned the EASTER RISING. Plunkett was a signatory to the proclamation of the Irish Republic and was executed on May 4, 1916, shortly after he married his fiancée, Mary Gifford.

Plunkett, Oliver (1625–1681)
archbishop, saint

Born near Oldcastle, County Meath, he came from an OLD ENGLISH Catholic family. He left Ireland and went to Rome to study for the priesthood with the support of Father Pietro SCARAMPI, who had been a papal envoy to the CONFEDERATION OF KILKENNY. The anti-Catholic persecution following the conquest by Oliver CROMWELL prevented his return to Ireland and he remained after ordination as a lecturer in the College for the Propagation of the Faith in Rome. When persecution had eased after the restoration of the monarchy, he was appointed archbishop of Armagh in 1669 and returned to begin a reorganization of the church, imposing greater discipline and ordaining a great number of new priests. His policies incurred enemies. Although Plunkett had developed amicable relations with leading Protestants and took a nonconfrontational position regarding the Irish political situation and the status of Catholics, he was accused on very spurious grounds in the wake of the POPISH PLOT of participating in a treasonous conspiracy. No verdict was reached in a trial in Ireland, but he was brought to England where a more accommodating court found him guilty. He was hung, drawn, and quartered in 1681. Pope Paul VI canonized him in 1975.

Plunkett, Sir Horace (1854–1932)
agricultural reformer

Born in Gloustershire, a son of Lord Dunsany, and educated at Eton and at Oxford, Plunkett left his family estate in County Meath in 1878 for reasons of ill health to ranch in Wyoming. He returned to Ireland 10 years later and was saddened by the state of Irish agriculture. He was a Unionist member of parliament for South Dublin from 1892 to 1900. A proponent of "Constructive Unionism," he championed the establishment of a Department of Agriculture and Industries, which he headed from 1900 to 1907, and had been one of the founders of the Irish Co-Operative Movement in 1889 and a member of the CONGESTED DISTRICTS BOARD. Plunkett chaired the IRISH CONVENTION in 1917 that sought unsuccessfully to resolve the Irish national question. He was named to the SEANAD of the IRISH FREE STATE. His home was burned during the CIVIL WAR and he moved to England.

Ponsonby, John (1713–1789)
politician

Ponsonby's ancestor had come to Ireland accompanying Oliver CROMWELL. The family acquired enormous wealth and provided leading figures in Irish politics for several generations. He was one of the "UNDERTAKERS," members of parliament who commanded large factions of that body in the mid-18th century, who were relied upon by the government to get its business through the legislature. Not a PATRIOT as such, he was assertive of the power of the Undertakers to lead and managed many of the members of the parliament rather than the lord lieutenant. He served as Speaker of the House from 1755 until the 1770s, when Lord Lieutenant Charles Townsend began to more directly influence parliament and dispense with the need for the Undertakers.

Popish Plot

An alleged plot by Catholics to kill King Charles II in the late 1670s, the Popish Plot was fueled by the conversion of his brother and successor, James, to Catholicism and by a number of foreign and domestic accommodations Charles had made to the Catholic king of France, Louis XIV. Unfounded accusations, especially those of Titus Oates, fired the popular imagination and a severe persecution of Catholics was imposed for a time, including the execution of Oliver PLUNKETT, the archbishop of Armagh.

Poynings' Law

A law introduced to the parliament by the lord deputy, Sir Edward Poynings, and passed in 1494 that made the agenda of the Irish parliament and any measure it would consider subject to the prior approval of the king and his council. It was only repealed in 1782. The measure was inspired by apprehension that the Irish parliament might again give recognition to a rival pretender to the throne as the members had done a few years earlier.

Presbyterianism

Presbyterians came to Ireland from Scotland as part of the PLANTATION of ULSTER. Their theological position was Calvinist, that is, suspicious of hierarchy and liturgy and believing in election rather than good works as a means of attaining salvation. While their clergy assumed positions in the CHURCH OF IRELAND, they were inherently suspicious of "popish" features of the church. Permanent separation ensued with the religious test imposed following the restoration of the monarchy in the 1660's. However, practical considerations prompted later monarchs to award a *REGIUM DONUM* or subsidy to their clergy in view of their support of WILLIAM III in 1689 and after. Nonetheless, as religious non-conformists to the established church they suffered some religious and political disabilities. Those grievances and the suspicion of monarchy that drew from their theological hostility to episcopacy, or a church run by bishops nominated by kings, made them sympathetic to republicanism in the eighteenth century. Most of the Irish who went to the American colonies at the time were Presbyterians who were annoyed at the economic consequents of British mercantilism toward Ireland and supportive of the American quest for independence. Most of the rank and file of the UNITED IRISHMEN were Presbyterian. However, the sectarianism that developed in the Rising of 1798 ultimately made most Presbyterians supportive of the ACT OF UNION. During the nineteenth century there were internal struggles within Irish Presbyterians in which New Light advocates of a flexible and less than orthodox theology clashed with Old Light champions of orthodoxy. The later gained ascendancy. To this day the Presbyterian Church in Ireland has been more hesitant in ecumenical involvement than other Presbyterian churches internationally. It remains the largest non-Catholic religious denomination in Northern Ireland, exceeding in numbers the Church of Ireland, although its membership in the Irish Republic is relatively small.

Preston, Thomas (1585–1655)
military commander

A member of an OLD ENGLISH family, Preston had served in the Spanish army. He was made a general of one of the armies of the CONFEDERATION OF KILKENNY in 1642. He was a rival of Owen Roe O'NEILL, and their rivalry reflected the mutual distrust of the Old English and the Gaelic allies. He was uncertain as to whether to associate with the duke of ORMOND in the later stages of the war. Preston commanded the forces that would be defeated by the army of Oliver CROMWELL in Waterford and Galway. He was allowed to leave, together with his soldiers, to serve in Spain.

Progressive Democrats

A political party founded in 1985, its first leader was Desmond O'MALLEY. The party consisted primarily of members of FIANNA FÁIL who were hostile to the leadership of Charles J. HAUGHEY, although some members of FINE GAEL also joined. The party is pro-market or neo-liberal on economic issues, but more liberal on social issues. The party has also been flexible on the question of Northern Ireland in demonstrating a recognition of UNIONIST identity and expressed condemnation of the IRA. The party has never again matched its electoral accomplishments in the 1987 general election when it won 14 seats. However, Progressive Democrats served in the first coalition government ever entered into by Fianna Fáil after the 1989 election. It was also able to force the TAOISEACH, Haughey, from office in early 1992 stemming from his awareness years earlier of wiretapping of journalists. Later that year they forced his successor, Albert Reynolds, to call a general election when they withdrew from the coalition over irregularities in the government subsidization of the beef industry. Mary HARNEY, the first female party leader in Irish history, succeeded O'Malley in 1993. While the party gained 10 seats in that election, it did not join the new coalition of Fianna Fáil and LABOUR, or the RAINBOW COALITION that succeeded after its breakup a year later. The party's electoral fortunes have continued to dwindle, although it has been part of Fianna Fáil–led coalitions since 1997 and Harney has served as TÁNAISTE.

Protestant Ascendancy

The term refers to the political and social situation in Ireland from the late 17th century through the early 19th century in which the political,

social, economic, and cultural life of the country was dominated by Protestants, particularly members of the CHURCH OF IRELAND, due to their control of most of the land in the country and to the political, economic, social, and religious restrictions imposed on Catholics by the PENAL LAWS.

Provisional Government

The ANGLO-IRISH TREATY called for the parliament of Southern Ireland (whose membership, aside from the four members elected for TRINITY COLLEGE DUBLIN was identical to the membership of the second DÁIL ÉIREANN) to elect a Provisional Government to implement the treaty, to accept the transfer of power from the British government, and to draft a constitution for the Irish Free State. Michael COLLINS was selected as the chairman of the Provisional Government, although the anti-treaty members of the Dáil Éireann had not attended the meeting that selected him nor had acknowledged the legitimacy of the government. In order to provide a continuity to the Dáil Éireann and possibly to accommodate the opponents of the treaty, the Dáil elected the pro-treaty Arthur GRIFFITH its president in succession to Eamon DE VALERA. A cabinet was named and Dáil meetings continued to be held, although they possessed a primarily symbolic character.

Provisional IRA   See IRISH REPUBLICAN ARMY.

Provisional Sinn Féin

The breakaway members of the movement who challenged the leadership of the SINN FÉIN party in 1970 because of what was seen as its being unprepared for the violent confrontations of the previous summer and its internationalist and socialist agenda were labeled Provisional Sinn Féin. Ultimately the descriptive adjective disappeared as they became the predominant portion of the movement as OFFICIAL SINN FÉIN, the supporters of the leadership, shrank in following and eventually changed its character to a primarily political movement opposed to violence, even changing its name.

Puck Fair

Puck Fair is an annual festival held in Killorglin, County Kerry, in which a wild mountain goat is captured, crowned, and placed at the top of a tower in the center of the town "presiding" over a fair that lasts several days. The selling of cattle and horses, extensive musical and dancing entertainment, and liberal extensions of drinking hours are featured. The festival has become more of a tourist attraction than a fair as tens of thousands come to it annually. The origins of the fair are disputed, but the most popular stems from the suggestion that noise made by mountains goats alerted the people of the area to approaching English soldiers, and they made ready to either effectively defend themselves or go into hiding.

Q

Queen's Colleges

Queen's Colleges were colleges for Cork, Galway, and Belfast established by the Colleges Act of 1845 by which Prime Minister Robert PEEL hoped to satisfy Catholic and Presbyterian complaints about the absence of higher education facilities other than TRINITY COLLEGE DUBLIN, which was identified with the CHURCH OF IRELAND. However, the exclusion of theological education in the schools caused many in the Catholic hierarchy and among Daniel O'CONNELL and his supporters to oppose such "godless colleges." The YOUNG IRELAND movement, on the other hand, supported the institutions as a means of forging an Irish identity that crossed religious identities. The opposition inhibited the development of the school in Cork and Galway, which never drew more than a few hundred students until the 20th century and their incorporation as constituents of the NATIONAL UNIVERSITY OF IRELAND established by the Universities Act of 1908. The college in Belfast, however, was very successful.

Queen's University Belfast

When the Irish Universities Act of 1908 established the NATIONAL UNIVERSITY OF IRELAND to which the QUEEN'S COLLEGES of Cork and Galway, and a new University College Dublin (which had been the Catholic University) were constituent parts, Queen's College Belfast was not included out of deference to Protestant sensitivity in view of the de facto Catholic character of the new body. Instead it was transformed into a university itself. Ironically, today the majority of the students at Queens are Catholics.

Quin, Windham Thomas Wyndham, fourth earl of Dunraven   See DUNRAVEN, WINDHAM THOMAS WYNDHAM QUIN, FOURTH EARL OF.

Quinn, Edel (1907–1944)
missionary

Born in Kanturk, County Cork, and trained as a secretary, Quinn joined the Legion of Mary in Dublin. She aspired to enter the convent, but tuberculosis inhibited her doing so. However, when she recovered after a year and a half in a sanatorium, she resumed her involvement with the Catholic aid organization. She went to Wales briefly and to Africa in 1936, where, in the course of four years, she set up over 250 chapters of the Legion of Mary in Kenya, Uganda, Tanganyika, Nyasaland, and Mauritius. Ill health forced her to return in 1941, but after another year of convalescence, she returned to her work in Nairobi in 1943. Quinn died a year later. Her devotion and accomplishments have prompted many to campaign for her canonization.

Quinn, Ruairi (1946–   )
politician

Born in Dublin and educated at BLACKROCK COLLEGE and University College Dublin, Quinn was a LABOUR PARTY member of the DÁIL ÉIREANN for Dublin Southeast from 1977 to 1981 and from 1982 to the present, as well as a member of the SEANAD from 1976 to 1977 and 1981 to 1982. He served as minister of state for the Department of the Environment from 1982 to 1983, Minister for Labour, 1983 to 1987, in the FINE GAEL–Labour coalition, minister for enterprise and employment from 1993 to 1994 in the FIANNA FÁIL–Labour coalition, and minister for finance from 1994 to 1997 in the RAINBOW COALITION government. He became deputy leader of the Labour Party in 1989, and was leader of the party from 1997 to 2002. He is an architect and planning consultant in private life.

R

Radio Éireann   See Radio Telefís Éireann.

Radio Telefís Éireann (RTE)

The national broadcasting service began to operate in 1926. It changed its name in 1932 to Radio Éireann. Its studios were located at the General Post Office from 1928 until 1974, when it moved to its current location at Donnybrook, Dublin. Television service began on January 1, 1961, from Donnybrook and in 1966 the authority's name was changed to Radio Telefís Éireann. A second television channel began in 1978 and, in 1996, an Irish language channel was started. RTE is governed according to a series of broadcasting authority acts, which emphasize its need to provide programming in topics of community interest and culture, and especially the Irish language. The sale of television licenses and revenues from advertising finance the system. Radio service expanded in 1968 to 24 hours a day and, in 1972, an Irish language station was started. In 1979, a popular music station, 2FM, began and in 1999 a classical music, Lyric FM, station began. In recent years Radio Éireann has had to contend with competition from a number of private local stations and its television partners have had to compete with serious competition from British television channels, as well as satellite and cable television. Programming has necessitated unavoidable compromises, including importing reruns and popular game shows.

Raftery, Anthony (Antoine Ó Raifteiri) (1779–1835)

poet

Born in Kiltimagh, County Mayo, Raftery was blinded as a child by smallpox. He became a wandering bard, composing popular songs and ballads, usually about significant current events, including the Clare electoral victory of Daniel O'Connell. His poems and songs were preserved in the oral tradition until collected and edited by Douglas Hyde in 1903.

Rainbow Coalition

The term refers to the coalition government from late 1994 to 1997 that came to power when the Labour Party broke with its coalition partner, Fianna Fáil, over the appointment of the attorney general to the Supreme Court. When no confidence was voted in the government of Bertie Ahern, a coalition government emerged that comprised a broad ideological spectrum. The Taoiseach was the leader of Fine Gael, John Bruton. Another party in the government was the Labour Party, headed by Dick Spring, who was Tánaiste and minister for foreign affairs. His Labour Party colleague, Ruairi Quinn, was minister for finance. The other partner in the coalition was the Democratic Left, which had evolved from Official Sinn Féin. Its leader, Proinsias de Rossa, served as minister for social welfare. The government was able to overcome its ideological differences and pursue a policy of capital gains tax reduction, along with some social welfare improvements including extended free education to the university or third level, as well as contend with the resumption of violence by the IRA in early 1996. The government supported a successful campaign to amend the constitution to allow divorce.

Raleigh, Sir Walter (1552–1618)
planter, adventurer

Born in Devon, Raleigh was one of the military leaders who suppressed the second Desmond rebellion in Munster, remembered especially for the massacre of Spanish and Italian prisoners at Smerwick, County Kerry. He was rewarded by Queen Elizabeth I with a grant of 42,000 acres in the Munster PLANTATION in 1586. Early efforts by him to plant colonies in North America were unsuccessful. In 1602 he sold his estates, which had been devastated during the wars of rebellion led by the northern earls, Hugh O'NEILL and

Sir Walter Raleigh *(Library of Congress)*

Hugh O'DONNELL, to Richard BOYLE for a fraction of their earlier value. In 1603 Raleigh was imprisoned for life for plotting against James I. He was executed in 1618, accused of plotting after having been released earlier.

Rea, Stephen (1948–)
actor

Born in Belfast, Rea has performed in a number of films, several with Irish themes, particularly *The Crying Game* (1992), *Michael Collins* (1996), and *The Butcher Boy* (1997). He won an Oscar nomination for his role in *The Crying Game* and a Tony Award for his role in the Broadway play *Someone Who'll Watch over Me* (1993). He is married to Dolores Price, who had served time for her bombing in 1973 of the Old Bailey Court building in London.

Rebellion of 1798   See UNITED IRISHMEN.

Rebellion of 1848   See YOUNG IRELAND.

recusancy

The term refers to persistent adherence to and attendance at services of the Catholic Church in the face of fines and political and social disabilities beginning in the 16th and continuing through the 18th centuries. The penalties particularly affected titled and land-owning Catholics, who were subject to various fines for nonconformity to the established CHURCH OF IRELAND and to political, professional, and socioeconomic disabilities.

Red Hand of Ulster

A red right hand is the central symbol on the flag of the province of Ulster, which had been on the coat of arms of the earls of Tyrone, and is on the coat of arms of the government of Northern Ireland. It is reputed to be taken from the legend that rival giants in prehistoric times engaged in a swimming race from Scotland to Ulster with the one who first touched land receiving the province as a prize. One of the contestants cut off one of his hands and threw it ashore and thereby won. LOYALIST groups in particular have employed the symbol for their cause.

Redmond, Captain William A.
(1886–1932)
soldier, politician

Born in Waterford, William Redmond was the eldest son of John REDMOND, and was educated at CLONGOWES WOOD COLLEGE and at TRINITY COLLEGE DUBLIN. He was called to the bar in 1910 and was also elected as an IRISH PARLIA-MENTARY PARTY member of parliament for Tyrone East from 1910 to 1918. He served in the Irish Guards during the First World War and was decorated for his service. In 1918 he was elected to succeed his father in parliament as member for the city of Waterford and held his seat until 1922. In the 1923 general election he was elected for Waterford to the DÁIL ÉIREANN as an independent. In 1926 he formed a National League Party, which gained eight seats in the June 1927 election and which was ready to join with FIANNA FÁIL and LABOUR in moving no confidence in the CUMANN NA NGAEDHEAL government. However, the effort failed by one vote when one of his party members, John Jinks of Sligo, absented himself from the vote. In the election called immediately afterward, his party's numbers in the Dáil fell to two and he joined Cumann na nGaedheal in 1931.

Redmond, John (1856–1918)
politician

Born in Ballytrent, County Waterford, and educated at CLONGOWES WOOD COLLEGE and TRINITY COLLEGE DUBLIN, he was elected to parliament for Waterford as a member of the IRISH PARLIA-MENTARY PARTY from 1881 to 1918. He was a supporter of Charles Stewart PARNELL in the leadership crisis of 1890 and led the minority of Parnellites for the next decade. He became the leader of the reunited party in 1900 and delicately balanced the diverse factions, although

having to bear with secessions by independent figures such as William O'BRIEN and Tim HEALY. His greatest chance of achieving the central goal of the party, HOME RULE, came following the 1910 elections in which the Irish party provided the clear majority to the governing Liberals. The passage of the House of Lords reform measure, which ended the absolute veto power of the upper house, seemed to ensure that a Home Rule measure would be passed within several years. The measure became law in 1914 despite the threat of violent UNIONIST resistance, however, its application was postponed by the outbreak of the First World War. Earlier in 1914, Redmond had successfully absorbed the newly formed IRISH VOLUNTEERS under the direction of the party by insisting that he nominate half the members of its ruling committee. When the war started he was able to persuade the overwhelming majority of the Volunteers to join the NATIONAL VOLUNTEERS that he had formed to support the British war effort. Only a minority remained opposed to supporting the war, but they retained the title of Irish Volunteers. The repressive treatment of the leaders of the EASTER RISING began to erode support for Redmond and his party among the Catholic and nationalist population of Ireland, which was demonstrated in the success of SINN FÉIN in a series of by-elections in 1917 and 1918. In 1918 Redmond died during the IRISH CONVENTION, which was held to attempt to achieve a solution for the governance of Ireland.

Redmond, William H. K. (Willie H. K. Redmond) (1861–1917)
politician, soldier

Born in Wexford and educated at CLONGOWES WOOD COLLEGE, Redmond was an IRISH PARLIA-MENTARY PARTY member of parliament for Wexford from 1883 to 1885, for Fermanagh from 1885 to 1892, and for East Clare from 1892 to 1917. He supported his brother in the split in the party over Charles Stewart PARNELL, and made fund-raising trips to the United States and Australia in 1902 and 1905 when his brother had become leader of the reunited party. Although refused a commission when he sought to join the British army at the outset of the First World War, he enlisted as a private and rose in rank to major. He was killed in action on the western front in 1917, opening his seat to a by-election, which was won by Eamon DE VALERA for SINN FÉIN.

Regency Crisis

When King George III suffered a mental break down, the Irish parliament in February 1789 petitioned that the prince of Wales, the future George IV, be named regent for the duration of the king's instability. In such a position the prince of Wales was assumed to be more likely to appoint the Whigs, who were more favorably disposed to accommodating the demands of the Irish parliament, to government. However, the question became academic when the king recovered and the government of William Pitt continued in power.

Regium Donum

This was a sum of money given to the Presbyterian Church in Ireland by the king as a gesture of appeasement in view of the established status of the CHURCH OF IRELAND. The first king to provide funds was Charles II and monies continued with increases until 1802, when Presbyterian ministers were given a direct sum from the government itself up until the disestablishment of the Church of Ireland in 1869. At that point the Presbyterian Church was given a final lump-sum payment.

repeal

The term means repeal of the ACT OF UNION. The cause became increasing identified with the Catholics of Ireland, especially in view of the failure to advance Catholic emancipation after the union had been established. On the other hand, there were always a certain number of Protestants who were sympathetic to repeal.

Daniel O'CONNELL employed the issue when he believed other reforms he desired were unlikely to be achieved; actually moving for repeal in the House of Commons in 1834, but receiving only one other supporting vote besides the handful of his own followers who were members from Ireland. He made repeal the central issue in the mass movement he started in the 1840s and during the Conservative government of Robert PEEL, and he was supported by the YOUNG IRELAND movement, many of whom were Protestants. But Peel banned the last demonstration and the movement failed. The HOME RULE movement can be considered a continuation of the effort to repeal the Act of Union, and the establishment of the Irish Free State can be considered to have marked the achievement of repeal in most of Ireland. In a way the provincial self-rule obtained by NORTHERN IRELAND by the GOVERNMENT OF IRELAND ACT of 1920 could be considered a partial repeal. However, the continued presence of members of the Westminster parliament elected from Northern Ireland would imply that union still continues, and the present direct rule pending the reestablishment of a devolved provincial government further reinforces the union.

republicanism

In Ireland, republicanism means a commitment to a sovereign independent Ireland separate from Britain and its monarchy. Its origins lie in the UNITED IRISHMEN movement and it has been the central doctrine that has moved Irish revolutionaries, including the YOUNG IRELAND participants in the mid-19th century, their successors in the FENIAN or IRISH REPUBLICAN BROTHERHOOD movement, and the participants in the EASTER RISING and the WAR OF INDEPENDENCE. Significantly, the SINN FÉIN movement originally supported a concept of dual monarchy, whereby a self-governing Ireland would share a monarch with Britain. The major issue in the debate over the ANGLO-IRISH TREATY and in waging the subsequent CIVIL WAR centered on whether the Irish Free State should adopt dominion status in the

British COMMONWEALTH, which necessitated acknowledging the monarch's position as head of that organization. Only in 1949 did Ireland formally withdraw from the Commonwealth, although monarchist references and oaths had earlier been removed from its constitution. The current Sinn Féin and IRA demand that Britain withdraw from its connection with Northern Ireland is a statement of adherence to that republican faith, although it has not inhibited the continuance of a cease-fire or forbidden Sinn Féiners from serving in Northern Ireland governmental posts and receiving compensation from Britain. Sinn Féiners elected to the Westminster parliament from Northern Ireland refuse to serve, but they accept salary, reimbursement for expenses, and office space.

Restoration of Order in Ireland Act, 1920

This act was passed by parliament in 1920 to empower the commander in chief of the military in Ireland, where the WAR OF INDEPENDENCE was ongoing, to arrest those suspected of participation in and support of the war and subject them to secret military tribunals and to suppress coroner's inquests. The passage of the act was followed by increased activities by the AUXILIARIES and by the BLACK AND TANS.

revisionism

A term used in contemporary Ireland to label a historical perspective that had developed, especially in the 1960s and 1970s, that viewed Irish history in less clear-cut terms as solely a national struggle between Ireland and Britain and in seeing significant positive consequences from the connection with Britain. Although the concept did not deny the significance of the achievement of national self-determination, revisionism was especially important in balancing a popular Irish tendency to ignore the reality of a UNIONIST identity in NORTHERN IRELAND at the beginning of the modern difficulties there.

Reynolds, Albert (1932–)
politician

Born in County Sligo and educated at Summerhill College, Sligo, Reynolds was a businessman who promoted dance halls and sold pet food. He was elected to the Longford County Council as a member of FIANNA FÁIL in 1974 and in 1977 was elected to the DÁIL ÉIREANN for Longford. He supported Charles J. HAUGHEY in his successful bid to succeed Jack LYNCH as TAOISEACH and party leader in 1979 and was made minister for posts and telegraphs and transport from 1979 to 1981. In Haughey's third ministry, he served as minister for industry and commerce from 1987 to 1988 and for finance from 1988 to 1991. He resigned in November 1991 after having supported an attempt to force Haughey from power. When Haughey did resign the following February after it was discovered that he had been aware of official wiretapping of journalists, Reynolds was selected as his successor as Taoiseach and party leader. Since 1989 Fianna Fáil had held office in a coalition with the PROGRESSIVE DEMOCRATS. Later that year the PD's withdrew from the coalition after Reynolds and their leader, Desmond O'MALLEY, clashed over the issue of alleged corruption in government support of the beef industry. In an election called immediately afterward, Fianna Fáil failed to secure an absolute majority and formed a coalition with the LABOUR PARTY, which had gained its highest ever number of seats, 33. A year later Reynolds and British prime minister John Major issued the DOWNING STREET DECLARATION in which both parties emphasized the need for consent in any change in the status of NORTHERN IRELAND, the British indicated the absence of any strategic interest in Northern Ireland, and both parties expressed an openness to negotiations. The declaration was viewed as paving the way toward the cease-fire declaration by the IRA in August 1994. But the following November, Reynolds had to resign as Taoiseach and party leader when Labour withdrew from the coalition when it challenged his appointment of the attorney general as president of the High Court and a vote of no confidence was passed. Bertie AHERN temporarily succeeded Reynolds. Shortly after John BRUTON and the RAINBOW COALITION formed a government. Since then Reynolds has been very successful in various corporate activities.

Ribbonism

This term is used to describe early 19th-century adherents to the practice, beliefs, and style of the secret Catholic groups, the DEFENDERS, who were inspired by prophecies of a Catholic cleric named Pastornini about the imminent collapse of Protestantism. They were especially active at the time of agitation against tithes in the 1830s and were numerous in the counties of Laois, Tipperary, Kilkenny, Limerick, and Monaghan. Political authorities attributed certain crimes, especially agrarian crimes such as cattle maiming and burning of crops and occasionally murder, to Ribbonism.

Rice, Edmund Ignatius (1762–1844)
educator, founder of religious order

Born in Callan, County Kilkenny, Rice was educated at a hedge school. His wife died shortly after the birth of their daughter. He was successful in the exporting business and distributed much of his fortune to help the sick, the poor, and imprisoned debtors. Rice opened a school for the poor at Mount Sion, Waterford, in 1802 with the assistance of Charles BIANCONI, whom he had taught English. He went on to establish other schools in Clonmel, Dungarvan, and Cork. Having taken vows with eight others in 1808, Rice and his group received papal recognition as the Religious Brothers of the Christian Schools in 1820. He remained superior of the order until 1838. In 1996 Pope John Paul II beatified him.

Rightboys

The Rightboys were an 18th-century secret agrarian group, primarily Catholics, who acted against tithes and sought to intimidate landlords and some clergy. Many of them would become

DEFENDERS and their movement was comparable to RIBBONISM.

Ring, Christopher (Christy Ring) (1920–1979)
athlete

Born in Cloyne, County Cork, Ring was one of the greatest players in the sport of HURLING. He began playing with the Cork senior team in 1939 and he continued playing until he was 47 years of age. Cork won eight Hurling All Ireland matches while he was playing with them from 1941 to 1944, in 1946, and 1952 to 1954, and four National League championships, 1940–41, 1948, and 1953, and he was the top scorer in 1959, 1961, and 1962.

Rinuccini, Giovanni Battista (1592–1653)
archbishop, diplomat

Rinuccini served as the papal nuncio to the CONFEDERATION OF KILKENNY from October 1645 to February 1649. He disapproved of an agreement made by the ruling council of the confederation with the lord lieutenant, James Butler, duke of ORMOND, because its concessions did not go far enough to meet Catholic demands, particularly with regard to church property and reestablishment of the church in Ireland. He ordered the members who signed to be excommunicated. He had the support of Owen Roe O'NEILL and the leaders capitulated to him. Ormond then sought to come to terms with the parliamentary army. However, major defeats and internal disputes between the confederate military leaders led to a renewal of efforts to again reach an accord with Ormond and Rinuccini fled Ireland. The alliance proved to be too late as the forces of Oliver CROMWELL began their conquest of Ireland before the end of 1649.

Rising of 1641

Ulster Catholics, led by Sir Phelim O'NEILL, staged an insurrection in various parts of Ulster in which great numbers of Protestant settlers were killed. The numbers would be enormously magnified over the years and provide an important component of Ulster UNIONIST historical memory. The uprising was put down throughout Ulster by the end of November. An attack planned for the same time on DUBLIN CASTLE failed when the authorities got knowledge of it through the loose talk of a drunken would-be participant. The uprising could be seen as the opening shot in what would be called the "War of Three Kingdoms," as parliamentary forces in Britain interpreted the uprising as tolerated by or acquiesced in by King Charles I and they began taking steps against his authority, which culminated in a civil war. On the other hand, within Ireland, royalists remained loyal to the king, but opposed both the Catholic insurgents and parliamentary aspirations. Finally, OLD ENGLISH Catholics and the Gaelic Irish overcame their mutual suspicions to combine in the CONFEDERATION OF KILKENNY.

Rising of 1798   See UNITED IRISHMEN.

Rising of 1916   See EASTER RISING.

Riverdance

A dancing and musical spectacular that began as an interval act for the 1994 Eurovision Song Contest. It was expanded into a two-hour show performed at the Point Theatre in Dublin in 1995. The music and lyrics were by Bill Whelan, and it was produced by Moya Doherty and directed by John McColgan. Leading performers included the dancers Michael Flatley and Jean Butler, and the singing was performed by Anuna. The show has been performed worldwide before millions, and its cast has changed significantly as its stars have done separate programs of their own with similar success.

Robinson, Esmé Stuart Lennox (Lennox Robinson) (1886–1958)
writer, dramatist

Born in Douglas, County Cork, Robinson was a producer and manager of the ABBEY THEATRE, where more than 20 plays written by him were produced. Many of his works dealt with comic presentations of small-town life. The titles included *The Whiteheaded Boy* (1916), *The Round Table* (1922), *The Big House* (1926), and *Church Street* (1934). He also edited *Lady Gregory's Journals 1916–1930* (1946) and *The Oxford Book of Irish Verse* (1956).

Robinson, Mary (née Bourke) (1944–   )
barrister, politician, president of Ireland

Born in Ballina, County Mayo, Mary Robinson was educated at TRINITY COLLEGE DUBLIN, the KING'S INN, and Harvard University. She was professor of law at Trinity from 1969 to 1975 and a member of the SEANAD from 1969 to 1989. She was involved in numerous constitutional cases before Irish and European courts dealing with such issues as a woman's right to serve on juries, legal aid accessibility, and the decriminalization of homosexual acts. She joined the LABOUR PARTY in 1977, but left the party in protest at the Anglo-Irish Agreement signed at HILLSBOROUGH in 1985 by the Irish coalition government that included the Labour Party because she believed it was negotiated without the participation of the UNIONISTS of Northern Ireland. Nonetheless, that party nominated her for the Irish presidency in 1990. She was elected on the second count, getting the transfer votes of the FINE GAEL candidate Austin Currie and defeated the earlier expected favorite, Brian LENIHAN of FIANNA FÁIL. She was the first woman to be president of Ireland. She greatly increased the public profile of the presidency, especially from an international perspective. Robinson was much more active, giving her veiled endorsement, to the degree that she could within the restraints of her office, to various humanitarian and libertarian causes. She was the first Irish president to visit the queen of England and she conversed

Mary Robinson *(Mark Baker/Reuters/Landov)*

with Gerry ADAMS of SINN FÉIN while on a visit to Belfast to the consternation of many in the government. She resigned from the presidency a few weeks before the end of her term in 1997 to assume the post of High Commissioner for Human Rights with the United Nations, which she held until 2002. Among her present activities includes a professorship at Columbia University and work with human rights organizations.

Robinson, Peter (1948–)
politician
Born in Belfast and educated at the Annadale Grammar School, Belfast, Robinson became the general secretary of the DEMOCRATIC UNIONIST PARTY in 1975. He failed in his election bid that year to the Northern Ireland Constitutional Convention, running for Belfast East, but was returned for the same constituency to the West-

minster parliament in 1979 and ever since. He was also elected for Belfast East to the NORTHERN IRELAND ASSEMBLY in 1982. Robinson has been twice elected to the Northern Ireland Assembly called for by the GOOD FRIDAY AGREEMENT and served as a minister in the off-and-on-again power-sharing ministry selected by that assembly. In 1986 he was arrested and fined when he took part in a LOYALIST march into County Monaghan. In more recent times his views appear to reflect a more pragmatic side to the Democratic Unionists.

Roche, Adrienne (Adi Roche) (1955–)
antinuclear campaigner, presidential candidate
Born in Clonmel, County Tipperary, Roche worked for AER LINGUS for eight years, before taking voluntary redundancy in 1986 to be a full-time volunteer for the Irish Campaign for Nuclear Disarmament. Earlier she had been active in protesting a proposal to build a nuclear power station at Carnsore Point in County Wexford. She began in 1990 the Chernobyl Children's Project to assist children suffering from the effects of the radioactive fallout that was a result of the explosion in the Chernobyl nuclear reactor. The project has brought hundreds of children from the area to Ireland for holidays and for medical treatment and recuperation, and has supplied humanitarian aid to hospitals and orphanages in the region affected by the disaster. She co-produced the documentary *Black Wind, White Land* about the disaster and its effects and has written a book *The Children of Chernobyl* (1996), which was a best seller in Ireland. Roche was made the European Person of the Year in the same year. The next year, she ran unsuccessfully as the LABOUR PARTY candidate for the presidency of Ireland to succeed Mary ROBINSON. Mary McALEESE of FIANNA FÁIL won the election.

Roche, Sir Boyle (1743–1807)
soldier, politician
Born in Dublin of ANGLO-NORMAN extraction, Roche distinguished himself in service in the

British army, particularly in the American War of Independence. He returned to Ireland and served in the Irish parliament for several constituencies, including Gowran, County Kilkenny, 1777–83; Portarlington, County Laois, 1783–90; Tralee, County Kerry, 1790–97; and Old Leighton, County Carlow, 1797–1800. He opposed Catholic emancipation and favored the ACT OF UNION. He was renowned for his malapropisms, such as, "Why should we do anything for posterity? What has posterity done for us?" and "the cup of Ireland's misery has been overflowing for centuries and is not yet half full," and that his love for Ireland and England was such that he wished "to have the two sisters embrace like a brother."

Roche, Stephen (1959–   )
cyclist

Born in Ranelagh, Dublin, Roche won cycling's three biggest races, the Tour de France, the World Championship, and the Giro d'Italia, all in the same year, 1987, for which he was made a freeman of the city of Dublin. Earlier, as an amateur, he had won Ireland's Ras Tailteann in 1979 and had finished 24th in the Moscow Olympics of 1980.

Ros, Amanda McKittrick (1860–1939)
novelist, poet

Born in Drumaness, County Down, Ros wrote a number of novels as well as poetry of a very melodramatic and verbose style, employing much alliteration. Her works include *Irene Iddlesleigh* (1897), *Delina Delaney* (1898), *Poems of Puncture* (1912), and *Fumes of Formation* (1933), and the posthumously published *Bayonets of Bastard Sheen* (1949), *St. Scandalbags* (1954), and *Helen Huddleston* (1969).

Roscommon

Roscommon is an inland county in Connacht with a population of over 53,000 and an area of 950 square miles. Bounded on the east by Lough Rea and on the west by the counties of Sligo,

Galway, and Mayo, it consists primarily of a plateau with the Curlew Mountains on its north. Much of its drumlin topography is interspersed with peat. The legendary Queen Maeve launched *Tain Bo Cuailnge* (The cattle raid of cooley) on its plains. The names of the county and of the county town come from the Irish *Ros Comain,* which means the wood of Coman, an early saint. It contained the site for the inauguration of the ancient kings of Connacht, particularly the O'Connors, whose family home is Clonalis House, near Castlerea. Major industries include agriculture, bacon and pork production, cannery production, and dairy food manufacturing and processing. Major towns besides the county town are Boyle, Castlerea, Elphin, and Strokestown. The latter has a celebrated Famine Museum on the estate of a local landlord identified with subsidized emigration of famine victims from a county that was especially hard hit by the Great FAMINE. Celebrated natives of Roscommon include Douglas HYDE, Percy FRENCH, Turlough O'Carolan, and Maureen SULLIVAN.

Rosse, William Parsons, third earl of
astronomer

Born in York and educated at TRINITY COLLEGE DUBLIN and Magdalen College, Oxford, the earl of Rosse was a member of parliament for King's (Offaly) County from 1831 to 1834. Afterward, he devoted himself to scientific pursuits, most notably the construction on his father's estate at Birr Castle of what would be from 1848 to 1878 the largest telescope in the world. He designed the structure and directed its construction, especially its reflector, which was a remarkable engineering achievement. The telescope gave observers the ability to peer into space to depths never before reached, and from it he was able to discover, among other things, that the galaxies were spherical in shape. He was a member of numerous learned societies, including the Imperial Academy of St. Petersburg. He was made chancellor of the University of Dublin (Trinity College) in 1862. Parson succeeded his father as the earl of Rosse in 1841, and in 1845 he was elected as one of the representative Irish peers in the House of Lords. His record as a landlord was a good one as he devoted all of the revenues from his property during the Great FAMINE to the relief of distress.

Rowan, Archibald Hamilton
(1751–1834)
United Irishman
Born in London in a family from County Down, Rowan was educated at Westminster School and at Queen's College, Cambridge. He settled in Rathcoffey, County Kildare, in 1784 after having been in France and America. He inherited a considerable fortune. Nonetheless he joined the IRISH VOLUNTEERS that year, and soon was a member of the radical Northern Whig Club. In 1791 he joined the UNITED IRISHMEN. In 1794 he was convicted of sedition and sentenced to two years imprisonment, even though defended by James Philpot CURRAN. However, he escaped shortly afterward and made his way to France where he became a friend of Mary Wollstonecraft. The next year, 1795, he went to America. His experiences in France had turned him away from revolutionary violence and he moved to Hamburg in 1800. In 1803, upon receipt of a pardon, Rowan returned to Ireland, settling on the family estate in Killyleagh Castle, County Down. He was a supporter of Catholic emancipation.

Royal Irish Academy
Ireland's leading learned society, it was founded in 1785 by James Caulfied, the earl of CHARLEMONT, to promote the study of science, polite literature, and antiquities. Its governing council has included representatives from the sciences and the humanities and has sponsored conferences, discourses, and research. It published its *Transactions* from 1786 to 1907 and since 1830 has published its *Proceedings,* which continues to appear in three sections dealing, respectively, with mathematics, biology, and the environment. Celebrated participants in the work of the academy in the past have included Irish archaeologist George PETRIE, scientist William Rowan HAMILTON, and genealogists

Charles O'CONOR, Eugene O'CURRY, and John O'DONOVAN. Nonscientific work it has sponsored in recent times includes a *Dictionary of the Irish Language* (1913–76), and the ongoing *New History of Ireland* and a *Dictionary of Irish Biography.* There are less than 300 members elected to the academy, some of whom are honorary members, and a permanent staff of about 40. It receives a government grant.

Royal Irish Constabulary
Original formed as the County Constabulary in 1822 as the first formal police force for maintaining law and order in Ireland, as opposed to grand jury–summoned posses responsive to and reflective of landlord and gentry sentiment, it became a national force in 1837 at the behest of reform-minded Whig undersecretary Thomas DRUMMOND. In 1867 the force was given the title "royal" in recognition of its service in combating the FENIAN rising. Most of its rank and file was drawn from the Catholic population. The force performed its assigned responsibilities in enforcing evictions, combating the land league, and restraining other types of agitation. A career in the constabulary was sought by many in the community, which was closely linked to the force until the WAR OF INDEPENDENCE, when the IRA made its members the particular objects of its violent campaign. There followed an inevitable massive resignation from the force, which prompted the government to recruit as substitutes the BLACK AND TANS and an auxiliary force called the AUXILIARIES.

Royal Ulster Constabulary
This was the police force formed for Northern Ireland by the parliament of Northern Ireland in 1922. Originally it was hoped that its members would include Catholics in proportion to the Catholic portion of the population, but relatively few joined. Many of its members had served earlier in the ROYAL IRISH CONSTABULARY. In contending with the IRA, still involved in action in Northern Ireland after the ANGLO-IRISH TREATY,

the force's numbers were supplemented by auxiliary special forces, who were notoriously sectarian. The first serious efforts to deal with sectarianism existing in the force came after the issue of a parliamentary commission report in 1969. However, the intensification of the IRA campaign in the 1970s and 1980s worked to inhibit Catholic recruitment and saw instances of abusive behavior by the police in the form of maltreatment of prisoners, collaboration with LOYALIST groups, and instances of "shoot to kill" tactics. On the other hand, several hundred of its members were killed by the IRA, often while not on duty but in their own homes. Since the GOOD FRIDAY AGREEMENT and following the recommendations of the Patten Commission the force has been renamed the Police Service of Northern Ireland and a policy of discrimination in favor of Catholic recruits to achieve parity in the force has been implemented.

Russell, George William ("AE") (1867–1935)
editor, poet, mystic

Born in Lurgan, County Antrim, and trained at the Metropolitan School of Art, Dublin, Russell began contributing to *The Irish Theosophist* in 1892 and shortly afterward became involved in the Agricultural Organization Society that sponsored the cooperative movement as he edited its journal *The Irish Homestead.* He served as vice president of the ABBEY THEATRE and was a sponsor of many young writers. He was a critic of employers during the 1913–14 Dublin lockout and took part in the IRISH CONVENTION, 1917. Russell refused a seat in the SEANAD of the IRISH FREE STATE. Instead he started a weekly paper *The Irish Statesman,* which ran from 1923 to 1930. His writings ranged from mysticism (*The Candle of Vision* [1919]) to economics (*The Building of a Rural Civilization* [1910]) to politics (*The National Being* [1916]).

Russell, Seán (1893–1940)
republican revolutionary

Born in Dublin, educated at the IRISH CHRISTIAN BROTHERS' School, Fairview, Russell was a member of the IRISH VOLUNTEERS and took part in the EASTER RISING. He was a participant in the WAR OF INDEPENDENCE and opposed the ANGLO-IRISH TREATY. He remained in the anti-treaty IRA and disapproved of the founding of FIANNA FÁIL by Eamon DE VALERA. Russell opposed the left-wing elements in the IRA, who were led by Peadar O'DONNELL and Frank RYAN, as he placed primary emphasis on the national question. He called for a national war against Britain as a member of the Army Council of the IRA, of which he became chief of staff. It participated in one of the BOMBING CAMPAIGNS IN BRITAIN undertaken by Irish nationalist revolutionaries, with a series of bombings in 1939. He made his way to the United States seeking aid for his cause and from there through Italy to Nazi Germany. From there he joined with his old antagonist from the left-wing of the movement, Frank Ryan, on a 1940 U-boat mission to Ireland to recruit IRA activists for further action. However, he died on the way and was buried at sea west of Galway. Ryan returned to Germany, where he died before the war ended.

Russell, Thomas (1767–1803)
United Irishman

Born in County Cork, Russell had served as an officer in the British army, but resigned his commission after meeting Theobald Wolfe TONE with whom he founded the UNITED IRISHMEN in 1791. In 1796 he was arrested, but released on condition that he leave Ireland. He went to France. In 1803 Russell joined the uprising led by Robert EMMET, but he was arrested, convicted, and hanged in October.

Ryan, Dr. James (1891–1970)
politician

Born in Tomcoole, County Wexford, Ryan was educated at St. Peter's College, Tomcoole, and at University College Dublin, where he qualified as a doctor. While still a medical student he took part in the EASTER RISING and was interned afterward. He was elected for Wexford South to the first DÁIL ÉIREANN, and for Wexford to the second Dáil. He was imprisoned for a while during the WAR OF INDEPENDENCE, while also serving on the Wexford County Council. He opposed the ANGLO-IRISH TREATY and was one of the occupants of the FOUR COURTS. He went on hunger strike when imprisoned by the PROVISIONAL GOVERNMENT. Not elected to the third Dáil, he was elected for Wexford to the fourth in 1923 while a prisoner. Ryan was an abstentionist, but became a founding member of FIANNA FÁIL in 1926. He was reelected in 1927, took his seat with the other Fianna Fáil members that August, and was reelected in every election until his retirement in 1965. He became minister for agriculture in 1932 and held the post until 1947, when he became minister for health and social welfare. He served as minister for finance in subsequent Fianna Fáil governments, 1951–1954 and 1957 to 1965, until his retirement from the Dáil. Ryan was subsequently selected for SEANAD ÉIREANN, where he served until 1969.

Ryan, Frank (1902–1944)

republican revolutionary

Born in Elton, County Limerick, and educated at St. Colman's College, Fermoy, and at University College Dublin, Ryan interrupted his studies to take part in the WAR OF INDEPENDENCE. Although opposed to the ANGLO-IRISH TREATY, he completed his studies and became a teacher, while continuing a connection with the IRA. He was associated with left-wing leaders in the movement, such as Peadar O'DONNELL, and was a founder of SAOR ÉIRE. He organized Irish volunteers for the Republican cause in the Spanish Civil War, during which he was wounded. While home in Dublin recuperating he sat unsuccessfully for a DÁIL ÉIREANN seat for Dublin South in the 1937 general election. Ryan then returned to the war in Spain where he became an adjutant to a Republican general. The Nationalists captured him in 1938. He was spared sentence of death by the intervention of Eamon DE VALERA. In 1940 he was released and went to Germany. The same year he joined an abortive U-boat mission to Ireland to stimulate IRA action. The vessel returned after Russell died. Ryan himself died in Germany in 1944 as his health deteriorated.

Ryan, William Patrick (1867–1942)

journalist

Born near Templemore, County Tipperary, Ryan worked as a journalist in England for the *Catholic Times*, the *Sun*, the *Weekly Sun*, the *Morning Leader*, and the *Daily Chronicle*. He returned to Ireland and in 1905 became the editor of the *Irish Peasant*. His socialist and anticlerical views in a widely read paper incurred hierarchical outrage and the paper was closed in 1906. He tried to revive it with the same name in 1907 and with a different name, the *Irish Nation*, from 1908 to 1910, but his efforts failed and he returned permanently to England where he continued to work as a journalist. His writings include *The Pope's Green Island* (1912) and *The Irish Labour Movement* (1919).

S

Sadleir, John (1814–1856)
politician

Born in Shrone Hill, County Tipperary and educated at CLONGOWES WOOD COLLEGE, Sadleir was originally a solicitor, but he turned to business speculation, including involvement in a joint-stock bank and a number of railway companies. He was elected a member of parliament for Carlow from 1847 to 1853 and was one of the IRISH BRIGADE, a group whose members were committed to preserving their independence and their collective power by not taking office in any government, After the government of Lord Derby had been brought down, he broke his pledge and helped bring about the demise of the brigade by accepting office as a junior lord of the Treasury in the Aberdeen government. He was subsequently returned for Sligo. However, when speculation with the funds of investors in a bank he had started failed, he committed suicide in 1856.

St. Edna's

This was the school for boys started by Patrick PEARSE in Ranelagh, Dublin, in 1908 as an alternative to the "murder machine," as he labeled the Irish educational system with its emphasis on examinations and rote learning. Irish folklore and mythology served as the guiding inspiration of the school, in which the Irish language was taught. The school was continually beset with financial difficulties, although it did draw well over 100 students and boasted as either teachers or occasional lecturers such notables as Pearse himself, his brother William, Thomas MACDON-AGH, William Butler YEATS, Eoin MACNEILL, and Douglas HYDE. In 1910 the school moved to 50-acre site, the Hermitage, Rathfarnham, and survived on contributions, many of which came from Irish-American sources, especially from CLAN NA GAEL. Some of the preparations for the EASTER RISING took place in the school, which was kept open by Pearse's mother and sister after he and his brother were executed following the rising. The school closed permanently in 1935. It was bequeathed to the Irish state in 1969 by Pearse's sister upon her death.

Sands, Bobby (1954–1981)
revolutionary, hunger striker

Born in Rathcoole, Belfast, Sands became active in the IRA soon after his own family had been forced from their home by LOYALISTS. He was arrested and imprisoned twice for IRA activities. On the second imprisonment he quickly joined the protest for special status as political prisoner. He was the leader of the imprisoned IRA members who had called off an earlier HUNGER STRIKE on the mistaken impression that their demands had been met. Accordingly, when the second strike was begun on March 1, 1981, he insisted on being the first striker in a protest that was deliberately designed so that individual strikes would begin periodically to enable the strike to continue following the death of any one participant. While on strike his name was placed in nomination to fill a parliamentary vacancy in a by-election for the parliamentary seat for Fermanagh–South Tyrone. The SOCIAL DEMOCRATIC AND LABOUR PARTY did not run a candidate for the seat and Sands was elected in April, although a prisoner. His death on May 5, 1981, was followed by extensive disturbances during which many from both Northern Ireland communities were killed. Several others hunger strikers would follow him to the their deaths before the strike was called off in September. The strike probably brought more international sympathy to the IRA than any other action during the three decades of campaign that marked the modern troubles. Probably his electoral success was one of the major factors in prompting SINN FÉIN's resort to electoral politics in subsequent elections, although the organization did not reject the use of violence until its cease-fire in 1994.

Saor Éire

Saor Éire was a movement formed by left-wing members of the IRA in 1931 to combine the nationalist objective with the class objective of combating capitalism. Leading figures in the movement included Peadar O'DONNELL, Frank RYAN, and Seán MACBRIDE. The movement was condemned by the Catholic hierarchical and the CUMANN NA NGAEDHEAL government succeeded in outlawing it. The organizations subsequently collapsed, although its memory was invoked by some in the 1960s.

Sarsfield, Patrick (c. 1655–1693)
soldier
Born in Kildare, Sarsfield served in the army of Louis XIV, but advanced in the British army when James II enabled Catholics to do so. He remained supportive of James after the Glorious Revolution and became a brigadier in the JACOBITE forces in Ireland. His attack on the cavalry of the forces of William II at Ballyneety, County Limerick, in 1690 prevented an earlier siege of Limerick. However, the following year Sarsfield capitulated and negotiated the Treaty of Limerick, which confirmed the defeat of the Jacobites and of Gaelic Ireland and whose conciliatory terms were disregarded with the passage of the PENAL LAWS.

Saunderson, Edward (1837–1906)
politician
Born in Ballinmallard, County Cavan, Saunderson was a Liberal member of parliament for Cavan from 1865 to 1874. He became disillusioned with the Irish program of William Gladstone as prime minister. He joined the ORANGE ORDER and was elected as a Conservative for North Armagh in 1885 and he held his seat until his death. Saunderson was the leader who brought Ulster members of parliament who opposed HOME RULE into a single group known as the UNIONIST Party, which subsequently affiliated with the Conservative Party.

Saurin, William (1757–1839)
politician
Born in Belfast and educated at TRINITY COLLEGE DUBLIN, Saurin was a barrister and a member of the Irish parliament for Blessington, County Wicklow. He opposed Catholic relief and served as a prosecutor of UNITED IRISHMEN. He also opposed the ACT OF UNION, but he did accept the post of solicitor general for Ireland, which he held from 1807 to 1822. He was the particular object of scorn of Daniel O'CONNELL in his harangues against the judicial and political system, especially in delivering a four-hour closing statement in the trial of publisher John Magee whose conviction for sedition was a foregone conclusion. After he was removed from his post by Arthur Wellesley, the duke of WELLINGTON, because of his intemperate attitudes, Saurin returned to private practice, although continuing in opposition to Catholic emancipation and to O'Connell.

Sayers, Peig (1873–1958)
storyteller
Born in Dunquin, County Kerry, Sayers married and lived on Great BLASKETT ISLAND off the coast of Kerry. She had 10 children, six of whom died in childhood and another as an adult. She was not literate in Irish, but told a remarkable number of Irish stories and was visited by numerous

scholars and Irish language revivalists. She dictated her memoirs to her son, which were published as *Peig: A Sceal Féin* (1936) and *Machnamh Seana-Mhna* (1939). She left the island in her later years.

Scarampi, Pietro
papal envoy

Scarampi served as the papal envoy to the CON-FEDERATION OF KILKENNY from 1643 to 1645. He brought money and stores to assist the cause. He argued against a truce with the royalist forces led by the duke of ORMOND, but the confederation agreed to such. He was succeeded by Giovanni Battista RINUCCINI.

Schomberg, Friedrich Herman, duke of (1615–1690)
general

Born in Heidelberg, Germany, Schomberg was a Protestant and became a celebrated mercenary soldier having served in the Dutch, Swedish, and French military. He resigned from the rank of Marshall of France after the revocation of the Edict of Nantes and the ending of religious freedom for non-Catholics in 1685. William III named him general of his army in 1688. He led an army of 14,000 to Ireland and captured Carrickfergus. He moved south as far as Dundalk, where he camped. The damp conditions in the area resulted in 6,000 of his men dying from disease. Schomberg rallied the Huguenot regiments in the Battle of the BOYNE, at which he lost his own life.

Scots-Irish

The term refers to the tens of thousands of Ulster Protestants who immigrated to America in the 18th century and who settled primarily in the Appalachian Mountains region. The term Scots-Irish developed in the 19th century as a means by which to distinguish these individuals from those arriving in a later immigration from Ireland, who were primarily Catholics, especially before and during the Great FAMINE.

Scullabogue

Scullabogue, County Wexford, was the site of an atrocity committed on June 6 during the Rising of 1798 when about 100 LOYALISTS, many of them children and noncombatants, were burned to death by rebels on their way to the battle at New Ross.

Seanad Éireann

The upper house in the Irish legislature with a limited power in delaying legislation, the Seanad was first established by the constitution of the Irish Free State in part to guarantee the participation and inclusion of the UNIONIST minority in the new state. Half of the membership was to be named by the president of the Executive Council with the express purpose of including groups or parties not represented in the DÁIL ÉIREANN. The other half was to be selected by the Dáil according to proportional representation. The entire membership, by lot, were to be given terms of either three, six, nine or 12 years to insure that a quarter of the membership would be up for reelection every three years. All elected in subsequent elections were to serve 12 years. Those nominated to the first Seanad included Oliver St. John GOGARTY, Andrew JAMESON, the earl of DUNRAVEN, and William Butler YEATS. In subsequent elections, all citizens of 30 years of age and over could vote from a panel of candidates, one-third nominated by the incumbent Seanad and two-thirds by the Dáil, that would consist of three times the number as there were seats open. The turnout was at first poor and nominations were of those less distinguished. In subsequent years the Séanad and the Dáil were to each nominate as many candidates as there were places to fill and the election was to be by a joint vote of both bodies. The FIANNA FÁIL Party was always antagonistic to the Seanad, especially because it included a number of unionists. When Eamon DE VALERA came to power in 1932 one of his objectives was to abolish the Seanad, especially since the body delayed other legislation he was promoting in his efforts to undo much of the ANGLO-IRISH TREATY. He moved for its abolition in 1934 and the enabling legislation was passed in 1936. De Valera reestablished a Seanad in the 1937 constitution, which continues today. The term of the Seanad runs concurrent with the term of the Dáil. It has 60 members, 11 of whom are named by the Taoiseach, three are elected by the alumni of the NATIONAL UNIVERSITY OF IRELAND, three by the alumni of TRINITY COLLEGE DUBLIN, and the remainder are elected by county councils from five panels: cultural and education, agricultural, labor, industrial and commercial, and administrative. The panels marked a concession to the corporatist thinking of the 1930s, but in fact the nominees are invariably regular politicians, usually recently defeated candidates or candidates aspiring to eventual election to the Dáil. The Seanad has a very restricted suspensive veto power.

Services, Industrial, Professional, and Technical Union

The largest trade union in Ireland with more than 200,000 members, it was formed in 1990 with the amalgamation of the IRISH TRANSPORT AND GENERAL WORKERS' UNION and the smaller Federated Workers' Union of Ireland. James LARKIN had formed the former in 1909. When he returned from America in the 1920s, he was dissatisfied with the conservatism of the union under William O'BRIEN and started the rival workers' union. However, by the 1970s and 1980s, the ideological clashes had disappeared and rationalization prevailed in union organization.

Settlement Act

The Settlement Act passed by parliament in 1652 gave effect to the legislation of the Long Parliament in 1642 calling for ADVENTURERS to help finance the parliamentary cause with compensation to come from confiscation. The 1652 legislation determined those individuals in Ireland who were to be subjected to forfeiture of their landed estates. Exempt from any pardon were participants in the early rebellion, Roman

Catholic hierarchy who had supported the rebellion, and all who had killed civilians or all civilians who had killed English soldiers, and any still in arms who had not submitted. To make sure no one would escape, 104 individuals were specifically named in the act to be ineligible for pardon. Others, who had shown "constant good affection to the commonwealth of England" during the rebellion, would suffer partial forfeiture of between one-fifth and one-third of their estate depending on their degree of delinquency, and might be required to accept alternate property in other sections of Ireland in exchange for those portions of their estate still left to them. This is the origin of the celebrated "To Hell or to Connacht" policy. Obviously the legislation applied to the landed classes among the Catholics, not to the rank and file of the population. But many of those who were tenants invariably followed their lords when they were expelled from their property. A subsequent "Act of Satisfaction" was passed by the parliament in 1653 to regularize the policy of distributing forfeited property that Oliver CROMWELL had dictated. That policy was to use forfeited land in 10 counties to be divided, half to compensate Adventurers and half to compensate soldiers. Forfeited lands in other counties were placed at the government's disposal to meet public debts, to make grants to leaders, and to meet deficiencies in the compensation of Adventurers and soldiers. A later Act of Settlement, passed in 1662, after the restoration of the monarchy, confirmed a body of commissioners established by Charles II to allow restoration of land to those who fought on the side of the CONFEDERATION OF KILKENNY and who had abided by the treaties with the royalists in 1646 and 1649, to those who had served the king abroad while he was in exile, and to those who had been innocent of involvement in the rebellion. At the same time the lands conferred to Adventurers and soldiers were confirmed. Obviously there was not enough land left to be distributed equitably, and, in 1663, an Act of Explanation put a stop to any additional claims by the dispossessed from being heard and one-third of the property of soldiers and Adventurers was surrendered to meet the valid restoration claims. The effect of the whole process, in spite of the amelioration offered by the Act of Settlement in 1662, was to change the proportion of land owned by Catholics in Ireland from three-fifths in 1641 to one-fifth in 1663.

Shackleton, Ernest (1874–1922)
explorer

Born in Kilkea, County Kildare, Shackleton's family moved to Dublin when he was six and four years later permanently to London. He was educated at Dulwich College. He joined the merchant service rather than the Royal Navy because of limitations on his family's finances. He accompanied Captain Robert Scott on an Antarctic expedition in 1901. In 1907 he led his own expedition that came within 100 miles of reaching the actual South Pole, although he did reach the magnetic pole. He was knighted in 1909. In 1914, after the First World War had started, Shackleton led another expedition to Antarctica. He failed to achieve his goal of crossing the continent, but photographs taken of the expedition gained him worldwide fame. Even more extraordinary was the rescue he achieved of his crew of 28 after their ship *Endurance* was trapped in ice. He and five of the crew, including Thomas Crean, set out in a small boat on a treacherous 800-mile trip to the island of South Georgia seeking aid. They returned and successfully rescued the entire crew. After serving in an expeditionary force to northern Russia in 1918 and 1919, he returned on another expedition to the Antarctic, but he died in South Georgia, where he is buried.

Shannon, Henry Boyle, earl of (1682–1764)
politician

Born in Castlemartyr, County Cork, he was a member of the Irish parliament for Midleton from 1707 to 1713, for Kilmallock from 1713 to 1715, and for Cork from 1715 to 1753. He successfully resisted government efforts to appropriate a revenue surplus for the exchequer. He was one of the UNDERTAKERS, who the lord lieutenant was required to rely upon to manage the government's business through the parliament. He was speaker of the house from 1733 to 1753. He was rewarded with a pension for life and was created the earl of Shannon in 1756.

Shaw, George Bernard (1856–1950)
playwriter, man of letters

Born in Dublin, the son of a grain merchant father and an artistically inclined mother, Shaw left school at 16 and worked as a clerk in a land agent's office. He went to London in 1876 and made that his permanent residence. He tried his hand unsuccessfully at writing novels, but turned to journalism and reviewing. Accepting socialism, he became a member of the Fabian Society, which sought to advance socialism gradually by slowly converting the leaders of society

George Bernard Shaw *(Library of Congress)*

to individual aspects of the program. He then began writing plays with a political message, as he was influenced by the work of Henrik Ibsen. The objects of his criticism included middle-class hypocrisy, economic exploitation, and the military. Among his then controversial titles were *Widowers' Houses* (1892), *Mrs. Warren's Profession* (1894), and *Arms and the Man* (1894). He married an independently wealthy Irish woman, Charlotte Payne-Townsend, in 1898, and turned exclusively to playwriting. Among his plays in the beginning of the 20th century were *Man and Superman* (1903), *John Bull's Other Island* (1904), and *Major Barbara* (1905). He usually wrote a lengthy introduction to his plays in which he espoused his notions of societal responsibility for hardship and progressive human evolution. Beginning with *The Shewing-Up of Blanco Posnet* (1909), his plays began to appear at the ABBEY THEATRE, even his *John Bull's Other Island* that had originally been refused. From 1905 on he began to spend his summer holidays at Parknasilla, County Kerry. He approved the EASTER RISING, opposed the execution of Roger CASEMENT, opposed British involvement in the First World War, but also opposed Irish separatism, as he though NATIONALIST sentiment worked against progressive evolution. Later plays included *Back to Methuselah* (1921) and *Saint Joan* (1923). He was awarded the Nobel Prize in literature in 1925. Like many talented writers he was uncritical in his judgment of some foreign leaders, as he wrote and spoke approvingly at times of Mussolini, Stalin, and Hitler. He also wrote political tracts such as *Fabianism and the Empire* (1900) and *The Intelligent Women's Guide to Socialism and Capitalism* (1928) and took part in frequent public debates with English controversialists Hilaire Belloc and G. K. Chesterton.

Shaw, William (1823–1895)
politician
Born in Cork, Shaw was a minister in the Congregational Church from 1846 to 1850. Then he turned to business as a bank director and finally was elected to parliament as a member for Ban-

don (1868–74) and then for County Cork (1874–85). A member of the IRISH PARLIAMENTARY PARTY, he succeeded Issac BUTT when the latter died in 1879, but was defeated by Charles Stewart PARNELL for the leadership the following year. He and 11 other members left the party. However, he continued to support William Gladstone and HOME RULE.

Shee, Sir Martin Archer (1769–1850)
portrait painter
Born in Dublin to an impoverished Catholic gentry family, Shee studied at the Dublin Society and began at a young age to make a living doing portrait paintings. In 1788 he went to London and attended the Royal Academy. He came under the influence of Sir Joshua Reynolds and Gilbert Stuart. By 1800 he had established himself as a portrait painter and was elected president of the Royal Academy in 1830.

Sheehy, Nicholas (1728–1766)
priest
Born in Clonmel, County Tipperary, Sheehy was educated at Santiago and at Salamanca and ordained a priest in 1750. He served first in the city of Waterford and then in the parishes of Shanraghen and Templetenny. Siding with his parishioners in disputes over rents and tithes, he was accused of involvement in WHITEBOY crimes. Successfully petitioning for a change of venue from a suspected packed jury in the Clonmel court, he was acquitted in a trial before the King's Bench in Dublin. However he was rearrested and charged with murder in the Clonmel court, convicted, and hung on March 15, 1766.

Sheehy Skeffington, Francis (1878–1916)
journalist, socialist, pacifist
Born in Bailieborough, County Cavan, Sheehy was educated at University College Dublin and served as its registrar from 1902 to 1904 until he resigned in a dispute over female academics. A

committed feminist, he added his wife's surname, Sheehy, to his own upon marriage in 1903. He had been a friend of James JOYCE while a student. He edited the suffragist paper the *Irish Citizen*, and was an editor of the *Nationalist*. He also published a biography of Michael DAVITT in 1908. He was a pacifist, although he was for a while a member of the IRISH CITIZEN ARMY, but was a close friend of many involved in the NATIONALIST struggle and was even hosted by CLAN NA GAEL while on a lecture tour of the United States in 1915. He disapproved of the EASTER RISING and ironically was arrested while attempting to discourage looting. The arresting officer, a Captain J. C. Bowen-Colthurst, held an arbitrary court-martial and had him executed. The same captain was subsequently convicted of murder for the action, but escaped penalty on grounds of insanity.

Sheehy Skeffington, Hannah (1877–1946)

feminist, political radical

Born in Loughmore, County Tipperary, Sheehy was the daughter of David Sheehy, an IRISH PARLIAMENTARY PARTY member of parliament. She was married to Francis SHEEHY SKEFFINGTON and was supported by him in founding the Irish Women's Suffrage League. She was imprisoned for destructive behavior in suffrage protests in 1912. During the WAR OF INDEPENDENCE she supported SINN FÉIN and made international appeals for their cause, including a meeting with President Woodrow Wilson. She also served on the revolutionary DÁIL ÉIREANN courts that had replaced the regular judiciary in Ireland during the war. She opposed the ANGLO-IRISH TREATY and visited the United States campaigning on behalf of its REPUBLICAN opponents. She visited the Soviet Union and was imprisoned for a month for republican activism in Newry, Northern Ireland, in 1933. Her sister, Mary, was married to Thomas KETTLE, and her sister, Kathleen, was married to Cruise O'Brien. The latter were the parents of Conor Cruise O'BRIEN.

Sheil, Richard Lalor (1791–1851)

politician

Born in Drumdowney, County Kilkenny, Sheil was educated at Stonyhurst and at TRINITY COLLEGE DUBLIN. Although called to the bar in 1814, he supported himself at first by writing plays until his practice improved. He clashed with Daniel O'CONNELL as he was willing to accept the veto by the government on hierarchical appointments in return for Catholic emancipation. However, he later supported him in his campaign for the same and was himself elected to parliament in 1830 for a constituency in England and subsequently sat for County Louth from 1831 to 1833, County Tipperary from 1833 to 1841, and for Dungarvan from 1841 on. He helped bring about the Lichfield House Compact between O'Connell and the Whigs in 1835. From then on he secured for himself a number of sinecures, such as vice president of the Board of Trade in 1839, judge advocate in 1841, and master of the Mint from 1846 to 1850, and became ambassador to Tuscany in 1851. He died in Florence.

Sheridan, Jim (1949–   )

film director, writer

Born in Dublin and educated at University College Dublin, Sheridan had several plays produced in Dublin before becoming the director of the Irish Arts Center in New York, where he also studied at New York University. His adaptation of the Christy Brown autobiography *My Left Foot* into a film in 1989 won several Academy Award nominations and Oscars for two of the actors. Other successful films were *The Field* (1990) with Richard HARRIS and *In the Name of the Father* (1993), about the falsely imprisoned GUILDFORD FOUR, which won a Berlin Film Festival award and several Oscar nominations. Other films he helped write include *Into the West* (1992) and *Some Mother's Son* (1996), about the HUNGER STRIKE of 1981.

Sheridan, Richard Brinsley (1751–1816)

playwright, politician

Born in Dublin, Sheridan's family settled in Bath, England. He eloped in 1771 with the beautiful and musically talented Elizabeth Linney. Instead of allowing her to sing professionally, he turned to playwriting to make a living and to support an extravagant lifestyle. He achieved remarkable success with plays such as *The Rivals* (1775) based on his elopement, *The School for Scandal* (1777), and *The Critic* (1779). His success enabled him to buy the Drury Lane theatre. In 1780 he was elected to parliament for Stafford and was associated with the Whigs, particularly Charles James Fox and Edmund BURKE, and delivered remarkable orations in support of the impeachment of Warren Hastings, the governor-general of the East India Company. He was also supportive of American grievances at the time of the American Revolution. He opposed the ACT OF UNION. Sheridan lost his seat in 1811. The theatre he owned burned in 1809, which, coupled with enormous debts incurred by his lavish spending, subjected him to arrest for debt. He died in 1816 and was given an impressive funeral by his friends in Westminster Cathedral.

Sheridan, Thomas (1719–1788)
actor

Born in Quilca, County Cavan, Sheridan's father was an educator and his godfather was Jonathan SWIFT. He was educated at TRINITY COLLEGE DUBLIN. He performed at the Smock Alley Theatre in 1743 and soon became its manager. He also appeared in Drury Lane and in Covent Garden. He taught elocution, wrote a volume on the educational system, *British Education: Source of Disorder* (1756), compiled *A General Dictionary of the English Language*, 2 vols. (1780), and edited *The Works of Swift, with Life*, 18 vols. (1784). He was the father of Richard Brinsley SHERIDAN.

Shields, Arthur (1896–1970)
actor

Born in Dublin, Shields acted at the ABBEY THEATRE. He served in the IRISH VOLUNTEERS and took part in the EASTER RISING, after which he was interned at Frongoch for several months.

Upon release he resumed acting. His brother, William, was more famous, performing under the stage name of Barry FITZGERALD. He went to America in 1936 to play in a film version of the Seán O'CASEY play *The Plough and the Stars*. Shields remained in California for the rest of life, believing that the dry climate was more appropriate for his health, and he continued to act in movies and on television.

Silken Thomas   See KILDARE, THOMAS (SILKEN THOMAS) FITZGERALD, THE 10TH EARL OF.

Simnel, Lambert (1475–1522)
pretender to the English throne

Lambert Simnel was trained to impersonate the Earl of Warwick, the nephew of the late Edward IV, in a challenge to Henry VII. He went to Ireland in 1487 where the ANGLO-IRISH community supported his cause and recognized him as king. When he led an expeditionary force to England he was defeated and spent the rest of his life as a servant in the court of Henry VII.

Sinn Féin

Arthur GRIFFITH proposed Sinn Féin as a national policy in 1905 and started a newspaper with the same name in 1906. In 1907 a number of distinct political groups, including the Duncannon Clubs and CUMANN NA NGAEDHEAL joined with Griffith's National Council to form Sinn Féin as a political party. The strategy of the movement was to elect members to the Westminster parliament who would refuse to attend and instead meet in Ireland and proclaim a distinct Irish parliament without waiting for HOME RULE legislation. Griffith's ultimate strategy aimed to secure a self-governing Ireland that would retain as its king the ruling monarch is Britain, much like the same monarch ruled as emperor in Austria and king in Hungary. His policy called for economic protection and self-sufficiency. The party did not do well in by-elections or in the general elections of 1910, but it did gain some places in local governmental bodies. Many members of the movement were also members of other nationalist political and cultural movements of the time ranging from the GAELIC LEAGUE through the IRISH REPUBLICAN BROTHERHOOD, although Sinn Féin from the beginning was neither violent nor entirely separatist or REPUBLICAN. A common misconception among British commentators was to regard the 1916 EASTER RISING as a Sinn Féin effort. In 1917 the character of the movement changed when Eamon DE VALERA was elected its president and replaced Griffith. It went from success to success in a series of by-elections in 1917 and 1918 and virtually eliminated the IRISH PARLIAMENTARY

Propaganda poster for Sinn Féin *(Library of Congress)*

PARTY in the 1918 general election. Its elected members, who were neither in jail nor on the run, gathered in Dublin's Mansion House to form the DÁIL ÉIREANN as the government of Ireland. Soon clashes between the IRISH VOLUNTEERS and the ROYAL IRISH CONSTABULARY intensified into the WAR OF INDEPENDENCE as the Dáil considered the Irish Volunteers to be the Army of the Irish Republic, or the IRA. The Sinn Féin movement split over acceptance or rejection of the ANGLO-IRISH TREATY and the split eventually resulted in the CIVIL WAR. The supporters of the treaty, who formed the PROVISIONAL GOVERNMENT and what would soon be the Irish Free State, formed a new party called CUMANN NA NGAEDHEAL in order to attract support from the many in Ireland who had never supported Sinn Féin, whereas the opponents of the treaty and supporters of the IRREGULARS in the civil war retained the name of Sinn Féin. Its successful candidates in elections to the third and fourth Dáils refused to take their seats, as they regard those and all subsequent Dáils as illegitimate for having been created by authority of the British and in violation of the original Dáil oath to uphold the Irish Republic. By 1926 the leader of Sinn Féin, de Valera, broke with his own party on the issue of abstention, as he supported a willingness to serve in the Dáil if the offensive oath to the king was removed. Most of the leading figures in Sinn Féin followed him into a new party, FIANNA FÁIL, and they took their seats in 1927 when threatened with legislation that would have deprived them of their seats if they did not take the oath and enter the chamber. A minority remained in the Sinn Féin Party and the few elected continued to abstain from their places in the legislature. The party was also closely linked with the IRA, which it supported in occasional violent campaigns, particularly during the late 1930s and in the late 1950s and early 1960s. When the leadership of the party began to emphasize social more than national questions in the late 1960s and turned more to intellectual debate than to military organization, a split developed. The more nationalist and militarist members, disappointed at the movement's lack of preparedness for the violent community confrontations in Northern Ireland in 1969, started a separate organization called the PROVISIONAL SINN FÉIN and also a Provisional IRA. The organization itself called itself the OFFICIAL SINN FÉIN and the OFFICIAL IRA. It did not at first foreswear the use of violence, but soon abandoned it, and within a few years called itself Sinn Féin the Workers' Party, and later the Workers' Party. A further split saw a majority form the democratic left, which later merged with the LABOUR PARTY. Provisional Sinn Féin soon called itself simply Sinn Féin. Tasting political success with the election of Bobby SANDS, while on HUNGER STRIKE, to parliament in 1981, the movement, led by Gerry ADAMS, began to take electoral politics in Northern Ireland more seriously, while not rejecting the continued use of violence. Its success in NORTHERN IRELAND ASSEMBLY elections, local government elections, and ultimately Adams's own election to parliament in 1983, created a major shift in attitudes. At first the slogan was "the ballot box and the armalite," but by the mid-1990s the IRA agreed to proclaim a cease-fire, although it did not cease to exist. In this period elected Sinn Féiners have refused to take their seats in the Westminster parliament, although insisting on and receiving compensation and expense money, as well as office space. However, they have taken their places in local governmental bodies, in the European Parliament, and in the Northern Ireland Assembly formed as part of the GOOD FRIDAY AGREEMENT. The willingness of Sinn Féin candidates to take their seats in the Dáil Éireann caused a further split as a small minority of more traditional members, calling themselves Republican Sinn Féin, refused to abandon the generations' held view of the Dáil as constituting the so-called government of Ireland. Later, others dissatisfied with the cease-fire formed a 32 County Sovereignty Movement. However, Sinn Féin has gone on to achieve considerable success, including having held seats in a power-sharing government in Northern Ireland, surpassing the SOCIAL DEMOCRATIC AND LABOUR PARTY, as the largest non-UNIONIST party in Northern Ireland, electing several members to Dáil Éireann and increasing its presence in a number of local government bodies in the Irish Republic, especially in urban areas. However, at this writing, the reestablishment of a power-sharing executive in Northern Ireland is being held up by Unionist distrust of its abandonment of violence. Also, parties in the Republic of Ireland refuse to accept Sinn Féin as a coalition partner so long as it retains its ties with the IRA.

Sirr, Henry Charles (1764–1841)
army officer, police official
Born in Dublin, Sirr served in the British army from 1778 to 1791. In 1796 he obtained the same post his father had held as town-major head of the police, which gave him a residence in DUBLIN CASTLE. He was central to the counterinsurgency efforts of the government, particularly in the arrest of Lord Edward Fitzgerald in 1798 and Robert EMMET in 1803. He retired in 1826. Sirr was also an art and antique collector.

Sisters of Mercy See McAULEY, CATHERINE.

Skeffington, William (died 1535)
lord deputy of Ireland
He was lord deputy from 1530 to 1532 and from 1534 to 1535. He defeated the forces of "Silken Thomas" or Lord Thomas Fitzgerald, the 10th earl of KILDARE at Maynooth and who accepted his surrender in 1535. He had earlier obtained the acquiescence of the O'Neills and the O'Donnells in Ulster.

Skelligs, the
Two islands about seven miles off the coast of County Kerry, one of which had been the site of an early Irish monastery, until VIKING raids forced the relocation to the mainland. The ruins of its beehive huts still exist. The larger island,

which rises about 700 feet above the sea, is also the site of a lighthouse. Both are important bird sanctuaries, especially for gannets.

Sligo

A maritime county of Connacht bounded by the counties of Leitrim, Roscommon, and Mayo, Sligo has a population of over 58,000 and an area of 695 square miles. The county's farms are small and feature primarily beef and sheep but with some dairy cattle in the south of the county. Its natural beauty, particularly the mountain Benbulbin served as a source of inspiration for William Butler YEATS, who is buried nearby, and his artist brother, Jack B. YEATS. Near the west Sligo town of Carrowmore is the largest Megalithic cemetery in Ireland, which predates NEWGRANGE. Inishmurray Island, six miles off the northwest coast, features the ruins of an ancient Christian monastery destroyed by the VIKINGS. The county is replete with sites connected to ancient folklore, including the burial place of Queen Maeve. The name comes from the Irish *Sligeach,* meaning river of shells, possibly connected to the shellfish of Sligo Bay. The largest town, Sligo Town, has a population of over 18,000 serves as the cathedral town of the diocese of Elphin. It lies near lands granted in the 13th century to the ANGLO-NORMAN Maurice Fitzgerald, who built a castle and a Dominican friary. In the far north is the seaside resort of Mullaghmore where Lord Mountbatten was assassinated in 1979. Celebrated natives of Sligo, in addition to the Yeats brothers, include the fiddler Michael Coleman, Countess Constance MARKIEVICZ, and poet Tadhg Dall Ó hUiginn.

Sloane, Sir Hans (1660–1753)
physician

Born at Killyleagh Castle, County Down, Sloane studied medicine at Paris, Montpelier, and at the University of Orange. He served as physician to the governor of Jamaica between 1687 and 1689. He collected 800 plant species there and published a catalogue. Sloane became a successful doctor in

London, was appointed physician to King George II, and was president of the Royal Society in 1727. He accumulated a library of over 50,000 volumes and thousands of manuscripts, which he left to the British nation and which became the nucleus of what would become the British Museum.

Smiddy, Timothy A. (1875–1962)
economist, diplomat

Born in Cork and educated at QUEEN'S COLLEGE Cork, at Paris and in Cologne, Smiddy was professor of Economics at University College Cork for 1909 to 1924. He was the envoy and fiscal agent of the Irish Free State to the United States from 1922 to 1924, envoy extraordinary and minister plenipotentiary in Washington from 1924 to 1929, and high commissioner in London from 1929 to 1930. Other positions he held included chairman of the Free State Tariff Commission from 1931 to 1933, director of the Central Bank of Ireland from 1943 to 1955, and chairman of the Commission on Post-Emergency Agricultural Policy in 1947.

Social Democratic and Labour Party (SDLP)

Various activists in the civil rights campaign of the preceding years formed this political party on August 27, 1970. The first leader was the republican Labour Party member of parliament for West Belfast, Gerry FITT. Other figures included John HUME, Austin Currie, and Ivan Cooper. Although not limited to Catholics, the party became in fact the major constitutional and political voice of the Catholic minority population, and replaced the older Nationalist Party led by Eddie McATEER. It withdrew from the Northern Ireland PARLIAMENT in August 1971 in protest at the policy of INTERNMENT. It joined in the power-sharing government formed in 1973 and confirmed by the SUNNINGDALE AGREEMENT, but which collapsed after the LOYALIST general strike the following May. In 1979 Fitt withdrew from the party because of its increasing NATIONALIST or "Green" line and John Hume became the leader. The party held its position as the leading nationalist party in the 1980s despite SINN FÉIN's entry into electoral politics. It cooperated closely with the British and Irish governments in the preliminaries to the HILLSBOROUGH AGREEMENT of 1985. Leader John Hume engaged in a series of conversations with Sinn Féin leader Gerry ADAMS that helped bring Sinn Féin and the IRA to agree to a cessation of violence and proclaim a cease-fire in 1994. Since then, Sinn Féin continued to gain electorally at the expense of the SDLP, a price Hume was willing to pay to advance the prospects for peace. Seamus MALLON, a SDLP member of parliament for Armagh, served as the minister in the power-sharing government headed by David TRIMBLE of the UNIONIST Party as called for by the GOOD FRIDAY AGREEMENT. Mark Durkan replaced Hume as leader in 2001. In the 2002 general election Sinn Féin increased its numbers elected to the Westminster parliament, and in the 2003 elections for the NORTHERN IRELAND ASSEMBLY surpassed the SDLP in the number of seats gained. In 2004 a Sinn Féin candidate also was elected to the European Parliament seat that John Hume had held.

Social Partnership

The term refers to the ongoing agreements reached, starting in the mid-1980s, between the Irish government and major economic interests in society, including management and labor, and later, in 1997, voluntary and community organizations, regarding pay, welfare, and tax issues, with the purpose of minimizing labor disputes and similar confrontations at a time of needed government retrenchment. Fewer labor disputes and lower taxes, plus the inclusion of a number of social policy issues, such as extension of paternal benefits, contributed to creating the atmosphere in which the economic boom of the late 1990s and early 2000s flourished.

Somerville and Ross (Edith Somerville and Violet Martin [Martin Ross]) (1858–1949 and 1862–1915)
writers

These were the pen names of second cousins from an ANGLO-IRISH PROTESTANT ASCENDANCY background. They collaborated in writing a number of travelogues, essays, and novels that gave a fascinating picture of rural Ireland and its gentry in the late 19th and early 20th centuries. Major titles include *The Real Charlotte* (1894) and *Some Experiences of an Irish R.M.* (1899). Edith Somerville, who was born in Corfu but educated at home in Castletownshend, County Cork, was an activist for women's rights and a sportswoman. She continued to write and used the dual pen name even after the death of her cousin in 1915. Her cousin, Violet Martin, was born in County Galway, and was a descendant of an ANGLO-NORMAN family, but lived for a while in Dublin and then in London, where she met her cousin. She combined sympathy for UNIONISM with an interest in women's suffrage.

Souperism

The term refers to the willingness of some Catholics during the Great FAMINE to agree to convert to Protestantism in return for food and other assistance offered by Protestant groups. It was not a condition for aid from most Protestant agencies, but may have been imposed by some. Also, some Catholic recipients might have been inclined to convert as a means to enhance their prospects of receiving aid.

Southern Ireland

Southern Ireland refers to the parliament and government that were to be created by the GOVERNMENT OF IRELAND ACT of 1920 that gave HOME RULE to both sections of Ireland and created PARTITION. All of the 128 members elected to the parliament of Southern Ireland except for the four elected for TRINITY COLLEGE DUBLIN refused to sit and met instead as the second DÁIL ÉIREANN. However, those who supported the ANGLO-IRISH TREATY of December 1921 did agree to meet with those four and, as the parliament of Southern Ireland, approve the treaty and select the PROVISIONAL GOVERNMENT to which power was transferred from the British.

Special Powers Legislation See EMER-
GENCY POWERS LEGISLATION.

Spenser, Edmund (1552–1599)
poet, political administrator

Born in London and educated at Pembroke Hall, Cambridge, Spenser was a secretary to Lord Leonard Grey, lord deputy of Ireland, and was a witness to the brutal massacre of continental supporters of the Munster Irish at Smerwick, County Kerry, in 1580. He was rewarded with 3,000 acres of land at Kilcolman, County Cork, as part of the PLANTATION of Munster. His poem *The Fairie Queen* (1590–96) earned him repute as a leading Elizabethan poet. However, he also wrote *A View of the Present State of Ireland* (1596) that was quite critical of Irish society and culture and that argued that the Irish must be subdued "by the sword, for all evils must first be cut away with a strong hand before any good can be planted." Not surprisingly his own estate was destroyed in 1598 during the O'Neillite rebellion, and he fled to England.

Spring, Dick (1950–   )
politician

Born in Tralee and educated at the Cistercian College, Roscrea, County Tipperary, at TRINITY COLLEGE DUBLIN, and at the KING'S INN, Spring qualified as a barrister. He was a celebrated rugby player. Elected to the DÁIL ÉIREANN in 1981 for North Kerry as a member of the LABOUR PARTY, he succeeded his father who had held the seat since 1943. The following year he was elected as the party leader in succeeding Michael O'Leary in a contest in which the party was divided between supporters of Barry Desmond and Michael D. Higgins. In the coalition government led by Garret FITZGERALD, he served as TÁNAISTE and minister for the environment and for energy. He was closely involved with the NEW IRELAND FORUM and the negotiations leading to the HILLSBOROUGH AGREEMENT. His opposition to the budget led to his party's departure from the coalition government, neces-

sitating a general election in 1987. In opposition he promoted the Labour Party's selection of former member Mary ROBINSON as its successful presidential candidate and he led his party to its greatest-ever electoral success in the 1992 general election, when it gained 33 seats in the Dáil. Spring led his party into a coalition with the FIANNA FÁIL Party led by Albert REYNOLDS and became Tánaiste again, as well as minister for foreign affairs. Within two years his party split with Reynolds over the issue of a judicial appointment and the resulting vote of no confidence was followed by the creation of the RAINBOW COALITION government headed by John BRUTON of FINE GAEL in which Spring was again Tánaiste and minister for foreign affairs until the government was defeated in the 1997 general election. He resigned as party leader subsequent to the election and in the 2002 general election lost his own seat in the Dáil for North Kerry.

Stack, Austin (1880–1929)
republican politician

Born in Tralee, County Kerry, Stack was a member of the IRISH VOLUNTEERS and was a member of the mission that ought have met Roger CASEMENT and weaponry at the time of the EASTER RISING. He was imprisoned afterward for over a year. He was returned for West Kerry to the first DÁIL ÉIREANN and was made substitute minister for home affairs in 1920. He was returned to the second Dáil for Kerry and Limerick West in 1921 and became minister for home affairs. He was closely associated with Cathal BRUGHA in hostility to Michael COLLINS and the IRISH REPUBLICAN BROTHERHOOD, believing in a more clear-cut revolutionary approach in contrast to Collins's guerrilla warfare tactics. He opposed the ANGLO-IRISH TREATY, was reelected to the third Dáil Éireann in 1922, but did not take his seat as he supported the IRREGULARS in the CIVIL WAR. He was captured in April 1923 and went on HUNGER STRIKE for several weeks while imprisoned. He was returned as an abstentionist member of SINN FÉIN in the 1923 and the June 1927 elections, but did not run in the September 1927 election.

Stalker, John (1939–)

police officer

Born in Manchester and educated locally, he joined the Manchester Police Force and became its deputy chief constable in 1984. The same year he was appointed to conduct an investigation into alleged illegal killings by the ROYAL ULSTER CONSTABULARY. Shortly after he submitted his interim report, he himself became the subject of an investigation regarded allegations of corruption and was suspended as director of the Northern Ireland investigation. An investigation undertaken by a West Yorkshire chief constable, Colin Sampson, ultimately exonerated him, but he resigned from the police force nevertheless in 1987. Sampson assumed the direction of the investigation of the RUC and arrived at much the same conclusion as had Stalker, namely, that some members of the RUC were involved in a "shoot to kill" policy. Official reluctance to allow immediate release of the reports was attributed to a desire to maintain morale in the force, which was confronted with the task of restraining LOYALIST and ORANGE protests against the HILLSBOROUGH AGREEMENT and the new phase of cooperation between the British and Irish governments that had ensued.

Statute of Westminster

This statute, passed in 1931 by the Westminster parliament, gave legal status to the 1926 British Commonwealth Conference recommendations that the dominions possessed legal autonomy from Britain and that they have the power to void Westminster legislation which effected them. It essentially gave the Irish Free State the right to void parts of the ANGLO-IRISH TREATY, which the British regarded as deriving its legitimacy from having been legislatively sanctioned by the Westminster parliament, if it chose. Paradoxically, CUMANN NA NGAEDHEAL took the position that alterations to the treaty, as an international agreement, required the consent of both signing parties. The party subsequently opposed Eamon DE VALERA's successful attempts to eliminate offensive treaty provisions from the Free State constitution.

Steele, Richard (1672–1729)

writer

Born in Dublin, Steele was educated at Oxford and earned a commission in the Coldstream Guards. He wrote the devotional manual *The Christian Hero* (1701) out of remorse for having seriously wounded a fellow officer in a duel. He turned to playwriting and in 1705 married a wealthy widow who died two years later. He left the army, remarried, and began editing the *Gazette* in 1707. In 1709 he and his close friend, Joseph Addison, founded the periodical the *Tatler.* In 1711 they founded the *Spectator* and in 1713 the *Guardian.*

Stephens, James (1825–1901)

founder of the Fenians

Born in Kilkenny and educated at St. Kieran's College, Stephens took part and was wounded in the rising in 1848 by members of YOUNG IRELAND. He fled to Paris. He returned to Ireland and in 1858, with Thomas Clarke LUBY, founded the IRISH REPUBLICAN BROTHERHOOD, or the FENIAN movement. Going about Ireland he successfully recruited thousands in a secret organization formed into "Circles" of 820 men, whose setup followed a formula by which there was one sergeant for every nine men and nine sergeants reported to nine captains, who in turn reported to a colonel, with theoretically no single member having direct contact with or knowledge of anyone other than those of his own rank, his immediate superior, or those under him. He also founded a supporting newspaper the *IRISH PEOPLE,* along with Luby, Thomas KICKHAM and John O'LEARY. He fell out with American supporters because of his delay in calling for a rising. Stephens himself was arrested in Ireland the same year, but he escaped to France and later to America. The hostility of American Fenians drove him back to Paris, where he lived by writing until a final return and settlement in Ireland in Blackrock, Dublin, in 1886.

Stephenson, Sam (1933–)

architect

Born in Dublin and educated at the Dublin Institute of Technology, Stephenson designed the

ESB offices in Fitzwilliam Street (1968). The construction required the destruction of a row of Georgian houses, the Central Bank (1976), and the Civic Offices at Wood Quay (1982), which incurred great outrage on the part of archaeologists and medievalists.

Sterne, Laurence (1713–1768)
novelist

Born in Clonmel, County Tipperary, Sterne's mother was Irish and his father was a British army officer. He spent only his childhood in Ireland and became an Anglican clergyman in Yorkshire. Sterne wrote the classic comic novels *The Life and Opinions of Tristram Shandy, Gentleman* (1759–67) and *A Sentimental Journey* (1768), which were noted for their depictions of rural life.

Stewart, Robert, Viscount Castlereagh and second marquis of Londonderry

See CASTLEREAGH, ROBERT STEWART, SECOND MARQUIS OF LONDONDERRY AND VISCOUNT.

Stoker, Abraham (Bram Stoker) (1847–1911)
novelist

Born in Dublin, Stoker was educated at TRINITY COLLEGE DUBLIN and entered the civil service. He also wrote unpaid theatre reviews for the *Evening Standard.* He moved to London in 1878 to become the manager of an actor friend, Henry Irving, until the later died in 1905. Stoker wrote a number of novels, the most famous of which was *Dracula* (1897), which was inspired by a tale of vampirism by Sheridan LE FANU, and which inspired plays, movies, and even comic strips.

Stokes, George Gabriel (1819–1903)
mathematical physicist

Born in Skreen, County Sligo, the son of a Church of Ireland clergyman, Stokes was educated at Pembroke College, Cambridge, where he took a first in mathematics and where he became professor of mathematics. His work

included deriving the equations of motion for the internal friction of fluids and the motion for the behavior of waves in electric solids. He formulated what became known as Stokes law, about the movement of a body through viscous fluids of various densities. He provided an explanation of fluorescence. His work on elliptically polarized light provided the standard way of describing light emitted in experiments in modern atomic and optical physics.

Strafford, Thomas Wentworth, first earl of (1593–1641)
politician

Born in London, Wentworth was a supporter of King Charles I in his struggles with parliament. He was made lord deputy in Ireland in 1632 and pursued a policy of "thorough," which sought to assert royal power against various local interests, increase revenue, and impose an Anglican religious orthodoxy on the church in Ireland. He played off the hostilities of the OLD ENGLISH Catholics and the New English Protestants against each other and alienated both, in spite of promises of concessions, such as the GRACES, which were never completely granted. Calvinist influences in the established CHURCH OF IRELAND were inhibited and many Catholic landowners, especially in Connacht, lost land because of judicial "discovery" of title weaknesses. Wentworth personally enriched himself while lord deputy. His downfall began with his support of the war against Scotland in 1639. Granted the title of earl in reward for his service to the king, he pursued policies, especially recruitment of an army in Ireland for future use against Scotland and, the parliamentarians feared, against parliament, which resulted in his impeachment and execution under a bill of attainder in 1641, to which the king, out of fear for himself and his family, assented.

Stuart, Francis (1902–2000)
novelist

Born in Australia of Ulster parents, Stuart was educated at Rugby School, Warwickshire. He married Iseult Gonne, the daughter of Maud GONNE. Stuart supported the Irish WAR OF INDEPENDENCE and the anti-treaty side in the Irish CIVIL WAR. He wrote a book of poetry, *We Have Kept the Faith* (1924), and a number of novels such as *Pigeon Irish* (1932), *The White Hare* (1936), and *The Coloured Dome* (1936), which received some acclaim. He converted to Catholicism and, in 1939, accepted a position as lecturer at a university in Berlin. During the war his broadcasts on German radio were interpreted as pro-Axis propaganda and he was interned for a year by the English after the war and declared "outside the diplomatic protection of his own government" by the Irish Department of External Affairs. He only returned to Ireland in 1959. He wrote a number of novels after the war, including *The Pillar of Cloud* (1948), *Redemption* (1949), and the autobiographical *Blacklist, Section H* (1971).

Stuart, Henry Villiers, first baron (1803–1874)
landlord, politician

Stuart was educated at Eton. He was a landlord who agreed to run for parliament as a champion of Catholic emancipation in a by-election in County Waterford in 1826, where, with support from Daniel O'CONNELL and the CATHOLIC ASSOCIATION he defeated the incumbent candidate, Lord George Beresford, several of whose own tenants deserted him.

Sullivan, Alexander Martin (A. M. Sullivan) (1830–1884)
journalist, politician

Born in Bantry, County Cork, Sullivan was educated locally and joined the staff of the *NATION*, which he began editing in 1855 and of which he became sole proprietor in 1858 following Charles Gavan DUFFY's departure for Australia. He was a constitutional NATIONALIST and met the opprobrium of the FENIANS whose council called for his assassination, but the high regard in which he was held by the rank and file inhibited such. He

was actually imprisoned for six months by the authorities for writing an article about the MANCHESTER MARTYRS. Upon release he insisted that a 400-pound tribute raised for him be used instead to erect a statue of Henry GRATTAN in College Green, Dublin. One of the founders of the IRISH PARLIAMENTARY PARTY, Sullivan was a member of parliament for County Louth from 1874 to 1880 and for County Meath from 1880 to 1881. Called to the Irish bar in 1876 and the English bar in 1877, he gave over the editorship of the *Nation* to his brother, Timothy Daniel SULLIVAN. When his health broke in 1881 he resigned from parliament and died in Dublin in 1884. His *History of Ireland* (1870) was widely read.

Sullivan, Timothy Daniel (T. D. Sullivan) (1827–1914)
politician

Born in Bantry, County Cork, Timothy Sullivan had supported YOUNG IRELAND and was a contributor to the *NATION* that was edited by his brother, Alexander Martin SULLIVAN. He became its editor in 1877 and employed his nephew, Tim HEALY, on the staff. As a member of the IRISH PARLIAMENTARY PARTY he sat for County West Meath from 1880 to 1885, for Dublin from 1885 to 1892, and for West Donegal from 1892 to 1900. He was also lord mayor of Dublin from 1886 to 1887. Sullivan was the leader of a faction of the Irish party called "the Bantry Band," and he supported Charles Stewart PARNELL at first, even being prosecuted in 1880 for involvement with LAND LEAGUE agitation. He was also a leading figure in the PLAN OF CAMPAIGN in the later 1880s, which was not favored by Parnell. While traveling as a member of a delegation raising funds for the party in America, he opposed Parnell in the split over his leadership following the divorce and Liberal Party insistence on his being removed as a condition for continued cooperation with the Irish. Sullivan wrote a number of songs, including "God Save Ireland," a tribute to the MANCHESTER MARTYRS, which became the virtual anthem of the nationalists, and "Ireland Boys Hurray" that was sung by Irishmen fighting on both sides in the American Civil War, as well as collections of poetry, such as *Greenleaves* (1885), *Lays of the Land League* (1887), and *Poems* (1888), and memoirs, *Recollections of Troubled Times in Ireland, 1843–1904* (1905). He was the maternal grandfather of Kevin O'HIGGINS.

Sunningdale Agreement

This agreement was formulated at a conference in Sunningdale in December 1993 that was attended by representatives of the British and Irish governments and leaders of the three Northern Ireland political parties, the UNIONISTS, the SOCIAL DEMOCRATIC AND LABOUR PARTY, and the ALLIANCE PARTY, that were willing to join a power-sharing coalition government selected by a NORTHERN IRELAND ASSEMBLY elected the previous June. The agreement endorsed the power-sharing concept, accepted the principle that the constitutional status of Northern Ireland was not to be changed without the consent of its people, and called for the formation of a COUNCIL OF IRELAND in which representatives of Ireland and Northern Ireland would participate for dealing with and harmonizing mutual concerns. More militant unionist and LOYALIST opposition, especially to the latter concept, the following spring manifested itself in a general strike, which resulted in the resignation of the Unionist Party members of the executive and in the suspension of the power-sharing government. Many of the terms of the GOOD FRIDAY AGREEMENT of 1998 were comparable to what was sought at Sunningdale.

Surrender and Regrant

A policy adopted in the 1540s by which the English monarchy sought to secure the acceptance of its authority by the various Irish lords. In return for surrendering their Irish or Gaelic claims to their land and acknowledging their fealty to the king, they would be given their lands back as a royal grant and be made peers. Naturally they were also expected to advance English laws, customs, and socioeconomic practices of land cultivation and development, to

provide military service to the king, and to pay royal rents for the land they held. The process was carried out with varying success through the rest of the 16th century and into the 17th century. Frequently, lords would disregard the surrender and regrant and base their titles on native Irish grounds, which would often be followed by their defeat in a military encounter and their territory being subject to PLANTATION.

Sutherland, Peter (1946–   )
politician, barrister, businessman
Born in Dublin and educated at Gonzaga College, University College Dublin, and the KING'S INN, Sutherland was called to the bar in 1969, and later admitted to the New York State bar and to practice before the Supreme Court of the United States. He served as attorney general in the coalition government in 1981–82 and from 1982 to 1984. He advised the TAOISEACH, Garrett FITZGERALD, to oppose the constitutional amendment, which passed, barring abortion, as he argued that it might actually create a situation allowing abortion, a fear that was born out by a Supreme Court decision several years later allowing abortion in cases when the mother threatened suicide. From 1985 to 1989 he served as a member of the European Commission with specific responsibility for competition policy. He subsequently became director of a number of private companies. In 1993, as director-general of the General Agreement on Tariffs and Trade, he supervised the formulation of a new trade agreement between the European Community and the United States. He became director-general of the World Trade Organization in 1995. Sutherland has been visiting fellow or professor at Harvard, University College Dublin, and at the Centre for European Studies in Brussels. In 2005 he became goodwill ambassador for the United Nations Industrial Development Organization.

Sweetman, Gerard (1908–1970)
politician
Born in Dublin and educated at TRINITY COLLEGE DUBLIN, Sweetman became a successful solicitor.

He failed twice running as a FINE GAEL candidate for the DÁIL ÉIREANN: for Carlow-Kildare in 1937 and for Kildare in 1943. He sat in the SEANAD from 1943 to 1948 and was elected to the Dáil for Kildare in 1948 and served until his death in 1970. He was the chief whip during the 1948 to 1951 coalition government and served as the minister for finance during the 1954 to 1957 coalition. He adhered to an orthodox economic perspective in introducing deflationary budgets. Later in opposition he distanced himself from the liberal voices emerging in the Fine Gael Party. He died in an automobile accident in 1970.

Swift, Jonathan (1667–1745)
writer, dean of St. Patrick's Cathedral
Born in Dublin and educated at Kilkenny College and at TRINITY COLLEGE DUBLIN, Swift went to England in 1689 as did most students and fellows from Trinity during the brief period of JACOBITE domination in Ireland. In London he became secretary to Sir William Temple and met Esther Johnson ("Stella"), who followed him to Ireland and to whom he remained attached for life. In 1695 he was ordained a priest in the CHURCH OF IRELAND and made a curate in Kilroot in County Antrim, a Presbyterian stronghold. Finding life unpleasant there, he returned to London until Temple's death. He returned to Ireland as vicar of Laracor, near Trim, County Meath. At this time he wrote his *Tale of a Tub* (1704), a satire that attacked corrupt church figures and modern writers. He also traveled between Dublin and London acting on behalf of the interests of the Church of Ireland. His ties were originally with the Whigs, but he later swung toward allegiance to the Tories in writing for the new periodicals of the time like the *Tatler* and the *Examiner*. He became closely associated with such literary figures and habitués of clubs and coffee houses as Addison, Congreve, and Pope. When the Tory ministry fell in part because for the rivalry of Robert Harley and Viscount Bolingbroke, Swift returned to Dublin and became dean of St. Patrick's, a position that he viewed as a disappointment in having expected

Jonathan Swift *(Library of Congress)*

a greater reward such as a bishopric for his services. In Dublin he took up his pen as an Irish PATRIOT, urging in his *Proposal for the Universal Use of Irish Manufacture* (1720) that English goods be boycotted and in his *Drapier's Letters* (1724) that the Irish not accept new coinage, "Wood's ha'penny," that had been imposed on them by the English government as a favor to a friend of the king's mistress. On his return from England in 1713, another young woman, Esther Vanhomrigh ("Vanessa"), followed him. She was infatuated with him, and her arrival caused Stella some distress. She died in 1723 of consumption. Swift continued to write remarkable satirical prose, including *Gulliver's Travels* (1726), a fantasy concerned with human depravity, and *A Modest Proposal* (1729), a suggestion that the suffering of the Irish people be relieved by the sale of their children as food for the rich. The death of Stella increased his discontent, and his health and mental stability weakened. In 1742 he was committed to the care of guardians and he died in 1745. Swift is buried in St. Patrick's churchyard next to Stella.

Synge, John Millington (1871–1909)
playwright

Born in Rathfarnham, County Dublin, into an Anglo-Irish family, Synge studied at TRINITY COL-LEGE DUBLIN. His reading of Charles Darwin weakened his religious faith, causing him to clash with his evangelical widowed mother and to lose the affection of his fiancée, who was a devout member of the Plymouth Brethern. He developed an enthusiasm for pagan Celticism and was urged by William Butler YEATS to go to the Aran Islands to experience the life about which he was so fascinated. He went regularly from 1898 through 1902 and later to West and South County Kerry. From his travels he developed not only a command of the Irish language that he had studied at Trinity but also an ability to master the Hiberno-Irish dialect, that is, the manner of speaking in English while thinking in Irish. This ability manifested itself in the series of plays he wrote and which were produced in the ABBEY THEATRE. The plays were not filio-pietistic idealizations of Irish Catholic peasants that many NATIONALISTS wanted, but rather realistic portraits of rural life, warts and all. The most controversial, *THE PLAYBOY OF THE WESTERN WORLD* (1907), provoked a riot, but many found equally disturbing his *The Shadow of the Glen* (1903), about the wife in a loveless marriage who runs away with a homeless tramp. Other plays include *Riders to the Sea* (1904) and *Deirdre of the Sorrows* (1910). He died of Hodgkin's disease in 1909.

T

Talbot, Matthew (1856–1925)

laborer

Born in Dublin and having earned only a primary-level education, Talbot was a casual laborer who from his teenage years had become addicted to alcohol. In 1884 he took a pledge of total abstinence, which he reinforced with mortifications, fasting, frequent attendance at Mass, and other religious devotions. He kept his fasting and mortifications private, some of which, like wearing penitential chains on parts of his body, were discovered only after his death. He continued to work regularly as a laborer until the day before he died, but he gave much of his earnings to charity. His remains have been enshrined in the Church of Our Lady of Lourdes in Sean MacDermott Street, Dublin, and the cause of his canonization by the Catholic Church is well advanced.

Talbot, Richard, earl of Tyrconnell

See TYRCONNELL, RICHARD TALBOT, EARL OF.

Tánaiste

Tánaiste is the title of the deputy head of government in Ireland, who acts for the TAOISEACH during a temporary absence or if he becomes incapacitated or should die until a new Taoiseach is selected. The name derives from the medieval title *tanaiste ri*, which referred to the heir apparent to a king, not automatically the eldest son, but a relation of the incumbent. Its modern use derives from the 1937 constitution.

Tandy, James Napper (1740–1803)

revolutionary nationalist

Born in Dublin, Tandy was an ironmonger and then a land agent and rent collector. He joined the IRISH VOLUNTEERS at the time of the campaign for parliamentary independence in the early 1780s and was an early member of the UNITED IRISHMEN. He fled to America in 1793 to escape prosecution for having taken the oath of the DEFENDERS. He went to Paris in 1798 and was appointed a general in the French army and went to Donegal to command a small force that was to act in conjunction with the French landing at KILLALA. When he heard of Jean-Joseph HUMBERT's defeat, he left for Norway. He was eventually captured in Hamburg, handed over to the British, and tried, convicted, and sentenced to death, but he was released as a precondition of Napoleon's acceptance of the Peace of Amiens in 1802. Tandy settled in Bordeaux where he died the next year.

Taoiseach

Taoiseach is the title of the head of government, or prime minister, in Ireland. The president appoints as Taoiseach whoever has been nominated by the DÁIL ÉIREANN, inevitably the leader of a party with a majority of the members, or the leader of a coalition. The Taoiseach names the other members of government and up to 11 members of SEANAD ÉIREANN, and can call for a general election, but not if he or she has lost the confidence of the Dáil Éireann. Prior to adoption of the 1937 constitution, the name given to the comparable figure in government was president of the Executive Council. The word was used in medieval times to identify the head of a tribe or family in the Gaelic system.

Tara

Tara is the name of a hill about 500 feet above sea level in County Meath, which provides a panoramic view of the Central Plain of Ireland. It served as a seat of power in ancient Ireland and the site of the inauguration of kings. Geological surveys and aerial photography have substantiated its ancient importance, especially by the presence of numerous burial sites, monuments, and ring forts.

Tate, Nahum (1652–1715)
poet

Born in Dublin and educated at TRINITY COLLEGE DUBLIN, Tate moved to England where he wrote plays and poetry. One of his plays, an adaptation of Shakespeare's *King Lear,* was popular until the middle of the 19th century. Dryden commissioned him to write the second part of "Absalom and Architophel," and he did other translation and editing work, besides his own poetry. He was England's Poet Laureate in 1692.

Tenant League   See IRISH TENANT LEAGUE.

Test and Corporation acts

These were legislative acts passed by the Westminster and Irish parliaments in the early eighteenth century requiring reception of the sacraments in the established CHURCH OF IRELAND as a requirement for public office. It was superfluous in terms of excluding Catholics, but also excluded Presbyterians and other nonconformist Protestants.

Thompson, William (1775–1833)
radical economist

Born in Rosscarbery, County Cork, Thompson had inherited a large fortune. Influenced by his observation of the French Revolution and his travels on the Continent and England, he developed a radical perspective on society. He was a friend of Jeremy Bentham, David Ricardo, and Robert Owen, and wrote a number of books, including *An Inquiry into the Distribution of Wealth Most Conducive to Human Happiness* (1824), which predated Marxism, and *An Appeal of One Half of the Human Race* (1825), which advocated equality of the sexes. He wrote proposals for the establishment of communes in his *Practical Directions for the Establishment of Communes* (1830), and he started a cooperative farm on his lands in Cork. He left his wealth to cooperative societies in Ireland, to the disgruntlement of his relatives.

Three F's   See LAND ACTS.

Tierney, Michael (1894–1975)
academic

Born in Ballymacward, County Galway, Tierney was educated at University College Dublin (UCD) and studied classics at the Sorbonne, Athens, and Berlin. He was married to one of the daughters of Eoin MACNEILL. He lectured in classics at UCD from 1915, became professor of Greek in 1923, and was president of the school from 1947 to 1964. As a member of CUMANN NA NGAEDHEAL, he contested a seat for Galway unsuccessfully in the 1923 general election and unsuccessfully for Mayo North in a 1924 by-election, but he was successful in a by-election in the same constituency in 1925. He was also elected for the National University of Ireland in the September 1927 general election, and he served as a member of the SEANAD ÉIREANN from 1938 to 1942. Tierney was associated with the intellectual brain trust of Cumann na nGaedheal and FINE GAEL, and championed the corporatist view of society being paid lip service to by the BLUESHIRT movement, although he quickly distanced himself from the excesses of its leader Eoin O'DUFFY. The purchase of a site for a new campus for UCD in the then suburban area of Belfield in the years of his presidency marked perhaps his greatest achievement. The site now houses a thriving modern academic institution in territory that has become choice real estate.

Tinkers

The word is the common, but politically incorrect, used to describe the more than 20,000 native Irish itinerants, also referred to as Travellers, usually members of a limited number of families, possibly descended from people disposed in the 17th and 18th centuries, who supported themselves by traveling about doing tin smith work and other odd work. More recently their major source of income has been as traders, very often of antiques. They have also come to gravitate more toward major cities and are not as widely dispersed through the rural countryside as in earlier times. Serious efforts have been made to encourage them to accept a permanent residency, but many itinerants have been reluctant to part with their customary ways. In certain areas, often against much popular opposition, halting sites have been marked out for their use.

Tipperary

Tipperary is the only county in Munster that lies inland. It is the only county in Ireland that is divided into two ridings, North and South, for administrative purposes. The population equals over 140,000 and the area comprises 1,644 square miles. The Shannon River on the north and the Suir River on the south drain the county. There are several mountain ranges, including the Silvermines in the northwest and the Galtees and the Knockmealdowns in the south, while the central plain forms part of the agriculturally rich Golden Vale that also extends into County Limerick, making dairy farming a major industry, along with food and meat processing and assorted manufacturing. Major towns are Nenagh and Clonmel, the respective riding capitals, as well as Cahir, Cashel, Roscrea, and Thurles. There are many historic sites and ruins, particularly the Rock of Cashel, from

where the kings of Munster ruled until the ascendancy of Brian Boru. After the Normans arrived, the county was under the control of the Butlers. But the Cromwellian plantation displaced most of the older landowners. Understandably the county was the center of agricultural agitation, ranging from the 18th-century Whiteboys through the early 19th-century Ribbonmen and the Fenians to the Irish Republican Army (IRA) in the War of Independence and the Civil War. The Gaelic Athletic Association was founded in Thurles. Celebrated natives include Charles Bianconi, cardinal Michael Browne, Patrick Browne or Pádraig de Brún, Charles Kickham, Theobold Mathew, and Thomas MacDonagh.

Titanic, RMS

The *Titanic* was a White Star liner built in the shipyards of Harland and Wolff in Belfast and launched on May 31, 1911. It sank on April 14, 1912, on its maiden voyage from Southampton to New York when it struck an iceberg. Over 1,500 lives were lost, and there were over 700 survivors. At Queenstown (Cobh), 123 Irish passengers had boarded, of whom 44 survived. At the time of its launching it was the world's largest vessel.

tithes

These were taxes imposed on the producers of agricultural produce by the clergy that had begun in the medieval period. By the 17th and 18th centuries tithes constituted a tax imposed to support the clergy of the minority established Church of Ireland and was understandably resented by Catholics and other denominations of Protestants. The issue became more intense in the 18th century when pasture lands were exempt from the tithe, leaving the burden on tillage land, which was the type of land occupied primarily by Catholics. There were violent outbreaks of land agitation by, respectively, the Whiteboys and the Ribbonmen and, together with the more formal protests and expressions of refusal to pay tithes, occasional outbreaks of violence into the 1830s. Legislation in 1838 changed the character of the tithes to a rent charge on landlords, which partially eased popular annoyance, but the problem was not completely resolved until the DISESTABLISHMENT of the Church of Ireland in 1869.

Tod, Isabella (1836–1896)
suffragist

Born in Edinburgh, Tod moved to Belfast and worked as a journalist. She was very involved in the temperance cause, serving as an official, in turn, of the British Women's Temperance Association and of the Irish Women's Total Abstinence Union. She championed women's rights, especially equality in education and voting rights. She organized the first society promoting women's suffrage in Ireland in 1871. Tod was an opponent of HOME RULE and made defense of the union her primary political concern as she was the only woman on the executive committee of the Ulster Liberal Unionist Association. She started the Ulster Women's Liberal Unionist Association in 1888.

Toland, John (1670–1722)
controversialist

Born in Donegal, Toland abandoned Catholicism as a teenager, entered the CHURCH OF IRELAND, and studied in Glasgow, Edinburgh, and Leiden. He ultimately challenged all established Christian churches in his book *Christianity Not Mysterious* (1696), which called for a rational religion and which depicted the clergy as exploiting the mysteries of religion to dominate the laity. The book was condemned by the Irish parliament as atheistic and it was ordered burned. He had to flee Ireland at that time, but found favor from William III who gave him the mission of bringing notice of the Act of Succession, which guaranteed Protestant succession to the Crown of England (and ultimately specifically to her descendants). Toland traveled on the Continent, engaging in debate, promoting Freemasonry, denouncing the Catholic Church especially, but

other established churches as well, and sympathizing with persecuted minorities such as Jews and Huguenots. He wrote about pre-Christian Ireland in *A History of the Druids* (1722) and was a native Irish speaker.

Toler, John, first earl of Norbury   See
NORBURY, JOHN TOLER, FIRST EARL OF.

Tone, Theobald Wolfe (1763–1798)
nationalist revolutionary

Born in Dublin and educated at TRINITY COLLEGE DUBLIN and at the Middle Bar in London, Theobald Wolfe Tone was called to the Irish bar in 1789. He was not inclined to practice, however, and instead turned to political agitation. In 1791 he led a group that included Thomas RUSSELL and William DRENNAN, which became the UNITED IRISHMEN. The same year he wrote a

Theobald Wolfe Tone *(Library of Congress)*

pamphlet *An Argument on Behalf of the Catholics of Ireland,* which reassured Irish Protestants that the dangers of Catholicism were receding and that they should be open to allying with Irish Catholics in the pursuit of reforming objectives. The CATHOLIC COMMITTEE employed him as its secretary and he organized a convention in which they petitioned for Catholic relief. Tone found the Catholic Relief Act of 1793, which enfranchised Catholics, unsatisfactory, and, influenced by the revolution in France, he began to turn toward actual revolution in Ireland with the goal of a separate republic in which distinction of creed would be irrelevant. In 1794 he entered into negotiations with the French government to consider the feasibility of a French invasion of Ireland. The intermediary, a clergyman named William Jackson, was arrested and Tone's involvement was discovered. He was allowed to leave Ireland. He went to Philadelphia and immediately met with French representatives in the United States, who gave him an introduction to French officials in Paris. He arrived in 1796 and, within a year, he had successfully persuaded the French both to send a fleet with an army of 15,000 men to land in Ireland under the command of General Lazare Hoche and to make him an adjutant-general in the French army. However, bad weather made it impossible for that part of the force that had reached Bantry Bay to land and the invasion was called off. In 1798, when the United Irishmen rising took place, Tone was able to secure French agreement for a number of landings in Ireland, the foremost of which took place at KILLALA. He himself led another force of 3,000 men, which was captured by the British off Lough Swilly in Donegal on October 12. Tone, who had accepted rank in the French army, was tried by court-martial and sentenced to death by hanging, although he would have preferred the soldier's death of a firing squad. He committed suicide by slashing his throat rather than face the gallows. Tone's grave in Bodenstown, County Kildare, remains a site for annual pilgrimages by Irish republicans of all varieties, including members of SINN FÉIN and FIANNA FÁIL.

Townsend, George, first marquis of (1724–1807)
politician

He served as lord lieutenant of Ireland from 1767 to 1772. His difficulties in getting the parliament and the UNDERTAKERS to secure certain measures, particularly financing of the British army in Ireland, prompted his decision to change the style of managing the parliament. Rather than rely on the Undertakers to secure passage of measures in parliament, he took up residency in Ireland and made DUBLIN CASTLE the center of political power, particularly by means of distributing favors and patronage, thereby bringing the dominance of the Undertakers to an end.

Traynor, Oscar (1886–1963)
politician

Born in Dublin, Traynor was a member of the IRISH VOLUNTEERS. He took part in the EASTER RISING, for which he was interned. After release he became active in SINN FÉIN and was a brigade commander in the IRA during the WAR OF INDEPENDENCE and led the attack on the Customs House in May 1921. He was among those on the anti-treaty side in the CIVIL WAR. Elected to the DÁIL ÉIREANN as an abstentionist Sinn Féiner for Dublin North in a 1925 by-election, he was one of the founders of the FIANNA FÁIL Party in 1926, and was returned for the same constituency as a Fianna Fáil candidate in the June 1927 general election, taking his seat the following August. Traynor ran again unsuccessfully for the same constituency in a March 1929 by-election, but was returned in the 1932 and 1933 general elections, and from 1937 to 1961 sat for Dublin Northeast. He served as minister for posts and telegraphs from 1936 to 1939, minister for defense from 1939 to 1948 and from 1951 to 1954, and minister for justice from 1957 to 1961. An excellent football (soccer) player in his youth, he was also president of the Football Association of Ireland from 1948 until his death in 1963.

Treacy, Seán (1895–1920)
republican soldier

Born in Solohead, County Tipperary, Treacy was active in the GAELIC LEAGUE and the IRISH REPUBLICAN BROTHERHOOD, and also joined the IRISH VOLUNTEERS in 1913. He took part in the attack on the ROYAL IRISH CONSTABULARY at Soloheadbeg in January 1919, the first action in the WAR OF INDEPENDENCE. He was active in various other raids, primarily in Dublin, but was killed in a gun battle in Talbot Street in October 1920.

Trench, Richard Chenevix (1807–1886)
archbishop

Born in Dublin and educated at Harrow and at Trinity College, Cambridge, Trench was professor of divinity at King's College from 1846 to 1858 and dean of Westminster from 1856 to 1864, when he became archbishop of Dublin. He opposed the DISESTABLISHMENT of the CHURCH OF IRELAND in 1869 and guided the church in the difficult period immediately following enactment. He published poetry and devotional works, including sermons.

Trevelyan, Sir Charles Edward (1807–1886)
civil servant

Born in Taunton, Trevelyan served in the East India Company and in 1838 returned to England where he became assistant secretary to the Treasury. He directed the relief works for Ireland during the Great FAMINE. Sharing the free trade perspective of the Whig government of Lord John Russell and his chancellor of the exchequer, Charles Wood, he was parsimonious in the distribution of public relief, even taking the position that the famine was providential in view of Irish overpopulation. Later he contributed to a report that inspired reforms on which the modern civil service was formed. Trevelyan again served in India from 1859 to 1865.

Trevor, William (1928–)
writer

Born in Mitchelstown, County Cork, Trevor dropped his family name of Cox and kept his first and middle names as his pen name. He was educated at TRINITY COLLEGE DUBLIN and lived in England since 1953. His novels and short stories deal with the contrast between normal society and eccentricity and most deal with English society, such as *The Old Boys* (1964), *Mrs. Eckdorf in O'Neill's Hotel* (1968), and *The Children of Dynmouth* (1976). But he has also turned to Ireland as the site for his writings, including his treatment of violence and the Anglo-Irish big house in works such as *The Silence in the Garden* (1988) and *Fools of Fortune* (1988). One of his many short stories, "The Ballroom of Romance," became the basis for a television program. His work has twice won the prestigious Whitbread Prize. Later work has included his autobiography, *Excursions in the Real World* (1993), and *The Story of Lucy Gault* (2002).

Trimble, David (1944–)
politician

Born in Belfast and educated at Bangor Grammar School and at QUEEN'S UNIVERSITY Belfast, where he became a lecturer in law, he was a member in the 1970s of the militant VANGUARD movement and supported the loyalist strike that brought down the SUNNINGDALE AGREEMENT. In 1978 he joined the ULSTER UNIONIST PARTY, the mainline unionist group, and in 1990 was elected to the House of Commons for Upper Bann, although he continued to take a strong, uncompromising stand on the issue of negotiations with SINN FÉIN. In 1995 he walked with Ian PAISLEY in support of an ORANGE ORDER march down the Garvaghy Road in Portadown and a few months later was selected as the leader of the Ulster Unionist Party as the successor to James MOLYNEUX. Since then he has displayed a remarkable pragmatism demonstrated in his willingness to include Sinn Féin in negotiations that led to the GOOD FRIDAY AGREEMENT, for which he shared a Nobel Prize with John HUME in 1998. He was elected first minister of a devolved Northern Ireland government by the Assembly created by the agreement, but delayed the formation of a government because of IRA reluctance to decommission its weaponry. Even after the Assembly's formation in late 1999, he forced its suspension because of the IRA's continued failure to move on decommissioning in 2000 and its threat to do the same again in 2001, except for a partial gesture of decommissioning in the fall of that year. The Northern Ireland government was again suspended in 2002 because of alleged Sinn Féin espionage in the Northern Ireland office. In late 2003 elections for a second-term NORTHERN IRELAND ASSEMBLY were held and they resulted in the DEMOCRATIC UNIONIST PARTY led by Rev. Ian Paisley winning a number of seats equal in size to the hitherto predominant Unionist Party in the Assembly. When three members of the latter joined the DUP, Trimble's party found itself to be the smaller of the unionist parties. He lost his seat in the 2005 general election in which Ulster Unionists lost all their places but one and he subsequently resigned as leader of the party.

Trinity College Dublin

The institution was founded in 1592, on the site of an Augustinian house that had been suppressed in 1538 to provide instruction for which students might otherwise have gone to the Continent, where they would have been infected with Popery. The college was primarily founded to educate the clergy of the established CHURCH OF IRELAND, although Catholics were allowed to attend at first. However, they were soon barred, until 1793 when they were admitted by the Catholic Relief Act, although still forbidden from receiving scholarships or fellowships. In the 19th and most of the 20th centuries the Catholic hierarchy discouraged the faithful from attending because of the institution's Protestant character. But since the 1970s that discouragement has been abandoned and the overwhelming majority of current students are at least nominally Catholic. Alumni of the university include so many of the great and famous in all aspects of Irish life that a list of them here would duplicate a large portion of those cited in this volume. The size of the current student body is nearly 10,000.

Trollope, Anthony (1812–1882)
novelist

Born in London, this celebrated English novelist worked for a number of years as a Post Office official. There he met his wife and wrote his first novel, *The Macdermotts of Ballycloran* (1847). Several other novels featured locales in Ireland, such as *The Kellys and the O'Kellys* (1848), *Castle Richmond* (1860), and the incomplete *The Landleaguers* (1883).

Troy, John Thomas (1739–1823)
archbishop

Born in Porterstown, County Dublin, Troy went to Rome when 15 years of age to enter the Dominican Order. He was ordained in 1762, became prior of St. Clement's in Rome in 1772, and bishop of Ossory in Ireland in 1776. Ten years later he became archbishop of Dublin. He was very conservative and condemned the WHITEBOYS and attacks on constitutional authority, even criticizing the severity of agitation by the CATHOLIC COMMITTEE. Troy feared the prospect of Catholic seminarians studying in the revolutionary atmosphere on the Continent and was able to secure government subsidization of a domestic seminary at MAYNOOTH. He condemned the UNITED IRISHMEN rising of 1798 and the DEFENDERS. Together with his hierarchical colleagues, he was supportive of a governmental veto on hierarchical appointments in return for the awarding of Catholic emancipation, although the delay in its eventual achievement allowed Daniel O'CONNELL to successfully dissuade the Irish hierarchy and the papacy from agreeing to such a concession. Troy laid the foundation stone for the Dublin Pro-Cathedral in 1815.

Tudor, Hugh H. (1871–1965)
general, police commissioner

Born in Exeter, Tudor served in both the Boer War and the First World War. He became the chief of police in Ireland responsible for both the DUBLIN METROPOLITAN POLICE and the ROYAL IRISH CONSTABULARY, and, when they were formed, the BLACK AND TANS and the AUXILIARIES, which had been recruited to replace the depleted ranks of the RIC and which had a notorious record of brutality. He later served with the British forces in Palestine.

Tyndall, John (1820–1893)
physicist

Born in Leighlinbridge, County Carlow, and educated by a local teacher, Tyndall worked first with the ORDINANCE SURVEY and after at the Royal Institution of Great Britain. There he researched infrared transmission in the atmosphere, meteorology, and bacteriology, as well as diamagnetism and glaciology. His inventions include the fireman's respirator, the fiber optic, and the infrared analyzer, and he worked on measures to control bacterial infection. He was an early enthusiast of Alpine mountain climbing, which he undertook as part of his research. Several mountain peaks throughout the world are named in his honor, as is the explanation of the coloring of the sky, known as the Tyndall effect.

Tyrconnell, Richard Talbot, earl of (1630–1691)
military leader

Born in Mahahide, County Dublin, and a member of an OLD ENGLISH Catholic family from County Meath, he fought with the Royalist army and was wounded in the defense of Drogheda at the time of the siege by Oliver CROMWELL. He escaped to the Continent and served in the regiment commanded by the duke of York, the future King James II. After the Restoration he returned to Ireland and was given land as well as compensation from Catholics whom he had helped to recover some of their lands. He became a leading spokesperson for Catholics in the 1670s in efforts to further amend their grievances. When James II became king, he made Talbot the commander of the army in Ireland with independence from Lord Clarendon, the lord lieutenant. He used his position to advance Catholics within the army and, when made lord lieutenant himself in 1687, he appointed Catholics to various positions, such as sheriffs and magistrates. His actions were a major factor in provoking Irish Protestant fears of James II and advancing their readiness to support William of Orange. Tyrconnell was a commander at the Battle of the BOYNE and, following the JACOBITE defeat, he went to France. He returned to Ireland with promises of further French aid in terms of money and men. However, he died in the summer of 1691 prior to the final capitulation by the Jacobite cause in the Treaty of LIMERICK.

Tyrone

Tyrone is the largest of the counties in Northern Ireland. An inland county, it has a population of over 152,000 and an area of 1,220 square miles. The name comes from Tir Eoghan, which meant the land of Eoghan, the son of the legendary Niall of the Nine Hostages. In the Middle Ages and after, it formed part of the territory of the Ui Neill, or the O'Neills, but, following the Flight of the Earls in 1607, the county constituted part of the Ulster PLANTATION. The Sperrin Mountains are located in the northwest whereas the west consists of a plateau, and the east and south contain the more fertile land. Agriculture and various forms of food and meat processing are among the major industries, and major towns include Cookstown, Dungannon, Omagh, and Strabane. Important and often tragic events in the history of Tyrone include the Battle of BENBURB in 1646 when Owen Roe O'NEILL defeated the army of General Henry MUNRO, the IRISH VOLUNTEER convention at Dungannon in 1782 demanding LEGISLATIVE INDEPENDENCE, and the Real IRA bombing of Omagh in 1998, which wrought the greatest number of deaths of any incident in the Northern Ireland troubles. Famous natives of Tyrone include Charles Gavan DUFFY, writers Patrick KAVANAGH and Ben KIELY, and political activist Bernadette Devlin MCALISKEY.

Tyrone, Conn O'Neill, first earl of (c. 1484–1559)
Lord of Tyrone

Conn O'Neill became the chieftain or lord of the O'Neills of Tyrone in 1519. He was an ally of

Gerald Fitzgerald, the ninth earl of KILDARE, and joined in the Geraldine rebellion of 1534 to 1539. In September 1542 he made peace with Henry VIII and accepted the position of earl of Tyrone as part of the SURRENDER AND REGRANT policy of securing the adherence of the Gaelic leaders to the monarchy. His son Shane and other members of the family resented this and challenged his authority and his designation of another son, Matthew, as successor. Matthew was killed and Conn fled to the PALE for safety.

Tyrone, Hugh O'Neill, second earl of (1550–1616)

Gaelic earl

The grandson of Conn O'Neill, first earl of TYRONE and the son of Matthew O'Neill who had been murdered by his half-brother, Shane, he was taken into protection by Lord Deputy Henry Sidney and raised by English patrons in the anticipation of his becoming earl of Tyrone. When he returned to Ireland in 1568 he served Queen Elizabeth against the Geraldine revolt in Munster. Later his loyalties became more ambiguous. He was hostile to his cousin, Turlough O'Neill, who had become leader of the O'Neills, and he was married to the daughter of the English military commander, Marshall Bagenal. However, he had given hospitality to

refugees from the Spanish Armada, and, on the death of Turlough O'Neill, he succeeded to the leadership of the O'Neills in all its Gaelic symbolism. When his wife died, he married Catherine Magennis, and took up arms against the English, winning major victories in the battles of Clontibret in 1595 and Yellow Ford in 1598. At the latter, his former father-in-law was killed. The strength of his army was such that he was a virtual "king of Ireland" and Robert Devereux, earl of ESSEX, the special commander whom Queen Elizabeth sent to confront him, was compelled to consent to a truce in 1600. When Charles Blount, Lord MOUNTJOY, came to Ireland to resume the struggle, O'Neill and Hugh O'DONNELL led their forces south to relieve an allied force of Spaniards who were being besieged. The relief failed at the Battle of KINSALE on Christmas Eve 1601. O'Neill retreated with his greatly reduced army to Ulster, and, in March 1603, kept unaware that Queen Elizabeth had died, submitted to Mountjoy at Mellifont in County Louth. In contrast to Mountjoy's more accommodating attitude, the government harassed the earl, inhibiting his control of great tracts of his land. Accordingly, he and the nephew of O'Donnell, left Ireland in September 1607—the Flight of the Earls—with the hope of attaining continental support for a recovery of their position Ireland. He died in exile in Rome.

U

U2

rock group

Formed in Dublin in 1976, the group of four became not only Ireland's most successful rock band but also one of the more successful in the world. The members are Bono (Paul David Hewson, b. 1960) on vocals and guitar, The Edge (David Howell Evans, b. 1961) on guitar, piano, vocals, and bass, Adam Clayton (b. 1960) on bass and guitar, and Larry Mullen Jr. (b. 1960) on drums. Their manager is Paul McGuinness. Their first single, *U2-3,* which topped the Irish charts, was released in 1979. The following December they did their first shows outside of Ireland in London. Earlier releases between 1979 and 1982 were favorably reviewed, but they sold relatively

Bono (right) and The Edge from the Irish rock group U2 perform at a concert in Dublin, 2005. *(EPA/Aidan Crawley/Landov)*

poorly. Their first appearance on U.S. television was on June 4, 1981. The 1983 albums, *War* and *U2 Live: Under a Blood-Red Sky*, marked their breakthrough, especially in the American market. One of their songs "Sunday Bloody Sunday" dealt with the Northern Ireland situation, particularly the BLOODY SUNDAY incident of 1972. The song disowns violence and anger and calls for Christians to stop fighting each other. "New Year's Day" was U2's first international hit single, reaching the 10th position on the United Kingdom charts and the Top 50 in the United States. Their album *The Unforgettable Fire* (1984), named after a series of paintings made by survivors of the atomic bombs at Hiroshima and Nagasaki, featured a tribute to Martin Luther King, Jr. The single from the album reached the U.K. Top 5 and the U.S. Top 50. They were called the "Band of the 80s" by *Rolling Stone* magazine. They were a major act in the 1985 Live Aid concert for Ethiopian famine victims and went on a tour for Amnesty International in 1986 across the United States, which helped Amnesty International triple its membership in the process. Later releases and tours that sold out worldwide include *The Joshua Tree* (1987) and *Rattle and Hum* (1988). The band played in Belfast three days before the public voted in favor of the Northern Ireland Peace Accord in 1998. That same year, they released the first greatest hits compilation, *The Best of 1980–1990*. They won several Grammys in 2001 for the album *All That You Can't Leave Behind*. In 2002 they released *The Best of 1990–2002*. In 2004, another album, *How to Dismantle an Atomic Bomb* (2004) was the number one hit in 32 countries. In March 2005 U2 was inducted into the Rock and Roll Hall of Fame in their first year of eligibility. They began a world tour in San Diego, California, in March 2005 and in an appearance at Croke Park, Dublin, they broke Irish records with ticket sales of 150,000. They also participated in a Live 8 concert in July 2005 promoting world consciousness of African poverty.

Ua Buachalla, Domhnall (1865–1963)

governor-general of Ireland

Born in County Cork, Ua Buachalla was a native Irish speaker. He took part in the EASTER RISING and was imprisoned, but released in 1917. He was elected as a member of SINN FÉIN to the first DÁIL ÉIREANN for Kildare North, and to the second Dáil for Kildare-Wicklow. He was not elected from the same constituency in the 1922 election when he opposed the ANGLO-IRISH TREATY, nor in that of 1923. However, he was successful in winning election for Kildare in the June and September 1927 general elections, in both cases as a candidate for FIANNA FÁIL. In 1932 in the election in which that party came to power, he failed to be elected for Kildare. In November 1932 he was appointed GOVERNOR-GENERAL to replace James MACNEILL, who had retired in protest at what he thought was disrespect by the government of Eamon DE VALERA. On de Valera's instructions and in keeping with his desire to downplay the role of the office, Ua Buachalla did not live in the Vice Regal lodge in PHOENIX PARK, or make any public appearance, or participate in social functions. Rather, he performed only legally required functions, such as signing legislation, until the office was abolished by the 1937 constitution.

Ulster

One of the four historic provinces of Ireland, Ulster is often incorrectly identified with NORTHERN IRELAND. However, only six of the nine counties of Ulster are in Northern Ireland. They are ANTRIM, ARMAGH, DERRY, DOWN, FERMANAGH, and TYRONE. Three others, CAVAN, DONEGAL, and MONAGHAN, are in the Republic of Ireland. Ironically, Malin Head, which is the northernmost point in the island, is in Donegal and not in Northern Ireland. The name derives from a pre-Christian kingdom or tribe, *Uladh*, and it was the site of many of the heroic epics of ancient times. The dominant family was the Ui Neill (O'Neill), whose roots in and dominance of the area date from mythical times, and whose presence persisted throughout the Middle Ages and in the late 16th and early 17th centuries in giving leadership to Irish resistance to increasing English control. The ultimate departure of the O'Neills was followed by the PLANTATION. The population of Northern Ireland is approximately 1,700,000 with an area of 5,452 square miles, while the three counties in the republic have a population of a quarter of a million and an area of 3,093 square miles.

Ulster-American Folk Park

This is a museum near OMAGH, County Tyrone, which celebrated the role of emigrants from ULSTER to North America, particularly that portion of the emigration whose descendants regard themselves as SCOTS-IRISH. Major emphasis is given to the number of American presidents who had Ulster antecedents.

Ulster Custom   See LAND ACTS.

Ulster Defence Association

One of the largest of the LOYALIST paramilitary groups, it was founded in 1971 and played a major role in the 1974 general strike that brought down the provincial power-sharing government approved at SUNNINGDALE. The organization was responsible for killing a number of Catholics, supposedly in retaliation for IRA actions, in the 1970s and with increased vigor through an associated group, the Ulster Freedom Fighters, in the early 1990s. The group accepted the GOOD FRIDAY AGREEMENT and had a political wing, the Ulster Democratic Party. Various breakaway and more locally organized loyalist groups continue to engage in some violence and criminality.

Ulster Defence Regiment (UDR)

The UDR was formed in 1972 as an auxiliary military force to assist the British army in maintaining law and order in Northern Ireland. It served as a replacement for the discontinued and notoriously sectarian "B Specials," an auxiliary police force. In spite of the hope to recruit Catholics, few joined and the force became de facto Protestant. Its size reached close to 9,000

and approximately 250 of its members or former members were killed by the IRISH REPUBLICAN PARTY (IRA), often while on duty and sometimes in their own homes in sight of their families. Some in the organization had links with various LOYALIST groups and were involved in violent crimes against Catholics. In 1992 the group was merged with a regular army unit, the Royal Irish Rangers, to form a new group, the Royal Irish Regiment.

Ulster Plantation   See PLANTATION.

Ulster Unionist Party

Unionism, that is, opposition to HOME RULE, had a following throughout Ireland, and was not limited to the northeast of the island. In 1886 an Irish Unionist Party of members of parliament, most of whom, but not all, represented Ulster constituencies, was formed to work with the Conservative Party to oppose Home Rule. However, by 1904, unionists in the North were apprehensive that unionists in the rest of Ireland, a decided minority in their counties, were not as determined in their resistance to Home Rule and were beginning to consider steps toward devolution. Accordingly, the Ulster Unionist Council of 200 members was formed in December 1904 to keep the unionist organizations in the province in line in the struggle against potential rule from Dublin. That group, which over the years expanded in size to nearly 1,000, but in more recent times has been reduced to 600, called into being the Ulster Unionist Party in 1905, and remains to this day the governing body of that party. The party was made up of representatives from constituency associations and from the ORANGE ORDER as well as unionist members of parliament. The first leader was Edward SAUNDERSON and when he died in 1906, the English politician, Walter Long, succeeded him. In 1910 Sir Edward CARSON became the leader until 1921, when NORTHERN IRELAND was created. James CRAIG, the first prime minister, succeeded him

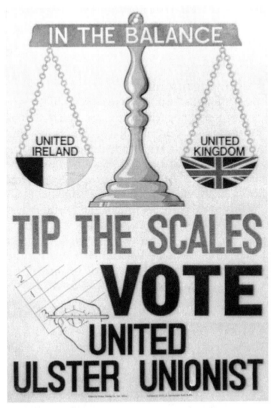

Propaganda poster for the Ulster Unionist Party
(Library of Congress)

and remained leader until 1940. The party constituted the dominant majority in the Northern Ireland parliament from 1921 until its prorogation in 1972. Since then, in all elections to the variety of assemblies and parliaments that have been attempted, including the contemporary NORTHERN IRELAND ASSEMBLY, it was the largest unionist group until most recently when the DEMOCRATIC UNIONIST PARTY surpassed it. Leaders of the party after Craig include John ANDREWS from 1940 to 1943, Basil Brooke, Lord BROOKE-BOROUGH, from 1943 to 1963, Terence O'NEILL from 1963 to 1969, James CHICHESTER-CLARK from 1969 to 1971, Brian FAULKNER from 1971 to 1974, Harry WEST from 1974 to 1979, James MOLYNEAUX from 1979 to 1995, and David TRIMBLE from 1995 to 2005. He was succeeded

by Reg Empey. All except the last four served as prime minister as well, and Trimble served as first minister in the frequently suspended power-sharing government set up in accordance with the GOOD FRIDAY AGREEMENT.

Ulster Volunteer Force (UVF)

The Ulster Unionist Council formed the Ulster Volunteer Force in 1913 as a means to resist by violence implementation of HOME RULE legislation, the passage of which appeared imminent. The group grew to 100,000 in number, many of them had signed the Solemn League and Covenant in September 1912 indicating a willingness to fight to resist Home Rule. The organization was able to draw on the support and leadership of numerous retired British army officers. In September 1913 the UVF was designated as the Army of Ulster when the Ulster Unionist Council appointed the Provisional Government of Ulster. The organization's blatant disregard for legality in setting up a private army prompted Irish NATIONALISTS to emulate them in forming the Irish Volunteers the same year. Their most notorious action was in April 1914 when 25,000 rifles and 3,000,000 rounds of ammunition were openly landed at various ports in Northern Ireland, particularly at Larne. Their efforts were further encouraged by the mutiny at the CURRAGH when several score officers in the British army were not disciplined for threatening to resign rather than take part in potential action against Ulster. When the First World War started and the enforcement of the Home Rule Act was postponed, tens of thousands of the UVF were enlisted as units and became the Ulster Division. The same group suffered a very high number of casualties at the Battle of the Somme. However, that loss of life worked to intensify the loyalty and commitment to the union with Britain by the survivors. Many of its members became recruits to the various Special Constabularies that were set up to aid the ROYAL ULSTER CONSTABULARY after the Northern Ireland government was established.

In 1966 LOYALISTS formed a new Ulster Volunteer Force to protest the liberal reforms promoted by Prime Minister Terence O'Neill. From the outset they, and comparable groups, engaged in brutal sectarian assaults and murders. They were especially active in the 1970s. One particularly brutal gang was nicknamed the "Shankill Butchers," and was responsible for killing three members of a popular Irish music group, the Miami Showband. In 1994 six Catholics watching a World Cup Soccer match in a bar in Loughlinisland, County Down, were killed. In 1994 a political party affiliated with the UVF emerged and called itself the Progressive Unionist Party. It worked to bring about loyalist acceptance of a cease-fire and elected several candidates to the NORTHERN IRELAND ASSEMBLY in 1998.

Ultimate Financial Agreement

Following the December 1925 agreement abrogating the report of the BOUNDARY COMMISSION and exempting the IRISH FREE STATE from the ANGLO-IRISH TREATY obligations of paying a proportionate part of the imperial debt, a supplemental agreement was made between the British government and the Irish Free State by which the latter agreed to assume responsibility for paying both the land ANNUITIES deriving from the various land purchase acts and the pensions of former members of the ROYAL IRISH CONSTABULARY.

Undertakers

The term describes leading political figures in the 18th-century Irish parliament who "undertook" to promote the government's agenda. They wielded the power of patronage necessary to guarantee appropriate voting by their followers. The lord lieutenants were so frequently absent from Ireland, as were the chief secretaries, that the use of the Undertakers was the most effective means to manage the parliament. Leading Undertakers included William CONNOLLY and Henry Boyle, earl of SHANNON. The use of undertakers come to an end when Charles Townsend served as lord lieutenant

(1767–72), as he began the practice of remaining in Ireland and assuming the management of parliament directly.

unionism/unionist

Historically the term refers to support of the ACT OF UNION and opposition to HOME RULE. Generally unionists came from the Protestant and ANGLO-IRISH minority of the population of Ireland. Since the attainment of political independence by the Irish Free State in 1922, the term has come to refer to those who wish to maintain the link between Great Britain and Northern Ireland regardless of whatever political affiliation they might have, whether the ULSTER UNIONIST PARTY, the DEMOCRATIC UNIONIST PARTY, the United Kingdom Unionist Party, or one of the smaller LOYALIST groupings.

United Irishmen

The society was founded in Belfast in October 1791 by Theobald Wolfe TONE, William DRENNAN, Thomas RUSSELL, and others to promote political reform, especially to expand the franchise, then very limited. They were inspired by the course of the American Revolution and, perhaps more so, by the revolution occurring in France. Although they drew most of their original support from Ulster Presbyterians, many of the leaders, especially when they attracted a following in Dublin, had CHURCH OF IRELAND background. Also, they were committed to gaining rights, including the franchise, for Catholics, as the name of the organization itself implied the unification of Irishmen regardless of creed. The organization was proscribed in 1794 after war broke out between Britain and revolutionary France. Soon the group turned to revolutionary goals—those of seeking assistance from France and making Ireland a separatist republic that would be religiously nonsectarian. When the authorities became aware of contacts being made with the French, arrests followed. Tone was given the option, which he took, of leaving Ireland. But when abroad, he was able to convince the French to come to the aid of revolution in Ireland. However, bad weather forestalled an invasion planned for December 1796. Ships with thousands of men had actually arrived in Bantry Bay off Cork. In 1797, United Irish weapons were seized in Ulster and there a general repression was imposed by General Gerard LAKE. In early 1798, a number of United Irish leaders in Dublin were arrested and further repressive measures prompted an actual rising in May and June. By this time the United Irishmen had secured alliance with the primarily Catholic DEFENDERS, a group adhering to an uncertain ideology other than the desire to see the overthrow of the current PROTESTANT ASCENDANCY and a return to an idealized Gaelic past. Most of the leaders in Dublin including Lord Edward Fitzgerald, were arrested. The rising in the southeast, especially in Wexford, was put down with brutality after some initial successes that saw the commission of some sectarian crimes. A rising in Mayo, following a landing by the French at KILLALA, was also put down after initial success, particularly at Castlebar. The French invaders were allowed to return to France, but the United Irishmen and their Defender allies were brutally repressed. Tone himself was captured when attempting to land in Donegal in September 1798. He committed suicide just prior to the execution by hanging to which he had been sentenced. Pockets of United Irishmen continued for some years, especially in the Wicklow Mountains, and Robert EMMET staged a rising in Dublin in 1803, which failed. Nonetheless, the movement was venerated and admired by many Irish nationalists, although not Daniel O'CONNELL, and it served especially as a source of inspiration for those Irish who sought to achieve political independence by violent means, such as the IRISH REPUBLICAN BROTHERHOOD and the IRA. Elements of the ideology of the United Irishmen , including separatism from Britain and political REPUBLICANISM, that is, no monarchy or hereditary titles, have made the society an object of idealization by many Irish, including the largest contemporary political party, FIANNA FÁIL.

university colleges

Legislation in 1845 established three QUEEN'S COLLEGES, in Belfast, Cork, and Galway, as alternatives to TRINITY COLLEGE DUBLIN. The institutions met the displeasure of the Roman Catholic hierarchy because of their failure to include specific religious and theological curricula. Accordingly, only the school in BELFAST thrived, although the other two continued with a small number of students. The Catholics established a Catholic University in DUBLIN in 1851 with John Henry NEWMAN as its president. The Jesuits later administered the institution. Legislation in 1879 created the Royal University to act as an examining body to grant degrees to students from nonrecognized institutions, specifically the Catholic University, upon the passing of certain exams. Finally, in 1908, further legislation created a NATIONAL UNIVERSITY OF IRELAND, which would include the Queen's Colleges in Cork and Galway and the Catholic University in Dublin as constituent colleges (Queen's College Belfast became a separate QUEEN'S UNIVERSITY BELFAST), which were nonsectarian but in fact Catholic. The term *university college* derives from that time and, for most of the 20th century, the institutions were known as UCC, UCD and UCG, respectively. In 1910 the Catholic seminary in MAYNOOTH was also recognized by the National University and made a fully constituent college in 1967. However, legislation in 1997 gave independent university status to all four, and they are formally titled National University of Ireland, Cork; National University of Ireland, Dublin; National University of Ireland, Galway; and National University of Ireland, Maynooth. Other universities in the Irish Republic include the University of Dublin (Trinity College Dublin), Dublin City University, and the University of Limerick.

Ussher, James (1581–1656)
archbishop, scholar

Born in Dublin, he was one of the first students to attend TRINITY COLLEGE DUBLIN, where he became a professor of divinity and vice provost between 1607 and 1621. He was bishop of Meath from 1621 to 1625 and archbishop of Armagh and primate of all Ireland from 1625 to 1656. He was more a scholar than an administrator. Although primate of Ireland, he moved to England in 1640 and was away from Ireland during the war of the three kingdoms, which pitted Catholic and Protestant and royalist and parliamentarian against each other. In England, he was a supporter of the monarchy and the high church, but was appreciative of Puritan views. Ussher used much of his scholarly energies to argue against Catholicism, the Counter-Reformation, and a feared Spanish support of a native rising in Ireland. He corresponded with scholars throughout Europe, including Catholics, and amassed a library of 10,000 volumes for Trinity. Ussher sought to calculate the date of creation, which he put at 4004 B.C.

V

Vanguard

William CRAIG, who had served as Northern Ireland minister for home affairs, formed this group in February 1972 to defend the Northern Ireland PARLIAMENT and to resist the unification of the island, which he feared was a prospect, especially following suspension of the parliament in March of that year. His group held demonstrations and parades, which had a militaristic flavor. That and his rhetoric about attacking the enemy provoked accusations of fascism. The movement also considered the notion of an independent Northern Ireland. Under the name of the Vanguard Unionist Progressive Party they gained a few seats in the NORTHERN IRELAND ASSEMBLY elected in 1973, but they refused to support the power-sharing government created by that body and endorsed by the SUNNINGDALE AGREEMENT and worked with the general strike to bring it down. Later, the movement split when Craig talked about an emergency coalition with the SOCIAL DEMOCRATIC AND LABOUR PARTY. He eventually returned to the ULSTER UNIONIST PARTY.

viceroyalty   See LORD LIEUTENANT.

Vikings

Invaders from Scandinavia who raided Ireland and various other parts of Western Europe from the late eighth through the 10th centuries. The Vikings first arrived in Ireland in 795. Their primary targets were monastic sites. They also sought livestock and slaves. From the middle of the ninth century the Vikings began to establish bases in Ireland from which to launch their raids. These bases eventually developed into the first Irish cities, as Vikings began to interact commercially and socially with the Irish, indeed even intermarrying and becoming Christians. The Viking position in Ireland was weakened during the 10th century at the hands of various Irish kings, culminating with their defeat at the Battle of Clontarf in 1014 by the forces of Brian Boru. The struggle against the Vikings strengthened the process of centralizing royal authority in Ireland.

Vinegar Hill

A campsite on a hill overlooking Enniscorthy and central Wexford used by the rebel forces in 1798. The rebels achieved a series of victories in May, but, on June 21, the government forces under General Gerard LAKE successfully attacked the campsite and dispersed the rebels, changing the momentum of the struggle and leading to the ultimate collapse of the revolt.

W

Wadding, Luke (1588–1657)
priest, scholar

Born to a merchant family in Waterford, Wadding went to Portugal at 14 years of age and studied under the Jesuits. He subsequently joined the Franciscans and was ordained a priest in 1613. He became a professor of theology at the Irish University in Salamanca in 1617, but in 1625 he was sent to Rome by King Philip III to promote the doctrine of the Immaculate Conception. He remained thereafter in Rome where he founded in 1625 a college for Irish Franciscans and in 1627 another college for Irish secular or diocesan clergy. He was responsible for having March 17 liturgically recognized as the feast of St. PATRICK. He published a 36-volume history of the Franciscans and a critical edition of the works of Duns Scotus. He served in various curial offices, including the Congregations of Rites, Propaganda, and the Index, and was a promoter of the Catholic CONFEDERATION OF KILKENNY, securing papal support, including the sending of Giovanni Battista RINUCCINI as nuncio to Ireland in 1645. He rejected all honors, including elevation to cardinal, remaining a simple priest until his death.

Walker, George (1646–1690)
governor of Derry

Born in County Tyrone, Walker was the CHURCH OF IRELAND rector at Donoughmore, County Tyrone. He raised a Protestant force in late 1688 to resist the JACOBITE army, but was forced to take refuge in the walled city of DERRY the following spring. Among those critical of Robert LUNDY for being willing to bargain with Jacobites, he and Major Henry Baker, the joint governors

of the city, gained credit for successfully withstanding the siege. His diary of the events, *A True Account of the Siege of Londonderry* (1689) won him great applause, especially when he reported on the event in London. Other contemporary accounts dispute his central role, particular that by Presbyterian minister John Mackenzie, *Narrative of the Siege of Londonderry* (1690). Nonetheless Walker was made bishop of Derry, but he was killed at the Battle of the BOYNE in 1690.

Walsh, Maurice (1879–1964)
writer

Born in Listowel, County Kerry, Walsh joined the civil service in 1901 and served as an excise officer in Scotland, England, and the west of Ireland until 1923, when he joined the service of the Irish Free State government. He retired from the civil service in 1933, but even before had begun to write novels. His first, *The Key above the Door* (1926), was bought by a publisher for 100 pounds, but later sold 150,000 copies. Other volumes include *While Rivers Run* (1928), *The Small Dark Man* (1929), and *The Road to Nowhere* (1934). He wrote short stories as well, the most celebrated, *The Quiet Man,* which appeared in the collection *The Green Rushes* (1935) and for which a film version was produced by John Ford, starring John Wayne and Maureen O'HARA.

Walsh, Peter (circa 1600–1670)
priest

Walsh was a Franciscan priest who had led clerical opposition to the influence of papal nuncio Giovanni Battista RINUCCINI on the Catholic CONFEDERATION OF KILKENNY in the 1640s. At the time of the restoration, in the early 1660s, he advocated that Irish Catholics agree to a loyal remonstrance, or declaration of loyalty, to the king in which they disavowed any allegiance to the papacy in temporal matters and rejected the papal right to depose monarchs. The hierarchy rejected his proposal.

Walsh, William (1841–1921)

archbishop of Dublin

Born in Dublin, Walsh was educated at the Catholic University and at MAYNOOTH, where he became a professor of theology from 1867 to 1878, then vice president from 1878 to 1880, and president from 1880 to 1885. He became archbishop of Dublin in 1885. He was sympathetic to the LAND LEAGUE and to Charles Stewart PARNELL, and he worked to mitigate the implications of papal condemnation of the PLAN OF CAMPAIGN. He was a supporter of bimetallism, that is, a joint gold and silver basis for currency, and wrote a book on the subject. Committed to Catholic education on primary, secondary, and advanced levels, he served in numerous public appointed posts, which facilitated his efforts to further that goal. They included commissioner of intermediate education (1892 to 1918), commissioner of national education (1895–1901), and first chancellor of the NATIONAL UNIVERSITY OF IRELAND. A contributor to numerous periodicals, such as *FREEMAN'S JOURNAL, Contemporary Review,* and *Dublin Review,* he wrote a number of books on a variety of subjects, including *Harmony of the Gospels* (1879), *Grammar of Gregorian Music* (1885), *The Irish University Question* (1897), and *O'Connell and Archbishop Murray and the Board of Charitable Donations and Bequests* (1916). He was sympathetic to SINN FÉIN and opposed the GOVERNMENT OF IRELAND ACT of 1920. Possibly his outspoken political views as a NATIONALIST inhibited his becoming a cardinal, as had his two predecessors.

Walton, Ernest Thomas Sinton (1903–1995)

physicist

Born in Dungarvan, County Waterford, Walton was educated at Cookstown Academy, Banbridge Academy, and Methodist College, Belfast, TRINITY COLLEGE DUBLIN, and Cambridge. While working with Ernest Rutherford in Cambridge, he and J. D. Cockcroft produced an instrument with which they were able to "split the atom," and for which they were awarded the Nobel Prize in 1951. He returned to Trinity in 1934 and became the Erasmus Smith Professor of Natural and Experimental Philosophy. Walton also became head of the physics department. He was an official in the ROYAL IRISH ACADEMY.

war of independence

Sometimes called the Anglo-Irish War, the war began with an assault on the ROYAL IRISH CONSTABULARY in Soloheadbeg, County Tipperary, by members of the IRISH VOLUNTEERS. It occurred about the same time SINN FÉIN members elected to the Westminster parliament in the 1918 general election were meeting in Dublin to form the DÁIL ÉIREANN. The first phase of the war consisted of attacks by Irish Volunteers on RIC barracks throughout the countryside, which achieved the purpose of inducing massive numbers of resignations from the force. The Dáil Éireann came to regard the Irish Volunteers as the Army of the Irish Republic, or the IRA. The Dáil also approved the establishment of a rival court system to supplant the existing judiciary and succeeded in getting most of the local and popularly elected authorities to recognize it as the government of Ireland, even at the cost of losing essential grants from the British. The British response to what was happening was mixed, at times treating it as a matter of law enforcement, but at other times as a war. The army presence was reinforced. Replacements for the depleted RIC were found in the notorious BLACK AND TANS and an equally outrageous force of AUXILIARIES. An important figure in the war on the Irish side was Michael COLLINS, who held the official title of minister for finance, but who, more importantly, served as director of intelligence and head of the IRISH REPUBLICAN BROTHERHOOD. A rival was Cathal BRUGHA, minister for defense, whose authority was largely ignored by Collins in directing, through the IRB, the guerrilla war campaign. Particular bitter incidents took place in November 1920, when Collins's squads killed several British agents in Dublin and on the same day the Black and Tans and Auxiliaries retaliated by firing on a crowd at a football match in Dublin. There were several retaliatory burnings and sackings of towns by the Auxiliaries and a dramatic, ultimately fatal, hunger strike by Terence MacSwiney, the Sinn Féin lord mayor of Cork. Soon after one major assault on the Customs House, which failed, in response to the demands of Brugha for a more conventional form of warfare, peace feelers began and in July 1921 a truce took place with existing forces allowed to keep their respective positions and abstain from confrontation. Subsequent negotiations resulted in the Anglo-Irish Treaty of December 1921.

Waterford

Waterford, which is in the province of Munster, is a maritime county bounded on the south by the Celtic Sea, on the west by Cork, on the north by Tipperary and Kilkenny, and on the east by Wexford. The population stands at slightly more than 100,000 and it has an area of 710 square miles. The northern part of the county contains two mountain ranges, the Comeraghs and the Knockmealdowns, while the east is low lying. Farming and fishing are common activities in the county, although there are several towns that have harbors, such as the county town, Dungarvin, and Tramore. But most significant is the city of Waterford, an inland port near the meeting of the Barrow and the Suir Rivers. Founded in the 10th century by the Vikings, it was captured by the Normans in 1170, and for

The town of Dunmore in County Waterford *(Library of Congress)*

the remainder of the medieval and early modern period, it was the second city of Ireland. Its economy featured shipbuilding and trade, notably exportation of wool and hides to Flanders and other continental ports and importation of wines. The city vigorously resisted efforts to impose Protestantism in the reign of Elizabeth I. Identified closely with the Catholic CONFEDERATION OF KILKENNY, the city was subjected to a siege by CROMWELL in 1649 and was subsequently dominated by a Protestant oligarchy. Domination by the PROTESTANT ASCENDANCY led to modernization of the town with the removal of medieval walls and the construction of Georgian streets and buildings. Catholics predominated in the countryside and in the later 18th and early 19th centuries became part of the flourishing middle class of the city, when the export of bacon and flour became important. However, as the 19th century advanced, development of Waterford remained stagnant. Even a crystal business started in 1783 was forced to close. The population of the town dropped from 40,000 in 1800 to 23,000 in 1841 and barely climbed to 27,000 in 1900. Residents were not drawn to the nationalist revolutionary spirit of the early 20th century, as they continued to return the IRISH PARLIAMENTARY PARTY candidate in 1918 when SINN FÉIN swept all before it in much of Ireland. The revival of the crystal industry in 1947 paved the way for development and expansion, including extensive urban renewal and revitalized trade with the Continent.

Wellesley, Arthur, duke of Wellington

See WELLINGTON, ARTHUR WELLESLEY, DUKE OF.

Wellesley, Richard Culley (1760–1842)

politician

Born in County Meath, Wellesley was the elder brother of the Duke of Wellington. He served as governor-general of India from 1798 to 1805 and LORD LIEUTENANT of Ireland from 1821 to 1828 and from 1833 to 1834. He was sympathetic to Catholic emancipation, for which reason he was

recalled by his brother in 1828. He placed restrictions on ORANGE ORDER demonstrations, which prompted a bottle being thrown at him in the theater. During his second tenure he dealt with the tithe agitation of the WHITEBOYS and suspended habeas corpus. However, he also worked to remove bigots from the magistracy and the police.

Wellington, Arthur Wellesley, duke of (1769–1852)

soldier, politician

Born in Dublin, Wellesley spent most of his career as a British military commander, serving with exceptional prominence in the wars against Napoleon, and then as a politician, serving in various cabinets and as prime minister. He sat in the Irish parliament for Trim from 1790 to 1795 and supported the Catholic relief bill of 1793. He was chief secretary from 1807 to 1809, but devoted his attention to his military commitments elsewhere. As prime minister he originally opposed Catholic emancipation, but acquiesced in its adoption after Daniel O'CONNELL's electoral success in Clare in 1828.

Wentworth, Thomas, earl of Strafford

See STRAFFORD, THOMAS WENTWORTH, FIRST EARL OF.

Wesley, John (1703–1791)

clergyman

Born in Epworth, Lincolnshire, and educated at Oxford, Wesley was ordained a priest in the Church of England in 1728. He was disturbed by the absence of religious enthusiasm in the church in the mid-18th century as bishoprics and vicarages were increasingly filled with political appointees, a deistic temperament seemed to prevail, and the lack of availability of religious service for many, especially in the increasingly populated centers of industry and mining where popular needs were not met by parish boundaries organized according to a rural social structure. His criticisms of the church and his "revivalist" style of services created great animosity toward him, but he never broke with the church, although his followers did so after his death in establishing the Methodist Church. He was also very critical of Calvinism and Catholicism. Hostility toward the latter was a partial reason for his making 21 missions to Ireland to further his concept of religious enthusiasm. After his death there were 15,000 Methodists in Ireland.

West, Harry (1917–2004)
politician

Harry West was a member of the Northern Ireland PARLIAMENT for Enniskillen from 1954 to 1972 and was Northern Ireland minister for agriculture from 1960 to 1966 and 1971 to 1972. He opposed Brian Faulkner's policy of power sharing and replaced him as leader of the ULSTER UNIONIST PARTY in 1974, when he led the party into a United Ulster Unionist Coalition, joining the Vanguard Progressive Unionist Party and the DEMOCRATIC UNIONIST PARTY in putting up single anti-SUNNINGDALE Unionist candidates in all 12 constituencies. He himself was elected to parliament for Fermanagh–South Tyrone as he benefited from a split in the NATIONALIST vote in that constituency. However, he lost in the October vote when a single nationalist candidate ran. He replaced Brian Faulkner as leader of the Ulster Unionist Party. West was elected to the NORTHERN IRELAND ASSEMBLY in 1973 and to the Northern Ireland Constitutional Convention in 1975, in both instances for Fermanagh–South Tyrone, but was not elected to the European Parliament in 1979, after which he resigned his leadership of the party. He lost in a by-election to fill the Westminster seat for Fermanagh–South Tyrone in April 1981 to Bobby SANDS, the candidate HUNGER STRIKE. He remained an active member of the Ulster Unionist Council.

Westmeath

A midlands county in LEINSTER, Westmeath has a population of 72,000 and an area of 679 square miles. It shares boundaries with the river Shannon, Lough Ree, and with the counties of Longford and Roscommon. Important towns are Athlone to the west and the county town, Mullingar, to the west. Originally intended to be part of the Norman settlement, most of it slipped out of the PALE and remained Gaelicized, assuming an almost frontier-like character. In 1542 it was designated a separate county from Meath. Its topography is primarily gentle pasture area with some raised bogs. The 19th-century Royal Canal, linking Dublin with the Shannon, dissects the county. The town of Athlone was besieged three times by the Williamite forces in 1690. Famous natives of the county include the tenor John MCCORMICK and the novelist Brinsley MACNAMARA. One of the county's larger lakes, Lough Derrevaragh, was the site of the ancient legend about the Children of Lir.

Wexford

A county at the southeast corner of Ireland, Wexford has population of over 116,000 and an area of 907 square miles. The county is bounded by St. George's Channel on the east, by the River Barrow on the west, and by the Celtic Sea on the south. The Slanney River bisects the county. The county town, Wexford, was founded by the VIKINGS and further developed by the Normans. It is one of the more intensively tillaged counties in Ireland, while its coast features dunes, sandbanks, and some erosion. Its port of Rosslare serves as the ferry gateway to Britain and the Continent. Besides farming, the county has a variety of manufacturing industries and is a major center for freight forwarding, haulage, and shipping. The town was sacked by Cromwell in 1649 and the county was the scene of major action in the Rising of 1798. Famous natives include the politician James DILLON, the Arctic explorer Robert John Le Mesurier McClure, and IRISH PARLIAMENTARY PARTY political figures John and William REDMOND.

Whaley, Thomas (1766–1800)
politician, eccentric

Born in Dublin, Whaley inherited a massive fortune as a teenager. He was a member of the Irish parliament for Newcastle, County Down, in 1785 and later for Enniscorthy. He accepted bribes from both sides in the debate over the ACT OF UNION, which he first voted for and then against. Whaley was a notorious gambler who accumulated enormous debts. However, his victory in a wager that he could travel to Jerusalem and return within a year marked one of his celebrated winnings.

Wheatley, Francis (1747–1801)
painter
Born and trained in London, Wheatley was a portrait and a landscape painter. He visited Ireland in 1767 and returned in 1779 to escape creditors. He was soon employed to paint portraits. He also painted a number of subjects that would be of historical importance. Celebrated works include *A View of the College Green with the Meeting of the Volunteers on the 4th of November 1779, The Irish House of Commons in 1780,* and *Henry Grattan Urging the Claim of Irish Right.* He returned to London, and exhibited paintings with Irish subjects, many done from sketches he had made while in Ireland, such as *Donnybrook Fair.* Wheatley became a member of the Royal Academy in 1791.

Whitaker, T. K. (Thomas Kenneth Whitaker) (1916–)
economist, public servant
Born in Rostrevor, County Down, Whitaker was educated at the IRISH CHRISTIAN BROTHERS' School in Drogheda and later obtained a B.A. in mathematics, economics, and Celtic studies and subsequently a M.Sc. in economics from the University of London. He did extremely well in civil service examinations and advanced rapidly in the Department of Finance, where he became secretary of the department at the age of 39. In that position he organized a detailed study of the then stagnant Irish economy and drafted a *Programme for Economic Expansion,* which was published as a white paper in November 1958. The program, which called for abandonment of a protectionist and primarily agricultural economy and for the acceptance of free trade, international competition, and industrialization, became the guide for the economic rejuvenation and modernization that began during the government of Seán LEMASS. Whitaker also organized the breakthrough exchange of visits between Lemass and Terence O'NEILL in 1965. He left the Department of Finance in 1969 and became governor of the Central Bank until 1976. He was named to the SEANAD from 1977 to 1982. He chaired several public bodies including the National Industrial and Economic Council (1963 to 1967), the Economic and Social Research Institute (1974–87), the Council of the Dublin Institute of Advanced Studies (1980), president of the ROYAL IRISH ACADEMY (1985–87), chairman of the Committee of Enquiry into the Penal System (1983–85), and chancellor of the National University of Ireland (1976–96). He received honorary degrees from the National University of Ireland, TRINITY COLLEGE DUBLIN, QUEEN'S UNIVERSITY BELFAST, and the University of Ulster.

Whiteboys
The Whiteboys were participants in an agrarian protest movement, primarily in the 1760s, that started in Tipperary, and spread to Limerick, Waterford, Cork, Kilkenny, and later to Laios, Carlow, and Wexford. They wore white sheets over their regular clothing at their assemblies and threatened landlords and their agents, whose property they attacked in protest over enclosures of common land, the encroachment of pasture on tillage land, tithes, and evictions. The nickname of the movement, "Whiteboys," became the common name for agrarian protest and was the name given to legislation, which even listed certain offenses as capital, passed to restrain them.

Wicklow
Wicklow is a maritime county in Leinster, bordered on the north by Dublin, on the south by

Wexford, on the west by Kildare and Carlow, and on the east by the Irish Sea. It has a population of over 114,000 and an area of 784 square miles. Much of the county consists of mountain ranges, including the second highest mountain in Ireland, Lugnaquilla, and strikingly beautiful landscapes, such as those seen at the Glen of the Downs, Glendalough, Glenmacnass, and the Vale of Avoca. Glendalough is the site of an early Christian monastery founded by St. Kevin. The mountains were places of refuge for rebels, especially after the Rising of 1798. The county contains many stately homes of the era of the PROTESTANT ASCENDANCY, such as the ruins of Powerscourt and Russborough House (which houses the Alfred Beit art collection). Another attraction is Avondale House, the home of Charles Stewart PARNELL. Besides agriculture and various forms of food processing, the county has numerous other industries, including computer software, refrigeration motors, pharmaceutical chemicals, veterinary products, and telecommunications equipment. The county town is Wicklow and other towns, mainly on the coast, are Bray, Greystones, and Arklow. Important natives besides Parnell include Robert BARTON, Robert Erskine CHILDERS, and the 1798 rebels Michael DWYER and Joseph HOLT.

Wilde, Oscar (1854–1900)
writer

Born in Dublin, the son of a celebrated surgeon and a feminist poet, Wilde was educated at TRINITY COLLEGE DUBLIN and at Magdalen College Oxford as a scholar of the classics. He was influenced by the aesthetics of John Ruskin and Walter Pater. Wilde settled in London in 1879 and became a writer, lecturer, and critic. He established a reputation as a dandy and as a wit, and even went on a lecture tour of the United States in 1882 to accompany and act as a foil to the touring Gilbert and Sullivan musical *Patience*, which satirized the aesthetic movement. He returned from America, married, and had two sons. He edited a women's magazine, *Women's World*, wrote essays, such as "The Critic as Artist"

and "The Truth of Masks," and plays, which were a study of manners and which satirized high society, such as *Lady Windermere's Fan* (1891), *The Importance of Being Earnest* (1895), and *An Ideal Husband* (1895). One play, *Salome* (1893) was banned, but later performed in Paris. His celebrated novel, *The Picture of Dorian Grey* (1891), about a hedonist who retains his youth while his portrait manifests his personal decay, provoked great praise and rebuke. In 1895 he sued the Marquis of Queensberry for libel, when the later accused him of being a sodomite, as he was having a homosexual affair with his son, Lord Alfred Douglas. The libel suit backfired as the extent of Wilde's involvement in the homosexual world of the time became public. He was subsequently convicted and imprisoned for two years for gross indecency. He wrote *The Ballad of Reading Gaol* (1896) about his experience in prison. Upon release, broken in spirit and ill, he drifted to Paris, where he died from meningitis. While in prison he wrote a letter to Douglas, *De Profundis*, an autobiographical apologia that was published in 1905.

Wild Geese

The Wild Geese refers to the thousands of Irish men and women who went to the Continent in the 16th, 17th, and 18th centuries, usually fleeing imposition of the new order being imposed on Ireland, especially in religious matters, but also in the holding of land. They were of both OLD ENGLISH and Irish backgrounds. Since many of them were from a noble position in Ireland, they gained positions in various continental armies, especially those of the great Catholic powers, originally Spain, but later Austria and France. A substantial number arrived after the defeat of the JACOBITE forces in 1691. The role of the Irish in several victories by continental armies against the English, especially during the mid-18th century wars, was a source of great satisfaction for the exiles. The Irish often brought their families with them and drew further relatives in subsequent years. They played important roles in continental European societies, military, political, and commercial, and actively supported the various Irish colleges on the Continent that educated clergy for Ireland, especially during the era of the PENAL LAWS. Some Irish sided with the monarchy during the French Revolution and others served in the Napoleonic armies.

William III (1650–1702)
king of England

William was the son of the Prince of Orange, ruler of the Netherlands, and of Mary, the sister of Charles II and James II of England. He married Mary, the daughter of James II and his first wife, in 1677. When James, who had converted to Catholicism, succeeded to the throne in 1685, anxieties mounted among Protestants. They intensified and spread to the ordinarily loyalist "Tories" who accepted a Catholic king as a temporary measure preferable to the election of a ruler who might usher in a return to the republicanism of the era of CROMWELL. However, when James became increasingly impolitic in his awarding of position and favors to co-religionists, especially in Ireland, a coalition of Whigs and Tories invited William and his wife Mary to assume the throne. James fled, but challenged the coup d'état from exile. The Irish parliament, summoned by his LORD LIEUTENANT, and predominantly Catholic in membership, the PATRIOT PARLIAMENT, continued to regard James as King of Ireland. Ireland became the focal point of what was becoming a grand alliance against Louis XIV of France, who was a patron of James. Both William and James confronted each other at the Battle of the BOYNE, with William's forces triumphing. James fled Ireland and several years the Williamite forces prevailed. William's success guaranteed the position of the PROTESTANT ASCENDANCY in Ireland, as the Irish parliament undertook the passage of what would be called the PENAL LAWS for the purpose of permanently inhibiting any prospects of a Catholic revival and challenge to the political domination and control over most of the land by Protestants, who were usually settlers or descendants of settlers who had come to Ireland no earlier than the middle of the 16th century. William, himself, although temperamentally a Calvinist and scarcely sympathetic to Catholicism, was also a political pragmatist. That pragmatism made him unsympathetic toward a punitive peace with the Irish Catholics, but it also inhibited him from interfering with the policies of his Irish Protestant allies. Accordingly, he acquiesced in the passage by the Irish parliament in 1697 of a mutilated confirmation of the Treaty of Limerick that had ended the war in Ireland in 1691. Ignored were guarantees that Catholics who accepted William were to be entitled to the same liberties as they had under Charles II. Accordingly, a significant number of Catholics had their lands confiscated, reducing Catholic ownership from 22 to 14 percent of the land in Ireland. The triumph at the Battle of the Boyne and the guaranteeing of the Protestant Ascendancy made William a natural figure of celebration in Protestant circles and an object of scorn among Catholics, a position that he would not necessarily have sought. Developments in Ireland were a tragic contradiction of the liberal and constitutional rational for the "Glorious Revolution" that brought William to power. He outlived his wife, died childless, and was succeeded by his sister-in-law, Mary, the other Protestant daughter of James II.

Williams, Betty (1943–)
peace activist

Betty Williams was one of the founders of the Peace People in 1976, a popular movement that conducted marches protesting the violence in Northern Ireland. The movement was formed in response to the death of three children in the same family. They were killed by a joy-riding car driver, who had ignored an order to stop and had been shot by the army. She shared in the Nobel Prize in 1976 with Mairead CORRIGAN. Several years later she divorced her husband and left Northern Ireland for the United States where she married James T. Perkins. She has lectured extensively in the United States. She was Visiting Professor in Political Science and

History at Sam Houston State University in Huntsville, Texas, where she worked to unite ethnic and cultural groups on campus and in the local community and heads the Global Children's Foundation. The awards she has received include the Eleanor Roosevelt Award of the International Platform Association, the Carl Von Ossietsky Medal for courage from the Berlin section of the International League of Human Rights, and an honorary doctorate in law from Yale University.

Wilson, Henry (1864–1922)
soldier, politician

Born in Currygrane, County Longford, Wilson was commissioned in the Longford militia. He served in the Royal Irish Brigade in Burma and in South Africa during the Boer War. Attached to the headquarters staff, he became a brigadier general in 1907 and was attached to the war office. He became the assistant chief of the General Staff of the British forces in France at the beginning of the First World War. Wilson was sympathetic to UNIONIST resistance to HOME RULE and was supportive of those involved in the mutiny at the CURRAGH. Lloyd George looked favorably on him and he was made chief of the Imperial General Staff in February 1918. In 1919 he was knighted and made field marshall. He was supportive of strong measures against the insurgents in the WAR OF INDEPENDENCE, although he was also critical of the criminality of the BLACK AND TANS, whose employment he had advised against. He retired in 1922 and was elected in a February by-election as a Unionist member of parliament for North County Down. On June 22, 1922, he was shot dead by two Irish gunmen. Speculation continues as to who ordered his assassination, whether it was an order given much earlier by Michael COLLINS that he had failed to rescind, it was an independent action, or, as the British assumed at the time, it was done at the orders of the anti-treaty IRISH REPUBLICAN ARMY (IRA). At any rate, it served to increase pressure on the PROVISIONAL GOVERNMENT to take firm action against the IRREGULARS who were occupying the FOUR COURTS, which started the CIVIL WAR.

Workers' Party See OFFICIAL IRA.

Wyndham, George (1863–1913)
politician

Born in London, and the great grandson of Lord Edward Fitzgerald, Wyndham served as private secretary to Arthur Balfour. He was elected to parliament for Dover as a Conservative in 1889 and was chief secretary for Ireland from 1900 to 1905. Supportive of what was called constructive UNIONISM, he supported a continuation and expansion of the reform programs commenced by Balfour when he was chief secretary. His most celebrated accomplishment was the 1903 Land Purchase Act that was based on recommendations of the Land Conference of 1902 chaired by his cousin, Lord DUNRAVEN. The act went very far in almost completing the process of tenant land purchase. He incurred the suspicions of many UNIONISTS for his generous response to Irish concerns, including political devolution and university reform, and resigned his position 1905. See also Land Purchase acts.

Wyse, Thomas (1791–1862)
politician

Born in County Waterford into the Catholic gentry, Wyse was educated at Stonyhurst and TRINITY COLLEGE DUBLIN. He was a major activist supporting the CATHOLIC ASSOCIATION and the successful campaign to overturn the Beresford interest in County Waterford and elect Villiers Stuart, a supporter of Catholic emancipation, in an 1826 by-election. He sat in parliament himself for Tipperary from 1830 to 1832 and for Waterford from 1835 to 1847. He disliked Daniel O'CONNELL and did not support REPEAL of the ACT OF UNION. Wyse chaired a commission on education, which recommended developing intermediate education and local third-level colleges, or what would become the QUEEN'S COLLEGES. He held ministerial office in the Whig governments from 1839 to 1841 and from 1846 to 1847 and in 1849 became British ambassador to Greece.

Y

Yeats, Jack Butler (1871–1957)
painter

Born in London, the youngest son of the artist John Butler Yeats and the brother of the writer William Butler YEATS, Jack Yeats was born in London, but he spent much of his youth with his mother's relatives in Sligo. He returned to London and studied at the Westminster School of Art and began working as an illustrator for various papers. He married, and he and his artist wife settled in Devon where he completed landscapes in watercolors. He traveled as well to Paris, to the west of Ireland, and to New York, where the collector John Quinn arranged an exhibition of his watercolors. In 1905 John Millington SYNGE commissioned him to do illustrations for some articles and for his *Aran Islands*. From then on he settled in Ireland, first at Greystones, County Wicklow, and then in Dublin, and he began doing landscapes in oil that reflected the influence of impressionism. Yeats became a member of the Royal Irish Academy in 1915. Much of his work was based on memory and it increasingly reflected the events and life of the times in which he lived in Ireland. Later his work turned toward expressionism, often of a romantic character and leaning toward fantasy, as colors tended to disregard form. He also wrote plays and novels, such as *The Amaranthers* (1936) and *The Careless Flower* (1947), as well *Life in the West of Ireland* (1912), a collection of his sketches and paintings.

William Butler Yeats *(Library of Congress)*

Yeats, William Butler (1856–1939)
poet, playwright

Possibly the greatest English-language poet of the 20th century, Yeats was born in Dublin, the son of the artist John Butler Yeats. His mother, Susan Pollexfen, came from a Sligo merchant family. He spent his childhood summers in rural western Ireland. He failed to gain admittance to TRINITY COLLEGE DUBLIN, but studied at the Metropolitan School of Art. Although from a Protestant background, he became drawn to Irish nationalist circles, being especially influenced by the Fenian John O'LEARY, acquiring an infatuation for Maud GONNE, and becoming acquainted with George RUSSELL and Douglas

HYDE. His early work drew from Irish mytholog-ical and nationalist themes, as in *The Wanderings of Oisin* (1889) and *The Wind among the Reeds* (1899). He moved to London in 1887 and was drawn to the mysticism of Madame Blavatsky's Theosophical Society, attending its séances. His play *The Countess Cathleen* appeared in Dublin in 1899 and soon after he became a central fixture in the theatrical world of the city as a founder of the Irish Literary Theatre, which later became the ABBEY THEATRE. His incendiary play *Cathleen ni Houlihan* appeared in 1902, and he gave much of his energies for the next decade to the theater, although summering at the Galway home of Lady GREGORY, Coole Park. Other plays of his during the period include *On Baile's Strand* (1904), the opening play of the Abbey, and *The Death of Cuchulainn*. In addition he wrote several volumes of poems, including *In the Seven Woods* (1903), *The Green Helmet* (1908), and *Responsibilities* (1914). He spent the years of the First World War in London, but continued to write of Irish things, including particularly his "Easter 1916." He married Georgie Hyde-Lees in 1917. His later poetry became increasing more personal and of a spiritualist and psychological character. His book *A Vision* (1925) mixes stories, poems, and prose to comment on history and on personal-ity. Other poems, which some regard as his greatest, include *The Tower* (1928) and *The Wind-ing Stair* (1933), which deal with the interrela-tionship of the feminine and the masculine and with war and peace. Yeats was a member of the SEANAD of the IRISH FREE STATE from 1922 to 1928 where he was best remembered for his criticism of the prohibition on divorce, which he saw as a Catholic assault on the ANGLO-IRISH. His views became increasingly aristocratic and skep-tical of the excesses of democracy and he was drawn to authoritarian political figures such as Eoin O'DUFFY. He received the Nobel Prize in lit-erature in 1923. Ill health necessitated his spending much time in the warmer climate of southern France during the later 1930s, and he died and was buried there, although later rein-terned in Drumcliff Churchyard in Sligo, "under Ben Bulben."

Yellow Ford

Yellow Ford was a battle in north County Armagh in 1598 where the Irish under Hugh O'NEILL inflicted the greatest defeat of the 16th century on the English forces under Henry Bagenal. The victory gave O'Neill access to the midlands and to his ultimate quest to undo the Munster plantation. Bagenal and many of his officers were killed and only about 1,500 of his force of 4,000 survived the attack by the Irish from the cover of the natural terrain on the advancing English column, which was marching northward to strengthen other positions.

Yelverton's Act

This 1782 act of the Irish parliament asserted Irish parliamentary independence by removing the POYNINGS' LAW requirement that the agenda of the parliament be set by the Privy Council. Legislation passed by both houses of parliament would proceed directly to the monarch for royal assent.

Yeomanry

The Yeomanry was an auxiliary military force of civilians formed in 1796 primarily to counter the UNITED IRISHMEN and the DEFENDERS. Recruits soon numbered 30,000. They were officered by landlords in rural areas and were organized by professions and trades in cities. Most members were Protestants and they played an important, and brutal, role in suppressing the uprising of 1798. The force remained in existence during the Napoleonic Wars, when they were regarded as a useful deterrent to invasion. Highly sectar-ian and linked to the ORANGE ORDER, it was dis-banded in 1834.

Young, Arthur (1741–1820)
agriculturalist

Born in London, Young took up farming and then began writing about agricultural subjects and his travels to various areas in England. He visited Ire-land in 1776 and returned the next year to

Mitchelstown, County Cork, as the agent for Lord Kingborough, and stayed for two years, traveling extensively about the country. He published a report on his visit in 1780. Titled *A Tour in Ireland,* it was regarded as one of the most informed studies of the country at the time as it gave thorough information on agricultural practices and statistical information. He later wrote a study, *Travels in France* (1792), which dealt with his visit there at the time of the French Revolution.

Young Ireland

Young Ireland constituted a group of young intellectuals, primarily middle class and including Protestants, who espoused a romantic vision of Irish NATIONALISM comparable to the nationalist movements in existence at the time in various parts of the Continent. Leading figures included Thomas DAVIS, John Blake DILLON, and Charles Gavan DUFFY, and they published a paper, the *NATION,* which espoused their ideals. They were associated with Daniel O'CONNELL in the REPEAL movement of the early 1840s and concurred with his decision to call off the monster meeting scheduled for Clontarf after the government had prohibited it. Differences with O'Connell later developed, partly on the basis of personality as the older leader had a natural suspicion of younger possible rivals, but also over issues such as the Colleges Bill. They supported the measure introduced by Robert PEEL to establishing non-

sectarian colleges as a means to enhance a non-sectarian Irish identity, while O'Connell sided with the Catholic hierarchy in seeking Catholic institutions as an alternative to Protestant TRINITY COLLEGE DUBLIN. Davis died in 1845, but O'Connell then forced an antiviolence resolution through the repeal organization. While not advocating violence, the Young Irelanders did not want to foreclose on its possible use if necessary. O'Connell wanted to make clear his absolute disapproval of such as a prerequisite to an alliance he was formulating with the Whigs, who had returned to power. The next year the Young Irelanders formed a rival organization, the Irish Confederation. However, even within their ranks there was division between the more moderate Gavan Duffy and William Smith O'BRIEN and John MITCHEL, who advocated radical land reform. By the next year even Smith O'Brien turned radical, inspired by the revolution in France. Soon Mitchel was convicted and sent to transportation in Australia. Smith O'Brien joined with a small number in a futile rising in County Tipperary. Many of the leaders were subjected to transportation. Others escaped and achieved prominence in the United States. Some from the rank and file would start the FENIAN movement a decade later. While they proved politically ineffective, their writings provided a rhetoric of nationalism and their actions served as a source of emulation for later generations of nationalists, both constitutional and revolutionary.

CHRONOLOGY

8000 B.C.
First people in Ireland.

3000 B.C.
New stone age in Ireland, construction of New Grange.

300 B.C.
Celts arrive in Ireland.

432
Patrick begins his mission to Ireland.

548
Monastery at Clonmacnoise is founded.

558
Brendan founds monastery at Clonfert and later undertakes voyages possibly as far as North America.

563
Columba founds monastery at Iona.

590
Columbanus undertakes mission to Gaul.

598
Kevin founds monastery at Glendalough.

664
Synod of Whitby accepts Roman rather than Irish ecclesiastical style.

795
The beginning of Viking raids on Ireland.

850–77
John Scotus Eriugena teaches at the court of Charles the Bald, the Frankish king.

852
The Norse settle at Dublin.

914
Second wave of Viking raids begin.

1005
Brian Boru visits Armagh and is recognized as High King of Ireland.

1014
Battle of Clontarf in which Brian Boru defeats Vikings and their Irish allies, but is killed himself.

1132–48
Malachy exerts reforming influence on church in Ireland.

1142
First Cistercian house established in Ireland at Mellifont.

1154
Synod of Kells approves church reform.

1169
Strongbow and Normans come to Ireland at request of Dermot MacMurrough, king of Leinster, who wanted assistance in dispute with the king of Breifne and with Rory O'Connor, overlord of Ireland.

1171
Henry II comes to Ireland.

1172
Pope awards Ireland to Henry II.

1175
Treaty of Windsor whereby the Irish High King, Rory O'Connor, acknowledges Henry II as his overlord.

1177
Henry II's son, Prince John, is made lord of Ireland.

1185
Prince John visits Ireland.

1210
King John visits Ireland.

1224
Dominicans (Order of Preachers) come to Ireland.

1230
Franciscans (Order of Friars Minor) come to Ireland.

1282
Augustinian Friars come to Ireland.

1299

Beginning of Irish parliament.

1315–18

Edward Bruce unsuccessfully wages war trying to be king of Ireland.

1348

Black death arrives in Ireland.

1366

Statutes of Kilkenny are passed.

1394–95

King Richard II visits Ireland.

1399

King Richard II again visits Ireland.

1478

Garret Mor, the eighth earl of Kildare, begins the period of Kildare ascendancy.

1485

Richard III is killed at the Battle of Bosworth and is succeeded as king of England by Henry (Tudor) VII.

1487

A pretender, Lambert Simnel, is crowned as king of England in Dublin (May), but is defeated and captured by Henry VII the next month.

First recorded use of firearms in Ireland.

1488

Earl of Kildare (Garret Mor) acquires six handguns for his personal guard.

General pardon is granted to Irish supporters of Simnel, as Irish lords and English lords in Ireland (including Kildare, who remains chief governor) submit to Henry.

1491

Another pretender to the English throne, Perkin Warbeck, arrives in Ireland and originally receives some support from Kildare and Desmond. However, Kildare clears himself by 1493 when he sends his son as hostage to the king.

1494

Edward Poynings is appointed as lord deputy in Ireland. Pardon is granted to Irish supporters of Warbeck. The Irish parliament approves "Poynings' Law," which severely limits its autonomy.

1496

Earl of Kildare replaces Poynings as deputy and marries Elizabeth St. John, a cousin of the king.

1497

Control of Irish finances is given to nominees of the Earl of Kildare.

Warbeck comes to Ireland in July, raises supporters who follow him to Cornwall in September, but is defeated and captured in October. He is executed two years later.

1503

The son of the earl of Kildare (Garret Og) marries a royal ward, Elizabeth Zouche.

1506

Henry VII considers invading Ireland with 6,000 men, but does not do so.

1508

Garret Og is appointed treasurer.

1509

Henry VIII succeeds his father on the English throne.

1510

Earl of Kildare again is confirmed as deputy.

1513

Earl of Kildare (Garret Mor) dies from gunshot wounds (September) and is succeeded by his son (Garret Og), who is also appointed deputy (November).

1516

Kildare is reconfirmed as deputy with power to appoint all officials.

1517

Martin Luther presents his 95 theses at Wittenburg: origins of Protestant Reformation.

1520

Thomas Howard, earl of Surrey, as lord lieutenant, arrives in Ireland with 500 men (March), campaigns in Leinster, Ulster, and Munster, inducing the submission of O'Cearbhaill, O'Neill (July), and O'Donnell (August), and McCarthy Mor and McCarthy Reagh (October), while Kildare is forced to remain in London until November.

1521

Surrey proposes plan of thorough conquest of Ireland to Henry VIII (June), even though the king had advised to subdue the Irish lords by "amiable persuasions" rather than by "strength or violence." When his proposals are not accepted, he requests and receives his recall (December).

1522

Piers Ruadh Butler, the earl of Ormond, becomes deputy (March).

The earl of Desmond communicates with the king of France, Francis I.

1524

Earl of Kildare is reappointed deputy, and the earl of Ormond is appointed treasurer.

1528

Piers Ruadh Butler, the eighth earl of Ormond, is created earl of Ossory, and Thomas Boleyn, son-in-law of the seventh earl of Ormond, becomes earl of Ormond (February) and is made deputy (August).

An envoy of the earl of Desmond negotiates with the Holy Roman Emperor.

1529

Reformation parliament meets at Westminster (November).

1530

William Skeffington is appointed deputy (June).

1531

Henry VIII is recognized as "supreme head of the Church in England" by convocation at Canterbury (February) and later York (May).

Skeffington invades Ulster and achieves submission of O'Neill (February) and O'Donnell (May).

Earl of Desmond accepts the government (September).

1532

Earl of Kildare (Garret Og) appointed deputy and James Butler, the son of the earl of Ossory, is appointed treasurer (July).

1533

Henry VIII marries Anne, the daughter of Sir Thomas Boleyn, the earl of Ormond and Wiltshire (January).

Parliament at Westminster approves restraining appeals to Rome (February).

Henry VIII excommunicated by Pope Clement VII (July).

1534

Earl of Kildare, summoned to the court in England, appoints his son Thomas as his deputy (February).

Thomas ("Silken Thomas") repudiates allegiance to Henry VIII, and the earl of Kildare is imprisoned in the Tower of London (June).

Kildare dies in the Tower and Silken Thomas besieges Dublin (September).

Skeffington is appointed deputy (July) and arrives in Dublin with troops (October).

1535

Skeffington secures support of O'Neill and Ossory and prevents support for Silken Thomas by Desmond and the O'Briens.

Skeffington takes Maynooth castle from Silken Thomas (March).

Silken Thomas surrenders to Skeffington and is taken prisoner to London by Lord Leonard Grey, the marshall of the army (August).

1536

Five uncles of Silken Thomas are sent to England (February).

Grey is appointed deputy, as Skeffington had died the previous December (February).

"Reformation" session of Irish parliament approves attainder of Silken Thomas and his uncles and recognizes Henry VIII as "supreme head in earth of the whole church in Ireland" and forbids appeals to Rome (May).

1537

Silken Thomas and uncles are executed at Tyburn (February).

Irish parliament approves the suppression of monasteries, and acts against the authority of the bishop of Rome and for the promotion of the English language (October–December).

1538

Piers Butler, the earl of Ossory, is restored as earl of Ormond.

Grey wages a military campaign against the Irish in Offaly, Munster, Connacht, and Ulster that will last for two years.

1540

Grey leaves for England (May).

Sir Anthony St. Leger becomes deputy as part of a new policy of conciliation.

1541

Irish parliament declares the king of England to be the king of Ireland (June).

Grey is executed in the Tower of London (June).

1542

First mission of Jesuits arrives in Ireland (February–March).

Conn O'Neill becomes earl of Tyrone.

1545

Council of Trent opens (December).

1547

Henry VIII dies and is succeeded by his minor son, Edward VI (January). Earl of Hertford becomes protector and is created duke of Somerset (February).

Sir Edward Bellingham is sent with military reinforcements to restore order in Ireland (May).

1548

Bellingham replaces St. Leger as deputy (May).

1549

First Book of Common Prayers ordered to be used in Ireland (June).

Somerset deposed as protector (October).

1550

St. Leger reappointed as deputy (September).

1553

Edward VI dies and is succeeded by his half-sister Mary (July).

1554

Earldom of Kildare is restored to Gerald Fitzgerald, the nephew of Garret Og (May).

Mary I marries Philip (July), the son of the Holy Roman emperor Charles V, who becomes King Philip II of Spain (January 1556).

1556

Thomas Radcliffe (becomes earl of Sussex in February 1557) replaces St. Leger as deputy (May).

1557

Irish parliament approves plantation of Leix and Offaly as Queen's and King's Counties, repeals statutes against the papacy, and declares royal power in Ireland be vested in the queen (June–July).

Sussex campaigns against the O'Connors of Offaly (July) and Shane O'Neill (October).

1558

O'More and O'Connor attacks on Maryborough are blocked (May).

Mary I dies and is succeeded by half sister Elizabeth I (November).

Shane O'Neill, son of the earl of Tyrone, has his illegitimate half-brother Matthew, baron of Dungannon, who was designated successor to the earl of Tyrone, killed (December).

1559

Shane O'Neill succeeds his father Conn, the first earl of Tyrone, in O'Neill lordship (July).

1560

Irish parliament restores royal supremacy in matters ecclesiastical, authorizes the use of the second prayer book of Edward VI, and requires attendance at parish churches under pain of fine (January–February).

Sussex elevated to lord lieutenant (May).

1561

Shane O'Neill proclaimed a traitor and Sussex campaigns against him (June–July).

1562

Shane O'Neill acquiesces to Elizabeth (January).

Brian O'Neill, the second baron of Dungannon, is killed by Turlough O'Neill, the tanist to Shane O'Neill. Brian's brother Hugh is taken to England by Sir Henry Sidney, the vice treasurer (April).

1563

Sussex campaigns against Shane O'Neill, who finally submits (September).

Council of Trent concludes (December).

1564

O'Connors and O'Mores rise in Offaly and Leix (February).

1565

Shane O'Neill defeats the MacDonnells, capturing Sorley Boy McDonnell (May).

Sir Henry Sidney replaces Sussex as lord lieutenant (October).

1566

Shane O'Neill again proclaimed traitor (August).

Sidney campaigns in Ulster (September–November).

1567

Shane O'Neill defeated by Hugh O'Donnell near Letterkenny (May) and is killed by the McDonnells in Antrim (June).

Turlough O'Neill becomes the lord of the O'Neills (June).

Earl of Desmond becomes a prisoner in London (December).

1568

Hugh O'Neill recognized as baron of Dungannon (March).

James Fitzmaurice, as "captain" of the Desmond Fitzgeralds, attacks Thomas Fitzmaurice, baron of Kerry and Lixnaw (July).

1569

James Fitzmaurice and MacCarthy Mor, the earl of Clancare, and others rebel in Munster, sending envoys to the king of Spain, ravaging leased lands in Cork, and Edmund Butler, brother of the earl of Ormond, rebels in Carlow. Sidney campaigns in Leinster and Munster against both, with Humphrey Gilbert placed in command of Munster operations.

1570

Elizabeth I is excommunicated by Pope Pius V in the bull *Regnans in excelsis* (February).

Edmund Butler submits (February).

John Perrot appointed president of Munster (December).

1571

Spanish fleet commanded by Don John of Austria defeats Turks at Lepanto (October).

William Fitzwilliam replaces Sidney as deputy (December).

1572

Philip II of Spain rejects proposed invasion of Ireland (January).

Huguenots massacred in Paris (August).

1573

James Fitzmaurice submits to Perrot (February).

Earl of Desmond imprisoned in Dublin (March).

Elizabeth gives the earl of Essex rights to colonize Antrim, and then he is given the "general captaincy" in all Ulster. He is opposed by Brian O'Neill and Turlough O'Neill, but assisted by Hugh O'Neill, earl of Dungannon (July–October).

1574

Although he escaped from imprisonment, Desmond submits to Fitzwilliam (September).

Essex imprisons Brian O'Neill, and he is executed (November).

1575

Although Elizabeth withdraws support for his colonization of Ulster, Essex gains Turlough O'Neill's submission (June) and massacres the inhabitants of Rathlin Island (July).

Sidney returns again and replaces Fitzwilliam as deputy (August).

1576

Sidney establishes four counties in Connacht: Galway, Mayo, Roscommon, and Sligo (April).

1577

Pope Gregory XIII approves an expedition to Ireland by James Fitzmaurice (February).

Massacre of the O'Connors and O'Mores by English soldiers in Mullaghmast, County Kildare (November–December).

1578

Sidney leaves Ireland (September).

1579

James Fitzmaurice arrives in Dingle with papal legate and builds fort, Dun an Oir, at Smerwick (July).

Humphrey Gilbert is commissioned to attack Fitzmaurice, who is killed in a skirmish in Limerick (July–August).

Desmond is proclaimed a traitor (November).

1580

Lord Grey is appointed deputy (July).

Sir James of Desmond captured (August) and executed (October).

Spaniards and Italians land at Smerwick (September), but are successfully attacked by Grey and are massacred (November).

1581

Grey wages a campaign against the Kavanaghs in Leinster (June).

1582

Sir John of Desmond killed (January).

Pardon offered to Munster rebels who submit (August).

1583

Earl of Desmond killed (November).

1584

John Perrot replaces Grey as deputy (January).

Hugh O'Neill, the baron of Dungannon, made tanist of Turlough O'Neill (March).

Survey is made of lands forfeited by Munster rebels (September–November).

1585

Composition of Connacht takes places confirming existing Irish landowners, but subject to the queen.

Plantation of Munster planned (December).

1587

Walter Raleigh is given grant of territory in Cork and Waterford (February).

Hugh O'Neill formally given title of earl of Tyrone (May).

Hugh Roe O'Donnell kidnapped and imprisoned in Dublin Castle (September).

1588

William Fitzwilliam replaces Perot as deputy (February).

More than a score of ships from the defeated Spanish Armada wrecked off the Irish coasts (September).

1590

Earl of Tyrone is at the English court (March–July).

Hugh Roe O'Donnell escapes from Dublin Castle, but is recaptured (December).

1591

The earl of Tyrone marries Mabel Bagenal, the sister of Henry Bagenal, the marshal of the army (August).

Hugh Roe O'Donnell successfully escapes from Dublin Castle (December).

1592

Hugh Roe O'Donnell succeeds his father Hugh, who retires, as Lord of Tyrconnell (May).

Philip II of Spain supports Irish College at Salamanca (July).

Catholic bishops assemble at Tyrconnell (December).

1593

Catholic archbishop of Tuam, James O'Hely, represents O'Donnell before Philip II of Spain (April).

1594

William Russell replaces Fitzwilliam as deputy (May).

O'Donnell and Hugh Maguire, lord of Fermanagh, besiege Enniskillen that had been captured by an English force. Maguire defeats an English force coming to relief of Enniskillen, but Russell ultimately succeeds in gaining town (June–August).

1595

O'Donnell and Maguire retake Enniskillen (May).

Tyrone defeats the forces of Bagenal at Clontibret, County Monaghan (June).

Tyrone and O'Donnell offer kingship of Ireland to Archduke Albert, the governor of the Spanish Netherlands (August), and the next month ask Philip II for help.

Tyrone and O'Donnell submit to a truce with the government (October).

1596

Tyrone calls on Lords of Munster to join against the English (July).

Spanish arms arrive at Killybegs, County Donegal (September).

Spanish ships aiming for Ireland are dispersed by storm off Finisterre (October).

1597

Lord Burgh replaces Russell as deputy (March) and begins campaign against Tyrone.

Burgh dies of typhus and Ormond becomes military commander (October) and Tyrone submits to a truce with Ormond (December).

1598

Bagenal is killed when his forces are defeated by Tyrone, O'Donnell, and Maguire at the Yellow Ford (August).

James Fitzthomas Fitzmaurice becomes earl of Desmond and attacks the Munster plantation (October).

1599

Robert Devereux, second earl of Essex, becomes lord lieutenant (March) and campaigns in Leinster and Munster (May–July).

Spanish ships bring arms to Lough Foyle (May).

Essex and Tyrone reach a truce, and Essex leaves Ireland (September).

1600

Charles Blount, Lord Mountjoy, becomes deputy (January) and campaigns against Tyrone in Connacht, Leinster, and Ulster (May–October).

George Carew becomes president of Munster (March) and campaigns in Limerick (May–June).

1601

Essex is executed in Tower of London (February).

Earl of Desmond is captured and sent to the Tower of London (May), where he dies six years later.

Spanish fleet arrives at Kinsale, County Cork, and Mountjoy comes to take charge of moves against them (September).

O'Donnell and Tyrone begin separate marches south to Munster (October).

More Spanish ships arrive at Kinsale and O'Donnell and Tyrone meet at Bandon, County Cork, but in the Battle at Kinsale both are defeated as O'Donnell leaves for Spain and Tyrone retreats to Ulster (December).

1602

The Spanish commander at Kinsale surrenders to Mountjoy (January) and leaves for Spain (March).

Mountjoy moves to Ulster and destroys the O'Neill inaugural chair at Tullaghoge, County Tyrone (June–September).

Hugh O'Donnell dies in Spain and his brother, Rory O'Donnell, submits to Mountjoy (December).

1603

Elizabeth directs Mountjoy to offer pardon to Tyrone if he were to submit. Tyrone submits unaware Elizabeth had died in the meantime (March).

James I succeeds Elizabeth I.

Tyrone accompanies Mountjoy to England, as George Carey is appointed deputy (May).

John Davies becomes solicitor general (November) and later attorney general and sheriffs are appointed for Counties Donegal and Tyrone.

1605

Arthur Chichester becomes deputy (February).

All persons are declared free subjects of the king and not of any lords or chieftains (March).

Jesuits are ordered to leave Ireland (July).

Gunpowder plot in Westminster by Catholics fails (November).

Deputy mandates certain citizens to attend established church and fines and imprisons noncompliers, as well as those petitioning for freedom of religion (November–December).

1606

The Irish custom of *gavelkind,* namely, equal distribution of inheritance, is declared illegal and a commission examines defective land titles (January–July).

1607

Rather than comply with a summons to London, Tyrone, joined by Tyrconnell and others, sails from Lough Swilly (September). The earls and their associates are indicted on grounds of high treason and their lands declared forfeited (December).

1608

The Irish system of designating successors, tanistry, is declared illegal.

Tyrone and Tyrconnell arrive in Rome (April), but Tyrconnell dies in July.

A commission surveying six Ulster counties—Donegal, Coleraine, Tyrone, Armagh, Fermanagh, and Cavan—determines they are almost entirely escheated to the king (July–September).

1609

Plantation plans are drawn up for the escheated lands in the six counties (January–September).

1610

The Privy Council and the city of London agree on the plantation of the city of Derry and the county of Coleraine (January) and three years later Derry will be chartered as the city of Londonderry and Coleraine will become the county of Londonderry, most of which will be controlled by the Irish Society of London, that is, the London planters (March 1613).

1613

First Irish parliament of James I is elected, but when Catholic members withdraw in dispute over election of Speaker, it is prorogued and a commission appointed to inquire into allegations of illegality in its election (April–August).

1614

James makes some concessions to Catholics on make up of parliament (August), which then meets (October–November).

1616

Earl of Tyrone dies in Rome (July).

1622

Viscount Falkland becomes deputy (September).

Court of wards and liveries established which would enable king to assume wardship over minor children of deceased nobility, aimed especially at Old English Catholics (December).

1623

Oath of Supremacy required of all city and town officials (June).

1625

James Ussher, who demanded severe measures against Catholics, becomes archbishop of Armagh (March).

James I dies and is succeeded by his son, Charles I (March).

1626

Charles I offers concessions or "Graces" to the Irish in return for subsidies for his army (September).

1627

George Downham, bishop of Derry, opposes suggested toleration for Catholics (April).

Irish College in Rome opens (December).

1628

Charles I meets with an Irish delegation of eight Old English and three New English and issues "Graces" in return for a subsidy (January–May).

1632

Viscount Wentworth becomes deputy (July).

1634

Charles I's first Irish parliament is elected and holds four sessions between July of 1634 and April 1635 in which very major concessions in the form of the Graces are passed, but in which other legislation enhances royal power and furthers Wentworth's policy of "thorough" whereby the king's government in Ireland and its military become self-financing. A statute of uses enforces fulfillment by landowners of feudal dues to the king and royal justices are empowered to impose charges on localities for repair of highways (December), imprisonment is mandated for beggars and vagabonds, and licenses are required for ale houses (April 1635).

1635

Under pressure from Wentworth, juries award title to the king of contested lands in Connacht (July).

1636

Galway jury yields to threat of fine and imprisonment and reverses decision not granting title to the king for certain lands (December).

1638

Scots take national covenant against high church policies Charles seeks to impose on them (March).

1639

War is fought by Charles I against the Scots for their opposition to his high church policy. It ends with treaty (May–June).

1640

Wentworth created earl of Strafford (January).

Charles I's second Irish parliament meets (February–March).

Wentworth leaves Ireland (April).

"Short parliament" meets in England (April 13–May 5).

Second war with Scots begins with Scottish victory near Newcastle-upon-Tyne (August).

Irish parliament meets again and sends petition of remonstrance to England (October–November).

Truce between English and Scots (October).

"Long Parliament" meets in England and calls for proceeding with impeachment of Wentworth (November).

1641

William Parsons and John Borlase become lords justices (February).

Impeachment trial of Wentworth begins at Westminster, but a bill of attainder is passed, and he is executed (March–May).

Irish parliament comments on Poynings' Law to king (May).

Rebellion takes place in Ulster with many Protestant deaths in the next few months (October).

Attempted seizure of Dublin Castle blocked (October).

Earl of Ormond made lieutenant general of royal army (November).

1642

English parliament passes Adventurers Act that offers Irish land as compensation to contributors of funds for the repression of the rebellion in Ireland (March).

A Scottish army led by Robert Munro lands in Carrickfergus (April).

Catholic clergy and laity meet in Kilkenny (March).

Catholics draw up an oath of association in Kilkenny (June).

Owen Roe O'Neill lands in Donegal (July).

Thomas Preston lands in Wexford (September).

Catholics hold first general assembly of Catholic Confederation in Kilkenny (October–November).

1643

Pier Francesco Scarampi arrives as papal envoy to Catholic Confederates (July).

On royal instructions Ormond negotiates with Catholic Confederation concluding in a one-year truce (September).

Marquis of Ormond becomes lord lieutenant (November).

1644

Charles gives plenary powers to English Catholic earl of Glamorgan to treat with Catholic Confederates (April).

Ormond is also instructed to negotiate with Confederates (June).

Royalist army defeated by parliamentary army and Scots at Marston Moor (July).

Lord Inchiquin joins the parliamentary side (July).

1645

Royalists defeated by New Model Army at Naseby (June).

Secret treaty made between Glamorgan and the Confederates (August).

Archbishop Giovanni Rinuccini, new papal envoy to Confederates, arrives in Ireland (October).

Glamorgan and Confederates arrive at second treaty directed by Rinuccini (December).

1646

Confederates and Ormond agree to peace (March).

Charles I surrenders to Scots (May).

Owen Roe O'Neill defeats Munro's army at Benburb, County Tyrone (June).

Confederates proclaim peace with Ormond, but it is condemned by Rinuccini (August).

Rinuccini presides over new council of Confederation (September).

1647

Charles I is seized by parliamentary army at Holmby (June).

Parliamentary army under Michael Jones lands near Dublin, and Ormond surrenders Dublin to parliamentary commissioners (June). He leaves for England (July).

Inchiquin sacks Cashel and defeats Confederate Army of Munster near Mallow (September–November).

Charles I and Scots sign an agreement to war against the parliamentary forces (December).

1648

Truce between Inchiquin and Confederates condemned by Rinuccini, but his condemnation is appealed by the Council of the Confederation to Rome (May).

Oliver Cromwell defeats the Scots at Preston (August).

Supreme Council of Confederation condemns Owen Roe O'Neill (September).

Ormond returns to Ireland (September).

1649

Ormond and Confederates again make a peace treaty (January).

Charles I is executed (January).

Rinuccini leaves Ireland (February).

Owen Roe O'Neill aids parliamentary army in Derry being besieged by Scots (April).

Jones's army defeats Ormond forces in Dublin (August).

Cromwell lands in Dublin with parliamentary commission to exercise civil and military power in Ireland (August).

Cromwell attacks Drogheda and massacres garrison (September).

Cromwell takes Wexford and also massacres the garrison (October).

Treaty agreed between Ormond and Owen Roe O'Neill (October).

Owen Roe O'Neill dies (November).

1650

Cromwell continues to take various Irish towns, including Fethard, Kilkenny, and Clonmel until he leaves Ireland with Henry Ireton becoming his deputy (May).

Carlow and Waterford surrender to Ireton (July–August).

Ormond, Inchiquin, and others leave Ireland.

1651

Navigation Act limits shipping of goods to England, Ireland, and colonies to English ships (October).

Ireton dies after Limerick surrenders and Edmund Ludlow is appointed commander (October–December).

1652

Charles Fleetwood becomes commander in chief in Ireland (July).

Act for settling of Ireland passed by parliament categorizing degrees of guilt of opponents of parliament in Ireland (August).

1653

Act of Settlement is passed by the Little or Barebones Parliament, which Cromwell called into being to replace the Rump of the Long Parliament that he had expelled. The act allots seized Irish land to adventurers and settlers and reserves most of Connacht and Clare for Irish landowners expelled from other areas (September).

Cromwell becomes Lord Protector under the Instrument of Government, the written constitution. Ireland is united with England in a single parliament and is allotted 30 members (December).

1654

Fleetwood is designated as deputy (August).

William Petty is directed to map forfeited Irish lands to be distributed to soldiers (December).

Henry Cromwell is appointed to the Irish Council (December).

1655

Catholic priests in the custody of the government are ordered to be shipped to Barbados (January).

The celebration of Easter is prohibited (April).

1657

Cromwell is given increased powers by a new constitution (May).

Legislation confirms the settling of land in Ireland and requires suspected Catholics to take an oath rejecting the papacy and denying the doctrine of transubstantiation or forfeit two-thirds of their property (June).

Henry Cromwell becomes deputy (November).

1658

Oliver Cromwell dies and is succeeded as Lord Protector by his son Richard (September).

1659

The Rump of the Long Parliament reassembles, forces Richard Cromwell to resign, recalls Henry Cromwell from Ireland, and nominates a commission to govern Ireland (May–July).

Edmund O'Reilly, consecrated as Catholic archbishop of Armagh in Brussels in May, returns to Ireland (October).

1660

Lord Broghill, Charles Coote, and William Bury become commissioners for Ireland (January).

General George Monck forces the Rump of the Long Parliament to admit excluded members, and the parliament then dissolves itself, while a convention meets in Dublin (February–March).

Charles II returns as king to London and is proclaimed king in Dublin (May).

Charles II confirms soldiers and adventurers in their ownership of land in Ireland but also promises return of land to "innocent papists" and supporters of the monarchy (November).

1661

Catholics draw up a remonstrance proclaiming allegiance to king and denying papal authority to disallow the same (December).

1662

Duke of Ormond becomes lord lieutenant of Ireland (February).

Act of Settlement confirms Charles II's declaration on Irish land and seeks to resolve conflicting claims (July).

Plot by Colonel Thomas Blood and other Cromwellians to seize power in Dublin fails (May).

English Navigation Act restricts Irish trade with colonies and the importation of Irish cattle into England (July).

Court of Claims issues 566 decrees of innocence to Catholics, but many other claims are not heard (August).

1665

Act of Explanation requires Cromwellians to give up one-third of their holdings so that Catholics may have lands available (December).

1666

Irish Catholic bishops and clergy accept remonstrance of 1661 pledging allegiance to king, but make no reference to papal authority to disallow such (June).

1667

English law prohibits importation of Irish cattle to England (January).

1669

Peter Talbot consecrated Catholic archbishop of Dublin (April).

George Fox organizes Quaker meetings in Ireland (May–August).

Lord Robartes replaces Ormond as lord lieutenant (September).

Oliver Plunkett consecrated Catholic archbishop of Armagh (November).

1670

Charles II agrees in secret Treaty of Dover to become a Catholic in return for French subsidy (May).

1671

English Navigation Act prohibits imports from colonies to Irish ports (April).

John Brenan consecrated Catholic bishop of Waterford (August).

1672

Charles II issues declaration of indulgence to suspend penal laws against nonconformist Protestants and recusant Catholics (March).

Earl of Essex becomes lord lieutenant (August).

Regium Donum granted to Presbyterian ministers (October).

1673

Charles forced to withdraw declaration of indulgence, which House of Commons declares to be illegal (February–March).

Test Act passed requiring officeholders to take communion in the Church of England (March).

James, duke of York, marries his second wife, Mary of Modena (September).

1676

Charles II enters secret treaty with Louis XIV to enter no alliance without French consent in return for French subsidy (February).

1677

Ormond returns as lord lieutenant (August).

1678

Titus Oates makes charges of popish plot before Privy Council (September).

Archbishop of Dublin Peter Talbot arrested (October).

1679

House of Commons considers Exclusion Bill to bar James, duke of York, from succession to throne (May).

Archbishop of Armagh, Oliver Plunkett, arrested (December).

1680

Plunkett's trial ends without indictment (July).

Talbot dies imprisoned in Dublin Castle (November).

1681

Plunkett tried and convicted of high treason in London and executed (May–July).

1684

Dublin Philosophical Society established by William Molyneux (January).

1685

Charles II dies and is succeeded by his brother James II (February).

Catholics, Justin MacCarthy and Richard Talbot, are exempted from Oath of Supremacy and given command of regiments (March).

Talbot is created earl of Tyrconnell (June).

Louis XIV revokes Edict of Nantes of 1598, which had granted religious liberties to Protestants in France (October).

1686

Earl of Clarendon replaces Ormond as lord lieutenant (January).

Tyrconnell is made commander of army in Ireland (June).

Tyrconnell and Richard Nagle campaign in England for redress of Catholic grievances (August–October).

1687

Tyrconnell becomes lord deputy (February).

Tyrconnell is empowered to issue new city and corporate town charters (June).

Tyrconnell's governance is satirized by Protestant song "Lillibullero."

1688

James II's wife gives birth to a son (June).

Episcopal bishops acquitted of charges for not publishing James's declaration of indulgences for Catholics and nonconformists (June).

Coalition of Tories and Whigs invites William of Orange to come to England (June).

Irish regiments sent to England (October).

William arrives in England (November).

James leaves England (December).

1689

William of Orange and wife, Mary, accept Bill of Rights and become king and queen of England and Ireland (February).

James II arrives in Ireland with French and Jacobite officers (March).

Siege of Derry by Jacobite forces begins (April).

James II's Irish parliament (the Patriot Parliament) meets and passes act repealing the land settlement but drops act to repeal Poynings' Law (May–July).

Williamite ships break boom on river Foyle and relieve besieged Derry (July).

Marshall Schomberg and force lands in Bangor, County Down, in support of William and take Carrickfergus (August).

James II's army advances toward Schomberg near Dundalk, but does not engage him, although

Schomberg's forces suffer heavy loses from sickness (September–October).

1690

Irish regiments go to France (April).

William III arrives near Carrickfergus (June).

William increases *Regium Donum* for Presbyterian clergy (June).

William's army defeats James's forces at the Battle of the Boyne. James leaves for France and William enters Dublin (July).

William returns to England, and Tyrconnell and French army leave for France (September).

Earl of Marlborough takes Cork and Kinsale (September–October).

1691

Tyrconnell returns to Ireland (January).

French general, Marquis de Saint-Ruth, lands at Limerick (May).

Williamite general, Baron von Ginkel, takes Athlone (June).

Jacobite army is defeated by von Ginkel at Aughrim, County Galway, with thousands of losses, including Saint-Ruth (July).

Ginkel takes Galway (July).

Tyrconnell dies in Limerick, which Ginkel begins to besiege (August).

After a truce in siege of Limerick, a treaty is signed allowing Irish army to go to France to continue to serve James II and promising the Catholics remaining in Ireland the religious rights they had under Charles II (October).

1692

Viscount Sidney becomes lord lieutenant (September).

First Irish parliament under William III claims exclusive right to prepare money bills (October).

1694

Mary II dies (December).

1695

Lord Capel becomes lord lieutenant (May).

Second Irish parliament of William III meets and passes penal legislation against Catholics, including prohibition against sending their children abroad for education, teaching school in

Ireland, keeping arms, or owning horses valued at £5 or more (August–December).

1696

English legislation permits duty free import of Irish linen (April).

1697

English legislation bans export of Irish woolen goods (April).

Reassembled second Irish parliament requires Catholic bishops and regular clergy (members of religious orders) to leave Ireland and confirms the Treaty of Limerick without clauses guaranteeing Catholic rights (September).

1698

William Molyneux publishes a tract challenging the English parliament's right to legislate for Ireland (January).

1699

The second Irish parliament of William III imposes duties on export of wool from Ireland and prohibits Catholics from becoming solicitors (January).

English legislation prohibits export of wool from Ireland to anywhere other than England (May).

1701

James II dies, and his son James III is recognized by Louis XIV (September).

Earl of Rochester becomes lord lieutenant (September).

The first public library in Ireland, Marsh's, is built.

1702

William III dies and is succeeded by his sister-in-law, Anne (March).

1703

Second duke of Ormond becomes lord lieutenant (June).

First Irish parliament of Anne meets (September–March).

1704

Irish parliament prohibits Catholics from buying land or acting as guardians, requires reception of communion in the established church as a test for public officials, and requires the Catholic clergy to register (March).

1705

English legislation permits export of Irish linen to American colonies (March).

1707

English and Scottish parliaments are united (May).
Earl of Pembroke becomes lord lieutenant (June).

1709

Earl of Wharton becomes lord lieutenant (April).
Hundreds of Palatine Protestant families come to Ireland (September).

1711

Second duke of Ormond is again lord lieutenant (July).

1713

Jonathan Swift becomes dean of St. Patrick's Cathedral (June).
Duke of Shrewsbury becomes lord lieutenant (October).

1714

Queen Anne dies and is succeeded by her Hanoverian cousin, George I (August).

1715

Duke of Ormond joins James III in Paris and is condemned by an act of attainder (July–August).
First Irish parliament of George I meets and elects William Connolly as Speaker of House of Commons (November).
Jacobite force lands in Lancashire and James III lands in Scotland (November–December).

1716

James III returns to France (February).

1719

Toleration act exempts nonconforming Protestants from requirement to attend established church (November).

1720

Declaratory Act by British parliament asserts its right to legislate for Ireland (April).

1721

Duke of Grafton becomes lord lieutenant (August).

1722

William Wood gets monopoly for coining copper halfpence in Ireland (July).

1724

Jonathan Swift publishes his *Drapier's Letters.*
Lord Carteret becomes lord lieutenant (October).

1725

Wood's monopoly is given up (September).

1726

Swift's *Gulliver's Travels* published (October).

1727

George I dies and is succeeded by his son, George II (June).

1728

Irish parliament deprives Catholics of parliamentary franchise (May).

1729

Swift's *Modest Proposal* published (October).

1731

British legislation permits direct importation from American colonies to Ireland of goods not specifically prohibited (May).
Irish parliament meets in new building for the first time (October).

1733

Henry Boyle elected Speaker of the Irish House of Commons (October).

1734

Converts to the established church whose wives are Catholic are prohibited from educating their children as Catholics or as serving as justices of the peace (April).

1737

Duke of Devonshire becomes lord lieutenant (September).

1738

Turlough Carolan, poet, composer, and harpist, dies (March).

1739

British legislation removes duty on Irish woolen yarn entering Great Britain (June).

Frost, after very wet and unproductive summer, results in severe famine (December).

1740

Bad summer and autumn with poor crop production, followed by frost, brings another famine (December).

1742

Handel's *Messiah* is performed for the first time, Dublin (April).

1743

Radical Charles Lucas publishes a pamphlet about infringements on the rights of the citizens of Dublin (April).

1745

Irish exiles in a brigade play important role in French victory over the British and the Dutch at the Battle of Fontenoy (April).

Charles Edward, son of James III, lands in Scotland (July). His forces have some success, including an advance into England, but they retreat from Derby (December).

1746

Jacobites are defeated at Culloden, and Charles Edward leaves Scotland (April).

1747

John and Charles Wesley first visit Ireland (August–September).

1749

Charles Lucas flees from being committed for prosecution as an enemy of the country (October).

1751

Laying of cornerstone of Rotunda Hospital, the first maternity hospital in Ireland (July)

Duke of Dorset becomes lord lieutenant (September).

Legislation authorizes applying revenue surplus to national debt (December).

1752

Gregorian calendar takes effect in British dominions, as September 2 is followed by September 14.

1753

House of Commons rejects bill to apply revenue surplus to reduction of debt (December).

1756

John Ponsonby elected Speaker of the Irish House of Commons (April).

1757

Duke of Bedford becomes lord lieutenant (September).

1758

British legislation permits importation of salted beef, pork, and butter from Ireland (June).

1759

British legislation allows importation of Irish cattle into Great Britain (April).

Henry Flood enters parliament (November).

Arthur Guinness leases brewery (December).

1760

Meeting of Catholics results in formation of "Catholic Committee" (March).

George II dies and is succeeded by his grandson, George III (October).

1761

Charles Lucas returns to Dublin (March)

Popular violent groups, the "Whiteboys," begin in Munster.

1762

Catholic nobility and gentry send address of support to George III in war with Spain (February).

1763

Popular violent groups, the "Hearts of Oak," are involved in Ulster disturbances.

Newspaper, *Freeman's Journal*, first appears (September).

1766

James III dies (January).

Catholic priest, Nicholas Sheehy, is executed at Clonmel for alleged instigation of "Whiteboy" crimes (March).

1767

Viscount Townsend becomes lord lieutenant (October).

1768

Life of parliament limited to eight years by Octennial Act (February).

Irish House of Commons rejects request by lord lieutenant to increase size of army (May).

1769

Popular violent group, "Hearts of Steel," engages in disturbances in Ulster (July).

1771

Charles Lucas dies (November).

1772

Legislation allows Catholics to rent bog land on 61-year leases (June).

Earl of Harcourt becomes lord lieutenant (November).

1775

Henry Flood accepts position of vice treasurer (October).

Irish House of Commons approves sending 4,000 troops to America (November).

Nano Nagle establishes the Presentation Order of teaching sisters (December).

1776

American colonies issue Declaration of Independence (July).

1777

Earl of Buckinghamshire becomes lord lieutenant (January).

1778

American naval figure, John Paul Jones, raids Belfast Lough (April).

Gardiner Act allows Catholics to take leases for up to 999 years and to inherit property similarly to Protestants (August).

1779

Irish Volunteers, a popular militia, parades in Dublin demanding lessening of commercial restrictions on Ireland (November).

1780

British legislation allows free trade between Ireland and British colonies in America, West Indies, and Africa (February).

British parliament repeals Test Act inhibiting Protestant nonconformists from public positions by requiring reception of sacrament in established church (May).

British legislation allows Ireland to trade with American colonies, the West Indies, and Africa on equal terms with Great Britain (February).

British parliament repeals requirement to receive sacrament in established church for officeholders as gesture to Protestant nonconformists (May).

Earl of Carlisle becomes lord lieutenant (December).

1781

Laying of foundation stone of Custom House, Dublin, designed by James Gandon (August).

Earl Cornwallis surrenders to Americans at Yorktown (October).

1782

Irish Volunteers convention at Dungannon demands legislative and judicial independence for Ireland and relaxation of penal laws against Catholics (February).

Marquis of Rockingham becomes prime minister and includes Irish-born Edmund Burke in his government (March).

Duke of Portland becomes lord lieutenant (April).

Henry Grattan moves in Irish parliament a declaration of legislative independence carried unanimously (April).

Gardiner Act allows Catholics to acquire land other than in parliamentary boroughs (May).

Irish House of Commons votes that Grattan be awarded 50,000 pounds (May).

British parliament repeals the Declaratory Act (June).

Poynings' Law, which inhibited Irish legislative independence, is amended (July).

Legislation allows Catholics to teach school and to act as guardians (July).

Earl of Temple becomes lord lieutenant (September).

1783

British parliament recognizes that Irish parliament has exclusive right to legislate for Ireland (April).

Earl of Northington becomes lord lieutenant (June).

Irish Volunteers convention at the Rotunda in Dublin proposes parliamentary reform, but the

Irish House of Commons refuses to accept it (November).

William Pitt the Younger becomes prime minister (December).

1784

William Drennan publishes letters in *Belfast Newsletter* asking for parliamentary reform (November).

1785

Radical reform congress meets in Dublin (January–February).

William Pitt forwards proposals for free trade between Ireland and Britain, which are approved by Irish House of Commons (February).

Royal Irish Academy has first meeting (May).

Irish House of Commons does not deal with revised version of Pitt's free trade proposals (August).

John Foster elected Speaker of Irish House of Commons (September).

Renewed disturbances by "Whiteboys" in Munster.

1786

Laying of cornerstone of Four Courts, Dublin, designed by James Gandon (March).

1787

Legislation against rioting and interference with collection of tithes passed (March).

Marquis of Buckingham becomes lord lieutenant (December).

1789

Irish parliament petitions that prince of Wales assume regency in view of insanity of George III (February).

1790

Earl of Westmoreland becomes lord lieutenant (January).

Edmund Burke publishes *Reflections on the Revolution in France* (November).

1791

Thomas Paine publishes *Rights of Man* (March).

Second anniversary of fall of Bastille in Paris is commemorated with Dublin and Belfast demonstrations (July).

Wolfe Tone publishes *An Argument on Behalf of the Catholics of Ireland* (August).

United Irishmen founded in Belfast (October).

Earl of Kenmare and other conservatives withdraw from Catholic committee (December).

1792

Northern Star, United Irishmen paper, first appears in Belfast (January).

Edmund Burke publishes *A Letter . . . on the Subject of the Roman Catholics of Ireland* (February).

House of Commons rejects Catholic Committee petition for parliamentary franchise (February).

Legislation allows Catholics to practice as lawyers (April).

Wolfe Tone becomes agent for the Catholic Committee (July).

Catholic convention sends delegates via Belfast to London to present petition to king (December).

Dublin United Irishmen call for revival of Volunteers (December).

1793

Louis XVI is executed, and France declares war on Great Britain (January–February).

Relief Act extends parliamentary franchise to Catholics, allows them to hold civil and military offices (with some exceptions), and to obtain university degrees (April).

Militia established at strength of 15,000 (April).

Convention Act prohibits gatherings to prepare petitions to the king or parliament (August).

1794

Archibald Hamilton Rowan, United Irishman, is fined and imprisoned for distributing seditious paper (January).

Rev. William Jackson arrested as agent for French government (April).

Rowan escapes to France (May).

Dublin United Irishmen suppressed (May).

William Drennan tried for seditious libel, but acquitted (June).

1795

Earl Fitzwilliam becomes lord lieutenant (January).

Fitzwilliam begins to dismiss leading political appointees in Protestant Ascendancy (January).

Grattan introduces measure for Catholic emancipation (right to sit in parliament) (February), which is rejected.

Fitzwilliam is dismissed (February).

Earl Camden becomes lord lieutenant (May).

Grattan motion to allow Catholics to sit in parliament is rejected by Irish House of Commons (May).

An act passed providing for the support of a Catholic seminary (June), which opens in Maynooth, County Kildare (October).

Wolfe Tone leaves for America (June).

Confrontation takes place near Loughgall, County Armagh, between Protestant Peep o' Day Boys and Catholic Defenders, the Battle of the Diamond (September).

1796

Wolfe Tone arrives in France (January).

Insurrection Act passed to inhibit illegal oaths and to impose curfew and arms searches in districts that are proclaimed as disturbed (March).

Newly formed Orange Order holds parades in Ulster (July).

United Irishmen figures such as Thomas Russell and Samuel Neilson are arrested in Belfast (September).

Act allows suspension of habeas corpus (October).

French fleet carrying invasion force comes to Bantry Bay, County Cork, but inclement weather prevents landing (December).

1797

General Gerard Lake orders surrender of arms in Ulster (March).

Militia breaks up the presses of the *Northern Star* (May).

Election to what would be the last Irish parliament (July–August).

Sir Ralph Abercromby appointed commander in chief in Ireland (November).

1798

French army captures Rome and Pope Pius VI arrested (February).

Most of the leaders of the United Irishmen are arrested in Dublin (March).

Martial law imposed on Ireland (March).

General Gerard Lake succeeds Abercrombie as commander in chief in Ireland (April).

Lord Edward Fitzgerald, United Irishman, is arrested and subsequently dies from wounds received at arrest (May).

United Irishmen rebel in Leinster, as insurgents, primarily Defenders, take Wexford, although they are later defeated at Arklow and finally at Vinegar Hill, near Enniscorthy (May–June).

United Irishmen rebel in Ulster including an attack on Antrim town led by Henry Joy McCracken and an attack at Ballynahinch led by Henry Munro, both of which fail and both leaders are executed (June).

Marquis Cornwallis becomes lord lieutenant (June).

French force of 1,000 lands at Killala, County Mayo, advances as far as Castlebar, where it routs government forces, but then surrenders to Cornwallis at Ballinamuck, County Longford (August–September).

Banishment act pardons rebels who will leave British dominions (October).

French invasions squad captured outside Lough Swilly and Wolfe Tone, who accompanied it, was arrested (October).

Tone is convicted by court-martial and is sentenced to be hung, but commits suicide (November).

1799

Pitt advocates union of Ireland with Great Britain (January).

Leaders of United Irishmen are interned at Inverness (April).

1800

Orange lodges oppose proposed union with Great Britain (February–March).

British parliament passes Act of Union (July).

Irish parliament passes Act of Union (August).

1801

Union of Great Britain and Ireland comes into effect (January 1).

Pitt resigns as prime minister because of the refusal of George III to accept Catholic emancipation as had been expected to follow union and is succeeded as prime minister by Henry Addington (March).

1802

Peace of Amiens between United Kingdom and France (March).

United Irishmen at Inverness are released and go to the Continent (June).

1803

War resumes between United Kingdom and France (May).

Rising in Dublin led by Robert Emmet fails (July).

Legislation allows suspension of habeas corpus (July).

Emmet executed for treason (September).

Thomas Russell executed for treason (October).

United Irishman Michael Dwyer surrenders in Wicklow Mountains and will go into exile in New South Wales (December).

1805

Henry Grattan makes his maiden speech in House of Commons (May).

1807

William Saurin becomes attorney general in Ireland (May).

Insurrection Act refines and amends that of 1796 (August).

1808

Proposal is made in House of Commons to grant Catholic emancipation in return for a royal veto on the appointment of Catholic bishops (May).

Edmund Rice founds a teaching order, the Christian Brothers (August).

Irish Catholic bishops reject royal veto proposal (September).

1809

Catholic Committee reestablished (May).

1811

Catholic Committee proposes to have representatives appointed by parish and diocese to advance petitions, but the proposal is proclaimed illegal under the 1793 Convention Act (July).

Kildare Place Society is formed to support nondenominational schools (December).

1812

Robert Peel becomes chief secretary for Ireland (August).

1813

Henry Grattan introduces a Catholic relief bill in the House of Commons, but it is defeated (April–May).

John Magee, editor of *Dublin Evening Post,* is tried, convicted, fined, and imprisoned for libeling the lord lieutenant (July–November).

1814

A letter favorable to the royal veto over Catholic bishops written by Msgr. Quarantotti is published in Dublin (May).

Jesuits open Clongowes Wood College (July).

Peace Preservation Act, advanced by Peel, is passed allowing the lord lieutenant to appoint a police force in disturbed areas that would be responsible to the central government (July).

Laying of cornerstone of General Post Office in Dublin (August).

Apprentice Boys formed.

1815

O'Connell warns pope and hierarchy of opposition of rank-and-file clergy and laity to the veto proposal (January).

O'Connell kills John D'Esterre in duel (February).

Laying of foundation stone of Catholic procathedral in Dublin (March).

Charles Bianconi begins coach service (July).

Catholic bishops inform papacy of their opposition to veto proposal (August).

1816

Legislation amalgamates British and Irish exchequers (July).

1818

Protestant missionaries form society to proselytize through the Irish language.

1819

Grattan unsuccessfully advances Catholic emancipation in House of Commons (May).

Disturbances by Ribbonmen (irregular violent groups) occur from Dublin to Galway (October).

1820

George III dies and is succeeded by his son, George IV (January).

Henry Grattan dies (June).

1821

House of Lords rejects bill allowing Catholic emancipation subject to royal veto of Catholic hierarchical appointments

Census taken in Ireland: population of 6,801,827 (May).

George IV visits Ireland (August–September).

1822

Legislation establishes police force for all Irish counties controlled by local magistrates but regulated by central government (August).

Marquis of Londonderry (Castlereagh) commits suicide (August).

1823

Catholic Association is formed (May).

1824

Daniel O'Connell proposes making Catholic Association a mass organization with universal membership of Irish Catholics with a penny a month dues (January).

Legislation removes duties on manufactured articles imported to Great Britain from Ireland and vice versa (April).

1825

Legislation curtails petitioning organizations like the Catholic Association (March).

After being dissolved (March), the Catholic Association is reformed under a different name (July).

1826

O'Connell and the Catholic Association campaign on behalf of pro–Catholic emancipation candidates in four constituencies and succeed in all (June–July).

1828

Duke of Wellington becomes prime minister (January).

Daniel O'Connell is elected to parliament from Clare in a by-election (July).

Anti–Catholic emancipation Brunswick clubs are started (August).

1829

Catholic emancipation is approved by parliament, allowing Catholics to enter parliament and hold virtually all civilian and military offices (April).

County franchise requirement is raised from 40 shillings to £10 (April).

O'Connell, after being denied entry to the House of Commons until he would stand again for office, is returned unopposed (May–July).

1830

O'Connell takes his seat in parliament (February).

George IV dies and is succeeded by his son, William IV (June).

Revolution in Paris forces Charles X to abdicate. He is replaced by Louis-Philippe (July).

General election results are hostile to Tories, and Wellington and Earl Grey form a Whig government (August–November).

Polish nationalists revolt (November).

Belgian secession from The Netherlands is recognized by great powers (December).

1831

O'Connell arrested under Insurrection Act (January).

Parliamentary reform bill introduced in House of Commons (March).

General election strengthens Grey government (May).

Chief secretary Edward Stanley moves to have 30,000 pounds available for a national system of education in Ireland (September).

Catherine McAuley establishes the Sisters of Mercy (December).

Twelve policemen killed in disturbances connected with tithe collection in Kilkenny (December).

Census in Ireland: Population is 7,767,401.

1832

Parliamentary reform allows increase in Irish membership in House of Commons from 100 to 105 and imposes standard 10 shilling franchise requirement in boroughs, allowing increase of electorate to over 90,000 or 1.2 percent of population (August).

Tithe Composition Act passed (August).

General election returns 42 O'Connellites from Ireland (December).

1833

Church Temporalities Act lessens number of bishops in established Church of Ireland (August).

Tithe Arrears Act gives relief to tithe owners who had not collected tithes (August).

1834

O'Connell unsuccessfully moves for repeal of the Act of Union (April).

Viscount Melbourne becomes prime minister (July).

John McHale becomes bishop of Tuam (July).

Robert Peel becomes prime minister (December).

1835

O'Connell reaches a political understanding with the Whigs at Lichfield House (February).

Melbourne becomes prime minister (April).

Thomas Drummond becomes undersecretary for Ireland (July).

1836

Drummond appoints commission on construction of railways in Ireland (October).

1837

William IV dies, succeeded by niece Victoria (June).

Conservatives (Tories) gain in general election, O'-Connellites obtain 30 seats, but Melbourne continues as prime minister (July–August).

Fergus O'Connor starts a radical newspaper in Leeds, the *Northern Star* (November).

1838

Rev. Theobald Matthew, O.F.M.Cap., starts total abstinence movement (April).

Drummond tells landlords "property has its duties as well as its rights" (May).

Poor Relief Act extends English poor relief system to Ireland (July).

Legislation changes tithes into rent charges and reduces them (August).

1840

Laying of foundation stone of Catholic cathedral in Armagh (March).

National Association of Ireland (later called Loyal National Repeal Association) formed (April).

Irish municipal reform act is passed (August).

Archbishop McHale joins the Loyal National Repeal Association (August).

1841

Thomas Davis joins the Loyal National Repeal Association (April).

Census in Ireland: Population is 8,175,124 (June).

General election results in a conservative victory with O'Connellites getting 20 seats (July).

Peel becomes prime minister.

O'Connell is elected lord mayor of Dublin (October).

1842

National Repeal Convention in America splits on the issue of slavery (February).

The *Nation,* edited by Charles Gavan Duffy, appears (October).

1843

Monster repeal meeting held at Trim (March).

Monster repeal meeting held at Hill of Tara (August).

O'Connell cancels monster meeting scheduled for Clontarf after proclamation prohibits the same (October).

1844

O'Connell and associates are tried and found guilty of conspiracy (January–February) and sentenced to imprisonment and fine (May).

Legislation calls for construction of railway lines (Great Southern & Western Railway) that will eventually serve Limerick and Cork (August).

House of Lords reverses judgment on O'Connell and associates (September).

1845

Irish Colleges bill is introduced in House of Commons, but O'Connell and Davis differ on it within the Repeal Association (May).

Irish Catholic bishops oppose the colleges bill (May).

Peel's Maynooth College Act passes and provides increased capital and annual grants (June).

Irish Colleges Act passes (July).

Potato blight reported (September).

Thomas Davis dies (September).

Peel orders purchase of Indian corn for Ireland (November).

1846

Public works act for Ireland is passed to encourage piers, harbors, and other works (March).

Corn laws are repealed as encouraged by Peel against the wishes of most of his own Conservative Party (June).

Lord John Russell becomes prime minister (June).

Potato crop failure reported (July).

Split within Repeal Association between O'Connell and Young Irelanders develops on principle of employing violence (July).

Russell announces in House of Commons policy of noninterference with regular sale of grain in Ireland and Trevelyan writes Malthusian memo about the food situation in Ireland (August).

Relief works to be financed by treasury loans authorized in Ireland (August).

Irish Quakers organize a relief committee (November).

1847

James Fintan Lalor advocates agrarian reform, national independence, and the use of physical force (January).

Irish Confederation formed (January).

O'Connell makes last appearance in House of Commons pleading for relief for Ireland (February).

Legislation calls for soup kitchens for the poor. Also approved is outdoor poor relief (to those not in workhouses) to be financed out of local rates (February).

O'Connell dies in Genoa (May).

Poor relief legislation allows outdoor relief to the aged, sick, infirm, widows with two or more children, and for limited periods to the able-bodied, but excludes from benefit those holding more than a quarter of an acre of land (June).

Reports appear that potato harvest is sound but small because so many seed potatoes were consumed the previous year (July).

1848

John Mitchell starts the *United Irishman* (February).

William Smith O'Brien and Thomas Francis Meagher advocate physical force at meeting of Irish Confederation (March).

Fergus O'Connor presents Chartist petition to House of Commons (April).

Under treason Felony Act passed in April, John Mitchell is arrested, tried, convicted, and sentenced to transportation (May).

William Smith O'Brien, Terence Bellew McManus, and other members of the Irish Confederation clash with police near Ballingarry, County Tipperary (July).

Blight continues to affect potato crop (July–September).

Smith O'Brien, Meagher, McManus, and Patrick O'Donohue are found guilty of high treason and sentenced to execution (October).

1849

Sentences of Smith O'Brien and others commuted to transportation for life to Van Dieman's Land (June).

Encumbered Estates Act facilitates sale of encumbered estates (July).

Queen Victoria and Prince Albert visit Ireland (August).

Nation resumes publication (September).

Queen's Colleges at Belfast, Cork, and Galway are opened (October).

James Fintan Lalor dies (December).

1850

Paul Cullen becomes archbishop of Armagh (February).

Irish Tenant League formed (August).

1851

Census of Ireland: Population is 6,552,385 (a decline of almost 20 percent).

Ecclesiastical Titles Act prohibits Catholic hierarchy in England and Wales that the pope had reestablished from assuming the existing territorial titles of the established church (August).

Catholic Defence Association of Great Britain and Ireland formed in Dublin in opposition to Ecclesiastical Titles Act (August).

1852

Archbishop Cullen transferred from Armagh to Dublin (May).

John Henry Newman delivers in Dublin his lectures on university education (May).

Liberal M.P.'s from Ireland agree to remain independent from any government that doesn't respond to the tenant-right cause (September).

Two Irish M.P.'s, John Sadleir and William Keogh, break with pledge and accept positions in coalition government formed by Lord Aberdeen (December).

1853

John Mitchell escapes from Van Dieman's Land and heads toward the United States (July).

Queen Victoria and Prince Albert visit Dublin (August–September).

1854

John Mitchell's "Jail Journal" begins to appear in the *Citizen,* and will later appear in book form (January).

Catholic University is opened in Dublin with John Henry Newman as rector (November).

1855

Catholic cathedral in Killarney, designed by Augustus Pugin, is consecrated (August).

Charles Gavan Duffy leaves Ireland for Australia (November).

1856

James Stephens, 1848 rebel, returns to Ireland from France (January).

1857

Sectarian rioting in Belfast related to preaching by Rev. Hugh Hanna (September).

1858

Founding of Irish Republican Brotherhood (IRB) by James Stephens (March).

1859

John O'Mahony organizes the Fenian Brotherhood in the United States to correspond with the IRB in Ireland (April).

1860

Holy Ghost Fathers open college that would later be called Blackrock College (September).

1861

Census in Ireland: Population is 5,798,967, a decrease of $11^1/_2$ percent (April).

Queen Victoria and Prince Albert visit Ireland (August).

Funeral held in Dublin of Terence Bellew McManus, who had died in exile in San Francisco in January (November).

1862

Harland and Wolff shipbuilding firm is founded in Belfast (January).

1863

Legislation calls for registration of births and deaths in Ireland (April).

Legislation calls for registration of marriages in Ireland (July).

Irish People appears, owned by Thomas Clarke Luby, published by Jeremiah O'Donovan Rossa, and edited by John O'Mahony (November).

1864

National Association of Ireland starts to advance agrarian reform, church disestablishment, and Catholic education (December).

1865

Laying of foundation stone of Methodist College in Belfast (August).

Police suppress *Irish People* (September).

James Stephens is arrested, but escapes to France (November).

1866

Fenians raid Canada unsuccessfully (April–May).

Archbishop Cullen made the first Irish cardinal (June).

Transatlantic cable completed between Valentia, County Kerry, and Newfoundland (July).

James Stephens deposed as head of Fenian Brotherhood in the United States (December).

1867

Fenian rebellion in Kells, County Kerry, suppressed and condemned by David Moriarty, bishop of Kerry (February).

Fenian rebellions in Dublin and in Munster are suppressed (March).

Clan na Gael founded in New York (June).

IRB selects Colonel Thomas J. Kelly to succeed Stephens as leader (August).

A police sergeant is killed when two Fenian prisoners, Colonel Thomas J. Kelly and Captain Timothy Deasy, are released from police van in Manchester by Fenians (September).

William Allen, Michael Larkin, and Michael O'Brien are executed for the killing of the sergeant (November).

Explosion resulting from attempted release of Fenian prisoners in Clerkenwell Jail, London, causes numerous deaths and injuries (December).

1868

Benjamin Disraeli becomes prime minister (February).

Parliamentary reform act expands franchise in borough constituency (July).

William Gladstone becomes prime minister after Liberal victory in general election (December).

1869

Forty-nine Fenian prisoners are given amnesty (March).

Church of Ireland is disestablished (July).

Friedrich Engels visits Ireland (September).

Jeremiah O'Donovan Rossa elected to parliament from Tipperary, but is denied seat since he was an imprisoned felon (November).

1870

Gladstone's first Irish land act passed (August).

First meeting held of Home Government Association, Dublin (September).

1871

Thirty-three Fenian prisoners, including John Devoy and Jeremiah O'Donovan Rossa, are amnestied (January).

Census in Ireland: Population is 5,412,377.

1872

Ballot Act makes voting secret (July).

Legislation requires licensing for sale of liquor (August).

1873

Home Rule Confederation of Great Britain is formed after Issac Butt speaks in Manchester (January).

Gladstone resigns after his university bill for Ireland (opposed by Irish Catholic bishops) is defeated (March).

Legislation ends religious tests at Trinity College (May).

Home Rule League founded in Dublin (November).

1874

Conservatives win general election, but Home Rulers get 60 seats in Ireland (February).

Joseph Gillias Biggar and others begin to use obstructionist tactics in House of Commons to advance Home Rule cause, but are opposed by leader Issac Butt (July).

1875

John Mitchell elected in Tipperary by-election, but is unseated as a convicted felon (February).

He is again elected, but dies soon after (March).

1876

Fenian convicts escape from prison in Western Australia and get to New York via the *Catalpa* (April–August).

Home rule motion by Butt defeated in House of Commons (July).

Clan na Gael and IRB form joint revolutionary directory (August).

IRB Supreme Council withdraws support of Home Rule movement (August).

1877

Jeremiah O'Donovan Rossa succeeds John O'Mahony as head of Fenians (January).

Supreme Council of IRB calls for resignation of four IRB home rule MP's, but two, Biggar and O'Connor Power, refuse to do so and are expelled from movement (March–August).

Obstructionist Home Rulers prolong meeting of House of Commons for over 24 hours (July–August).

Charles Stewart Parnell replaces Butt as president of Home Rule Confederation of Great Britain (August).

Three years of bad harvests and agricultural depression begin.

1878

Cardinal Cullen, archbishop of Dublin, dies (October).

Michael Davitt and John Devoy meet in America and forward new departure proposals for cooperation of Fenians with Home Rulers and Land League (September–December).

1879

Davitt and Devoy meet with Parnell in Dublin (April).

Land agitation organized by Davitt begins in Irishtown, County Mayo (April).

Parnell addresses land meeting at Westport, County Mayo (June).

Legislation dissolves Queen's University in Ireland and replaces it with an examining university (August).

Founding of National Land League in Castlebar, County Mayo (August).

Marian apparitions occur at Knock, County Mayo (August).

Irish National Land League founded and elects Parnell as its president (October).

1880

Parnell addresses House of Representatives in Washington and visits President Rutherford B. Hayes (February).

General election returns the Liberals to power under Gladstone, while returning 63 Home Rulers from Ireland (March–April).

Parnell is elected as chairman of Irish Parliamentary Party (May).

Parnell calls for moral coventry tactic in speech at Ennis, County Clare (September)

"Moral Coventry," or "boycott" of Captain Charles Boycott, land agent, in County Mayo, begins (September).

1881

Davitt arrested (February).

Coercion legislation to deal with agrarian disturbances is passed (march).

Census of Ireland: Population is 5,174,836 (April).

Second Irish land act of Gladstone is passed (August).

Parnell and other Land League leaders arrested (October).

No-rent manifesto issued from Kilmainham Gaol by Parnell and other imprisoned Land League figures (October).

Archbishop John McHale of Tuam, County Mayo, dies (November).

1882

Kilmainham Treaty allows release of Parnell, Davitt, and others from jail in return for withdrawal of no rent manifesto. Chief Secretary C. S. Forster resigns (May).

Lord Frederick Cavendish, new chief secretary, and Thomas Burke, undersecretary, are assassinated in Phoenix Park, Dublin (May).

Arrears of Rent Act passed to meet complaints of Land Leaguers (August).

1883

Tom Clarke and other IRB dynamiters are tried and sentenced to life imprisonment (April–June).

Phoenix Park assassins are tried and executed (April–June).

1884

Catholic bishops have Irish Parliamentary Party press church claims in education (October).

Gaelic Athletic Association is formed in Thurles, County Tipperary (November).

Legislation broadens the franchise (December).

1885

Edward Cardinal McCabe, archbishop of Dublin, dies (February).

William Walsh appointed archbishop of Dublin (June).

Marquis of Salisbury becomes prime minister pending election (June).

Legislation redistributes parliamentary seats, ending borough seats, and having relatively uniform constituencies (June).

Land Purchase (Ashbourne) Act passed (August).

General election returns 86 Irish Parliamentary Party members equaling the number the Conservative majority exceeds the Liberal membership of parliament; Parnell had urged supporters in Britain to vote against the Liberals (November–December).

Gladstone's son, Herbert, announces his father acceptance of Home Rule, which announcement was nicknamed the "Hawarden kite" (December).

1886

Gladstone becomes prime minister after defeat of Salisbury on no confidence vote (February).

Irish Catholic bishops approve home rule (February).

Randolph Churchill speaks at anti–Home Rule meeting in Ulster Hall, Belfast, after telling associate that "the orange card would be the one to play" if Home Rule was pushed by Gladstone (February).

Home Rule bill is defeated in House of Commons as 93 Liberals oppose it (June).

Conservatives win general election with the Irish Parliamentary Party getting 85 seats and Salisbury returns as prime minister (July).

Another rent withholding campaign, the Plan of Campaign, begins, but is proclaimed as a criminal conspiracy (October–December).

1887

Arthur Balfour becomes chief secretary (March).

The *Times* of London publishes articles linking Parnell with crimes, especially the Phoenix Park assassinations (April–May).

Legislation toughening criminal law and procedure in Ireland is passed (July).

The National League is proclaimed under same legislation (August).

1888

Vatican document condemns the Plan of Campaign (April).

Legislation establishes a commission to enquire into charges against Parnell (August).

1889

Richard Pigott is exposed as a forger of anti-Parnell documents and commits suicide (February–March).

The Total Abstinence League is founded (June).

Special commission meets for last time (November) pending exoneration of Parnell in its report.

Captain William O'Shea sues his wife Katherine, Parnell's mistress, for divorce (December).

1890

O'Shea wins divorce case unopposed (November).

Parnell unanimously reelected as chairman of the Irish Parliamentary Party, although Gladstone states Parnell's leadership would jeopardize alliance with Liberals (November).

Split occurs in Irish Parliamentary Party as majority breaks with Parnell (December).

Parnell supporter is defeated in North Kilkenny by-election (December).

1891

Parnell supporter is defeated in North Sligo by-election (April).

Census in Ireland: Population is 4,705,750 (April).

Parnell marries Katharine O'Shea (June).

Parnell supporter is defeated in Carlow by-election (July).

Further land purchase legislation is passed, and the Congested Districts Board is established (August).

Parnell dies at Brighton (October).

1892

Irish Education Act is passed, making national school education free of fees and compulsory for children (June).

General election allows return to power by Gladstone because of 80 nationalist seats (71 anti-Parnellites and nine Parnellites) (July).

Douglas Hyde delivers his speech "On the necessity for de-anglicising the Irish people" (November).

1893

Archbishop of Armagh, Michael Logue, is created a cardinal (January).

Eoin MacNeill convenes the Gaelic League (July).

Home Rule passes House of Commons, but is defeated in House of Lords (September).

1894

Gladstone resigns as prime minister and is succeeded by the earl of Rosebery, who declares that Home Rule would have to require consent of not just the majority of the House of Commons, but of the members from England (March).

Horace Plunkett forms Irish Agricultural Organization (April).

1895

East Wicklow by-election is won by anti-Parnellite (April).

General election gives clear majority to Conservative-Unionist alliance with 81 Irish Parliamentary Party members elected from Ireland (69 anti-Parnellites and 12 Parnellites) and one from England (July). Salisbury is again prime minister.

1896

John Dillon succeeds Justin McCarthy as leader of anti-Parnellites in Irish Parliamentary Party (February).

Maynooth College becomes a pontifical university (March).

1898

William O'Brien starts the United Irish League in Westport, County Mayo, to promote land distribution to small farmers (January).

Local Government (Ireland) Act calls for popularly elected local government councils in Ireland (August).

James Connolly issues the first number of *Workers' Republic* (August).

Tom Clarke is released from Portland prison (September).

1899

John Dillon resigns as chairman of anti-Parnellite Irish parliamentary party (February).

Arthur Griffith's *United Irishman* first appears (March).

Gaelic League paper, *An Claidheamh Soluis*, edited by Eoin MacNeill, first appears (March).

1900

Irish Parliamentary Party is reunited with John Redmond as leader (January).

Queen Victoria visits Ireland (April).

D. P. Moran's journal, the *Leader*, first appears (September).

General election returns Conservative-Unionists to power as the Irish Parliamentary Party has 76 members returned from Ireland, along with 5 independent nationalists, and one member from England (October).

George Wyndham becomes the chief secretary (November).

1901

Queen Victoria dies and is succeeded by her son, Edward VII (January).

Census in Ireland: Population is 4,458,775 (March).

1902

Cathleen ni Houlihan by William Butler Yeats has its first performance (April).

Arthur Balfour becomes prime minister (July).

Sir Antony MacDonnell becomes undersecretary (November).

Conference of landlord and tenant representatives meets at Mansion House, Dublin (December).

1903

Edward VII visits Ireland (July–August).

Irish Land Act (Wyndham Act) passes (August).

1904

Anti-semitic episodes occur in Limerick (January).

Edward VII again visits Ireland (April–May).

Lord Dunraven forms Irish Reform Association and advocates devolution (August).

Ulster Unionist MP's gather in Belfast to form what will become the Ulster Unionist Council (December).

Abbey Theatre opens in Dublin (December).

1905

Wyndham resigns as chief secretary (March).

Arthur Griffith purposes a policy called Sinn Féin (November).

Conservative government, in anticipation of an election, resigns, expecting Liberal disunity to insure Conservative victory. Henry Campbell-Bannerman, who had indicated support for Home Rule, becomes prime minister (December).

James Bryce becomes chief secretary (December).

1906

General election results in a Liberal landslide with Irish Parliamentary Party securing 81 seats in Ireland, along with one independent nationalist and one member from England (January).

Arthur Griffith is the editor of *Sinn Féin*, which first appears (May).

Walter Long is elected leader of the Irish unionists in the House of Commons (November).

The 1881 coercion legislation is allowed to expire (December).

1907

Riots accompany first performance in Abbey Theatre of John M. Synge's *The Playboy of the Western World* (January).

Augustine Birrell becomes chief secretary (January).

Sinn Féin League is formed at Dundalk uniting Dungannon Clubs and Cumann na nGaedheal (April).

James Larkin organizes strike by dockers at Belfast Steamship Company (May) and organizes a Dublin branch of Dock Workers Union (August).

The Sinn Féin League amalgamates with Arthur Griffith's National Council under the name of Sinn Féin League (September), later changed to just Sinn Féin.

Tom Clarke returns to Ireland from the United States (December).

1908

In North Leitrim by-election, a parliamentary party candidate easily defeats the Sinn Féin candidate (February).

H. H. Asquith becomes prime minister (April).

New Irish universities legislation establishes the National University of Ireland (which includes university colleges in Cork, Dublin, and Galway that were de facto Catholic) and Queen's University in Belfast (August).

Patrick Pearse opens St. Edna's school for boys in Rathmines, Dublin (September).

James Larkin forms the Irish Transport Workers' Union (December).

1909

The House of Lords rejects the budget approved by the House of Commons prompting a general election (November).

1910

General election gives Liberals a plurality of two seats over Conservative-Unionists, giving the 82 nationalists (70 Irish Parliamentary Party, one from England, and 11 independent nationalists from Ireland) the balance of power (January).

Sir Edward Carson becomes leader of the Irish unionists in the House of Commons (February).

Edward VII dies and is succeeded by his son, George V (May), which allows the major parties to engage in a conference seeking to form a national coalition that could bypass inclusion of the Irish and consideration of Home Rule (May).

The conference fails largely on the Home Rule issue and another general election is held with both major parties tied in seats, giving the nationalists (one from England, 73 Irish Parliamentary Party, and 10 independents) the balance of power (December).

1911

Census in Ireland: Population is 4,381,951 (April).

George V visits Dublin (July).

Legislation is passed restricting the veto power of the House of Lords to a two year suspension, which will mean probable success of Home Rule (August).

Irish Women's Suffrage Federation is formed (August).

Thousands of Orangemen and unionists demonstrate (September).

Balfour resigns as leader of Conservatives and is replaced by Andrew Bonar Law (November).

1912

Winston Churchill gives a pro–Home Rule address in Belfast (February).

Andrew Bonar Law in Belfast pledges support of unionist resistance to Home Rule (April).

RMS *Titanic* sinks on maiden voyage (April).

Daniel Mannix, president of Maynooth College, becomes coadjutor bishop of Melbourne (July).

Thousands in Ulster sign Solemn League and Covenant to resist Home Rule (September).

1913

Home rule is passed in the House of Commons, but is defeated in the House of Lords (January).

The private, paramilitary Ulster Volunteer Force is formed (January).

Home Rule is again passed by the House of Commons, but is defeated by the House of Lords (July).

Tramway men in Dublin, members of Irish Transport and General Workers' Union, strike in Dublin, amidst serious disturbances (August–January).

Ulster unionists organize a provisional government to function in event of passage of Home Rule legislation (September).

Eoin MacNeill advocates a nationalist counterpart to the Ulster Volunteer Force and the Irish Volunteers are soon after formed (November).

1914

Striking tramway workers return to work (January).

Commander and 57 of 70 army officers at Curragh, County Kildare, indicate preference to be dismissed from service rather than be ordered to enforce Home Rule in the north of Ireland (March).

Guns are successfully landed at Larne and other spots in Ulster for the Ulster Volunteer Force (April).

Home Rule bill passes the House of Commons for the third time (May).

Governing committee of Irish Volunteers accepts John Redmond's demand that it include 25 nominees of his party (June).

Government proposes temporary exclusion of parts of Ulster from Home Rule legislation, while House of Lords passes a measure to allow permanent exclusion of all of Ulster, but unionists, nationalists, the government and the opposition fail to reach an agreement on the issue at a Buckingham Palace conference (June–July).

Rifles are landed at Howth, County Dublin, for the Irish Volunteers, troops fire on hostile crowd in

Bachelors Walk, Dublin, killing four and wounding several more (July).

United Kingdom declares war on Germany following German invasion of Belgium. Redmond pledges support of Britain and calls on employment of Irish and Ulster Volunteers in defense of Ireland (August).

Legislation is passed suspending implementation of passed Home Rule law (September).

Redmond asks Irish Volunteers to serve in the war effort (September).

MacNeill and the convention of the Irish Volunteers repudiate Redmond (October).

James Larkin goes to the United States and James Connolly succeeds him as acting secretary of the ITGWU (October).

1915

Submarine sinks *Lusitania* off of Old Head of Kinsale (May).

Asquith forms a national coalition cabinet, which includes Carson. Redmond refuses to be included (May).

Douglas Hyde steps down as president of the Gaelic League (July).

Military council of the IRB is formed (December).

1916

Supreme Council of IRB decides to initiate an uprising as soon as possible and James Connolly joins its military council (January).

German vessel, *Aud*, unable to land with weapons near Tralee, is scuttled off Queenstown when stopped by the British. Roger Casement is arrested after landing at Banna Strand off of German submarine (April).

Eoin MacNeill cancels Irish Volunteers maneuvers ordered for Easter Sunday by Pearse, but military council of IRB orders them to take place the next day, Easter Monday. The General Post Office and several public buildings in Dublin are seized and an Irish republic is proclaimed, although the commanders surrender the following Saturday after a week of fighting in which over 450 were killed and 3,000 injured. General Sir John Maxwell becomes commander in chief in Ireland where martial law is proclaimed (April).

Over 400 Irish Volunteers are interned in camps in Britain, 15 leaders of the rebellion are executed following trial by courts-martial (May).

Somme offensive results in 20,000 British deaths, many from Ulster (July–November).

Roger Casement is convicted of high treason and is executed (June–August).

Negotiations under David Lloyd George to have immediate implementation of Home Rule with temporary exclusion of six Ulster counties fail as Redmond rejects proposal (July).

Lt. General Sir Bryan Mahon replaces Maxwell as commander in chief in Ireland (November).

Lloyd George becomes prime minister of national coalition government (December).

Interned Irish prisoners are released from Frongoch and Reading camps (December).

1917

George Noble Count Plunkett, whose son Joseph Mary Plunkett was one of the executed Easter Week leaders, as Sinn Féin candidate wins a North Roscommon parliamentary by-election (February).

Joseph P. McGuinness, a Sinn Féin candidate, wins South Longford parliamentary by-election (May).

Remaining Irish prisoners serving sentences for role in Easter rebellion are released (June).

Eamon de Valera, as Sinn Féin candidate, wins East Clare parliamentary by-election (July).

Irish convention of all political parties summoned by Lloyd George to produce a system of Irish self-government and chaired by Horace Plunkett meets. Sinn Féin refuses to attend (July–April).

William T. Cosgrave, Sinn Féin, wins Kilkenny city by-election to parliament (August).

Thomas Ashe dies after forcible feeding while on hunger strike (September).

De Valera is elected president of Sinn Féin at its *ard-heis* and of the Irish Volunteers (October).

1918

Legislation extends right to vote to all men over the age of 21 and to women over 30 and constituencies are made equal in electorate size (February).

Lloyd George seeks power to extend conscription to Ireland (April).

Irish Parliamentary Party, Sinn Féin, and the Catholic bishops join forces in condemning conscription for Ireland (April–May).

Dozens of Sinn Féin figures are interned on basis of alleged "German plot" (May).

Arthur Griffith, Sinn Féin, wins East-Cavan parliamentary by-election (June).

Armistice ends First World War (November).

Legislation allows women to serve in the House of Commons (November).

General election sees overwhelming victory by Conservatives and coalition Liberals and Lloyd George remaining as prime minister of a primarily Conservative government; from Ireland Sinn Féin wins 73 seats, while the Irish Parliamentary Party gets six (in addition to one from England), and the unionists get 26 (December).

1919

Sinn Féin MP's, who have refused to take their seat in Westminster, and aside from 36 who were in prison, meet in Mansion House, Dublin, and hold first meeting of Dáil Éireann, adopt a provisional constitution, a declaration of independence, and a democratic program, and elect Cathal Brugha as acting president (January).

Ambush by Irish Volunteers results in two RIC men being killed (January).

De Valera escapes from jail in England (February).

De Valera is elected president of Dáil Éireann (April).

De Valera leaves for the United States (June).

Legislation approves proportional representation in Irish local authority elections (June).

Dáil Éireann establishes arbitration courts as alternatives to existing judiciary (June).

Sinn Féin, Irish Volunteers, the Gaelic League, and similar bodies are suppressed in various counties (July–September).

Dáil Éireann requires Irish Volunteers to swear allegiance to the Dáil and the Irish Republic (August).

Dáil Éireann is declared illegal (September).

1920

Recruitment occurs in Britain of thousands of RIC replacements, who would be nicknamed the "Black and Tans" because of their mixed uniforms, and who would gain notorious reputation for atrocities (January).

Sinn Féin and nationalist and Labour allies win control of 172 of 206 councils in urban local government elections in Ireland (January).

RIC kills Tomas MacCurtain, lord mayor of Cork and IRA commandant (March).

Hamar Greenwood becomes chief secretary (April).

Sinn Féin is successful in most county council and rural district elections (June).

Formation of auxiliary division of the RIC, recruited from former army officers. It gains reputation similar in notoriety to that of "Black and Tans" (July).

Dáil Éireann starts boycott of Belfast products to protest intimidation of Catholics (August).

Terence MacSwiney, lord mayor of Cork, dies on hunger strike while imprisoned (October).

Michael Collins orders the killing of 14 suspected British agents in Dublin and, on same day, the Black and Tans fire on crowd in at football match in Croke Park, killing 12, and auxiliaries shoot two IRA commanders (November).

IRA ambush auxiliary patrol at Kilmichael, near Macroom, County Cork (November).

Cork city sacked by Black and Tans and Auxiliaries (December).

Government of Ireland Act passed, calling for two separate Home Rule parliaments, one for Northern Ireland and one for Southern Ireland (December).

1921

Carson resigns as leader of Ulster unionists and is replaced by Sir James Craig (January).

Viscount Fitzalan becomes lord lieutenant, the first Catholic since reign of James II (May).

All candidates to the parliament of Southern Ireland (124 Sinn Féin, four independents from Dublin University) are returned unopposed; 40 unionists, six parliamentary nationalists, and six Sinn Féiners are elected to parliament of Northern Ireland (May).

King George V opens Northern Ireland parliament (June), but only four of the 128 members of the Southern Ireland House of Commons attend its opening (June), as the Sinn Féiners will gather as the second Dáil Éireann (August).

Truce signed between the British army and the IRA (July).

Frank Duff organizes the group that would become the Legion of Mary (August).

Conference between delegates selected by Dáil Éireann and the British government begins (October).

Anglo-Irish Treaty signed (December).

1922

Dáil Éireann approves Anglo-Irish Treaty by a 64-57 vote and de Valera resigns as president being replaced by Arthur Griffith (January).

Parliament of Southern Ireland elects a provisional government for the Irish Free State with Michael Collins as chairman (January).

Two abortive peace pacts are made between James Craig and Michael Collins aimed at lessening maltreatment of Catholics in Northern Ireland and restraining the IRA (January and March).

Sinn Féin *ard-fheis* agrees to postpone decision on treaty (February).

IRA convention is held against wishes of Provisional Government minister of defense Richard Mulcahy, and is dominated by anti-treatyites (March).

Anti-treaty IRA members seize the Four Courts, Dublin (April).

Pact between Collins and de Valera for pro- and anti-treaty factions run candidates proportionate to their respective membership in the existing Dáil in a forthcoming election and that a coalition government be formed from both factions (May).

British object to pact and to the "republican" flavor of tentative Irish Free State constitution (May–June).

Collins withdraws from electoral pact. Election returns 58 pro-treaty Sinn Féin, 36 anti-treaty Sinn Féin, 17 Labour, seven farmers, and 10 independents (June).

Field Marshall Sir Henry Wilson is assassinated in London by IRA members (June), who are apprehended, tried, and executed (August).

Provisional Government attacks Four Courts after kidnapping of pro-treaty General J. J. O'Connell, which begins civil war (June).

Arthur Griffith dies of cerebral hemorrhage and Michael Collins is assassinated (August).

William T. Cosgrave becomes chairman of Provisional Government and third Dáil Éireann assembles as constituent assembly of the Irish Free State, although anti-treaty deputies refuse to attend or acknowledge its legitimacy (September).

Dáil Éireann resolution approves emergency powers for the military courts including execution (September).

Catholic bishops condemn violent opposition to the Provisional Government (October).

Andrew Bonar Law replaces Lloyd George as prime minister (October).

Dáil Éireann approves constitution of the Irish Free State (October).

Conservatives win decidedly in United Kingdom general election (November).

Executions begin under emergency powers resolution, including Erskine Childers (November).

Irish Free State constitution is approved by Westminster parliament. Anti-treaty IRA announces policy of assassination against members of the Dáil who voted for the emergency resolution and kill one member and wound another. The Irish Free State government gives its consent to the army retaliating by executing four republican prisoners, Rory O'Connor, Liam Mellows, Joseph McKelvey, and Richard Barrett (December).

Tim Healy becomes the first governor-general of the Irish Free State (December).

The parliament of Northern Ireland votes against inclusion in the Irish Free State (December).

1923

Anti-treaty IRA burns homes of several Irish Free State senators (January).

Several atrocities are committed against anti-treaty prisoners by the Irish Free State army in County Kerry (March).

Liam Lynch, commander of the anti-treaty IRA, is killed. Eamon de Valera, president of rival government to the Free State, calls on his followers to give up the armed struggle (April–May).

Bonar Law resigns as prime minister because of incurable cancer and is succeeded by Stanley Baldwin (May).

Northern Ireland legislation calls for establishment of nondenominational local authority schools (June).

Public Safety or Emergency Powers legislation allows Irish Free State government to continue detention without trial (August).

Unarmed police force, the Garda Síochána, is given legislative sanction by Dáil Éireann (August).

Land legislation (Hogan Act) gives land commission authority over all tenanted land (August).

Irish Free State general election returns 63 Cumann na nGaedheal (pro-treaty), 44 Sinn Féin (anti-treaty), 14 Labour, 15 Farmers Party, and 17 independents and others. Sinn Féiners refuse to recognize legitimacy of this fourth Dáil Éireann (August).

Irish Free State joins the League of Nations (September).

Hunger strike by hundreds of detainees in Irish Free State ends after two participants die (October–November).

William B. Yeats wins Nobel Prize in literature (November).

United Kingdom general election leaves conservatives with just a plurality and James Ramsay MacDonald will be able to form the first Labour Government (December).

1924

Demobilization of Irish Free State army and dissatisfaction with government moderation prompts a mutiny by some officers. Mutiny is called off and promise is made for an enquiry into the management of the army and the police commissioner, Eoin O'Duffy, is made commander of the military. Unauthorized and premature arrest of mutineers prompts government to dismiss the army chief of staff, adjutant general, and quartermaster general. In turn Minister for Defense Richard Mulcahy, resigns. The vice president of the Irish Free State, Kevin O'Higgins, is the main mover of the steps, which would see the exclusion from the army of both the more militant "old IRA" and the IRB (March).

Old age pensions are reduced (June).

Boundary commission to adjust boundary between Irish Free State and Northern Ireland is formed with Richard Feetham, South African jurist as British designee and chairman, and Eoin MacNeill, Irish Free State minister for education, as Irish Free State member. Since Northern Ireland refuses to nominate a member, legislation by both the Irish Free State and the United Kingdom is required to enable the British to nominate a member for Northern Ireland, who is a Northern Irish jurist, J. R. Fisher (June–October). Commission begins to work (November).

Conservatives return to power under Baldwin after another U.K. general election (October–November).

1925

Dáil Éireann votes to exclude by standing orders the consideration of private legislation to award divorce, to which Seanad member, W. B. Yeats, objects (February–April).

Legislation amalgamates the Dublin Metropolitan Police Force and the Garda Síochána (April).

A Shannon hydroelectric scheme is authorized by legislation (July).

Morning Post leaks impending boundary commission award, which includes transfer of persons and territory both ways. Outrage in the Irish Free State prompts conference, which results in agreement to maintain existing boundary and the ending of Irish Free State liability for its share in 1921 of the British public debt (November–December).

IRA convention asserts its autonomy from antitreaty Sinn Féin (November).

1926

De Valera resigns from Sinn Féin after its *ard-fheis* narrowly rejects his motion to consider entering the Irish Free State Dáil Éireann if the oath to the monarch is removed (March).

Census in Irish Free State: 2,9771,992; in Northern Ireland: 1,256,5621 (April).

De Valera forms the Fianna Fáil Party (May).

Imperial conference in London confirms the autonomy of the dominions, including the Irish Free State; Irish Free State vice president O'Higgins suggests a kingship of Ireland as a means to unite the island (October–November).

1927

Intoxicating liquor legislation reduces hours of opening of public houses and begins process of reducing the number of such establishments (May).

Irish Free State general election results: Cumann na nGaedheal (government) 47, Fianna Fáil 44, Labour 22, Farmers 11, National League (Redmonite) 8, Sinn Féin 5, and independents 16. Cumann na nGaedheal is able to form a government with a plurality as Fianna Fáil refuses to take the required oath and cannot take its seats (June).

Kevin O'Higgins, Irish Free State vice president, minister for external affairs, and minister for justice is assassinated (July).

Government proposes strong public safety legislation and legislation requiring candidates to the Dáil to be willing to take the oath (July).

De Valera leads his Fianna Fáil TD's in signing the oath and entering the Dáil (August).

A motion of no confidence in the government fails by reason of the Speaker's tie-breaking vote (August).

Irish Free State general election results: Cumann na nGaedheal 62, Fianna Fáil 57, Labour 13, Farmers 6, National League 2, independents 13 (September).

James MacNeill becomes second governor-general of the Irish Free State (December).

1928

Dáil and Seanad approve constitutional amendments removing initiative and referendum from constitution, changing method of electing members of the Seanad, and extending the suspensory period of the veto power of the Seanad (July).

1929

Proportional representation is ended for elections to Northern Ireland parliament (April).

General election in the United Kingdom results in Labour victory as Ramsay MacDonald becomes prime minister again (May–June).

Legislation establishes a board empowered to censor or ban publications in the Irish Free State (July).

1930

Northern Ireland education legislation allows former managers to have representation on local authority schools; allows public financing of 50 percent of construction and equipping costs of voluntary schools; and requires local authority schools to provide nondenominational Bible education for children of parents wanting such (June).

1931

Ramsay MacDonald forms a national coalition government (August).

A Fianna Fáil newspaper, *Irish Press,* appears (September).

Irish Free State declares the IRA, Saor Éire (radical socialist republican group), and several other groups illegal and Catholic bishops also condemn them (October).

U.K. general election gives massive victory to Conservatives, but Ramsay MacDonald remains prime minister (October).

Constitutional amendment establishes military tribunals to try sedition and illegal organization membership (October).

Statute of Westminster acknowledges that U.K. legislation cannot impede legislative power of dominions, which can change any U.K. legislation that effects them (December).

1932

Irish Free State general election results: Fianna Fáil 72, Cumann na nGaedheal 57, Labour 7, Farmers 3, and independents 14, and de Valera is elected president of the executive council, with Sean T. O'Kelly becoming vice president, Seán MacEntee minister for finance, Frank Aiken minister for defense, and Seán Lemass minister for justice (February–March).

Executive Council suspends the public safety amendment of the previous year (March).

The International Eucharistic Congress is held in Dublin (June).

Constitutional amendment to remove the oath is approved by the Dáil, but rejected by the Seanad (June), causing a delay of 270 days before the Dáil's approval will go into effect.

Irish Free State withholds payment of land annuities (June).

British impose 20 percent duty on two-thirds of Irish Free State exports to the United Kingdom (July).

Legislation is passed allowing Executive Council to vary duties on imports from certain countries (July).

Following controversy over discourtesies shown to the governor-general by some ministers, de Valera requests and obtains his replacement by Domhnall Ua Buachalla (July–November).

1933

General election returns absolute majority for Fianna Fáil: Fianna Fáil 77, Cumann na nGaedheal 48, Centre Party 11, Labour 8, others 9 (January).

The police commissioner, General Eoin O'Duffy, is dismissed (February).

Removal of the oath takes effect (May).

O'Duffy is elected leader of the Army Comrades Association (group of ex-army members founded in January 1932), which group had adopted a blueshirt as its uniform (gaining the nickname of "Blueshirts") (March) and which changes its name to National Guard (July).

The government prohibits a march by the National Guard commemorating Griffith, Collins, and O'Higgins and proclaims the group to be illegal (August).

A new party, Fine Gael, is formed uniting Cumann na nGaedheal, the Centre Party, and the National Guard and O'Duffy is selected as its president. O'Duffy forms Young Ireland Association out of the National Guard (September).

Constitutional amendments are passed removing from the governor-general the power to withholding assent to legislation and recommend appropriation, and abolishing the right of appeal to the Privy Council (November).

Northern Ireland general election: unionists 36, independent unionists 3, nationalists 9, Labour 2, republicans 1, and independents 1 (November).

When Young Ireland Association is outlawed, it is reformed as the League of Youth (December).

1934

Seanad rejects constitutional amendments abolishing the Seanad and university seats in the Dáil (June–July).

Legislation gives military pensions to members of the anti-treaty forces in the civil war (September).

O'Duffy resigns leadership of Fine Gael Party and of the Blueshirts (September).

Anglo-Irish cattle and coal agreement is reached (December).

1935

Richard More O'Ferrall, the son of a land agent, is killed in Edgeworthstown, County Longford, where a land dispute occurs (February).

Legislation requires court licenses for dance halls (February).

Legislation prohibits sale and importation of contraceptives (February).

Judicial committee of the Privy Council acknowledges right of Irish Free State to prohibit appeals to Privy Council (June).

Stanley Baldwin replaces Ramsay MacDonald as prime minister of the United Kingdom (June).

De Valera tells Assembly of League of Nations that the Irish Free State will invoke sanctions against Italy because of invasion of Ethiopia (September).

U.K. general election is a massive Conservative victory (November).

1936

George V dies and is succeeded by his son, Edward VIII (January).

IRA assassinates retired admiral Henry Somerville in Cork because he wrote reference for Irish youths seeking to join the British navy (March).

Constitutional amendments ending university representation in the Dáil and abolishing the Seanad go into effect nine months after original rejection by the Seanad (April–May).

Irish Free State outlaws the IRA (June).

O'Duffy leads a group of followers to Spain as volunteers on the side of the Spanish Nationalists, while Frank Ryan of the IRA leads others to support the Spanish Republicans (November–December).

Edward VIII abdicates and is succeeded by his brother, George VI (December).

Dáil Éireann at an emergency meeting enacts a constitutional amendment removing all reference to the governor-general from the constitution and an external relations act acknowledging only a diplomatic representational role for the Crown for Ireland (December).

1937

Neville Chamberlain replaces Baldwin as prime minister (May).

Irish Free State general election results: Fianna Fáil 69, Fine Gael 48, Labour 13, others 8; referendum approves new constitution for Ireland by vote of 685,105 to 526,943 (July).

New constitution comes into effect (December).

1938

Northern Ireland general election results: unionists 39, independent unionists 3, nationalists 8, independent labour 1 (February).

Anglo-Irish agreement settles land annuities and tariff issue and gives naval ports at Berehaven, Cobh, and Lough Swilly to the government of Ireland (April).

Irish general election: Fianna Fáil 77, Fine Gael 45, Labour 9, others 7 (June).

Douglas Hyde becomes the first president of Ireland (June).

De Valera becomes president of the Assembly of the League of Nations for the session (September).

1939

IRA issues ultimatum for the British to withdraw from Northern Ireland and commences bombing campaign in Britain (January).

Dáil passes Offences against the State legislation allowing military tribunals and internment without trial and a treason act, which allows death penalty (May–June).

IRA bomb in Coventry kills five and wounds scores (August).

Dáil passes legislation declaring a national emergency, which allows constitutional rules for wartime to apply even when Ireland is not a participant in the war declared by Britain and France on Germany (September).

1940

IRA prisoners in Ireland go on hunger strike in which two die before strike ends (February–April).

Winston Churchill replaces Chamberlain as prime minister (May).

Frank Ryan, left-wing republican, and Seán Russell, IRA chief of staff, approach Ireland in a German submarine, but Russell dies, and Ryan returns in sub to Germany (August).

De Valera is unwilling to lease "treaty ports" to Britain during war (November).

Lord Craigavon dies and is succeeded as prime minister of Northern Ireland by J. M. Andrews (November).

John Charles McQuade becomes Catholic archbishop of Dublin (December).

1941

German bombs mistakenly dropped in places in Ireland (January).

British restrict shipping to Irish ports (January).

German air raids on Belfast kill close to 1,000 and wound hundreds. Fire brigades from Dublin and other towns in Ireland come to aid (April–May).

German bombing in Dublin kills 34 and injures 90 (May).

German government apologizes for bombing and promises compensation (June).

1942

United States troops arrive in Northern Ireland, where an American naval base is established in Derry (January–February).

Irish government forbids use of radio transmitter by German embassy (February).

James Dillon, Fine Gael deputy leader, resigns leadership following criticism of his advocacy of support for Americans in war (February).

IRA attacks on RUC in Tyrone and Belfast (April).

1943

Basil Brooke succeeds J. M. Andrews as prime minister of Northern Ireland (April).

Irish general election results: Fianna Fáil 67, Fine Gael 32, Labour 17, Clann na Talmhan 10, Farmers 5, independents 7 (June).

1944

Split in Irish Labour Party occurs as five TD's, associated with the Irish Transport and General Workers' Union, form a National Labour Party (January).

Richard Mulcahy is selected to replace the resigning Fine Gael leader, William T. Cosgrave (January).

De Valera refuses request made by U.S. minister David Gray to have German and Japanese missions in Ireland recalled (February).

Legislation establishes children's allowances in Ireland (February).

Irish general election results: Fianna Fáil 76, Fine Gael 30, Clann na Talmhan 11, Labour 8, National Labour 4, Farmers 2, others 7 (May).

A public corporation, Coras Iompar Eireann, is established to take over the Great Southern Railways Co. and the Dublin United Transport Co. (December).

1945

The Irish Transport and General Workers' Union and other unions, previously members of the Irish Trade Union Congress, and others form a Congress of Irish Unions (April).

De Valera calls on German representative in Dublin to express official condolences on death of Hitler (May).

Churchill, in victory speech upon end of war in Europe, praises role of Northern Ireland and condemns the Irish approach to the war. De Valera responds three days later (May).

Northern Ireland general election results: unionists 33, independent unionists 2, nationalists 10, Labour 2, independent labour 1, Commonwealth labour 1, socialist republicans 1, independents 2 (June).

Sean T. O'Kelly elected president of Ireland, defeating Seán McEoin (Fine Gael) and Patrick MacCartan (Independent) (June).

Labour Party wins British general election and Clement Attlee succeeds Churchill as prime minister (July).

1946

Northern Ireland welfare benefits are made similar to those in Britain (February).

Teachers strike in Dublin (March–October).

Census in Ireland: population 2,955,107 (May).

Bord na Mona is established as public company to develop peat industry (June).

A radical republican party, Clann na Poblachta, is formed and Seán MacBride is selected as its leader (July).

Irish application for United Nations membership is rejected by the Soviet Union (August).

1947

Secondary education is made available for all in Northern Ireland and school leaving age is raised to 15 and construction and maintenance grants for voluntary schools (primarily Catholic) is increased from 50 to 65 percent of costs (March).

Shannon Airport becomes a duty-free area (April).

Clann na Poblachta wins two of three Dublin by-elections (October).

1948

Irish general election results: Fianna Fáil 68, Fine Gael 31, Labour 14, National Labour 5, Clann na Poblachta 10, Clann na Talmhan 7, others 12, and a coalition government is formed headed by John A. Costello of Fine Gael (February).

De Valera tours United States, Australia, New Zealand, and India (March–June).

Ireland becomes a member of the newly formed Organization for European Economic Development (April).

Costello, visiting Canada, announces intention to proclaim Ireland a republic (September).

Legislation repeals External Relations Act of 1936 and arranges for the proclamation of republican status for Ireland (December).

1949

All political parties agree to a church gate collection for an anti-partition fund (January).

Northern Irish general election results: unionists 37, independent unionists 2, anti-partition league 9, independent labour 1, socialist republicans 1, independents 2 (February).

Seán MacBride, minister for external affairs, states that British occupation of Northern Ireland makes Irish participation in Atlantic alliance impossible (February).

Ireland becomes a republic and leaves the Commonwealth (April).

British legislation declares that Northern Ireland will not cease being part of the United Kingdom without consent of its parliament and it also declares that Ireland, although a republic outside the Commonwealth, is not a foreign country nor are its citizens aliens (June).

1950

United Kingdom general elections return a narrow Labour Party victory (February).

Labour and National Labour Parties reunite under William Norton (June).

Irish Supreme Court upholds pre-marriage agreements regarding religious education of children (August).

1951

Catholic hierarchy condemn the "Mother and Child" scheme in proposed national health legislation and Dr. Noel Browne, the minister for health, resigns his position and his membership in Clann na Poblachta (April).

Census in Ireland: 2,960,593; census in Northern Ireland: 1,370,921 (April).

Irish general election: Fianna Fáil 69, Fine Gael 40, Labour 16, Clann na Talmhan 6, Clann na Poblachta 2, others 14 (May).

De Valera becomes Taoiseach in a Fianna Fáil government (June).

United Kingdom general election results in Conservative victory and Churchill becomes prime minister (October).

1952

George VI dies and is succeeded by his daughter Elizabeth II (February).

Social insurance system is established (June).

Sean T. O'Kelly begins his second term as president. His selection is unopposed (June).

Adoption legislation requires both adopters to be of the same religion as the child and its parents, and, if mother is unmarried, of her religion (December).

1953

Irish representatives are absent from garden party at British embassy on occasion of queen's coronation and anti-partitionists picket the same (June).

Northern Ireland general election: unionists 38, independent unionists 1, anti-partition league 7, independent nationalists 2, other labour and independents 4 (October).

Mother and child benefits are extended to all persons insured under the existing social insurance system (October).

1954

Flags and Emblems Act by Northern Ireland parliament allows police removal of flags other than Union Jack to preserve peace (April).

Irish general election: Fianna Fáil 65, Fine Gael 50, Labour 19, Clann na Talmhan 5, Clann na Poblachta 3, independents 5 (May).

John A. Costello of Fine Gael becomes Taoiseach in a second coalition government (June).

IRA attacks on military barracks in Armagh and Tyrone (June and October).

1955

Anthony Eden becomes U.K. prime minister (April).

Conservatives win U.K. general election, but two convicted IRA members are elected from Northern Ireland along with 10 unionists (May).

Ireland is admitted to the United Nations (December).

1956

Census in Ireland: 2,898,264 (almost 3% decline) (April).

IRA begins a campaign with number of attacks in Northern Ireland (December).

1957

Funeral of Sean South, IRA member killed in raid on police barracks in Fermanagh, Northern Ireland, takes place in Limerick with massive public attendance (January).

Harold Macmillan becomes U.K. prime minister (January).

Irish general election: Fianna Fáil 78, Fine Gael 40, Labour 12, Clann na Talmhan 3, Clann na Poblachta 1, others and independents 13; de Valera becomes Taoiseach (March).

Irish government applies war emergency powers against the IRA (July).

Gaeltarra Eireann established to run small enterprises in Gaeltacht areas (December).

1958

Northern Ireland general election: unionists 37, nationalists 7, independent nationalists 1, Northern Irish Labour Party 4, independent labour 1, republican labour 1, independents 1 (March).

Aer Lingus begins to fly to the United States (April).

Irish UN delegation votes to allow debate on issue of admission of Peoples' Republic of China to membership (September).

A study *Economic Development* by T. K. Whittaker, secretary of the department of finance, appears (December).

1959

Irish Trade Union Congress and the Congress of Irish Unions combine as the Irish Congress of Trade Unions (February).

De Valera is elected president of Ireland defeating Seán McEoin, but referendum on the same day rejects Fianna Fáil proposal to end proportional representation; Seán Lemass is selected as Taoiseach (June).

Conservatives win U.K. general election, while unionists win all 12 seats from Northern Ireland (October).

Legislation ends required Sunday closing of rural public houses (October).

Television service begins in Northern Ireland (October).

James Dillon replaces Richard Mulcahy as leader of Fine Gael (October).

1960

Brendan Corish succeeds William Norton as head of Labour Party (March).

Transfer of University College Dublin to Bellfield is approved (March).

A Radio Éireann authority is established to direct radio and television service (April).

Irish military goes to Congo to serve United Nations mission (July).

Irish ambassador, Frederick H. Boland, is elected president of the United Nations General Assembly (July).

Ten Irish soldiers are killed in Congo ambush (November).

1961

Census in Ireland: 2,818,341 ($2^1/_4$% decline); census in Northern Ireland: 1,425,042 (3.9% increase) (April).

Ireland applies to join European Economic Community (EEC) (August).

Irish general election: Fianna Fáil 70, Fine Gael 47, Labour 16, Clann na Talmhan 2, National Progressive Democratic Party 2, Clann na Poblachta 1, others 6; Lemass remains as Taoiseach (October).

Conor Cruise O'Brien resigns United Nations position in Congo (December).

Telecasts by Radio Telefís Éireann begin (December).

1962

IRA calls off its border campaign (January).

Northern Ireland general election: Unionists 34, Nationalists 9, Northern Irish Labour Party 4, independent labour 1, republican labour, Irish labour 1, independents 2 (May).

Gay Byrne's program, *The Late, Late Show,* first appears on RTE (July).

First motorway in Northern Ireland, the M1, opens from Belfast to Lisburn (July).

1963

Captain Terence O'Neill succeeds Viscount Brookeborough as prime minister of Northern Ireland (March).

John F. Kennedy, president of the United States, visits Ireland (June).

Sir Alex Douglas-Home renounces his peerage and become prime minister succeeding Harold Macmillan (October).

1964

Fine Gael approves Declan Costello's "Just Society" program (May).

Labour Party wins United Kingdom general election and Harold Wilson become prime minister; Unionists gain all 12 parliamentary seats from Northern Ireland (October).

1965

Seán Lemass and Terence O'Neill meet in Belfast (January) and in Dublin (February).

Nationalist Party agrees to be the official opposition in the Northern Irish parliament (February).

Irish general election: Fianna Fáil 72, Fine Gael 47, Labour 22, Clann na Poblachta 1, others 2; Lemass remains as Taoiseach (April).

Liam Cosgrave succeeds James Dillon as leader of Fine Gael (April).

New Roman Catholic cathedral consecrated in Galway (August).

Northern Ireland general election: Unionists 36, Nationalists 9, National Democratic Party 1, Northern Irish Labour Party 2, republican labour 2, liberals 1, independents 1 (November).

Anglo-Irish free trade agreement signed (December).

Legislation guarantees that widows receive one-third of estate and one-half where there are no children (December).

1966

Labour wins United Kingdom general election; Harold Wilson remains prime minister; Unionists win 11 seats from Northern Ireland and republican labour wins one (March).

Census in Ireland: 2,884,002 ($2 \, ^1/_3$% increase) (April).

Bank strike in Ireland runs from May through August.

De Valera reelected president over Thomas O'Higgins of Fine Gael (June).

Rev. Ian Paisley convicted of disturbance of peace and is imprisoned when refusing to pay fine or post bond (July).

Irish minister for education Donough O'Malley proposes free post-primary education (September).

Northern Ireland census: 1,484,775, 4.2 percent increase (October).

Lemass retires as Taoiseach and is succeeded by Jack Lynch (November).

1967

Northern Irish Civil Rights Association is formed (January).

Ireland and the United Kingdom reapply for EEC membership (May).

Legislation removes from censorship books banned for more than 12 years (August).

Taoiseach Jack Lynch and Northern Ireland prime minister Terrence O'Neill meet in Belfast (December).

1968

Lynch and O'Neill meet in Dublin (January).

Squatters protest discriminatory allocation of housing by local authority in Tyrone (June).

Civil rights marchers defy forceful police restriction on processions in Derry (October).

Referendum in Ireland to end proportional representation is defeated (October).

Nationalists withdraw from being official opposition in Northern Ireland parliament (October).

Terrence O'Neill announces Northern Ireland reform program to end extra vote for businesses in local government elections, to allocate public housing fairly, to replace Derry Council with a commission, to establish an ombudsman to hear grievances against government, and to review the Special Powers Act (November).

1969

Militants, with auxiliary police complicity, attack student protest group, People's Democracy, marching from Belfast to Derry, at Burntollet Bridge (January).

Northern Ireland general election: Unionists 36 (24 pro-O'Neill, 12 anti-O'Neill), independent unionists 3, nationalists 6, Northern Irish Labour Party 2, Republican Labour 2, independents 3 (February).

Bernadette Devlin is returned to House of Commons as Unity candidate of anti-Unionists in Mid-Ulster by-election (April).

O'Neill resigns as Northern Ireland prime minister and is succeeded by James Chichester-Clark (April).

Irish general election: Fianna Fáil 75, Fine Gael 50, Labour 18, independent 1 (June).

Disturbances in Belfast and in Derry (especially at August 12 Apprentice Boys parade) leads to sectors of cities coming under siege, burning of houses, and many fleeing, with ultimate British military assumption of peacekeeping role (August).

Assorted commissions issue reports on disturbances in Northern Ireland (Cameron) and on the police (Hunt) (September–October).

Samuel Beckett awarded Nobel Prize in literature (October).

Legislation lowers Northern Ireland franchise age requirement to 18 and removes restrictions on franchise in local government elections (November).

Ulster Defence Regiment is established as an auxiliary security force under army control (December).

1970

Split occurs in Sinn Féin (and the IRA) between the "Provisionals," traditionally nationalist and supportive of continuance of policy of parliamentary abstention, and the "Officials," a more left-wing group concerned with socioeconomic issues (January).

Bank officials go on strike in Ireland (March–November).

Alliance Party, a moderate group of liberal Catholics and Protestants, is formed in Northern Ireland (April).

"B" Specials, controversial Northern Ireland police auxiliary force, is disbanded (April).

Charles Haughey, Neil Blaney, and Kevin Boland leave Irish cabinet in controversy over supplying arms to the Provisional IRA (May).

United Kingdom general election results in Conservative victory; results in Northern Ireland: Unionist 8, Protestant unionist 1, republican labour 1, unity 2. Edward Heath become prime minister (June).

Catholic bishops end prohibition on Catholic attendance at Trinity College (June).

Social Democratic and Labour Party formed in Northern Ireland; leaders include Gerry Fitt, Ivan Cooper, Austin Currie, Paddy Devlin, John Hume, and Paddy O'Hanlon (August).

1971

Rioting and clashes with police in both Protestant and Catholic sections of Belfast; first British soldier is killed by the Provisional IRA (January–February).

Irish and British currencies go decimal (February).

Chichester-Clark resigns as Northern Ireland prime minister and is succeeded by Brian Faulkner (March).

Legislation reorganized Northern Ireland local government into 26 districts (March).

Census in Ireland: 2,978,248 (3.3% increase);census in Northern Ireland: 1,536,065 (3.45% increase) (April).

SDLP withdraws from Northern Ireland parliament in protest at lack of inquiry into the army's shooting of two men in Derry (July).

Internment without trial reintroduced in Northern Ireland as hundreds are apprehended and rioting ensues (August).

Jack Lynch and Heath meet, and later both meet with Faulkner (September).

1972

Ireland and the United Kingdom join the European Economic Community (January).

"Bloody Sunday," paratroopers kill 13 civilians at civil rights march in Derry; subsequent protests include the burning of the British embassy in Dublin (January–February).

British government suspends Northern Ireland parliament and imposes direct rule on the province from Westminster and William Whitelaw becomes secretary of state for Northern Ireland (March).

Widgery inquiry absolves military from "Bloody Sunday" shootings (April).

Referendum in Ireland endorses entry into EEC nearly five to one (May).

Irish government invokes 1939 Offences against the State legislation to allow special juryless criminal courts with three judges (May).

Whitelaw announces special category for certain interned prisoners in response to hunger strike (June).

Provisional IRA announces cease-fire and talks take place between their leaders and Whitelaw in London (June).

Provisional IRA calls off cease-fire and two weeks later, on "Bloody Friday," 22 explosions of bombs planted by the IRA in Belfast kill 11 and injure scores (July).

Provisional IRA leader Sean MacStiofain is sentenced to six months imprisonment for membership in IRA by Irish special court (November).

Bombs in Dublin kill two and injure over 100, which is followed by passage of amendment to the Offences against the State Act allowing a garda's statement that accused is a member of an unlawful organization to suffice as evidence and allowing certain meetings to be declared unlawful if presumed to be interfering with justice (December).

Diplock Commission recommends, in cases dealing with terrorist offenses, putting onus of proof on defense in certain matters, allowing soldiers to arrest and detain for limited times, and having juryless trials (December).

1973

Ruairi O'Bradaigh, president of Provisional Sinn Féin, is sentenced to six months' imprisonment for IRA membership, and Sean MacStiofain, imprisoned IRA commander, ends his 58 day hunger strike (January).

Irish general election: Fianna Fáil 69, Fine Gael 54, Labour 19, independents 2 (February), enabling Liam Cosgrave (Fine Gael) to form first coalition government since 1957 with Garret FitzGerald as minister for foreign affairs, Richie Ryan as minister for finance (both Fine Gael), Brendan Corish as Tánaiste, and Conor Cruise O'Brien as minister for posts and telegraphs (both Labour) (March).

The *Claudia,* a vessel carrying weapons and several IRA members, is seized off Waterford coast (March).

Erskine Childers (Fianna Fáil) wins Irish presidential election defeating Thomas F. O'Higgins (Fine Gael) (May).

Results of elections to new Northern Ireland district councils: Unionists 201, SDLP 76, loyalists (Democratic Unionist Party and Vanguard Unionists) 74, Alliance 59 (May).

Election results for new Northern Ireland Assembly: official Unionists 23, other unionists 10, SDLP 19, Alliance 8, DUP 8, Vanguard Unionist 7, other loyalists 2, Northern Ireland Labour Party 1 (June).

Northern Ireland Emergency Provisions Act implements the Diplock recommendations and allows single judge and juryless trials for designated terrorist offenses (July).

Official Unionists, Alliance, and SDLP parties in Northern Ireland Assembly agree to form a "power-sharing" coalition executive with Brian Faulkner as leader (November).

Sunningdale Conference of British and Irish governments and Northern Ireland executive agree that there will be no change of status for Northern Ireland without consent of majority of province, that a Council of Ireland will be set up with representatives of Northern Ireland and Ireland with both a Council of Ministers and a consultative Assembly, and that prisoners who have committed crimes of violence in Ireland should be tried where they are located (December).

Irish Supreme Court rules that prohibition of importation of contraceptives is unconstitutional (December).

1974

United Kingdom general elections results in Labour victory; results in Northern Ireland: Unionists 7, DUP 1, Vanguard Unionists 3, SDLP 1 (February); Harold Wilson becomes prime minister again and Merlyn Rees becomes secretary of state for Northern Ireland (March).

Ulster Workers Council declares general strike in Ulster against Sunningdale Agreement, a state of emergency is proclaimed, Unionist members resign from the executive, and the assembly is prorogued and direct rule from Westminster is restored (May).

Car bomb explosions in Dublin and Monaghan kill 31 and injure over 100 (May).

The IRA kidnap the earl and countess Donoughmore from their Tipperary home for five days (June).

Cosgrave votes against his own government's bill to allow sale of contraceptives, which is defeated (July).

Nineteen IRA prisoners escape from Portlaoise prison (August).

Bomb in public houses in Guildford kill five and injure 65 (October).

Bomb in public houses in Birmingham kill 21 and injure 182 (November).

United Kingdom general election results in Labour victory; Northern Ireland results: Unionists 6, DUP 1, Vanguard unionists 3, SDLP 1, and independent 1 (Conservative Party figure Enoch Powell is one of the Unionist victors) (October).

Irish language is removed as a requirement for entry to or promotion in Irish civil service (November).

Erskine Childers, Irish president, dies (November).

United Kingdom Prevention of Terrorism Act allows deportation from and prohibition of entry into Great Britain of suspected terrorists (November).

Cearbhall O'Dalaigh is selected as president of Ireland without opposition (December).

1975

Ireland assumes presidency of the EEC for six months (January).

Feuding occurs within loyalist and republican groups in Belfast (March and April).

Northern Ireland convention elected; results: Unionists 19, Vanguard Unionists 14, DUP 12, independent loyalists 1, SDLP 17, Alliance 8, Unionist Party of Northern Ireland 5, Northern Irish Labour Party 1, independent 1 (May).

Dutch businessman Tiede Herrema kidnapped by IRA, but released a month later unharmed after a siege (October–November).

Oliver Plunkett is canonized by Pope Paul VI (October).

Northern Ireland convention approves unionist rejection of power sharing (November).

Internment without trial ends in Northern Ireland (December).

Irish Supreme Court rules legislation exempting women from jury service unconstitutional (December).

1976

Five Catholics and 10 Protestants are killed in Armagh within two days (January).

Frank Stagg dies in Wakefield prison after a 60-day hunger strike and he is buried in Ballina, County Mayo (February).

Northern Ireland convention dissolves (March).

James Callaghan succeeds Wilson as prime minister of the United Kingdom (April).

Bank officials strike in Ireland (June–September).

Legislation in Ireland removes requirement that adoptive parents be of same religion as natural parents (July).

Christopher Ewart-Biggs, U.K. ambassador to Ireland, is killed by land mine near his residence (July).

Provisional IRA supporters attack home of SDLP leader Gerry Fitt (August).

Death of three children hit by car fleeing army prompts formation of "Peace People" by Mairead Corrigan and Betty Williams, which conducts massive protests against violence (August).

European Commission of Human Rights finds the United Kingdom guilty of torture of republican prisoners (September).

Emergency Powers legislation, allowing detention for up to seven days, is accepted as constitutional by the Irish Supreme Court, to which it had been referred by President O'Dalaigh prior to his signing. His invoking of the privilege of such referral prompts the minister for defense, Patrick Donegan (Fine Gael), to label the president "a thundering disgrace," in response to which remark the President resigns to protect the dignity of the office (October).

Patrick Hillery is selected unopposed to succeed O'-Dalaigh as president (November).

Founders of the Peace People, Betty Williams and Mairead Corrigan, win the Nobel Peace Prize (November).

1977

Brian Faulkner dies in riding accident (March).

Taoiseach Liam Cosgrave's attack on a journalist as a "blow-in" at Fine Gael conference backfires politically (May).

Irish general election: Fianna Fáil 84, Fine Gael, 43, Labour 17, others 4. Jack Lynch returns as Taoiseach (June).

1978

Sixteen killed in Le Mon Hotel bomb in Belfast (February).

Radio Telefís Éireann establishes a second television station (November).

1979

Oil tanker explosion at Whiddy Island, Cork, kills 50 (January).

Ireland joins the European Monetary System thereby ending the parity between the Irish punt and sterling (March).

Census in Ireland: 3,368,405 (April).

British general election results in Northern Ireland: Unionists 5, Democratic Unionists 3, SDLP 1, other unionists 2, other nationalist 1. Conservatives win and Margaret Thatcher becomes prime minister (June).

Elections to European Parliament: Ireland: Fianna Fáil 5, Fine Gael 4, Labour 4, others 2; Northern Ireland: Ulster Unionists 1, DUP 1, SDLP 1.

Referendum passes measures protecting adoption system in Ireland and altering university representation in the Seanad (July).

Earl Mountbatten and three others are killed in boat explosion at Mullaghmore, County Sligo, and 18 soldiers are killed in an IRA ambush at Warrenpoint, County Down (August).

Pope John Paul II visits Ireland (September).

John Hume replaces Gerry Fitt as leader of the SDLP (November).

Jack Lynch steps down as Taoiseach and Fianna Fáil leader. His candidate for successor, George Colley, loses to Charles Haughey (December).

1980

Two Irish soldiers serving in UN peacekeeping mission in Lebanon are killed (March).

Charles Haughey and Margaret Thatcher meet in London (May).

Hunger strike for special political status by seven republican prisoners in the Maze near Belfast begins (October).

Haughey and Thatcher meet at Dublin Castle (December).

Hunger strike is called off (December).

1981

Fire in Stardust Ballroom in Artane, Dublin, kills 48 (February).

Another hunger strike for political status for prisoners begins, this time there are intervals between each individual commencement of strike. Bobby Sands is the first (March).

Hunger striker Sands is elected to House of Commons in a Fermanagh–South Tyrone by-election (April).

Census in Ireland: 3,443,405; census in Northern Ireland: 1,4081,959 (April).

Sands dies on hunger strike, disorders ensue with several deaths (May).

General election in Ireland: Fianna Fáil 78, Fine Gael 65, Labour 15, Workers' Party 1, others (including two hunger strikers) 7. Fine Gael and Labour form coalition government with Garret FitzGerald as Taoiseach (June).

Nine other hunger strikers die, while 64 are killed in disturbances following the deaths (May–August).

Hunger strike is called off with some veiled concessions (September).

FitzGerald and Thatcher meet in London and establish an Anglo-Irish Intergovernmental Council (November).

1982

Charles Haughey fails to have critic T.D., Charles McCreevy, expelled from Fianna Fáil Party (January).

Independents vote against budget proposed by Minister for Finance John Bruton. Government loses and FitzGerald asks for a dissolution of the Oireachtas and a general election (January).

Haughey argues against dissolution as associate Brian Lenihan asks the president not to grant such (January).

Irish general election results: Fianna Fáil 81, Fine Gael 63, Labour 15, Workers' Party 3, others 4. Fianna Fáil under Haughey forms government (February).

Desmond O'Malley fails in attempt to challenge Haughey's leadership of the Fianna Fáil Party (March).

Irish criticism of British role in Falklands War and neutrality on European and UN resolutions supportive of the British cause diplomatic difficulties (April–May).

In Dublin by-election to fill seat of Richard Burke, Fine Gael member appointed by Haughey as a European commissioner, Fine Gael candidate wins and Haughey's electoral agent is arrested for personation, allegedly having voted at two places (May).

IRA attack on the Household Cavalry in London results in the death of eight (July).

Attorney general Patrick Connolly resigns after his apartment mate was arrested for murder. Haughey calls the incident "grotesque, unprecedented, bizarre, unbelievable," which resulted in the derisive acronym GUBU being used by anti-Haughey journalists (August).

Election to Northern Ireland Assembly: Unionists 26, SDLP 14, Alliance 10, Sinn Féin 5. It is the beginning of a new campaign by Sinn Féin to combine electoral politics with support for the armed campaign of the IRA (October).

Support by independents and by the Workers' Party deputies is withdrawn from Haughey, who loses a no confidence vote (November).

Irish general election results: Fianna Fáil 75, Fine Gael 70, Labour 16, Workers' Party 2, others 3. Fine Gael and Labour form a coalition government with Garret FitzGerald as Taoiseach (November).

Irish National Liberation Army bomb kills 17 in a Derry bar (December).

1983

New Ireland Forum holds first meeting at Dublin Castle (May).

Northern Ireland results in British general election: Unionist 11, Democratic Unionists 3, SDLP 1, Sinn Féin 1, other 1 (Gerry Adams is the first modern Sinn Féiner elected to Westminster); Conservatives returned to power under Margaret Thatcher (June).

Referendum approves amendment to Irish constitution that prohibits abortion by 66.9 percent majority (September).

Thirty-nine IRA inmates break out of Long Kesh Prison in Northern Ireland, but 20 are recaptured (September).

1984

New Ireland Forum publishes its report (May).

U.S. president Ronald Reagan visits Ireland (June).

Results of elections to the European Parliament: in Ireland, Fianna Fáil 8, Fine Gael 6, others 1; in Northern Ireland: SDLP 1, Unionists 1, DUP 1 (June).

IRA bombing of hotel in Brighton, England, during Conservative Party conference kills five. Cabinet members and prime minister narrowly escape injury (October).

1985

Nine killed in IRA mortar attack on Newry, County Down, RUC station (February).

Terrorist bomb causes crash of Air India jet off Kerry-Cork coast, 329 are killed (June).

Commercial flights from Knock Airport in County Mayo commence (October).

Anglo-Irish Agreement signed at Hillsborough Castle (November).

Anglo-Irish Intergovernmental Conference established by agreement has first meeting (December).

Progressive Democrats are formed as a political party in Ireland (December).

1986

Results of parliamentary by-elections in Northern Ireland necessitated by resignations of unionist MP's in protest at Anglo-Irish Agreement: Unionists 10, DUP 3, SDLP 1, others 1 (January).

Ireland signs European Convention on Suppression of Terrorism (February).

Census in Ireland: 3,540,643 (April).

Proposed constitutional amendment allowing divorce is rejected by 63.5 percent in referendum (June).

1987

Revelation appears that large number of Irish hemophiliacs contacted HIV through transfusions of contaminated blood (January).

Irish general election results: Fianna Fáil 81, Fine Gael 51, Progressive Democrats 14, Labour 12, Workers' Party 4, others 4. Sinn Féin announces new policy of willingness to take seats in Dáil Éireann, although none are elected. Fianna Fáil forms government under Charles Haughey (February).

Alan Dukes replaces Garret FitzGerald as leader of Fine Gael (March).

Haughey government introduces an austerity budget to counter inflation and public indebtedness (March).

Irish government begins a national lottery (March).

Eight members of the IRA and one passer-by are killed in a British army ambush at Loughall, County Armagh (May).

The Single European Act is approved by 69.9 percent of the voters in a referendum (May).

Northern Ireland results of British general election: Unionists 9, DUP 3, SDLP 3, Sinn Féin 1, other unionist 1 (June).

An IRA bomb at Memorial Day service in Enniskillen, County Fermanagh, kills 11 (November).

John McMichael, leader of the Ulster Defence Association, a loyalist group, is assassinated (December).

Legislation is passed allowing extradition in accord with the European Convention on the suppression of terrorism. Attorney general retains right to determine extradition of IRA suspects to the United Kingdom (December).

1988

Irish Supreme Court rules that political motivation for alleged crime is insufficient grounds to refuse to extradite IRA members to Northern Ireland (January).

British government decides not to prosecute RUC members for alleged complicity in earlier shoot-to-kill incidents (January).

John Hume, SDLP leader, and Gerry Adams, Sinn Féin leader, meet (January).

Three IRA members are killed by the SAS in Gibraltar. Three mourners are killed at their funeral in Belfast. Two British soldiers are killed at subsequent funeral procession (March).

Eight British soldiers killed by IRA bomb in Ballygawley, County Tyrone (August).

British introduce broadcasting ban of supporters of paramilitary organizations (October).

Attorney General John Murray refuses to extradite IRA member, who was already extradited from Belgium to Ireland, to Northern Ireland because of reservations about prospects of a fair trial (December).

1989

Belfast solicitor Patrick Finucane, a Catholic, is murdered. Loyalists who colluded with the security forces are suspected (February).

Church of Ireland General Synod approves ordination of women (May).

Irish general election results: Fianna Fáil 77, Fine Gael 55, Progressive Democrats 6, Labour 15, Workers' Party 7, others 6 (June).

Election to European Parliament: in Ireland, Fianna Fáil 6, Fine Gael 4, Labour 1, Workers' Party 1, Progressive Democrats 1, others 2; in Northern Ireland: Unionists 1, SDLP 1, DUP 1 (June).

Fianna Fáil and Progressive Democrats coalition forms a government with Charles Haughey as Taoiseach (July).

IRA bomb kills 10 Royal Marines in Deal, Kent (September).

The "Guildford Four," convicted of a 1975 terrorist bombing, have their sentences quashed and are released (October).

1990

Meetings of Northern Ireland parties take place, but only while Anglo-Irish Conference is not meeting (January).

Irish Supreme Court rejects Ulster Unionist test suit asserting that the 1985 Anglo-Irish Agreement was contrary to the Irish constitution (March).

Irish Supreme Court rules against extradition to Northern Ireland of escaped IRA prisoner, who feared retaliation by prison officers (March).

Stevens inquiry reports collusion between the Ulster Defence Regiment and loyalist paramilitaries (May).

Peter Brooke, secretary of state for Northern Ireland, announces a three-tier series of talks; Northern Ireland parties, British and Irish governments, and Northern Ireland parties and Irish government (June).

Brian Lenihan, Fianna Fáil candidate for the Irish presidency, is dismissed as Tánaiste after it appeared he inappropriately sought to influence the president to not dissolve the Dáil in 1982 (October).

Mary Robinson, candidate of the Labour Party, is elected president of Ireland on second count. Lenihan, Fianna Fáil, had 44 percent, Austin Currie, Fine Gael, had 17 percent, and Robinson had 39 percent on first count (November).

Alan Dukes resigns as leader of Fine Gael and is replaced by John Bruton (November).

John Major replaces Margaret Thatcher as prime minister and leader of the Conservative Party (November).

1991

IRA mortar bombs hits 10 Downing Street in London (February).

"Birmingham Six" have the sentences that convicted them of the 1974 bombing quashed and they are released from prison (March).

Census: Ireland 3,523,401; Northern Ireland 1,577,836 (April).

First of three-tier talks called by Peter Brooke on Northern Ireland, chaired by Sir Ninian Stephens, begin (April).

Three talks end (July).

Official inquiry into public corruption in state assistance to beef industry begins (October).

Charles Haughey survives effort by Sean Power, Pádraig Flynn, and Albert Reynolds to oust him as leader of Fianna Fáil (November).

1992

Sean Doherty, former minister for justice, alleges that Charles Haughey as Taoiseach knew of taping of journalists' phone conversations in 1982 (January).

IRA bomb kills eight workers in van at Teebane, County Tyrone (January).

Progressive Democrats require that Haughey resign if they are to continue in coalition. He does and Albert Reynolds succeeds him as Taoiseach. All of Haughey cabinet is replaced except for the two who are Progressive Democrats (February).

President Mary Robinson visits Secretary of State for Northern Ireland Peter Brooke, in Belfast (February).

Split occurs within Workers' Party after revelations that funds had been received from the Soviet Union and a new party, Democratic Left, is formed (February).

Irish Supreme Court overturns injunction acquired by attorney general to prevent an unnamed 14-year-old ("x") traveling to England to have an abortion (February).

Five Catholics killed outside bookmaker's on Ormeau Road, Belfast (February).

British general election results in Northern Ireland: Unionists 9, SDLP 4, DUP 3, other unionist 1 (Gerry Adams, Sinn Féin, loses seat for West Belfast) (April).

Eamon Casey, bishop of Galway, resigns when it is revealed he had fathered a son years earlier when bishop of Kerry and had used church funds to support the child (May).

Referendum in Ireland approves Maastricht Treaty to establish European Union (June).

Progressive Democratic leader Desmond O'Malley demands public inquiry into corruption in state support for beef industry (June).

Taoiseach Reynolds accuses Desmond O'Malley of dishonesty in his charges regarding beef industry corruption. O'Malley demands withdrawal of accusation (October).

Progressive Democrats withdraw from coalition when Reynolds refuses to withdraw statement and government calls for a general election (November).

Talks in Northern Ireland among parties collapse (November).

Irish general election results: Fianna Fáil 68, Fine Gael 45, Labour 33, Progressive Democrats 10, Democratic Left 4, others 6. Fianna Fáil and Labour form coalition government with Albert Reynolds as Taoiseach (November).

Referendum on three constitutional amendments approves right to receive information about abortion (59.9%) and right to travel abroad to secure abortion (62.4%), but rejects amendment excluding threat of suicide as a health justification for abortion (65.4%) (November).

1993

Popular outrage is expressed after IRA bomb in Warrington, England, kills two children (March).

John Hume and Gerry Adams issue a joint statement on the future of Northern Ireland (April).

President Mary Robinson makes the first visit by an Irish head of state to the Queen (May).

President Mary Robinson visits Belfast and meets briefly with Gerry Adams, leader of Sinn Féin (June).

Legislation allows the sale of condoms in Ireland and another legalizes homosexual activity by those over 17 years of age. This conforms to a 1988 European Court of Human Rights ruling that the existing legislation violated the European Convention on Human Rights (June).

Tribunal of inquiry into beef industry ends (July).

IRA bomb kills 10 on Shankill Road, Belfast, and a week later loyalists kill seven in a pub in Greysteel, County Derry (October).

Desmond O'Malley resigns as leader of Progressive Democrats and Mary Harney replaces him, becoming the first woman to lead a political party in Ireland (October).

Taoiseach Albert Reynolds and Prime Minister John Major issue the Downing Street Declaration on Northern Ireland (December).

1994

Irish government revokes the ban on broadcasting of statements by supporters of paramilitary groups (January).

U.S. president Bill Clinton disregards advice of State Department and CIA and grants a visa to Gerry Adams, leader of Sinn Féin, for a 48-hour visit to the United States to participate in a forum on Northern Ireland (February).

European Parliament election results: Ireland, Fianna Fáil 7, Fine Gael 4, Green Party 2, Labour 1, Independent 1; Northern Ireland, Unionists 1, SDLP 1, DUP 1 (June).

Six killed in loyalist attack on bar in Loughlinisland, County Down (June).

IRA proclaims a cease-fire (August).

Gerry Adams given an unrestricted visa to visit the United States (September).

Loyalist groups proclaim cease-fire (October).

Labour Party withdraws from coalition over appointment of Attorney General Harry Whelehan to Supreme Court because of displeasure at his not extraditing a priest accused of pederasty to Northern Ireland (November).

Following vote of no confidence, Reynolds is replaced by Bertie Ahern as caretaker Taoiseach (November).

A "Rainbow" coalition of Fine Gael, Labour, and the Democratic Left forms a new government with John Bruton as Taoiseach and Dick Spring as Tanaiste and minister for foreign affairs (December).

1995

Taoiseach John Bruton and Prime Minister John Major issue a Frameworks Document on the future of Northern Ireland (February).

U.S. president Bill Clinton allows Gerry Adams and Sinn Féin figures to raise funds in the United States and to attend White House celebration of St. Patrick's Day (March).

The *Irish Press* ends publication (May).

RUC first prevents Orange Order march down the Garvaghy Road, Portadown, County Down, but two days later allows the same without bands (July).

David Trimble replaces James Molyneaux as leader of the Unionist Party (September).

Seamus Heaney receives Nobel Prize for literature (October).

Constitutional amendment allowing divorce is approved by referendum (50.28%) (November).

U.S. president Bill Clinton visits Northern Ireland and Ireland (November).

Prime Minister John Major visits Dublin (December).

International panel chaired by former U.S. senator George Mitchell meets to consider preliminaries to negotiations for a Northern Ireland settlement (December).

1996

Mitchell panel recommends all-party talks occurring simultaneous with decommissioning and with all parties renouncing violence (January).

British government proposes the election of an assembly as a framework for such talks (January).

IRA breaks cease-fire with bombing of Canary Wharf in London (February).

Census in Ireland: 3,621,035 (April).

Elections to Northern Ireland Forum: Unionists 30, DUP 24, SDLP 21, Sinn Féin 17, Alliance 7, independent unionists 7, Labour 2, others 2 (May).

Multiparty talks chaired by Senator George Mitchell begin at Stormont. Sinn Féin refused entry because of continued IRA campaign (June).

Veronica Guerin, a journalist who investigated criminal activities, is murdered (June).

RUC bans Orange march along Garvaghy Road in Portadown and then reverses decision, resulting in intense rioting (July).

SDLP withdraws from Northern Ireland Forum (July).

Radio Telefís Éireann begin an Irish-language channel, Telifís na Gaeilige (October).

Referendum approves (74.8%) denial of bail to likely reoffenders (November).

Michael Lowry, minister for transportation, resigns following allegations of having received favors (November).

1997

British general election results in Northern Ireland: Unionists 10, SDLP 3, Sinn Féin 2, DUP 2, other unionist 1. Labour wins the election and Tony Blair becomes prime minister (May).

Alban Maginness of the SDLP becomes the first nationalist lord mayor of Belfast (June).

Irish general election results: Fianna Fáil 77, Fine Gael 54, Labour 17, Progressive Democrats 4, Workers' Party 4, Green Party 2, Sinn Féin 1, other 7. Fianna Fáil and Progressive Democrats form a coalition government with support of independents (June).

Public commission chaired by Judge Brian McCracken hears of extensive off-shore accounts of monies received as gifts by Charles Haughey before and while Taoiseach (June).

Haughey admits receipt of gifts but insists management of them was entirely in the hands of his late accountant (July).

Rioting follows RUC allowing Orange march along Garvaghy Road in Portadown (July).

IRA resumes cease-fire (July).

Sinn Féin admitted to multiparty talks at Stormont after accepting the "Mitchell" principles professing nonviolence (September).

Mary Robinson resigns as president of Ireland to become United Nations High Commissioner for Human Rights (September).

International panel on decommissioning headed by General John de Chastelain begins (September).

Ray Burke, minister for foreign affairs, resigns following allegations of receipt of gifts in return for influencing local planning decisions and is succeeded by David Andrews (October).

Mary McAleese is elected president of Ireland defeating three other women candidates, Mary Banotti (Fine Gael), Adi Roche (Labour), and Dana Rosemary Scallion (Independent), and one male independent, Derek Nally (October).

Dick Spring resigns as leader of the Labour Party and is succeeded by Ruairi Quinn (November).

Gerry Adams leads the first Sinn Féin delegation to talks at 10 Downing Street (December).

In the Maze Prison in Northern Ireland imprisoned members of the Irish National Liberation Army kill another prisoner, Billy Wright, a loyalist leader (December).

1998

Good Friday Agreement reached between British and Irish governments and the leaders of the Unionist, SDLP, Alliance, and Sinn Féin Parties to establish a Northern Ireland Assembly and power-sharing government, to create cross-border and cross-channel bodies, to remove territorial claims in the Irish constitution, to have the status of Northern Ireland determined by consent, to reform police, to begin release of prisoners, and to move toward decommissioning of weapons by paramilitary organizations (April).

Referenda in both Northern Ireland (71.1%) and in Ireland (94.4%) accept the Good Friday Agreement. The referendum in Ireland approves changes in articles 2 and 3 of the constitution (May).

Election results to Northern Ireland Assembly: Unionists 28, SDLP 24, DUP 20, Sinn Féin 18, Alliance 6, United Kingdom Unionist Party 1, Northern Ireland Unionist Party 4, Northern Irish Women's Coalition 2, Progressive Unionist Party 2, others 3 (June).

Independent commission on policing in Northern Ireland is named (June).

Parades committee reroutes Orange march away from Garvaghy Road in Portadown (June).

Firebomb of their home kills three young Catholic brothers in Ballymoney, County Antrim (July).

Last of the loyalist paramilitary groups, the Ulster Volunteer Force, announces a cease-fire (August).

Bomb set by "Real IRA" in Omagh, County Tyrone, kills 29 (August).

Irish National Liberation Army announces a cease-fire (August).

President Clinton visits Ireland and Northern Ireland, including Omagh (September).

John Hume, SDLP leader, and David Trimble, Unionist leader, are jointly awarded the Nobel Peace Prize (October).

President McAleese and Queen Elizabeth open a tower in Mesen, Belgium, commemorating Irish who died in the First World War (November).

Labour and Democratic Left Parties vote to merge (December).

1999

European Union commissioner Pádraig Flynn accused of treating as personal gifts political donations received in 1989 while he was minister for the environment (January).

Comptroller general reports that 30 percent of bank deposits in November 1998 were in nonresident accounts and that about one-half of the nonresidency addresses were bogus (January).

Four IRA members plead guilty to charge reduced to manslaughter for the killing of Garda Jerry McCabe and are sentenced to terms of 11 to 14 years (February).

Rosemary Nelson, a solicitor who represented nationalists in celebrated cases, is murdered in a car-bomb explosion in Belfast (March).

Supreme Court justice Hugh O'Flaherty resigns after the chief justice issued a report critical of his intervention in a case involving dangerous driving that caused a death (April).

Journalist Terry Keane reports that she had an affair for several years with former Taoiseach Charles Haughey (May).

The body of Eamonn Molloy, who disappeared 24 years ago, is discovered just south of the border. IRA admits they killed him and eight others whose remains were still missing (May).

European Parliament election results: Ireland, Fianna Fáil 6, Fine Gael 4, Labour 1, Green Part 2, Independents 2; Northern Ireland, SDLP 1, DUP 1, Unionists 1 (June).

British and Irish governments issue a document *The Way Forward* that sets forth a mechanism for selecting ministers in the Northern Ireland government and establishing a mechanism for its suspension if decommissioning of weapons and establishment of devolved government were not in place by May 2000 (July).

Non-attendance of unionists made the selection of ministers by the Northern Ireland Assembly academic and Assembly adjourned (July).

Brian Meehan is convicted of the murder of Veronica Guerin (July).

The IRA is linked to a plot to smuggle arms from America that is interrupted by the Federal Bureau of Investigation (July).

IRA issues a death threat to allegedly unruly teenagers who go abroad or in hiding (August).

Senator George Mitchell begins review of Good Friday Agreement, as both Unionists and Sinn Féin agree to participate but not to meet each other directly. The DUP does not participate but gives its views to Mitchell (September).

A commission chaired by Christopher Patten issues a report on police reform that calls for the renaming of the RUC and devolution of numerous police procedures and organization (September).

Sinn Féin and the Unionists meet directly with Mitchell (September).

Peter Mandelson replaces Marjorie Mowlam as secretary of state for Northern Ireland (October).

Senator Mitchell issues a report calling for the reestablishment of devolved institutions on the basis of the IRA's willingness to send a representative to the Independent International Commission on Decommissioning. The ruling council of the Unionist Party agrees to talk part in the government and the reconvened Northern Ireland Assembly elects a 10-member Executive Council according to the d'Hondt rules of proportional selection (November).

Power is transferred to the Northern Ireland Executive from Westminster and the territorial claims to Northern Ireland are removed from the Irish constitution (December).

2000

McCracken Tribunal (now chaired by Justice Michael Moriarty) hears that Denis Foley, North Kerry Fianna Fáil T.D., had large offshore bank account (January).

Gerry Adams, Sinn Féin leader, dismisses report of imminent IRA decommissioning (January).

IRA is given a deadline on February 4 to commence decommissioning by February 11 (February).

Northern Ireland government is suspended and direct rule from Westminster is restored following IRA failure to commence decommissioning (February).

Tribunal headed by Justice Feargus Flood hears testimony from Frank Dunlop, former Fianna Fáil government press secretary, that he gave thousands to Dublin county councilors to influence planning decisions (April).

Northern Ireland Executive and Assembly are restored following IRA offer to initiate process to put arms beyond use (May).

Moriarty tribunal hears that Charles Haughey received gifts exceeding 8 million pounds (May).

Liam Lawlor resigns from Fianna Fáil Party following party report critical of his lack of cooperation regarding investigation of his activities (June).

Coalition government narrowly survives no-confidence vote (June).

Charles Haughey appears before Moriarty tribunal giving evidence (July).

2001

Fine Gael parliamentary party passes a no-confidence vote in party leader John Bruton, who is replaced by Michael Noonan (January).

John Reid replaces Peter Mandelson as Secretary of State for Northern Ireland (January).

Tribunal headed by Justice Feargus Flood hears testimony that former minister for foreign affairs Ray Burke held money in offshore accounts while a minister (March).

Charles Haughey is admitted to hospital suffering a heart attack after finishing giving evidence to the Moriarty Tribunal (March).

The Flood Tribunal hears further testimony that Burke, while minister for commerce and industry in 1989, had made representations for a construction company to the revenue commissioners and that money given to him came from other offshore accounts rather than from fund-raising events (May).

The Moriarty Tribunal hears testimony that 33,000 pounds were transferred to the account of the Fine Gael Party from the chairman of Esat Digifone, which firm was seeking a license for mobile phones (May).

Referenda results: 62.1 percent approve removal from the constitution of all reference to capital punishment and prohibition of any further legislation allowing the same; 64.2 percent approve the establishment of an International Criminal Court for crimes against humanity; and 53.9 percent reject the Treaty of Nice regarding changes in the votes of member states in the European Union (June).

British General Election results in Northern Ireland: Unionists 6, DUP 5, Sinn Féin 4, SDLP 3 (June).

David Trimble, Unionist leader, resigns his post as first minister in the Northern Ireland government because of the absence of any independent confirmation of decommissioning of IRA weapons, and Reg Empey assumes role of acting first minister (July).

Joint British-Irish governmental proposals fail to meet the satisfaction of Northern Ireland parties, but British government suspends the Northern Ireland Assembly for 24 hours, to allow a further six-week delay in the necessity to appoint a permanent first minister (August).

Unionist and DUP ministers resign from the Northern Ireland Executive, but five days later the IRA began a process of putting a substantial amount of weapons beyond use, which was witnessed by the Independent International Commission on Decommissioning, and the Unionists and DUP ministers reassumed their posts (October).

Testimony to the Flood Tribunal indicates that Ray Burke had received more than 400,000 pounds from a construction company (November).

When David Trimble fails to receive the needed votes from the unionist parties to be elected as first minister, the Alliance Party is designated as unionist to give him the needed votes (November).

Mark Durkan replaces John Hume as leader of the SDLP and is elected as deputy first minister, succeeding Seamus Mallon (November).

2002

Allegations are made that the IRA stole documents from Special Branch offices in Belfast (March).

Irish general election results: Fianna Fáil 81, Fine Gael 31, Labour 21, Progressive Democrats 8, Sinn Féin 5, Greens 6, Socialists 1, Independents 13 (May).

Database is discovered in possession of the IRA listing judges, politicians, and members of the security forces (June).

Michael Noonan resigns as leader of Fine Gael and is replaced by Enda Kenny (June).

Fianna Fáil and Progressive Democrats form a coalition government with Bertie Ahern as Taoiseach and Mary Harney as Tainaiste (June).

European Union heads of state summit in Seville, Spain, issues a declaration limiting Irish participation in any military action by the European Union to operations sanctioned by the United Nations (June).

IRA apologizes for deaths and injuries of noncombatants in the 30-year struggle (July).

Another referendum on the Nice Treaty is approved by 62.9 percent of the voters (October).

Ulster Unionist Council announces that it would withdraw Unionist ministers from the Northern Executive in January if the IRA and Sinn Féin had not demonstrated their commitment to nonviolence and democracy (September).

Sinn Féin offices are raided by the police in an investigation into republican intelligence-gathering and on suspicions of infiltration of the Northern Ireland Office (October).

Northern Ireland institutions are suspended and direct rule from Westminster is restored until Sinn Féin agrees to end all links with the IRA (October).

Paul Murphy replaces John Reid as Secretary of State for Northern Ireland (October).

2003

The Irish Supreme Court rules that non-national parents and siblings of children born in Ireland were not entitled to Irish residency (January).

Feuding between loyalist paramilitary organizations in Belfast results in the death of senior members of the Ulster Defence Association (January–February).

A government resolution allows the use of Shannon Airport by the armed forces of the United States taking part in the military conflict in Iraq passes in the Dáil Éireann (March).

U.S. president George W. Bush meets with Prime Minister Tony Blair in Northern Ireland to discuss the military campaign in Iraq and with the parties supportive of the Good Friday Agreement (April).

The British and Irish governments issue a Joint Declaration relating to the restoration of Northern Irish institutions with proposals to reduce the size of security forces and repeal anti-terrorist legislation specific to Northern Ireland, the establishment of an International Monitoring Commission to assess breaches of the Good Friday Agreement, and a call for the permanent cessation of paramilitary activity, including punishment attacks (May).

David Trimble secures a narrow victory within the Ulster Unionist Council against a proposal by Jeffrey Donaldson to reject the Joint Declaration. Jeffrey Donaldson, Rev. Martyn Smyth, and David Burnside subsequently resign from the Unionist Party in Westminster (June).

Four members are appointed to the International Monitoring Commission on compliance with the Good Friday Agreement (September).

David Trimble considered an act of decommissioning by the IRA, witnessed by General John de Chastelain, as insufficiently transparent and he refuses to consider power sharing with Sinn Féin without a full inventory of IRA weapons and a timetable for their decommissioning (October).

Results of Northern Ireland Assembly election: DUP 30, Unionists 27, Sinn Féin 24, SDLP 18, others 9 (November).

2004

Ireland assumes presidency of European Commission (January).

Smoking ban is imposed in all pubs, restaurants, and work places under direction of Minister for Health, Micheál Martin (March).

Dublin hosts the admission of ten new member-states of European Union (May).

European parliament elections: Ireland, Fianna Fáil 4, Fine Gael 5, Labour 1, Sinn Féin 1, Others 2; Northern Ireland: DUP 1, Unionists 1, Sinn Féin 1 (June).

U.S. President George Bush meets with European Union leaders near Shannon Airport (June).

Constitutional amendment that does not guarantee citizenship simply on the basis of birth in Ireland is passed by 79.17% of the voters (June).

Charlie McCreevy, Minister for Finance, is appointed European Commissioner (July).

Former Taoiseach John Bruton becomes European Union ambassador to the United States (September).

Mary McAleese is re-elected unopposed for a second term as President of Ireland (October).

Margaret Hassan, an Irish-born aid worker, is murdered by her capturers in Iraq (November).

Negotiations to restore power-sharing institutions in Northern Ireland fail when Sinn Féin and the DUP fail to agree on mechanisms to confirm decommissioning of weapons, specifically its being photographed (December).

Bogotá's Columbian Supreme Court gives lengthy jail sentences to the "Columbia Three", Niall Connolly, Martin McCauley and James Monaghan, for training local rebels, but they are reported to have fled (December).

£22,000,000 is stolen from Northern Bank in Belfast (December).

2005

Police Service of Northern Ireland concludes that the December bank robbery was done by the Provisional IRA. The Irish Governments concurs in the judgment (January).

Robert McCartney is murdered outside a bar in Belfast and IRA members are suspected of involvement (January).

Former Minister for Foreign Affairs, Ray Burke, is jailed for six months for tax evasion (January).

Several people are apprehended and £2,300,000 is recovery in Cork in relation to the Belfast bank robbery in December (February).

Sinn Féin President, Gerry Adams, asks the Provisional IRA, to consider decommissioning and disbanding as a military organization (March).

The sisters and partner of murdered Robert McCartney meet with U.S. President George Bush and other American political figures in campaign to draw attention to alleged IRA intimidation of potential witnesses of murder (March).

Cian O'Connor loses his Olympic gold medal after ruling that his horse, Waterford Crystal had banned substances in its system during the 2004 Olympics (March).

President Mary McAleese and Taioseach Bertie Ahern attend the funeral of Pope John Paul II (April).

At its annual congress the Gaelic Athletic Association agrees to allow soccer and rugby to be played in Croke Park under certain circumstances (April).

Results of British general election in Northern Ireland: DUP 9, Official Unionists 1, Sinn Féin 5, SDLP won 3. David Trimble, who lost his own seat, resigns as party leader of the Unionists. Peter Hain is appointed as Secretary of State for Northern Ireland (May).

Results of local government elections in Northern Ireland: DUP 182, Sinn Féin 126, Unionists 115, SDLP 101, Alliance 30, others 28 (June).

The European Union grants official status as a working language to Irish (June).

Taoiseach Bertie Ahern has a private audience with Pope Benedict XVI in Rome (July).

Provisional IRA announces the end of the armed campaign, orders units to dump arms, and instructs members to engage in peaceful democratic politics (July).

Three Irish women challenge Irish constitutional ban on abortion in the European Court of Human Rights (August).

Former Secretary of State for Northern Ireland Mo Mowlaw dies at 55 (August).

Head of the Independent International Commission on Decommissioning, General John de Chastelain, reports the decommissioning by the Provisional IRA of their weapons, including ammunition and explosives, which was witnessed by Catholic priest, Alec Reid, and Methodist minister, Harold Good (September).

An official Irish government inquiry reports on child sexual abuse by twenty-one priests in the Diocese of Ferns between 1962 and 2002 prompting demands for similar inquiries about other dioceses (October).

APPENDIXES

Appendix I
Irish Leaders from 1922 to 2005

Appendix II
Maps

APPENDIX I

Irish Free State

Governor-General:

Tim Healy	1922–1928	
James MacNeill	1928–1932	
Domhnall Ua Buachalla	1932–1937	

President of the Executive Council:

William T. Cosgrave	1922–1932	Cumann na nGaedheal
Eamon de Valera	1932–1937	Fianna Fáil

Ireland or Eire

President:

Douglas Hyde	1938–1945	no party
Sean T. O'Kelly	1945–1959	Fianna Fáil
Eamon de Valera	1959–1973	Fianna Fáil
Erskine Childers	1973–1974	Fianna Fáil
Cearbhall O'Dalaigh	1974–1976	Fianna Fáil
Patrick Hillery	1976–1990	Fianna Fáil
Mary Robinson	1990–1997	Labour
Mary McAleese	1997–	Fianna Fáil

Taoiseach:

Eamon de Valera	1937–1948	Fianna Fáil
John A. Costello	1948–1951	coalition (Fine Gael–Labour–Clann na Poblachta–Clann na Talmhan)
Eamon de Valera	1951–1954	Fianna Fáil
John A. Costello	1954–1957	coalition (Fine Gael–Labour–Clann na Talmhan)
Eamon de Valera	1957–1959	Fianna Fáil
Seán Lemass	1959–1966	Fianna Fáil
Jack Lynch	1966–1973	Fianna Fáil
Liam Cosgrave	1973–1977	coalition (Fine Gael–Labour)
Jack Lynch	1977–1979	Fianna Fáil
Charles J. Haughey	1979–1981	Fianna Fáil
Garret FitzGerald	1981–1982	coalition (Fine Gael–Labour)
Charles J. Haughey	1982	Fianna Fáil

IRISH LEADERS FROM 1922 TO 2005 *(continued)*

Garret FitzGerald	1982–1987	coalition (Fine Gael–Labour)
Charles J. Haughey	1987–1989	Fianna Fáil
Charles J. Haughey	1989–1992	coalition (Fianna Fáil–Progressive Democrats)
Albert Reynolds	1992	coalition (Fianna Fáil–Progressive Democrats)
Albert Reynolds	1992–1994	coalition (Fianna Fáil–Labour)
John Bruton	1994–1997	coalition (Fine Gael–Labour–Democratic Left)
Bertie Ahern	1997–	coalition (Fianna Fáil–Progressive Democrats)

Northern Ireland

Governor-General:

Duke of Abercorn	1922–1945
Vice Admiral Earl Granville	1945–1952
Lord Wakehurst	1952–1964
Lord Erskine of Rerrick	1964–1968
Lord Grey of Naunton	1968–1973

Prime Minister:

James Craig	1921–1940	Unionist
John M. Andrews	1940–1943	Unionist
Basil Brooke	1943–1963	Unionist
Terence O'Neill	1963–1969	Unionist
James Chichester-Clark	1969–1971	Unionist
Brian Faulkner	1971–1972	Unionist

Secretary of State for Northern Ireland:

William Whitelaw	1972–1973
Francis Pym	1973–1974
Merlyn Rees	1974–1976
Roy Mason	1976–1979
Humphrey Atkins	1979–1981
Jim Prior	1981–1984
Douglas Hurd	1984–1985
Tom King	1985–1989
Peter Brooke	1989–1992
Patrick Mayhew	1992–1997
Mo Mowlam	1997–1999
Peter Mandelson	1999–2001
John Reid	2001–2002
Paul Murphy	2002–2005
Peter Haim	2005–

IRISH LEADERS FROM 1922 TO 2005 *(continued)*

Chief Minister Northern Ireland Executive*:
Brian Faulkner   1974   Unionist

First Minister for Northern Ireland**:
David Trimble   1999–2002   Unionist

Deputy First Minister for Northern Ireland**:
Seamus Mallon   1999–2001   SDLP
Mark Durkan   2001–2002   SDLP

*The Northern Ireland Executive, a power-sharing experiment in devolved government, collapsed, as did the Northern Ireland Assembly, to which it was responsible, in May of 1974 after a general strike by the Ulster Workers' Council.
** On several occasions the Northern Ireland Assembly to whom these ministers were responsible was suspended because of disputes about IRA decommissioning of weapons and other alleged illegalities, and remains suspended at this writing.

APPENDIX II

MAPS

Ireland, 2005

Ireland, 650

Ireland, c. 950

Ireland, 1300

Ireland, 1450

Plantations in Ireland, 1550–1610

Catholic Land Ownership in Ireland Before and After Cromwell

The 1798 Rebellion in Ireland

Poverty in Ireland, 1841

The Great Famine in Ireland, 1845–1849

Population Change in Ireland, 1841–1851

Distribution of Protestants in Ireland, 1861 and 1991

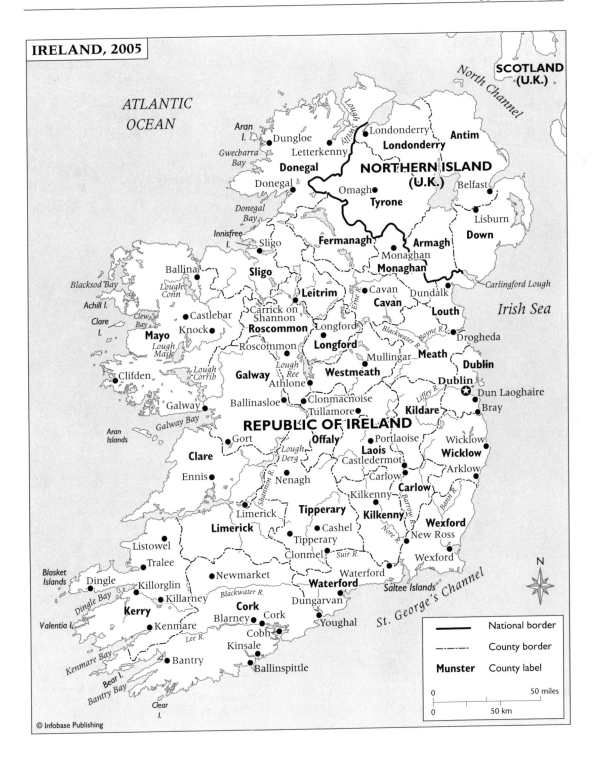

IRELAND, 2005

SCOTLAND (U.K.)

North Channel

ATLANTIC OCEAN

Aran I.
Dungloe
Gwecbarra Bay
Letterkenny
Londonderry
Londonderry
Antim
Donegal
Donegal
Omagh
Tyrone
NORTHERN ISLAND (U.K.)
Belfast
Donegal Bay
Lisburn
Innisfree I.
Sligo
Fermanagh
Monaghan
Monaghan
Armagh
Down
Carlingford Lough
Sligo
Ballina
Blacksod Bay
Lough Conn
Sligo
Leitrim
Cavan
Cavan
Dundalk
Irish Sea
Achill I.
Castlebar
Carrick on Shannon
Louth
Clare I.
Clew Bay
Knock
Roscommon
Longford
Longford
Blackwater R.
Boyne R.
Drogheda
Mayo
Lough Mask
Roscommon
Mullingar
Meath
Lough Corrib
Lough Ree
Athlone
Westmeath
Dublin
Clifden
Galway
Clonmacnoise
Liffey R.
Dublin
Galway
Ballinasloe
Tullamore
Dun Laoghaire
Aran Islands
Galway Bay
REPUBLIC OF IRELAND
Kildare
Bray
Gort
Offaly
Portlaoise
Wicklow
Clare
Lough Derg
Laois
Castledermot
Wicklow
Ennis
Nenagh
Carlow
Arklow
Shannon R.
Kilkenny
Carlow
Barrow R.
Bann R.
Limerick
Tipperary
Kilkenny
Wexford
Limerick
Cashel
New Ross
Listowel
Tipperary
Nore R.
Tralee
Clonmel
Suir R.
Wexford
Blasket Islands
Newmarket
Waterford
Saltee Islands
Dingle
Killorglin
Blackwater R.
Waterford
St. George's Channel
Dingle Bay
Killarney
Dungarvan
Kerry
Cork
Cork
Valentia I.
Kenmare
Blarney
Youghal
Lee R.
Cobh
Kinsale
Kenmare Bay
Bantry
Ballinspittle
Bear I.
Bantry Bay
Clear I.

N

National border
County border
Munster County label

0   50 miles
0   50 km

© Infobase Publishing

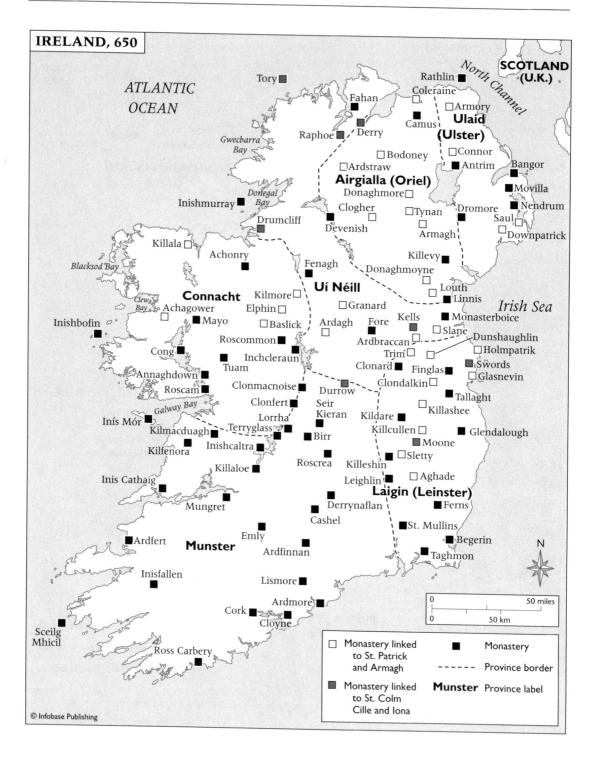

IRELAND, 650

SCOTLAND (U.K.)

ATLANTIC OCEAN

North Channel

Tory

Rathlin

Coleraine

Fahan

Armory

Camus

Ulaid (Ulster)

Raphoe   Derry

Gwecbarra Bay

Bodoney

Connor

Antrim

Bangor

Ardstraw

Movilla

Airgialla (Oriel)

Nendrum

Donaghmore

Donegal Bay

Clogher

Tynan

Dromore

Saul

Inishmurray

Devenish

Armagh

Downpatrick

Drumcliff

Killevy

Killala

Donaghmoyne

Achonry

Fenagh

Donaghmoyne

Louth

Blacksod Bay

Uí Néill

Linnis

Irish Sea

Kilmore

Granard

Connacht

Elphin

Fore

Kells

Monasterboice

Clew Bay

Achagower

Ardagh

Slane

Mayo

Baslick

Ardbraccan

Dunshaughlin

Inishbofin

Roscommon

Trim

Holmpatrik

Cong

Inchcleraun

Clonard

Swords

Tuam

Finglas

Glasnevin

Annaghdown

Clonmacnoise

Durrow

Clondalkin

Roscam

Clonfert

Seir Kieran

Killashee

Galway Bay

Lorrha

Kildare

Tallaght

Inís Mór

Terryglass

Killcullen

Glendalough

Kilmacduagh

Birr

Moone

Kilfenora

Inishcaltra

Sletty

Inis Cathaig

Killaloe

Roscrea

Killeshin

Aghade

Leighlin

Laigin (Leinster)

Mungret

Derrynaflan

Ferns

Ardfert

Emly

Cashel

St. Mullins

Munster

Ardfinnan

Begerin

Inisfallen

Taghmon

Lismore

N

Ardmore

Cork

0   50 miles

Cloyne

0   50 km

Sceilg Mhicil

Ross Carbery

□ Monastery linked to St. Patrick and Armagh   ■ Monastery

▣ Monastery linked to St. Colm Cille and Iona   ----- Province border

Munster Province label

© Infobase Publishing

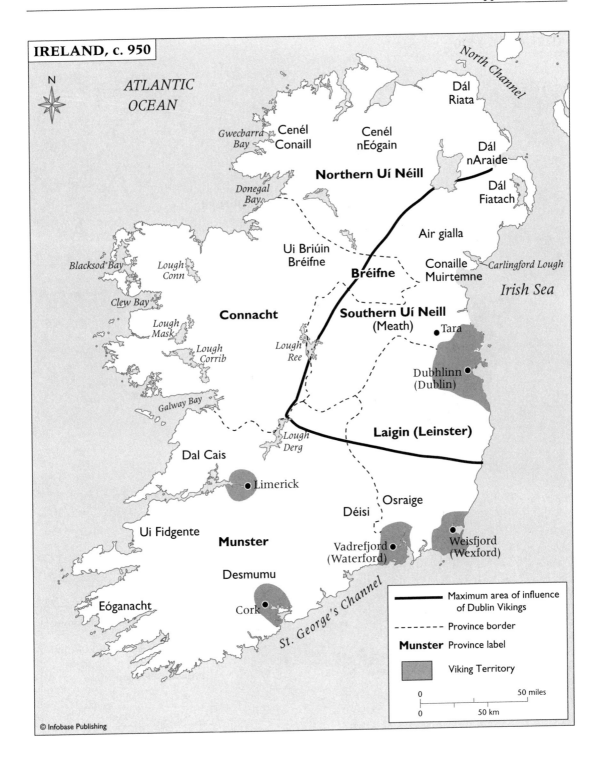

IRELAND, c. 950

N

ATLANTIC
OCEAN

North Channel

Dál
Riata

*Gwecbarra
Bay*
Cenél
Conaill

Cenél
nEógain

Dál
nAraide

*Donegal
Bay*

Northern Uí Néill

Dál
Fiatach

Air gialla

Ui Briúin
Bréifne

Bréifne

Conaille
Muirtemne

Carlingford Lough

Blacksod Bay
*Lough
Conn*

Irish Sea

Clew Bay

Connacht

Southern Uí Neill
(Meath)

● Tara

*Lough
Mask*

*Lough
Corrib*

*Lough
Ree*

Dubhlinn
(Dublin) ●

Galway Bay

*Lough
Derg*

Laigin (Leinster)

Dal Cais

● Limerick

Osraige

Déisi

Ui Fidgente

Munster

Vadrefjord
(Waterford) ●

Weisfjord
(Wexford) ●

Desmumu

Eóganacht

Cork ●

St. George's Channel

	Maximum area of influence of Dublin Vikings
	Province border
Munster	Province label
	Viking Territory

0   50 miles

0   50 km

© Infobase Publishing

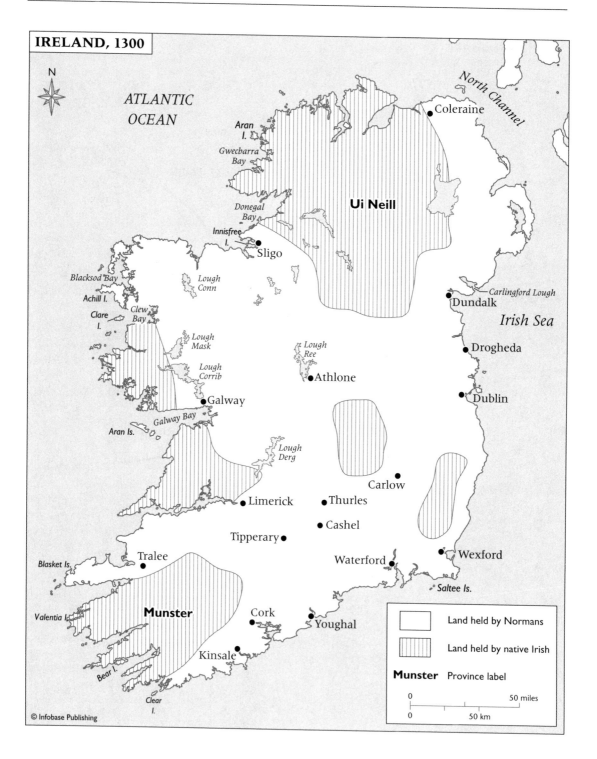

IRELAND, 1300

N

ATLANTIC
OCEAN

North Channel

● Coleraine

Aran
I.

Gwecbarra
Bay

Ui Neill

Donegal
Bay

Innisfree
I.

● Sligo

Blacksod Bay

Lough
Conn

Carlingford Lough

● Dundalk

Achill I.

Irish Sea

Clare
I.

Clew
Bay

Lough
Mask

● Drogheda

Lough
Corrib

Lough
Ree

● Dublin

● Galway

● Athlone

Galway Bay

Aran Is.

Lough
Derg

● Carlow

● Limerick

● Thurles

● Tipperary

● Cashel

Blasket Is.

● Tralee

● Waterford

● Wexford

Valentia I.

Munster

● Cork

Saltee Is.

● Youghal

● Kinsale

Bear I.

Clear
I.

© Infobase Publishing

	Land held by Normans
	Land held by native Irish
Munster	Province label

0   50 miles

0   50 km

IRELAND, 1450

N

ATLANTIC
OCEAN

North Channel

Mac-
Donnells

Earldom
of Ulster

O'Donnell

*Donegal
Bay*

O'Neill

Mayo

O'Rourke

Magennis

Irish Sea

Burkes

O'Reilly

O'Connor

O'Farrell

The Pale

O'Flaherty

Burkes

Dempsey

Earldom of Kildare

Galway Bay

Aran Is.

MacMurrough

O'Brien

Earldom of
Ormond

Blasket Is.

Wexford
Lordship

Earldom of
Desmond

Mac Carthy Mor

	Land held by Anglo-Irish lords
	Land held by English king
	Land held by native Irish
– – –	Borders
O'Brien	Clan name

0   50 miles

0   50 km

© Infobase Publishing

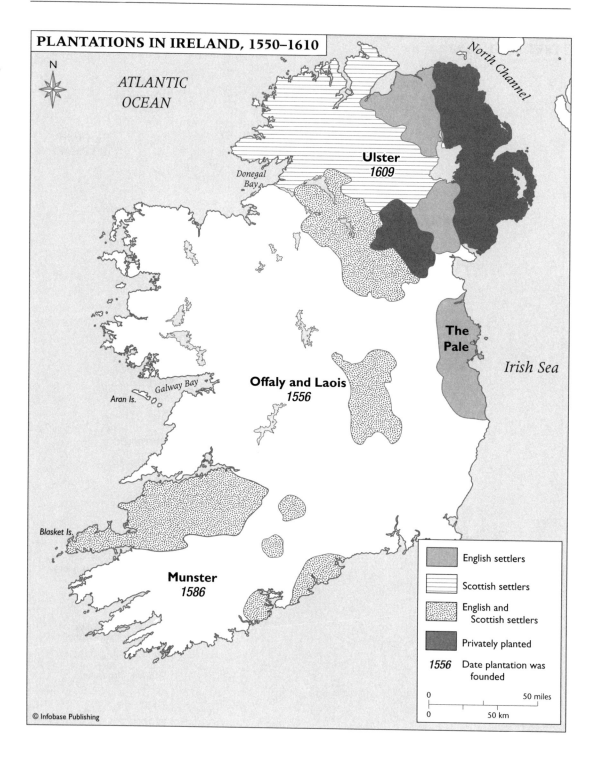

PLANTATIONS IN IRELAND, 1550–1610

N

ATLANTIC
OCEAN

North Channel

Donegal
Bay

Ulster
1609

The
Pale

Irish Sea

Galway Bay

Aran Is.

Offaly and Laois
1556

Blasket Is.

Munster
1586

English settlers

Scottish settlers

English and
Scottish settlers

Privately planted

1556   Date plantation was
founded

0   50 miles

0   50 km

© Infobase Publishing

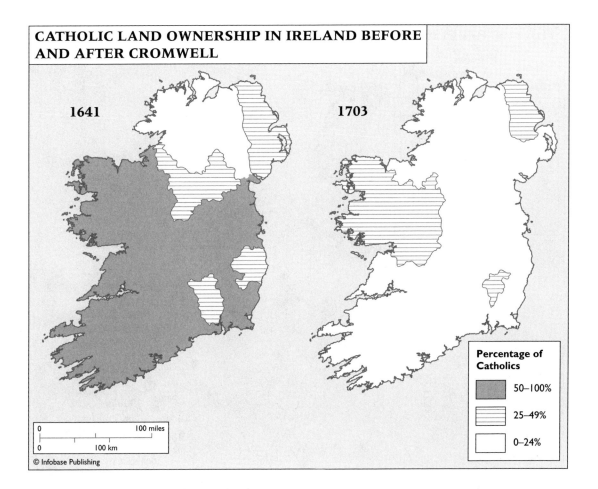

CATHOLIC LAND OWNERSHIP IN IRELAND BEFORE AND AFTER CROMWELL

1641

1703

0   100 miles
0   100 km

© Infobase Publishing

Percentage of Catholics

50–100%

25–49%

0–24%

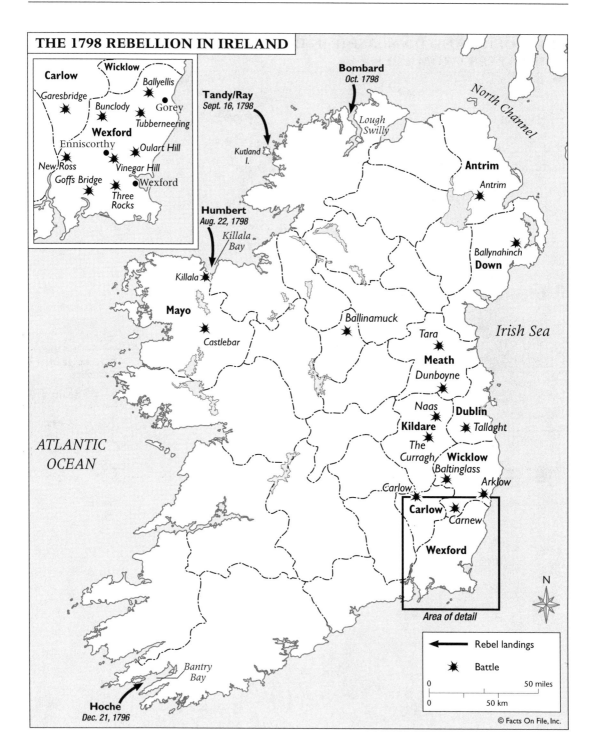

THE 1798 REBELLION IN IRELAND

Carlow

Wicklow

Garesbridge

Ballyellis

Bunclody

● *Gorey*

Tubberneering

Wexford

Enniscorthy ●

Oulart Hill

New Ross

Vinegar Hill

Goffs Bridge

● *Wexford*

Three Rocks

Bombard
Oct. 1798

Tandy/Ray
Sept. 16, 1798

Lough Swilly

Kutland I.

Antrim

Antrim

Humbert
Aug. 22, 1798

Killala Bay

Killala

Mayo

Castlebar

Ballinamuck

Ballynahinch

Down

North Channel

Tara

Meath

Dunboyne

Irish Sea

Naas

Kildare

Dublin

Tallaght

The Curragh

Wicklow

Baltinglass

ATLANTIC OCEAN

Carlow

Arklow

Carlow

Carnew

Wexford

Area of detail

N

Bantry Bay

← *Rebel landings*

Hoche
Dec. 21, 1796

✷ Battle

0   50 miles

0   50 km

© Facts On File, Inc.

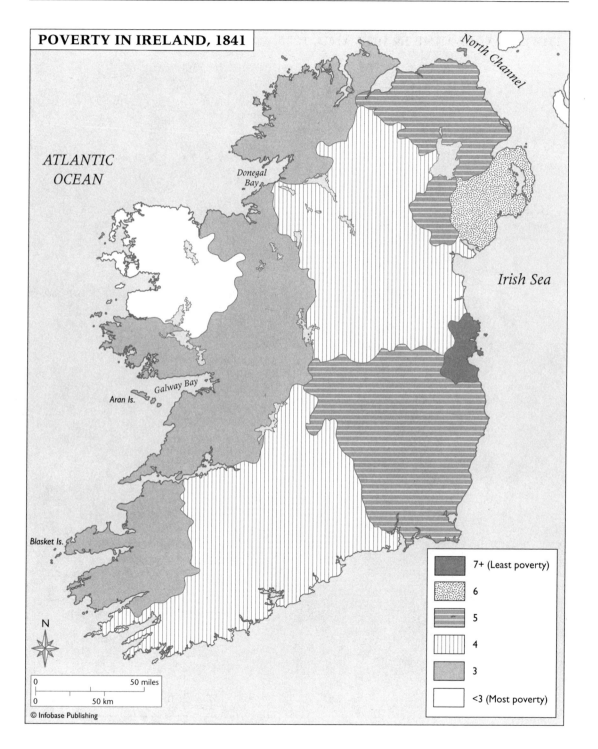

POVERTY IN IRELAND, 1841

ATLANTIC
OCEAN

North Channel

Donegal
Bay

Irish Sea

Galway Bay

Aran Is.

Blasket Is.

N

| 0 | | 50 miles |
| 0 | | 50 km |

© Infobase Publishing

7+ (Least poverty)	
6	
5	
4	
3	
<3 (Most poverty)	

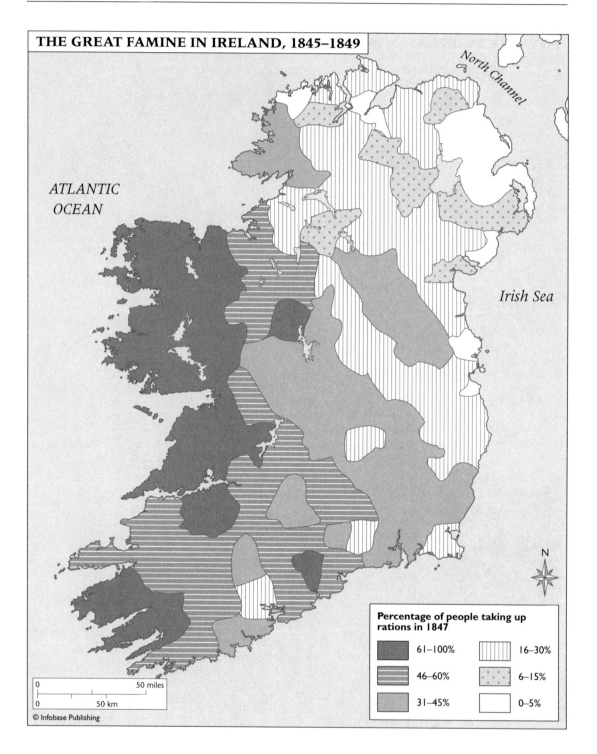

THE GREAT FAMINE IN IRELAND, 1845–1849

ATLANTIC
OCEAN

North Channel

Irish Sea

N

Percentage of people taking up
rations in 1847

▓ 61–100%	▥ 16–30%
▤ 46–60%	⸬ 6–15%
▦ 31–45%	☐ 0–5%

0   50 miles
0   50 km

© Infobase Publishing

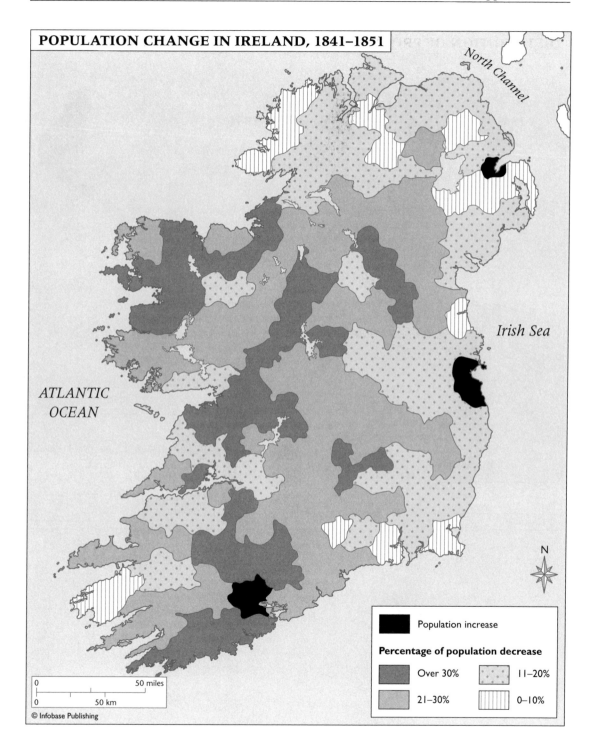

POPULATION CHANGE IN IRELAND, 1841–1851

North Channel

Irish Sea

ATLANTIC OCEAN

N

0   50 miles

0   50 km

© Infobase Publishing

Population increase

Percentage of population decrease

Over 30%   11–20%

21–30%   0–10%

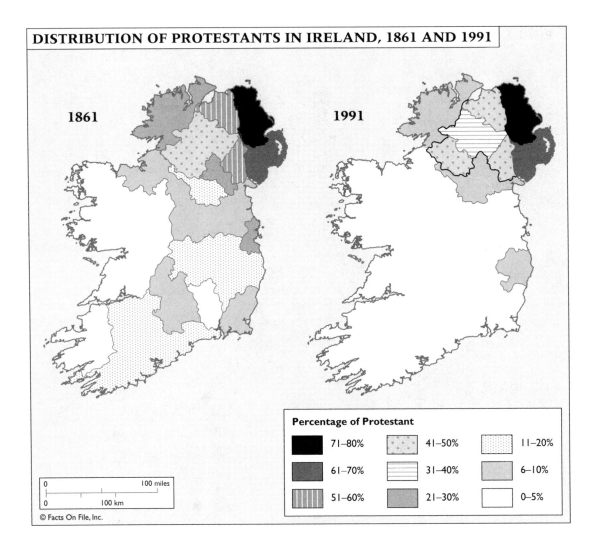

DISTRIBUTION OF PROTESTANTS IN IRELAND, 1861 AND 1991

1861

1991

Percentage of Protestant

71–80%   41–50%   11–20%

61–70%   31–40%   6–10%

51–60%   21–30%   0–5%

0   100 miles
0   100 km

© Facts On File, Inc.

BIBLIOGRAPHY

The titles in this bibliography include published works available in many general reference libraries. General reference and surveys are followed by listings according to chronological sections. Titles that cover several periods are listed with general surveys. Consult sections immediately before and after as the subject matter of some titles overlaps the period designations in this volume.

GENERAL REFERENCE

Chronologies, Dictionaries, Encyclopedias, Maps

Aalen, F. H. A., Kevin Whelan, and Matthew Stout, eds. *Atlas of the Rural Irish Landscape*. Toronto: University of Toronto Press, 1997.

Boylan, Henry, ed. *A Dictionary of Irish Biography*. New York: Barnes and Noble, 1978.

Connolly, S. J., ed. *The Oxford Companion to Irish History*. 2nd ed. Oxford: Oxford University Press, 2002.

Curley, Helen, ed. *Local Ireland Almanac and Yearbook of Facts 2000*. Dublin: Local Ireland, 1999.

Duffy, Sean, ed. *Atlas of Irish History*. Dublin: Gill and Macmillan, 2000.

Edwards, Ruth Dudley. *An Atlas of Irish History*. London: Metheun, 1981.

Hickey, D. J., and J. E. Doherty, eds. *A Dictionary of Irish History since 1800*. Totowa, N.J.: Barnes and Noble, 1981.

Lalor, Brian, ed. *The Encyclopedia of Ireland*. Dublin: Gill and Macmillan, 2003; New Haven, Conn.: Yale University Press, 2003.

MacArt, Pat, and Donal Campbell, eds. *Irish Almanac and Yearbook of Facts, 1997*. Derry: Artcam, 1996.

———, Colm McKenna, and Donal Campbell, eds. *Irish Almanac and Yearbook of Facts, 1998*. Burt, Donegal: Artcam, 1997.

McRedmond, Louis, ed. *Modern Irish Lives: Dictionary of 20th Century Biography*. Dublin: Gill and Macmillan, 1998.

Moody, T. W., F. X. Martin, and F. J. Byrne, eds. *A Chronology of Irish History to 1976: A Companion to Irish History, Part I*. Oxford: Clarendon Press, 1982.

———, *Maps, Genealogies, Lists: A Companion to Irish History, Part II*. Oxford: Clarendon Press, 1984.

Power, Patrick. *The Timechart History of Ireland*. London: Worth Press, 2001.

Ruckenstein, Lelia, and James A. O'Malley, eds. *Everything Irish*. New York: Ballantine Books, 2003.

Shannon, Michael O., ed. *Irish Republic (World Bibliographical Series)*. Oxford: Clio Press, 1986.

———. *Northern Ireland (World Bibliographical Series)*. Oxford: Clio Press, 1991.

Vaughan, W. E., and A. J. Fitzpatrick. *Irish Historical Statistics: Population, 1821–1971*. Dublin: Royal Irish Academy, 1978.

Walker, Brian M. *Parliamentary Election Results in Ireland, 1801–1922*. Dublin: Royal Irish Academy, 1978.

———, ed. *Parliamentary Election Results in Ireland, 1918–92*. Dublin: Royal Irish Academy, 1992.

Wallace, Martin. *100 Irish Lives*. Totowa, N.J.: 1983.

General Surveys

Bardon, Jonathan. *A History of Ulster*. Belfast: Queen's University Press, 1992.

Bartlett, Thomas, and Keith Jeffrey, eds. *A Military History of Ireland*. New York: Cambridge University Press, 1996.

Beckett, J. C. *The Making of Modern Ireland*. New York: Knopf, 1969.

Bradley, Anthony, and Valiulis Maryann Gialanella, eds. *Gender and Sexuality in Modern Ireland*. Amherst: University of Massachusetts Press, 1997.

Brooke, Peter. *Ulster Presbyterianism: The Historical Perspective, 1610–1970*. New York: St. Martin's Press, 1987.

Boyce, D. George. *Nationalism in Ireland*. Baltimore, Md.: Johns Hopkins University Press, 1982.

———, R. Eccleshall, and V. Geoghegan, eds. *Political Thought in Ireland since the Seventeenth Century*. London: Routledge, 1993.

Clark, S., and J. Donnelly, eds. *Irish Peasants, Violence and Political Unrest 1780–1914*. Madison: University of Wisconsin Press, 1983.

Corish, Patrick J. *The Irish Catholic Experience: An Historical Survey*. Wilmington, Del.: Michael Glazier, 1985.

Cullen, L. M. *An Economic History of Ireland since 1600*. London: Batsford, 1972.

Daly, Mary E. *Social and Economic History of Ireland since 1800*. Dublin: The Educational Company, 1981.

Deane, Seamus, ed. *The Field Day Anthology of Irish Writing*. 3 vols. New York: Norton, 1991.

Drudy, P. J., ed. *The Irish in America: Emigration, Assimilation, and Impact*. Cambridge: Cambridge University Press, 1985.

Edwards, Ruth Dudley. *The Faithful Tribe: An Intimate Portrait of the Loyal Institutions*. London: HarperCollins, 1999.

Elliott, Marianne. *The Catholics of Ulster: A History*. New York: Basic Books, 2001.

Foster, R. F. *Modern Ireland, 1600–1972*. New York: Viking Penguin, 1988.

Foster, R. F., ed. *The Oxford Illustrated History of Ireland*. New York: Oxford University Press, 1989.

Hachey, Thomas E., Joseph M. Hernon, and Lawrence J. McCaffrey. *The Irish Experience, A Concise History*. Armonk, N.Y.: M. E. Sharpe, 1996.

Jackson, Alvin. *Ireland, 1798–1998*. Oxford: Blackwell, 1999.

Kee, Robert. *The Green Flag: A History of Irish Nationalism*. New York: Delacorte, 1972.

Lydon, James. *The Making of Ireland from Ancient Times to the Present*. New York: Routledge, 1998.

Lyons, F. S. L. *Ireland since the Famine*. London: Weidenfield and Nicolson, 1971.

McCaffrey, Lawrence J. *The Irish Diaspora in America*. Washington, D.C.: Catholic University of America Press, 1984.

MacCurtain, Margaret, and Donncha O'Corrain, eds. *Women in Irish Society. The Historical Dimension*. Dublin: Arlen House, 1978.

MacDonagh, Oliver. *Ireland*. Englewood Cliffs, N.J.: Prentice Hall, 1968.

———. *States of Mind: A Study of Anglo-Irish Conflict, 1780–1980*. Boston: George Allen and Unwin, 1983.

Moody, T. W., and F. X. Martin, eds. *The Course of Irish History*. Cork: Mercier, 1966.

Norman, Edward. *A History of Modern Ireland, 1800–1969*. London: Penguin, 1969.

O'Connor, Emmet. *The Labour History of Ireland, 1824–1960*. Dublin: Gill and Macmillan, 1993.

O'Farrell, P. *England's Irish Question: Anglo-Irish Relations 1534–1970*. New York: Schocken Books, 1972.

O'Grada, Cormac. *Ireland: A New Economic History, 1780–1939*. Oxford: Clarendon, 1994.

Stewart, A. T. Q. *The Narrow Ground: Aspects of Ulster 1609–1969*. London: Faber and Faber, 1977.

Valiulis, Maryann Gialanella, and Mary O'Dowd, eds. *Women in Irish History*. Dublin: Wolfhound Press, 1997.

Ward, Alan J. *The Irish Constitutional Tradition: Responsible Government and Modern Ireland*. Washington, D.C.: Catholic University of America Press, 1994.

Historiography

Boyce, D. G., and Alan O'Day, eds. *The Making of Modern Irish History: Revisionism and the Revisionist Controversy*. London: Routledge, 1996.

Brady, Ciaran, ed. *Interpreting Irish History: The Debate on Historical Revisionism*. Dublin: Irish Academic Press, 1994.

EARLY AND MEDIEVAL IRELAND

Barry, Terry, ed. *A History of Settlement in Ireland*. London: Routledge, 2000.

Bieler, Ludwig. *Ireland: Harbinger of the Middle Ages*. London: Oxford University Press, 1963.

———. *St. Patrick and the Coming of Christianity*. Dublin: Gill, 1967.

Byrne, F. J. *Irish Kings and High Kings*. Dublin: Four Courts, 2001.

Chadwick, Nora. *The Age of the Saints in the Early Celtic Church*. London: Oxford University Press, 1961.

Cosgrove, Art, ed. *A New History of Ireland*. Vol. II: *Medieval Ireland, 1169–1534*. Oxford: Clarendon Press, 1993.

Curtis, Edmund. *A History of Medieval Ireland from 1086 to 1513.* London: Methuen, 1938.

De Paor, Maire, and Liam De Paor. *Early Christian Ireland.* London: Thames and Hudson, 1978.

Dolley, Michael. *Anglo-Norman Ireland.* Dublin: Gill and Macmillan, 1972.

Duffy, Sean. *Ireland in the Middle Ages.* London: St. Martin's Press, 1997.

Flanagan, Marie Therese. *Irish Society, Anglo-Norman Settlers, Angevin Kingship: Interactions in Ireland in the Late Twelfth Century.* Oxford: Clarendon, 1989.

Flower, Robin. *The Irish Tradition.* Oxford: Clarendon, 1947.

Frame, Robin. *English Lordship in Ireland, 1318–1361.* Oxford: Oxford University Press, 1981.

Greene, David, and Frank O'Connor, eds. *A Golden Treasury of Irish Poetry, AD 600 to 1200.* London: Macmillan, 1967.

Hanson, R. P. C. *St. Patrick: His Origins and Career.* Oxford: Clarendon, 1968.

Henry, Françoise, ed. *Irish Art in the Early Christian Period.* Ithaca, N.Y.: Cornell University Press, 1965.

———. *Irish Art during the Viking Invasions, 800–1020 AD.* Ithaca, N.Y.: Cornell University Press, 1967.

———. *Irish Art in the Romanesque Period, 1021–1170 AD.* Ithaca, N.Y.: Cornell University Press, 1970.

Hughes, Kathleen. *The Church in Early Irish Society.* Ithaca, N.Y.: Cornell University Press, 1966.

Lydon, J. F. *Church and Society in Ireland, AD 400–1200.* London: Variorum Reprints, 1987.

———. *The Lordship of Ireland in the Middle Ages.* Toronto: University of Toronto Press, 1972.

Lydon, James. *Ireland in the Later Middle Ages.* Dublin: Gill and Macmillan, 1972.

MacNiocaill, Gearoid. *Ireland before the Vikings.* Dublin: Gill and Macmillan, 1972.

O'Corrain, Donncha. *Ireland before the Normans.* Dublin: Gill and Macmillan, 1972.

O'Croinin, Daibhi. *Early Medieval Ireland, 400–1200.* London: Longman, 1995.

Otway-Ruthven, A. J. *A History of Medieval Ireland.* New York: St. Martin's Press, 1980.

Richter, Michael. *Medieval Ireland: The Enduring Tradition.* New York: St. Martin's Press, 1988.

Simms, Katharine. *From Kings to Warlords: The Changing Political Structures of Gaelic Ireland in the Later Middle Ages.* Woodbridge: Boydell, 2000.

Watt, John. *The Church and the Two Nations in Medieval Ireland.* Cambridge: Cambridge University Press, 1970.

———. *The Church in Medieval Ireland.* Dublin: University College Dublin Press, 1998.

ANGLICIZATION OF IRELAND

Bradshaw, Brendan. *The Dissolution of the Religious Houses in Ireland under Henry VIII.* Cambridge: Cambridge University Press, 1974.

———. *The Irish Constitutional Revolution of the Sixteenth Century.* Cambridge: Cambridge University Press, 1979.

Brady, Ciaran. *The Chief Governors: The Rise and Fall of Reform Government in Tudor Ireland.* Cambridge: Cambridge University Press, 1994.

Canny, Nicholas. *From Reformation to Restoration, 1543–1660.* Dublin: Helicon, 1987.

———. *The Elizabethan Conquest of Ireland: A Pattern Established, 1565–1576.* New York: Barnes and Noble, 1976.

Ellis, Steven. *Reform and Revival: English Government in Ireland, 1470–1534.* New York: St. Martin's Press, 1986.

———. *Ireland in the Age of the Tudors, 1447–1603: English Expansion and the End of Gaelic Rule.* New York: Longmans, 1998.

———. *Tudor Ireland, 1470–1603.* New York: Longman, 1985.

Lennon, Colm. *Sixteenth Century Ireland: The Incomplete Conquest.* Dublin: Gill and Macmillan, 1994.

MacCurtain, Margaret. *Tudor and Stuart Ireland.* Dublin: Gill and Macmillan, 1972.

McCarthy-Murrough, Michael. *The Munster Plantation: English Migration to Southern Ireland, 1583–1611.* Oxford: Oxford University Press, 1986.

Moody, T. W., F. X. Martin, and F. J. Byrne, eds. *New History of Ireland.* Vol. 3: *Early Modern Ireland, 1534–1691.* Oxford: Clarendon Press, 1984.

Morgan, Hiram. *The Battle of Kinsale.* Bray, Ireland: Wordwell, 2004.

———. *Political Ideology in Ireland, 1541–1641.* Dublin: Four Courts, 1999.

Quinn, D. P. *The Elizabethans and the Irish, 1536–48.* Ithaca, N.Y.: Cornell University Press, 1966.

Silke, John J. *Kinsale: The Spanish Intervention in Ireland at the End of the Elizabethan Wars.* Dublin: Four Courts, 2004.

STUART ERA, 1603–1691

Barnard, T. C. *Cromwellian Ireland: English Government and Reform in Ireland, 1649–1660.* Oxford: Oxford University Press, 1975.

Bottigheimer, Karl. *English Money and Irish Land: The Adventurers in the Cromwellian Settlement of Ireland.* Oxford: Oxford University Press, 1971.

Canny, Nicholas. *Kingdom and Colony: Ireland in the Atlantic World, 1560–1800.* Baltimore, Md.: Johns Hopkins University Press, 1988.

———. *Making Ireland British, 1580–1650.* New York: Oxford University Press, 2001.

———. *The Upstart Earl: A Study of the Social and Mental World of Richard Boyle, First Earl of Cork, 1566–1643.* Cambridge: Cambridge University Press, 1982.

Clarke, Aidan. *The Old English in Ireland, 1625–1642.* Dublin: Four Courts, 2000.

Corish, Patrick. *The Catholic Community in the Seventeenth and Eighteenth Centuries.* Dublin: Helicon, 1981.

Dickson, David. *New Foundations: Ireland 1660–1800.* Dublin: Helicon, 1987.

Ford, Alan. *The Protestant Reformation in Ireland, 1590–1641.* Frankfort-on-Main: Peter Lang, 1985.

Gillespie, Raymond. *Colonial Ulster: The Settlement of East Ulster, 1600–41.* Cork: Cork University Press, 1985.

———. *Devoted People: Belief and Religion in Early Modern Ireland.* Manchester: Manchester University Press, 1997.

Kilroy, Phil. *Protestant Dissent and Controversy in Ireland, 1660–1714.* Cork: Cork University Press, 1994.

Pawlisch, Hans. *Sir John Davies and the Conquest of Ireland: A Study in Legal Imperialism.* Cambridge: Cambridge University Press, 1983.

Robinson, Philip. *The Plantation of Ulster: British Settlement in an Irish Landscape, 1600–1670.* New York: St. Martin's Press, 1984.

Simms, J. G. *Jacobite Ireland, 1685–91.* London: Routledge and Kegan Paul, 1969.

———. *The Jacobite Parliament of 1689.* Dundalk: Dundalgan Press, 1975.

———. *William Molyneux of Dublin, 1656–1698.* Dublin: Irish Academic Press, 1982.

ASCENDANCY IRELAND, 1691–1800

Bartlett, Thomas. *The Rise and Fall of the Irish Nation: The Catholic Question, 1690–1830.* Dublin: Gill and Macmillan, 1992.

———, Kevin Dawson, and Daire Keogh. *The 1798 Rebellion.* Niwot, Colo.: Roberts Rinehart, 1998.

Burns, Robert E. *Irish Parliamentary Politics in the Eighteenth Century.* Vol. I: *1714 1734;* Vol. II: *1734–1760.* Washington, D.C.: Catholic University of America Press, 1989, 1990.

Connolly, S. J. *Religion, Law, and Power: The Making of Protestant Ireland, 1660–1760.* Oxford: Clarendon Press, 1992.

Cullen, L. M. *Hidden Ireland: Reassessment of a Concept.* Dublin: Lilliput Press, 1988.

Curtin, Nancy. *The United Irishmen: Popular Politics in Ulster and Dublin, 1791–1798.* Oxford: Clarendon Press, 1992.

Dickson, David. *New Foundations: Ireland 1660–1800.* Dublin: Helicon, 1988.

———, ed. *The Gorgeous Mask: Dublin, 1650–1850.* Dublin: Trinity History Workshop, 1987.

———, Hugh and Gough, eds. *Ireland and the French Revolution.* Dublin: Irish Academic Press, 1990.

———, Daire Keogh, and Kevin Whelan, eds. *The United Irishmen: Republicanism, Radicalism, and Rebellion.* Dublin: Lilliput, 1993.

Doyle, David N. *Ireland, Irishmen and Revolutionary America, 1760–1820.* Dublin: Mercier, 1981.

Elliott, Marianne. *Wolfe Tone: Prophet of Irish Independence.* New Haven, Conn.: Yale University Press, 1989.

Johnston, Edith M. *Great Britain and Ireland, 1760–1800: A Study in Political Administration.* London: Oliver and Bond, 1989.

———. *Ireland in the Eighteenth Century.* Dublin: Gill and Macmillan, 1974.

Keogh, Daire. *The French Disease: The Catholic Church and Irish Radicalism, 1790–1800.* Dublin: Four Courts, 1994.

McDowell, R. B. *Ireland in the Age of Imperialism and Revolution, 1760–1800.* Oxford: Clarendon Press, 1979.

———. *Irish Public Opinion, 1750–1800.* London: Faber and Faber, 1944.

McGuire, N. A., ed. *Kings in Conflict: The Revolutionary War in Ireland and Its Aftermath, 1689–1750.* Belfast: Blackstaff, 1990.

Malcomson, A. P. W. *John Foster: The Politics of the Anglo-Irish Ascendancy.* Oxford: Oxford University Press, 1978.

Miller, Kerby, Arnold Schrier, Bruce Boling, and David N. Doyle. *Irish Immigrants in the Land of*

Canaan: Letters and Memoirs from Colonial and Revolutionary America, 1675–1815. Oxford: Oxford University Press, 2003.

O'Brien, Gerard. *Anglo-Irish Politics in the Age of Grattan and Pitt.* Dublin: Irish Academic Press, 1987.

Pakenham, Thomas. *The Year of Liberty: The Great Irish Rebellion of 1798.* Dublin: Hodder and Stoughton 1969.

Smyth, Jim. *The Men of No Property: Irish Radicals and Popular Politics in the Late Eighteenth Century.* Dublin: Gill and Macmillan, 1992.

Whelan, Kevin. *The Tree of Liberty: Radicalism, Catholicism and the Construction of Irish Identity, 1760–1830.* Cork: Cork University Press, 1996.

NINETEENTH-CENTURY IRELAND

Akenson, Donald H. *Small Differences: Irish Catholics and Irish Protestants, 1815–1922.* Montreal: McGill-Queen's University Press, 1988.

———. *The Irish Educational Experiment.* Toronto: University of Toronto Press, 1970.

Bew, Paul S. *C. S. Parnell.* Dublin: Gill and Macmillan, 1981.

Bew, Paul. *Land and the National Question in Ireland, 1858–1882.* Dublin: Gill and Macmillan, 1978.

Bowen, Desmond. *Paul Cardinal Cullen and the Making of Modern Irish Catholicism.* Dublin: Gill and Macmillan, 1983.

Boyce, D. George. *Nineteenth Century: The Search for Stability.* Dublin: Gill and Macmillan, 1991.

Boyle, John W. *The Irish Labour Movement in the Nineteenth Century.* Washington, D.C.: Catholic University of America Press, 1988.

Broeker, Galen. *Rural Disorder and Police Reform in Ireland, 1812–1836.* Toronto: University of Toronto Press, 1970.

Brown, Thomas N. *Irish-American Nationalism, 1870–1890.* Philadelphia: J. B. Lippincott, 1966.

Clarke, Sam. *Social Origins of the Land War.* Princeton, N.J.: Princeton University Press, 1979.

Comerford, R. V. *The Fenians in Context: Irish Politics and Society, 1842–1882.* Atlantic Highlands, N.J.: Humanities Press, 1985.

Connolly, S. J. *Priests and People in Pre-famine Ireland, 1780–1845.* New York: St. Martin's Press, 1982.

Daly, Mary E. *The Famine in Ireland.* Dundalk: Dublin Historical Association, 1986.

———. *Social and Economic History of Ireland since 1800.* Dublin: Educational Company of Ireland, 1981.

Davis, Richard. *Young Ireland Movement.* Dublin: Gill and Macmillan, 1988.

Donnelly, James S. *Landlord and Tenant in Nineteenth Century Ireland.* Dublin: Gill and Macmillan, 1973.

Edwards, R. Dudley, and T. Desmond Williams, eds. *The Great Famine: Studies in Irish History, 1845–1852.* Dublin: Browne and Nolan, 1956.

Feingold, William. *Revolt of the Tenants: The Transfer of Local Government in Ireland, 1872–1886.* Boston: Northeastern University Press, 1984.

Geary, Laurence M. *The Plan of Campaign, 1886–1891.* Cork: Cork University Press, 1987.

Harmon, Maurice, ed. *Fenians and Fenianism.* Seattle: University of Washington Press, 1970.

Hoppen, K. T. *Elections, Politics and Society in Ireland, 1832–1885.* Oxford: Clarendon, 1984.

———. *Ireland since 1800: Conflict and Conformity.* London: Longmans, 1989.

Jenkins, Brian. *Era of Emancipation: The British Government of Ireland, 1812–1830.* Montreal: McGill–Queen's University Press, 1988.

Keenan, Desmond J. *The Catholic Church in Nineteenth Century Ireland.* New York: Barnes and Noble, 1983.

Larkin, Emmet. *The Historical Dimensions of Irish Catholicism.* Washington, D.C.: Catholic University of America Press, 1984.

———. *The Making of the Roman Catholic Church in Ireland, 1850–1860.* Chapel Hill: University of North Carolina Press, 1980.

———. *The Consolidation of the Roman Catholic Church in Ireland, 1860–1870.* Chapel Hill: University of North Carolina Press, 1987.

———. *The Roman Catholic Church and the Emergence of the Modern Irish Political System, 1874–1878.* Washington, D.C.: Catholic University of America Press, 1996.

———. *The Roman Catholic Church and the Home Rule Movement in Ireland, 1870–1874.* Chapel Hill: University of North Carolina Press, 1990.

———. *The Roman Catholic Church and the Modern Irish State, 1878–1886.* Philadelphia: American Philosophical Society, 1975.

———. *The Roman Catholic Church and the Plan of Campaign, 1886–1888.* Cork: Cork University Press, 1978.

———. *The Roman Catholic Church in Ireland and the Fall of Parnell, 1888–1891.* Chapel Hill: University of North Carolina Press, 1979.

Lee, Joseph. *The Modernization of Irish Society, 1848–1918*. Dublin: Gill and Macmillan, 1972.

Loughlin, James. *Gladstone, Home Rule, and the Ulster Question, 1882–1893*. Atlantic Highlands, N.J.: Humanities Press, 1987.

Lyons, F. S. L. *Charles Stewart Parnell*. London: Oxford University Press, 1977.

McCartney, Donal. *The Dawning of Democracy: Ireland 1800–1870*. Dublin: Helicon, 1987.

———, ed. *The World of Daniel O'Connell*. Cork: Mercier Press, 1980.

MacDonagh, Oliver. *The Emancipationist: Daniel O'Connell, 1830–1847*. London: Weidenfeld and Nicolson, 1989.

———. *The Hereditary Bondsman: Daniel O'Connell, 1775–1829*. London: Weidenfield and Nicolson, 1988.

McDowell, R. B. *Public Opinion and Politics in Ireland, 1801–1846*. London: Faber and Faber, 1952.

———. *The Irish Administration, 1801–1914*. London: Routledge and Kegan Paul, 1964.

Miller, Kerby, *Emigrants and Exiles: Ireland and the Irish Exodus to North America*. New York: Oxford University Press, 1985.

Molkyr, Joel. *Why Ireland Starved: A Quantitative and Analytical History of the Irish Economy, 1800–1852*. Boston: George Allen and Unwin, 1983.

Moody, T. W. *Davitt and Irish Revolution, 1846–1882*. New York: Oxford University Press, 1982.

Murphy, David. *Ireland and the Crimean War*. Dublin: Four Courts Press, 2002.

Nowlan, Kevin, and Maurice O'Connell, eds. *Daniel O'Connell: Portrait of a Radical*. Belfast: Appletree Press, 1984.

O'Brien, Conor Cruise. *Parnell and His Party, 1880–1890*. Oxford: Clarendon Press, 1960.

O'Broin, Leon. *Fenian Fever: An Anglo-American Dilemma*. New York: New York University Press, 1971.

O'Faolain, Sean. *King of Beggars: A Life of Daniel O'Connell*. Dublin: Poolbeg Press, 1986.

O'Ferrall, Fergus. *Catholic Emancipation: Daniel O'Connell and the Birth of Irish Democracy, 1820–1830*. Dublin: Gill and Macmillan, 1985.

———. *Daniel O'Connell*. Dublin: Gill and Macmillan, 1981.

O'Grada, Cormac. *Ireland before and after the Famine: Explorations in Economic History, 1800–1925*. Manchester: Manchester University Press, 1988.

———. *The Great Irish Famine*. Cambridge: Cambridge University Press, 1995.

O'Neill, Kevin. *Family and Farm in Pre-famine Ireland*. Madison: University of Wisconsin Press, 1984.

O'Tuathaigh, Gearoid. *Ireland before the Famine, 1798–1848*. Dublin: Gill and Macmillan, 1972.

Solow, Barbara Lewis. *The Land Question and the Irish Economy, 1870–1903*. Cambridge, Mass.: Harvard University Press, 1971.

Thornley, David. *Issac Butt and Home Rule*. London: Ambassador Press, 1964.

Townsend, Charles. *Political Violence in Ireland: Government and Resistance since 1848*. New York: Oxford University Press, 1983.

Trench, Charles Chevenix. *The Great Dan: A Biography of Daniel O'Connell*. London: Jonathan Cape, 1984.

Vaughn, W. E. *Landlords and Tenants in Ireland, 1848–1904*. Dublin: Gill and Macmillan, 1984.

———, ed. *A New History of Ireland*. Vol. V: *Ireland under the Union, 1801–1870*. Oxford: Clarendon Press, 1989.

Ward, Alan J. *The Irish Constitutional Tradition, Responsible Government and Modern Ireland, 1782–1992*. Dublin: Irish Academic Press, 1994.

Whyte, John. *The Independent Irish Party, 1850–1859*. London: Oxford University Press, 1858.

ACHIEVING INDEPENDENCE

Andrews, C. S. *Dublin Made Me*. Dublin: Lilliput, 2001.

Bew, Paul. *Conflict and Conciliation in Ireland, 1890–1910*. Oxford: Clarendon Press, 1987.

Boyce, D. G. *Englishmen and Irish Troubles: British Public Opinion and the Making of Irish Policy, 1918–1922*. Cambridge, Mass.: M.I.T. Press, 1972.

———. *The Irish Question and English Politics, 1868–1986*. London: Macmillan, 1988.

Buckland, Patrick. *Irish Unionism*. Vol. I: *The Anglo-Irish and the New Ireland, 1885–1922*. Dublin: Gill and Macmillan, 1972.

———. *Irish Unionism*. Vol. II: *Ulster Unionism and the Origins of Northern Ireland, 1886–1922*. Dublin: Gill and Macmillan, 1972.

Callanan, Frank. *T. M. Healy*. Cork: Cork University Press, 1996.

Carroll, Francis M. *American Opinion and the Irish Question, 1910–1923*. New York: St. Martin's Press, 1978.

Caufiled, Max. *The Easter Rebellion.* London: Frederick Muller, 1964.

Coffey, Thomas. *Agony at Easter.* Baltimore: Penguin, 1969.

Coogan, Tim Pat. *The Man Who Made Ireland: The Life and Death of Michael Collins.* Niwot, Colo.: Roberts Rinehart, 1992.

Costello, Francis. *The Irish Revolution and Its Aftermath, 1916–1923.* Dublin: Irish Academic Press, 2003.

Curran, Joseph. *The Birth of the Irish Free State, 1921–1923.* University: University of Alabama Press, 1980.

Curtis, L. P., Jr. *Anglo-Saxons and Celts: A Study in Anti-Irish Prejudice in Victorian England.* Bridgeport, Conn.: Conference on British Studies, 1968.

———. *Apes and Angels: The Irishman in Victorian Caricature.* Newton Abbot, U.K.: David and Charles, 1971.

Dangerfield, George. *The Damnable Question.* Boston: Little, Brown, 1976.

Doyle, David N. *Irish Americans, Native Rights, and National Empires: The Structure, Divisions, and Attitudes of the Catholic Minority in the Age of Expansion, 1890–1901.* New York: Arno Press, 1976.

Edwards, Ruth Dudley. *Patrick Pearse: The Triumph of Failure.* Boston: Faber and Faber, 1979.

Fallis, Richard. *The Irish Renaissance.* Syracuse, N.Y.: Syracuse University Press, 1977.

Farrell, Brian. *The Founding of Dail Eireann.* Dublin: Gill and Macmillan, 1971.

Farrell, Sean. *Patrick Pearse and the Politics of Redemption. The Mind of the Easter Rising, 1916.* Washington, D.C.: Catholic University of America Press, 1994.

Fitzpatrick, David. *The Two Irelands, 1912–1939.* Oxford: Oxford University Press, 1998.

Gailey, Andrew. *Ireland and the Death of Kindness: The Experience of Constructive Unionism, 1890–1905.* Cork: Cork University Press, 1987.

Garvin, Tom. *The Evolution of Irish Nationalist Politics.* Dublin: Gill and Macmillan, 1972.

———. *Nationalist Revolutionaries in Ireland, 1858–1928.* Oxford: Clarendon Press, 1987.

———. *1922: The Birth of Irish Democracy.* Dublin: Gill and Macmillan, 1996.

Goldring, Maurice. *Faith of Our Fathers: The Formation of Irish Nationalist Ideology—1890–1920.* Dublin: Respol, 1987.

Harkness, D. W. *The Restless Dominion: The Irish Free State and the British Commonwealth of Nations, 1921–1931.* Dublin: Gill and Macmillan, 1969.

Harris, Mary. *The Catholic Church and the Foundation of the Northern Irish State.* Cork: Cork University Press, 1993.

Holt, Edgar. *Protest in Arms, The Irish Troubles, 1916–1923.* New York: Coward-McCann, 1961.

Hopkinson, Michael. *Green against Green: The Irish Civil War.* Dublin: Gill and Macmillan, 1988.

Hutchinson, John. *The Dynamics of Cultural Nationalism: The Gaelic Revival and the Creation of the Irish Nation State.* London: Allan and Unwin, 1987.

Kissane, Bill. *Explaining Irish Democracy.* Dublin: University College Dublin Press, 2002.

Laffan, Michael. *The Partition of Ireland, 1911–1925.* Dundalk: Dundalgan, 1983.

Larkin, Emmet. *James Larkin, Irish Labour Leader, 1876–1947.* Cambridge, Mass.: M.I.T. Press, 1965.

Lyons, F. S. L. *Culture and Anarchy in Ireland: 1890–1939.* Oxford: Clarendon Press, 1979.

MacCaffrey, Lawrence J. *The Irish Diaspora in America.* Washington, D.C.: Catholic University of America Press, 1984.

McCarthy, John P. *Kevin O'Higgins, Builder of the Irish State.* Dublin: Irish Academic Press, 2006.

Martin, F. X., and J. F. Byrne, eds. *The Scholar Revolutionary: Eoin MacNeill, 1867–1945, and the Making of the New Ireland.* New York: Barnes and Noble, 1973.

Matthews, Kevin. *Fatal Influences: The Impact of Ireland on British Politics, 1920–1925.* Dublin: University College Dublin Press, 2004.

Miller, David. *Church, State, and Nation in Ireland, 1898–1921.* Pittsburgh: University of Pittsburgh Press, 1973.

———. *Queen's Rebels: Ulster Loyalism in Historical Perspective.* New York: Barnes and Noble, 1978.

Mitchell, Arthur. *Revolutionary Government in Ireland: Dail Eireann, 1919–1922.* Dublin: Gill and Macmillan, 1995.

Morrissey, Thomas J., S.J. *Toward a National University: William Delany, S.J., 1835–1924.* Atlantic Highlands, N.J.: Humanities Press, 1985.

Murphy, Cliona. *The Women's Suffrage Movement and Irish Society in the Early Twentieth Century.* Philadelphia: Temple University Press, 1989.

Nolan, Janet A. *Ourselves Alone: Women's Emigration from Ireland, 1885–1920.* Lexington: University of Kentucky Press, 1989.

O'Brien, Conor Cruise. *Ancestral Voices: Religion and Nationalism in Ireland.* Dublin: Poolbeg Press, 1994.

O'Brien, Joseph V. *Dear Dirty Dublin: A City in Distress, 1899–1916.* Berkeley: University of California Press, 1982.

———. *William O'Brien and the Course of Irish Politics, 1881–1918.* Berkeley: University of California Press, 1976.

O'Halpin, Eunan. *The Decline of the Union: British Government in Ireland, 1892–1920.* Syracuse, N.Y.: Syracuse University Press, 1987.

Paseta, Senia. *Before the Revolution: Nationalism, Social Change and Ireland's Catholic Elite, 1879–1922.* Cork: Cork University Press, 1999.

Regan, John M. *The Irish Counter-Revolution, 1921–1936.* Dublin: Gill and Macmillan, 1999.

Shannon, Catherine. *Arthur Balfour and Ireland, 1874–1922.* Washington, D.C.: Catholic University of America Press, 1988.

Stewart, A. T. Q. *Edward Carson.* Dublin: Gill and Macmillan, 1981.

———. *The Narrow Ground: Aspects of Ulster, 1609–1969.* London: Faber and Faber, 1977.

Ward, Alan J. *The Easter Rising: Revolution and Irish Nationalism.* Arlington Heights, Ill.: AHM Publishing, 1980.

———. *Ireland and Anglo-American Relations, 1880–1921.* London: Weidenfeld and Nicolson, 1969.

Younger, Carlton. *Ireland's Civil War.* London: Fontana, 1968.

ASSERTING INDEPENDENCE

Andrews, C. S. *Man of No Property.* Dublin: Liliput, 2001.

Barrington, Ruth. *Health, Medicine and Politics in Ireland 1900–1970.* Dublin: Institute of Public Administration, 1987.

Bell, James Bowyer. *The Secret Army: History of the Irish Republican Army, 1916–79.* Dublin: Academy, 1979.

Bew, Paul, Peter Gibbon, and Henry Patterson. *The State in Northern Ireland, 1921–1972: Political Forces and Social Classes.* Manchester: Manchester University Press, 1979.

———, and Henry Patterson. *Sean Lemass and the Making of Modern Ireland, 1945–1966.* Dublin: Gill and Macmillan, 1982.

Bowman, John. *De Valera and the Ulster Question, 1917–1973.* Oxford: Clarendon Press, 1982.

Brown, Terence. *Ireland: A Social and Cultural History, 1922 to the Present.* Ithaca, N.Y.: Cornell University Press, 1985.

Buckland, Patrick. *A History of Northern Ireland.* Dublin: Gill and Macmillan, 1981.

Canning, Paul. *British Policy towards Ireland, 1921–1941.* Oxford: Clarendon Press, 1985.

Carroll, Joseph T. *Ireland in the War Years, 1939–1945.* Dublin: Gill and Macmillan, 1976.

Coogan, Tim Pat. *De Valera: Long Fellow, Long Shadow.* London: Hutchinson, 1993.

Duggan, John P. *Neutral Ireland and the Third Reich.* Dublin: Lilliput Press, 1989.

Dwyer, T. Ryle. *De Valera's Darkest Hour, In Search of National Independence, 1919–1932.* Dublin: Mercier, 1982.

———. *De Valera's Finest Hour: In Search of National Independence, 1932–1959.* Dublin: Mercier, 1982.

———. *De Valera: The Man and the Myths.* Dublin: Poolbeg, 1991.

———. *Irish Neutrality and the USA, 1939–1947.* Dublin: Gill and Macmillan, 1977.

Fanning, Ronan. *Independent Ireland.* Dublin: Helicon, 1983.

Farrell, Brian. *Chairman or Chief: The Role of the Taoiseach in Irish Government.* Dublin: Gill and Macmillan, 1971.

———. *Sean Lemass.* Dublin: Gill and Macmillan, 1983.

Ferriter, Diarmaid. *The Transformation of Ireland, 1900–2000.* London: Profile, 2004.

Fisk, Robert. *In Time of War: Ireland, Ulster and the Price of Neutrality.* London: Andre Deutsch, 1983.

Gaughan, James Anthony. *Thomas Johnson: 1872–1963: First Leader of the Labour Party in Dail Eireann.* Dublin: Kingdom Books, 1980.

Harkness, David. *Northern Ireland since 1920.* Dublin: Helicon, 1983.

Keatinge, Patrick. *The Formulation of Irish Foreign Policy.* Dublin: Institute of Public Administration, 1973.

Kennedy, Keiran A., Thomas Gilbin, and Deirdre McHugh. *The Economic Development of Ireland in the Twentieth Century.* London: Routledge, 1988.

Keogh, Dermot. *Ireland and Europe, 1919–1989.* Cork: Hibernian University Press, 1989.

———. *Twentieth Century Ireland: Nation and State.* Dublin: Gill and Macmillan, 1994.

————. *The Vatican, the Bishops, and Irish Politics 1919–1939.* Cambridge: Cambridge University Press, 1986.

Lee, Joseph, ed. *Ireland, 1945–70.* Dublin: Gill and Macmillan, 1979.

————. *Ireland, 1912–1985.* Cambridge: Cambridge University Press, 1989.

————, and O'Tuathaigh, Gearoid, eds. *The Age of de Valera.* Dublin: Ward River, 1982.

McMahon, Deirdre. *Republicans and Imperialists: Anglo-Irish Relations in the 1930's.* New Haven, Conn.: Yale University Press, 1984.

Murphy, John A. *Ireland in the Twentieth Century.* Dublin: Gill and Macmillan, 1972.

Nowlan, Kevin B., and T. Desmond Williams. *Ireland in the War Years and After, 1939–1951.* Dublin: Gill and Macmillan, 1969.

O'Brien, Conor Cruise. *States of Ireland.* New York: Vintage Books, 1973.

O'Buachalla, Seamus. *Educational Policy in Twentieth Century Ireland.* Dublin: Wolfhound, 1988.

O'Carroll, J. P., and John A. Murphy, eds. *De Valera and His Times.* Cork: Cork University Press, 1983.

O'Grada, Cormac. *A Rocky Road: The Irish Economy since the Mid-1920s.* Manchester: Manchester University Press, 1997.

O'Halpin, Eunan. *Defending Ireland: The Irish State and Its Enemies since 1922.* Oxford: Oxford University Press, 1999.

Pilkington, Lionel. *Theatre and State in Twentieth Century Ireland: Cultivating the People.* London: Routledge, 2001.

Rose, Richard. *Governing without Consensus: An Irish Perspective.* London: Faber and Faber, 1971.

Schmitt, David E. *The Irony of Irish Democracy.* Lexington, Mass.: Heath, 1973.

Shore, Bernard. *The Emergency: Neutral Ireland, 1939–45.* Dublin: Gill and Macmillan, 1978.

Sinnot, Richard. *Irish Voters Decide. Voting Behavior in Elections and Referenda since 1918.* Manchester: Manchester University Press, 1995.

Skelly, Joseph Morrison. *Irish Diplomacy at the United Nations, 1945–1965: National Interests and the International Order.* Dublin: Irish Academic Press, 1997.

Townshend, Charles. *Ireland in the 20th Century.* New York: Oxford University Press, 1998.

Whyte, John. *Church and State in Modern Ireland.* New York: Barnes and Noble, 1971.

TROUBLESOME THIRTY YEARS

Akenson, D. H. *Conor: A Biography of Conor Cruise O'Brien.* Ithaca, N.Y.: Cornell University Press, 1994.

Ardagh, John. *Ireland and the Irish: Portrait of a Changing Society.* London: Hamish Hamilton, 1994.

Arnold, Bruce. *What Kind of Country: Modern Irish Politics, 1968–1983.* London: Jonathan Cape, 1984.

Birrell, Derek, and Alan Murie. *Policy and Government in Northern Ireland: Lessons of Devolution.* Dublin: Gill and Macmillan, 1980.

Boyle, Kevin, and Tom Hadden. *Ireland: A Positive Proposal.* Harmondsworth, U.K.: Penguin Books, 1985.

————. *Northern Ireland: The Choice.* London: Penguin, 1994.

Breen, R., ed. *Understanding Contemporary Ireland: State, Class and Development in the Republic of Ireland.* Dublin: Gill and Macmillan, 1990.

Darby, John, ed. *Northern Ireland: The Background to the Conflict.* Belfast: Appletree, 1983.

Dunlop, John. *A Precarious Belonging: Presbyterians and the Conflict in Ireland.* Belfast: Blackstaff, 1995.

English, Richard. *Armed Struggle: The History of the IRA.* Oxford: Oxford University Press, 2003.

Finnegan, Richard B., and Edward T. McCarron. *Ireland: Historical Echoes, Contemporary Politics.* Boulder, Colo.: Westview, 2000.

Galligan, Yvonne, Ward Ellis, and Rick Wilford, eds. *Contesting Politics: Women in Ireland, North and South.* Boulder, Colo.: Westview, 1999.

Gibbons, Luke. *Transformations in Irish Culture.* Cork: Cork University Press, 1996.

Harrington, John P., and Elizabeth J. Mitchell, eds. *Politics and Performance in Contemporary Northern Ireland.* Amherst: University of Massachusetts Press, 1999.

Hayes, Maurice. *Minority Verdict: Experiences of a Catholic Public Servant.* Belfast: Blackstaff, 1995.

Keatinge, Patrick. *A Place among the Nations: Issues of Irish Foreign Policy.* Dublin: Institute of Public Administration.

————, ed. *Ireland and EC Membership Evaluated.* New York: St. Martin's Press, 1991.

Kennedy-Pipe, Caroline. *The Origins of the Present Troubles in Northern Ireland.* New York: Longman, 1997.

McCarthy, John P. *Dissent from Irish America.* Lambert, Md.: University Press of America, 1993.

McGarry, John, and Brendan O'Leary, eds. *The Future of Northern Ireland.* Oxford: Clarendon Press, 1990.

Mitchell, George. *Making Peace.* New York: Knopf, 1999.

O'Malley, Padraig. *The Uncivil Wars: Ireland Today.* Boston: Beacon, 1997.

O'Toole, Fintan. *The Exiles of Erin: Images of Global Ireland.* Dublin: New Island Books, 1996.

Peillon, Michel, and Eamon Slater, eds. *Encounters with Modern Ireland.* Dublin: Institute of Public Administration, 1998.

Savage, Robert. *Irish Television: The Political and Social Origins.* Cork: Cork University Press, 1996.

Twomey, D. Vincent. *The End of Irish Catholicism.* Dublin: Veritas, 2003.

Wichert, Sabine. *Northern Ireland since 1945.* London: Longman, 1999.

Wilson, Andrew J. *Irish America and the Ulster Conflict, 1968–1995.* Washington, D.C.: Catholic University of America Press, 1995.

INDEX

Note: *Italic* page numbers indicate illustrations; **boldface** page numbers indicate major discussion of a topic; *m* indicates map; *n* indicates footnote

A

Abbey Theatre 107, **181**
  Carroll, Paul Vincent 212
  Fitzgerald, Barry 266
  Gregory, Isabella Augusta 280
  Macken, Walter 345, 346
  McKenna, Siobhán 346
  MacNamara, Brinsley (John Weldon) 346
  O'Casey, Sean 373
  Robinson, Esme Steward 422
abortion 163, 165, 266
absentees 12, 87, **181**
abstentionism **181–182**
Achill Head *352*
Act of Explanation (1663) 49
Act of Explanation (1665) 44
Act of Satisfaction (1653) 431
Act of Settlement (1662) 44, 49, 66, 431
Act of Supremacy (1537) 19
Act of Uniformity 21, 35, 45
Act of Union (1801) **72–75**, **182**
  Castlereagh, Robert Stewart, Viscount 213–214
  economic effects of 75
  Langrishe, Hercules 324
  Norbury, John Toler, first earl of 366
  O'Connell, Daniel 80, 82, 84–85, 86–87, 375, 376, 419
  opposition to 72–73
  repeal of 73, 80, 84–85, 375, 376, 406, **419**
  Whaley, Thomas 469
actors *See* film; television; theater
Acts of Attainment 24

Adams, Gerry 161, 167, 168, 169, 178, **182–183**, *183*, 293
Adventurers 37, 40, **183**, 233, 431
Aer Lingus **183**
agrarian violence 65, 81–82, 83, 323, 421, 449–450
Agricultural Credit Corporation (ACC) **183**
Agricultural Organization Society 105
agriculture *See also* land/land reform
  agrarian violence 65, 81–82, 83, 323, 421, 449–450
  Agricultural Credit Corporation (ACC) **183**
  annuities **186**
  cattle 45–46
  cooperatives 105, 426, 448
  Devon Commission 243
  Farmer's Party 260
  mercantile restrictions 57
  Plunkett, Horace 410
  tithes 81–82, 449–450
  Young, Arthur 474–475
Ahern, Bertie 168, 170, 172, *183*, **183–184**, 263
Aiken, Frank 144, **184**
airline (Aer Lingus) **183**
aisling poems 396, 398
Alderdice, John 168, **184**
Aldershot Military Barracks bombing 200
Allen, William Philip 350
Alliance Party of Northern Ireland 153, **184**, 364, 444
American Association for the Recognition of the Irish Republic 343
American Revolution 61
Ancient Order of Hibernians (AOH) **184**
An Claideamh Solus (newspaper) 110, 273, 347, 394, 405

Andrews, D. S. (Todd) **184–185**
Andrews, Eamon **185**
Andrews, John Miller **185**
Anglo-Irish 12*n*, 53*n*, **185**, 460
Anglo-Irish Agreement *See* Hillsborough Agreement; Sunningdale Agreement
Anglo-Irish Intergovernmental Council 160
Anglo-Irish Treaty (1921) 120–123, **186** *See also* Irish Free State
  Aiken, Frank 184
  Barton, Robert Childers 191
  Boundary Commission **201–202**
  Childers, Robert Erskine 217
  civil war 218
  Collins, Michael 223
  de Valera, Eamon 241
  Document No. 2 245
  Duffy, George Gavin 250
  governor-general 278–279
  Griffith, Arthur 281
  Irregulars 307
  O'Higgins, Kevin 389
  Provisional Government 412
  Sinn Féin 436
  Statute of Westminster 441
  Ultimate Financial Agreement 460
Anglo-Irish War *See* war of independence
Anglo-Normans **186**
  absentees 181
  Kildare (county) 317
  Old English 390
  Pale, The 11, 13, 186, 317, **401**, 543*m*, 544*m*
  Statute of Kilkenny 318
Annals of the Four Masters **186**
Anne (queen of Great Britain and Ireland) 54–55
annuities **186**
"An Seabhac" *See* Ó Siochfhradha, Padraig